T0215790

Communications
in Computer and Information Science   1421

More information about this series at http://www.springer.com/series/7899

Constantine Stephanidis ·
Margherita Antona · Stavroula Ntoa (Eds.)

HCI International 2021 - Posters

23rd HCI International Conference, HCII 2021
Virtual Event, July 24–29, 2021
Proceedings, Part III

 Springer

Editors
Constantine Stephanidis
University of Crete and Foundation
for Research and Technology – Hellas
(FORTH)
Heraklion, Crete, Greece

Margherita Antona
Foundation for Research
and Technology – Hellas (FORTH)
Heraklion, Crete, Greece

Stavroula Ntoa
Foundation for Research
and Technology – Hellas (FORTH)
Heraklion, Crete, Greece

ISSN 1865-0929   ISSN 1865-0937 (electronic)
Communications in Computer and Information Science
ISBN 978-3-030-78644-1   ISBN 978-3-030-78645-8 (eBook)
https://doi.org/10.1007/978-3-030-78645-8

This Springer imprint is published by the registered company Springer Nature Switzerland AG
The registered company address is: Gewerbestrasse 11, 6330 Cham, Switzerland

Foreword

Human-Computer Interaction (HCI) is acquiring an ever-increasing scientific and industrial importance, and having more impact on people's everyday life, as an ever-growing number of human activities are progressively moving from the physical to the digital world. This process, which has been ongoing for some time now, has been dramatically accelerated by the COVID-19 pandemic. The HCI International (HCII) conference series, held yearly, aims to respond to the compelling need to advance the exchange of knowledge and research and development efforts on the human aspects of design and use of computing systems.

The 23rd International Conference on Human-Computer Interaction, HCI International 2021 (HCII 2021), was planned to be held at the Washington Hilton Hotel, Washington DC, USA, during July 24–29, 2021. Due to the COVID-19 pandemic and with everyone's health and safety in mind, HCII 2021 was organized and run as a virtual conference. It incorporated the 21 thematic areas and affiliated conferences listed on the following page.

A total of 5222 individuals from academia, research institutes, industry, and governmental agencies from 81 countries submitted contributions, and 1276 papers and 241 posters were included in the proceedings to appear just before the start of the conference. The contributions thoroughly cover the entire field of HCI, addressing major advances in knowledge and effective use of computers in a variety of application areas. These papers provide academics, researchers, engineers, scientists, practitioners, and students with state-of-the-art information on the most recent advances in HCI. The volumes constituting the set of proceedings to appear before the start of the conference are listed in the following pages.

The HCI International (HCII) conference also offers the option of 'Late Breaking Work' which applies both for papers and posters, and the corresponding volume(s) of the proceedings will appear after the conference. Full papers will be included in the 'HCII 2021 - Late Breaking Papers' volumes of the proceedings to be published in the Springer LNCS series, while 'Poster Extended Abstracts' will be included as short research papers in the 'HCII 2021 - Late Breaking Posters' volumes to be published in the Springer CCIS series.

I would also like to thank the Program Board Chairs and the members of the Program Boards of all thematic areas and affiliated conferences for their contribution towards the highest scientific quality and overall success of the HCI International 2021 conference.

This conference would not have been possible without the continuous and unwavering support and advice of Gavriel Salvendy, founder, General Chair Emeritus, and Scientific Advisor. For his outstanding efforts, I would like to express my appreciation to Abbas Moallem, Communications Chair and Editor of HCI International News.

July 2021   Constantine Stephanidis

HCI International 2021 Thematic Areas and Affiliated Conferences

Thematic Areas

- HCI: Human-Computer Interaction
- HIMI: Human Interface and the Management of Information

Affiliated Conferences

- EPCE: 18th International Conference on Engineering Psychology and Cognitive Ergonomics
- UAHCI: 15th International Conference on Universal Access in Human-Computer Interaction
- VAMR: 13th International Conference on Virtual, Augmented and Mixed Reality
- CCD: 13th International Conference on Cross-Cultural Design
- SCSM: 13th International Conference on Social Computing and Social Media
- AC: 15th International Conference on Augmented Cognition
- DHM: 12th International Conference on Digital Human Modeling and Applications in Health, Safety, Ergonomics and Risk Management
- DUXU: 10th International Conference on Design, User Experience, and Usability
- DAPI: 9th International Conference on Distributed, Ambient and Pervasive Interactions
- HCIBGO: 8th International Conference on HCI in Business, Government and Organizations
- LCT: 8th International Conference on Learning and Collaboration Technologies
- ITAP: 7th International Conference on Human Aspects of IT for the Aged Population
- HCI-CPT: 3rd International Conference on HCI for Cybersecurity, Privacy and Trust
- HCI-Games: 3rd International Conference on HCI in Games
- MobiTAS: 3rd International Conference on HCI in Mobility, Transport and Automotive Systems
- AIS: 3rd International Conference on Adaptive Instructional Systems
- C&C: 9th International Conference on Culture and Computing
- MOBILE: 2nd International Conference on Design, Operation and Evaluation of Mobile Communications
- AI-HCI: 2nd International Conference on Artificial Intelligence in HCI

List of Conference Proceedings Volumes Appearing Before the Conference

38. CCIS 1420, HCI International 2021 Posters - Part II, edited by Constantine Stephanidis, Margherita Antona, and Stavroula Ntoa
39. CCIS 1421, HCI International 2021 Posters - Part III, edited by Constantine Stephanidis, Margherita Antona, and Stavroula Ntoa

http://2021.hci.international/proceedings

23rd International Conference on Human-Computer Interaction (HCII 2021)

The full list with the Program Board Chairs and the members of the Program Boards of all thematic areas and affiliated conferences is available online at:

http://www.hci.international/board-members-2021.php

HCI International 2022

The 24th International Conference on Human-Computer Interaction, HCI International 2022, will be held jointly with the affiliated conferences at the Gothia Towers Hotel and Swedish Exhibition & Congress Centre, Gothenburg, Sweden, June 26 – July 1, 2022. It will cover a broad spectrum of themes related to Human-Computer Interaction, including theoretical issues, methods, tools, processes, and case studies in HCI design, as well as novel interaction techniques, interfaces, and applications. The proceedings will be published by Springer. More information will be available on the conference website: http://2022.hci.international/:

General Chair
Prof. Constantine Stephanidis
University of Crete and ICS-FORTH
Heraklion, Crete, Greece
Email: general_chair@hcii2022.org

http://2022.hci.international/

Contents – Part III

Interacting and Playing

Interacting and Driving

Digital Wellbeing, eHealth and mHealth

Interacting and Shopping

HCI, Safety and Sustainability

HCI in the Time of Pandemic

Interacting and Learning

Interaction and Everyday Life

Learning Interactions: Robotics Supporting the Classroom

Giovana Barros, Beatriz Motta, Vitor Teixeira, Alexandre Gravatá,
Sérgio Silva Júnior[✉], Leandro de Sá, Marília Amaral, and Leonelo Almeida

Federal University of Technology, Curitiba, Paraná, Brazil
{giovanabarros,beatrizmotta,vittei.2000,alexandregravata,
sergiojunior.2018,leandrosa}@alunos.utfpr.edu.br, {mariliaa,
leoneloalmeida}@utfpr.edu.br

Abstract. Programming teaching can improve children's skills in logical-mathematical concepts. This learning process can benefit from the use of artifacts that value principles of Human-Computer Interaction and the area of early childhood education. From the Interaction Design, Visibility, Constraints, Consistency and Affordance principles were addressed together with the design principles adapted for children's technology, such as Literacy, Feedback and Guidance, Mental Development, Imagination, Motor Skills, Tangibility, Motivation and Engagement, Social Interaction and Collaboration, to plan an artifact designed to assist the introduction to learning programming logic for children. The artifact is also based on concepts related to ludic activities and imagination in education. Given this context, this paper intends to present a ludic artifact, the *Roboquedo*, to support this teaching of programming aimed at children. The development stages of *Roboquedo* are presented, based on the Interaction Design process and the characteristics of the artifact, combined with the Interaction Design area, introductory teaching of programming and ludic education.

Keywords: Interaction design · Education · Children · Robotics

1 Introduction

Logical mathematical reasoning and introductory programming teaching can be interesting resources to be inserted in early childhood education. Nevertheless, this preliminary education for children and young people points to possible improvements in the development of mathematical logic [1, 4, 10] and even social and emotional aspects [9], especially when principles of Human-Computer Interaction (HCI) are added to the elements of early childhood education. However, it is not trivial to start this type of teaching, and one of the possible approaches involves practical and ludic aspects, which provide collaboration and autonomy to students.

According to Leite [5] "It is through the act of playing that transition paths to higher levels of mental development are opened, allowing the child to restructure, and re-elaborate their way of understanding, thinking, feeling and interacting with reality".

C. Stephanidis et al. (Eds.): HCII 2021, CCIS 1421, pp. 3–10, 2021.
https://doi.org/10.1007/978-3-030-78645-8_1

Henceforth, this article presents the development of a ludic artifact which follows the principles of Interaction Design, to support the introductory teaching of programming for children, the *Roboquedo* (in Portuguese, "*Robô + Brinquedo*", combination of the words Robot and Toy), developed by PET - CoCE[1].

The *Roboquedo* has as differentials, in face of the existing options, the low financial cost, the use of free technologies and the possibility of using it in a collaborative way. This toy has the following elements: a turtle-shaped robot, a physical map to suggest robot activities, and two forms of directional control of the robot, one tangible (acrylic table with arrows to indicate directions to the robot), and one through a mobile device (with a software to indicate directions to the robot), which will be detailed in Sect. 4 of this article.

This article is divided into five sections. Section 2 presents the theoretical foundation, Sect. 3 presents the research steps, while in Sect. 4 we present the *Roboquedo* artifact and its elements, followed by Sect. 5 with the final considerations and next steps of the research, which is in progress.

2 Theoretical Foundation

Vigotski [9] establishes that the toy appears as an activity when children develop necessities that are not possible to be realized immediately. Necessity, for the author, is defined as "everything that is a reason for action". It would be in the toy, therefore, that children find the possibility to satisfy these necessities. At this stage, imagination is a new psychological process, since younger children are restricted to the impositions of the environment [8]. It can be said that the imagination, for children, would be the toy without action [9]. Thus, Vigotski [9] differentiates the act of playing from other activities as being the imagination in action since the toy does not derive only from any unrealizable desire formed in children. The toy makes it possible to create a zone of proximal development, that is, the transition from one development stage to another, by providing support for the separation between meaning and object, when it is used as a toy and by imposing rules with the imagination making the children submit to them as the purpose of play [9].

To think ludic artifacts with the aim of introducing programming teaching (sequence of commands, input, processing and output) [1], in addition to considering the characteristics of ludic education it is important to understand how children interact with these artifacts. In this regard, the concepts of Interaction Design [6], covered in HCI, offer principles, methods, theories and approaches for the development of aspects related to children's interactions with *Roboquedo*. Regarding the principles, the classics can be listed: Affordance, Feedback, Visibility and Consistency [6]. Besides these, Chiasson and Gutwin [3] suggest the addition and adaptation of some principles, considering the context of children's use, based on three categories of child development, namely: cognitive development, physical development and social and emotional development.

---

[1] A PET group (Tutorial Education Program) is formed by university students under the tutelage of a member of the faculty, with the objective of providing actions for students to carry out activities that fall within the pillars of research, extension and teaching, aiming at a differentiated formation of its members.

In the first category, the presence of four principles is pointed out: Literacy, Feedback and Guidance, Mental Development and Imagination. In the second category, two principles: Motor Skills and Tangibility. The third has three principles: Motivation and Engagement, Social Interaction and Collaboration. For the development of *Roboquedo*, all the principles of Preece, Rogers and Sharp [6] and Chiasson and Gutwin [5] were followed.

3   Research Steps

The steps for the development of this artifact followed the steps stipulated in the Interaction Design process by Preece [6]: a) Identify needs and establish requirements; b) Develop alternative designs; c) Build interactive versions; d) Evaluate designs.

At first, as already explained in Sect. 1 of this article, the research context was established, and with this definition, the requirements for *Roboquedo* were listed, among them:

1. Data entry must be done through a tangible medium and a digital device;
2. The turtle robot must obey the commands given in the input and data medium;
3. The turtle robot must follow the direction (right – left) indicated by the user;
4. The turtle robot must walk for 5 s with each move request;
5. The displacement time of the turtle robot must be possible to change;
6. The turtle robot should work via Bluetooth;
7. The map must contain a route with beginning, proposed activities and end.

Thus, with the set of requirements, alternative *Roboquedo* designs were built, as shown in Fig. 1.

Fig. 1. Alternative designs for the table and the robot.

In the third step of the Interaction Design process, interactive versions were built, both tangible and digital, as presented in detail in Sect. 4 of this article. The fourth step "Evaluate Design" involved an assessment of the artifact, carried out by the team itself, regarding compliance, safety and resistance. This evaluation followed the NBR NM 300-1, which has existed since 2004 in Brazil [2]. In this evaluation it was understood that the *Roboquedo* meets the following topics: does not have sharp edges, has non-toxic paint and responded smoothly to the drop and throw test.

Since the beginning of the project, four versions of *Roboquedo* have been created and since improved, following the principles of Interaction Design [3, 6] and the characteristics of low cost, usability and compliance with safety standards [2]. It is worth noting that *Roboquedo* was presented at public events for children, teachers and family members, as a demonstration, but they have not yet been held based on interaction with the intended audience. This step will be carried out in the future and will have all the necessary care.

4 The Roboquedo

As already mentioned, *Roboquedo* was developed with the intention of inserting logical reasoning and the introduction of programming teaching in early childhood education in a practical and ludic way [1, 9]. It consists of the following elements: a turtle-shaped robot, a physical map for suggesting robot activities, and two forms of directional control of the robot, one tangible (acrylic table with arrows to indicate directions to the robot), and one through a mobile device (software to indicate directions to the robot).

The ludic objective of the artifact is to make the turtle robot scroll through the map either through the tangible interface or through the mobile device. To start the activity, the turtle robot must be positioned at the beginning of the map; the child, or the group of children, (via the mobile device or the table) indicates the sequence of directions that he wants the artifact to make on the map. Then, the robot moves to a certain "stage" of the map, which has a written action to be performed by the children. The dynamics are repeated until the robot covers the entire path. This activity promotes the exploration of concepts such as: commands, data input, processing and laterality, and in addition, collaboration/cooperation concepts can be worked on.

The next subsections present the details of each element of *Roboquedo*.

4.1 Turtle Robot

The turtle-shaped robot consists of an Arduino board, two motors, a controller board for the motors and a Bluetooth module, in addition to three wheels and an internal acrylic structure to receive the components.

Through the Bluetooth module, the Arduino receives commands: go forward, backward, turn left or turn right, from the table (tangible interface) or from the mobile device, and start the motors by means of the controller board according to the command. In each command the motors move for a predefined time for each action. With each command, the *Roboquedo* moves for 5 s, however, such speed conditions can be regulated according to the target audience.

These technical characteristics support the Consistency principle [6], through the movements performed from the commands requested on the input devices. The turtle shape of the carcass, made on a 3D printer, has its design inspired by a platform game known to children, as can be seen in Fig. 2. As its appearance is reminiscent of a toy, the robot stimulates the presence of the Imagination principle [3, 9]. It is also possible to emphasize the presence of Tangibility [3] since there is also physical interaction of children with the robot.

Fig. 2. The turtle robot.

4.2 Map

The map on which the actions of the turtle robot are developed is a square physical "mat" with 2.5 m on its side, positioned on the floor for the robot to follow the indicated path through the control interfaces (table and application). Figure 3 shows the design of this map/carpet (a) and the carpet in use (b).

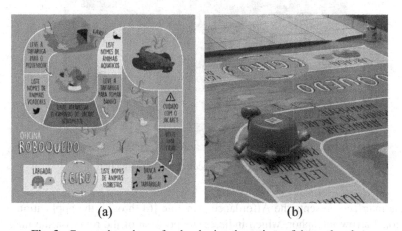

(a)   (b)

Fig. 3. Carpet-shaped map for developing the actions of the turtle robot.

It is possible to observe that the map presents "stages" and that in each one it is proposed, in simple language and presentation, according to the principle of Literacy

[4], an action to be performed by the children. Among them we have list animal names, dance, make the turtle spin and position the turtle in the lake. When going through all the stages (there are 12 in total) the turtle must reach the final stage, which is the arrival at its home.

The map clearly shows the beginning and end of the game, as well as what is the path to be taken from one point to another, taking into account the principle of Consistency and Visibility [6]. The actions taken by the children in each stage are related, in a ludic way, to the shape of the robot's turtle, according to the Imagination principle [3, 9]. In the controls, in each stage, there is the stimulus for physical movements performed only by the children (dancing) or performed by the children using the robot (placing the robot on the lake, on the map) thus promoting the principles of Tangibility and Motivation and Engagement [3]. Tangible interactions encourage Collaboration [3] and, as a result, stimulate children's communication "increasing the degree to which children have to externalize their thoughts, increasing their awareness of the experience" [7], also encouraging the principle of Social Interaction [3]. The turtle performs on the map the requested action on the data input device, presenting the principle of Feedback and Guidance [3, 6].

4.3 Mobile Device Interface

One of the forms of directional control of the robot is an application for mobile device. This application is based on the use of Bluetooth technology through an Arduino board. The interface of the mobile device consists of buttons in the shape of arrows. Each arrow or button pressed will indicate the direction the robot should take on the map/mat. Figure 4 shows the interface of the mobile device with this arrow control.

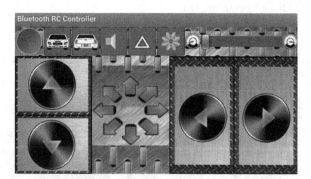

Fig. 4. Application interface for turtle robot control.

The interface presents the Affordance principle [6] through the application of the directional arrow metaphor, which indicate the position of the robot on the map. The robot performs the action defined by the selected arrow immediately, considering the principles of Feedback and Guidance [3, 6]. These technical characteristics support the actions of the robot, promoting the principles of Literacy and Mental Development [3], that is, a visual interface, without predominance of texts and with metaphors (drawing the arrows representing its actions) to aid the robot's navigation on the map. In this way it is possible to combine such interactions with the preliminary concepts of teaching programming (command, command sequence, processing, data entry and exit) and rules in ludic education [9].

4.4 Tangible Interface

The table is made of acrylic with rounded corners (Fig. 5), respecting safety standards [2]. The transparent material was chosen on purpose to awaken in children an interest in the functioning of the internal components of the device.

Fig. 5. Table interface for the turtle robot control.

The table meets the principles of Tangibility, Literacy and Mental Development [3], offering children physical interaction with the arrows referring to the directions chosen during the route on the map. The acrylic structure provides as inputs only the fittings in the shape of the arrows, in compliance with the principles of Motor Skills [3], Constraints and Visibility [6]. As in the map, the tangible interface promotes Collaboration [3, 7]. The arrow shape of the data input refers to the shape of plug-in toys, demonstrating the Imagination principle [3, 9].

5   Final Considerations and Next Steps

Robotics in education provides new experiences, perspectives, and a rich environment for individual and collective learning in the classroom [1]. When considering the introduction of programming concepts during early childhood education, it is essential to use principles of Interaction Design, combined with ludic education, to stimulate the interest of this audience [1].

When considering tangible, imaginable and interactive aspects [10], *Roboquedo* can be considered an option to address initial programming concepts such as commands, data entry, data processing and output, for an early childhood introduction to programming. Concepts present in Interaction Design [3, 6] are relevant allies to the area of education, since the principles cover aspects for observation and improvement of the learning process with the aid of the artifact.

The *Roboquedo* is still under development, and one of the next steps to be followed is to analyze the current artifact and raise improvements and ideas for features, which can be added to *Roboquedo* to provide new forms of interaction. The team is already considering some ideas that consist of modifications both in hardware and software, such as the addition of a gyroscope and a spin counter in the engine to refine the robot's position on the map. Furthermore, the addition of speech recognition as a new command method is also being studied.

We expect as future actions, in the post-COVID19 pandemic period, to have interactions with children, family members and teachers. For this, the project will be submitted to a research ethics committee. In addition, we expect to make the entire contents of the *Roboquedo* project freely and openly available in a web repository, so that it is accessible to others who want to reuse this project. Another future objective is to carry out studies on accessibility and ergonomics of the artifact.

Acknowledgements. To Tutorial Education Program – Connections of Knowledge – Ministry of Education (MEC), Secretariat of Higher Education (SESu) and Secretariat of Continuing Education, Literacy and Diversity (SECAD).

References

1. Amaral, M.A., Sdroievski, N.M., de Oliveira, L.C., Castelini, P.: Sobre experiências, críticas e potenciais: computação física educacional e altas habilidades. In: Barbosa, R., Blikstein, P. (eds.) Robótica educacional: experiências inovadoras na educação brasileira, pp. 251–275. Penso, Porto Alegre (2020)
2. Associação Brasileira de Normas Técnicas. NBR NM 300-1: Segurança de Brinquedos (2004)
3. Chiasson, S., Gutwin, C.: Design principles for children's technology. Technical report HCI-TR-05-02, Saskatchewan Computer Science Department (2005)
4. Kazakoff, E.R., Sullivan, A., Bers, M.U.: The effect of a classroom-based intensive robotics and programming workshop on sequencing ability in early childhood. Early Childhood Educ. J. **41**(4), 245–255 (2013)
5. Leite, E.C.R., Ruiz, J.B., Ruiz, A.M.C., Aguiar, T.F.: O brinquedo na educação infantil: contribuições de Piaget, Vigotsky e Vallon. Akrópolis **13**(1), 13–21 (2005)
6. Preece, J., Rogers, Y., Sharp, H.: Interaction Design: Beyond Human-Computer Interaction. Wiley, Indianapolis (2011)
7. Price, S., Rogers, Y., Scaife, M., Stanton, D., Neale, H.: Using 'tangibles' to promote novel forms of playful learning. Interact. Comput. **15**(2), 169–185 (2003)
8. Rego, T.C.: Vygotsky: uma perspectiva histórico-cultural da educação, 25nd edn. Vozes, Petrópolis (2020)
9. Vigotski, L.S.: A formação social da mente, 7nd edn. Martins Fontes, São Paulo (2007)
10. Wang, D., Zhang, C., Wang, H.: T-Maze: a tangible programming tool for children. In: Proceedings of the 10th International Conference on Interaction Design and Children (IDC 2011), pp. 127–135. ACM, New York (2011)

Technological Intervention Through the Virtual Assistant Alexa in the Development of Linguistic Skills of a New Language

Omar Cóndor-Herrera[1] , Janio Jadán-Guerrero[1] , Pamela Acosta Rodas[2] ,
and Carlos Ramos-Galarza[1,2(✉)]

[1] Centro de Investigación en Mecatrónica y Sistemas Interactivos MIST/Carrera de Ingeniería
en Ciencias de la Computación/Maestría en Educación Mención Innovación y Liderazgo
Educativo/Carrera de Psicología, Universidad Tecnológica Indoamérica,
Av. Machala y Sabanilla, Quito, Ecuador
{omarcondor,janiojadan,carlosramos}@uti.edu.ec
[2] Facultad de Psicología, Pontificia Universidad Católica del Ecuador,
Av. 12 de Octubre y Roca, Quito, Ecuador
{mpacosta,caramos}@puce.edu.ec

Abstract. Nowadays, technological advances have made possible the constant innovation of education, adding resources, tools, and technological devices that are rapidly updated, and improved, is in this scenario where it is proposed to take advantage of the benefits that technology offers, plus the set of informatic abilities that current students have developed from early stages, in benefit of education, since these abilities make easier for teachers to introduce tools, and technological devices into the teaching-learning process. The present research consisted on a technological intervention using the virtual assistant Alexa, with the aim of working on linguistic abilities to learn a new language. The study was conducted with a sample of 32 children aged between 9 and 12 years old. The procedure consisted in the application of an initial assessment (pre-test), then, along 6 weeks an intervention based on the application of Alexa virtual assistant was made, and, at the end of the intervention, a post-test was applied. The intervention focused on four abilities: vocabulary, comprehension of English language, communication skills, and skills of meaning. As results, in vocabulary, there were found statistically significant differences between the pre (M = 4.06), and post-test (M = 7.19); in the comprehension of English language, pre (M = 2.38), and post-test (M = 3.47); regarding communication skills, pre (M = 2.28), and post-test (M = 3.09); and, in skills of meaning, the mean obtained in the pre-test was (M = 3.31), and post-test (M = 4.66); these results contribute with empirical evidence about the improvement in learning a new language. From this research, it is proposed to continue using, and discovering the benefits of different innovations in educative context.

Keywords: Artificial Intelligence · Innovation · ICTs · IoT · Skills in English language · Virtual assistants

© Springer Nature Switzerland AG 2021
C. Stephanidis et al. (Eds.): HCII 2021, CCIS 1421, pp. 11–16, 2021.
https://doi.org/10.1007/978-3-030-78645-8_2

1   Introduction

Recently, Artificial Intelligence (AI) has showed a significative progress, its potentiality is increasing day by day, through clouds computing model, and, the use of the internet of thing (IoT), voice assistants have been incorporated to AI, allowing like this, voice assistants to communicate with usures in a natural language, making easy its usage, and it is the main reason of millions of devices that are incorporated in homes nowadays [1].

There is an extensive variety of electronic devices that count with an integrated voice assistance, as in the case of cellphones, and intelligent speakers, that are sub-utilized in its basic functions only, although, in current scenarios these, and many other technological devices, have started to be used at schools and universities with educative objectives [2], for example, in learning a new language, as it is reported in a recent study, where students learning a new language are supported by a voice Russian assistant called "Alice", for practicing speaking, obtaining satisfactory results [3]. Also, these assistants can work as virtual teachers, maintaining an interactive conversation with the user, being capable of answer doubts, and explaining some topics. Thus, the present investigation shows the results of a technological intervention based on the usage of "Alexa" virtual assistant, with the aim of working on linguistic skills when learning a new language [2].

1.1   Benefits of Using Technology in Education

Using resources, devices, and another technological elements, into the educational context have allowed to find new ways of knowledge production, representation, diffusion, and accessibility [4], innovating teaching process.

Implementing these technological resources, and devices have made possible to propose novel educative interactions, different to those traditional ones [5], like this, students get involved, enjoying their learning process, increasing also, success on team works [6], emerging on them their intrinsic motivation, considering that, when a student enjoy doing a task, there is involved a positive intrinsic motivation, therefore, their learning experience improves significantly [7, 8].

1.2   Technological Proposal of Alexa Virtual Assistant to Develop Linguistic Skills in the Process of Learning a New Language

As it has been previously analyzed, virtual assistants are evolving fast, and taking an important part of our daily life, its utility goes from supporting elderly people [9], in medical field to help pronunciation, real time translations, and virtual communication to find possible explanations to symptoms present in foreign people [10], in the educational field, current investigations have incorporated a prototype of a virtual assistant named "FENNChat", which is directed to offer automatic answers to students enrolled in an English course with educative objectives [11]. Therefore, our investigation proposes the incorporation of the virtual assistant Alexa, created by Amazon, into the educational process to develop linguistic skills of a new language.

Traditionally, assistants are used as dialogue systems (conversational), based on text or voice, or combining both, on the intervention made for this study, it was taken as a reference point this interaction to work in different abilities necessary to learn a new language. The intervention was conducted along 6 weeks in different working sessions, students interacted directly with "Alexa" virtual assistant, through different commands, at the beginning, to work vocabulary, simple commands such as "Alexa how (an X word) is pronounced in English?", or "Alexa, what is the meaning of (an X word) in Spanish? were used; to work on writing, and vocabulary, commands used were such as, "Alexa how does (X word) is written?", or, "Alexa spell (X word)". Afterwards, interactive conversations between students and "Alexa" virtual assistant, were simulated.

Among the abilities trained, are skills of meaning, vocabulary, comprehension of English, and communication skills, equivalents to a level of English A1, according to the Common European Framework of Reference for Languages [12].

2   Hypothesis of Investigation

Based on the intervention made, it is projected that the students benefited by the techno-logical intervention into the educational process, will improve their skills in, vocabulary, comprehension, communication skills, and skills of meaning, when comparing pre and post-test measurements.

2.1   Methodology

This study is quantitative, pre-experimental, and the main measurements used are pre and post-test. The sample was composed by 32 participants (16 females, and 16 males), aged between 9, and 12 years old, belonging to Ecuador educational system. The intervention process conducted, lasted 6 weeks, with frequency of 1 session per week. An instrument Ad-hoc was built, where vocabulary, comprehension, communication skills, and skills of meaning variables were evaluated.

The data analysis consisted on descriptive techniques of central tendency, and dis-persion. To prove the hypothesis, a T-Test was applied, among the pre and post-test values obtained by the group. It is important to stress that throughout this study, ethical standards of research with human beings were followed, as well as an informed consent of volunteer participation was obtained with the signature of the participants and their legal guardians.

3 Results

Tables 1, 2, 3 and 4 show the descriptive results obtained from each variable measured with the application of pre and post-test. The comparison made between the values obtained show a statistical signification in favor of the hypothesis made, and, in these four variables valued, improvements in English learning are evidenced (Fig. 1).

Table 1. Descriptive results of vocabulary

	Mean	N	Std. deviation	Std. error mean	t	p
Vocabulary pre-test	4.06	32	2.08	.37	−7.60	< .001
Vocabulary post-test	7.19	32	.82	.15		

Table 2. Descriptive results of English comprehension

	Mean	N	Std. deviation	Std. error mean	t	P
Comprehension pre-test	2.38	32	1.16	.20	−5.53	< .001
Comprehension post-test	3.47	32	.67	.12		

Table 3. Descriptive results in communicative skills

	Mean	N	Std. deviation	Std. error mean	t	p
Communication Skills pre-test	2.28	32	1.28	.23	−3.12	.004
Communication Skills post-test	3.09	32	.818	.14		

Table 4. Descriptive results in skills of meaning

	Mean	N	Std. deviation	Std. error mean	t	P
Skills of meaning pre-test	3.31	32	1.51	.27	−4.38	< .001
Skills of meaning post-test	4.66	32	1.00	.18		

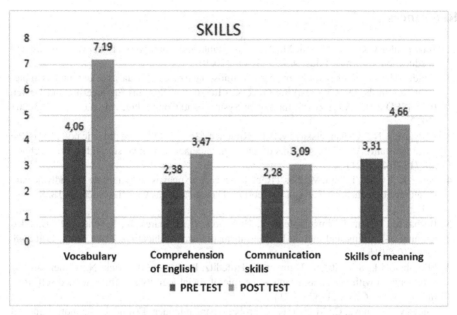

Fig. 1. Graphic representation of the comparison among pre, and post-test values

4 Conclusions

This article reports an investigation aiming to analyze the impact of a technological intervention protocol to improve the teaching-learning process of English as second language. It is important to highlight that in Latin America, and, especially in Ecuador, country where this study was conducted, it is necessary to develop resources that help to improve the performance in English as a second language in our students, since this knowledge, is one of the weakest one at the local educational process.

In the presented technological intervention, "Alexa" virtual assistant was used, it allowed an interaction between students and the proposed process, creating like this, an enjoyable learning environment, contributing to the acquisition of skills in English language, which is complex to work with, in a South American country, such as Ecuador, where English language is an artificial skill, and not motivating for students belonging to the public educational system.

Differences found between pre and post-test values, highlight the benefits offered when using this type of technological strategies, contributing the teaching-learning process. These innovator practices generate a challenge into the educational process, because is necessary to change from the traditional schooling to the new ways of teaching, using technology, and all the innovator tools, and resources that are currently offered.

The research team plans, as future investigation, to contribute to other skills when learning English as second language, as well as, to create more activities that can benefit to the greatest number of students belonging to Latin American countries.

References

1. Terzopoulos y, G., Satratzemi, M.: Voice assistants and smart speakers in everyday life and in education. Informat. Educ. **9**(3), 473–490 (2020)
2. Cóndor- Herrera, O., Jadán-Guerrero y, J., Ramos-Galarza, C. «Virtual assistants and its implementation in the teaching-learning process.,» In: Human Systems Engineering and Design III. IHSED 2020. Advances in Intelligent Systems and Computing, vol. 1269, pp. 203–208 (2020)
3. Al-Kaisi, A.N., Arkhangelskaya y, A.L., Rudenco-Morgun, O.I.: The didactic potential of the voice assistant "Alice" for students of a foreign language at a university, Educ. Inf. Technol. **26**, 715–732 (2021)
4. Pérez de A y, M., Tellera, M.: Las TIC en la educación: nuevos ambientes de aprendizaje para la interacción educative. Revista de Teoría y Didáctica de las Ciencias Sociales **18**, 83–112 (2012)
5. Borba, M., Askar, P., Engelbrecht, J., Gadanidis, G., Llinares, S., Sánchez, M.: Blended learning, e-learning and mobile learning in mathematics education. ZDM Math. Educ. **48**, 589–610 (2016)
6. Mirbabaie, M., Stieglitz, S., Brunker, F., Hofeditz, L., Ross y, B., Frick, N.: Understanding collaboration with virtual assistants – the role of social identity and the extended self. Bus. Inf. Syst. Eng. **63**(1), 21–37 (2021)
7. Anaya y, A., Anaya, C.: Motivar para aprobar o para aprender? Estrategias de motivación del aprednizaje para los estudiantes. Tecnol. Ciencia Educ. **25**(1), 5–14 (2010)
8. Cóndor -Herrera, O., Ramos-Galarza, C.: The impact of a technological intervention program on learning mathematical skills. Educ. Inf. Technol. **26**, 1423–1433 (2020)
9. Corbett, C., et al.: Virtual home assistant use and perceptions of usefulness by older adults and support person dyads. Int. J. Environ. Res. Public Health **18**(3), 1–13 (2021)
10. Drydakis, N.: Mobile applications aiming to facilitate immigrants' societal integration and overall level of integration, health and mental health. Does artificial intelligence enhance outcomes? Comput. Hum. Behav. **117,** 106661 (2021)
11. Ckaka y C., Nkhobo, T.: The use of a virtual personal assistant (FENNChat) as a platform for providing automated responses to ODL students' queries at UNISA. In: 13th International Conference on Interactive Mobile Communication, Technologies and Learning (IMCL 2019), vol. 1192, pp. 289–296 (2021)
12. Cambridge: Cambridge Assessment. [En línea]. https://www.cambridgeenglish.org/es/exams-and-tests/cefr/. Último Acceso: 29 Jan 2021

Implementation of Virtual Learning Objects in the Development of Mathematical Skills: A Qualitative Analysis from the Student Experience

Omar Cóndor-Herrera[1] , Carlos Ramos-Galarza[1,2]([⊠]) ,
and Pamela Acosta-Rodas[2]

[1] Centro de Investigación en Mecatrónica y Sistemas Interactivos MIST/Maestría en Educación Mención Innovación y Liderazgo Educativo/Carrera de Psicología, Universidad Tecnológica Indoamérica, Av. Machala y Sabanilla, Quito, Ecuador
{omarcondor,carlosramos}@uti.edu.ec
[2] Facultad de Psicología, Pontificia Universidad Católica del Ecuador, Av. 12 de Octubre y Roca, Quito, Ecuador
{caramos,mpacosta}@puce.edu.ec

Abstract. This article reports a research of a qualitative methodology that analyzed narratives of students aged between 10 and 14 years old, who received a learning technological program based on Virtual Learning Objects. As results, it was found that the program applied propitiate significant willingness, happiness, motivation, and innovation towards learning mathematics. There is discussed about the need of the implementation of this methodology in benefit of learning mathematics.

Keywords: Virtual learning objects · VLOs · Mathematics · Qualitative research · Education

1 Introduction

Virtual Learning Objects, from now on VLOs, are a series of technological elements that allow to accomplish the teaching-learning process, through the proposal of a dynamic, and motivating context for students [1]. The application of this didactical methodology seeks to overcome limitations of traditional education, it proposes to students a real learning environment, which is according to the current technological advances, taking advantage of motivation, attention and interest that the technological usage generates in students, as a support to transit towards a teaching model that allow to take advantage of the possibilities that technology offers, as [2].

This new teaching practices are built cyclically in the interaction between teachers-students, students-teachers, and student-student, since in individual and group experiences that every participant had with technology, it was possible to find an adequate technological tool, which allowed building learning environments according to nowadays student's needs.

© Springer Nature Switzerland AG 2021
C. Stephanidis et al. (Eds.): HCII 2021, CCIS 1421, pp. 17–30, 2021.
https://doi.org/10.1007/978-3-030-78645-8_3

Like this, the adequate application of technological resources makes possible to bring traditional education towards a technological digital environment, at the same time, it generates the conditions to go beyond the physical barrier that traditional classrooms offer, to a broader space for the acquisition, and assimilation of knowledge in environments out of classrooms [3].

However, changes in educational practice require a general change in every school aspect, among those, the methodology will be analyzed. From this break of the conventional space, where the classroom is the only environment that allows the development of a teaching-learning process, it is proposed a teaching methodology that will allow to potentiate the benefits of the technological usage, such as the flipped classroom methodology, that allow students to generate from home the acquisition and assimilation processes of theoretical and practical knowledge, which are complemented with analytic, and feedback processes in class, focusing on the analysis or doubts, and questions that students can have about the topic under study [4].

From above, this article presents to the reader a qualitative analysis about the data collected from a technological group intervention, which worked on a specific topic through the implementation of virtual learning objects (VLOs) into the teaching process, at the same time, there was a control group, that studied the same topic proposed for the intervention group, but this last one worked in the traditional classroom. Following, a revision of essential concepts of this research are presented, after this, the qualitative results found once the study ended, are detailed.

1.1 VLOs Conceptualization

The 2.0 web gives place to the emergence of uncountable digital and multimedia resources such as videos, educative softwares, educative games, learning gamification, among others, which are used in the educative teaching process as supporting material, since it is possible to count in the web with diverse, and varied resources that allow even to assemble resources among them with a learning objective, emerging like this, the conceptualization of VLO. One of the main characteristics of a VLO is the possibility to add resources to its structure, just as it happens when using LEGOS blocks, in the same way it is possible to assemble the VLOs differently, inserting with the aid of specialized softwares normalized learning blocks in their structures as a puzzle, which can be used in many educative processes [1].

[5, 6] points out that a VLO can be defined as the union of digital resources such as videos, activities on-line, images, diagrams, among others, with an educative objective, which allows the students to work in determined topic autonomously, because of its structure.

1.2 VLOs Characteristics

[1, 7, 8] highlight aspects such as flexibility, personalization, modularity, durability, reutilization, and adaptability, as characteristics of a VLO. For example, a VLO can be used in a variety of scenarios because of its flexibility, since it can be updated easily, managing its content, and with the aid of metadata that makes possible to find it.

The personalization of a VLO allows that its content structure, and modularity to adequate to different needs presented by students, as it was already mentioned, to count with diverse and free web access resources, it is possible to adapt a content to a determined group of students, as well as to different levels, such as higher or lower one [7]. For example, if a study topic is extensive, it is possible to design the VLO modulated and in sequences, facilitating students' assimilation and learning [9].

Adaptability is the characteristic that allows a VLO to be attached as an autonomous component, according to contextual information about the students' learning rhythm, as well as designing VLOs adapted to the students' different learning styles, as it has been affirmed in several articles [10]. This characteristic also makes reference to a platform where can be used, since these can be inserted in a virtual learning environment VLE, or directly might be used from a computer or a mobile device.

According to a VLO's time of utility, it may be pointed that its durability is extensive, while those resources with ones the VLOs were built still in the network, and can be reused unlimitedly, and, in the case that a resource is not available, it can be replaced with a new resource or activity for the VLO, which extends even more its durability [8].

1.3 Virtual Learning Environments Adapted with VLOs for Teaching Mathematics

The design of learning environments is a field that is being currently investigated on a larger scale, because of it, teachers are becoming aware that the quality of a learning environment is highly important, since it affects directly students' satisfaction and learning [11].

As it has been highlighted previously, emerging teaching-learning methodologies, such as the flipped classroom, which uses technological resources, allows students going through their learning process on virtual environments (VLE), which implies the use of technology to burst on the traditional educative activities, improving the educative process [12].

In this context, the usage of VLO as part of a VLE, allows teachers to present dynamically the contents to students, it explains the interest of investigating the impact of using this type of technologies in the teaching-learning process of numerical skills, analyzing the best usage of computers, softwares and communicational technology in teaching and learning this science [13]; since the VLO is considered as a technological resource, and its adaptation to students' personality, learning style, and rhythm, it allows the interaction of individuals and the VLOs, being more dynamic, obtaining the students' interest, influencing in their motivation, thus, it makes possible to improve their learning experience, because it encourages different dynamics, and heuristic processes, which are useful for students' logical, and constructivist formation [14].

1.4 VLOs and m-Learning

The advance of wireless technologies, the development of applications, and educative resources for mobile devices have experimented an exponential increase, it explains why, for many teachers, mobile learning is a strategic topic in current education [15].

As it was described above, one of the VLOs characteristics is its adaptability, which allows to insert easily within its modular structure, resources, applications, educative games, and another technological resources, that can be used in mobile devices, and, in this manner, using resources that technology offers in educative processes [16], which can be exploited and improve students' interaction from their mobile devices, that in the case of this research, made possible to interact in the conceptualization of topics belonging to mathematics area, and the resolution of applied problems, obtaining an increased autonomy to manage their own learning rhythm [17].

Regarding to the accessibility to a VLO, it is important to mention that its functionality is not limited to computers, since it is possible to be accessed from mobile devices by students, who currently count at least with a smartphone or a tablet.

1.5 VLOs and Gamification

Learning through games is a teaching manner that bases on constructivist and contextual learning theories, which identify dynamic and interrelated interactions between mind, and environment, to promote the active knowledge acquisition process [18]. At the beginning, gamification was used with board games, although nowadays these games are digital, and the activities that a VLO proposes are in app lications, softwares, serious games, among others. Besides the multimedia resources presented, research highlight that student's exposure to multimedia resources, and interactive videogames, promote higher motivated and positive learning environments, also these improve students' participation in math, and allow to expand their significant learning [19, 20].

1.6 Benefits of a VLO in Learning

Within the benefits that VLOs offer, is the possibility to access learning in an environment that overcomes the physical barriers of a classroom, which extends to a digital environment, implying to consider an environment outside classroom, such as home or any other determined place, which benefits students when working autonomously and in their own learning rhythm, since the VLO is reusable, it allows students to go over again its contents until accomplishing the adequate assimilation of a specific topic, this resource responds to a methodology that can be used in a wide range of methods, allowing students to learn reflexively [21].

Previous investigation about the implementation of VLO, as the research conducted by Lizcando [22], evidence a general improvement after the implementation of the VLO, comparing the pre and post -tests measurements, that can be explained considering that the game consisted in evoking mathematical concepts and repeating them. At the same time, as the VLO counts with the resources already mentioned, plus current students characteristics, it is important to motivate students to learn different to the traditional way, although, to obtain higher benefits, once the VLOs are implemented, it is important to consider students perspectives and their feedback about the experience of learning with VLO, which serves to improve planification errors, design, development, and elements if necessary [23].

2 Methodology

2.1 Research Problem

From the context described, it merges as interest for the research team to analyze the impact of the application of VLOs in learning process, in areas demanding innovation processes to improve their academic performance, such as mathematics. As a contribution to this line of research, it is proposed as problem of investigation to analyze in this study, how is the user experience learning mathematics using VLOs. Trying to answer this question, following, it is reported a study of qualitative methodology that identified the students' subjective construction based on learning through VLOs.

2.2 Participants

Sample was composed by 34 males and 20 females, aged between 10 and 14 years old (Mage $= 11.11$, SD $= .79$). Participants were divided into two groups: the first group, had some mathematics classes based on VLOs, and the second group had mathematics classes traditionally. Exogenous variables such as gender, socioeconomic status, age, and academic level, were controlled in both groups. The group that learnt mathematics through VLOs, was composed by 26 students with an average age of 11.07 years old (SD $= .84$), and the group of learning mathematics traditionally was composed by 28 students with an average age of 11.14 years old (SD $= .76$).

2.3 Data Collection Techniques

In-depth interviews were applied, questions asked valued aspects related to students' like or dislike of the class based on VLOs technology, difficulties or improvements when this methodology was applied in learning process, perceived differences between the traditional class and the one based on technology, perception of joy, and many other aspects that allowed to deepen on students' experience about the type of learning proposed in this research. Another element used for registering the information was the field bitacora, aiming to incorporate the observations, as well as the notes obtained throughout the field study.

2.4 Data Analysis Plan

For the analysis of the linguistic content, open codification technique was used, which allow to identify different categories that emerged from participants' speeches about learning mathematics based on VLOs, as well as learning in the traditional way [24].

2.5 Procedure

Once the investigation was approved by the Ethical Committee and authorities of the institution where this study was conducted, teaching mathematics based on VLOs and traditional education began. Once this process concluded, the next step was to conduct the in-depth interviews with both groups, as well as the qualitative phase reported in this paper.

This study followed with every ethical standard for research with human beings declared in Helsinki and Nuremberg in 1964 [25]. An informed consent, about volunteer participation was signed by legal representatives of the students participating in this study, before beginning with the intervention, every obtained data was managed with absolute confidentiality, students and representatives (parents) were informed about the purpose of this study, as well as their right to withdrawn from the study at any moment, without any penalty [26].

2.6 Results

Applying the procedure of open codification, constant comparison and its respective association between participants' narratives allowed to identify the categories that built a substantive description of the resultant phenomenon about the application of the VLOs to learn mathematics, which are presented as follows: innovator learning environment, adaptation to a new learning methodology, learning joy, willingness to learn, and expectations about education; linguistic analysis will focus on these.

Innovator Learning Environment. The first session with students of the group intervention with VLOs was essential for this research, since in this session there was visualized the first significant break in the students teaching learning process in relationship with the traditional learning environment.

At the beginning of the intervention for the group of learning with VLOs, it was mentioned to participants that the working sessions were going to take place on the computer's laboratory, which created expectation about what was going to happen in the next mathematics class. Once in the lab, the teacher presented general directions, and for the first time the VLOs and their content elements were presented (Fig. 1).

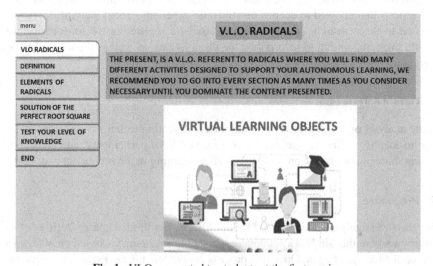

Fig. 1. VLOs presented to students at the first session

Immediately, it was possible to observe the students' expectations, a group of them started to express their first positive impressions about VLOs.

– *What is it teacher? It looks so cool, looks like a game, we are not going to work with books, I do want to play with it, teacher. (10 years old, male student).*

In this first interaction of students with the VLOs, it was observed a first breaking point in relation to the students' learning environment, since it has been introduced to the educative process a technological innovator resource, which takes its attention from the application beginning. Subsequently, the definition of the VLO was explained, as well as its function in their learning process, is in this point where students started a process of questioning about the learning process they knew, showing surprise facing the dilemma that using books is not the only method through which a class would be developed, and, when it was explained the VLO's functionality and pointed that this resource could be used from a computer or even from their mobile autonomously.

This type of education brought to students a new learning environment, which has the characteristic of a virtual environment, which goes beyond the physical classroom space, and naturally, since, nowadays, technology is immerse in every human activity.

Adaptation to a New Learning Methodology. Even though, these technological resources offer a significant benefit in the teaching-learning process, it is necessary to understand that these resources are the means, but not the process itself, it explains why it is indispensable that these resources go along with learning methodologies mediated by technology, taking into account that this generation has been exposed to technology devices from early stages of life, it has allowed them to develop abilities in the management of technological resources.

At the end of the intervention, it was asked to the group of students if they have had worked any time with the VLOs, or if working with them was difficult, students answered as following:

– *We have never worked with this material, but it is easy for me to work with these objects (…). (12 years old, male student).*

As it was analyzed previously, even when students used VLOs for first time, it is easy for the students to interact with those, and, overall, it generates interest in students to work with those, improving like this, their motivation and interest, that was observed in students during the intervention.

– *I liked to work with the VLOs, because we are able to go over and over again the content (…), (12 years old, male student)*
– *also, we are able to learn having fun and joy (…). (11 years old, male student).*

From the answers obtained in this category, it is possible to identify two aspects that explains that this methodology, based in learning through VLOs, generates students' interest and motivation, the first one relates to the characteristics of reusing the VLO, which makes possible for the student to work on the VLOs content the times that consider necessary until understand the content presented, and in his/her own rhythm.

In the first approach to VLOs, students made activities of concept internalization through a video-quiz, allowing to watch an explanation about a specific topic, meanwhile it is observed by students, there are pauses in the video, where the student must answer some questions about the explanations already made. If he/she chooses a wrong answer, this resource offers instant feedback, which allows the student to realize about the mistake made and to correct the answer (Fig. 2).

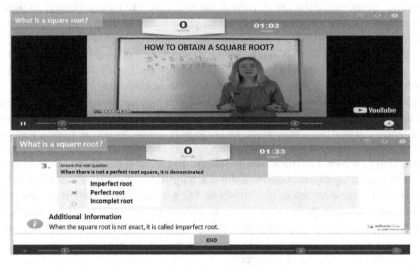

Fig. 2. VLOs video-quiz

Following statements were obtained from the interaction between the teacher -researcher- and students, where are highlighted students' perceptions about the characteristics of the VLOs.

- *Teacher: ¿Which are the differences do you find between traditional classes, in comparison with those that we have worked lately?*
- *Student 1: we are able to work with technology, its like we are playing.*
- *Student 2: that we can go back to the topics already reviewed, and make again the exercises, the video quiz allowed us to go more than once over the content.*
- *Student 3: that in the video, it was possible to watch a little piece and then a question popped up, if the answer was wrong, the right answer came up, and it gives you feedback about what you did wrong.*

The second aspect makes reference to students' motivation generated through technological games designed with an educative aim, allowing them to learn in a funny and joyful way.

Joyful Learning. The mathematical class based on technology began with a high expectative, students were counting down the minutes until the class started, also were willing to work again with the VLOs. The experience with the resources incorporated in the VLO resulted very pleasant for students, in the new working session with the VLO, activities aiming to measure the comprehension of the topic, and designed through the tool Quizizz, were presented.

To use this resource, it was designed a competition dynamic at the class, it consisted in diving students into three different groups, challenging each other by solving individually a Quizizz assigned, looking for one winner by group. Finally, winners of each group were challenged again, solving a new Quizizz individually, looking for a final winner, such as a mathematical virtual championship (Fig. 3).

Fig. 3. Quizizz about radicals applied to students.

This activity was not proposed to students as an evaluation, but based on gamification, a championship between students was developed, it allowed them to enjoy the activity freely, without the pressure that an evaluation brings. Instead, in the development of this activity, students were happy and dynamic, while winner students were competing, the others, autonomously started to cheer up their classmates with claps, cheers, etc. At the end of the activity, it was projected the name of the student that obtained the first place to the whole class, everybody answered it with claps and congratulations to the champion effusively (Fig. 4).

Even when the activity was not planned as evaluation for students, for the researcher had this objective, since the tool incorporated in the VLO registered right and wrong answers by every student, which allowed to conduct an evaluation different to the traditional one.

In the next statements, a dialogue between researcher and students is presented, where narratives allowed to identify students' joy and happiness while learning.

– *Teacher: ¿Which task would you like the most, to solve a video-quiz in a VLO, or to solve a normal task -pencil, paper-?*
– *Student 1: Video-quiz, because there, while we are playing, we are learning, it is faster and fun.*

Fig. 4. Recognition to the champion by classmates through clapping effusively.

- *Student 2: Also, we can repeat if we get an answer wrong.*
- *Teacher: ¿Which class is better for you in terms of joy and fun, the class that we usually have, or the one that we had using VLOs?*
- *Student 1: The class that we had in the computer's laboratory.*
- *Student 2: Yes, because we were learning while we were playing, also we were able to compete, please teacher, ¿can you do that activity for us again?*

"Please teacher, ¿can you do that activity for us again? (…)", expressed a student during the in-depth interview, which leaded us to analyze that besides the fun and dynamism evidenced in the students along the development of this intervention, a factor of vital importance for educative objectives arose, since the teaching-learning process mediated by technological resources generated a significant willingness to learn in the group, following, this factor is analyzed.

Willingness to Learn. As it has been mentioned throughout this work, with the application of this technological resource, it was generated an increased level of motivation in students, since it allowed them to learn while were having fun, and their willingness to learn improved significantly. It is important to mention that mathematical activities are not pleasant for every student, because of the complexity that it represents most of the time, although, when questioning the students about their desire of continue working with VLOs at school or even from home, and how much time they would spend at home working with VLOs, they answered as next:

- *I would love to continue working with VLOs (…), well, I would work between two to three hours at home, because it is entertained and fun (…).*
- *In my case, 4 h.*

With the aim of improving VLOs about different topics, it was asked to students, what type of activities or resources they would like future VLOs to have. The answers are presented next, without a specific order:

- *Student 1: More games*
- *Student 2: More activities*
- *Student 3: More of those videos that pauses and pops up questions (video-quiz)*
- *Student 4: Some riddles can be added*
- *Student 5: More video-quiz*

Expectations About Education. The group of students that did not have the intervention classes with VLOs, also made an interview about their abilities of working with technological resources, and, to their criteria, which activities they would like to be included in classes to make those more dynamic and enjoyable, they answered as following.

- *There can be included drawings, technology, games, internet, team works, playing games in the mobile device, or in computers (…)*
- *I do know how to use a computer (…)*
- *It is easy to use a computer and mobile phone (…)*

From our experience, it is very easy for students to work on technological devices such as computers, smartphones, tablets, web sites, etc. Similar, when are using resources that are new for them, such as applications, software's, etc., it is important to highlight that the adaptation to these resources is usually fast.

Finally, it was proposed to the students from the group that received the traditional class, the possibility to work on the computers' laboratory, using technology, the answer was favorable y they were excited about the proposal. Following, there is showed a final fragment from the dialogue obtained at the end of the interview.

- *Teacher: ¿if you could have the class in the computers' laboratory, with the computers and internet, would you like it?*
- *Student 1: Yes*
- *Student 2: Of course, we would love that (…)*

3   Conclusions

In this article it was reported a study that identified subjective narratives about learning mathematics through a technological innovation program based on VLOs. The methodology applied for this investigation was qualitative and it was found that the usage of technology contributes significantly in aspects as motivation, willingness, and emotion, which are involved when learning mathematical skills.

One of the arguments that cont ributes explaining the relationship to the results found in this investigation, is about the management of the class that is done in favor of learning mathematics, since, it has been reported that a teacher who is interested in students' behavior and learning, is a factor that influences positively in the students' mathematical performance, as it was possible to observe in this investigation, since students that received this new method of teaching-learning mathematics based on VLOs technology, improved their levels of motivation, and initiative to learn [27].

Another aspect in favor of the results of this study, which is also taken as a significant contribution in the learning process, makes reference about the implementation of technological resources as VLOs that allow, not just to improve students' behavior, but allows to transform the learning environment, and to move it from a traditional physical space (classroom), towards a digital one, where the teaching-learning process is mediated by the usage of technology [28, 29].

It was evidenced also, that the interactions with VLOs allows students to enjoy their teaching-learning process, being more dynamic, which at the same time, improves students' motivation and willingness to learn. In this point, it is important to mention that, the fact that the student learns in an enjoyable way has a positive impact, and it is a revolutionary change in the educative process, since, in general, learning mathematics involves higher anxiety levels, these negatively influence the student behavior towards learning, obtaining unsatisfactory results [30]. Instead, in this research, for the group of students that had classes based on VLOs, it was possible to observe joy and happiness while learning, decreasing, like this, anxiety levels.

It is important to highlight that the resources utilized, even when these are helpful to improve the teaching-learning process, these are the means, but not the process itself to transform the educative process, to this to occur, it must go hand to hand with a teaching methodology, that based on its functionality and its adequate management, allow to explode to the maximum, the possibilities that technology offers.

Finally, as future investigation, the research team plans to implement the usage of VLOs in different areas, and in the different levels of mathematics formation, applying quantitative methodologies that allow to measure the differences between pre- and post-technological intervention in favor of learning.

References

1. Callejas, M., Hernández, E., Pinzón, J.: Learning objects, a state of the art. Entramado **7**(1), 176–189 (2011). https://www.redalyc.org/pdf/2654/265420116011.pdf
2. Karabatak, S., Polat, H.: The effects of the flipped classroom model designed according to the ARCS motivation strategies on the students' motivation and academic achievement levels. Educ. Inf. Technol. **25**(3), 1475–1495 (2019). https://doi.org/10.1007/s10639-019-09985-1
3. Kokko, A.K., Hirsto, L.: From physical spaces to learning environments: processes in which physical spaces are transformed into learning environments. Learn. Environ. Res. **24**(1), 71–85 (2020). https://doi.org/10.1007/s10984-020-09315-0
4. Zownorega, S.: Effectiveness of flipping the classroom in a honors level, mechanics-based physics class. Unpublished Master's thesis, Eastern Illinois University (2013). https://thekeep.eiu.edu/theses/1155
5. Cóndor, O.: Virtual learning objects in the mathematical educational process of elementary school students. Master's thesis, Universidad Tecnológica Indoamérica (2020). http://repositorio.uti.edu.ec//handle/123456789/1520
6. Cóndor-Herrera, O., Jadán-Guerrero, J., Ramos-Galarza, C.: Virtual learning objects' of math educative process. In: Karwowski, W., Ahram, T., Etinger, D., Tanković, N., Taiar, R. (eds.) IHSED 2020. AISC, vol. 1269, pp. 192–197. Springer, Cham (2021). https://doi.org/10.1007/978-3-030-58282-1_31
7. Logmire, W.: A primer on learning objects (2000). http://files.kennison.name/learning/learning-object-design.pdf

8. Latorre, C.: Design of NTIC-Based Educational Environments (2008). https://es.calameo. com/read/0006789930e290c3165b5
9. Morales, M., Luz, Y., Ariza, L.: Guide for the design of virtual learning objects (OVA). Application to the process. Rev. Cient. Gen. José María Córdova **14**, 127–147. https://www. redalyc.org/pdf/4762/476255360008.pdf
10. Mosquera, D., Guevara, C., Aguilar, J.: Adaptive learning objects in the context of eco-connectivist communities using learning analytics. Heliyon **5**(11), e02722 (2019). https:// doi.org/10.1016/j.heliyon.2019.e02722
11. Casanova, D., Huet, I., Garcia, F., Pessoa, T.: Role of technology in the design of learning environments. Learn. Environ. Res. **23**(3), 413–427 (2020). https://doi.org/10.1007/s10984-020-09314-1
12. Adefila, A., Opie, S., Bluteau, P.: Students' engagement and learning experiences using virtual patient simulation in a computer supported collaborative learning environment. Innov. Educ. Teach. Int. **57**(1), 50–61 (2020). https://doi.org/10.1080/14703297.2018.1541188
13. Sokolowski, A., Li, Y., Willson, V.: The effects of using exploratory computerized environments in grades 1 to 8 mathematics: a meta-analysis of research. Int. J. STEM Educ. **2**(1), 1–17 (2015). https://doi.org/10.1186/s40594-015-0022-z
14. Kerimbayev, N.: Virtual learning: possibilities and realization. Educ. Inf. Technol. **21**(6), 1521–1533 (2015). https://doi.org/10.1007/s10639-015-9397-1
15. Mohamed, A., Blázquez, J.: What is the future of mobile learning in education? Univ. Knowl. Soc. J. **1**(11), 142–151 (2014). https://doi.org/10.7238/rusc.v11i1.2033
16. Donnelly, D., Linn, M., Ludvigsen, S.: Impacts and characteristics of computer-based science inquiry learning environments for precollege students. Rev. Educ. Res. **84**(4), 572–608 (2014). https://doi.org/10.3102/0034654314546954
17. Arango, J., Gaviria, D., Valencia, A.: Differential calculus teaching through virtual learning objects in the field of management sciences. Procedia Soc. Behav. Sci. **176**, 412–418 (2015). https://doi.org/10.1016/j.sbspro.2015.01.490
18. Kim, S.J., Bacos, C.: Wearable stories for children: embodied learning through pretend and physical play. Interact. Learn. Environ. 1–13 (2020). https://doi.org/10.1080/10494820.2020. 1764979
19. Chipangura, A., Aldridge, J.: Impact of multimedia on students' perceptions of the learning environment in mathematics classrooms. Learn. Environ. Res. **20**(1), 121–138 (2016). https:// doi.org/10.1007/s10984-016-9224-7
20. Engerman, J.A., Carr-Chellman, A.A., MacAllan, M.: Understanding learning in video games: a phenomenological approach to unpacking boy cultures in virtual worlds. Educ. Inf. Technol. **24**(6), 3311–3327 (2019). https://doi.org/10.1007/s10639-019-09930-2
21. Goedhart, N.S., Blignaut-van Westrhenen, N., Moser, C., Zweekhorst, M.B.M.: The flipped classroom: supporting a diverse group of students in their learning. Learn. Environ. Res. **22**(2), 297–310 (2019). https://doi.org/10.1007/s10984-019-09281-2
22. Lizcano, A.: Prototipo de objeto virtual de aprendizaje para la ejercitación en matemáticas de primer grado de. Revista Colombiana de Educación (58), 96–115 (2010). https://www.red alyc.org/pdf/4136/413635664005.pdf
23. Bisol, C., Valentini, C., Karen, R.: Teacher education for inclusion: can a virtual learning object help? Comput. Educ. **85**, 203–210 (2015). https://doi.org/10.1016/j.compedu.2015. 02.017
24. Ramos-Galarza, C.: El abandono de la estadística en la psicología de Ecuador. Revista Chilena de Neuro-psiquiatría **55**(2), 135–137 (2017). https://www.redalyc.org/pdf/3315/331552284 008.pdf
25. Manzini, J.: Declaración De Helsinki: Principios Éticos Para La Investigación Médica Sobre Sujetos Humanos. Acta bioethica **6**(2), 321–334 (2000)

26. Nathanson, V.: Revising the declaration of Helsinki. BMJ **346**, 1–2 (2013)
27. Ahmad, A., Eka, S.: Clasroom management in mathematics class: university student's perception. Talent Development y Excellence **12**(1), 429–442 (2020). http://sersc.org/journals/index.php/IJAST/article/view/9782
28. Cóndor-Herrera, O., Ramos-Galarza, C.: The impact of a technological intervention program on learning mathematical skills. Educ. Inf. Technol. **26**(2), 1423–1433 (2020). https://doi.org/10.1007/s10639-020-10308-y
29. Cóndor-Herrera, O., Oña-Simbaña, J., Bonilla-Guachamin, J., Llumiquinga-Simbaña, M., Ramos-Galarza, C.: Innovaciones educativas del nuevo milenio (2020). Quito. http://repositorio.uti.edu.ec//handle/123456789/1685
30. Ramos-Galarza, C.: Introducción a la investigación, entre anecdotas musicales y científicas. Universidad Internacional SEK, Quito (2017)

A Chatbot that Uses a Multi-agent Organization to Support Collaborative Learning

Mateus da Silveira Colissi[1]([✉])[ID], Renata Vieira[2][ID], Viviana Mascardi[3][ID], and Rafael H. Bordini[1][ID]

[1] School of Technology, Pontifical Catholic University of Rio Grande do Sul, Av. Ipiranga, 6681, Porto Alegre, RS, Brazil
`Mateus.Colissi@edu.pucrs.br`, `rafael.bordini@pucrs.br`
[2] CIDEHUS, University of Évora, Palácio do Vimioso Largo do Marquês de Marialva, no. 8, Évora, Portugal
`renatav@uevora.pt`
[3] Department of Informatics, Engineering, Robotics and Systems Engineering, University of Genova, Via Dodecaneso, 35, 16146 Genova, GE, Italy
`Viviana.mascardi@unige.it`

Abstract. This work investigates and apply the use of a multi-agent system to assist in the coordination of group tasks, specifically in educational environments, in which the interaction occurs indirectly, that is, asynchronously. The system has a web interface integrated with a chatbot for more natural interaction. The chatbot communicates with the multi-agent system that is responsible for the organization of the group, that is, it contains information about the tasks and members of the groups, in addition to restrictions that can be imposed according to the organization of the group, and it is also able to return the requested information in natural language through the chatbot. This approach was validated in a practical undergraduate course of software engineering. The students assessed the functionalities and usability of the system while working in groups in order to develop software collaboratively. Our system was used to assist students in a real project. With this assessment, it was found that the system was able to support the development of the group tasks, ensuring quick and consistent responses to the student's request.

Keywords: Multi-agent system · JaCaMo · Chatbot · Dialogflow · Group coordination

1 Introduction

Institutions use different types of learning methods, such as classroom learning and virtual learning. However with different learning methods, we need different learning approaches. To assist these learning methods, several techniques and tools are being used in virtual environments, such as: chats, conversational agents

© Springer Nature Switzerland AG 2021
C. Stephanidis et al. (Eds.): HCII 2021, CCIS 1421, pp. 31–38, 2021.
https://doi.org/10.1007/978-3-030-78645-8_4

and others. With the use of virtual learning environments, concerns arise for example regarding collaboration between people in learning techniques such as groupwork.

According to King [11], collaborative learning may motivate studies more than individual study, so in educational environments it is important to promote collaborative learning to enable group participation and interaction in various tasks, where knowledge is built through dialogues that enable the sharing of ideas and information within the group [12]. Also, it can provide important feedback for the teacher to know how were the interactions and discussions made by the group, as well as the individual contribution of students in problem solving [1].

However, there are various causes of inefficiencies in groupwork such as poor capacity balance, incorrect team dynamics, poor communication or difficult social situations [2]. Solving these inefficiencies for virtual teams would help improve the relationship of team members in their online learning environment, allowing them to complete tasks daily, improving collaboration, productivity, and task tracking.

One way to support the management of group learning is to create environments that facilitate knowledge sharing and other valuable learning attitudes, helping to promote student discussion and interaction skills [7]. With the advancement of Artificial Intelligence (AI), there is growing use of conversational agents such as chatbots to aid learning. However, most of the work in this area are for individual learning.

In a functional group, each member is responsible for one or more tasks. One of the main requirements for group work to perform well is that its members operate in harmony. Contributing toward solutions for the problem of groupwork coordination, this work aims mainly to: improve information sharing among group members; increase group productivity; improve overall performance in collaborative tasks; and to allow the person responsible for the groups to be aware of noteworthy events during the performance of the tasks.

This work explores the use of virtual assistants in a collaborative environment, where agents represent their users as part of a groupwork project, and they also assist in the organization and communication between users. The communication is done through the chatbot and not directly. This multi-agent system has the main objective of facilitating the dissemination of information about the current status of the project and allowing the person in charge of the group to monitor performance during the execution of tasks without disturbing the individual members. In particular, the focus is on academic environments, where it is very important that the group members as well as the lecturers are aware of how the project is evolving.

2   Related Work

Islam et al. [10] proposed a browser-based client interface approach with Express and SocketIO framework, Node.js, Jade and AngularJS, that can be accessed using only a web browser available on PCs, tablets, laptops, or mobile devices.

The teacher uploads the lecture to the site for students to study/solve by collaborating in pairs. Collaborative peer activities were proposed where students collaborated synchronously or asynchronously in conjunction with the teacher's lecture.

Tegos and Demetriadis [14] proposed a prototype dialogue support system, acting as an instant messaging application, in order to accomplish one or more learning tasks in an online activity, with a conversation agent that uses text-to-speech to read its interventions, offering academically productive talk (APT). To encourage collaboration, the agent introduces concepts into the group discussion displaying outside the main chat frame using the Levenshtein-based string similarity algorithm and a WordNet lexicon for synonyms to calculate a proximity score for each identified concept.

Paikari et al. [13] proposed a chatbot called Sayme to address the detection and resolution of possible code conflicts that may arise in the development of parallel software. Sayme is implemented using Python, MySQL, and Google Cloud Platform. Slack is used as the chat channel to communicate with developers. In addition, the chatbot operates autonomously, initiating conversations with developers based on information collected from Git. Sayme also monitors when developers save files using Git commands to automatically extract files that are being changed and on which lines they are being changed. To detect possible indirect conflicts between files, all files are analyzed using the Abstract Syntax Trees (AST) library.

Sayme provides information about potential direct and indirect conflicts, helping developers to resolve those conflicts. Its main function is to proactively detect possible conflicts between developers working in parallel, notifying them before the conflicts become too complex. Its secondary function is to respond to a variety of requests that help developers understand the state of work of other developers.

Unlike other approaches in the literature, our architecture allows a formal representation of the group organization through a MAS, managing multiple groups simultaneously, in which each group has different roles and tasks for members to carry out. This improves the management of knowledge related to the proposed organization in collaborative work. On the other hand, there are challenges in the use of these systems in collaborative educational environments, for example, due to the efforts required in the construction of agent organizations, in which roles and tasks must be well defined and explicitly represented within the system.

3   Our Approach

The overall architecture of the proposed system involves software development in different environments to allow better user interaction and coordination. Our system is able to receive requests in the form of questions (about the state of the organization) or actions to be performed (register new tasks, select new tasks, among others) and return a coherent answer with the user's group through plans in the JaCaMo multi-agent systems development platform [3].

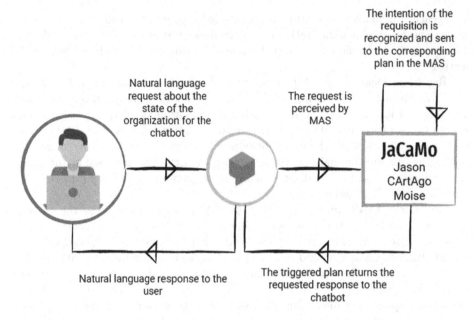

Fig. 1. Our approach

Figure 1 shows our approach. The student makes a request in natural language about the tasks they need to complete and the chatbot returns information from the MAS. The tasks that students had to achieve were related to software development, that is, front-end and back-end development tasks, among others. The following are examples of tasks to be performed: modeling the persistence layer, generating the initial physical and logical database schema, creating the POST method to receive the registration data, creating the GET endpoint in the users API, and creating the profile screen and user route management.

A website was developed to define permission levels and assist in the identification of agents in JaCaMo, in addition to allowing the leader to register/delete users and make requests to the chatbot. The website was developed using the Angular frontend framework, for the backend Firebase was used with the Real-time Database. To coordinate the groups, the JaCaMo system is able to collect information from the database to initialize the groups according to commands from the leaders. The information generated at runtime by the organization is not stored in the database, but in the JaCaMo artifact for each group. For the development of the chatbot, the Dialogflow platform was used. The next sections present the details of the architecture components mentioned above.

3.1 Chatbot

To communicate with the JaCaMo MAS, *intents* were created in Dialogflow for each question to be answered about the group's organization and for each action to be performed. To organize requests made by users, intents were trained using parameters. The phrases were trained with a parameter name (*@name*) for queries of the type "name_last-name_discipline_role Question". The *@name* parameter was created to identify the agent in MAS and is managed by an entity that recognizes a pattern through regular expressions.

3.2   Multi-agent System

The system was implemented on the JaCaMo platform using a Dialogflow integration developed by Engelmann et al. (available in https://github. com/DeboraEngelmann/helloworld_from_jason/wiki). The available JaCaMo-Dialogflow integration was adapted to suit the needs of our project.

JaCaMo enables the integration of three multi-agent programming dimensions: agents, organizations, and environment. A JaCaMo system consists of the following platforms: Jason [5] for agent programming, CArtAgO [4] for environment programming, and Moise [8] for programming organizations. JaCaMo integrates these three platforms for a uniform and consistent programming model, with the goal of simplifying the combination of these dimensions when programming MAS [3].

Organizations can be used to ensure coordination in multi-agent systems. Coordination is related to agents' social skills, where agents communicate with each other to share data, beliefs, goals, and plans [5]. With coordination, agents can achieve joint objectives and plans that otherwise would not be possible, and ensure that tasks are performed consistently and efficiently by synchronizing their actions and interactions with other agents [6,9].

In JaCaMo, agents who are members of a group play various roles, each with a set of distinct missions that must be fulfilled for the project to be completed. These roles and missions must be part of a Moise scheme, previously organized, usually before the system started. Note that such schemes must be developed according to the instructions and needs of the responsible teacher for each application.

For the development of the JaCaMo MAS, three types of agents were used:

Request coordinator is the agent who focuses on the artifact related to the requests from Dialogflow. It has plans to deal with each Dialogflow intent, that is, for each chatbot intent there is a corresponding plan. As it receives all requests from Dialogflow, it is responsible for the communication between the real user and the respective agent, that is, it forwards the information to the respective agent. It also has plans responsible for starting a leader agent at runtime, sending the necessary beliefs for that agent to start a group.

Leader is the agent that is responsible for starting a group at runtime, creating the members of the team dynamically with the information provided by the request coordinator. It has plans responsible for: initializing and defining the team's workspace, group, and initial tasks; in addition to initializing team members, it is also responsible for assigning missions and roles to these agents; and finally it is responsible for answering the questions regarding the group, that is, organizing the group's information and forwarding it to the request coordinator according to the requests.

Student is the agent that has plans to dynamically join a group and workspace as directed by the group leader. It also has plans related to the tasks to be completed for the resolution of the group project, that is, the plans are related to the situation of the tasks in relation to the Moise scheme, such as: selecting, dropping, and completing tasks. Finally, it is also able to directly answer the request coordinator's queries regarding tasks.

Table 1 shows the commands available in the system. The `command` operation has two representations in the system, one for leaders that shows: tasks [register task, remove task, list tasks, tasks not being performed and uncompleted tasks], group [group members, list due date for tasks, remove member and mark project as complete], log and members' productivity and one for students: tasks [list registered tasks, select task and list unfinished tasks], my tasks and group [group members and project status (completed or not completed)].

Table 1. System commands

Command	Description	Responsible agent
`commands`	Show the commands available in the system	Leader and student
`create group`	Initialize the group in the MAS	Leader
`tasks`	Show commands for tasks	Leader and student
`group`	Show commands for groups	Leader and student
`log`	Show the group log	Leader
`productivity`	Show group productivity	Leader
`update`	Show the last update made by the group	Leader and student
`objective`	Show the project description	Leader and student
`delivery date`	Show the due date for tasks	Leader and student
`completed project`	Mark the project as completed	Leader
`how long to deliver the task`	Show how much time is left before the delivery date	Student
`project`	Show the state of completion of the project	Student
`concluded`	Mark task as complete	Student

4   Experiment Results and Analysis

Our system was evaluated during two months of tests with students in an undergraduate course on software engineering. It was tested with two groups (two software development projects), in which the groups consisted of eighteen students and a lecturer responsible for the group. The students performed several sprints during the development of the project; with each sprint, new tasks were added to the MAS, specifically in the Moise organization, as well as corrections and improvements in the system's response.

The students' questions and answers were checked through the Dialogflow platform itself to assess whether the chatbot was able to correctly identify and trigger the desired intent. Of the 577 requests made to the chatbot, only 54 were incorrectly identified.

The MAS was able to deliver quick responses (which is necessary due to the time that Dialogflow waits for a query to be answered) and consistent with the group and its representation in the system. The exchange of messages between the agents of the system to consult information about the group was an interesting approach regarding the organization, since all information about a group was stored in one place, specifically with the group leader.

The most important reason for using MAS is the possibility to create multiple domains. In particular, if there are different people or organizations with different objectives and proprietary information, the MAS is capable of handling those interactions effectively, and possibly efficiently, e.g., when decentralised coordination is required. That is, MAS are able to model an organization's internal affairs in unified approach, avoiding the need to develop an organization that encompasses all representations of roles and tasks, but rather to develop different organizations that are accessible in a single system with its own capabilities and priorities.

5   Conclusion and Future Work

Increasingly, remote (non face-to-face) learning has been used in the education or training of people through digital resources to acquire new knowledge, to develop professionally by acquiring new skills and abilities of the most diverse types, among others. With reasonable technological support, management systems play a large role in collaborative groups and can mainly assist in online education, which is being used as an alternative to face-to-face activities to continue education amid the restrictions imposed by the pandemics of COVID-19.

In this context, online education allows people who do not have access to information in physical environments (for social reasons or for a specific situation, such as the pandemic) to easily, quickly, and dynamically use personalized and efficient knowledge from a digital platform. Although this form of learning has so many good points, it is still far from being the ideal method. There are concerns about the collaborative distance learning method, in which the main problems to be solved in this approach are: balance of skills within a group, incorrect group dynamics, lack of communication in the group and difficulty with social situations.

Our work provides initial evidence that an approach based on multi-agent systems are adequate, in particular with the JaCaMo platform, because it allows us to create and control an organization in terms of members and the management of task assignment. Communication with the user through a chatbot aims to allow a more effective and natural communication with the system. As future work, we intend to work on the chatbot's pro-activity in interaction with the group, thus making it an active member in group decision making.

Acknowledgments. This work was partially funded by the Portuguese Foundation for Science and Technology, project UIDB/00057/2020. The authors also gratefully acknowledge partial support from CAPES and CNPq.

References

1. Allaymoun, M.H., Trausan-Matu, S.: Analysis of collaboration in computer supported collaborative learning chat using rhetorical schemas. In: Proceedings of the International Conference on Information and Communication Systems, pp. 39–44 (2016)
2. Andrejczuk, E., Rodríguez-Aguilar, J.A., Roig, C., Sierra, C.: Synergistic team composition. In: Proceedings of the Conference on Autonomous Agents and Multiagent Systems, pp. 1463–1465 (2017)
3. Boissier, O., Bordini, R.H., Hübner, J.F., Ricci, A., Santi, A.: Multi-agent oriented programming with JaCaMo. Sci. Comput. Program. **78**, 747–761 (2013)
4. El Fallah Seghrouchni, A., Dix, J., Dastani, M., Bordini, R.H. (eds.): Multi-Agent Programming. Springer, Boston (2009). https://doi.org/10.1007/978-0-387-89299-3
5. Bordini, R.H., Hübner, J.F., Wooldridge, M.: Programming Multi-Agent Systems in AgentSpeak using Jason. Wiley, Hoboken (2007)
6. Brazier, F.M.T., Mobach, D.G.A., Overeinder, B.J., Wijngaards, N.: Supporting life cycle coordination in open agent systems. In: Proceedings of the MAS Problem Spaces Workshop at AAMAS, pp. 1–4 (2002)
7. Ferschke, O., Tomar, G., Rosé, C.P.: Adapting collaborative chat for massive open online courses: lessons learned. In: Proceedings of the International Conference on Artificial Intelligence in Education, pp. 13–18 (2015)
8. Hübner, J.F., Sichman, J.S., Boissier, O.: Developing organised multiagent systems using the MOISE+ model: programming issues at the system and agent levels. Int. J. Agent-Oriented Softw. Eng. **1**, 370–395 (2007)
9. Huhns, M.N., Stephens, L.M.: Multiagent Systems and Societies of Agents, chap. 2, pp. 79–120. Massachusetts Institute of Technology Press, Cambridge (1999)
10. Islam, A.B.M.T., Flint, J., Jaecks, P., Cap, C.H.: A proficient and versatile online student-teacher collaboration platform for large classroom lectures. Int. J. Educ. Technol. High. Educ. **14**(1), 1–13 (2017). https://doi.org/10.1186/s41239-017-0067-9
11. King, A.: Structuring peer interaction to promote high-level cognitive processing. Theory Pract. **41**, 33–39 (2002)
12. Neto, A.J.M., Fernandes, M.A.: Chatbot and conversational analysis to promote collaborative learning in distance education. In: Proceedings of the International Conference on Advanced Learning Technologies, pp. 324–326 (2019)
13. Paikari, E., et al.: A chatbot for conflict detection and resolution. In: Proceedings of the 1st International Workshop on Bots in Software Engineering, pp. 29–33 (2019)
14. Tegos, S., Demetriadis, S.N.: Conversational agents improve peer learning through building on prior knowledge. Educ. Technol. Soc. **20**(1), 99–111 (2017)

Reciprocity in Reviewing on Fanfiction.Net

Niamh Froelich[✉], Arthur Liu[✉], Ruoxi Shang[✉], Zile Xiao[✉], Travis Neils[✉], Jenna Frens[✉], and Cecilia Aragon[✉]

University of Washington, Seattle, WA 98195, USA

{niamhf,rxshang,zilex,neilstra,jfrens,aragon}@uw.edu,
artliu@cs.washington.edu

Abstract. The recent rise in online education and the accompanying difficulties encountered by both students and educators demonstrate the value of better understanding how online environments can facilitate learning and community. Fanfiction websites contain an enormous amount of original creative writing, primarily written by young people, offering an opportunity to examine informal learning within an online community. Previous research has shown that fanfiction encourages this informal learning through "distributed mentoring," which occurs when members of an online community quickly and asynchronously receive abundant feedback, while giving others feedback in turn [1]. However, not all interaction in online communities has such a positive nature, as a study of massive open online courses found students who received longer feedback became less likely to reciprocate with similar effort when leaving peer reviews [4]. This study looked at reciprocity between fanfiction reviewers and found a moderate, statistically significant correlation between the quality of reviews given and received by fanfiction authors. These findings are valuable in understanding the ways in which members of online communities interact and learn from each other, an area that would benefit from further research.

Keywords: Online learning · Learning environments · Online community · Peer feedback

1   Introduction

Writing fanfiction, a hobby that is especially popular with young people, allows people to connect over their shared enjoyment of movies, video games, books, and other entertainment. Fanfiction websites such as fanfiction.net support vibrant communities that encourage informal learning through "distributed mentoring," a term which refers to the scenario where members of an online community can quickly and asynchronously receive feedback from many people, while giving others feedback in turn [1]. The distributed mentoring in fanfiction communities has been shown to have measurable benefit as receiving reviews increases the lexical diversity, a measure of vocabulary, of fanfiction writers over time [3]. Additionally, receiving reviews is beneficial for motivating continued participation in the fanfiction community [2].

© Springer Nature Switzerland AG 2021
C. Stephanidis et al. (Eds.): HCII 2021, CCIS 1421, pp. 39–44, 2021.
https://doi.org/10.1007/978-3-030-78645-8_5

However, interaction in online communities is not always mutually beneficial or even positive. A study of massive open online courses (MOOCs) found that students exhibit anti-reciprocal behavior, where receiving a longer peer review leads to students giving shorter peer reviews on the following assignment [4]. The goal of our analysis was to identify whether fanfiction writers have reciprocal reviewing behavior - does receiving high quality reviews make an author more likely to give high quality reviews to others? Additionally, this study looked at whether there are differences in reviewing behavior for authors who primarily write stories and those who primarily write reviews.

2 Methods

The reviews in the data set had previously been labeled as either targeted or non-targeted, where targeted reviews provided specific feedback: "I loved this!" is not targeted, but "Great character development in this chapter!" is targeted. These labels had been applied using a machine learning model created with BERT, which was trained with a data set of reviews qualitatively coded by a team of student researchers. Linear regression was used to look at the relationship between the proportion of targeted reviews to total reviews an author received in a given month and the proportion of targeted reviews to total reviews the author gave in the following month.

This analysis was first performed on the entire group of authors. Then, the authors were divided into groups of primarily-readers and primarily-authors based on whether they largely gave or received reviews (Table 1).

Table 1. Summary of each linear regression.

Trial number	Independent	Dependent	R-squared	P-value	Fig.
1 (all authors)	Ratio of targeted received to total in the previous month	Ratio of targeted given to total in the current month	0.388	2.2e−16	2
2 (writers)	Ratio of targeted received to total in the previous month	Ratio of targeted given to total in the current month	0.372	2.2e−16	4
3 (readers)	Ratio of targeted received to total in the previous month	Ratio of targeted given to total in the current month	0.399	2.2e−16	5

3 Results

Initially, we looked at whether authors who tend to receive a large percentage of targeted reviews out of their total received reviews also give a large percentage of targeted reviews. We found that the Pearson correlation coefficient is 0.481, with a p-value of 6.384e−105. Authors who wrote fewer than 10 targeted reviews total were not included. This shows a moderate, statistically significant correlation (Fig. 1).

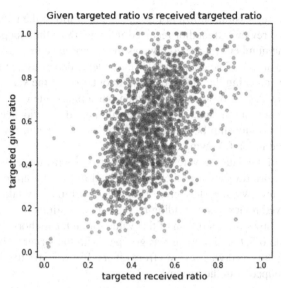

Fig. 1. A scatter plot showing the ratio of received targeted reviews to total received reviews for each author on the x-axis and their ratio of targeted given reviews to total given reviews on the y-axis.

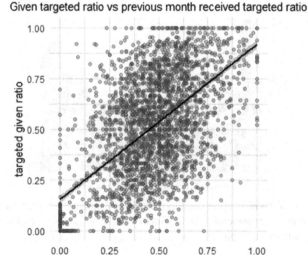

Fig. 2. A scatter plot showing the ratio of targeted reviews received to total reviews received in the previous month for each author on the x-axis and their ratio of given targeted reviews to total given reviews in the current month on the y-axis. The regression line is overlaid on the scatter plot.

The first linear regression, shown in Fig. 2, used the ratio of the number of targeted reviews to the total reviews an author received in a month as the independent variable and the ratio of the number of targeted reviews the author gave in the following month as the dependent variable. The coefficient of the independent variable was 0.768. The r-squared is 0.388, meaning the model explains about 39% of the variation in the data. As the p-value was 2.2e−16, which is less than our alpha value of 0.05, we consider this result statistically significant. This can be interpreted as evidence that there is a moderate-strength relationship between the proportion of targeted reviews given in a month and received in the following month.

Next, authors in the data set were divided into two groups: those that are primarily readers and give more reviews than they receive, and those who are primarily writers and receive more reviews than they give. This was determined by taking the count of the author's received reviews and dividing by the sum of both their given and received reviews. Figure 3 shows the histogram of this value for all the authors. If this value was strictly greater than 0.5, the individual was grouped with the writers since the majority of their participation is receiving reviews from others. If it was strictly less than 0.5, the individual was grouped with the readers.

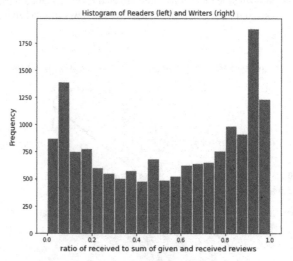

Fig. 3. A histogram of the ratio of received to the sum of given and received reviews for each author. A low ratio indicates someone who is primarily a reviewer, while a higher one indicates someone who is primarily an author.

For each group of authors, the same linear regression using the ratio of the number of targeted reviews to the total received reviews an author received in a month as the independent variable and the ratio of the number of targeted reviews the author gave in the following month was repeated. This regression is shown in Fig. 4. For readers, the coefficient of the independent variable was 0.739 and the r-squared was 0.399. The regression coefficient had a standard error of 0.03, while the first regression analysis had a coefficient of 0.768 with a standard error of 0.02, so there is no evidence that readers have different reciprocal reviewing habits compared to authors overall.

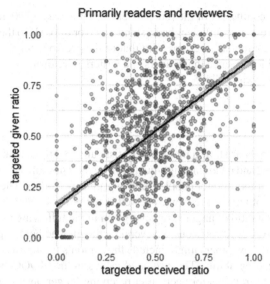

Fig. 4. A scatter plot showing the ratio of targeted reviews received to total reviews received in the previous month for each author on the x-axis and their ratio of targeted reviews given to total reviews given in the current month on the y-axis. The regression line is overlaid on the scatter plot. These authors are primarily reviewers, although they have received reviews as well.

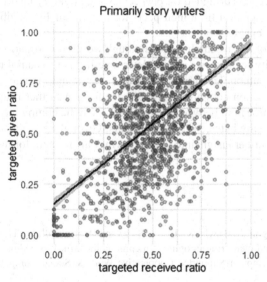

Fig. 5. A scatter plot showing the ratio of targeted reviews received to total reviews received in the previous month for each author on the x-axis and their ratio of targeted reviews given to total reviews given in the current month on the y-axis. The regression line is overlaid on the scatter plot. This plot is for authors who are primarily story writers.

For writers, the coefficient of the independent variable was 0.790 and the r-squared was 0.372. The regression coefficient had a standard error of 0.03, so the margin of error for this regression coefficient overlaps with that of the previous regression for readers. This does not provide evidence that readers and writers have different reviewing habits. This regression is shown in Fig. 5.

4 Conclusion

The results of this analysis show a moderate, statistically significant, and positive correlation between giving and receiving high-quality reviews. This holds true both for people who are primarily authors and for people who are primarily readers. The r-squared value shows that the ratio of targeted reviews received in the previous month explains 38.8% of the variation in the ratio of targeted reviews given in the following month, suggesting that quality of received reviews is one of several factors in whether people take the time to write a detailed review; others might include the person's familiarity with the fandom and their critical reading ability. The r-squared values in the MOOCs study that found students wrote shorter reviews for peers after receiving longer ones were between 0.47 and 0.52 depending on the model, which are comparable to the r-squared values in this study. However, the direction of the effect found in the MOOCs study was opposite to the one found in this study: the MOOC students demonstrated anti-reciprocal behavior while the fanfiction community's behavior was reciprocal. To encourage reciprocity, online learning interfaces designed for peer reviewing might try incorporating ways for students to gain recognition from their peers for leaving quality feedback and to build community in their classes.

One limitation of this research is that although we show correlation between giving and receiving quality reviews, we cannot determine if this is a causal relationship. The motivation behind authors leaving high-quality reviews and the nature of relationship building in the fanfiction community would benefit from further research. While this study looks at reciprocation between the individual and the community, future research could assess reciprocity between pairs of authors. Given the benefits of peer feedback and collaboration, further insight into these areas may also benefit formal online learning environments.

References

1. Campbell, J., Aragon, C., Davis, K., Evans, S., Evans, A., Randall, D.: Thousands of positive reviews: distributed mentoring in online fan communities. In: Proceedings of the 19th ACM Conference on Computer-Supported Cooperative Work & Social Computing, pp. 691–704. ACM (2016)
2. Fowler, J., Frens, J., Sharma, N., Fan, W., Aragon, C.: Towards a model of engagement in online communities: how reviews predict continued participation on FanFiction.net, in Press
3. Frens, J., Davis, R., Lee, J., Zhang, D., Aragon, C.: Reviews matter: how distributed mentoring predicts lexical diversity on Fanfiction.net. In: Proceedings of the 2018 Connected Learning Summit (2018)
4. Kotturi, Y., Du, A., Klemmer, S., Kulkarni, C.: long-term peer reviewing effort is anti-reciprocal. ACM Learning at Scale (2017)

STEM Excellence and Equity in K-12 Settings: Use of Augmented Reality-Based Educational Experiences to Promote Academic Achievement and Learner Success

Patrick Guilbaud[1]([⊠]), Eric Bubar[2], and Elizabeth Langran[3]

[1] Graduate School/Learning Technology, Winthrop University, Rock Hill, SC, USA
guilbaudp@winthrop.edu
[2] Physics Marymount University, Arlington, VA, USA
ebubar@marymount.edu
[3] Education Marymount University, Arlington, VA, USA
elangran@marymount.edu

Abstract. This exploratory paper examines the degree to which Extended Reality (XR) and more specifically, Augmented Reality (AR) technology along with experiential learning pedagogy, can be used to facilitate academic readiness, engagement, and motivation of underserved populations in the STEM fields. We examine the literature and approaches currently being used to help students and other learners gain the technical and behavioral skills needed to succeed in STEM-related courses. We specifically pay attention to studies involving teachers' use and integration of XR/AR applications and other advanced technology tools and applications, even at the exploratory level, to determine readiness and ease of use of those applications as part of regular school activities. We outline some pedagogically-grounded ideas and suggestions to promote excellence and equity in K-12 STEM education, teacher training, and professional development.

Keywords: Augmented Reality · STEM education · K-12 · Equity · BIPOC

1   Introduction

Continued gaps in academic access, readiness, and achievement in the STEM fields persist in US K-12 education. Underserved US students and most specifically Black, Indigenous, and people of color (BIPOC) populations exhibit higher levels of under-performance in secondary school, low college matriculation, and sub-optimal career choices than their majority counterparts [1, 2]. Research shows that a major reason for the persistence of the gaps in STEM educational attainment or participation by many student groups can be traced to the lack of direct exposure or regular contact to role models (parents, family members and other accessible adults) with backgrounds and practices in those fields [3, 4]. As a result, many BIPOC students are unable to link or contextualize the study of STEM-related topics to regular issues or problems that they see or encounter in their everyday lives.

© Springer Nature Switzerland AG 2021
C. Stephanidis et al. (Eds.): HCII 2021, CCIS 1421, pp. 45–50, 2021.
https://doi.org/10.1007/978-3-030-78645-8_6

The recent advances in Extended Reality (XR) technologies to include Augmented Reality (AR), Mixed Reality (MR) and Virtual Reality (VR) indicate a tipping point in the possibility of leveraging those technologies to enhance education and training [5, 6]. Specifically, XR technologies offer the possibility to move past traditional instructional approaches to the use of complex physical, social, and collaborative learning activities and interactions in realistic complex environments to better engage students in the learning process [7]. AR-based applications in particular offer instructors the chance to develop student-centered and "sticky" learning experiences that can both improve academic performance and elicit change in behavior and self-efficacy.

Via this paper, we are hypothesizing that using the AR technologies in a real-world context will provide a safe learning space with the necessary affordances that result in more effective skill development and academic performance by all students. We also argue that the focus on anchoring and connecting learning activities to real-life situations will allow BIPOC populations to make sense of phenomena and problems being examined in their courses. Thus, we propose that use of AR with sound pedagogy can help them overcome the prohibitive barriers and social challenges (e.g., inadequate funding, low resources, lack of support and other disparities) that keep them from moving forward academically and achieving success in school. In the next sections of the paper, we present a brief overview of current approaches being used to improve STEM education in the US. We then delineate key XR technologies that are deployed in various learning contexts to facilitate stronger learners' participation, engagement, and content retention. We then argue that a focus on strengthening the learning experience of students with XR technology can help both improve student achievement and address the manifest equity issues in the STEM fields.

2 Related Work

2.1 Traditional Approaches to STEM Instruction

Many U.S. middle and high school students very often come to the classroom with inadequate STEM preparation and exposure as well as analytical and critical thinking skills [4, 7]. This gap between academic preparation and readiness presents a major challenge for secondary school science teachers and curriculum designers who often must conduct heavy lecture and light laboratory duties due to resource limitations [10]. More specifically, data shows that BIPOC students and other underserved communities are very often unprepared academically, emotionally, and socially for the rigors of scientific study and as a result often fail to grasp foundational concepts of biology, human anatomy and physiology, and nursing [3, 5, 6]. This is because mastery of a new topic often involves high demand cognitive tasks and use of several layers of skills and abilities such as, understanding terminology, analyzing data to determine the type of problem faced, and then interpreting the results. Some students have the capacity for example to learn health concepts such as connection or interaction between nutrition and metabolism quickly, while others require more direction, guidance, and practice [2, 3]. Moreover, many young learners are unfamiliar or inexperienced with the practice of making decisions based on reflective inquiry, data analysis, and reasoned judgment [8–10].

Afterschool and summer programs have been used by many academic institutions for quite some time to help underperforming students overcome challenges that they face with learning STEM by bringing the topic to life in ways that are both engaging and relevant to the learners background and perspectives. While these programs provide a path to increasing academic development, they are unable to offer the scaffolding and dedicated support and mentoring to BIPOC students, which are needed to help them overcome unique cognitive challenges and socio-cultural barriers that they face.

Yet, pedagogically grounded methods, techniques, and approaches such as inquiry-based learning and repeated practice have been used effectively as heuristics to facilitate the development of metacognitive skills and reflective thinking as well as self-efficacy that students need for persistence and tenacity to succeed when completing high-order tasks [1, 3, 9]. Further, innovative and targeted use of technology can be a catalyst or enabler for including high-impact practices in a course and enhancing students' participation and engagement in the learning process.

2.2 Extended Reality Technologies and Education

Extended reality (XR) technologies to include augmented reality (AR), mixed-reality (MR), and virtual reality (VR) have been widely adopted in a variety of professional environments and settings such as healthcare/medical training, construction and product design [see 11–13]. Table 1 presents a brief overview of the unique characteristics, opportunities, and challenges that each of these technologies presents for K-12 education and STEM learning contexts.

Table 1. XR characteristics and opportunities for education

XR	Characteristics	Opportunities/Challenges for K-12 Education and STEM Learning
VR	Allows users to be fully-immersed into a computerized environment; Offers one form of extended reality experience through use of headsets – Oculus Quest/Quest 2 headset is the "gold standard" offers fully immersive virtual reality experiences at a reasonable cost	- VR headset offers a higher quality VR experience, which helps visualization STEM topics, such as Physics, Biology, Chemistry, and Construction - Some set-ups require VR headsets to be tethered to a high-power PC with advanced graphics capabilities - Concerns with VR-induced motion sickness suggest that ubiquitous adoption for young learners may be a major hurdle
MR	Offers experiences that couple the real world with virtual elements in work settings where simulations can be combined with real objects	- There are many applied MR options available, for example in healthcare/nursing and logistics-related training - MR solutions are available at a variety of price-points and experience levels
AR	Like MR offers experiences that couple the real world with virtual elements have perhaps the greatest potential e.g., Pokémon Go or Wizards Unite	- Virtual learning environment for Science projects can be achieved via use of a smartphone - Ease of use allow developers to design effective learning experiences Interface that's familiar to learners

The recent drop in the cost of hardware along with wider availability of open-source software now allow hobbyist creators and novice educators to experiment with all types of XR-related technologies. For example, teachers and academic support personnel with a rudimentary computer science knowledge can essentially utilize game development engines (like e.g. Unity, Unreal etc.) to create a variety of immersive simulated environments. Traditional scripting in C# or block-based programming utilities have lowered the barrier for non-programmer educators to create gaming content. Video sharing platforms abound with free tutorial content for aspiring developers to create gaming experiences that can be utilized to improve student learning by increasing student engagement. These free tools, coupled with the ubiquity of mobile devices capable of interacting with this content make them an excellent resource for bringing high-technology interactives to all students and particularly BIPOC students. Further, when XR-related technologies and applications are combined with appropriate pedagogies, they can serve as a bridge to bring greater equity in the types of learning experiences that are offered in K-12 settings and contexts [14, 15].

2.3 XR/AR and Implications for K-12 Education

The healthcare, safety, military, logistics fields have been early adopters of XR technologies, particularly in the context of education and training [5, 6, 9]. As these technologies have matured, the cost of associated hardware and peripherals to use them have decreased. Specifically, AR offers the opportunity to improve access and equity in K-12 education and STEM learning because of its low footprint. For example an AR-based activity that uses a smartphone can offer the context, meaning, and tailored guidance that BIPOC students need to better engage in a learning experience.

Below are some of examples of opportunities and implications to leveraging AR and related technologies in K-12 education.

1. Hands-on Experiences: Use of AR allows students to explore education topics and contents when they cannot physically be there. This may be due to the impracticality or impossibility such as visiting an international city or undersea location, or students who are differently abled and cannot be on-location. Using Global Positioning Systems (GPS) applications, learning experiences that are offered can be collaborative irrespective of the participants' location [16].
2. Guided Inquiry: Inquiry-based pedagogical approaches orient students to direct their own learning. As AR technology can be used as a supplement to offline learning, it can be leveraged to provide prompts and parameters to make sure that the learner is properly scaffolded as part of their educational experience.
3. Adaptive Learning: AR helps students visualize a place or an object and thus can bridge the divide between abstract concepts and real-world application. One of the barriers for BIPOC students who sometimes struggle with reading is their challenges in visualizing what is being described in the text [17]. Recent research supports the view that students have better recall when employing XR-based learning environments [18].

4. Mastery of practical skills. AR is being used in learning and training activities because it allows a low-stakes attempt at a task. This capability provides learners time on task to master a specific skill and gain confidence before attempting it in real life. AR thus reduces risk by ensuring skills mastery before an individual works in the situations e.g., using an expensive equipment or operating on a patient, where mistakes would be costly.

3   Conclusion

The integration of virtual elements into a realistic environment, particularly through AR, can provide meaningful educational interventions for any learner with access to low-cost smartphone technologies. Thus, it is widely anticipated that the use of AR will continue to grow. While new AR applications have yet to reach the popularity of Pokémon Go or Wizards Unite, numerous small educational projects currently allow users to develop location-based mixed reality games and activities on mobile storytelling platforms [14–16]. Loco-Matrix, for example, is a tool that allows players to move through "virtual archeology" and use the application to "discover" and "dig" ancient sites whether in Europe or Africa without leaving their schools. Thus, AR can be used to support learning on location when it is not possible to be there. Furthermore, implementing new technologies such as artificial intelligence and machine learning algorithms along with AR can result in scalable virtual learning experiences. These can also be designed to be adaptable to students from a wide range of academic experiences, cultural backgrounds, personal interests, and learning preferences. Therefore, AR technology is ideally suited for K-12 education, where BIPOC and other underserved students oftentimes need tailored support to pursue programs of studies or careers in STEM-related fields. Hands-on and active learning with XR technologies holds the potential to address key deficiencies with traditional learning models.

References

1. Anderson, R.: Reforming science teaching: What research says about inquiry. J. Sci. Teacher Educ. **13**(1), 1–12 (2002)
2. Chemers, M.M., Zurbriggen, E.L., Syed, M., Goza, B.K., Bearman, S.: The role of efficacy and identity in science career commitment among underrepresented minority students. J. Soc. Issues **67**, 469–491 (2011). https://doi.org/10.1111/j.1540-4560.2011.01710.x
3. Connell, G.L., Donovan, D.A., Chambers, T.G.: Increasing the use of student-centered pedagogies from moderate to high improves student learning and attitudes about biology. CBE Life Sci. Educ. **15**(1), ar3 (2016). https://doi.org/10.1187/cbe.15-03-0062
4. Bybee, R.W., Powell, J.C., Trowbridge, L.W.: Teaching Secondary School Science: Strategies for Developing Scientific Literacy. Merrill Prentice Hall, Upper Saddle River (2008)
5. Lindner, C., Andreas, R., Carsten, J.: Augmented reality applications as digital experiments for education–an example in the earth-moon system. Acta Astronaut. **161**, 66–74 (2019)
6. Yoon, S.A., Elinich, K., Wang, J., Steinmeier, C., Tucker, S.: Using augmented reality and knowledge-building scaffolds to improve learning in a science museum. Int. J. Comput.-Support. Collab. Learn. **7**(4), 519–541 (2012)
7. Herrington, J., Oliver, R.: An instructional design framework for authentic learning environments. Educ. Tech. Res. Dev. **48**(3), 23–48 (2000)

8. Potvin, P., Hasni, A.: Interest, motivation and attitude towards science and technology at K-12 levels: a systematic review of 12 years of educational research. Stud. Sci. Educ. **50**(1), 85–129 (2014). https://doi.org/10.1080/03057267.2014.881626

9. Armbruster, P., Patel, M., Johnson, E., Weiss, M.: Active learning and student-centered pedagogy improve student attitudes and performance in introductory biology. CBE Life Sci. Educ. **8**(3), 203–213 (2009). https://doi.org/10.1187/cbe.09-03-0025

10. Flick, L.B.: Cognitive scaffolding that fosters scientific inquiry in middle level science. J. Sci. Teacher Educ. **11**(2), 109–129 (2000)

11. Hsieh, M.C., Lee, J.J.: Preliminary study of VR and AR applications in medical and healthcare education. J. Nurs. Health Stud. **3**(1), 1 (2018)

12. Li, X., Yi, W., Chi, H.L., Wang, X., Chan, A.P.: A critical review of virtual and augmented reality (VR/AR) applications in construction safety. Autom. Constr. **86**, 150–162 (2018)

13. Wolfartsberger, J.: Analyzing the potential of Virtual Reality for engineering design review. Autom. Constr. **104**, 27–37 (2019)

14. Brown, M., et al.: 2020 Educause Horizon Report Teaching and Learning Edition. EDUCAUSE, Louisville (2020)

15. Langran, E., DeWitt, J.: Navigating Place-Based Learning: Mapping for a Better World. Palgrave Macmillan, London (2020)

16. Bursztyn, N., Walker, A., Shelton, B., Pederson, J.: Increasing undergraduate interest to learn geoscience with GPS-based augmented reality field trips on students' own smartphones. GSA Today **27**(5), 4–11 (2017)

17. Wilhelm, J.D.: You Gotta BE the Book, 3rd edn. Teachers College Press, New York (2016)

18. Krokos, E., Plaisant, C., Varshney, A.: Virtual memory places: immersion aids recall. Virtual Reality **23**, 1–15 (2018)

Technological Pedagogical and Content Knowledge (TPACK): Higher Education Teachers' Perspectives on the Use of TPACK in Online Academic Writing Classes

Doaa Hamam[1] [iD] and Ajrina Hysaj[2][✉] [iD]

[1] Higher Colleges of Technology, Dubai, UAE
dhamam@hct.ac.ae
[2] UOWD College, University of Wollongong in Dubai, Dubai, UAE
Ajrinahysaj@uowdubai.ac.ae

Abstract. This paper revisits the technological, pedagogical and content knowledge (TPACK) framework and its use in Higher Education, especially in the online writing classes. The framework for teaching with technology was described by Mishra and Kohler [19], who mentioned that it was built on Shulman's [27] theory of "pedagogical content knowledge". The framework describes the logic behind the technology used in teaching. So it equips teachers with the knowledge they need to design or use activities while teaching with technology. The study aims at exploring the Higher Education teachers' level of mastery of the framework and their perspectives about using it in online academic writing classes. A survey was designed based on the framework and sent to higher education TESOL teachers to explore their perspectives on the utilisation of the TPACK framework in writing classes. The sample was comprised of (n = 43) university teachers. The study concluded that Higher Education teachers have positive views towards using the TPACK framework in online classes. Besides, the study discussed some pedagogical implications that can be useful for various educational stakeholders and policymakers.

Keywords: Academic writing · Online platform · TPACK framework

1 Introduction

The utilisation of the technological, pedagogical, and content knowledge is crucial in adapting to the online platform, considering the requirements of the education system, students' needs, and the capacities of educators. According to studies by Mishra and Koehler [19], as well as Koehler et al. [15], the Technological Pedagogical Content Knowledge (TPACK) serves as a guiding concept that demonstrates the interdependency between instructors' technology (T), pedagogy (P), and content (C) knowledge which encompasses effective teaching practices. This simply enables teachers to know the logic behind the technology they are using in their teaching. While the necessity of

© Springer Nature Switzerland AG 2021
C. Stephanidis et al. (Eds.): HCII 2021, CCIS 1421, pp. 51–58, 2021.
https://doi.org/10.1007/978-3-030-78645-8_7

analysing the utilisation of TPACK in Higher Education has become more imminent due to the circumstances imposed by the 2020 pandemic, its framework, to date, has not had adequate implications in the Higher Education [2, 9, 15, 21]. We decided that it is of utmost importance to explore and understand the theoretical and practical impacts that TPACK can have on Higher Education and especially EAP writing classes at the undergraduates level. These implications will be considered from the perspectives of university teachers. Also, we wanted to explore the level of mastery of the TPACK framework among university teachers.

2 Literature Review

2.1 Teacher's Awareness and Mastery of the TPACK Framework

According to Straumsheim, Jaschik and Lederman [26], the percentage of Higher Education faculty with experience in online teaching was 33%, and the percentage of faculty with experience in blended learning was 40%. The guidance framework of TPACK provides a platform where the effectiveness of online teaching practices within the context of Higher Education [20, 21] and their pedagogical implications [19] create multilayers of online teaching experience for instructors and students. Understandably, the degree of instructors' knowledge and curriculum designers may serve as a starting point towards utilising the basic tenets of TPACK that are pedagogical, content and technological knowledge. For instance, instructors who are aware of the subjects they teach tend to recognise the necessity of acknowledging students' needs and applying pedagogical knowledge to create inclusiveness and active engagement in their classrooms. When the classrooms are in the online platform, then technological knowledge becomes an indispensable tool, and it is added to the list of tools, substantial for a successful teaching and learning experience [1, 2, 24].

Finally, to validate the use of the framework among educators, the study of Castéra et al. [3] aimed to empirically identify the seven factors that comprise the base of the TPACK framework and other elements like context, age and gender. The study sample comprised 574 teacher educators from different schools in six countries who were given a Likert-scale questionnaire. The study's findings were divided into four aspects: first, the model's stability had seven factors in the participating countries. Second, there were differences between teacher educators in Asia and Europe. Third, there was a link between age and TPACK, and finally, there was no independence of gender and academic level concerning the framework. The study led to critical pedagogical implications in understanding teachers' mastery and knowledge of the TPACK framework.

2.2 The Significance of the TPACK Framework

Previous empirical and theoretical studies conducted in Higher Education have focused on understanding the importance of pedagogical approaches [20, 30], the effectiveness of technology integration [25] and the understanding the roles of online instructors [16]. Notably, these studies are consistent with the unique concepts that encompass the integrated TPACK framework. Nevertheless, despite researchers and educators' continuous call about the value that TPACK holds for the effective development of online teaching practices [20], minimal research has been conducted on the use of TPACK itself as a guide within online Higher Education [9].

Finger et al. [6] argued that in Australia, most teacher education programs are built on Shulman's theory [27]. The authors of the study claim that this is inadequate with the current advances in teaching with technology as several other factors should be put into practice, and the TPACK framework ideally describes these. They described TPACK as "the total package" to reveal the frame's comprehensiveness and importance. In China, Xu and Sun [31] too reported on the development and validation process of the TPACK framework for ESP teachers in Higher Education.

Moreover, the study of Habibi, Yusop and Razak [7] examined language pre-service teacher's use of ICT tools during their teaching practice in Indonesia. The TPACK framework was used and the study aimed at exploring the validity of the framework to assess the teachers' use of information and communication technology. The study concluded that the framework was valid to explain the pre-service UICT in their practice. Furthermore, Durdu and Dag [4] attempted to check the pre-service teachers' TPACK knowledge by joining a course that was designed based on the framework. The teachers' knowledge was assessed through the teachers' microteaching performance tests' scores, and the findings revealed that the used instructional process had a positive impact on the teachers' development of TPACK knowledge. This finding is also in line with other studies [2, 23], and this reflects the importance and the significance of the TPACK framework as it is essential now for teachers to use technology in their teaching practice. We conclude that a successful university teacher should be proficient in all the framework subscales to be able to improve his/her instruction in the classroom.

2.3 Academic Writing in the Online Platform as the Focus of the Study

The study's focus is academic writing due to its importance in any university setting. Academic writing is critical as it is considered an inseparable part of almost every assignment, even in the students' major subjects [8]. In a study by Hysaj and Hamam [13] to explore the students' perceptions of using the online platform, students preferred to continue studying online during the pandemic. With the shift to the online platform, both students and teachers have the opportunity to work differently within the TPACK framework. This framework should facilitate online writing classes and improve its delivery, and it should make the classes more engaging and exciting for the students. Looking at the previous literature, it is evident that there are not many studies about the TPACK framework use in academic writing. Therefore, we analyse some recent studies from the literature in this section.

Tai, Pan and Lee [29] wanted to apply the TPACK model to create an English writing course for nursing students to be delivered online, and the target was to see the course's impact on students' performance. The study also aimed at measuring the students' satisfaction level with the course. The researchers collected quantitative data and discovered that the students' performance improved dramatically after the course. The study concluded that the TPACK framework led to effective teaching and learning and enhanced English writing skills; therefore, it was advised to continue to use the framework. Based on this, it seems that the TPACK framework provides a solid ground for teaching EAP writing courses using technology [5, 18].

Furthermore, Schmidt [28] stated that to provide effective instruction based on technology, language teachers must mix their knowledge of language instruction and technology in their teaching. He also confirmed that many teachers are struggling to do that. Schmidt [28] focused on a case study that describes three language teachers' knowledge of the TPACK framework by digitally creating a reflective portfolio. Data were collected from classroom observations, online surveys, interviews, and instructional material. The study's findings showed that the TPACK framework significantly impacted how the teachers utilised different technological tools in their instruction of composition classes. However, the use of the framework was constrained by pedagogical beliefs of the impact of technology on students' teaching and learning and their extent of engagement. Therefore, the study findings are important as they guide language teachers in a world that is becoming more and more dependent on technology. The overall literature on the TPACK framework and teaching language skills in the online platform give promising results for using it in the future.

3   Methods

The study focused on higher education teachers' perspectives on the use of the TPACK framework in academic writing online classes. A survey was designed and distributed to higher education teachers who teach/taught online academic writing classes. The chosen teachers' eligibility criteria were 1) They need to be specialised in TESOL/Writing/EAP or a relevant discipline 2) They can be holders of a master's degree or a PhD degree. 3) They must have experience in teaching with technology 4) they must have taught online academic writing classes in a higher education setting. The sample was a purposive sample that was carefully chosen based on the eligibility criteria mentioned above. The sample size was 43, and the teachers were given one week to fill in the survey. All teachers were assured anonymity and confidentiality of their identity and the collected information. The data collected from surveys revealed positive perspectives by teachers on the use of the TPACK framework in the online academic writing classes and gave insights on their knowledge of the framework.

4   Results

The results were extracted from the survey platform, and it included 23 Likert scale items, and the percentage for each answer is 1-Strongly agree, 2 = Agree, 3 = Neutral, 4 = Disagree, and 5 = Strongly disagree. The survey items were selected to gauge educators' perceptions of their individual technological knowledge, pedagogical knowledge and content knowledge regarding the utilisation of digital tools and their corresponding pedagogical usefulness in a discipline related subject, in this case: EAP and specifically academic writing. The survey aimed at understanding the educators' readiness to teach online and their professional preparedness to utilise digital tools considering the TPACK framework under imposed remote learning due to the pandemic of COVID 19.

The teachers' survey's overall results revealed that an overwhelming 90% of teachers were comfortable with the utilisation of technology and aware of its respective benefits with regards to teaching and learning. Furthermore, around 60% of teachers were self-aware of the encouraging pedagogical prospects of teaching academic writing in the online platform using technology, with around 50 per cent acknowledging the positive aspects of probing to scaffold academic writing tasks as practice tasks and as assessment tasks. Interestingly, teachers had been able to understand students' most common errors and had experimented with the utilisation of audio and video formative feedback in addition to the written feedback.

The survey revealed that some teachers were for the most part unable to fix technical issues while in the online platform, or were not very confident in dealing with class-room management issues. This could be due to the inability to be present in the same geographical space as their students. However, the teachers indicated that they enjoyed teaching online and were enthusiastic about the possibility of teaching academic writing in a variety of ways that were not previously explored. Considering the time during which this paper is written, and the survey is conducted, it is valuable to mention that based on the data collected, teachers preferred to consider online teaching as a very competitive alternative to face-face teaching. Furthermore, the data analysis highlights the teachers' passion for exploring different ways to teach academic writing in the online platform while giving utmost importance to students' learning prospects.

5   Discussion

The teachers' surveys' overall results showed that most teachers were comfortable with online teaching and noticed that online tools could facilitate high levels of teaching and learning effectiveness if the TPACK framework is utilised. Furthermore, teachers noticed an improvement of their pedagogical strategies regarding teaching academic writing skills in the online platform.

This study revealed that although the online platform did not hinder teaching and learning, its benefits and drawbacks need to be explored and analysed, as they are both equally valuable for a successful teaching and learning experience. However, the data revealed the passion that teachers have for teaching and their self-driven attitude towards positive change. The study's findings are in-line with the findings of previous research [11, 13]. Therefore, creating a supportive/communicative environment in the online platform between the teachers and students is equally important to the one present in a face-to-face platform. According to a study by Hysaj et al., [11], students consider the rapport with their tutors as substantial, which was reflected in their academic success. Moreover, students as social beings require individual and group connections which are facilitated through teacher-student relationship and student-student relationship in the online platform. These relationships are equally valuable for achieving a successful learning experience; hence teachers are required to facilitate group work, individual formative feedback and consider students' academic and personal development as the core of their online teaching. Therefore, all the specific measures explained in the TPACK framework should be taken into consideration when adapting the curriculum to suit the online learning platform; aiming to guarantee a successful learning experience.

6   Conclusion

The study findings reflected the extent of the teachers' mastery of the TPACK framework and their degree of satisfaction of the framework implementation in online writing classes. These findings lead to discovering the benefits and the challenges of using the framework in online writing classes. Since successful learning is a combination of individual and teamwork, naturally online teaching requires the consideration of both to facilitate students' accumulation of discipline-specific knowledge parallelly with the development of cognitive and multicultural knowledge related skills [12, 14, 17, 22]. Further research is needed to analyse the psychological factors associated with online teaching and learning. Another factor that was not taken into consideration in this study was the teachers' multiculturalism although multiculturalism has been very important to teaching and learning in the different settings [10, 12, 22, 32]. Due to the widespread of remote learning, the constant exploration of the critical success factors involved in the TPACK framework becomes crucial for its appropriate application and consideration by educators to benefit all stakeholders involved in the education sector.

References

1. Baran, E., Canbazoglu Bilici, S., Albayrak Sari, A., Tondeur, J.: Investigating the impact of teacher education strategies on pre-service teachers' TPACK. Br. J. Edu. Technol. **50**(1), 357–370 (2019)
2. Benson, S.N.K., Ward, C.L.: Teaching with technology: using TPACK to understand teaching expertise in online higher education. J. Educ. Comput. Res. **48**(2), 153–172 (2013)
3. Castéra, J., et al.: Self-reported TPACK of teacher educators across six countries in Asia and Europe. Educ. Inf. Technol. **25**(4), 3003–3019 (2020). https://doi.org/10.1007/s10639-020-10106-6
4. Durdu, L., Dag, F.: Pre-Service teachers' TPACK development and conceptions through a TPACK-based course. Aust. J. Teacher Educ. **42**(11), 10 (2017)
5. Farikah, F., Al Firdaus, M.M.: Technological pedagogical and content knowledge (TPACK): the students' perspective on writing class. Jurnal Studi Guru dan Pembelajaran **3**(2), 190–199 (2020)
6. Finger, G., Jamieson-Proctor, R., Albion, P.: Beyond pedagogical content knowledge: the importance of TPACK for informing preservice teacher education in Australia. In: Reynolds, N., Turcsányi-Szabó, M. (eds.) KCKS 2010. IAICT, vol. 324, pp. 114–125. Springer, Heidelberg (2010). https://doi.org/10.1007/978-3-642-15378-5_11
7. Habibi, A., Yusop, F.D., Razak, R.A.: The role of TPACK in affecting pre-service language teachers' ICT integration during teaching practices: Indonesian context. Educ. Inf. Technol. **25**(3), 1929–1949 (2019). https://doi.org/10.1007/s10639-019-10040-2
8. Hamam, D.: A study of the rhetorical features and the argument structure of EAP essays by L1 and L2 students in the UAE. J. Asia TEFL **17**(2), 699–706 (2020)
9. Herring, M.C., Meacham, S. and Mourlam, D.: TPACK development in higher education. Handbook of technological pedagogical content knowledge (TPACK) for educators, 207 (2016)
10. Hysaj, A., Elkhouly, A., Qureshi, A.W., Abdulaziz, N.: Analysis of engineering students' academic satisfaction in a culturally diverse university. In: 2018 IEEE International Conference on Teaching, Assessment, and Learning for Engineering (TALE), pp. 755–760. IEEE, December 2018

11. Hysaj, A., Elkhouly, A., Qureshi, A.W., Abdulaziz, N.A.: Study of the impact of tutor's support and undergraduate student's academic satisfaction. Am. J. Hum. Soc. Sci. Res 3(12), 70–77 (2019)
12. Hysaj, A., Hamam, D.: Does delivery method matter for multicultural undergraduate students? A case study of an Australian University in the United Arab Emirates. In: Meiselwitz, G. (ed.) HCII 2020. LNCS, vol. 12195, pp. 538–548. Springer, Cham (2020). https://doi.org/10.1007/978-3-030-49576-3_39
13. Hysaj, A., Hamam, D.: Exploring the affordance of distance learning platform (DLP) in COVID19 remote learning environment. In: Stephanidis, C., et al. (eds.) HCII 2020. LNCS, vol. 12425, pp. 421–431. Springer, Cham (2020). https://doi.org/10.1007/978-3-030-60128-7_32
14. Hysaj, A. and Hamam, D.: Academic Writing Skills in the Online Platform- A success, a failure or something in between? A study on perceptions of Higher Education students and teachers in the UAE' In: IEEE International Conference on Teaching, Assessment and Learning for Engineering (TALE) pp. 334–339, IEEE (2020)
15. Koehler, M.J., et al.: Deep-play: developing TPACK for 21st century teachers. International Journal of Learning Technology 6(2), 146–163 (2011)
16. Martin, F., Budhrani, K., Kumar, S., Ritzhaupt, A.: Award-winning faculty online teaching practices: Roles and competencies. Online Learn. 23(1), 184–205 (2019)
17. McDermott, D.: Towards wellbeing and happiness: Positive psychology in an Australian English language centre in the UAE. Engl. Aust. J. 36(2), 5 (2020)
18. Mei, L.I.: Study on three-dimensional teaching mode of college english expansive course: EAP writing. J. Guangxi Vocat. Tech. College (2), 15 (2017)
19. Mishra, P., Koehler, M.J.: Technological pedagogical content knowledge: a framework for teacher knowledge. Teach. Coll. Rec. 108(6), 1017–1054 (2006)
20. Meyer, K.A., Murrell, V.S.: A national study of training content and activities for faculty development for online teaching. J. Asynchron. Learn. Networks 18(1), p.n1. (2014)
21. Meyer, K.A., Murrell, V.S.: A national study of theories and their importance for faculty development for online teaching. Online J. Dist. Learn. Adm. 17(2), 1–25 (2014)
22. Nada, C.I., Araújo, H.C.: When you welcome students without borders, you need a mentality without borders' internationalisation of higher education: evidence from Portugal. Stud. Higher Educ. 44(9), 1591–1604 (2019)
23. Nazari, N., Nafissi, Z., Estaji, M., Marandi, S.S., Wang, S.: Evaluating novice and experienced EFL teachers' perceived TPACK for their professional development. Cogent Educ. 6(1), 1632010 (2019)
24. Ouyang, F., Scharber, C.: Adapting the TPACK framework for online teaching within higher education. Int. J. Online Pedag. Course Des. (IJOPCD) 8(1), 42–59 (2018)
25. Sun, A. and Chen, X.: Online education and its effective practice: a research review. J. Inf. Technol. Educ. 15 (2016)
26. Straumsheim, C., Jaschik, S., Lederman, D.: Faculty Attitudes on Technology. Inside, Washington, DC (2015)
27. Shulman, L.S.: Knowledge and teaching: foundations of the new reform. Harv. Educ. Rev. 57(1), 1–22 (1987)
28. Schmidt, N.: Digital multimodal composition and second language teacher knowledge. TESL Can. J. 36(3), 1–30 (2019)
29. Tai, H.C., Pan, M.Y., Lee, B.O.: Applying Technological Pedagogical and Content Knowledge (TPACK) model to develop an online English writing course for nursing students. Nurse Educ. Today 35(6), 782–788 (2015)
30. Wu, Y.-T.: Research trends in technological pedagogical content knowledge (TPACK) research: a review of empirical studies published in selected journals from 2002 to 2011. Br. J. Edu. Technol. 44(3), E73-76 (2013)

31. Xu, X., Sun, Y.: A Technological Pedagogical Content Knowledge (TPACK) Framework for ESP teachers in tertiary education in China. Asian ESP J. **193** (2019)
32. Wilder, L.K., Sanon, D., Carter, C., Lancellot, M.: Narrative ethnographies of diverse faculty in higher education: "Moral" multiculturalism among competing worldviews. J. Ethnic Cult. Stud. **4**(2), 1–12 (2017)

The New Teacher Assistant: A Review of Chatbots' Use in Higher Education

Doaa Hamam[(✉)] [iD]

Higher Colleges of Technology, Dubai, UAE
dhamam@hct.ac.ae

Abstract. This paper aims at reviewing the use of chatbots in teaching and learning in higher education. Since AI and chatbots represent a rapidly-evolving field, a review of recent academic papers on the topic was needed. Through the systematic review method described by Kitchenham [3], academic papers written between 2018–2020 were reviewed to analyse the benefits and the limitations of using chatbots in the higher education field. The focus was on teaching and learning using chatbots, not on providing general services like customer service or answering students' general queries. The review findings reveal many benefits of using chatbots in higher education, such as improving teaching and learning, increasing students' engagement, and providing an individualised experience, especially for large classes. However, some limitations were also identified, such as technical and functionality issues and other privacy and security issues. To sum up, more research is needed to explore the benefits of chatbots in the field of higher education.

Keyword: Chatbot-higher education · Teaching with technology · Artificial intelligence

1 Introduction

Chatbots are AI tools that are used to assist people in particular tasks, and they are now used in several fields. People can communicate with chatbots through texting or even voice calls. Chatbots can offer tremendous opportunities in education, especially for large classes [15]. Chatbots now have very advanced features, and they can talk like humans producing a very logical and organised thought process. Scientists are also working on the emotional side of the conversation, so the chatbots appear more human when interacting with users. There are many benefits of chatbots in education. They could initiate a conversation with a student, ask about his/ her details like name, course, contact details, and others, then attempt to answer the student's query or forward it to the teacher if the chatbot did not have the answer. Another way can be feeding the chatbot with frequently asked questions to respond to students. Chatbots can also explain simple parts in the syllabus or provide assignments requirements like word count, deadline, and other details.

© Springer Nature Switzerland AG 2021
C. Stephanidis et al. (Eds.): HCII 2021, CCIS 1421, pp. 59–63, 2021.
https://doi.org/10.1007/978-3-030-78645-8_8

In general, chatbots can be excellent and cost-efficient teacher assistants. In addition to that, chatbots do not have working hours or office hours; they can respond to queries 24/7 during business days and days off. So, there are pedagogical and well as administrative benefits for chatbots. With the complete switch to online learning because of the COVID19 pandemic in several educational institutions, AI tools are becoming even more prominent and important. Several reviews were done on the use of chatbots in education and other fields, like the review of Winkler and Söllner [15]. However, no recent systematic reviews were found in the literature, focusing on teaching and learning in higher education.

2 Method

To review the recent articles about using chatbots in teaching and learning in higher education, I used the systematic literature review method described by Kitchenham [3], which was based on two steps. The first step is to develop a plan for the review, and this plan should include preparing a particular search protocol to use in the review. It also requires defining the research question(s) of the review. The second step is to identify the chosen articles' source according to their relevance and quality. Therefore, I formulated the following research question for the first step: What are the advantages and disadvantages of using chatbots in teaching and learning in higher education? To answer this research question, I decided to analyse the relevant articles between 2018–2020. The focus was on the benefits and limitations of using chatbots in the process of teaching and learning in higher education. Google scholar was the main research engine used to find the articles. The relevant articles found were fourteen (n = 14), and the focus was on empirical research in teaching and learning using chatbots. Other articles involving using chatbots to provide customer services or to perform other functions in a higher education setting were not included because they were out of the review's focus.

3 Literature Review

3.1 Benefits of Chatbots in Higher Education

Studente, Ellis and Garivaldis [11] reported using chatbots to develop four learning communities in a university setting with a diverse population. Using chatbot's focused on two main aspects; first, to help the students in their first year in the programme and second, increase their engagement. Both students and program leaders were given access to the chatbot through a mobile application. Data were collected through questionnaires and focus groups from both students and teachers at the end of the term. The purpose of the data collected was to identify the benefits and challenges of chatbots' use. The study's findings revealed a positive impact on the students' engagement with their subjects and with their peers and that it was easier to access the support offered by the programme leaders. The students even made more recommendations for improving the chatbot.

To make sure that chatbots are helpful in teaching and learning, Gonda et al. [9] developed several chatbot prototypes and decided to evaluate their educational efficiency according to the seven principles of good teaching described by Chickering and Gamson

[9]. The findings showed that the chatbots covered five of the seven principles of good teaching, and improved teaching in the course. This proves the pedagogical benefit of chatbots.

Sandu and Gide [10] examined the use of chatbots in higher education to enhance the students' learning experience. Data were collected from surveys given to some of the higher education institutions that utilise chatbots. The study concluded that that students preferred to use chatbots over any other type of communication methods. Another important finding was the stress that chatbots could efficiently facilitate student-centred learning and help students research and communicate better.

Fernoagă et al. [5] explored the use of chatbots as real-time assistants for teachers. In this experiment, the chatbots were designed to enhance interactivity with students at an individualised level. The authors mentioned that an individualised approach could add a high degree of personalisation to the students' learning experience because each student has his/her method of learning and comprehension abilities. The study's conclusion indicated that using chatbots as educational assistants improved the interaction between teachers and students in the classroom. In addition, Fleming, et al. [6] designed a study to explore the efficiency of chatbots' real-time responses to students' questions, and the findings revealed that chatbots were able to integrate within existing datasets and that they can respond to students' simple questions. Moreover, the study of Roos [13] described several benefits of using chatbots in higher education, such as answering students' queries 24/7, providing means to contact the teacher, giving suggestions about learning material, and many other benefits.

Furthermore, the study of Kim [2] described the benefits of a chatbot named "Elbot" in improving the students' language skills. The students had language pre-tests and post-tests before using the chatbot, and the findings revealed that students' reading and listening skills significantly improved because they engaged in chatting with the chatbot for 16 weeks.

Other studies revealed the students' willingness to use chatbots in the university setting. For example, the study of Von Wolff et al. [14], which concluded that chatbots are helpful in the university setting and that many students are interested in using them, and the study of Gupta, et al. [8], who mentioned that chatbots could be efficient tutors for students as they can answer questions and lead to a suitable environment for advanced learning. Also, Thomas [12] reviewed several studies about the use of chatbots in education and described several areas where chatbots could help teach and learn, such as customised learning, student-teacher interaction, language competency, and many others.

Finally, Georgescu [7] concluded that "chatbots may be cheap and easy to use educational tools, meant to be closer to nowadays students in a more pleasant way, adequate to modern styles of learning (p.95)." Chatbots can also be used to help in learning languages, according to Haristiani and Danuwijaya [1], who developed "Gengobot", which is a chatbot application that gives the meaning and explanation of words in three languages. The chatbot was functioning well and user friendly. It helped students with their Japanese grammar and provided basic language knowledge. The learners were able to use the chatbot and adjust it to their speed, which created an individualised learning experience and helped support teachers.

3.2 Limitations of Using Chatbots in Higher Education

Many studies explored the use of chatbots in higher education. However, some studies reported technical issues that hindered the use of chatbots. The study of Yang and Evans [16] looked at the use of chatbots within three areas; to support the university helpdesk, support the delivery of a master's course game and support a new education application. The study concluded that with too many challenging technical issues in using chatbots, they are not ready yet to be used. The authors hope if they fix these technical issues, chatbots can be very helpful in the education field, and educators will be inspired to use them.

Although Sandu and Gide [10] described the benefits of using chatbots in higher education, their study's findings also revealed that students were concerned about getting the wrong advice from the chatbots, and they were also worried about privacy issues. To measure the benefits and limitations of using chatbots. Lidén and Nilros [4] investigated the perceived advantages and disadvantages of chatbots from the students' perspective. The researchers interviewed students to explore their point of views. Four themes were identified based on the interviews: the first theme was minimising the obstacles that can be found while using chatbots, the second theme was improving the learning process, the third theme was the hesitance when it comes to chatbot's complexity, and the final theme was teachers' involvement in the process. The study suggested it is better to have basic features in the chatbots instead of complex AI features.

4 Conclusion

The review shows that chatbots could positively impact the field of teaching and learning in higher education; therefore, they can serve as good teachers' assistants. Several studies revealed that chatbots have pedagogical benefits and could enhance the process of teaching and learning. The review also concludes that chatbots can facilitate student-centred learning and create an individualised learning experience for students, especially for large classes. Chatbots can be beneficial to teachers and educational institutions as they are cost-effective and can save time and effort. However, further investigation is needed to consider the different factors that might affect the use of chatbots in education, such as technical and functionality issues, wrong advice, privacy and security issues. More research should be done in higher education, and more data should be collected from teachers and students to give better insights into their experiences of using chatbots, especially as teachers' assistants, to save time and efforts.

References

1. Haristiani, N.U.R.I.A., Danuwijaya, A.A.: Gengobot: A chatbot-based grammar application on mobile instant messaging as language learning medium. J. Eng. Sci. Technol. **14**(6), 3158–3173 (2019)
2. Kim, N.Y.: A study on chatbots for developing Korean college students' English listening and reading skills. J. Dig. Converg. **16**(8), 19–26 (2018)

3. Kitchenham, B.A.: Procedures for Undertaking Systematic Reviews, Joint Technical Report, Computer Science Department, Keele University (TR/SE0401) and National ICT Australia Ltd. (2004)
4. Lidén, A., Nilros, K.: Perceived benefits and limitations of chatbots in higher education. Linnaeus University (2020)
5. Fernoagă, V., Stelea, G.A., Gavrilă, C., Sandu, F.: Intelligent education assistant powered by Chatbots. In: The International Scientific Conference eLearning and Software for Education, vol. 2, pp. 376–383. "Carol I" National Defence University (2018)
6. Fleming, M., Riveros, P., Reidsema, C., Achilles, N.: Streamlining student course requests using chatbots. In: 29th Australasian Association for Engineering Education Conference 2018 (AAEE 2018), p. 207. Engineers Australia (2018)
7. Georgescu, A.A.: Chatbots for Education–Trends, Benefits and Challenges. In: Conference Proceedings of eLearning and Software for Education (eLSE), vol. 2, no. 14, pp. 195–200. "Carol I" National Defence University Publishing House (2018)
8. Gupta, S., Jagannath, K., Aggarwal, N., Sridar, R., Wilde, S., Chen, Y.: Artificially Intelligent (AI) Tutors in the Classroom: A Need Assessment Study of Designing Chatbots to Support Student Learning (2019)
9. Gonda, D.E., Luo, J., Wong, Y.L., Lei, C.U.: Evaluation of developing educational chatbots based on the seven principles for good teaching. In: 2018 IEEE International Conference on Teaching, Assessment, and Learning for Engineering (TALE), pp. 446–453. IEEE, December 2018
10. Sandu, N., Gide, E.: Adoption of AI-chatbots to enhance student learning experience in higher education in India. In: 2019 18th International Conference on Information Technology Based Higher Education and Training (ITHET), pp. 1–5. IEEE, September 2019
11. Studente, S., Ellis, S., Garivaldis, S.F.: Exploring the potential of chatbots in higher education: a preliminary study. Int. J. Educ. Pedagog. Sci. **14**(9), 768–771 (2020)
12. Thomas, H.: Critical literature review on chatbots in education. IJTSRD **4**(6), 786–788 (2020)
13. Roos, S.: Chatbots in education: A passing trend or a valuable pedagogical tool? (2018)
14. Meyer von Wolff, R., Nörtemann, J., Hobert, S., Schumann, M.: Chatbots for the information acquisition at universities – a student's view on the application area. In: Følstad, A., Araujo, T., Papadopoulos, S., Law, E.-C., Granmo, O.-C., Luger, E., Brandtzaeg, P.B. (eds.) CONVERSATIONS 2019. LNCS, vol. 11970, pp. 231–244. Springer, Cham (2020). https://doi.org/10.1007/978-3-030-39540-7_16
15. Winkler, R., Söllner, M.: Unleashing the potential of chatbots in education: a state-of-the-art analysis. In: Academy of Management Annual Meeting (AOM). Chicago, USA (2018)
16. Yang, S., Evans, C.: Opportunities and challenges in using ai chatbots in higher education. In: Proceedings of the 2019 3rd International Conference on Education and E-Learning, pp. 79–83, November 2019

Collaborative Spatial Problem-Solving Strategies Presented by First Graders by Interacting with Tangible User Interface

Jorge Hernán Aristizábal Zapata[1]($\boxtimes$) (iD) and Julián Esteban Gutíerrez Posada[2]($\boxtimes$) (iD)

[1] Gedes Research Group, Department of Education, University of Quindío, Armenia, Colombia
`jhaz@uniquindio.edu.co`
[2] Grid Research Group, Department of Engineering, University of Quindío, Armenia, Colombia
`jugutier@uniquindio.edu.co`

Abstract. Today's society alongside technological advancement requires people to work collaboratively, be better prepared and competent to deal with the diversity of problems, on the other hand, the use of technologies like Tangible User Interfaces (TUIs), allows people to explore different alternatives when they are faced with a problem situation, so this paper presents an investigation with the objective was to analyze the incidence of the different strategies collaborative in type spatial problem-solving that presented by first-grade boys and girls under the pretext of games. The research was carried out in a public primary school of low socioeconomic class in a region between mountains, called Córdoba, of Quindío State in country Colombia. The sample involved the first-grade course with 16 students randomly divided into groups. The methodology used was qualitative research by focusing on understanding the phenomena, exploring them from the perspective of the participants. Data collection is based on transcriptions and video analysis of student interaction during task execution with TUI in the educational scenario of the game. To develop this research 4 stages were planned, and two TUIs were built (an educational robot and a robot jeep-type vehicles) and an app for mobile phones. The results are related to the restructuring of children's thinking, the difficulties in solving the problem, and the resolution strategies that emerged within the groups, besides it the conflicts and agreements that arise in the interaction with classmates when proposing strategies of problem-solving.

Keywords: Collaborative spatial problem-solving strategies · Tangible User Interfaces · First-grade children · 21st century skills

1 Introduction

Actual society alongside requires people with a skill for the 21st-century, among these are creativity and innovation, problem-solving and critical thinking, communication and collaboration furthermore ICT literacy [1, 2] namely be better prepared to the diversity of problems that appear on the day by day.

21st-century skills are not only developed in college, but these skills must also be found since children in school or kindergarten.

C. Stephanidis et al. (Eds.): HCII 2021, CCIS 1421, pp. 64–71, 2021.
https://doi.org/10.1007/978-3-030-78645-8_9

Thus, children require new challenges that lead them to develop their think, opportunities to work collaboratively, learn problem-solving through games in class, and integrate technology into the teaching to explore different alternatives that allow them to develop these skills. Therefore, teachers should include in their classes the enriched environments that respond to an educational strategy. This implies the use of manipulable material, games, and technological tools such as Tangible User Interfaces (TUIs). This allows children through manipulation to explore different alternatives when faced with a problematic situation.

In this line, there are works like: [3] they developed Active Learning Environments with Robotic Tangibles for educational, in the context of free play and open-ended learning activities. They showed that these Learning Environments afford opportunities for young children to engage in spatial programming. [4] Who to observed and characterized heuristic resources and management processes developed by three pairs how of students of first school ages during the resolution of problems with the Bee-bot programmable robot.

This study was designed to determine Collaborative spatial problem-solving strategies or presented by first graders by interacting with Tangible User Interface. The structure of this paper is as follows: Sect. 2. Introduces the background of the research and shows the characteristics that support this research Sect. 3. The used methodology is briefly described. Sect. 4. Show the finding obtained in this study and discussion of the results Sect. 5. Presents the concludes this research.

2 Background

For the research "Collaborative spatial problem-solving strategies presented by first graders by interacting with Tangible User Interface" was necessary to design an enriched environment that included interaction with digital and tangible educational resources or TUI, the educational scenario of the game, and the strategies of the work-ing collaborative each of these elements is defined below.

2.1 Enriched Environment

We define an enriched environment as a scenario of actions with a pedagogical intention. That allows organizing mental schemes, through play, interaction with digital educational resources, and tangible materials. In order to enhance the development of skills, competencies, and dexterity of children, motivating discovery and conjecture through manipulation and exploration. Therefore, the enriched environment must motivate the desire to learn to facilitate the exchange and construction of knowledge in the teaching-learning process.

2.2 Tangible User Interfaces (TUIs)

The Tangible User Interfaces are manipulable materials that allow interaction between the physical object and digital information, making the technology invisible to the user besides the offers immediate feedback. Ishii suggests the (TUIs) aim to take advantage of the haptic interaction skills. The key idea of TUIs is to give physical forms to digital information through the manipulation of objects. Thus, the TUIs makes digital information directly manipulable with our hands, and perceptible through our peripheral senses by physically embodying [5]. Similarly, Gutierrez and other [6], in their study evidence that children using TUI a greater sense of motivation and joy than GUI. This allows them to believe in the potential of TUI to be used in educational contexts, hence "the use of TUI was capable of promoting a stronger and long-lasting involvement having a greater potential to engage children" [7, p. 1], for the above developing and implementing TUIs in a classroom allow empowering collaboration and learning taking advantage of digital technology on manipulating physical objects and digital materials [8]. Thus "tangible interfaces add new physical actions to the repertoire of computer-based learning activities" [9, p. 223].

2.3 Spatial Skill

Different research [10–14] show that Spatial skill is related to teaching mathematics and geometry. According to Gilligan, Flouri, and Farran in his model of Spatial skill have two theoretical distinctions intrinsic and extrinsic besides two representations, static and dynamic representations. The Intrinsic are those that relate to the size and orientation of an object, its parts, and its relationships. While the extrinsic relate to the location of an object, the relationship between objects as well as the relationship between objects and their reference frames. Thus, Dynamic representations require movement such as bending, moving, folding, scaling, or rotation [13].

2.4 Games

Game is a natural activity for people that allows organizing mental schemes mobilizing thought, language, and action, thus, the game enables learning through exploration. Game is necessary for child development besides stimulating and enhances strategies, and skills necessary for the development of various faculties such as cognition, psychomotor, affective, and social.

To Discuss the game, it is necessary to make the distinction between gamification, entertainment games, Educational games, learning games. Dörner, Göbel and Wolfgang [15] state that:

- Gamification means adding game elements to a non-gaming area.
- Entertainment games is a digital game that has the exclusive objective of entertaining the player.
- Educational games focus on formal learning and address the formal education sector from primary schools to higher education, vocational training, and collaborative training in the workplace.
- Learning games primarily address informal learning.

On the other hand, there are the Cooperative Games [16] where the participants with different skills contribute their best, helping the rest of the group to learn as well, creating relationships and positive social skills.

2.5 Collaborative Working

Collaborative working is a social process where needs to Interaction, communication, and collaboration of other people´s thus to get the problem-solving strategies type, thus it is essential the individual engagement. On the other hand, Wendel and Konert define "Collaborative learning is a situation in which two or more people learn, or attempt to learn, something together with various specific learning mechanisms"[17, p. 224]. Therefore, Search context is the collaborative strategies under the pretext of games in the classroom.

3 Methodology

3.1 Design

The research method used was qualitative according to Hernandez y Fernandez [18] research by focusing on understanding the phenomena, exploring them from the perspective of the participants in their natural environment, and concerning the context.

3.2 Population

The research was carried out in a public primary school of low socioeconomic class in a region between mountains, called Córdoba, of Quindío State in country Colombia. The sample involved the first-grade course with 16 students randomly divided into four groups (6 boys and 10 girls) aged between 5 to 7 years old. The intervention with children was carried out for six weeks with a duration of 2.5 h per session. Each session, a different activity was worked (see Fig. 1). Coding was used for Groups G1, G2, G3, and G4, for each member of the group with the letters a, b, c, and d. Furthermore, the problems were assigned T1, T2,…, T6. Each problem had different associated tasks. e.g. if group 1 did problem 5 and the leader of the moment was member c, it was coded "G1cT5". On the other hand, difficulties were also coded. SD = without difficulty. D1 = Change of direction (backward vs forwards). D2 = take a wrong turn and not know what to do. D3 = make a wrong turn but return around or turn several times. D4 = take a wrong turn and keep moving. D5 = passed over the obstacle. D6 = not find the shortest way. D7 = not finding all the paths. D8 = not find the solution (see Table 1).

3.3 Materials and Description

To develop this research was built an enriched environment which includes two TUIs an educational robot (see Fig. 2a). a Jeep-type vehicle robot (see Fig. 2b). an app for mobile phones (see Fig. 2c). and manipulative material (see Fig. 2d). where the educational scenario is under the game pretext, then were four stages planned for experimentation. (1) diagnostic stage: to inquire about the student's previous knowledge in terms of proposing and following algorithms, spatial location, and laterality. (2) feedback stage: where it was explained what teamwork consisted of through game, Aristizábal et al. in game as didactic strategy showed that "its dynamics puts into action the ability to reason, propose, communicate mathematically from orality and writing" [19, p. 118, 119] and,

Fig. 1. Different activity session work in group.

the TUI utilization because all technology substantially modifies the forms of knowledge construction and its nature [20]. (3) execution stage: an educational scenario for solving problems framed in the game and the utilization TUIs was implemented in the classroom, so an educational robot was used that stated the problems to the four groups. Thus, the children in each group will discuss and agree on a resolution strategy in a given time. Later each group introducing the strategy in an application mobile phone application designed in-app inventor to solve the problem posed. Consequently, a type-Jeep vehicle robot executes the actions entered on the mobile phone. The set of activities for each problem increases the level of difficulty. These activities are aimed at taking a jeep-type vehicle from a starting point A to a destination point B. Each group of four students had to discuss the sequence of steps to achieve the objective and propose it on a given paper template (see Fig. 2e)., before running it. According to the problem, the set of activities varies, that is to say, change the vehicle's starting position (see Fig. 3a)., make turns, and move the jeep with restriction of turns or movements (see Fig. 3b)., dodge obstacles (see Fig. 3c)., given a partial sequence of displacement, turns and the arrival point, complete the sequence (see Fig. 3d)., and given a sequence with instructions for displacement and turns, determine the destination point (see Fig. 3e)., and pose a problem to another team. (4) Evaluation stage: in it stage the information was collected, ordered, and classified in stage 3, to carry out the analysis and interpretation of the data, transcripts, and analysis of the videos taken in the interaction of the students with the TUIs.

(a)   (b)   (c)   (d)

Fig. 2. The enriched environment components

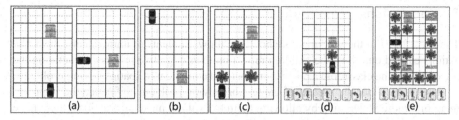

Fig. 3. Different activity spatial problems

4   Findings

The results found are related to the restructuring of children´s thinking, the spatial difficulties in solving the problem when changing orientation, the resolution strategies that emerged within the groups, on the other hand, the possible answers to questions are diverse but various groups agreed on one or more strategies, in addition to it show the conflicts and agreements that arise in the interaction with classmates when proposing spatial problem-solving strategies.

In problem T2C1 (Fig. 3b) it was observed that, despite the fact that the activity had different ways of resolution, the groups coincided in two paths (G1–G4, and G2–G3), while T3C1 (Fig. 3b) activity where it was restricted to three turns without obstacles, three different resolution were presented (G1–G3, G2, and G4).

It is observed that when the members of the same team agreed on the strategy, they wanted to be the first to go out to carry out the activity, while when they did not agree on the resolution, each one wanted to impose their solution, which caused more time in the development of the activity.

One of the difficulties observed with spatial problem-solving is the position of the child with respect to the jeep-type vehicles. Making the turn the jeep vehicles by children must imagine themselves as the driver of the vehicle. A fact that they do not when do start the activity because they pose the turns from the position in which they are. This causes sometimes jeep vehicles the turn to the opposite side G2dT2, G1cT3 and G4aT3 or instead of moving forward go back G1bT2. e.g., D1, D2, or D3 (see Table 1).

The collaboration includes dimensions as communication but also includes important individual contributions. G3dT4 presented difficulty in D3 because the student (d), despite having planned the strategy with his classmates, made out the procedure that he (d) considered appropriate thus generating a different route from the one agreed. This caused discussion in G3.

Table 1. Group performance vs problems.

	T1	T2	T3	T4	T5	T6
G1	ND	D1	D3	D1, D3	ND	D8
G2	ND	D2	D1, D3	D4	D7	D8
G3	ND	ND	ND	D3	ND	ND
G4	ND	D4	D3	ND	ND	ND

5 Conclusions

The use of TUI in the working collaborative allows students to immediately check the actions carried out, thus, the children reflect on their cognitive process. Generating the use of TUI in the classroom a positive impact at the moment of spatial solving problems.

Use TUIs under the pretext of games for solving problems influence the improvement of children's learning by allowing them to explore, make abstractions, then make conjectures, and interpretations around in group discussion, thus reach agreements and communicate them.

Various activities should be carried out within the framework of an enriched environment so that children at this age-old develop their spatial thinking.

References

1. Kereluik, K., Mishra, P., Fahnoe, C., Terry, L.: What knowledge is of most worth: teacher knowledge for 21st century learning. J. Digit. Learn. Teach. Educ. **29**(4), 127–140 (2013). https://doi.org/10.1080/21532974.2013.10784716
2. UNESCO: Documento de Trabajo E2030 : Educación y Habilidades para el Siglo 21. Doc. Trab., pp. 1–55 (2017). www.unesco.org/open-access/terms-use-ccbysa-sp
3. Burleson, W.S., et al.: Active learning environments with robotic tangibles: children's physical and virtual spatial programming experiences. IEEE Trans. Learn. Technol. **11**(1), 96–106 (2018). https://doi.org/10.1109/TLT.2017.2724031
4. Nebot, P.D.D., Vera, D.A., Calero Somoza, J.: Educación Matemática en la Infancia Elementos de resolución de problemas en primeras edades. **7**, 12–41 (2018)
5. Ishii, H.: From GUI to TUI Urp : An Example of TUI. Interfaces (Providence), pp. 1–17 (2006)
6. Gutiérrez Posada, J.E., Hayashi, E.C.S., Baranauskas, M.C.C.: On feelings of comfort, motivation and joy that GUI and TUI evoke. In: Marcus, A. (ed.) DUXU 2014. LNCS, vol. 8520, pp. 273–284. Springer, Cham (2014). https://doi.org/10.1007/978-3-319-07638-6_27
7. Sylla, C., Branco, P., Coutinho, C., Coquet, E.: TUIs vs. GUIs: comparing the learning potential with preschoolers. Pers. Ubiquitous Comput. **16**(4), 421–432 (2012). https://doi.org/10.1007/s00779-011-0407-z
8. Ishii, H., Ullmer, B.: Tangible bits: towards seamless interfaces between people, bits, and atoms. In: Proceedings of the 8th International Conference on Intelligent User Interfaces, no. March, p. 3 (1997). https://doi.org/10.1145/604045.604048
9. Schneider, B., Jermann, P., Zufferey, G., Dillenbourg, P.: Benefits of a tangible interface for collaborative learning and interaction. IEEE Trans. Learn. Technol. **4**(3), 222–232 (2011). https://doi.org/10.1109/TLT.2010.36
10. Güven, B., Kosa, T.: The effect of dynamic geometry software on student mathematics teachers' spatial visualization skills. Turkish Online J. Educ. Technol. **7**(4), 100–107 (2008)
11. Miller, D.I., Halpern, D.F.: Can spatial training improve long-term outcomes for gifted STEM undergraduates? Learn. Individ. Differ. **26**, 141–152 (2013). https://doi.org/10.1016/j.lindif.2012.03.012
12. Karakuş, F., Aydin, B.: The effects of computer algebra system on undergraduate students' spatial visualization skills in a calculus course. Malaysian Online J. Educ. Technol. **5**(3), 54–69 (2017). www.mojet.net
13. Gilligan, K.A., Flouri, E., Farran, E.K.: The contribution of spatial ability to mathematics achievement in middle childhood. J. Exp. Child Psychol. **163**, 107–125 (2017). https://doi.org/10.1016/j.jecp.2017.04.016

14. Rutherford, T., Karamarkovich, S.M., Lee, D.S.: Is the spatial/math connection unique? Associations between mental rotation and elementary mathematics and English achievement. Learn. Individ. Differ. **62**(January), 180–199 (2018). https://doi.org/10.1016/j.lindif.2018.01.014

15. Dörner, R., Göbel, S., Effelsberg, W., Wiemeyer, J.: Serious games, vol. 13, no. 6. Switzerland (2016)

16. Granado, N., Garayo, A.: Juegos cooperativos: Aprender a cooperar, cooperar para aprender. Barcelona (2015)

17. Wendel, V., Konert, J., Multiplayer Serious Games (2016)

18. del pilar Hernandez-Sampieri, . C.; Fernández-Collado, B.-L.M.: Metodología de la Investigación (2010)

19. Aristizábal, J. H., Colorado, H., Gutiérrez, H.: "El juego como una estrategia didáctica para desarrollar el pensamiento numérico en las cuatro operaciones básicas," *Sofia- sophia*, vol. 12, no. 1, pp. 117–127, 2016, doi: https://doi.org/10.18634/sophiaj.12v.1i.450.

20. Moreno, T.R.L.: Las nuevas tecnologias en el aula de matemáticas y ciencias. Av. y Perspect vol. 17 (1998)

A Study on the Promotion Strategy of the Taichung Learning City Project as the Development Process of the Culture Identity of a City

Chi-Sen Hung[1]([✉]) and Yun-Chi Lee[2]([✉])

[1] Department of Communication Design, National Taichung University of Science and Technology, Taichung, Taiwan
[2] Doctoral Program in Design, College of Design, National Taipei University of Technology, Taipei, Taiwan

Abstract. The definition of a learning city is defined by the European Lifelong Learning Initiative (ELLI), focusing on city development, vision, and the problem encountered at all stages of development. Citizens, through systematic learning processes, discovering questions, and mutual discussions, are able to reach consensus and work together on city development.

Since 2015, the Ministry of Education of Taiwan has promoted the learning city project, inviting the government worldwide to come up with suitable city development plans for regional cities. The Taichung city government launched the "Taichung city, a learning city" project during 2016 and 2019. Within four years, it has resulted effectively by the establishment of the city culture image of "Humanistic, Happiness and Livable, Taichung pro Learning and Beautiful;" this has become a model example for other county governments. To fully understand how Taichung city government promotes the identity of city culture by launching the learning city project, this study has taken the method of in-depth interview and participatory observation method. The interview began in 2016 with a total 25 interviewees from the project members and the execution team of the education bureau; while the practice of participatory observation method is by participating the 2019 Taichung learning city project for a year in order to analyze the promotion strategy of the Taichung learning city project.

Keywords: Learning city · Culture identity of a city · Taichung city

1 Introduction

The competition today has become even more globalized, while the competition advantages are dependent on the region. (Porter 1996). In the 80s, the United States and part of European countries began to put emphasis on "City Marketing" as a crucial development strategy. The perspective was based on re-evaluation and re-presentation in order to enhance city identity and to achieve the goal of building the harmonious city, so that the

© Springer Nature Switzerland AG 2021
C. Stephanidis et al. (Eds.): HCII 2021, CCIS 1421, pp. 72–79, 2021.
https://doi.org/10.1007/978-3-030-78645-8_10

multidimensional developments may satisfy the needs of citizens, investors, and tourists (Avraham 2004). However, there are still differences between "City Marketing" and the concept of average product marketing; the goal of City Marketing might not be profiting, in most situation, it is associate with social welfare, infrastructure establishment, employment, wellbeing of all, and public goods; by combining each perspective of needs and establishing the city brand image, city marketing aims at different marketing needs.

Taichung City is located in central Taiwan and serves as a critical transportation junction. It has been the important place for sports, culture, education, politics, and even wars during the 1920s. Taichung city was praised as a "Cultural City" in the past. Nevertheless, after World War II with the modernization, development and business and industries activities, Taichung gradually lost its position and features. After 2010, to eliminate the negative image of Taichung city, the government has been actively emphasizing "culture" as the brand image for Taichung city in hope of restoring the fame of "Cultural City".

Landry (2008) is the first scholar who created the idea of a "learning city". He suggested that every city should base on learning; with this concept in mind, each city should ensure every citizen with the chance of constant learning opportunities. The mentioned learning includes not only the former academicals education, but also multiple learning forms offered by the society through various strategies. The development of the learning city in Taiwan was initiated in the 2010 National Education Conference. Taichung city in 2016 participated in the national project of learning city and launched the learning city project during 2016 and 2019. This study aims at the development strategy of city identity; and Taichung city was chosen as a case study for further understanding of how Taichung City through the promotion of learning city projects, gradually construct the image of a cultural city, while eventually establishing the identity of city brand.

2 Literature Review

2.1 Learning City

The development of a learning city associates with issues such as sustainable development and global citizenship (Morgan 2009); therefore, a learning city is also named as a lifelong learning city which citizens are encouraged to be a lifelong learner and the public sector, private units, and non-profit organizations cooperate to facilitate the city learning network. The United Nations Educational, Scientific and Cultural Organization (UNESCO) points out that comprehensive learning improves citizen's ability, social integration, economy development, cultural prosperity, and sustainable development. Professor Longworth, the chairman of European Lifelong Learning Initiative (ELLI) presented 14 characteristics of a learning city in "LEARNINGCITIS," an acronym stands for Leadership, Employment, Aspirations, Resources, Networks, Information, Needs, Growth, Change management, Investment, Technology, Involvement, Environment, and Strategies for the family (Longworth 1999) it can be discovered that the promotion of learning city will enhance citizens in various ways and improve the competitiveness of a city.

2.2   The Context of Promoting Learning City in Taiwan

The lifelong learning education in Taiwan began in 1988 as it was mentioned in the 6th National Education Conference that "the establishment of the adult education system as the goal of citizen education and lifelong education. Later in 1991, the "Developing and Improving Adult Education Five Years' Plan" was launched; and in 1995 the Ministry of Education (MOE) published "Republic of China Education Report: The Education Vision Towards 21th Century" that the lifelong learning has officially become one of the Taiwan education goal. After the announcement, MOE promoted multiple adult education policies and lifelong education policies; these policies are the cornerstones for future promotion of learning cities. In 1998, MOE published the "Community Lifelong Learning Program White Paper of: Towards the lifelong learning society," and quoted "the concept of lifelong learning is the key for human beings to enter 21th century" from the 1996 UNESCO published "Learning: the Treasure Within" as a manifesto to transform Taiwan's society into a learning society by publishing the "Towards Learning Society" white paper. MOE announced that the year 1998 was the "Lifelong Learning Year" (MOE 2020). In 2002, the promulgated Lifelong Learning Act became the source of law for Taiwan's lifelong learning development.

Promotion of the learning city is a social movement of lifelong education and learning. Before 2010, the Taiwan government had actively promoted various learning society and learning community policies. With the development of international lifelong learning ideas, the 8th National Education Conference in 2010 mentioned the "Progression in lifelong learning strategy and creating a learning society" to discuss the challenges and future development strategies for learning cities. The conference ends with selecting four exemplary learning cities which are Taipei City as the lifelong learning development city, Miao-Li County as the development of smart city, Chia-Yi County for tourism and recreation education development, and Tainan City for the development of a grand temple learning base. The four locations were expected to be the role models for the future development of Taiwan's communities. (Department of Lifelong Learning of MOE 2020).

In 2015, MOE launched a pioneer project of initiating nationwide learning cities. The pioneer project office was designated to host a national lifelong education forum, inviting each city and counties for experience sharing and with keynote speeches, research paper publishing, topical discussions, and workshops to create exchange opportunities for each region. In the same year, MOE selected 7 cities to subsidized the initiation of learning city; the regions were, Taipei City, Yilan city, Hsinchu County, Nantou County, and Chiayi County; In 2016, Taichung City, Changhua County, and Taitung County participated the project, which is a total 10 cities; in 2017, New Taipei City, Tainan City, and Pingtung County adds in, a total 13 cities in count; in 2018, Yunlin County and ChiaYi city participated and the count is 15 cities; in 2019, since Taipei City did not apply for MOE's fund, the count of project participants are 14 cities; in 2020, MOE had different funding policy and promoted the learning city funding policies into overall transformation policies. Taichung City, benefited from the four year learning city project experience, has a steady growing city lifelong education system with the connection of the academic lifelong education resources that forms a lifelong learning supporting network.

2.3 City Brand and City Identity

The trend of globalization prompts the city brand manager, which usually is the government of the city, to consider a city's unique culture, site, history, customs, architecture, and the cultural values of the above-mentioned subjects to build the city brand identification through systematically brand positioning, marketing analysis, and the combination of communication strategies as the powerful marketing strategy, so that the city might have the capability of competing with other international cities (Kavaratzis and Ashworth 2008).

The construction of city brands may enhance the city identity and these are the image of how people think of the city. The description of the image can be divided as designate image and appraisable image (Stern and Krakover 1993). The designate image describes the innate condition of a city such as the tangible or intangible facilities, services, constructions, sites, cultural behaviors and cultural activities; while the appraisable image tends to be the description of the value, impressions, and emotional bonds of a city (Kavaratzis and Ashworth 2008). However, the establishment of a city brand is not simply the work of the government, but should be the goal for all the citizens. As the learning city ideology, so as the practice of city brand marketing, after the vision established by the government, cooperation with private enterprises, non-government organizations, and each citizen will boost the competitiveness of a city as well as regional economy growth and bring forth social welfare. Gelder and Allan (2006) more specifically pointed out the process of city branding and the creation of brand value, must come from the constant accumulation of projects and events that may include business investments, economy development plans, urban landscape planning, and city activity marketing and communications; these will gradually create the emotional, psychological, and spiritual bondings between people and city (Kavaratzis 2008).

3 Method

This study adopts the in-depth interview methods, interviewing the staff that are responsible for the implementation of the plan from the Taichung City Bureau of Education from 2016 to 2019. The interviewees are as follows: a total of 3 public servants, the annual plan hosts of each cooperative unit, 4 university professors, 3 members of lifelong education organization, 5 teachers who participated in the project, and 17 students who participated in the project. The in-depth interviews were conducted between November and December 2019, and each interview was conducted in their work environment.

For Taichung City's learning city development and project results, we adopted the second-hand literature collection and text analysis strategies. Special thanks to the Taichung City Government Education Bureau for providing the content and project reports of the learning city plan from 2016 to 2019; and thanks for providing relevant information such as development strategy meetings, work meetings, progress tracking meetings, review meetings, etc. for the implementation of the plan. This study also collected various annual media related reports for collection, various course management materials, lecture notes, teaching plans, student feedback materials… and other materials.

In addition, the researcher conducted a participatory observation method by actually participating in the implementation of the "2019 Taichung Learning City Plan" from March 2019 to January 2020 so that in-depth understanding of the actual situation, problems, strategies and benefits of the operation team in the implementation of the learning city may be achieved.

4 Data Analysis

4.1 Taichung City Development Background

During the Japanese rule era, Taichung has been strategically planned by the Japanese government. The development of Green Canal, Willow Canal, Taichung Park, and Taichung Train Station have been expected to transform Taichung into the landscape of "petit Kyoto". In 1921 and 1934, the Taiwanese Cultural Association and Taiwan Art and literature League were founded to voice for the rights for Taiwanese and bring up the national identity of Taiwan. These movements and organizations encouraged the gathering of intellectuals and social movement activists; and with these aggregations, the cultural heritage of Taichung has become abundant. In recent years, Taichung have become the development junction among the 6 cities and with numerous infrastructure launched that brings the overall development of the central Taiwan living sphere. Especially, the government encouraged the initiation of Central Taiwan Science Park which leads to the Technology Corridor of the west Taichung city and high-tech talents were recruited, the employment opportunity become higher, bringing the high effectiveness industrial clustering. However, the rapidness of modernizations and urbanization resulted in the decaying of the praise of "cultural city" since Japanese rule era.

Nearly a decade, Taichung city government target at "restoring the culture city fame," as the city development and brand marketing principle. The government fervently invest in numerous cultural activities and constructions such as, National Taichung Theater, transportation rearrangement, hydrological constructions, and revitalize regional culture centers; the 2018 Taichung World Flora Exposition was held and large scale cultural activities were facilitated and the promotion of large scale youth entrepreneurship incubation projects were initiated. According to the statistics of the Ministry of Culture, in 2008, a total 4,409 art and cultural events were held and 14,166 people participated; in 2019 the art and cultural event grew in numbers times 1.43, which was a count of 6,317 events and the participants were 30,656 in total which is a 2.16 times growth in number (MOC 2020). It is seen that the promoting of cultural policies in Taichung city has gradually changed the lifestyle of citizens.

4.2 Project Development Goal, Strategy, and Structure

The directing unit of Taichung Learning City project is the department of lifelong learning of Taichung City Education Bureau. Each year, regional education units, community college, experts, and cross section government personnels are invited to plan for next year's project and later send to MOE for applying the funds. Since 2015 when MOE began to launch the learning city project, it was up to each city and county to apply; and in 2020 the funding policy changed by funding cities and counties with special features. Taichung city has facilitated the learning city project for 4 years from 2016 to 2019. The result of the interview shows that in 2016, the first year of learning city projects, the main idea was to restore the fame of Cultural City and emphasize on aesthetic education. Meanwhile, it was the year when Taichung City successfully being authorized the host right of the "2018 Taichung World Flora Exposition" by International Association of Horticultural Producers (AIHP). For the 2018 flora expo, Taichung City government speeded up each transportation construction, and promoted aesthetic education policies through the national education system. From the perspective of organizations that participated in the learning city project, during 2016–2017 there were mainly units of elementary schools, junior high schools, art museums, museums, and community colleges for cooperation. Till 2018–2019 the focus of learning city started to combine with the local universities and the project of University Social Responsibilities (USR), local enterprises, lifelong educations; the project of learning city emphasized on aspects of innovation, entrepreneurship, and passing on culture as the main focus of aesthetic education. The core goal of the four year participation of learning city projects has been consistent, while actual practicing the strategy and the targeting group have been different. The construction of an overall aesthetic education network system prompts the participants, mainly Taichung City Residents, to rediscover regional aesthetic and the characteristics, so that the recognition of city identity and the cultural image of the city can be generated.

Through in-depth interview with the project personnel of the Taichung Education Bureau, we understand that there is a clear yearly goal for the operation of learning city project and there is a yearly operation strategy being proposed. The project in 2016 was based on three strategic facets that are "Aesthetic Seeding," "Aesthetic Experience," and "Aesthetic Living," for achieving the goal of improving aesthetic education; in 2017, the strategic facets were "Fulfill Aesthetic Knowledge," "Enhancing Aesthetic Experience," and "Create Aesthetic Life" and targeted at "Humanistic as foundation, Happiness and Livable".

Year 2018 was a year of flourishing, with the experience and aesthetic education of the previous years, and the 2018 Taichung World Flora Exposition, the goal was "Co-create artistic city, Taichung well learned and beautiful" in hope of utilizing local life, culture, and materials to bring about aesthetic life and learning atmosphere and lead to industrial innovation developments and competitiveness. The year 2019, the Taichung City government had deepened the local cultural discovery in terms of exploring the old city's culture, heritages, artifacts, and food. At the same time, the purpose was to cope with the city development goals and head towards "Aesthetic experience economy, representing the charm of old city", so that a livable cultural city could be built and with the boosting of cultural industries' development, old city cultural brand could be established.

4.3 Strategy of Promoting City's Identity

The promotion of learning cities should be based on the vision of urban development. The city government should invest inter-ministerial resources to work together. The four years include the contribution of the central government's Ministry of Culture,

Ministry of Education, Ministry of Labor, and Transportation and Communications. The contribution includes each Taichung city government sections which are the Education Bureau, The Labor Affairs Bureau, the Cultural Affairs Bureau, the Tourism and Travel Bureau, the construction Bureau, the Social Affairs Bureau, the Information Bureau and other bureaus participated.

In addition to the top-down policy promotion, the interactive relationship between education and learning can also form a local grassroots force through the implementation of the plan, which promotes residents' re-recognition and recognition of local culture and forms a cohesive force. Longworth (2006) pointed out that partnerships between the public sector, enterprises, schools, and non-profit organizations, combined with the use of various types of social resources, are an indispensable basic element of a learning city. A strategic alliance member of the Taichung Learning City Project for the four years includes 19 elementary schools, 8 junior high schools, 5 high schools, 8 universities, 14 central and local government units, 16 private enterprises, 19 non-profit organizations, and 6 lifelong education units as strategic alliance partners. The total number of people participating in the learning program exceeds 15,000, and the number of marginal touches is estimated to be more than 1 million, which has a good effect on city brand marketing.

In terms of the implementation strategy of city branding and self-identification, the Taichung Learning City Project guides students to explore the local culture in depth through various experiential learning processes and introduces innovative, creative, and entrepreneurial thinking, while actively explores sustainable business models as well as the possibility of young people returning to their hometowns to start their own businesses. They also put forward the announcement that "every Taichung citizen is a guide in Taichung", looking forward to proposing an innovative economic model. The actual actions include: holding regional tourism development forums, local tour planning workshops, training local guide volunteers, inviting literary writers and historians to share local cultural stories, facilitating international seminars on local creation issues, and establishing tourism reservation information platform, holding exchanges and achievement exhibitions for more media exposure, teachers and students from colleges and universities to introduce design power to develop cultural and creative products for the place, setting up Taichung City Lifelong Learning Promotion Committee... etc.; the aforementioned are all important strategies for reshaping Taichung City as a "culture city" brand.

5   Conclusion and Suggestions

Since the Taiwan Learning City Funding Program was promoted by the Ministry of Education in 2015 and with 14 counties and cities participated in the process until 2019. Each has promoted lifelong education policies in accordance with urban development goals and positioning and resulted fruitfully. Taichung City has implemented a learning city plan for four years. Government departments, national education units, life-long social education units, private enterprises, and non-governmental organizations have jointly contributed to build a Learning City Network and work hard towards urban development goals. Taichung City adopts the method of a learning strategy to invite urban residents to re-explore the cultural heritage of the local area. Through the process of re-understanding and re-experiencing, it arouses residents' identification and cohesion with the city, thereby improving employment opportunities, information development, tourism economy, and even migrant population. Theses strategies have comprehensively and systematically enhance Taichung's cultural awareness and quality of life.

References

Porter, M.E.: Competitive advantage, agglomeration economies and regional policy. Int. Reg. Sci. Rev. **19**(1–2), 85–90 (1996)

Avraham, E.: Media strategies for improving an unfavorable image. Cities **21**(6), 471–479 (2004)

Landry, C.: The Creative City: A Toolkit for Urban Innovators. Stylus, Sterling (2008)

Morgan, A.D.: Learning communities, cities and regions for sustainable development and global citizenship. Local Environ. **14**(5), 443–459 (2009)

UNESCO Institute for Lifelong Learning: UNESCO Global Network of Learning Cities. Hamburg (2016)

Longworth, N.: Making Lifelong Learning Work: learning Cities for a Learning Century. Kogan Page Limited, London (1999)

Longworth, N.: Learning Cities. Learning Communities: Lifelong Learning and Local Government. Routledge, London (2006)

Ministry of Education (MOE). Taiwan. http://www.edu.tw/. Accessed 23 Oct 2020

Department of Lifelong Learning of MOE. Taiwan. https://depart.moe.edu.tw/. Accessed 15 Oct 2020

Kavaratzis, M., Ashworth, G.J.: Place marketing: how did we get here and where are we going? J. Place Manag. Dev. **1**(2), 150–165 (2008)

Stern, E., Krakover, S.: The formation of a composite urban image. Geogr. Anal. **25**(2), 130–146 (1993)

Gelder, S.V., Allan, M.: City Branding: How Cities Compete in the 21st Century. Primaveraquint, UK (2006)

Kavaratzis, M.: From city marketing to city branding: an interdisciplinary analysis with reference to Amsterdam, Budapest and Athens. Ph.D. thesis, University of Groningen (2008)

Ministry of Culture (MOC). Taiwan. https://www.moc.gov.tw. Accessed 20 Sep 2020

The Influence of Different Drawing Tools on the Learning Motivation and Color Cognition of the Fourth Grade Students at the Elementary School

I-Chen Lee[1](✉) and Pei-Jung Cheng[2](✉)

[1] Graduate Program in Digital Content and Technologies, National Chengchi University, Taipei, Taiwan
108462004@g.nccu.edu.tw
[2] Department of Advertising, National Chengchi University, Taipei, Taiwan

Abstract. Applying scientific and technological products to the domain of education has gradually become a trend. In the area of art education, using digital tools such as tablets and stylus not only help students freely create their imagination, but strengthen their ability to understanding the colors of the real objects. Therefore, in order to understand how the different digital drawing tools influence on the color cognition and learning motivation of the fourth grade students at the elementary school, we asked the students using "interactive electronic drawing pen", which can capture the colors of the object, "stylus" and "traditional drawing tool" to take the drawing task. Four-stage drawing experiment with 27 students from the fourth grade of elementary school were carried out, and the differences on the drawing outcome and color cognition of the students were compared for further discussion.

The result shows that: 1) Comparing the results of "drawing behavior analysis" and "the pre-test and post-test of their color cognition", we found that the students using "interactive electronic drawing pen" can improve their color cognition and depict objects with richer and more accurate colors than using the other drawing tools; 2) Through the analysis of their drawing behaviors, we found that the students frequently interacted with the drawing objects when using the "interactive electronic drawing pen", showing that "interactive electronic drawing pen" indeed helps to increase the chances for them to observing and realizing real objects; 3) Analyzing the result on the interviews of the students' learning motivation, 85% of the students consider that using the "interactive electronic drawing pen" to learn color is interesting; 63% of them believe that the "interactive electronic drawing pen" can trigger their curiosity on colors and enhance their learning motivation.

Keywords: Color cognition · Learning motivation · Drawing tools · Art education

1 Introduction

With the development of technology, mobile devices have gradually been applied to learning. Digital education has become a trend in learning areas today [8]. Learners

© Springer Nature Switzerland AG 2021
C. Stephanidis et al. (Eds.): HCII 2021, CCIS 1421, pp. 80–90, 2021.
https://doi.org/10.1007/978-3-030-78645-8_11

are no longer limited to reality factors. No matter where they are, they can use mobile devices to learn, enhancing their abilities [42]. Among the mobile devices, the tablet can provide an intuitive and multifunctional interface, and the operation methods are familiar with human gestures [28, 34], so it is more efficient to use in teaching. Not only providing learners with more learning opportunities, and also improving learners' learning motivation and effectiveness [4, 11, 19, 25, 27, 37].

With the popularization of tablets, the opportunities for children to use touch screens have increased [35, 43]. Therefore, to understand the impact of different drawing tools on children's color cognition and learning motivation, this research adopted three tools: "electronic drawing pen", which can capture the color of objects, and "stylus", "traditional drawing tool". And 27 students from the fourth grade of elementary school were invited to use these tools to conduct the experiment in the form of a within-subject design.

2   Literature Review

2.1   The Color Cognition of Children

Color is omnipresent in life and is closely related to our vision. Japanese chromatist Nomura pointed out that vision occupies the highest proportion (87%) of the five senses [29], and color is an important factor affecting vision. Its function is different from that of text and can further influence and express human emotions and psychology through symbolic meaning [15, 45, 46].

Color cognition refers to the process by which human recognize color. In addition to being affected by emotion and environment, this ability plays an important role in the process of cognition development [23]. With the growth of cognition ability, children's color cognition ability will grow, too. Not only improving the ability of color-using and aesthetic, but also presenting their thoughts and mental states better [10, 13, 48].

The intermediate grade of elementary school is an important stage developing plastic art ability, and is the golden age of creation [40], so learning chromatics is suitable for starting from the fourth grade [44]. However, many children have not yet observed subtle color changes [14], so if the children's color-mixing experience and color perception can be enhanced at this stage, their color cognition can be effectively enhanced [21].

2.2   Children's Drawing and Cognitive Development

In the book "Creative and Mental Growth", Lowenfeld and Brittain divided the development of children's drawing skills from 2 to 17 years old into six stages. Among them, children between 9 and 12 years old are called the "gang age". The color in children's paintings is closely related to their emotional experience. The shape and color in their creations are gradually realistic, and become more subjective [20]. In addition, according to Piaget's cognitive development theory, children aged 7 to 11 are called the "concrete operational stage". Children at this stage can solve problems based on their specific experience and use concrete objects to help thinking [12, 31]. It can be seen that as the mental state gradually grows, children's cognition and drawing skills gradually become concrete, and they can integrate actual experience to think and make more realistic depictions. Therefore, this research selected the fourth-grade students as the research subject.

2.3 Learning Motivation

The word "Motivation", literally means that moving or prompting to action. In other words, any stimulus can be regarded as motivation as long as it can contribute to an action [5]. The strength of learning motivation determines whether an individual takes action and the degree of persistence [3, 24]. Theories of learning motivation are mainly divided into four schools of cognitivism, behaviorism, social learning orientation, and humanism. Further, Keller [18, 22] integrated these theories and developed the ARCS motivation model. The ARCS motivation model includes: Attention, Relevance, Confidence, and Satisfaction. Using these four elements can arouse learners' learning motivation and achieve motivating effects.

2.4 Tangible User Interfaces for Education

Ishii and Ullmer proposed the concept of tangible user interface (TUI) in 1997, and advocated that users should directly manipulate digital information instead of using a keyboard or a mouse as mediation. In this way, digital information can be integrated into the physical environment and become an intuitive way of interaction, making it easier for users to learn [16]. At present, the concept of TUI has been widely used in various education and business fields. Many TUI prototypes are designed for educational purposes, which can integrate learning and entertainment, allowing users to learn and entertain themselves at the same time [6, 47]. What's more, it can promote learners' willingness to participate in learning, and strengthen their confidence [32, 36].

Taking the field of art education as an example, Ryokai and others launched a drawing tool "I/O Brush", which allowed users to pick up elements such as color and textures in daily life. They studied the use of this tool by kindergarten children and found that children could not only use brushes to create complex works, but also clearly discuss design elements [33]. In the field of scientific education, Morita and Setozaki developed an entity system which could help learners to learn about the solar system, allowing users to operate astronomical models by themselves. They experimented with this system in elementary school science courses, and found that students using this system can significantly improve their scores on comprehension tests in the Mental Rotation Test (MRT) [26]. In the field of English education, Fan et al. designed a physical reading system "PhonoBlocks". This system uses color-changing 3D physical letters to attract users to notice that adding other letters will change the sound, and then recognize the relevance between English letters and phonetics. They conducted a systematic test with 10 Chinese children as subjects, and found that through systematic guidance, the subjects did achieve significant learning results [9].

What's more, the "electronic drawing pen" in our research is also based on the concept of TUI. Color can be captured by turning the pen and pressing the button at the end of the pen. The purpose is allowing children to learn more abstract color cognition from specific operations.

3 Methods

3.1 Participants

Considering that the children participating in this task have great differences in their drawing abilities, all the children are asked to use the following "stylus", "electronic drawing pen" and "traditional drawing tool" to perform drawing tasks during the four weeks. In order to ensure the accuracy of drawing tasks and color cognition tests, children must have the normal visual ability before they perform experiments.

3.2 Tasks and Equipment

The four-week experiment in this research included formal drawing tasks for three times, drawing exercises for two times, color cognition tests before and after the drawing tasks, and a motivation interview afterward.

3.3 Procedure

The experiment lasts for four weeks, about 30 min per week. The process is recorded by photos and videos. The experiment consisted of 5-min color cognition tests (pre-test & post-test); 20-min formal drawing experiments (three times); practice stages for about 15 min; the motivation interview is about 10 min. The first week is the pre-test of the color cognition, and making subjects use tablet and stylus for drawing exercises. The second week is using tablet and stylus for formal drawing experiment, and the use of tablet and electronic drawing pen for drawing exercises. The third week is using tablet and electronic drawing pen for formal drawing experiment and color cognition post-test. The fourth week is using paper and traditional drawing tool for formal drawing experiment and motivation interview.

3.4 Research Tool

1. **Drawing Tools.** The drawing tools in this research are all physical (Fig. 1). The stylus and the electronic drawing pen [41] are the same pen. The purpose is to prevent the ergonomics problem from affecting the research results. Both of these drawing tools are paired with a 9.7-in. iPad Air 1 [1], and the drawing app is "ColorPen Sketch" [2]. The biggest difference is whether it could "Capture Color". If the battery isn't installed, it represents "stylus"; if the battery is installed and connected with the tablet via Bluetooth, we can use it to capture color, which represents "electronic drawing pen". The color captured by the electronic drawing pen comes from the physical object, and the way to capture color is by turning the pen and pressing the physical object. All the students should prepare traditional drawing tools they are familiar with, such as colored pencils, colored pens, crayons, etc., with 16K paper to conduct the experiment.

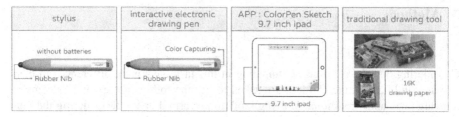

Fig. 1. Drawing tools

2. **The Pre-test and Post-test of Children's Color Cognition.** Figure 2 is the color sample of this research uses the Practical Color Co-ordinate System (PCCS). There are 149 colors in total, of which there are 12 colors, and each color can be divided into 12 colors, and achromatic has 5 colors. There are five questions in total, including: apple, sunflower, leaf, hand, eggplant. The PCCS color system is published by the Japan Color Research Institute in 1964. It combines the advantages of the Munsell Color System and the Ostwald System, and is a universal and practical color system [7, 17, 30, 39].

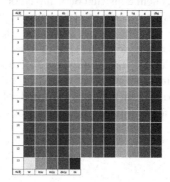

Fig. 2. The color sample of this research

3. **Motivation Interview.** The questions (Table 1) combine the ARCS Motivation Model proposed by Keller, and refer to the ARCS scale designed by Suen [38]. There are 36 questions in the original scale compiled by Suen. This research deleted questions that are not applicable to the field of art and repetitive questions with similar concepts, and considered the comprehension of the fourth grade students in elementary school and the time limit of the experiment, and revises the scale and the description of the questions. Finally, there are 15 questions, including 2 inverse questions, as the motivation interview questions. Each question has three drawing tools as options. The children should sort the three drawing tools according to their experience and explain the reasons why.

Table 1. The interview questions about ARCS model

Question number	Code name	Question description
1	R	This drawing tool is very useful when learning color
2	S	This drawing tool makes me very disappointed with learning color
3	A	This drawing tool can motivate my curiosity about color
4	A	This drawing tool can draw my attention to color
5	C	This drawing tool is very easy to operate when using color
6	R	It is very helpful to use this drawing tool in art class
7	A	This drawing tool is very interesting when learning color
8	S	This drawing tool gives me a sense of accomplishment in comprehending color
9	S	This drawing tool makes me very satisfied with learning color
10	A	This drawing tool can arouse my interest in color
11	C	This drawing tool meets my expectations in learning color
12	R	This drawing tool reminds me of my previous experience in learning color
13	C	This drawing tool gives me confidence when using color
14	A	This drawing tool cannot attract my attention to color
15	R	This drawing tool makes me more interested in observing color

A = Attention; R = Relevance; C = Confidence; S = Satisfaction

4. **Behavioral Coding Scheme.** In order to analyze their drawing behavior, we listed all the behavior characteristics, and then defined the behavior coding scheme after reviewing all the record videos, such as Table 2, as the basis for behavior analysis.

Table 2. Behavioral coding scheme

Behavior	Behavior (code)	Definition
Preparing a Draft	Drawing (DR)	Draw wireframe or applying color
	Moving the Canvas (MTC)	Move the tablet or paper
	Revising (RV)	Choose the eraser tool to modify what they have drawn Use an eraser to modify what they have drawn
	Adjusting the Stroke Width (ATSW)	Drag the slider to adjust thickness

(continued)

Table 2. (*continued*)

Behavior	Behavior (code)	Definition
	Changing Drawing Tools (CDT)	1. Choose the brush 2. Put the pen cap, put the pen back in the pencil box, take out of the pen from the pencil box, etc.
Thinking About Color	Adjusting the Colors (ATC) (use the color formally)	1. Choose the palette and adjust color on the palette 2. Choose the palette and use the slider to adjust the color depth and opacity
	Selecting A Color (SAC) (use the color formally)	1. Choose a color from the preset color sample 2. Check the record of the used color 3. Turn the pen to capture color 4. Replace the pen with different color
	Trying Out the Color (TOTC) (just test color)	1. Choose color or adjust color, but reject it in the end 2. Check color 3. Sketching on the blank space, but modified it with the eraser tool immediately
Observe	Interacting with the Objects (IWTO)	Pick up the object, or look at it closely, or touch it, or move it, etc.

4   Results

4.1   The Pre-test and Post-test of Children's Color Cognition

According to the results of the color cognition test (Fig. 3), "the number of colors selected in the post-test is more than the number of colors selected in the pre-test" accounts for 81.48% of all the students, "the number of colors selected in the pre-test and post-test are both the same" accounted for 11.11% of the total, and "the number of colors selected in the pre-test is more than the number of colors selected in the post-test" accounted for 7.4% of the total. It can be seen that when students use electronic drawing pens, the number of colors they choose is higher.

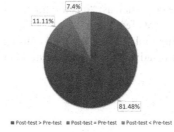

Fig. 3. Quantity statistics of the color cognition tests

4.2 Drawing Behavior Analysis

According to the statistical results of the number of drawing behaviors (Fig. 4). Among them, the number of times the color is officially used (ATC + SAC) is the interactive electronic drawing pen (688 times), the stylus (649 times), and the traditional drawing tool (516 times). The drawing tools with the highest number of observation times are the electronic drawing pen (522 times), the stylus (241 times), and the traditional drawing tool (77 times). Therefore, using the electronic drawing pen can help to improve students' color cognition and learning motivation.

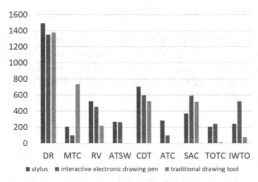

Fig. 4. Statistics of the number of drawing behaviors

4.3 Motivation Interview

According to the results of the interview, students have a high evaluation of the "color-capturing" function of the electronic drawing pen. Among them, 85% of the total think it is fun to use this pen to learn color; 63% of the total think this pen can inspire their curiosity about color and enhance their motivation to learn chromatics. They think that the electronic drawing pen is helpful to learn chromatics, and can draw more attention to color, and even feel that mastering color is a very rewarding thing; so, it can increase their interest in color. In contrast, the most dissatisfied drawing tool is the stylus. 67% of the total are disappointed with it. In addition to not having the function of capturing color, the shortcomings of the pen (such as: "it is too thick", or "the pen tip's material is not good", etc.) also make students feel that it is not as easy as traditional ones. As for the view on traditional drawing tool, 70% of the total consider it is easy to operate due to frequent use, but the main disadvantage is that the number of colors is low and it is not easy to be modified.

5   Conclusion

This research explores the impact of different drawing tools on students' color cognition and learning motivation. The results found that: 1) When using the electronic drawing pen, both the number of color selection and observation times are the most among the three tools. In particular, they have a good evaluation of the "Color-Capturing" function. 85% of the total think that learning chromatics is fun. 2) Regarding the number of color choices before and after color cognition, 81.48% of the total have more choice in the post-test than in the pre-test. Therefore, the electronic drawing pen helps to improve the students' color cognition. 3) According to the interview results, 67% of the total are dissatisfied with the stylus. They think it is not easy to use, and the function is slightly inferior to that of the electronic drawing pen. 4) As children can come into contact with many traditional drawing tools in their daily lives, 70% of them think that traditional drawing tool are easy to operate; but the disadvantage is that there are not enough colors to choose and it is relatively inconvenient to carry.

Acknowledgments. The author gratefully acknowledges the support provided by the Ministry of Science and Technology under Grant No. MOST 109-2410-H-004-036. Additional gratitude goes to the 27 students who participated in this study and their teacher Yi-Ling Dai and the four researchers, Tsung-Ju Ku, Shih-Ya Chou, Xiu-Ting Lin and You-Ying Huang, who assisted in the research process.

References

1. Apple Inc. iPad Air. https://support.apple.com/kb/SP692?locale=zh_TW. Accessed 20 Aug 2020
2. Apple Inc. Penpower Technology Ltd. ColorPen Sketch. https://apps.apple.com/us/app/col orpen-sketch/id1227358622. Accessed 8 Aug 2020
3. Ba, C.S.: The relationship between ethnic identity and ethnic language learning motivation in Paiwan elementary school students. Unpublished master's thesis, National Pingtung University, Pingtung, Taiwan (2019)
4. Butcher, J.: Can tablet computers enhance learning in further education? J. Furth. High. Educ. **40**, 207–226 (2016)
5. Chen, C.F., Tsai, Y.F., Hsiao, Y.H.: A study on the motivation, participation frequency and satisfaction of city farm participants in Taichung. Tour. Manag. Res. **5**(2), 157–171 (2005)
6. Cuendet, S., Dehler-Zufferey, J., Ortoleva, G., Dillenbourg, P.: An integrated way of using a tangible user interface in a classroom. Int. J. Comput.-Support. Collab. Learn. **10**(2), 183–208 (2015). https://doi.org/10.1007/s11412-015-9213-3
7. Color-site.com. PCCS tone map. https://www.color-site.com/pccs_tones. Accessed 20 Aug 2020

8. Ditzler, C., Hong, E., Strudler, N.: How tablets are utilized in the classroom. J. Res. Technol. Educ. **48**, 181–193 (2016)
9. Fan, M., Antle, A.N., Hoskyn, M., Neustaedter, C.: A design case study of a tangible system supporting young English language learners. Int. J. Child-Comput. Interact. **18**, 67–78 (2018)
10. Fan, H.H.: Research on children's color perception and creation of picture book. Unpublished master's thesis, Ming Chuan University, Taipei, Taiwan (2006)
11. Gasparini, A., Culén, A.L.: Children's journey with iPads in the classroom. In: Opportunities and Challenges when Designing and Developing with Kids@ School at the Interaction Design for Children Conference (IDC 2011), Ann Arbor, Michigan (2011)
12. Ginsburg, H.P., Opper, S.: Piaget's Theory of Intellectual Development. Prentice-Hall, Inc. (1988)
13. Huang, S.L., Shao, S.P.: The interaction of clothing color and emotion - Taiwan elementary school students as an example. Taiwan Text. Res. J. **27**(1), 65–79 (2017)
14. Huang, S.P.: E-book design and teaching - a case study in color discovery. Unpublished master's thesis, National Taipei University of Education, Taipei, Taiwan (2016)
15. Huang, C.Y.: Comparative study of pupils' expressional forms and attitudes when painting with computer media and traditional media. Unpublished master's thesis, Pingtung Teachers College, Pingtung, Taiwan (2002)
16. Ishii, H., Ullmer, B.: Tangible bits: towards seamless interfaces between people, bits and atoms. In: Pemberton, S. (ed.) Proceedings of the ACM Conference on Human Factors in Computing Systems (CHI 1997, Atlanta, GA, 22–27 March), pp. 234–241. ACM Press, New York (1997)
17. Japan Color Enterprise Co., Ltd. Homepage. http://www.sikiken.co.jp/home.html. Accessed 20 Jan 2021
18. Keller, J.M.: Motivational design of instruction. In: Instructional Design Theories and Models: An Overview of Their Current Status, vol. 1, pp. 383–434 (1983)
19. Knaus, T.: The potential of digital media: theoretical observations on the educational and didactic potential of tablets-and a conceptual outline of using them in schools. Teach. Work **14**, 40–49 (2017)
20. Lowenfeld, V., Brittain, W.L.: Creative and Mental Growth. Macmillan, New York (1987)
21. Lu, Y.C.: To learn the empirical development of children art. J. Aesthetic Educ. **69**, 11–26 (1996)
22. Lin, C.Y.: The effects of instructional strategies and goal orientation on elementary school students within an arcs integrated experiential learning activity. Unpublished master's thesis, National Taiwan Normal University, Taipei, Taiwan (2010)
23. Lu, L.: Inquiry on color in children's drawings. In: "Color & Life" Academic Conference. Collection of Theses, pp. 129–142 (1998)
24. Lu, C.W.: Situational mobile English learning system based on the ARCS motivation model. Unpublished master's thesis, Tamkang University, Taipei, Taiwan (2015)
25. McEwen, R.N., Dubé, A.K.: Engaging or distracting: children's tablet computer use in education. J. Educ. Technol. Soc. **18**, 9–23 (2015)
26. Morita, Y., Setozaki, N.: Learning by tangible learning system in science class. In: Kurosu, M. (ed.) HCI 2017. LNCS, vol. 10272, pp. 341–352. Springer, Cham (2017). https://doi.org/10.1007/978-3-319-58077-7_27
27. Mulet, J., Van De Leemput, C., Amadieu, F.: A critical literature review of perceptions of tablets for learning in primary and secondary schools. Educ. Psychol. Rev. **31**, 631–662 (2019)
28. Nichols, S.J.V.: New interfaces at the touch of a fingertip. Computer **40**(8), 12–15 (2007)
29. Nomura, J.: The Secret of Color. Bungeishunju Ltd., Japan (2015)
30. Nozawa2you. PCCS. https://sites.google.com/site/nozawa2you/colors/pccs. Accessed 22 Aug 2020

31. Piaget, J.: Cognitive development in children: Piaget. J. Res. Sci. Teach. **2**, 176–186 (1964)
32. Revelle, G., Zuckerman, O., Druin, A., Bolas, M.: Tangible user interfaces for children. In: CHI 2005 Extended Abstracts on Human Factors in Computing Systems, pp. 2051–2052 (2005)
33. Ryokai, K., Marti, S., Ishii, H.: I/O brush: drawing with everyday objects as ink. In: Proceedings of the SIGCHI Conference on Human Factors in Computing Systems, pp. 303–310 (2004)
34. Siegle, D.: iPads: intuitive technology for 21st-century students. Gift. Child Today **36**, 146–150 (2013)
35. Søby, M.: Children testing tablets and apps. Nordic J. Digit. Lit. **10**, 122–123 (2015)
36. Sylla, C., Branco, P., Coutinho, C., Coquet, E.: TUIs vs. GUIs: comparing the learning potential with preschoolers. Pers. Ubiquitous Comput. **16**, 421–432 (2012)
37. Sher, Y.J., Chou, C.H.: The effects of integrating tablet PCs into phonics instruction on English vocabulary for junior high school students with learning disabilities. Spec. Educ. Q. **140**, 1–10 (2016)
38. Suen, H.Y.: The effects of implementing different extent and quality of motivational strategies on elementary students' motivation in web-based instruction. Unpublished master's thesis, National Hualien Teachers College, Hualien, Taiwan (2000)
39. TOM's Web Site. Color code table. https://tomari.org/main/java/color/pccs.html. Accessed 22 Aug 2020
40. Tseng, C.P.: An action research on curriculum design of fine art using computer graphic for elementary school — a case study based on Kaohsiung ping-ding elementary school. Unpublished master's thesis, Pingtung Teachers college, Pingtung, Taiwan (2003)
41. Ufro Inc. ColorPillar. https://colorpillar.mystrikingly.com/. Accessed 10 Aug 2020
42. Vahey, P., Crawford, V.: Palm Education Pioneers Program: Final Evaluation Report. SRI International, Menlo Park (2002)
43. Woodward, J., Shaw, A., Aloba, A., Jain, A., Ruiz, J., Anthony, L.: Tablets, tabletops, and smartphones: cross-platform comparisons of children's touchscreen interactions. In: Proceedings of the 19th ACM International Conference on Multimodal Interaction, pp. 5–14 (2017)
44. Wang, W.C.: Research on the developmental stages of aesthetic sense in color–a review of the related documents. J. Aesthetic Educ. **94**, 23–32 (1998)
45. Wu, Y.H.: A framework of exploring children's color recognition through color-based story editing approach. Unpublished master's thesis, National Taichung University of Science and Technology, Taichung, Taiwan (2014)
46. Zhang, J.J., Fang, Y.H., Xie, S.S.: Interactive theory of color cognition and its evidence. Adv. Psychol. Sci. **20**, 949–962 (2012)
47. Zito, L., et al.: Leveraging tangible interfaces in primary school math: pilot testing of the Owlet math program. Int. J. Child-Comput. Interact. **27**, 1–14 (2021)
48. Zhung, Z.H.: The perception of color order from the elementary school children. Unpublished master's thesis, National Hsinchu Teachers College, Hsinchu, Taiwan (2002)

Sharing is Learning: Using Topic Modelling to Understand Online Comments Shared by Learners

Kok Khiang Lim[(✉)] and Chei Sian Lee

Wee Kim Wee School of Communication and Information, Nanyang Technological University, Singapore, Singapore
w200004@e.ntu.edu.sg, leecs@ntu.edu.sg

Abstract. Learners have utilised coding video tutorials to learn new programming languages or enhance their existing skillset. Past studies have focused on content creators' perspective (e.g. motivation to produce video tutorials) or understanding the learner perspective focusing on the outcome of the learning. However, the research on the learning process focusing on learners' sharing behaviour when and after watching the video tutorial was limited. This study aims to address this gap by analysing learners' online comments shared on the video hosting platform to infer learning behaviour from the self-regulated learning perspective. Learners' comments from 24 video tutorials were collected from a popular YouTube coding channel and analysed using the probabilistic topic modelling method. Ten latent topics were uncovered. The findings indicated the presence of three self-regulated learning behaviours. Interestingly, the learners' comments comprised a high proportion of comments related to sharing of coding-related questions, suggesting that learners not only use the commenting platform to provide feedback but also as a means to seek clarification. In addition, this finding also informed the content creators on the areas to engage the learners or refine course content.

Keywords: Online comment · Online learning · YouTube · Self-regulated learning · Video tutorial

1 Introduction

Coding video tutorial is typically produced using the digital video recording from the computer screen as the coding was typed on the screen along with audio narration to guide learners [1]. Coding video tutorial takes advantage of the rich media, visual and audio, afforded by the video to break down the complex procedural task of coding to support learning [2]. Learners would learn by observing the coding demonstration such as scripting, debugging and compiling the codes, and practising the coding as guided by the video. This form of learning has positive contributions to task relevance, self-efficacy and improve students' engagement [3, 4].

© Springer Nature Switzerland AG 2021
C. Stephanidis et al. (Eds.): HCII 2021, CCIS 1421, pp. 91–101, 2021.
https://doi.org/10.1007/978-3-030-78645-8_12

Not surprisingly, YouTube has become one of the popular video content sites to host video tutorials. It allows learners the flexibility and autonomy to search and access videos through its many dedicated learning channels [5]. In addition, as with most social network sites, the social features embedded in YouTube enable learners to publicly share their comments about their learning experiences or feedback on the video content [6, 7]. Consequently, these users-generated comments became a ready pool of large volume of data, enabling researchers to conduct studies such as users' behaviour and sentiments. Extant studies have examined the sentiments and toxicity expressed in the YouTube comments [8, 9], classified YouTube comments according to the thematic topics of interest [1, 10], and analysed the perceptions and behaviour of viewers [11].

However, the study on learners' learning behaviour after consuming the YouTube video tutorials is limited and little is known about what drives the learning behaviour. The characteristics of learning from an online environment, such as a video tutorial, require learners to adopt self-regulated learning (SRL) in order to achieve their learning outcome [12, 13]. Thus, this study will address this gap by analysing learners' comments shared on the video hosting platform. Specifically, YouTube comments will be collected and analysed using the probabilistic topic modelling method.

2 Related Work

2.1 Online Video Tutorial and Self-regulated Learning

Online video tutorials have become a prevalent teaching tool to deliver instructional content across various subjects such as languages [14] and health sciences [15]. In particular for coding, its popularity resides in the video tutorial's ability to demonstrate coding concepts [1, 5, 16, 17], convey the outcome of compiling and running a code [5, 17], and its interactivity that allows learners to search and navigate the video content [18, 19]. This form of learning has recently incorporated into online learning alongside mainstream online learning platforms, such as massive online open courses [20].

A main characteristic of online learning is that it requires learners' ability to self-regulate their learning to achieve a positive learning outcome. The influence of SRL in the online learning environment has been studied extensively, and the studies have shown positive results [13, 21, 22]. SRL strategies in an online learning environment can be broadly categorized into *goal setting*, *environment structuring*, *task strategies*, *help-seeking* and *self-evaluation* [23]. Goal setting requires the learner to set a learning goal and develop a plan to achieve that goal [24]. Environment structuring involves the selection or creation of effective and conducive condition for learning [24]. Task strategies refer to understanding tasks and identifying the appropriate approaches or methods to learn [24]. Help-seeking is defined as choosing an appropriate method to seek assistance in guiding oneself to learn [24]. Self-evaluation refers to the comparison between the attained performance against a standard and provides reasons for that success and failure [24].

Araka et al. [25] reviewed 30 past works of literature on the methods used to measure SRL in an online learning environment. The study found that the common methods used were self-reporting questionnaire and survey, and data mining and analytical methods on learners' activities [25]. However, the use of online comments with computational analysis to measure SRL in an online learning environment is few. Thus, this study proposed using online comments as a viable source of data that could be quickly harvested and analysed to understand learners' sharing behaviours from the lens of SRL.

2.2 Analysing YouTube Comments

YouTube comment is a form of publicly shared user-generated content on an online platform. It holds information or opinion that the user voluntarily contributes in a non-intrusive and unrestrictive manner [26, 27]. The online comments served as an important communications channel for the users to feedback and share their thoughts and opinions on their video consumption experiences [27, 28]. Various approaches have been taken to analyse, identify and categorise the YouTube comments. Obadimu et al. [9] used the Support Vector Machines (SVM), a supervised classification method, to automatically classify the comments to facilitate the filtering of unacceptable YouTube comments. Similarly, [1] used the SVM to effectively detect useful YouTube comments to help understand their viewers' concerns and needs. On the other hand, [10] utilised an off-the-shelf content analysis package, Text Miner (SAS Institute Inc.), to analyse YouTube comments to uncover healthy eating habits.

This study will adopt an increasingly popular unsupervised probabilistic topic modelling, Structural Topic Modelling (STM) [29]. STM extends from Latent Dirichlet Allocation [30] to incorporate documents metadata into its model in the form of covariates, for example, date and ratings of reviews, to enhance the allocation of words to the latent topics in the documents [29]. Reich et al. [31] have evaluated STM's utility and reliability to analyse a large volume of online learning data from discussion forums, surveys and course evaluations to "find syntactic patterns with semantic meaning in [the] structured text" (p. 156). In sum, topic modelling has the potential to identify latent topics related to learning behaviours and experiences from learners' comments.

3   Methodology

3.1 Sampling and Data Collection

Learners' comments were collected from one of the popular YouTube channels, the freeCodeCamp, which curates coding related video tutorials contributed by the coding community to help learners code. As of end-2019, freeCodeCamp has more than 3 million subscribers with over 1,200 videos in its channel. The videos were sorted according to their popularity. Those with more than a million views and published before 2019 were selected. The selection criteria imposed were to ensure that the data collected were representative of its popularity over one year. Due to the downloading limitation set by YouTube, the data collection via the Python v3.8 script was performed over three days, between 27 December 2020 to 29 December 2020. In total, 52,431 comments from 24 videos ($M = 2{,}185$, $SD = 3{,}437$) were collected (See Table 1). The collected data is pre-processed and analysed using R statistical software v4.0.

Table 1. Descriptive statistics for the 24 YouTube videos.

	Total	Mean	SD	Maximum	Minimum
Views	73,132,823	3,047,200	4,013,501	20,795,380	1,000,518
Comments	52,431	2,185	3,437	17,517	419

3.2 Data Pre-processing

Data pre-processing is performed before any computation analysis as it will help improve the overall data quality and the relevancy of the raw dataset. As YouTube comments is a form of user-generated content that is unstructured and free-text, this step is particularly important. Data pre-processing is used to (1) eliminate any data noises that were not meaningful (e.g. punctuation, numbers, non-alphanumeric characters and stop-words), unusual (e.g. 'cifoyimsye') or highly re-occurrence words (e.g. 'course') that might otherwise skew the analysis; (2) correct the misspelt words and typographic mistakes that were common in the user-generated content; (3) filter-off data that were not relevant to the study such as non-English language (R 'cld2' package), duplicates, empty or comments that were posted earlier than the year 2019; and (4) resolve words in the comments to its lemma (R 'textstem' package), that is, to convert the word to its based or dictionary form (e.g. from 'learning' to 'learn'). In addition, a total of 9,482 misspelt words were identified by R 'hunspell' package, of which 435 misspelt words (e.g. 'ecssssssssssssssssstatic') were unable to be resolved and thus, removed. The remaining misspelt words were auto-corrected. After pre-processing, 35,334 valid comments were used for topic modelling.

3.3 Topic Modelling

Before applying the STM to the dataset, the number of topics (k) needs to be defined. A range of k between 5 to 15, in intervals of 1, was applied to the model to estimate the best k for the dataset. The estimated k was evaluated based on three metrics: held-out likelihood estimation, semantic coherence and residuals [29, 32]. The held-out likelihood is a measure of the model's predictive power [29]. Semantic coherence is the words with the highest probability that occur together in a given topic [32]. Residuals measure whether there is an overdispersion of the multinomial variance in the STM method [29]. Thus, the best k would have a high held-out likelihood, high semantic coherence and low residuals measures [29, 32].

The best k was then further fine-tuned and evaluated to build the best fitting STM. The STM was then assessed based on exclusivity and semantic coherence [29]. Exclusivity in this instance measures the difference between topics based on the similarities of word distribution in the various topics, that is, a topic is considered exclusive if the top words do not appear in other topics. The fine-tuned k STM was applied to the dataset for the topic modelling analysis. The results were manually assigned with suitable labels to describe the topics based on their associated keywords and comments.

4   Results

The STM identified ten topics and computed its expected topic proportion (γ) within the dataset (See Appendix). The assignment of the labels was first performed by one researcher and then confirmed by the second researcher. The labelling was based on the logical association between the top keywords and their associated comments.

Four topics comprise Topic 4, 7, 9 and 10 represented coding-related questions and constituted about 33% of the overall expected topic proportion. The four topics were labelled as 'Sharing doubts and questions' ($\gamma = .077$), 'Sharing technical questions on coding' ($\gamma = .084$), 'Sharing programming questions' ($\gamma = .069$) and 'Sharing programming error messages' ($\gamma = .101$). Although the four topics were relatively similar, their associated comments revealed that the topics addressed different aspects of the coding video tutorial. For example, Topic 4 mainly shared how to execute the codes and set up the coding environment. Topic 7 was related to a database query. Topic 9 was associated with Python programming, and Topic 10 was related to general code debugging. Nonetheless, these were indicators that the learners were proactive in learning, reaching out to clarify their doubts and queries in response to their learning. Thus, Topics 4, 7, 9, 10 could be inferred as a form of help-seeking strategy from the SRL perspective [24].

Two topics (Topic 2 and 6) revealed that learners had exhibited positive learning behaviours. Topic 2, labelled as 'Sharing compliments', has the highest proportion ($\gamma = .186$) of comments with keywords such as 'thank', 'tutorial', and 'great'. Its associated comments "...I love your tutorials ... and all the knowledge it offers...", further implied that the topic is related to complimenting the instructors or video tutorials. Topic 6, labelled as 'Sharing learning practices' ($\gamma = .118$), had keywords on "good", 'understand' and 'help' and comment such as "...followed this course completely on Monday...bought exam and studied... passed the exam...", thus reflected how and what learners had achieved from the video tutorial. Topic 2 and 6, therefore, suggested that learning behaviours were reflective of SRL in both the self-evaluation and goal setting strategies [23]. By sharing compliments, learners attributed and explained their learning success as part of self-evaluation. The sharing of learning practices presented how learners learned and achieved their desired learning outcome in goal setting.

Next, three topics (Topic 1, 3 and 5) were observed to be feedback towards the video tutorial. Topic 1 and Topic 5 had a similar expected topic proportion ($\gamma = .075$) after rounded to three decimal places and were labelled as 'Sharing general feedback' and 'Sharing information on video segment' respectively. Topic 3 was labelled as 'Sharing specific feedback on video content' ($\gamma = .146$). In Topic 1, a learner commented that the used of multiple examples in the video was useful as it helped to reinforce the learning, while in Topic 5, learners shared the timing of the video segment much like a table of contents to ease in search of video content. Meanwhile, in Topic 3, learners were more targeted in their comments that included "in some parts of the video his voice sounds like Thor's voice, Walter Thor to the rescue!!!". Lastly, Topic 8 was labelled as 'Sharing of fun content' ($\gamma = .068$) and had the lowest expected topic proportion. This topic represented the sharing of functional codes by the learners in response to the video tutorials.

5   Discussion and Conclusion

This study is one of the earliest studies to examine learners' sharing behaviours from the lens of SRL. The topic modelling approach uncovered the latent topics and their associated comments that indicate how learners learn and how they share and interact with other learners. Out of the ten topics identified, six sharing behaviours are related to learning behaviours. Based on the SRL perspective, these behaviours are further categorised into three SRL strategies and inferred as goal setting, help-seeking and self-evaluation (See Table 2). However, it is important to note that the sharing behaviours are expected to change over time, according to evolving learners' needs. The other four topics identified were learners' feedback on the video tutorial.

Table 2. Relationship between SRL strategies and identified topics.

SRL strategies	Topics
Goal setting	6
Help-seeking	4, 7, 9, 10
Self-evaluation	2

Of interest is the category on sharing of coding-related questions comprises Topic 4, 7, 9 and 10, which were representative of a help-seeking SRL strategy. This result was unexpected as it was contrary to a past study showing that help-seeking was not effective in an online learning environment [33]. According to [23], help-seeking implies an in-person meeting or through email or online consultation with peers or instructors, while [24] defined help-seeking as "choosing specific models, teachers or books to help oneself to learn" (p. 79). In this finding, help-seeking appeared to be an effective dominating self-regulating coping behaviour. It presented a potential alternative definition of help-seeking in a social learning environment. Learners would seek help publicly through social features within the learning platform. Given that coding is a technical skill that often requires guidance and clarifications, it is not too surprising that learners would use social features as a means to "communicate" with instructors, peers or the public to seek help and guidance.

The results also found that learners do utilise the social features within the video hosting platforms to reflect on their learning experiences (Topic 2) and attribute their learning success (Topic 6). These sharing provided insights into learners' learning behaviours synonymous with self-evaluation and goal setting in the SRL strategies. On the other hand, Topics 1, 3, 5 and 8, while not typical of SRL, were feedback towards the coding video tutorial and content that could inform the content creators on the areas to engage the learners, address learners' concerns or refine the course content. Subtly, these topics represented an indirect form of environment structuring in SRL strategies. The topics address the softer aspect of the environment: video tutorial and content, rather than the physical environment.

In conclusion, this research provides a new perspective to the study of how sharing behaviours are associated with online learning behaviour. Specifically, this research demonstrated a feasible approach to use topic modelling such as STM to infer learning behaviour from user-generated content. Here, keywords were extracted, and together with their associated comments, were further evaluated for labelling. Furthermore, this research also gives an insight that learners do exhibit their learning activities in online comments. Though the number of learning behaviours extracted is small, it represents how the learners had reacted to consuming the video tutorials. Thus, it can hypothesize that different video tutorials could potentially vary learning behaviour.

Three limitations are identified in this study. First, the dataset was restricted to coding video tutorials and thus could not be generalized to other video tutorials as learners may exhibit different learning behaviours. Second, as this is a preliminary study on sharing behaviour from video tutorials, replies associated with learners' comments were not collected to reduce any potential differences that could arise during the computational analysis. Third, the labelling of the topic is manual and subjective to the researchers' interpretation. However, it should be noted that the two researchers participated in this exercise to reduce potential personal biases of the researchers.

Future work could expand the dataset to include other types of video tutorials (e.g. teaching language) that are less technical. Having video tutorials on different subjects would provide a contrasting comparison of the learning behaviour. Another limitation relates to the targeted audience in the sampled videos. The learners consuming the learning content in this study are general knowledge seekers who are interested in computer programming related content. Since YouTube is also a learning platform for other types of learners (e.g. children), it will be worthwhile to replicate this study with types of learners. With the findings from this study and the feasibility of using topic modelling on user-generated content, future work could further expand to include replies from its associated comments.

Appendix

See Table A-1.

Table A-1. Topic modelling results from YouTube comments.

Topic: Label*	Expected topic proportion (γ)	Top ten keywords	Extract of comments[#]
Topic 1: Sharing general feedback	0.075	follow, helpful, office, comment, example, step, note, reference, information, key	"Love this course! Learning coding and this is so simple and helpful, quick examples one right after the other gives quick imprinting and easy to remember information. 40 mins in and I feel really comfortable already"
Topic 2: Sharing compliments	0.186	thank, tutorial, great, love, awesome, beginner, free, amaze, video, basic	"I love you. I love your tutorials. I love free code camp and all the knowledge it offers. But I simply ask 2 things from you. atleast a banner ad so you guys make some money. and please please use dark theme…"
Topic 3: Sharing specific feedback on video content	0.146	video, like, watch, time, start, explain, finish, long, speed, subtitle	"In some parts of the video his voice sounds like Thor's voice, Walter Thor to the rescue!!!"
Topic 4: Sharing doubts and questions	0.077	know, app, project, read, website, lesson, idea, nothing, talk, wow	"I get this error when trying to run the "Hello World" "C++ Test Project - Debug": The compiler's setup (GNU GCC Compiler) is invalid, …" Does anyone know how to fix this???"
Topic 5: Sharing information on video segment	0.075	new, open, react, password, script, software, log, var, check, access	"00:04:22 comment your Javascript code 00:05:58 data types and variables 00:09:14 storing values with assignment … 00:11:33 initializing variables … 00:12:00 uninitialized variables …"
Topic 6: Sharing learning practices	0.118	good, understand, help, easy, job, exam, pass, useful, practice, excellent	"Booked exam on Sunday for Thursday. Followed this course completely on Monday, half of Tuesday. Bought practice exams and studied them through for Tue,Wed, half of Thurs. Studied for 5 hrs each dday. Passed the exam today ie Thursday. This course is excellent as beginner to understand AWS terminologies, but you shall need some practice exams as well to be confident when giving the exam."
Topic 7: Sharing technical questions on coding	0.084	work, text, world, database, late, channel, hard, hope, age, advance	"from tkinter import * root = Tk() myLabel = Label(root, text="Hello world") root.mainloop() I did this according to the video. But the "Hello world" did not appear on the window. Why is that?"

(continued)

Table A-1. (*continued*)

Topic		Keywords	Example
Topic 8: Sharing fun content	0.068	guess, word, console, game, count, friend, lose, leave, simple, enter	"Here's my animal guessing game. I had a little fun adding some features to it after doing a little research . This will tell you how many guesses you have left and also how many letters in your guess were correct. it also lets the user give up by typing "exit". import sys …"
Topic 9: Sharing programming questions	0.069	question, change, link, test, life, answer, color, confuse, image, bad	"can someone help with the multi quiz game from coding import Question question_prompts = ["What colour are apples?\n(a) Red/Green\n(b) Orange\n(c) Purple\n\n", "What colour are Bananas?\n(a) Teal\n(b) Magenta\n(c) Yellow\n\n", "What colour are strawberries?\n(a) Yellow\n(b) Red\n(c) Blue\n\n"]…"
Topic 10: Sharing programming error messages	0.101	error, help, create, user, problem, set, result, save, click, enter	"…elseif ($op == "*"){ echo $num1 * $num2; } else { echo "Invalid operator"; } What is wrong in this program? Can anyone please help?"

*Labels are manually assigned.
#Typos are inherent errors in the comments.

References

1. Poché, E., Jha, N., Williams, G., Staten, J., Vesper, M., Mahmoud, A.: Analyzing user comments on YouTube coding tutorial videos. In: IEEE/ACM 25th International Conference on Program Comprehension, Buenos Aires, pp. 196–206 (2017). https://doi.org/10.1109/ICPC.2017.26

2. Storey, M.-A., Singer, L., Cleary, B., Figueira Filho, F., Zagalsky, A.: The revolution of social media in software engineering. In: FOSE 2014: Future of Software Engineering Proceedings, New York, USA, pp. 100–116 (2014). https://doi.org/10.1145/2593882.2593887

3. van der Meij, J., van der Meij, H.: A test of the design of a video tutorial for software training. J. Comput. Assist Learn. **31**(2) (2014). https://doi.org/10.1111/jcal.12082

4. Carlisle, M.: Using YouTube to enhance student class preparation in an introductory Java course. In: SIGCSE 2010: Proceedings of the 41st ACM Technical Symposium on Computer Science Education, New York, USA, pp. 470–474 (2010). https://doi.org/10.1145/1734263.1734419

5. MacLeod, L., Bergen, A., Storey, M.-A.: Documenting and sharing software knowledge using screencasts. Empir. Softw. Eng. **22**(3), 1478–1507 (2017). https://doi.org/10.1007/s10664-017-9501-9

6. Dubovi, I., Tabak, I.: An empirical analysis of knowledge co-construction in YouTube comments. Comput. Educ. **156**, 103939 (2020). https://doi.org/10.1016/j.compedu.2020.103939

7. Zhou, Q., Lee, C.S., Sin, S.C.J., Lin, S., Hu, H., Ismail, M.F.: Understanding the use of YouTube as a learning resource: A social cognitive perspective. Aslib J. Inf. Manag. **72**(3), 339–359 (2020). https://doi.org/10.1108/AJIM-10-2019-0290

8. Lee, C.S., Osop, H., Goh, D., Kelni, G.: Making sense of comments on YouTube educational videos: a self-directed learning perspective. Online Inf. Rev. **41**(5), 611–625 (2017). https://doi.org/10.1108/OIR-09-2016-0274

9. Obadimu, A., Mead, E., Hussain, M.N., Agarwal, N.: Identifying toxicity within YouTube video comment. In: Thomson, R., Bisgin, H., Dancy, C., Hyder, A. (eds.) SBP-BRiMS 2019. LNCS, vol. 11549, pp. 214–223. Springer, Cham (2019). https://doi.org/10.1007/978-3-030-21741-9_22

10. Siersdorfer, S., Nejdl, W., Pedro, J.S.: How useful are your comments? Analyzing and predicting YouTube comments and comment rating. In: WWW 2010: Proceedings of the 19th International Conference on World Wide Web, Raleigh, North Carolina, USA (2010). https://doi.org/10.1145/1772690.1772781

11. Teng, S., Khong, K.W., Sharif, S.P., Ahmed, A.: YouTube video comments on healthy eating: descriptive and predictive analysis. JMIR Public Health Surveill. **6**(4) (2020). https://doi.org/10.2196/19618

12. Johnson, G., Davies, S.: Self-regulated learning in digital environments: theory, research, praxis. Br. J. Res. **1**(2), 1–14 (2014). http://hdl.handle.net/20.500.11937/45935

13. Zhou, Q., Lee, C.S., Sin, S.C.J.: Using social media in formal learning: investigating learning strategies and satisfaction. Proc. Assoc. Inf. Sci. Technol. **54**(1), 472–482 (2017). https://doi.org/10.1002/pra2.2017.14505401051

14. Brook, J.: The affordances of YouTube for language learning and teaching. Hawaii Pacific University TESOL Working Paper Series **9**(2), 37–56 (2011)

15. Burke, S., Snyder, S.: YouTube: an innovative learning resource for college health education courses. Int. Electron. J. Health Educ. **11**, 39–46 (2008)

16. Ellmann, M., Oeser, A., Fucci, D., Maalej, W.: Find, understand, and extend development screencasts on YouTube. In: SWAN 2017: Proceedings of the 3rd ACM SIGSOFT International Workshop on Software Analytics, New York, USA, pp. 1–7 (2017). https://doi.org/10.1145/3121257.3121260

17. MacLeod, L., Storey, M.A., Bergen, A.: Code, camera, action: how software developers document and share program knowledge using YouTube. In: Proceedings of the 23rd IEEE International Conference on Program Comprehension, Florence, Italy, pp. 104–114 (2015). https://doi.org/10.1109/ICPC.2015.19

18. Kim, J., Guo, P.J., Cai, C.J., Li, S.W., Gajos, K.Z., Miller, R.C.: Data-driven interaction techniques for improving navigation of educational videos. In: UIST 2014: Proceedings of the 27th Annual ACM Symposium on User Interface Software and Technology, New York, USA, pp. 563–572 (2014). https://doi.org/10.1145/2642918.2647389

19. Pavel, A., Reed, C., Hartmann, B., Agrawala, M.: Video digests: a browsable, skimmable format for informational lecture videos. In: UIST 2014: Proceedings of the 27th Annual ACM Symposium on User Interface Software and Technology, New York, USA, pp. 573–582 (2014). https://doi.org/10.1145/2642918.2647400

20. Swan, K.: Research on online learning. J. Asynchronous Learn. Netw. **11**(1), 55–59 (2007). https://doi.org/10.24059/olj.v11i1.1736

21. Jansen, R.S., van Leeuwen, A., Janssen, J., Conijn, R., Kester, L.: Supporting learners' self-regulated learning in massive open online courses. Comput. Educ. **146** (2020). https://doi.org/10.1016/j.compedu.2019.103771

22. Wong, J., Baars, M., Davis, D., Van Der Zee, T., Houben, G., Paas, F.: Supporting self-regulated learning in online learning environments and MOOCs: a systematic review. Int. J. Hum.-Comput. Interact. **35**(4–5), 356–373 (2019). https://doi.org/10.1080/10447318.2018.1543084

23. Barnard, L., Lan, W.Y., To, Y.M., Paton, V.O., Lai, S.L.: Measuring self-regulation in online and blended learning environments. Internet High. Educ. **12**, 1–6 (2009). https://doi.org/10.1016/j.iheduc.2008.10.005

24. Zimmerman, B.J.: Academic study and the development of personal skill: a self- regulatory perspective. Educ. Psychol. **33**(2), 73–86 (1998). https://doi.org/10.1080/00461520.1998.9653292

25. Araka, E., Maina, E., Gitonga, R., Oboko, R.: Research trends in measurement and intervention tools for self-regulated learning for e-learning environments—systematic review (2008–2018). Res. Pract. Technol. Enhanc. Learn. **15**(1), 1–21 (2020). https://doi.org/10.1186/s41039-020-00129-5

26. Naab, T.K., Sehl, A.: Studies of user-generated content: a systematic review. Journalism **18**(10), 1256–1273 (2016). https://doi.org/10.1177/1464884916673557

27. Yoo, K.H., Gretzel, U.: What motivates consumers to write online travel reviews? Inf. Technol. Tour. **10**(4), 283–295 (2008). https://doi.org/10.3727/109830508788403114

28. Boyd, D.M., Ellison, N.B.: Social network sites: definition, history, and scholarship. J. Comput.-Mediat. Commun. **13**(1) (2007). https://doi.org/10.1109/EMR.2010.5559139

29. Roberts, M.E., Stewart, B.M., Tingley, D., Airoldi, E.M.: The structural topic model and applied social science. Neural Information Processing Society (2013). http://scholar.harvard.edu/dtingley/node/132666

30. Blei, D.M., Ng, A., Jordan, M.: Latent dirichlet allocation. J. Mach. Learn. Res. **3**, 993–1022 (2003). https://www.jmlr.org/papers/volume3/blei03a/blei03a.pdf

31. Reich, J., Tingley, D., Leder-Luis, J., Roberts, M.E., Stewart, B.: Computer-assisted reading and discovery for student senerated text in massive open online courses. J. Learn. Anal. **2**(1), 156–184 (2014). https://doi.org/10.18608/jla.2015.21.8

32. Mimno, D., Wallach, H.M., Talley, E., Leenders, M., McCallum, A.: Optimizing semantic coherence in topic models. In: EMNLP 2011: Proceedings of the Conference on Empirical Methods in Natural Language Processing, pp. 262–272. Association for Computational Linguistics (2011)

33. Vilkova, K., Shcheglova, I.: Deconstructing self-regulated learning in MOOCs: in search of help-seeking mechanisms. Educ. Inf. Technol. **26**(1), 17–33 (2020). https://doi.org/10.1007/s10639-020-10244-x

Intuitive Visualization of Complex Diagnostic Datasets to Improve Teachers' Individual Support of Learners Based on Data Driven Decision Making

Imke A. M. Meyer[✉] and Karsten D. Wolf

University of Bremen, Bremen, Germany
{imeyer,wolf}@uni-bremen.de

Abstract. Being able to read and write properly is an important aspect of social participation. There are 6.2 million adults living in Germany who are considered to have low literacy levels. However, supporting people with low literacy is very time-consuming and personnel-intensive. For teachers in literacy courses, we have developed a dashboard for automated diagnosis as well as individual support and tested and evaluated it in the context of UX studies. The goal is to develop a tool that uses visualizations to present complex competence diagnostics in such a way that teachers can intuitively derive profound and individualized support measures for learners.

Keywords: UX research · Teaching · Data driven decision making · Literacy

1 Background: People with Low Literacy in Germany

Germany is populated by 6.2 million German-speaking adults with low literacy (Grotlüschen et al. 2019). These people have considerable problems reading and writing coherent texts, which presents them with major challenges in various life situations. Being able to read and write sufficiently is an important aspect for social participation. For those affected, it is possible to attend literacy courses at an adult education center, both free of charge and for a fee. In 2018, about 25,000 people attended such literacy courses (Reichart et al. 2019). However, diagnosing and supporting these individuals is often time- and staff-intensive. For use in a course context, the online diagnostic otu.lea was developed in the lea project (runtime: 2008–2010, BMBF) and will be adapted to current technical and didactic requirements in the lea.online project (runtime 2019–2021, BMBF). The otu.lea diagnostics enables learners to independently complete an online test, which provides a differentiated evaluation of their learning status. The evaluation is based on a competency model developed specifically for adults with low literacy in the areas of reading, writing, speaking fluency, and arithmetic. The evaluation of each participant is based on many sub-competencies, which together form a comprehensive competency diagnostic. Because skills in adults with low literacy are often not distributed in a linear fashion, small-step diagnostics and the individual support based on them are

© Springer Nature Switzerland AG 2021
C. Stephanidis et al. (Eds.): HCII 2021, CCIS 1421, pp. 102–108, 2021.
https://doi.org/10.1007/978-3-030-78645-8_13

particularly important. For literacy teachers, this means time-consuming and personal attention to each learner. Similarly, the Leo study makes statements about the highest vocational qualifications of low-literate adults. According to this, 38.3% have no vocational training, 5.3% are in vocational preparation measures, and 41.7% have completed an in-company apprenticeship or vocational school (Dutz and Kleinert 2019). It becomes clear that the majority of low-literate people have attended a vocational school, at least during their training. This results in the high importance of vocational schools to recognize and sustainably promote low literacy. Wolf and Koppel (2017) note that although digital support and diagnostic tools are currently available in the field of literacy, there is a lack of tools for linking support and diagnosis.

This is where the dashboard for course instructors, which is also being developed in the lea.online project, comes in. The goal is to develop a tool that enables course instructors in literacy courses as well as teachers at vocational schools to automatically and time-savingly recognize differentiated learning levels in the test results and at the same time to derive individual support needs.

2   Conceptual Development of the Dashboard

Since the effects of datafication (Cukier and Mayer-Schönberger 2013) have become an integral part of everyday professional and private life, we think that the evaluations and visualizations of complex data sets also offer great potential for the literacy field. The central question for the development is how the learners can be individually supported by the teachers based on data driven decision making. In combination with the user interface, data visualizations should provide information transport and enable even non-experts to explore and understand complex diagnostic contexts. Datnow and Hubbard (2016) note in an international literature review on data driven decision making in education that this is a growing area worldwide. They go on to describe that it is important that teachers also have the skills to analyze datasets and that these datasets provide a wealth of information about learning results and students.

Various diagnostic information is presented in the dashboard. First, an overall assessment is made for each user. This is done by assigning the user to a level. In the competence model, each individual sub-competence is assigned to a level. If a partial competence is tested sufficiently often in the test, it is integrated into the evaluation algorithm. 80% of all sub-competencies of a level must have been successfully completed for a test taker to be assigned to this level. This is useful to get an overview, but not helpful for concrete support. What is needed here is strength-oriented and fine-grained feedback that enables the course instructors to derive concrete support measures. The data visualizations of the sub-competencies serve on the one hand to represent (complex) correlations and to enable the user to explore and understand them (Schuhmann and Müller 2000) as well as to provide an information transport to the user (Fischer-Stabel 2018), which goes beyond the mere representation of the test results.

So far, there is little knowledge about the usage habits and media skills of teachers in literacy practice (Wolf and Koppel 2017). The goal is to develop a tool that can be learned quickly and used intuitively by teachers. User experience and usability are parts of the research on human-computer interaction. According to ISO 9241-210 (en) user experience is defined as "A person's perceptions and responses that result from the use and/or anticipated use of a product, system or service". Usability is defined as the "extent to which a system, product or service can be used by specified users to achieve specified goals with effectiveness, efficiency and satisfaction in a specified context of use" by the DIN EN ISO 9241-11. In current scientific literature, usability is often described as part of the user experience (Vermeeren et al. 2010). This approach is also used outside of science. The nngroup defines as follows: "User experience encompasses all aspects of the end-user's interaction with the company, its services, and its products". (Norman & Nielson n.d.). To ensure a high level of user-friendliness, usability criteria (DIN EN ISO 9241-11, Molich and Nielsen 1990) were taken into account in the conceptual and design development of the dashboard. The following goals, superior to the criteria, were essential for the development: (a) The dashboard provides a wide range of information. In order to make the functions of the dashboard as easy as possible to experience for the user, special attention was paid to the clarity of the user interface. (b) An evaluation of each learner's competency diagnostics should be presented in a differentiated and detailed manner. To achieve this, these points were taken into account in the design and conceptual development:

- *Clear design:* In order to make the functions of the dashboard as easy to experience as possible for the user, special attention was paid to clarity. The arrangement of elements was based on the laws of Gestalt from cognitive psychology (Anderson 2013) and colors were chosen based on color theories and the perceptual capabilities of the human brain in terms of physiological and cultural aspects (Wegman and Sahid 2011).
- *Present relevant information:* The data sets enable us to present a wide range of information. But which is really relevant for the users or which information is needed to make concrete diagnostic statements? The needs of the target group were determined and evaluated by analyzing the existing otu.lea test evaluation and expert interviews.
- *Individual usage options:* A filter system enables the user to obtain a comprehensive and at the same time clear overview of the competencies of the tested person. Didactically useful filter options, such as individual results, performance progressions and, among other things, levels of difficulty, can be viewed separately. In this way, the often heterogeneous literary competencies of learners in literacy courses (Koppel 2017) can be recorded and viewed in a differentiated manner.

A good design, the presentation of relevant information for the derivation of concrete support needs, and an individual filter system which allows significant reduction of complexity without the loss of important content should make the analysis of data and the recognition of correlations intuitively understandable for the user (Fig. 1 and Fig. 2). In this way, teachers with little media skills or experience in digital data analysis should also be able to make well-founded and data-supported decisions for the individual support of learners.

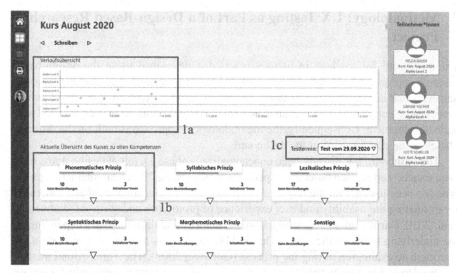

Fig. 1. Screenshot of a "course overview" page. 1a: Progress of each participant in a course, determined on different test dates. 1b: List of individual sub-competencies with results of each student, teacher can expand and collapse the lists. Each list contains several sub-competencies of one group. 1c: Selection of the test date for the list view.

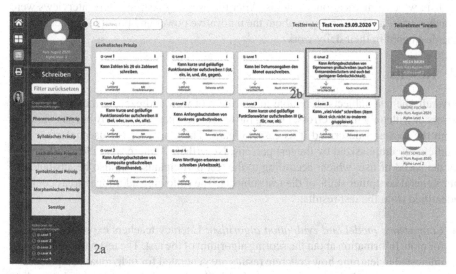

Fig. 2. Screenshot of a "student result" page. 2a: Filter system. Teachers can filter the competencies presented according to their own diagnostic needs. 2b: Each competence is presented on a card. Each card shows the learning level for that competency, the difficulty of the competency, and the student's learning progress.

3 Methodology: UX Testing as Part of a Design-Based Research Project

The dashboard for teachers in literacy practice is developed using the design-based research approach (Anderson and Shattuck 2012). This means that content is developed and evaluated iteratively in small steps. The target group is involved in the development process at an early stage, which is an important factor in the context of user-oriented software development. Consequently, the methodological approach is built on the different phases of the development of the dashboard.

The dashboard has already been conceptualized (phase 1), initial design drafts have been created and revised based on expert interviews (phase 2), and an interactive prototype has been tested with the target group (phase 3). There is a wide range of methods for evaluating the usability and user experience of prototypes and software (Vermeeren et al. 2010, Darin et al. 2019), which have advantages and disadvantages depending on the underlying goals of the study. The dashboard study is a formative evaluation, an intermediate evaluation during the process (Goodwin 2009). The Think Aloud method was used to conduct the usability tests. The users had to perform a previously defined set of tasks with the prototype and were encouraged to express their thoughts, feelings and opinions. Due to the Corona pandemic, testing was conducted digitally via the Zoom platform. All testing was screen-recorded. In total, the dashboard was tested with 12 teachers. Six of the test subjects were from literacy courses at an adult education center and six were from vocational schools. After the usability testing, short interviews were conducted with the test persons about the innovative power and possible applications of the dashboard in their daily work.

4 Results

Overall, the test subjects were able to use the tool well and execute the tasks without errors or with only minor errors. During the test, all test persons already became familiar with the tool and described it as easy to learn. The clarity of the user interface was particularly emphasized by the test persons. Nevertheless, there were clear differences in the speed of use, which, according to the test participants, can also be attributed to the general computer skills of the test subjects. The following additional areas could be identified from the test results:

- *Competence model and evaluation algorithm:* Literacy teachers expressed the need for more information about the scoring algorithm of the test. The test participants were interested in learning how concrete results are generated for individual competencies. On the other hand, teachers from vocational schools needed support in understanding the competency model. This group of people is much less familiar with competency diagnostic knowledge than teachers from literacy courses, which is a very important aspect for the use of the dashboard.
- *Learning materials:* Some teachers from literacy courses expressed the wish to have concrete task sets and/or learning materials suggested and provided in the dashboard on the basis of the test results, which they can then use in class with the learners. This wish was not mentioned by the teachers from the vocational school.

- *Learning progressions:* Especially the presentation of the learning progress of individual participants was mentioned by the test persons. The small-step presentation of partial competencies as well as the coarser feedback related to individual levels were positively emphasized.
- *Use in everyday work:* The vocational school teachers rated the tool as innovative and useful for use with learners. However, many test persons saw a problem with the actual use in the schools. Although many learners also in vocational schools show great problems with basic literacy skills, there is usually no time scheduled in the curriculum for special support for these students. The teachers mentioned on the one hand that they would like to use the dashboard and at the same time expressed concerns about how they can basically implement a literacy support for affected learners in their school, which goes beyond the normal lessons. The feedback regarding a possible use of the Dashboard in the daily work of teachers from literacy courses was consistently positive. The teachers saw the automated and at the same time small-step evaluation of the test results as a great added value for their own work practice. The individual filtering possibilities of results of sub-competencies were mentioned by the test persons as useful for deriving individual support measures.

5 Further Steps

The user experience tests with the think aloud method proved to be a useful tool for evaluating the interactive prototype of the dashboard. The short interviews conducted after the tests also brought good results. Potentials as well as weaknesses of the dashboard were revealed and can be revised in the upcoming project phase. The implementation of the tests as pure online sessions caused problems at various points. Poor internet connections as well as working with Zoom and the prototype at the same time led to interruptions and ambiguities at some points. Since these problems can be taken into account when evaluating the results, it was still a good way to conduct the tests.

In the next step, a first version of the complete usable software will also be tested in connection with the otu.lea test environment. The goal is to test the currently created revisions as well as the use of both tools together. After the release of the dashboard as well as the otu.lea test, usage data will be collected and evaluated as the last step of the surveys. In this way, the results of the qualitative UX surveys will be supplemented by quantitative analyses.

The tests with vocational school teachers have highlighted structural deficits in the support of people with low literacy in vocational schools. These should be examined more closely in further research projects in order to derive concrete approaches for action and reform for the work with people with low literacy in vocational schools.

Several steps can be derived for the use of the dashboard in literacy courses. On the one hand, a strategy must be developed to make the dashboard known and thus support a broad use of the tool. On the other hand, the tests have revealed potentials for further development of the dashboard. The diagnostics could be linked to concrete learning materials and task sets and thus be extended to a comprehensive tool for diagnosis, derivation of support measures as well as provision of task materials, execution and evaluation of these.

References

Anderson, T., Shattuck, J.: Design-based research: a decade of progress in education research? Educ. Res. **41**(1), 16–25 (2012). https://doi.org/10.3102/0013189X11428813

Wentura, D., Frings, C.: Kognitive Psychologie. BP. Springer, Wiesbaden (2013). https://doi.org/10.1007/978-3-531-93125-8

Cukier, K., Mayer-Schoenberger, V.: The rise of big data: how it's changing the way we think about the world. Foreign Aff. **92**(3), 28–40 (2013)

Darin, T., Coelho, B., Borges, B.: Which instrument should i use? supporting decision-making about the evaluation of user experience. In: Proceedings of the 21st HCI International Conference: Design, User Experience, and Usability Practice and Case Studies, pp. 49–67. Orlando/USA.s (2019)

Datnow, A., Hubbard, L.: Teacher capacity for and beliefs about data-driven decision making: a literature review of international research. J. Educ. Change **17**, 7–28 (2016). https://doi.org/10.1007/s10833-015-9264-2

Dutz, G., Kleinert, C.: Literalität und Weiterbildung (2019). https://www.alphadekade.de/files/2019%2005%2007%20Weiterbildung%20Gregor%20Dutz%20und%20Corinna%20Kleinert.pdf. 25 March 2021

Fischer-Stabel, P.: Datenvisualisierungen - Vom Diagramm zur Virtual Reality. UVK Verlag, München (2018)

Goodwin, K.: Designing for the Digital Age: How to Create Human-Centered Products and Services. Wiley Publishing, Indianapolis (2009)

Grotlüschen, A., Buddeberg, K., Dutz, G., Heilmann, L., Stammer, C.: LEO 2018 – Leben mit Geringer Literalität. Pressebroschüre. Universität Hamburg, Hamburg (2019)

International Organization for Standardization. ISO 9241-11:2018 (en), Ergonomics of human-system interaction — Part 11: Usability: Definitions and concepts (2018)

International Organization for Standardization. ISO 9241-210:2019 (en), Ergonomics of human-system interaction — Part 210: Human-centred design for interactive systems (2019)

Koppel, I.: Entwicklung einer Online-Diagnostik für die Alphabetisierung - Eine Design-Based Research-Studie. Springer VS, Wiesbaden (2017)

Molich, R., Nielson, J.: Improving a human-computer dialog. Commun. ACM **33**, 338–348 (1990)

Norman, D., Nielson, J. (n.d.): The Definition of User Experience (UX). https://www.nngroup.com/articles/definition-user-experience/. 26 Mar 2021

Reichart, E., Thomas, L., Huntemann, H.: Volkshochschul-Statistik. 57. Folge, Arbeitsjahr 2018. (DIE survey). Bielefeld: wbv (2019)

Schuhmann, H., Müller, W.: Visualisierung. Grundlagen und allgemeine Methoden. Springer Verlag, Berlin (2000)

Vermeeren, A.P., Law, E.L., Roto, V., Obrist, M., Hoonhout, J., Väänänen-Vainio-Mattila, K.: User experience evaluation methods: current state and development needs. In: Proceedings of the 6th Nordic Conference on Human-Computer Interaction: Extending Boundaries, pp. 521–530. ACM (2010)

Wegman, E., Said, Y.: Color theory and design. WIREs Comp. Stat. **3**, 104–117 (2011). https://doi.org/10.1002/wics.146

Wolf, K.D., Koppel, I.: Digitale Grundbildung: Ziel oder Methode einer chancengleichen Teilhabe in einer mediatisierten Gesellschaft? Wo wir stehen und wo wir hin müssen. In: Magazin Erwachsenenbildung.at 30, 11 S. - URN: urn:nbn:de:0111-pedocs-128864 (2017)

A Classification Method of the Learners' Queries in the Discussion Forum of MOOC to Enhance the Effective Response Rate from Instructors

Neha[✉] and Eunyoung Kim[✉]

School of Knowledge Science, Japan Advanced Institute of Science and Technology,
1-1 Asahidai, Nomi-shi, Ishikawa 923-1292, Japan
{neha11,kim}@jaist.ac.jp

Abstract. Although the quantity of online learning content in massive open online courses (MOOCs) has dramatically increased, there has been little focus on the discussion between learners and instructors regarding the course content itself.

This study proposes a classification method of the learners' queries in the discussion forum (DF) for enhancing the effective responses from instructors in video-based lectures. Different type of queries along with repetition causes confusion among learners and instructors. Therefore, analyzing the different types of queries was the basic task in this research.

We collected data from theoretical and practical courses in computer science with a duration of 12 weeks. The number of registered learners on the theoretical course was 11,973, while for the practical course this figure was 15,645. The number of participants in the DF was 11,555 on the theoretical course and 15,524 on the practical course. Following analysis, we conclude that there is a large number of enrolments on the courses. It can be very challenging for the instructors to answer all the queries. We found that the interest of learners varied and the ratio of content to non-content queries was significantly unbalanced between practical and theoretical courses.

To reduce the number of redundant tasks for the instructors and prevent them from having to answer repeated queries, we adopted a filtering method to identify non-content-related queries. This method uses the linguistic features from the queries of DF. Linguistic features showed a considerable role in extracting assignment-related (AR) and time-related (TR) queries. Classification of queries helps the instructor to give more attention to the main subject of study.

Keywords: Massive open online courses · Discussion forum · Classification method

1 Introduction

The current pandemic has implemented conventional classroom methods difficult in educational institutions because of lockdowns. Online learning has consequently displaced traditional classroom approaches in these contexts. Massive open online courses

© Springer Nature Switzerland AG 2021
C. Stephanidis et al. (Eds.): HCII 2021, CCIS 1421, pp. 109–115, 2021.
https://doi.org/10.1007/978-3-030-78645-8_14

(MOOCs) which combine course content with a discussion forum (DF), constitute one platform for E-learning. However, interaction in conventional classrooms and online learning is different. In virtual learning platforms, the interaction system can be real-time and cannot be. In both cases, interaction is difficult to control when the number of participants is large. Even it is more challenging to interact and access the DF if it is provided with pre-recorded learning videos. It is not only difficult for learners to access the information from the DF but also for the instructors to respond.

The platform of online studies creates confusion in the DF, hindering teacher-student interaction [1]. However, interaction and collaboration between learners are a necessary part of the DF of the online learning world [2]. There are several MOOCs platforms for learners such as Coursera, edX, FutureLearn. SWAYAM (Study Webs of Active Learning for Young Aspiring Minds) is an Indian-based platform with the facility of course credit transfer. It has a massive number of learners and offers courses for 9th grade to post-graduates' learners. However, there are only one or two instructors for each course [3]. If we compare this with traditional classroom learning, it is not surprising that many MOOC learners face difficulty when it comes to interacting with instructors. This paper focuses on the theoretical and practical DF with large number of enrolled learners in SWAYAM. It aims to find non-content-related queries by identifying the linguistic features of queries in the DF posts. Identification of non-content queries in the DF will automatically classify content-related queries that are focused on any DF.

2   Related Work

Eppa et al. compared student experiences and behavior's across different learning system designs, courses, and DF [4]. Jenny Bronstein et al. showed that personality traits, motivation, and interest towards the specific content of a person can be analyzed by looking at their participation in an online platform [5]. Past research focused on the structure of DF posts to understand the students' behavior better. Analysis of students' behavior can benefit learning analytics communication. In this research, the automatic extraction of data from the discussion forum has been done [6].

Diyi Yang et al. concluded, based on their findings, that MOOC discussion forums can give rise to confusing states which are mainly caused by not getting a response from the instructor in a timely manner [1].

Instructors can focus on specified queries and content-related queries after classification [7]. Hong et al. proposed a research technique that improved the system's performance in searching for questions and answers in the DF. They also proved that non-content features play a significant role in improving searching performance [8]. Yi Cui reported that content-related queries are less frequently answered by the instructor [9]. Feature selection is an important task in finding intention post in the DF [10]. Linguistic features can aid in detecting content-related and non-content-related queries so that the instructor can focus more on the former [11]. The community question answering system (CQA) can aid in finding relevant answers by the descriptive attributes of questions and classification of queries concerning the problem that is to be solved. This can be achieved with collaborative support from information technologies [12].

3 Research Procedure

3.1 Data Collection

The study was conducted based on data extracted from courses offered through SWAYAM (MOOC) in 2020 and goggle groups discussion forums of it. We compared two different courses to identify the similarities and differences between the DF posts of these courses, Table 1. The course materials included pre-recorded video lectures, transcripts, assignments, quizzes, and google groups DF. The course materials were in English. The category of both courses was computer science and engineering.

Table 1. Information about the two computer courses

Type of course	Theoretical course (TC)	Practical course (PC)
Course name	Computer networks	C and Cpp
Duration of course	12 weeks	12 weeks
Registered learners	11,973	15,645
Participant of DF	11,555	15,524

3.2 Data Coding

Data was received in text format from Google groups DF. In the DF of both the courses, our target was to analyze the various queries. Those queries included content-related queries (CR), assignment-related (AR) queries, and time-related (TR) queries. We found that mostly AR and TR were related to the inquiry. Therefore, we considered them as non-content-related (NCR) queries and the remaining queries were CR based on the query subject. Features were extracted for NCR queries. These features from the query subject were used to train a classification model as shown in Fig. 1.

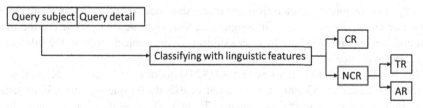

Fig. 1. Classification of queries for data coding

4 Results

4.1 Comparison of Learners' Queries and Their Interaction with Instructors

Despite the large, registered learners, there are few queries from the learner side for both the courses, as shown in Table 2. The ratio of CR queries to NCR is significant for the theoretical course, which is 8% to 91%. However, for the practical course, this ratio is 55% to 44%. Also, the total interaction including peer learning and instructor reply was 85 queries (75%) of all the threads in the theoretical course and 108 queries (78%) of all the threads in the practical course.

Table 2. Information on TC and PC

Type of course	TC	PC
Total queries	113 (till 17 sept.)	137 (till 30 sept.)
Total interactions	85 (75%)	108 (78%)
CR queries	10 (08%)	76 (55%)
NCR queries	103(91%)	61 (44%)

4.2 Peer Learning

In these two discussion forums, we observed less exchange of information among learners. For the TC, peer learning was 15%, while for the PC it was only 2%. There was a lack of knowledge sharing and collaborative learning. However, these two are important factors when it comes to interpreting the question-answering process in the CQA system [12]. Learners can communicate with each other on a specific identical question instead of asking the same question again. This can reduce instructor workload [10].

4.3 Role of Linguistic Features

The linguistic features extracted from the discussion forum queries for NCR are examination or exam, certificate, credit assignment, test, and question. These are the most commonly occurring words in the query subject. Query subject refers to the title of the query. We neglected the grammatical terms of queries.

For the TC, we were able to extract 90 (87%) queries out of 103 NCR queries. In contrast, we extracted 55 (90%) queries out of exactly 61 queries of NCR by using these linguistic features in PC, as shown in Table 3. The classification technique used the linguistic feature assignment for AR queries and TR queries, the technique used exam, examination, certificate, test, and credit as a linguistic feature. NCR queries were mostly related to inquiries. Table 4 shows the various words that were contained by NCR queries. These words were further classified as AR and TR query types. These features can be used to train a classification model for various queries. Extracted queries that were related to assignment in TC are represented in Fig. 2.

Table 3. Role of linguistic features in classifying queries

Linguistic feature	Query type	Frequency (TC)	Frequency (PC)
Assignment	AR	20	28
Exam or examination	TR	38	8
Certificate	TR	14	14
Test	TR	17	3
Credit	TR	1	2

Table 4. Words for classification

Query type	List of words for classification
AR	Submit, assignment, regarding, start, exam, submission, correct, answers, week
TR	Online, test, certificate, related, exam, regarding, examination, credit, points, issue, providing, change, centre, college, name, mistyped, eligibility, find, out, roll, number, procedure, not, yet, received, payment, fees, conduct, grading, showing, wrong, answer, email, question, where, due, date, course, type, closed

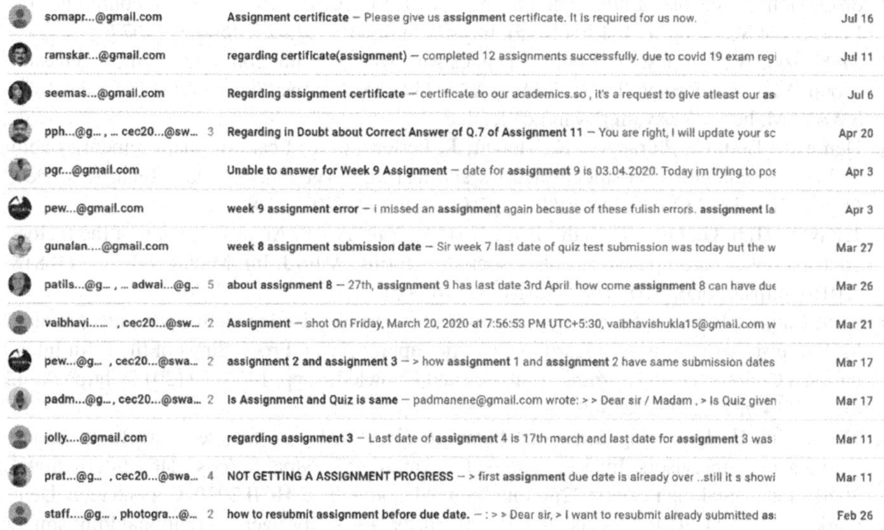

somapr...@gmail.com		**Assignment certificate** – Please give us **assignment** certificate. It is required for us now.	Jul 16
ramskar...@gmail.com		**regarding certificate(assignment)** – completed 12 assignments successfully. due to covid 19 exam reg	Jul 11
seemas...@gmail.com		**Regarding assignment certificate** – certificate to our academics.so , it's a request to give atleast our as	Jul 6
pph...@g... , ... cec20...@sw...	3	**Regarding in Doubt about Correct Answer of Q.7 of Assignment 11** – You are right, I will update your sc	Apr 20
pgr...@gmail.com		**Unable to answer for Week 9 Assignment** – date for **assignment** 9 is 03.04.2020. Today im trying to pos	Apr 3
pew...@gmail.com		**week 9 assignment error** – i missed an **assignment** again because of these fulish errors. **assignment** la	Apr 3
gunalan....@gmail.com		**week 8 assignment submission date** – Sir week 7 last date of quiz test submission was today but the w	Mar 27
patils...@g... , ... adwai...@g...	5	**about assignment 8** – 27th, **assignment** 9 has last date 3rd April. how come **assignment** 8 can have due	Mar 26
vaibhavi...... , cec20...@sw...	2	**Assignment** – shot On Friday, March 20, 2020 at 7:56:53 PM UTC+5:30, vaibhavishukla15@gmail.com w	Mar 21
pew...@g... , cec20...@swa...	2	**assignment 2 and assignment 3** – > how **assignment** 1 and **assignment** 2 have same submission dates	Mar 17
padm...@g... , cec20...@swa...	2	**Is Assignment and Quiz is same** – padmanene@gmail.com wrote: > > Dear sir / Madam , > Is Quiz given	Mar 17
jolly....@gmail.com		**regarding assignment 3** – Last date of **assignment** 4 is 17th march and last date for **assignment** 3 was	Mar 11
prat...@g... , cec20...@swa...	4	**NOT GETTING A ASSIGNMENT PROGRESS** – > first **assignment** due date is already over ..still it s showi	Mar 11
staff.....@g... , photogra...@...	2	**how to resubmit assignment before due date.** – : > > Dear sir, > I want to resubmit already submitted as:	Feb 26

Fig. 2. Screenshot of AR queries in TC

5 Conclusion

The results of this study showed that despite a large number of learners there were few queries. We observed that the instructor replied 70 to 80% of the queries. Analyzing the different types of queries was the basic task in this research. Detecting keywords and classifying them as content-related keywords and non-content-related keywords was a challenging task. Content-related queries contain keywords that are related to the content of the learning material. Since the material varies from course to course, it is difficult to find features for CR queries.

Most of the queries are from NCR class and it became a redundant task for the instructor to respond to similar queries. NCR queries are related to inquiries regarding the course. After classification, we concluded that most of the NCR queries are similar and can be further categorized into class. Therefore, we classified NCR queries into AR and TR. They can be marked as frequently asked questions to remove redundancy. Through this study, we could confirm that our classification method that filters NCR queries could organize DF with enhanced efficiency for learners and instructors.

However, our study has limitations in that it could not refine the list of words for each query type. Linguistic features can be found in NCR queries, but they cannot differentiate the queries exactly in AR and TR. Some words in the query subject also confused its query type. In our future research, more linguistic features of AR and TR will be refined to find detailed queries.

References

1. Yang, D., Wen, M., Howley, I., Kraut, R., Rosé, C.: Exploring the effect of confusion in discussion forums of massive open online courses. In: L@S 2015 - 2nd ACM conference on Learning@ Scale, pp. 121–130 (2015). https://doi.org/10.1145/2724660.2724677
2. McKenzie, W., Murphy, D.: I hope this goes somewhere: evaluation of an online discussion group. Australas. J. Educ. Technol. **16**(3), 239–257 (2000). https://doi.org/10.14742/ajet.1835
3. SWAYAM. https://swayam.gov.in/nc_details/
4. Demmans Epp, C., Phirangee, K., Hewitt, J., Perfetti, C.A.: Learning management system and course influences on student actions and learning experiences. Educ. Tech. Res. Dev. **68**(6), 3263–3297 (2020). https://doi.org/10.1007/s11423-020-09821-1
5. Jenny, B., Tali, G., Oren, P., Judit, B.-I., Noa, A., Yair, A.-H.: An examination of the factors contributing to participation in online social platforms. Aslib J. Inf. Manag. **68**(6), 793–818 (2016). https://doi.org/10.1108/AJIM-05-2016-0059
6. Ezen-Can, A., Boyer, K.E., Kellogg, S., Booth, S.: Unsupervised modeling for understanding MOOC discussion forums: a learning analytics approach. In: Proceedings of the Fifth International Conference on Learning Analytics and Knowledge, pp. 146–150 (2015). https://doi.org/10.1145/2723576.2723589
7. Neha, Kim, E.: Designing discussion forum in SWAYAM for effective interactions among learners and supervisors. In: Stephanidis, C., Antona, M., Ntoa, S. (eds.) HCI International 2020 – Late Breaking Posters: 22nd International Conference, HCII 2020, Copenhagen, Denmark, July 19–24, 2020, Proceedings, Part II, pp. 297–302. Springer International Publishing, Cham (2020). https://doi.org/10.1007/978-3-030-60703-6_38
8. Hong, L., Davison, B.D.: A classification-based approach to question answering in discussion boards. In: Proceedings of the 32nd International ACM SIGIR Conference on Research and Development in Information Retrieval, pp. 171–178 (2009). https://doi.org/10.1145/1571941.1571973
9. Cui, Y., Wise, A.F.: Identifying content-related threads in MOOC discussion forums. In: L@S 2015 - 2nd ACM Conference on Learning@ Scale, pp. 299–303 (2015). https://doi.org/10.1145/2724660.2728679

10. Liu, Y., Yin, C., Ogata, H., Qiao, G., Yano, Y.: A FAQ-based e-learning environment to support Japanese language learning. Int. J. Distance Educ. Technol. **9**(3), 45–55 (2011). https://doi.org/10.4018/jdet.2011070104
11. Chen, Z., Liu, B., Hsu, M., Castellanos, M., Ghosh, R.: Identifying intention posts in discussion forums. In: NAACL HLT 2013 - 2013 Proceedings of the Main Conference of the North American Chapter of the Association for Computational Linguistics: Human Language Technologies, pp. 1041–1050, June 2013
12. Srba, I., Bielikova, M.: A comprehensive survey and classification of approaches for community question answering. ACM Trans. Web **10**(3) (2016). https://doi.org/10.1145/2934687

The Relationship Between Student Attitudes Toward Online Learning and Environmental Factors During Covid-19 Pandemic: The Case of the University of Tetova

Ibrahim Neziri[1], Kushtrim Ahmeti[2], and Agon Memeti[3(✉)]

[1] Department of Psychology, University of Tetova, Tetova, North Macedonia
[2] Department of Philosophy, University of Tetova, Tetova, North Macedonia
[3] Department of Computer Sciences, University of Tetova, Tetova, North Macedonia
agon.memeti@unite.edu.mk

Abstract. During 2020, students and higher education institutions faced massive change regarding the online teaching/learning process, which evoked numerous debates within the institutions, teachers and students. The aim of this study is to verify the relationship between the attitudes towards online teaching and environmental factors, equipment, noise and distraction from other people, in the students of the State University of Tetova in North Macedonia.

Attitudes towards online learning are addressed in three specific dimensions, namely cognitive, affective and behavioral, while the environmental factors are focused on the conditions the learning process takes place, the noise, the technological equipment and distractions from other people during online learning.

The methodology used in this study is non-experimental correlational with quantitative data gathered through relevant instruments, with a sample of 801 University of Tetova students, in North Macedonia, whereas the most frequented age was 18–22 years.

The findings of the study, through relevant statistical tests, report slightly more emphasized negative student attitudes towards online learning, while the correlational analysis result as statistically moderate, with a negative direction between student attitudes towards online learning and environmental factors. The multiple regression analysis shows a statistically significant model for predicting the level of students' attitudes towards online learning by environmental factors such as: teaching conditions, noise and distractions from other people. Negative attitudes towards online learning are more associated with increasing difficulties of the environmental factors where online learning takes place.

Keywords: Attitudes · Online learning · Environmental factors

1 Introduction

During 2020, students and higher education institutions faced massive change regarding the online teaching/learning process, which evoked numerous debates within the institutions, teachers and students. We cannot say that this teaching form was easily accepted

© Springer Nature Switzerland AG 2021
C. Stephanidis et al. (Eds.): HCII 2021, CCIS 1421, pp. 116–121, 2021.
https://doi.org/10.1007/978-3-030-78645-8_15

by students, and due to this situation, different sides of opinions and beliefs towards online learning were created.

The purpose of this study resulted precisely from the idea of providing a scientific verification to the relationship between the attitudes towards online teaching and the factors of the environment, equipment, noise and distraction from other people, in the students of the State University of Tetova in North Macedonia.

Attitudes towards online learning are addressed in three specific dimensions, namely cognitive, affective and behavioral. The cognitive aspect includes the part of certain beliefs that students possess related to this teaching form, the affective part refers to emotional experiences and the behavior part is mainly treated in terms of concrete behaviors or actions that students have conducted during distance learning.

Regarding the environmental factors, the study is focused on the environmental conditions where online learning takes place, the noise, the technological equipment and distractions from other people during online learning, which were assessed as environmental factors related to attitudes towards online learning process by students.

The study offers higher education institutions data on the environmental factors' significance in relation to student attitudes towards online learning and their assessment of this form of learning during the pandemic. Certainly, the environmental factors addressed represent only a certain part that this study aimed to test.

2   Theoretical Framework

Student attitudes towards online learning vary based on many factors. The study of [1], accentuated that "students have a clearly expressed positive attitude towards distance learning, which means that they are more likely to accept it as a way of education. Most of them not only use ICT in their daily lives, but also want to actively use ICT in their education." Students are satisfied with online classes and are getting sufficient support from teachers, but they do not believe that online classes will replace traditional classroom lessons. Regardless of the fact that they face difficulties in conducting online lessons due to lack of proper training and development, the technical-related issues are usually the key issues impacting the effectiveness of online learning [2]. The study of [3], shows that out of 382 students, 76% of them used mobile devices for their e-learning. 77.4% of students showed a negative perception related to e-learning, of which 86% of students reported that e-learning has little impact on their learning. Most students preferred face-to-face learning rather than e-learning. The main finding score shows that students are still not ready for e-learning. The results of studies show that temperature, lighting and noise have significant direct effects on the academic performance of university students, where in conclusion it was verified that the three independent variables have an impact on the sustainability of university students [4]. Regarding environmental conditions, such as noise, negative correlations to student performance are reported [5].

3   Methodology

The methodology used in this study is non-experimental correlational to find the relationship between the environmental factors and the student attitudes towards online learning during the COVID-19 pandemic, since the nature of the data and the assessment with relevant instruments was the most appropriate to the method used.

The population of the study comprised of all University of Tetova active students in the summer semester 2019/20, with a sample selected from a total of 801 students according to the standard methodological procedures with a margin of error ±5 and 95% confidence level. The study sample was selected only within the University of Tetova faculties, and from the participants who responded positively to the survey, whereas the most frequented age was 18–22 years old, with a maximum age of 32–36 years. Based on the faculties' scientific fields, 265 are students of natural and applied sciences, 255 humanities and arts and 277 students of medical sciences. By gender, a total of 581 female and 220 male respondents participated (Table 1).

Table 1. Data on age and gender

		N	%
What is your age group?	18–22	464	57.93%
	23–25	304	37.95%
	26–38	17	2.12%
	29–31	10	1.25%
	32–36	6	.75%
Which is your gender?	Female	581	72.53%
	Male	220	27.47%
	Total	798	100.00%

3.1 Instruments

The student attitudes measuring instrument was created by the authors of the paper, going through the stages of face validity and finding a good internal statistical construct, adapted to the study population through factor reduction analysis. Bartlett's Sphericity Test showed statistically significant data that the data matrix resulted in an identity and KMO value sufficient for the sample.80. The internal intercorrelation analysis resulted in Cronbach's Alpha $\alpha = .71$ in 9 questions measuring attitudes. The attitudes level at this measurement scale is operationalized by the value of the score obtained from 1 (Never) to 3 (Very often).

The measurement of environmental factors was conducted through questions which included various environmental factors, such as: environmental conditions where online teaching takes place, equipment, noise and distraction from other people, assessed from 1 (Not at all) to 3 (A lot). The highest total of scores for all environmental factors resulted in the highest level of difficulties' presence that students face during online learning.

3.2 Data Collection and Ethics Criteria

The study data were collected online, through official emails of University of Tetova students enrolled in the summer semester 2019/20. During the data collection, the ethical criteria of anonymity and voluntary participation were respected, as well as the right to withdraw from the study. All the necessary filling instructions were detailed in the questionnaire. Due to the side effects, participants were not informed about the purpose of this study, namely about the relevant comparison of variables, but only about issues related to the assessment of online learning during the pandemic.

4 Results

The findings of the study, through relevant statistical tests, report slightly more emphasized negative student attitudes towards online learning (M = 17.37, SD = 2.99, N = 801, Skw = .218), respectively under average (Graph 1), while the assessment of environmental factors difficulties during online learning is assessed with (M = 7.57, SD = 1.52, N = 801, Skw = .02) (Graph 2).

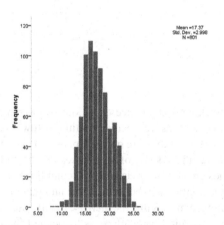
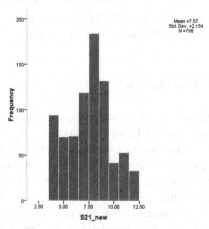

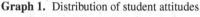

Graph 1. Distribution of student attitudes

Graph 2. Environmental factors toward online learning

The correlational analysis shows statistically significant moderately negative relationship (Table 2) between student overall attitudes toward online learning during the Covid-19 pandemic and environmental factors (r = −.465, p = .00). The multiple linear regression analysis of the enter method (Table 3), since the terms of use were met by the Durbin-Watson value for autocorrelation 1.96 and the value of VIF within the limits of .10, reported that environmental factors explain with statistical significance student attitudes towards online learning with 22.5% (R^2 = .225, $F(4,792)$ = 58.85, p < 0.01), where, the space where lessons take place is in the first place (β = .21, p < .001), second are the distractions from other people (β = .20, p < .001), and third is the noise (β = .16, p < .001), while the equipment was not a significant predictor of the model in statistical terms (p > .05).

Table 2. Correlation between student attitudes toward online learning during pandemic Covid-19 with environmental factors

	Environmental factors	Distract	Learning environment conditions	Noise	Equipment
Attitudes towards online learning	−.465**	−.357**	−.391**	−.381**	−.289**

** Correlation is significant at the 0.01 level / N = 801

Table 3. Regression model for predicting students' attitude towards online learning by environmental factors

Model	R	R Square	Adjusted R Square	Std. Error of the Estimate	Durbin-Watson
1	.479a	.229	.225	2.62717	1.964

a. Predictors: (Constant), Distract, Equipment, Learning environment conditions Noise

b. Dependent Variable: Students attitude
$(R^2 = .225, F(4,792) = 58.85, p < 0.01)$.

5   Conclusion

The findings of the study show the negative role or significance of the online learning environmental factors in students' beliefs, experiences, respectively attitudes towards the online learning process. Student attitudes in this study were more emphasized on the negative direction, a finding which is not in line with the study of [1]. The results showed that negative attitudes related to the difficulties created by environmental conditions are statistically valid. The negative direction of the relationship between environmental factors and student attitudes towards online learning, explains that the increase in difficulties related to environmental factors where online learning takes place, is associated by a more negative tendency of attitudes towards this form of teaching. Regarding the environmental conditions, the results of the study were similar to other studies, although studies of the same type were not found. Based on this conclusion, this study findings recommend that higher education institutions consider these environmental factors during online teaching, since they represent a part with significant effects on the students' approach to this form of the teaching/learning process.

References

1. Roumiana, F., Blagovesna, Y., Lyubka, A.: Factors affecting students' attitudes towards online learning - the case of Sofia University. In: AIP Conference Proceedings, vol. 2048, 020025 (2018). https://doi.org/10.1063/1.5082043. Published Online 11 Dec 2018

2. Kulal, A., Nayak, A.A.: Study on perception of teachers and students toward online classes in Dakshina Kannada and Udupi District. Asian Assoc. Open Univ. J. **15**(3), 285–296 (2020). https://doi.org/10.1108/AAOUJ-07-2020-0047

3. Abbasi, S., Tahera, A., Abdul, M., Shabnam, M.: Perceptions of students regarding E-learning during Covid-19 at a private medical college. Pak. J. Med. Sci. **36**(COVID19-S4), S57–S61 (2020). https://doi.org/10.12669/pjms.36.COVID19-S4.2766

4. Realyvásquez-Vargas, A., Maldonado-Macías, A.A., Arredondo-Soto, K.C., Baez-Lopez, Y., Carrillo-Gutiérrez, T., Hernández-Escobedo, G.: The impact of environmental factors on academic performance of university students taking online classes during the COVID-19 pandemic in Mexico. Sustainability **12**(21), 9194 (2020). https://doi.org/10.3390/su12219194

5. Diaco, S.B.: Effects of noise pollution in the learning environment on cognitive performances. Liceo J. Higher Educ. Res. (2014). https://doi.org/10.7828/ljher.v10i1.655

Digital Museums as Pedagogical Mediators in the Pandemic Crisis

Diana Palacios[1] , Janio Jadán-Guerrero[1,2(✉)] , and Carlos Ramos-Galarza[2,3]

[1] Maestría en Educación, Mención Innovación y Liderazgo Educativo, Universidad Tecnológica Indoamérica, Av. Machala y Sabanilla, Quito, Ecuador
janiojadan@uti.edu.ec
[2] Centro de Investigación en Mecatrónica y Sistemas Interactivos MIST/Carrera de Ingeniería en Ciencias de la Computación/Carrera de Psicología, Universidad Tecnológica Indoamérica, Av. Machala y Sabanilla, Quito, Ecuador
carlosramos@uti.edu.ec
[3] Facultad de Psicología, Pontificia Universidad Católica del Ecuador, Av. 12 de Octubre y Roca, Quito, Ecuador
caramos@puce.edu.ec

Abstract. As a result of social isolation due to the COVID-19 pandemic, museums around the world have closed their physical doors, but some of them have opened digital windows to be able to visit them through virtual tours. Through them, interactive and sensory experiences are created developing educational and training spaces, which constitute pedagogical mediators that help teachers make their virtual classes more innovative, creating the interest of their students. This article describes the interactive museums as pedagogical mediators that propose a fusion of knowledge and new experiences, which transport the student to a cultural environment fostering the interest of interacting, knowing and visiting museums; in this way they can renew and create new interactive and innovative experiences. Through interactive museums, it is intended to promote a different learning dynamic, and at the same time improve the student's disposition to receive new knowledge. This proposal contributes to the teaching-learning process with the use of innovative, interactive teaching resources that are at the same time consistent with the current environment in which children grow up. It is relevant to be able to encourage teachers to apply new educational strategies supported by technology, and thereby enrich their teaching management, achieve better teaching results with their students and seek other interrelationships. The study is also consistent and timely with current times, as teachers and students continue to interact in a virtual mode. The study delves into interactive museums and investigates the type of digital resources that can support the teaching-learning process in the area of Sciences. These ideas are intended to contribute to the design of innovative teaching resources that are based on the experiences of virtual visits to interactive museums, through which it is possible to take advantage of all the advantages and benefits they offer.

Keywords: Digital museums · Pedagogical mediator · Interactive resources · Science · Interactive museums

1   Introduction

There are approximately 341 children's museums in 22 countries. 23% of them are in the start-up phase, the reason is because it is a relatively new initiative in much of the world, it is not usual for the museums to be interactive or to be managed under a learning project. Based on the data, more than 30 million children and families annually visit museums of this type, acting as self-directed learning spaces as a nursery of creativity [1]. In addition, a study that addresses the topic of interactive museums shows that around the world there are approximately 15,000 museums of this type, not only oriented to children but also to visitors of any age [2]. These figures show that museums are spaces for learning about history, science, art and the nature of human life itself; and with the advancement of technology they become more and more interactive. However, they are spaces where students have to visit them in person or virtually in recent months of confinement caused by the pandemic. This effect has generated a process in a certain inverse way, since museums have looked for a way to enter homes through the internet. In addition, it should be noted that with the COVID-19 pandemic, according to the International Council of Museums ICOM, almost 94% of museums in the world closed, and at the same time many increased their digital activities [3]. In this way, it is the precise moment in which these resources can be used in the classroom, either virtual at the current moment when education is carried out online or post-pandemic when it returns to face-to-face in a new reality.

Interactive museums as a pedagogical medium can contribute greatly to the teaching-learning process, however, this requires not only the existence of these museums, but also the preparation that the teacher can assume to take advantage of these spaces and guide the students to the knowledge. In Latin America this practice is still limited, and having found little information in this regard, it is estimated that its application is also scarce [4, 7]. Therefore, the study seeks to explore the interactive resources of local museums in order to establish whether they can be brought to the classroom as pedagogical mediators in the teaching-learning process of Sciences.

2   Related Research

Various studies are approached in which the use of museums as pedagogical mediators have been investigated Varela and Stengler (2004) analyzed interactive museums as didactic resources, taking the Museum of Science and the Cosmos in Tenerife as a case study, Spain. The authors analyzed the activities that the museum proposes, and based on these they produced educational material for teachers and students. For these authors, the relevance of interactive museums lies in the fact that they are spaces of interest to communicate and learn scientific information in a fun and suggestive way [5].

Walz and Triano (2010) dealt with interactive science museums as a didactic medium and its relationship with technological literacy. For the authors it is important to revalue the environments where knowledge is manifested, so that both the teacher and the students can take advantage of them, the first guiding and motivating and the second, assimilating the knowledge in a meaningful way. However, they point out that one of the challenges is to promote in students a critical, investigative and analytical thinking and attitude about what they see or what they interact with [6].

Cambre (2017) has observed in his analysis of the interactive Museums of Science and Technology in Latin America that in this region the creation of interactive centers has been late compared to Europe and North America; however, he observes that interactive museums have grown in number and size in recent years. In this regard, he points out the relevance of networks in the process of change, mentioning the RedPOP in Latin America, which is the Network for the Popularization of Science and Technology in Latin America and the Caribbean, and which links various interactive centers and museums to share experiences, disseminate scientific information and generally promote a reflection on the Latin American reality in terms of production and dissemination of scientific knowledge [7].

One of the factors involved in the conceptualization of the interactive museum is that of the user or visitor, since without this there is no interactivity. According to Rivero (2009), the visitor's experience to a museum has varied over the years, demanding more and more, a greater amount of information and data about what they see, but simplified or summarized, that means, that the visitor wants to observe the exhibition faster and receive the most relevant information quickly, which is consistent with the way in which people currently interact with the information on the network. In inter-active museums this changes because the way in which information is received is participatory [8].

Therefore, communication with the visitor stops being passive, and becomes active, so that whoever attends an interactive museum becomes a user of it, according to Orozco (2005), for which it is no longer a question of a unilateral experience in which the visitor only observes or listens, but receives and participates in comprehensive and playful educational experiences to develop knowledge and skills [9].

3 Method

The purpose of this study is to identify the percentage of knowledge of teachers about museums and their use in the classroom. The data obtained allowed to propose alternatives or guidelines to include the use of interactive museums as pedagogical mediators. Being understood as an interactive museum, a space destined to provide experiences and stimuli related to science, scientific knowledge and the scientific method through the possibility of the user to interact with objects, phenomena, and people in a social, personal and physical context planned for learning as outlined in [10, 11].

For this, an educational resource based on an interactive digital museum was designed for its application in the virtual classroom that is still used today. Also, an assessment of the resource is made with a focus group with the participants.

3.1 Particpants

The study population consisted of 38 students and 12 teachers from a school located in Quito canton - Ecuador. In addition, the participation of two museum administrators from Ecuador and Costa Rica is included.

3.2 Materials

The museum must contemplate plans, programs and a design of its exhibition in accordance with the interests and motivation of the visitors, and that allow the concatenation of three contexts, personal, social and physical to generate an interactive museum experience which in itself has a pedagogical character.

One of the components that adds value or interactive museums, and that differentiates it from traditional museums experiences, is the use of technology to promote exhibitions in which the user can participate.

Among the technologies that can be found in museums, we can mention augmented reality, virtual reality, tangible interfaces, auditory interfaces, hepatic interfaces, and visual interfaces.

Regarding the techniques and instruments for data collection, those shown in Table 1 will be applied:

Table 1. Data collection techniques and instruments

Technique	Instrument	Subject	Objetive
Survey	Survey questionnaire	Teachers	Identify the percentage of teachers' knowledge about interactive museums and their use as pedagogical mediators
Interview	Interview guide	Representatives Administrators of Museums	To delve into the point of view of museum managers on the integration of museums within the educational process
Focus group	Group interview guidel	Students	Observe the effectiveness of the interactive museum use as pedagogical mediators in a test group of students

3.3 Procedure

The present investigation was carried out in three phases:

The first phase was to obtain information on interactive museums and their use as a pedagogical mediator, categorizing the educational resources used by museums with potential use in science teaching, a systematic search of scientific documents in databases was carried out. In English and Spanish related to museums, museums with potential use in science teaching were also identified and the IV National Meeting of Museum Educators [4] participated. The types of museums that exist in Ecuador were identified and two interviews were conducted with representatives of the Museum Network.

In the second phase, the educational strategies for the use of interactive educational resources in the Science classes within the School were determined, designing and validating the data collection instruments with the Cronbach's Alpha coefficient. A sample survey was carried out with 10 people and authorization was requested from the institution's authorities for the application of surveys to teachers. It can be mentioned that in this phase the search process was also made, the contact with administrators or museum representatives for the interview and application of the survey.

In the third phase, an interactive virtual museum was designed based on the experiences of virtual visits to museums. Objectives were established according to the contents of the Science subject. Strategies were developed for each objective and the resources were defined for each of the strategies. In addition, it was coordinated with the authorities of the institution to carry out a class applying the proposal, carrying out the evaluation through a focus group with students.

4   Design of a Virtual Interactive Museum

The virtual interactive museum consists of a website constituted as an interactive museum of l Science that functions as a pedagogical mediator to be used by teachers to work with their students, in which various strategies linked to both external sites and designed by the teacher. These strategies can be applied during a virtual class, or sent to students for practice at home.

The site is prepared by the introduction where the interactive museum is presented, six strategies are integrated that aim to provide mediation resources to teachers, all based on museum activity. These strategies are: Augmented reality, virtual tours, interactive games, interdisciplinary museums, home experiments, and student expositions.

It should be noted that the activities integrated in the Google Sites, work as an example. The expectation is that, as the platform works, it can be enriched with material referenced to other web pages and with unpublished content prepared, both by teachers and students. The six strategies are detailed below.

4.1 Strategy 1. Augmented Reality

Augmented reality provides interesting learning opportunities by allowing the student to observe 3D elements in their own environment. For this activity, the Google Images search engine has been considered with the function to present objects in augmented reality. In Fig. 1 an application of ARcore technology is shown, with which many objects or images can be visualized in 3D.

Fig. 1. Augmented reality presentation at the Interactive Museum

On the other hand, Google Expeditions was applied to promote the use of virtual reality on issues related to the Earth. An example of this technology is shown in Fig. 2.

Fig. 2. Google expeditions images

Finally, Chromville was applied to know the human body, through an App and downloadable and printable sheets. An example of use is shown in Fig. 3.

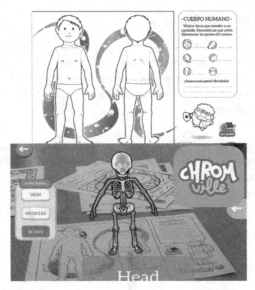

Fig. 3. Chromville images to understand the human body

4.2   Strategy 2: Interactive Games

The integration in the Interactive Museum of Sciences of interactive games related to Sciences subject is proposed. An example of interactive games related to science is shown in Fig. 4.

Fig. 4. Capture of the interactive games strategy

4.3   Strategy 3: Virtual Visits

Part of the inclusion of museums as pedagogical mediators is the use of exhibitions from real museums, through their virtual visits. Therefore, in this strategy, links to virtual tours of the following museums have been included: Smithsonian Museum of Natural History. American Museum of Natural History, Museum of Sciences, Madrid, Museum of the Desert, Saltillo and Coahuila, as shown in Fig. 5.

Fig. 5. Virtual visits

4.4   Strategy 4: Interdisciplinary Museums

In this case, it is the same activity presented in strategy three, referring to visits to virtual museums, however, interdisciplinary museums will be integrated here, in which other topics such as archeology, history, or the arts are addressed. Figure 6 shows the National Archaeological Museum of Spain.

Fig. 6. National archaeological museum of Spain

4.5   Strategy 5: Home Experiments

There are a large number of home experiments that can be found on YouTube or other sites, and that have been compiled in the Interactive Museum. However, it is important that teachers always review each experiment carefully before including it, to consider it safe and feasible by students without running any risk for them at home (Fig. 7).

Fig. 7. Home experiments

4.6 Strategy 6: Student Expositions

The last strategy was to show the results of the work or projects carried out by the students, which is used as an example and motivation for their experience in the interactive virtual museum.

5 Conclusions

Interactive museums as pedagogical mediators propose a fusion of knowledge and new experiences, which transport the student to an environment of culture, fostering the interest of interacting, knowing and visiting the museums; in this way they can renew and create new interactive and innovative experiences. In the validation with the focus group, it was possible to show the high motivation of the students and the interest in the interactive activities presented. In conclusion, it can be corroborated that pedagogical mediation through museums constitutes an evaluative dynamic in which a teacher guides with instructional supports that make it possible for a student to appropriate knowledge with experimental experiences [12].

Through interactive museums, it was possible to promote a different learning dynamic, and at the same time improve the student's disposition to receive new knowledge by contributing to the teaching-learning process, with the use of innovative, interactive and educational resources. at the same time consistent with the current environment in which children grow up. It is relevant to be able to encourage teachers to apply new educational strategies supported by technology, and thereby enrich their teaching management, achieve better teaching results with students and seek other interrelationships.

References

1. Cano, R.: La importancia de los museos para niños. Obtenido de EVE Museos e innovación (2018). https://evemuseografia.com/2018/06/13/la-importancia-de-los-museos-para-ninos/
2. Rodríguez, A.: Museos científicos abren sus puertas a través de la Internet. El Comercio, (2020)

3. ICOM: Museos, profesionales de los museos y COVID-19. Obtenido de Consejo Interna-cional de Museos (2020). https://icom.museum/wp-content/uploads/2020/05/Informe-museos-y-COVID-19.pdf
4. Universidad de Costa Rica: IV Encuentro Nacional de Educadores de Museos. Obtenido de Museo de la Universidad de Costa Rica (2020). https://vinv.ucr.ac.cr/sites/default/files/documentos/encuentro_museos.pdf
5. Varela, C., Stengler, E.: Los museos interactivos como recurso didáctico: El Museo de las Ciencias y el Cosmos. Rev. Elect. Enseñanza de las Ciencias 3(1), 32–34 (2004)
6. Walz, V., Triano, J.: Alfabetización Tecnológica. El museo interactivo de ciencias como medio didáctico para la comunicación pedagógica. In: Congreso Iberoamericano de Educación, págs. 1–8. Argentina (2010)
7. Cambre, M.: Centros y museos interactivos de ciencia en América Latina. En Massarani, L., Rocha, M. Aproximaciones a la investigación en divulgación de la ciencia en América Latina a partir de sus artículos académicos, págs. 108–138. Río de Janeiro, Brasil: Fiocruz-COC (2017)
8. Rivero, M.: Museos y didáctica on-line: cinco ejemplos de buenas prácticas. Rev. Hermes 1, 110–114 (2009)
9. Orozco, G.: Los museos interactivos como mediadores pedagógicos. Rev. Electr. Sinéct. 26, 38–50 (2005)
10. Terradas, R., Terradas, E., Arnal, M., Wagensberg, J.: Cosmocaixa: el museo total por conversación entre arquitectos y museólogos. SACYR, España (2006)
11. Falk, J., Dierking, L.: Learning from Museums: Visitor Experiences and the Making of Meaning. Altamira Press, Walnut Creek (2000)
12. Alzate, M., Arbeláez, M.: Intervención, mediación pedagógica y los usos del texto escolar. Rev. Iberoame. Educ. 37(3), 1–15 (2005)

A Trial of Active Learning Method for Business Management Education in Online Environment

Tomofumi Uetake[✉], Takashi Majima, Akimichi Aoki, and Sugio Baba

School of Business Administration, Senshu University, Kanagawa, Japan
{uetake,t-majima,aaoki,scbaba}@isc.senshu-u.ac.jp

Abstract. Recently, with the spread of active learning (AL), various types of teaching methods have been proposed in the field of business management education. However, in the current situation where face-to-face group work with a large number of people is restricted due to the influence of Coronavirus (COVID19) disaster, it is necessary to carry out such learning in an online environment, but the implementation method and effect are unknown. In this situation, we conducted a trial of an active learning method based on the PDCA cycle in order to draw out the active nature of the participants and to obtain learning effects through "dialogue" in an online environment. Furthermore, we conducted group work in an online environment for 48 university students, evaluated the effects, and considered the points when conducting such learning online.

Keywords: Active learning method · Business management education · Online environment

1 Introduction

In recent years, an educational method called "active learning" that encourages students to actively learn has been attracting attention, and many universities in Japan have begun to adopt it. And even in the field of business management education where it is necessary to experience the process of putting the theory into practice, active learning methods of these processes by conducting group work using business games, clay, skits, etc., have been proposed [1–4]. However, in the current situation where face-to-face group work with a large number of people is restricted due to the influence of Coronavirus (COVID19) disaster, it is necessary to carry out such learning in an online environment, but the implementation method and effect are unknown.

Therefore, in this study, we will conduct a trial of an active learning method in the field of business administration, which is conducted in an online environment using ICT tools.

2 Proposal

In this paper, we proposed an active learning method in order to draw out the active nature of the participants and to obtain learning effects through "dialogue" in an online environment.

C. Stephanidis et al. (Eds.): HCII 2021, CCIS 1421, pp. 132–137, 2021.
https://doi.org/10.1007/978-3-030-78645-8_17

2.1 Theoretical Framework

Our research is based on the concept of "transfer of learning" in the situated cognition perspective [5]. In this view, knowledge of any action is seen as being embedded in the context. Thus, people learn to do something through interplays with any other actors in the context [6, 7]. Based on this perspective, to understand the management theory fully, students should use the following three steps.

Step 1: Acquiring knowledge
Step 2: Structuralizing acquired knowledge
Step 3: Generalizing structuralized knowledge

At first, students can acquire knowledge by taking traditional style classes or reading books. This step is named "Acquiring knowledge". Then, students can structuralize acquired knowledge by trying to use and apply it to a certain situation through role-playing (e.g., group work, case study, internship). This step is named "structuralizing acquired knowledge". However, they cannot apply it in other or different settings. They just acquire a contextualized knowledge in this step. The next step is "generalizing structuralized knowledge". Students can generalize structuralized knowledge based on the similarity across many situations [8]. Our research project has been groping for a more suitable teaching method to promote step 2 and 3 in an online environment.

2.2 Implementation Method of Our Proposal

In this paper, we focused on "groupthink" that would be cultivated in organizational and group decision-making. We designed the group work based on the PDCA cycle (Fig. 1).

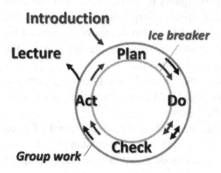

Fig. 1. Implementation method

Since the group work is conducted in a short period of time, we thought that an ice-breaker was essential to improve the quality of the group work, so we decided to conduct an ice breaker before the group work. After the group work, a lecture was given to explain what was learned in the group work.

2.3 Implementation Method of Our Proposal

We design a group work by using a team-building game for understanding basic management organization theory. This group work also aims for students to understand the importance of dialogue in organizing [9, 10]. So, in this group work, to increase the effectiveness of learning, communication with each group member is necessary.

The implementation method of our proposal is shown in Table 1.

Table 1. Implementation method of our proposal

Step 1	Self-introduction (Ice-breaker)
Step 2	Explanation and planning
Step 3	Group work 1 (Ice-breaker)
Step 4	Mutual inspection
Step 5	Reflection
Step 6	Explanation and planning
Step 7	Group work 2 (Team-building game)
Step 8	Mutual inspection
Step 9	Reflection
Step 10	Lecture

At first, we set a time for self-introduction (Ice breakier) to get to know the group members (Step 1).

Second, to get the participants to relax, we conduct a group work 1 (ice-breaker game: Steps 2–5). The task of this group work is to work together with group members to draw something that looks like it can be drawn but cannot be drawn. They worked cooperatively to draw a cartoon character at that time. After the ice-breaker, students can be more active in their assignments.

Third, they work on group work 2 (team-building game) as above (Steps 6 –9) (see also next chapter for detail). After finishing their work, every participated student evaluates the work of other teams.

After the group work, we explain the fundamental of management organization theory. We also explain the importance of understanding the environment around their own organization and creating good collaboration (enhancing psychological safety) in an organization (Step 10).

3 Experimental Class

In the experimental class, we used "Moon landing exercise: Ranking survival objects for the moon" as the subject of group work. This team-building game aims to reinforce the concept of using critical thinking in prioritization activities. It was originally developed by NASA.

To evaluate the effectiveness of our proposal, we conducted group work in an online environment. Data from this paper comes from a business management course at Senshu University in Japan. Data collection was conducted in June 2020 in COVID19 environment via online (see Fig. 2), and the final sample consists of 48 respondents (4 students × 12 groups) who were third year and fourth year (last year) students.

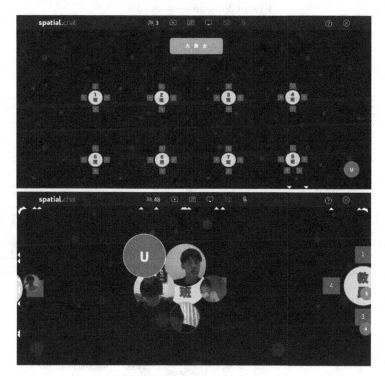

Fig. 2. Experimental class

As a meeting tool, we used "spatial.chat (https://spatial.chat/)". This meeting tool is a VR chatroom that translates speech in real time, while emotional analysis of the conversation unfolds via responsive, visually dazzling scenes and allows us to grasp the surrounding situation.

4   Results

We analysed the students' understanding, interest, needs for knowledge in management and ability to apply by using a questionnaire survey. Each variable was designed using 5-point Likert scale with answers of 1 "Low" and 5 "High". In addition, this questionnaire survey was conducted before and after the group work in order to analyze the effects of the group work.

Table 2 showed that there are some improvements in students' understanding and interest by applying our proposed method. Moreover, we also found some improvements in students' ability to apply learned management theory (Table 3).

Table 2. Results of the experimental class (1)

Understanding	4.5
Interest	4.4
Ability to apply	3.7
Ease of doing group work	4.3
Ease of communication	4.5

Table 3. Results of the experimental class (2)

step	Factor	ave.	incremental
Acquiring Knowledge	Understanding	2.89	—
	Interest	4.11	—
	Needs for Knowledge in Management	4.37	—
	Ability to Apply	3.59	—
Mediator Variable	Experience of Groupwork	3.81	—
	Ease of Doing Groupwork	4.54	—
	Ease of Communication	4.77	—
Generalizing Structuralized Knowledge	Understanding after Groupwork	3.31	0.42
	Interest after Groupwork	4.23	0.12
	Needs for Knowledge in Management after Groupwork	4.38	0.01
	Ability to Apply after Groupwork	3.65	0.06

Table 4. Results of the difference between good teams and bad teams.

	To be resolved through direct confrontation	To withhold judgment until all data is collected.	To use logical thinking	To have the disciplin to prove or dismiss them one by one
Bad Teams	4.83	4.00	4.83	4.17
Good Teams	3.91	3.55	4.18	3.73
Incremental	-2.58	-1.50	-1.58	-1.17
Standard Diviation	1.514	1.293	1.168	0.905

As a result, we confirm that our trial of an active learning method based on the PDCA cycle was effective in supporting students' understanding in an online environment since, each incremental value is positive.

We also analysed the differences between good teams and bad teams. Table 4 showed that good teams are don't to be resolved through direct confrontation, to withhold judgment until all data is collected, to use logical thinking and to have the discipline to prove or dismiss them one by one compared to bad team. That means good teams are flexible and not extremely rational.

5   Conclusion

In this paper, we focused on the active learning method which is conducted in an online environment using ICT tools for undergraduate students in understanding management theory. we proposed a group work method in order to draw out the active nature of the participants and to obtain learning effects through "dialogue" in an online environment. We also conducted an experimental class and demonstrated the effectiveness of our proposal. The results suggest that our proposed method works effectively for undergraduate students in understanding management theory in an online environment.

However, we have some issues that need to be overcome. In this study, as mentioned above, there was an improvement in understanding and interest in the theory and in the ability to apply it. On the other hand, however, the value of the applied ability was lower than the other items. Therefore, we should consider ways to increase the effectiveness of Step 3, and to better understand the effects of Step 3, we should conduct another survey after some time (after a few months or after graduation). Moreover, it would be necessary to refine the content of group learning and present an evaluation method in future studies.

References

1. Majima, T., Hashida, Y., Uetake, T.: Introduction of active learning method for management education. Bull. Senshu Univ. Inst. Inform. Sci. No. **87**, 17–24 (2016). (in Japanese)
2. Majima, T., Hashida, Y., Aoki, A., Uetake, T.: Proposal of teaching methods combining role-playing and metaphor in undergraduate business management education. Ireland International Conference on Education (2017). http://www.iicedu.org/Proceedings/IICE-2017-October-Proceedings.pdf
3. Shima, Y.: Learning cost management through the art of folding paper into a crane. Shokeigakuso J. Bus. Stud. **169**, 395–403 (2013). Tokyo (in Japanese)
4. Ushio, S.: Applying "Paper Tower" game in accounting education and its effectiveness. J. Acc. Educ. Res. **2,** 22–31 (2014). Tokyo (in Japanese)
5. Kagawa, S.: Expanding the situated learning. Cogn. Stud. **18**(4), 604–623 (2011). Tokyo, (in Japanese)
6. Lave, J., Wenger, E.: Situated Learning: Legitimate Peripheral Participation. Cambridge University Press, New York (1991)
7. Wenger, E., McDermott, R., Snyder, W.M.: Cultivating Communities of Practice. Harvard Business School Press, Boston (2002)
8. Nonaka, I., Takeuchi, H.: Knowledge Creating Company. Oxford University Press, Oxford (1995)
9. Weick, K.: The Social Psychology of Organizing, 2nd edn. Addison-Wesley, Reading, MA (1979)
10. Weick, K.: Sensemaking in Organizations. SAGE Publications Inc, Thousand Oaks, CA (1995)

Interacting and Playing

Three Methods for Adapting Physical Games to Virtual Formats in STEM Courses – Easy (Google Suite), Medium (Web GL Games in Unity) and Hard (Virtual Reality)

Eric Bubar[✉], Susan Agolini, Deana Jaber, and Amanda Wright

Marymount University, Arlington, VA 22207, USA
ebubar@marymount.edu

Abstract. The use of games in learning has demonstrably positive impacts on experiences in the classroom. At Marymount University, the STEM faculty in biology, chemistry and physics have long utilized a wide-variety of gamifying techniques to bring gameplay into the classroom to improve attitudes of students towards science. Methods utilized have included commercial game software (e.g. quizlet live, kahoot), taboo-style games to practice complex scientific terminology, creating 3D printed manipulatives to build biological molecules, using card games to understand chemical reactions and playing astronomy role-playing games. The onset of the global pandemic in 2020/2021 revealed the need to find tools to convert these experiences into a format for remote/virtual delivery. In this paper we discuss the games that we utilize in a variety of STEM content areas, provide workflow suggestions for content experts to collaborate with programming experts to convert games into a virtual format and showcase our work in this collaborative area by presenting three different styles of physical-virtual game adaptation; 1) the use of google sites/sheets/docs for playing astronomy-related role-playing games through Zoom, 2) the creation of a WebGL-based chemistry card game using the Unity game development engine and hosted on itch.io for widespread delivery and 3) the development of an interdisciplinary STEM Escape Room in virtual reality on the Oculus Quest 2. The open source nature of the tools used mean these techniques can all be adopted widely by interdisciplinary teams to create a diverse range of virtual gamified learning experiences.

Keywords: STEM · Gamification · Game-based learning · Virtual-reality

1 Background

Game based learning is becoming a more attractive model for education with the ubiquity of game creation tools, recognition of games as effective learning tools and growth of individuals who grew up with gaming into roles as teachers. The use of "serious games", which are primarily designed for education, traditional games, which can be considered as designed for entertainment and a more general process of game-based learning/gamification of education have all emerged as excellent tools for improving

C. Stephanidis et al. (Eds.): HCII 2021, CCIS 1421, pp. 141–147, 2021.
https://doi.org/10.1007/978-3-030-78645-8_18

educational outcomes [1, 2]. Successful game design, and educational design in general, requires effective planning upon a pedagogically sound framework [3]. In the pursuit of identifying effective methods for these gamified learning experiences, the MDA framework of using mechanics (i.e. algorithms, point systems, level structures, gameplay loops, reward/penalty systems), dynamics (actual physical gameplay processes) and aesthetics (how a game evokes emotional responses including games as sensation, fantasy, narrative, challenge, fellowship, discovery, expression or submission) emerges as a valuable set of characteristics, borrowed from game design theory, to practically apply in creating game based learning experiences [4]. While the first two pillars of the MDA framework can be considered the physical/digital tools/rules for building an effective game, equally important is the theory and psychology behind making games not just functionally effective, but enjoyable. A well-designed game must not only work properly, it must also have elements of fun to be an engaging experience that encourages players to return for repeated gameplay sessions. In many ways the aesthetics of the game could be qualitatively understood to represent the "fun" aspects of a game.

2 Methodology

Theoretically, the success of games in education can be traced to not just being built on a solid framework, but also on their effort to make learning more fun and engaging. To this end, [5] heuristically established four key game characteristics that make digital games fun: challenge, curiosity, fantasy and control. These interlinked aspects of the MDA framework could be considered as specific subsets of the aesthetics of the game.

In early game development processes, identifying the mechanics, dynamics and aesthetics of the game can be simplified by first gamifying in the form of traditional games adapted to match desired content. In this manner the instructor can concentrate on adapting content without the need to develop rules or design original games. Word puzzles, competitive card games, memory/matching games, board games or competitive jeopardy/quiz games are all effective efforts at gamification [6, 7]. In our use this has primarily taken the form quiz and/or matching games with subject-specific content using commercial "gamification" tools like kahoot (https://kahoot.com/) or quizlet (https://quizlet.com/latest).

Creating an effective, original game-based learning experience in a digital format requires designers to create a mechanically functional and interactive experience that invokes fun. We define three levels of complexity for game development and how three specific game examples utilize these aspects of effective game design. Identifying these aspects of a game during development is a necessary approach to creating and adapting effective virtual games for education.

3 Game Designs

3.1 Easy Game Development – Direct Conversion Using Google Suite

Exploring game development can begin with a relatively low effort task of converting traditional worksheets into a virtual format through readily available open source tools.

In this approach, google's suite of resources (google slides, sheets, forms and sites) were utilized in concert with Zoom to convert a previous handout-based game into a full virtual format of delivery (https://sites.google.com/view/astronomy-rpg/home). The game's rules, design, gameplay, etc. were all developed following the philosophy of the Reacting to the Past pedagogy [8]. The specific content was a set of astronomy worksheets centered around a role-playing game where students take on parts as historical figures that were present during Galileo's trial for his heretical views on heliocentrism. Students were assigned to one of nine parts who had a historically significant part in this trial.

The premise of this particular game was that students must either defend or prosecute Galileo in a simulated trial. In a classroom setting this involves presenting oral arguments and proof to refute or confirm scientific theories at the time. To convert to an online format, students utilized google slides to generate presentations and then completed their arguments virtually through Zoom during a synchronous class session. The key to effective delivery of this particular experience, however, was not in the content, but in the way the content is presented in a narrative format. The narrative of the game was setup so that three factions existed - the church, the scientists and the jury. Each faction was provided with a dedicated google site containing a range of period appropriate information to develop their defense or prosecution cases. Students were encouraged to cheer for their team and aggressively question the presentation of the opposing team. Providing this simple context, encouraging students to inhabit their roles with "period specific" dress, use of virtual backgrounds, encouraging competition to support and defend your group at the expense of other groups and generally interjecting humor into the narrative game format resulted in improved learning outcomes and opinions of students in the learning experience.

Our recommended conversion of resources involves taking prequiz and postquiz content and putting it into a google form and creating individual websites for each student to access faction-specific content that would normally be provided in a PDF document. Prior testing of the game in an in-person setting meant all materials were already in existence. The simplest conversion would be to simply upload materials to an LMS, but qualitative evaluation of students has shown they preferred conversion into a more immersive standalone website rather than simply uploading a set of pdf worksheets.

3.2 Medium Game Development

More traditional game content (like e.g. card, puzzle, word and board games) can be developed into a virtual format using formal game development tools. In this context a well-developed physical card game centered around practicing complex organic chemistry reactions was developed using the Unity Physics game engine. Indeed, chemistry courses have long utilized card games for delivery of content [9–13]. Their effectiveness is well established, however few attempts have been made to digitize these card games, despite computer games being effective tools for chem ed [13]. This game conversion was a direct study to explore the efficacy of a digital conversion of a prior publication of results from a physical card game [12].

Creating this more complex digital card game does require expertise in basic programming. Therefore, this was a collaborative effort between a chemist with expertise in the content and a physicist with basic expertise in computer programming using python.

Over approximately 1 month during winter break, the individual faculty collaborated on the game development with the chemistry professor advising on content and the physics professor developing the coding skills necessary to program a C# card game. An estimate of 10 h of development time was required to learn the basics of programming in C# to create the necessary game logic to recreate the physical card game rules. An additional 10 h of time was required to learn the basics of the Unity game development environment (e.g. sprite placement and user interface design). A range of freely available documentation on youtube was utilized to develop these skills. Over the span of this month of effort, a functional prototype adaptation of this physical card game into a virtual format was completed. To further simplify implementation in a classroom environment, Unity allows for conversion of games into a web-based delivery format so games can be deployed through a browser-based format - itch.io (https://ebubar.itch. io/chem-complete-ii-v3). Twenty student participants played the virtual card game this spring. Identical quizzes were administered to students before and after playing the game. Additionally, a survey was administered to the students before and after playing the game. The pre and post quizzes and surveys will help us assess the virtual card game as a teaching tool and to measure student learning. Data from quiz scores and survey responses will be published as soon as permissible by IRB restrictions within the study.

For individuals with time and interest, we would suggest this as an appropriate path to further game development. However, we note that a tremendous range of free tutorial content exists to create popular games that can be given a particular aesthetic theme to deliver desired content. An example might be to change card sprites in a matching game to display chemical elements and their atomic properties. In this manner, the game logic (mechanics and dynamics) are programmed using an existing tutorial and an instructor only needs to adapt the artistic assets.

3.3 Hard Game Development

The fundamentals of Unity game development provide any user with a powerful skill set for making engaging gaming learning experiences. The immersion possible with this method of learning can be further enhanced by using extended reality tools that truly have the potential to immerse learners in a completely new world. Extended reality, a catch-all term for virtual reality (users enter an entirely virtual world) and mixed/augmented reality (users combine elements of both the real and virtual worlds), is a relatively new technology to become available to consumers in large numbers, due largely to the release of low cost but high-quality consumer VR headsets like e.g. Oculus Quest and Playstation VR. Development of VR experiences does require a higher skill-set with Unity than a more basic re-theming approach of applying content specific frameworks to a pre-made game/tutorial. The ubiquity of VR headsets has led to a great increase in available resources for novice VR developers to more easily design and create these virtual worlds. Premade asset packages and SDK's from Unity, Oculus, Valve, Microsoft (MRTK), Android (ARCore) and iOS (ARKit) provide the basic tools needed to develop games in VR/AR. With these premade tools, users can create virtual worlds with a small learning curve.

A particularly simple, yet still powerful, genre of educational content that lends itself well to VR development is that of escape room-style puzzle games. In this genre, players are challenged to solve a variety of physical puzzles inside of a room in order to accomplish a task within a given time limit [14]. A particular advantage of this form of game for virtual/augmented reality is that the interactions are very natural and intuitive, thus minimizing concerns of nausea or motion sickness that can have a negative impact on VR user experiences [15–17]. Escape rooms are often based around some form of theme, with puzzles being general enough that non-content experts can still solve them. In an educational setting, the puzzles to be solved can be easily themed around a specific lesson or set of lessons [18–20].

In this work, an escape room themed on teaching the general population about interdisciplinary atomic theory was designed. Through this escape room, players learn about how atoms are studied from the perspective of a physicist, chemist, biologist, astronomer and geologist. The puzzles involved allow players to get a sense of scale of the different pieces of atoms (from the smallest quarks to the largest molecules), the structure of atoms and molecules, visualize the cloud-structure of electrons, build molecules responsible for forming DNA structures, etc. These experiences allow players to literally experience the different physical scales involved in applying atomic theory into different sciences that is not possible in a traditional classroom. The introduction of a narrative structure involving recruiting the player to work in an elite laboratory can improve science self-identity of players. The coding necessary for creating an engaging experience is more involved than for the more basic 2D games - approximately 40 h of study to learn the basics of designing VR movement, animations and user interactions. It is likely that solo-developed experiences also would require designers to utilize commercial graphical game assets, particularly 3D models of a desired theme. Basic models can be designed within the Unity game development engine, but more advanced models require more specific tools. We have begun exploring collaborations with the design programs within business/technology schools and art schools within the university to streamline the creation of these art assets.

4 Summary

Gamification of learning holds excellent potential for engaging learners with content in immersive educational experiences. The primary motivator for this gamified learning is to increase the enjoyment of a lesson, particularly powerful for students that are not interested in the subject matter of a course or are otherwise not motivated by more traditional forms of college level content delivery. By adding narrative, competitive/cooperative aspects, pleasing aesthetics and point structures any lesson can be given aspects of gaming to improve outcomes of learning. A traditional, physical game can be developed through basic worksheet structures. Digital conversion then be accomplished through a scaffolded approach of complexity. Simple tools like google sites/forms/sheets/etc. can be used to relatively easily convert traditional lecture activities into a virtual game format when combined with zoom. Structured google forms, in particular can be used to provide a choose-your-own-adventure style structure to a classroom activity very easily. For individuals with moderate technical/programming skills, a variety of freely available tutorials on sites like youtube, coursera, udemy, etc. offer lessons on creating basic 2 or 3-dimensional games. These games can be programmed with block-based tools or traditional C# scripting and can include engaging graphical effects, point structures, multiplayer support, etc. that can be easily deployed through webGL builds hosted on open source game-hosting platforms like e.g. itch.io. For the highly technical individual, these Unity tools can be used with a variety of advanced SDK packages to further immerse students in extended reality environments through virtual and augmented/mixed reality. As an introduction into the technology, we suggest puzzle-based escape rooms as an excellent first foray into the technology as they are conducive to using the default tools and examples included in the various hardware SDK's within Unity and the environment of an escape room naturally lends itself to VR interactions and limits the amount of motion sickness induced by more intense experiences.

References

1. Qian, M., Clark, K.R.: Game-based Learning and 21st century skills: a review of recent research. Comput. Hum. Behav. **63**, 50–58 (2016)
2. Kim, J.T., Lee, W.-H.: Dynamical model for gamification of learning (DMGL). Multimed. Tools Appl. **74**(19), 8483–8493 (2015)
3. Mora, A., Riera, D., Gonzalez, C., Arnedo-Moreno, J.: A literature review of gamification design frameworks. In: 2015 7th International Conference on Games and Virtual Worlds for Serious Applications (VS-Games), pp. 1–8 (2015)
4. Hunicke, R., LeBlanc, M., Zubek, R.: MDA: a formal approach to game design and game research. In: Proceedings of the AAAI Workshop on Challenges in Game AI, vol. 4, p. 1722 (2004)
5. Malone T.W.: Making learning fun: a taxonomic model of intrinsic motivations for learning, Conative and Affective Process Analysis (1987). https://ci.nii.ac.jp/naid/10020713867/. Accessed 9 Mar 2021
6. Moursund, D.G.: Introduction to Using Games in Education: A Guide for Teachers and Parents. D. Moursund (2006)
7. Bochennek, K., Wittekindt, B., Zimmermann, S.-Y., Klingebiel, T.: More than mere games: a review of card and board games for medical education. Med. Teach. **29**(9), 941–948 (2007)
8. Powers, R.G., et al.: Reacting to the past: A new approach to student engagement and to enhancing general education, White paper report submitted to the Teagle Foundation, (2010). https://reacting.barnard.edu/sites/default/files/inline-files/reacting_white_paper_tea glefoundation_0.pdf
9. Granath, P.L.R.: Using games to teach chemistry. 1. the old prof card game. J. Chem. Educ. **76**(4), 485–486 (1999)
10. Farmer, S.C., Schuman, M.K.: A simple card game to teach synthesis in organic chemistry courses. J. Chem. Educ. **93**(4), 695–698 (2016)
11. Gogal, K., Heuett, W., Jaber, D.: CHEMCompete: an organic chemistry card game to differentiate between substitution and elimination reactions of Alkyl Halides. J. Chem. Educ. **94**(9), 1276–1279 (Sep. 2017)
12. Camarca, M., Heuett, W., Jaber, D.: CHEMCompete-II: an organic chemistry card game to differentiate between substitution and elimination reactions of alcohols. J. Chem. Educ. **96**(11), 2535–2539 (Nov. 2019)
13. Rastegarpour, H., Marashi, P.: The effect of card games and computer games on learning of chemistry concepts. Procedia – Soc. Behav. Sci. **31**, 597–601 (Jan. 2012)
14. David, D., Arman, E., Hikari, E., Chandra, N., Nadia, N.: Development of escape room game using VR technology. Procedia Comput. Sci., **157**, 646–652 (2019)

15. Martirosov, S., Kopecek, P.: Cyber Sickness In Virtual Reality-Literature Review," Annals of DAAAM & Proceedings, vol. 28, (2017). https://www.researchgate.net/profile/Sergo_Mar tirosov/publication/321661932_Cyber_Sickness_in_Virtual_Reality_-_Literature_Review/ links/5a339e81aca2727144b7702f/Cyber-Sickness-in-Virtual-Reality-Literature-Review. pdf
16. Żukowska, M., Buń, P., Górski, F., Starzyńska, B.: Cyber sickness in industrial virtual reality training. In: Advances in Manufacturing II, pp. 137–149 (2019)
17. Chang, E., Kim, H.T., Yoo, B.: Virtual reality sickness: a review of causes and measurements. Int. J. Hum.-Comput. Interact. **36**(17), 1658–1682 (2020)
18. Peleg, R., Yayon, M., Katchevich, D., Moria-Shipony, M., Blonder, R.: A lab-based chemical escape room: educational, mobile, and fun! J. Chem. Educ. **96**(5), 955–960 (2019)
19. Yeasmin, S., Albabtain, L.A.: Escape the countries: a VR escape room game. In: 2020 3rd International Conference on Computer Applications Information Security (ICCAIS), pp. 1–6 (2020)
20. Pendit, U.C., Mahzan, M.B., Basir, M.D.F.B.M., Mahadzir, M.B., Binti Musa, S.N.: Virtual reality escape room: the last breakout. In: 2017 2nd International Conference on Information Technology (INCIT), pp. 1–4 (2017)

Constructing 3D Mesh Indoor Room Layouts from 2D Equirectangular RGB 360 Panorama Images for the Unity Game Engine

James C. P. Chan[(✉)] [iD], Adrian K. T. Ng[iD], and Henry Y. K. Lau[iD]

Department of Industrial and Manufacturing Systems Engineering, The University of Hong Kong, Pokfulam, Hong Kong
{U3007303,adriang}@connect.hku.hk, hyklau@hku.hk

Abstract. To accelerate digital 3D environments creation, we propose a workflow utilizing neural network systems to create 3D indoor room layouts in the Unity game engine from 2D equirectangular RGB 360 panorama images. Our approach is inspired by HorizonNet, which generates textured room layouts in point clouds using Recurrent Neural Network (RNN). However, it is not desirable in VR since data points can be visible at close ranges, and thus, break user immersion. Alternatively, we used 3D meshes that are connected with small triangular faces, which stitch together with no gaps in between, simulating realistic solid surfaces. We succeeded in converting room layout representations from point cloud to 3D mesh, by extracting rooms' metadata predicted by HorizonNet, and dynamically generating textured custom mesh in Unity. Mesh layouts can be directly applied into Unity VR applications. Users can take 360 images on their mobile phones and visualize room layouts in VR through our system. As our evaluations suggest, mesh layout representation improves frame rates and memory usage and does not affect the layout accuracy of the original approach, providing satisfactory room layout for VR development.

Keyword: Virtual reality · Room layout estimation · Artificial neural network · Point cloud · Mesh · Unity

1 Introduction

Virtual environments (VEs) are essential when developing virtual reality (VR) applications, as they help users immerse in the virtual world through visual feedback. However, creating VEs are time consuming because every environmental detail, such as surfaces and objects, must be handcrafted. With the rapid advancement of artificial neural networks, our goal is to accelerate VR application development by developing a network system that can take 2D RGB images of indoor rooms and convert them into 3D room layouts that are readily accessible for VR applications. Although various previous efforts have discussed different networks to predict room layouts, practicality issues may occur when deploying the generated VEs into VR applications. The following subsections will cover the issues regarding practical deployment of 3D room layouts from previous works, and how they were addressed across numerous approaches.

© Springer Nature Switzerland AG 2021
C. Stephanidis et al. (Eds.): HCII 2021, CCIS 1421, pp. 148–155, 2021.
https://doi.org/10.1007/978-3-030-78645-8_19

1.1 Issues Addressed in Previous Approaches

Surface Material. When displaying 3D room layouts, the color of individual surfaces can be represented by a single medoid color [3], or by the 2D texture extracted from the image directly [4, 5]. In the context of VR, the realness of VEs highly contributes to users' feeling of presence [6], which is responsible for inducing immersion [7]. Therefore, VEs should be as realistic as possible for VR Applications, and hence textured surface is more preferable than single medoid color.

Input Image Type. 2 popular types of input images are perspective images [8, 10], and 360 panorama images [2, 4, 5, 9]. Perspective images have a low field-of-view, so only a portion of the room can be constructed [10]. Conversely, entire room layouts can be generated with panorama images with their full range field of view (360° horizontal and 180° vertical). As VR users can freely look around VEs with 6DOF, using 360 panorama images as input is more desirable.

Structure of 3D Layout. Many previous approaches estimate room layouts under certain premises. A popular assumption is that all generated layouts are of cuboid structure, which means every 3D layout should only have at max 4 walls perpendicular to each other [4, 5, 8]. Although forcing non-cuboid layout images into cuboid structures decreases their realness and the induced immersion [6, 7], very few approaches managed to support non-cuboid layout structure [2, 9, 11].

1.2 Issues not Addressed in Previous Approaches

HorizonNet [2], CFL [9], and DuLa-Net [11] are one of the few approaches that addressed all the above practicality issues for VR applications. Among them, HorizonNet's performance is the most superior. However, two practicality issues, which are rarely discussed in previous works, remain present.

Layout Representation. VEs must be realistic to induce a feeling of presence and immersion [6, 7]. However, previous studies mainly used point clouds to visualize 3D layout results [2, 12]. Although point cloud is flexible in forming shapes, it is visually unpleasant due to the gaps between points, which decrease layout realness. An alternative layout representation method is needed for VR applications.

Representation Performance. Apart from being realistic, the new representation should also have high frame rate performance, as low update rates in VR can cause cybersickness [13], which discourages users to stay in the VR experience. It is also desirable for representation to consume less memory while rendering to the screen.

2 Methodology

Our proposed 3D layout generation system consists of multiple sub-modules (see Fig. 1). The following subsections will describe each of the sub-modules in the workflow.

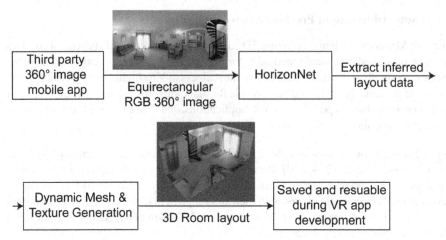

Fig. 1. Workflow of our mesh layout construction system

2.1 2D RGB Image Input

Obtaining a 2D equirectangular RGB 360 image is the first step of the workflow, which can be taken by any third party software. Users then save the image for HorizonNet's layout inference.

2.2 HorizonNet

HorizonNet is one of the few available approaches which supports textured surfaces, 360 panorama input, and non-cuboid layout structure (See Sect. 1.1). In terms of estimation performance, it introduced a 1D layout data representation which effectively shrink down its complexity. Their evaluations also suggest that their Pano Stretch Data Augmentation technique can improve inference accuracy by contributing more data for training [2]. It outperformed previous works [4, 14], as well as concurrent approaches [9, 11]. In practice, after the 360 panorama image input is received, the Unity game engine [1] triggers HorizonNet's preprocessing and inference algorithms, and the room corners' xyz coordinates, all surfaces' RGB texture array, and the floor/ceiling masks are extracted and stored in a .json file.

2.3 Mesh Representation of 3D Layout

Mesh representation is used to replace point cloud for visualizing generated 3D layouts. Points clouds are formed with individual data points that group together, so blank spaces between individual points may exist, which greatly hinders the realness of the representation. On the contrary, meshes are formed with small interconnected triangular surfaces. Therefore, mesh layouts appear as solid instead of scattered points, which increases layouts' realness. For the platform of visualization, the Unity game engine [1] is chosen because it supports custom mesh generation.

2.4 Conversion from Point Cloud to Mesh

After Unity deserializes the inferred layout data extracted from HorizonNet, custom mesh surfaces are created dynamically according to the extracted corner coordinates. At the same time, 2D textures for all surfaces are created in runtime according to the extracted RGB data. For floor and ceiling, RGB data from concave regions are masked from the texture. After all mesh and textures are generated, textures are assigned to their corresponding surfaces. Users can also save layout meshes and textures objects as Unity assets prefabs and load them before runtime to boost performance.

2.5 Integration with VR Application

Unity supports VR application development through external plug-ins, so developers can directly incorporate VR projects with the generated layouts.

3 Experiment

3.1 Setup

Layout Preparation. We first prepared the layouts for comparison by generating all the room layouts in mesh form from the test set of HorizonNet's dataset, including the test set from LayoutNet [14], and another 65 layouts that were re-annotated for fine-tuning non-cuboid layouts. In order to compare point cloud layout under different point cloud density against mesh layout, we generated two point cloud layouts for each image, one with 80 points-per-meter (ppm), and another with 300 ppm. 80 ppm is the default value used by HorizonNet. We also based on this value to create mesh layouts. Therefore, point cloud with 80 ppm (pc-80) can be considered a close equivalent to mesh layout in terms of performance. We also selected a higher density (300 ppm, pc-300) because point cloud is supposed to be as dense as possible for a high perceived quality [16]. The generated point cloud layouts were saved as .ply format for importing into Unity. Point sizes were adjusted such that no blank space is visible between individual points (0.015 for pc-80, 0.003 for pc-300). Finally, 3 distinct layouts were manually selected as test layouts from the 65 re-annotated layouts, based on different room sizes and color schemes (see Fig. 2a). In total, we had 9 test conditions (3 test layouts × 3 representations).

Custom Path Traversal. 3 Unity scenes were created, and each contained a mesh, a pc-80, and a pc-300 layout separated evenly within the VE. A VR character controller from VotanicXR [15] was imported and a custom path was set up for the VR character to follow in runtime (see Fig. 2b). The character controller passes all corners of the room (checkpoints). At each corner, it would look towards the center of the room and hold for 1 s. After traversing one layout, the VR character was teleported into the next one and follows the path again. We applied the same path sampling method in all test conditions.

(a)

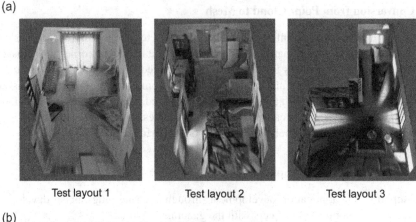

Test layout 1   Test layout 2   Test layout 3

(b)

Fig. 2. (a) 3 test layouts selected for experiment. (b) An example test path for VR character to traverse (long arrows, from light to dark). Short blue arrows indicate checkpoints. (Color figure online)

3.2 Hardware Specification

The experiment was conducted with a head mounted display (VIVE Pro; HTC, New Taipei City, Taiwan) with a 110° horizontal FOV. The HMD is connected to a 64-bit Windows 10 PC with Intel® Core™ i7-7700K CPU @4.20 Ghz processor, 16 GB RAM, and NVIDIA® GeForce® RTX 2080 Ti graphics card. Layouts were rendered with SteamVR (Valve, Bellevue, WA, United States) and developed in Unity 2018.4.6f1.

3.3 Procedure and Assessment

The HMD was physically fixed to the center of its play space. 3 scenes were executed in succession. When the VR character controller was traversing the paths, frame rate (in fps) and Mono Memory (in MB) were recorded at every frame.

4 Results

4.1 Realness of Representations

Figure 3 shows qualitative results of generated layouts with different representations. When inspected closely on small objects such as television, colored dots were clearly visible on pc-80 layouts, especially near the edge of objects where color deviates greatly, which decreased its quality and realness. Nevertheless, in layouts that have a darker color scheme such as test layout 3, the issue was less apparent. On the other hand, pc-300 layouts were hardly distinguishable from mesh representation under any color schemes, and surfaces from both layouts appeared smooth and more realistic.

(a) Mesh   (b) Point cloud: 80 ppm   (c) Point cloud: 300 ppm

Fig. 3. Appearance of small objects in different representations

4.2 Accuracy of Mesh Representation

As our mesh layouts are constructed by extracting the layout data originally used to generate point cloud layout, i.e., corner coordinates, texture array and its mask, without any postprocessing, the accuracy of mesh layouts is identical to that of the point cloud layouts.

4.3 Frame Rate and Memory Usage Comparison

During all paths along 3 test layouts, our mesh representations had a significantly higher frame rate than both pc-80 and pc-300, with an average of nearly 90 fps. pc-80 layouts had a mean frame rate of around 30 fps and around 7 fps for pc-300 (see Fig. 4), which is unacceptable for VR applications [13]. Both point cloud representations had performance spikes when passing through checkpoints, where more points must be rendered on the screen, while mesh layouts' frame rate was more consistent, with only a little fluctuation throughout the entire experiment.

3D layouts represented by mesh were also more memory efficient than both sets of point cloud layouts. On average, only 21.9 MB of mono memory was used for rendering mesh layouts without much performance spikes. For point cloud layouts, pc-80 layouts used slightly more memory, while pc-300 occupied significantly larger amount of memory. Its memory usage even increased while traversing test layout 3, presumably because it was the largest layout among the 3 test layouts.

The above results prove that layouts using our mesh representation performed better than point cloud representation in terms of frame rate and memory consumption.

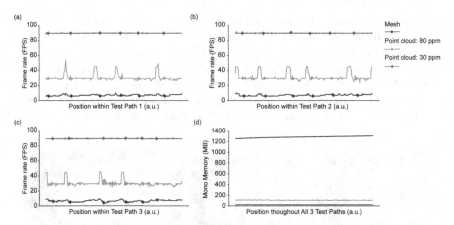

Fig. 4. Frame rate and overall memory usage in different representations

5   Conclusion

This paper introduced a workflow to construct 3D indoor mesh layouts from 2D equirectangular RGB 360 images, through the application of HorizonNet [2] and Unity's dynamic mesh generation. Although point cloud layouts with high point density were shown to possess similar realness against mesh layouts, evaluation shows mesh representation is more performant in terms of frame rate and memory usage, regardless of point density.

References

1. Unity. https://unity.com
2. Sun, C., Hsiao, C.W., Sun, M., Chen, H.T.: HorizonNet: learning room layout with 1D representation and pano stretch data augmentation. In: Proceedings of the IEEE CVPR, pp. 1047–1056. IEEE Press, New York (2019). https://doi.org/10.1109/CVPR.2019.00114
3. Izadinia, H., Shan, Q., Seitz, S.M.: IM2CAD. In: Proceedings of the IEEE CVPR, pp. 5134–5143. IEEE Press, New York (2017). https://doi.org/10.1109/CVPR.2017.260
4. Zhang, Y., Song, S., Tan, P., Xiao, J.: PanoContext: a whole-room 3D context model for panoramic scene understanding. In: Fleet, D., Pajdla, T., Schiele, B., Tuytelaars, T. (eds.) ECCV. LNCS, vol. 8694, pp. 668–686. Springer, Cham (2014). https://doi.org/10.1007/978-3-319-10599-4_43
5. Luo, C., Zou, B., Lyu, X., Xie, H.: Indoor scene reconstruction: from panorama images to CAD models. In: IEEE ISMAR-Adjunct, pp. 317–320. IEEE Press, New York (2019). https://doi.org/10.1109/ISMAR-Adjunct.2019.00-21
6. Schubert, T., Friedmann, F., Regenbrecht, H.: Embodied presence in virtual environments. In: Paton, R., Neilson, I. (eds.) Visual Representations and Interpretations, pp. 269–278. Springer, London (1999). https://doi.org/10.1007/978-1-4471-0563-3_30

7. Bohil, C., Owen, C., Jeong, E., Alicea, B., Biocca, F.: Virtual reality and presence. In: Eadie, W.F. (ed.) 21st Century Communication: A Reference Handbook. SAGE Publications, Thousand Oaks (2009). https://doi.org/10.4135/9781412964005.

8. Lee, C.Y., Badrinarayanan, V., Malisiewicz, T., Rabinovich, A.: RoomNet: end-to-end room layout estimation. In: IEEE ICCV, pp. 4865–4874. IEEE Press, New York (2017). https://doi.org/10.1109/ICCV.2017.521

9. Fernandez-Labrador, C., Facil, J.M., Perez-Yus, A., Demonceaux, C., Civera, J., Guerrero, J.J.: Corners for layout: end-to-end layout recovery from 360 images. IEEE Robot. Autom. **5**(2), 1255–1262 (2020). https://doi.org/10.1109/LRA.2020.2967274

10. Guo, R., Zou, C., Hoiem, D.: Predicting complete 3D models of indoor scenes. arXiv preprint (2015). https://arxiv.org/abs/1504.02437v3

11. Yang, S.T., Wang, F.E., Peng, C.H., Wonka, P., Sun, M., Chu, H.K.: DuLa-Net: a dual-projection network for estimating room layouts from a single RGB panorama. In: Proceedings of the IEEE CVPR, pp. 3358–3367. IEEE Press, New York (2019). https://doi.org/10.1109/CVPR.2019.00348.

12. Liu, C., Wu, J., Furukawa, Y.: FloorNet: a unified framework for floorplan reconstruction from 3D scans. In: Ferrari, V., Hebert, M., Sminchisescu, C., Weiss, Y. (eds.) ECCV. LNCS, vol. 11210, pp. 203–219. Springer, Cham (2018). https://doi.org/10.1007/978-3-030-01231-1_13

13. Jones, M.B., Kennedy, R.S., Stanney, K.M.: Toward systematic control of cybersickness. Presence. **13**(5), 589–600 (2004). https://doi.org/10.1162/1054746042545247

14. Zou, C., Colburn, A., Shan, Q., Hoiem, D.: LayoutNet: reconstructing the 3D room layout from a single RGB image. In: Proceedings of the IEEE CVPR, pp. 2051–2059. IEEE Press, New York (2018). https://doi.org/10.1109/CVPR.2018.00219

15. VotanicXR. https://www.votanic.com/votanicxr

16. Virtanen, J.P., et al.: Interactive dense point clouds in a game engine. ISPRS J. Photogramm. **163**, 375–389 (2020). https://doi.org/10.1016/j.isprsjprs.2020.03.007

The Rise of Video-Game Live Streaming: Motivations and Forms of Viewer Engagement

Fouad El Afi[⊠] [iD] and Smail Ouiddad

LRMMC, Hassan 1st University of Settat, ENCG Settat, Settat, Morocco
f.elafi@uhp.ac.ma

Abstract. Encouraged by the technological breakthrough of the hyper-modern era, social livestreaming has arisen as one of the most engaging communities in recent years, enabling live content production and instant based interaction. As a result, with the growing popularity of the gaming industry, video game live streaming is expected to induce a new and yet unprecedented surge in the digital landscape, especially with the development of online platforms, such as Twitch.TV, YouTube gaming and Facebook Gaming etc., allowing a real-time content dissemination and consumption. Therefore, with the proliferation of video game live streaming and the increasing number of gamers and professional players worldwide, this paper examines viewer engagement in live video-game streaming platforms. Although few researchers have addressed the subject, our aim is to outline users' motivations, as highlighted in the literature, as well as forms of engagement in these services through a case study of Twitch.TV and YouTube Gaming platforms. Moreover, as discussed in communication and social computing literature, we address the importance of chat messages through IRC in fostering simultaneous interaction with the streamer and other peers.

Keywords: Video-Game · Livestreaming · Engagement · Motivations · IRC

1 Introduction

Fueled by the lockdown in the entire globe, the video-game market achieved exponential results in 2020 and it is still continuing to grow. Recent data showed that the gaming industry will reach 189.3 billion dollars in 2021 across all devices (PC, PS, Xbox, Mobile etc.), with an estimation of 2.8 billion players around the world [1]. This increase in popularity pushed IT giants such as Google, Amazon, Facebook and Microsoft to rush for acquiring and developing their own live streaming platforms revolving around gaming content. These virtual and social spaces have been a growing trend in video gaming for more than a decade now, contributing to a spike in engagement. In their yearly reports, Stream-Hatchet[1] [2] provided some interesting insights related to the explosive growth of the big three (Twitch.TV, YouTube Gaming and Facebook Gaming). Numbers have skyrocketed of which the leading platform, Twitch.TV, accumulated nearly 180.6

---

[1] A Game streaming analytics and insights provider.

© Springer Nature Switzerland AG 2021
C. Stephanidis et al. (Eds.): HCII 2021, CCIS 1421, pp. 156–163, 2021.
https://doi.org/10.1007/978-3-030-78645-8_20

Billion of watched hours in 2020 with an estimation growth of viewership of 69%, While YouTube (6.2) and Facebook (3.64) respectively doubled and tripled their numbers.

The emergence of video-game live-streaming platforms has certainly accelerated many trends, setting the background to establish a significant number of changes in many fields, such as the rise of e-sports industry, and the adoption of reward and subscription-based approach as the main monetization system, instead of the traditional advertisement or pay-per-view model [3], which marks the fact that fans are ready to invest money and time to consume gaming content, therefore, they are willing to engage with the content producer on a deeper level.

The potential engagement, the gamification features and the widely acceptance of this technology by viewers, positioned video game live-streaming as a fertile area for research. Emphasizing the interactivity nature of this social media service is of high importance in order to understand viewers behavior [4]. Thereby, this paper examines the motivations as well as forms of viewer engagement in these virtual spaces.

2 Literature Review

2.1 Live-Streaming

From broadcasting live educational courses, to the Superbowl to watching NASA's Per-severance Rover land on Mars, it is undeniable that live streaming is changing the media ecosystem, by suppressing or at least decreasing information asymmetry. According to Ang et al. [5] livestreaming offers more authentic viewing experience than pre-recorded videos as it delivers a real time information. As a result, livestreaming platforms have emerged as one of the most engaging communities in recent years. This model enables the possibility of continuous interactivity between streamers and their audience. It is expected to induce a new and yet unprecedented surge in the digital landscape, bringing new forms of content generation and consumption [6]. This proliferation of social media livestreaming ignited scholars' interest to understand different behaviors of the implicated stakeholders. Thereby, various definitions came to light. Pires and Simon [7] indicated that *"User-Generated live video streaming systems are services that allow anybody to broadcast a video stream over the Internet"*. Other researchers tried to give a more in-depth definition to this new phenomenon. For instance, Cunningham et al. [8] defined Online livestreaming as *"a broadcast video streaming services provided by web-based platforms and mobile applications that feature synchronous and crossmodal (video, text, and image) interactivity"*. These definitions bring forward multiple factors that establish the very foundation of the emerging industry of livestreaming, namely Broadcast, live content, digital platforms and real-time interaction (between users and streamers and between users themselves).

2.2 Engagement Motivations

The existing literature is characterized by the scarcity of studies examining viewer engagement in live video-game streaming platforms [9]. However, the explosive growth of this media pushed scholars to investigate motivations underlying user implication, as it became a necessity in order to capture the essence of this emerging phenomenon.

Some preliminary work was carried out by applying the famous uses and gratifications theory given its importance in the field of media science. For instance, Sjöblom and Hamari [10] highlighted six aspects that influence consumers' behavior towards watching live game streaming, that is cognitive, personal, social, affective and hedonic drivers. They argue that spectators watch a live gameplay in order to release tension and stress, as well as acquiring information related to the game being streamed and learn about its strategies. In the same vein, Hilvert-Bruce et al. [9] explained the effect of social factors on users' psychological and behavioral dimensions. Results of their study outlined six motivations strongly associated to engagement, namely social interaction, sense of community, meeting new people, entertainment, information seeking, and a lack of external support in real life. They argue that for the sake of social support and hedonic purposes, users seek involvement with the platform, the streamer and other users. Following the discussion on the social settings, Lim et al. [11] argued that the awareness of belonging incorporated in the feeling of emotional connectedness with the caster and their peers, affects greatly users' participatory behavior. They believe that watching the gameplay while interacting through chat messages influences significantly their devotion towards the live-streaming game and the streamer.

Another line of research examined the impact of flow, entertainment, and endorsement on Twitch viewers' attitudes towards game live streaming [12]. They found that having fun is the main driver given the hedonic nature of the platform. It stands to reason considering the humoristic nature of interactions [13] and since the most of the chat messages are related to emotes. Moreover, the enabled sense of flow through a continuous concentration on the task, the recognition of the streamer as an influencer, and social interaction with them were found positively related to audience's attachment and intention to continue to watch.

3   A Case Study of Twitch.TV and YouTube Gaming

3.1   Forms of Engagement

According to the literature, engagement can take various forms in social media services. While researchers defined this concept from psychological perspective and the outcome of certain consumer behaviors, others argued that engagement is multidimensional construct comprising cognitive, affective and behavioral components. These three dimensions, supported by the proliferation of video-gaming platforms, are expressed through multiple forms such as emotional connectedness, like, share, subscription, donation, chat messages, etc.

On the account of the fact that streamers are broadcasting their personal experiences with their audience, a connection is created between them, allowing the acknowledgement of the streamers as micro celebrities [12, 14]. This phenomenon is translated by spending more time watching the gameplay content, learning game reviews, strategies, tactics and other useful directions [15]. This strong association leads viewers to seek information related to times of the broadcast, therefore it is important to subscribe to the channel, nevertheless, in the case of Twitch platform and YouTube Gaming, in order to complete this process, users need to pay some amount of money per month. In this regard, an alternative model has been offered based on following the caster instead of subscribing, however, some channels require a subscription in order to have access to game content and particular attributes such as exclusive emotes, badges and previous videos recorded and saved on their pages. As a matter of fact, it is predicted that the subscription model will change the streaming ecosystem as it proved its robustness and acceptance by users as well as its efficiency, replacing traditional paradigms such as pay-per-view model [3].

Generally speaking, subscribing is a sign that the displayed content got the attention of the spectator, leading eventually to a desire to support the channel which could be expressed by many means. While some spectators share the video, others choose to go a little further by providing monetary support through donations, allowing the streamer to be equipped with advanced material and the latest games in order to stream at high quality. Moreover, this donation mechanism could be used for social and charity purposes, for instance, the most popular YouTuber, by the alias *PewDiePie*, raised over 246 000 USD from donations while live streaming video-games on YouTube, in order to support Indian 9-year-old children. Furthermore, in their strategy dedicated to improve the experiences of both the streamer and the audience, Twitch invented another design named Bits, introducing a more flexible and gamified experience to their donation system. According to Twitch platform: *"Bits are a virtual good you can buy on Twitch that give you the power to encourage and show support for streamers"*. It endorses the streamer using cheers with Bits as a reward for their performance (Fig. 1).

Another similar practice has surfaced that is based on gift-giving. Viewers have the ability to support a channel by gifting subscriptions to their fellow viewers. Being aware of the importance of this behavior in enlarging his community base, the streamer acknowledges the benefactor's effort through the chat, or alerts (notification) stating his name and thanking him in the stream (Fig. 1).

Fig. 1. A live stream on Twitch.TV Platform

Twitch extended their user engagement experience strategy by allowing consumers to co-create value. Through a feature named "clip", viewers are able to create short videos of their best moments of a live stream and share it with other peers. Their role does not end here, considering the fact that the livestreaming ecosystem is built with the purpose to widen the community around the channel/streamer, managing the audience is a matter of high importance. As a result, larger channels tend to higher moderators by approaching the most active users. The moderator's job is to engage with the chatters and make sure that all regulations are well respected [16].

Fig. 2. A live stream on YouTube Gaming Platform

3.2   Chat Messages: An Instant-Based Engagement Mechanism

The chat is probably the most important feature that distinguishes live streaming platforms form other social media services, as it allows a real time engagement. Through IRC (Internet Relay Chat), users can connect with each other, socialize, share common interests, tease each other and discuss the gameplay. The streamer turns to chat in order to converse with his audience, with the purpose to answer their questions, thank them for their encouragements, or set up polls about the next game to stream etc. Therefore, it has been argued that chat rooms have a tremendous impact on building a community around the streamer as well as creating friendships and game partners [17]. Moreover, chat rooms are a great opportunity to acknowledge the users who made donations, by displaying their name and emphasizing their contributions (Fig. 1 and Fig. 2). For instance, a message written by a donator will be emphasized and displayed longer than regular messages (Fig. 2).

IRC has shown a promising research landscape where scholars can understand viewers' activities in such platforms. Following computer-mediated communication discussion, Ford et al. [18] found that chat messages are usually short, and consist mostly of emotes. The latter is an essential part of the language spoken in these spaces, and each one has a deeper meaning and a purpose (See Table 1). In addition to emotes predefined by the platforms, streamers are able to create their own emotes, and only subscribers are allowed to use them to enrich their engagement experience while watching the live stream as a part of a gamification encounter. Research has found that through emotes, viewers can express various emotions, such as complaint, boredom and frustration, sarcasm, enjoyment and amazement etc. [19, 20]. Therefore, streamers and channels are able to measure the impact of their content by reading the chat section directly, and make adjustments to meet their audiences' preferences.

Table 1. Example of Emotes predefined by Twitch.TV[a]

Emote Code	Emote	Meaning
:Kappa:		Sarcasm or wry humor. Kappa is our signature emote.
:HeyGuys:		A casual greeting. Used when joining chat, or when welcoming someone to a stream
:LUL:		Laughter. The emote version of Laugh Out Loud.
:CoolStoryBob:		A version of "Cool story, bro." Used sarcastically when someone is saying something unimportant or babbling.
:4Head:		:Laughter, but in a slightly mocking way. Often used as pity laughter when someone tells a lame/dad joke.

[a]https://www.twitch.tv/creatorcamp/en/learn-the-basics/emotes/

4   Future Directions

Our line of research to date, has outlined the literature review regarding engagement and empowerment in social livestreaming services. The next stage is to conduct a content analysis of the leading platforms, which we prefer to call the big three (Twitch.TV, YouTube Gaming and Facebook Gaming), through a large-scale analysis of the live videos offering a gameplay content, in order to fully capture the essence of this fast-growing trend. This phase is a three steps process:

1. Identify engagement forms and empowerment features by studying each platform's characteristics (continue to watch, donating, chatting etc.)
2. Conduct a quantitative content analysis.
3. And analyze the chat section.

The third step consists of two major parts. The first step is to extract chat messages from live videos. Considering the fact that the conversations are fast-paced and the number of exchanges displayed depends on the chat window size, it is necessary to resort to an IRC client such as chatty. However, since the latter does not support YouTube streaming services, we developed a python code in order to retrieve data of each video from both Twitch and YouTube platforms, creating log files (in the form of text/Excel/Jason).

The second step is to analyze the datasets. As the generated log files contain data from streams that last more than several hours (each video is longer than 4h), a great mass of data is presented, therefore, a probabilistic topic modeling is best suited for this analysis [21]. Consequently, we developed another python code in order to perform LDA text analysis[2]. Both codes are inspired from GitHub[3] community.

5   Conclusion

The magnified interest of video-games around the world led to a mushrooming of live streaming platforms, thereby, changing the media environment as we know it. From digitalization to gamification to experience customization, these platforms compile every feature supporting the nature of social media in satisfying users' gratifications, which can lead eventually to a deeper engagement and empowerment. Therefore, it is essential to decipher this emerging technology, in a way that users make the best out of this experience.

References

1. Newzoo: Global Games Market Report (2020), Newzoo (2020). https://newzoo.com/insights/articles/newzoos-games-trends-to-watch-in-2021/
2. Hatchet, S.: Video game streaming trends report 2020 yearly report. Stream Hatchet (2021). https://insights.streamhatchet.com/stream-hatchet-2020-yearly-report-1
3. Lin, J., Lu, Z.: the rise and proliferation of live-streaming in china: insights and lessons. In: Stephanidis, C. (ed.) HCI International 2017 – Posters' Extended Abstracts. CCIS, vol. 714, pp. 632–637. Springer, Cham (2017). https://doi.org/10.1007/978-3-319-58753-0_89
4. Gros, D., Wanner, B., Hackenholt, A., Zawadzki, P., Knautz, K.: World of streaming. motivation and gratification on Twitch. In: Meiselwitz, G. (ed.) Social Computing and Social Media. Human Behavior. LNCS, vol. 10282, pp. 44–57. Springer, Cham (2017). https://doi.org/10.1007/978-3-319-58559-8_5
5. Ang, T., Wei, S., Anaza, N.A.: Livestreaming vs pre-recorded: How social viewing strategies impact consumers' viewing experiences and behavioral intentions. Eur. J. Mark. 52(9/10), 2075–2104 (2018). https://doi.org/10.1108/EJM-09-2017-0576
6. Zhang, C., Liu, J.: On crowdsourced interactive live streaming: a twitch.TV-based measurement study. ArXiv150204666 Cs, February 2015. Accessed 24 Feb 24 2021. http://arxiv.org/abs/1502.04666
7. Pires, K., Simon, G.: YouTube live and Twitch: a tour of user-generated live streaming systems. In: Proceedings of the 6th ACM Multimedia Systems Conference, Portland Oregon, pp. 225–230, March 2015. https://doi.org/10.1145/2713168.2713195
8. Cunningham, S., Craig, D., Lv, J.: China's livestreaming industry: platforms, politics, and precarity. Int. J. Cult. Stud. 22(6), 719–736 (2019). https://doi.org/10.1177/1367877919834942

---

[2] A probabilistic topic model that extracts a number of topics from each document [21].

[3] https://github.com/

9. Hilvert-Bruce, Z., Neill, J.T., Sjöblom, M., Hamari, J.: Social motivations of live-streaming viewer engagement on Twitch. Comput. Hum. Behav. **84**, 58–67 (2018). https://doi.org/10.1016/j.chb.2018.02.013

10. Sjöblom, M., Hamari, J.: Why do people watch others play video games? An empirical study on the motivations of Twitch users. Comput. Hum. Behav. **75**, 985–996 (2017). https://doi.org/10.1016/j.chb.2016.10.019

11. Lim, S., Cha, S.Y., Park, C., Lee, I., Kim, J.: Getting closer and experiencing together: Antecedents and consequences of psychological distance in social media-enhanced real-time streaming video. Comput. Hum. Behav. **28**(4), 1365–1378 (2012). https://doi.org/10.1016/j.chb.2012.02.022

12. Chen, C.-C., Lin, Y.-C.: What drives live-stream usage intention? The perspectives of flow, entertainment, social interaction, and endorsement. Telemat. Inform. **35**(1), 293–303 (2018). https://doi.org/10.1016/j.tele.2017.12.003

13. Lu, Z., Xia, H., Heo, S., Wigdor, D.: You watch, you give, and you engage: a study of live streaming practices in China. In: Proceedings of the 2018 CHI Conference on Human Factors in Computing Systems, Montreal QC Canada, pp. 1–13, April 2018. https://doi.org/10.1145/3173574.3174040

14. Woodcock, J., Johnson, M.R.: Live streamers on twitch.tv as social media influencers: chances and challenges for strategic communication. Int. J. Strateg. Commun. **13**(4), 321–335 (2019). https://doi.org/10.1080/1553118X.2019.1630412

15. Li, Y., Wang, C., Liu, J.: A systematic review of literature on user behavior in video game live streaming. Int. J. Environ. Res. Public. Health **17**(9), 3328 (2020). https://doi.org/10.3390/ijerph17093328

16. Harpstead, E., Rios, J.S., Seering, J., Hammer, J.: Toward a twitch research toolkit: a systematic review of approaches to research on game streaming. In: Proceedings of the Annual Symposium on Computer-Human Interaction in Play, Barcelona Spain, pp. 111–119, October 2019. https://doi.org/10.1145/3311350.3347149

17. Recktenwald, D.: Toward a transcription and analysis of live streaming on Twitch. J. Pragmat. **115**, 68–81 (2017). https://doi.org/10.1016/j.pragma.2017.01.013

18. Ford, C., et al.: Chat speed OP PogChamp: practices of coherence in massive twitch chat. In: Proceedings of the 2017 CHI Conference Extended Abstracts on Human Factors in Computing Systems, Denver Colorado USA, pp. 858–871, May 2017. https://doi.org/10.1145/3027063.3052765

19. Bulygin, D., Musabirov, I., Suvorova, A., Konstantinova, K., Okopnyi, P.: Between an arena and a sports bar: online chats of Esports spectators. ArXiv180102862 Cs, December 2020. Accessed 26 Feb 2021. http://arxiv.org/abs/1801.02862

20. Kobs, K., et al.: Emote-controlled: obtaining implicit viewer feedback through emote-based sentiment analysis on comments of popular twitch.tv channels. ACM Trans. Soc. Comput. **3**(2), 1–34 (2020). https://doi.org/10.1145/3365523

21. Blei, D.M.: Probabilistic topic models. Commun. ACM **55**(4), 77–84 (2012). https://doi.org/10.1145/2133806.2133826

Emotions Driven Videogame Interactive Music System

Lluis Guerra Recas(✉)

Universitat Politècnica de València, 46002 Valencia, Spain

Abstract. The indisputable capacity of music to generate emotions has dragged along a research tradition studying the effects of music as a means of communication, expression or emotional induction. The observation of the effects caused by the emotions that music arouses, the type of most recurring emotions and the reasons why people experience emotions are aspects that have been broken down, often without reaching definitive conclusions.

The challenge of being able to lay the scientific bases for the correct measurement and study of emotions, approached firstly from Psychology, also implies the correct choice of the measurement methods used, both over the physiological and cognitive human reactions.

By transporting these methodologies to the field of film music, some authors have demonstrated the specific effects of music on the emotions and perception of the audiovisual viewer and at the same time the effectiveness of the measurement systems. Recently, the measurement of emotions related to music in the interactive environment (video games) has been approached in different works, evidencing the influence of music on the gaming experience and immersion.

This work aims to take advantage of the measurement of the physiological response to emotional stimuli (specifically through one of the methods that best respond in real time to changes in emotion, the Galvanic Skin Response), as a triggering element of the changes generated in the interactive music selection system used in video games. This way, the music of the game can change depending on the physiological reactions of the player, instead of responding to the state of the game or other variables of the action itself, thus generating a personalized experience for each individual.

So far, this system has proved to be a valid alternative way to generate interactive experiences that take in consideration the unconscious individual emotional reactions and add them to the gaming experience equation.

Keywords: Music emotions · Emotions medition · Interactive music system · Individualized gaming experience

1 Introduction

This work is part of a doctoral thesis, in which some of its parts are in progress. It addresses the Measurement of Emotions and how this can be used as a means to generate an individualized gaming experience in video games.

© Springer Nature Switzerland AG 2021
C. Stephanidis et al. (Eds.): HCII 2021, CCIS 1421, pp. 164–169, 2021.
https://doi.org/10.1007/978-3-030-78645-8_21

As stated by Schtachter and Singer [1], emotions consist of a physiological component in addition to a cognitive response. These are also key elements in the measurement of musical emotions, as suggested by Juslin [2] or Dainow [3].

The measurement of emotions in music has been used by several authors. Khalfa [4] observes differences in respiratory rhythm between a "happy" song and a "sad" song. Dainow [3] documents the effects of music on Galvanic Skin Response (GSR) measurements and underlines the importance of Dual Analysis. Watanabe et al. [5] verified the influence that the tempo of the music has on the heart rate (HR). Elrich et al. [6] proposed a looping system in which the brain's physiological response elicited by music is in turn reused to modify the music.

Taking into account the audiovisual element, Baumgartner et al. [7] verified that the images accompanied by music evoke cognitive responses of emotion and intense sensations. Thayer et al. [8], experimented with the visualization of a film with shocking scenes, and were able to measure alterations in the GSR and HR depending on whether the music accentuated those scenes or tried to minimize them. Koriat et al. [9] used films with dialogues after doing other previous desensitization processes (with and without music), using the measurement of cognitive experience. Thayer [8] observed the increase in stress due to particularly shocking images in a well-known documentary on occupational safety, depending on whether or not music was used, through HR and GSR.

Finally, in the most recent field of Videogames there have also been experiences with measuring emotions. Hébert et al. [10] verified the increase in the level of cortisol in the blood according to the use of music in a game. Ravaja et al. [11] used Dual Analysis with HR and electromyogram (EMG) to conclude that the interaction in the game with a real human player increases the emotional response. Cassidy & MacDonald [12] observed that the music known to the player creates a greater involvement of the player in the game. Williams [13] measured the effects that the use of Algorithmic Composition had on the subject in substitution of the original musical pieces in a video game. More recently, Granato [14] studied the design of a methodology for measuring emotions in video games, starting from physiological multi-analysis and suggesting the use of these systems for innovation in video games.

The present work wants to investigate whether it is possible to improve the individual game experience by integrating emotional physiological measurement into the Interactive Musical System (IMS), thus allowing the player's own emotions to determine the changes in mood reflected by the music. In this way, a loop is also generated between the music and the player's mood that can be used to create a more organic and immersive gaming experience. If compared to a conventional IMS, emotion driven IMS involves the actual player's psycho-emotional state in the music selection process, which in turn also affects the player's emotional state (see Fig. 1).

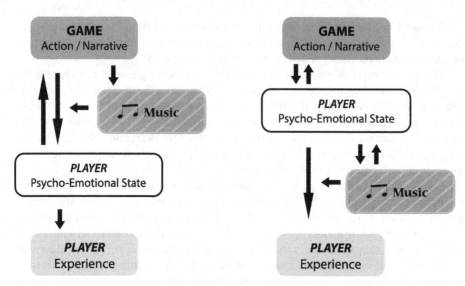

Fig. 1. Comparison of a conventional IMS (left) and the proposed emotion driven IMS (right).

2   Content and Methods

2.1   Interactive Music System (IMS) Design

The used IMS is conceived to work with a videogame level. It has an structure of 4 States that increase in intensity and stress level (E1_Calm, E2_Alert, E3_Danger, E4_Life_Or_Death). Four looped musical sequences of the same duration have been composed following a "compositive map" that allows smooth transitions between the sequences at any time. The music has been composed using musical characteristics that progressively generate more sensation of stress, found in scientific literature, such as the use of musical modes [15], harmonic tensions [15, 16], use of appoggiaturas and sequences [2] and Rythmic Roughness [15].

The IMS has two modes of use, depending on the trigger for changes in the State: Control_Mode (musical changes triggered by life level) and GRS_Mode (musical changes triggered by peaks in the GSR measurement).

2.2   GSR Emotion Sensor

Among the possible physiological meditions, GSR is selected due to its fast response and sensitivity. This brings the possibility of treating the data on real-time. An Arduino Nano is used with a GSR sensor attached to the player. Through UATTL Serial communication and the "Hairless Midi Serial" MIDI to serial bridge application, the Arduino sends MIDI messages that are received by the Middleware Wwise application, which manages the interactive music selection.

The Arduino code begins with a calibration period in which the player's average GSR value is registered. Then it is compared with the captured values in a quiet and relaxed state and finally with an "aroused" state by listening to several examples of exciting music from different genres for 2 min. The average between the maximum increase detected in each of the calm and aroused periods is taken as "emotion_jump". During the game, when the increase in the GSR measurement is greater than this value, Arduino sends a State change message (to the next state when positive or to the previous state if it is negative) and causes a state change in Wwise, creating a transition between one sequence and the next.

2.3 Experimentation

An environment of experimentation with a real game (Wolfestein 3D) is proposed, using the original sound effects of the game, but not the music. Instead, the music from the Wwise output is added to the sound mix the player hears. Players are asked to follow the instructions to do the calibration, and then they are asked to play the game twice. In the first game the GSR Mode is activated (there are only musical changes if there is an "emotion jump"). In a second game, the Control mode is used (music changes are made based on the character's level of life).

Before starting the game, the level of experience as a player is asked. The games are recorded and the ascending and descending jumps of emotion, the duration of the games and the score obtained in the games are monitored. A mic records the spontaneous verbal expressions and also a final interview where the subject is asked about the emotional experience and the differences he has noticed between the games.

2.4 Population

For this experimentation, partly due to the limitations demanded by the COVID pandemic situation, 14 random subjects without exclusion criteria were interviewed. With ages between 10 and 65 years, 40% of them being females and with different gaming experience (from null to professional).

Although it is suggested to observe the behavior of groups selected with narrower criteria in future research, working with such a heterogeneous group has facilitated the observation of certain aspects of the functioning of the system in diverse population profiles.

3 Results

During the pilot tests, the calibration and the choice of the game had to be adjusted until a balance was found between playability, difficulty, and duration of the game. Once stabilized, the system has worked on all occasions, although the physiological response of the players has been uneven (as expected).

In general terms, the numeric measurements have increased between the GSR game and the Control game (number of jumps: 9.68%, duration of games: 2.49%, score: 30.42%). During the first game (GSR Mode) 45% of the participants showed little physiological reactivity (low_response) with 1 or less emotion jumps, while 36% showed high-reactivity, experiencing between 7 and 19 emotion jumps (high_response).

During the final interview, some players admitted that they had no emotional reaction to the game for various reasons (no interest in video games, unchallenging game level, or even a conscious effort to control emotions). Most players recognized the effect that music causes on the experience of emotions, but were not able to differentiate one game from the other in this sense.

4   Discussion

While the important increment of the players' game scores in the second game could be explained by the advancement of the game's learning curve, emotion jumps and duration increases needed to be studied with more depth. Analyzing the two profiles according to the physiological response (low_response and high_response), there is a remarkable relationship between low responsiveness and low interest generated by the video game in the player.

All the players in the Low-response group who reported not having experience in video games experienced an increase of more than 80% in the number of GSR jumps in the second game, and for different reasons they felt more involved in the second game. In these cases, the control version offered the player more musical variety. This could suggest that music changes helped the players to get more into the game. The players in this group who reported having an important gaming experience didn't experience significant changes in the number of jumps between one game and the other. A particular case explained that due to his high level of knowledge of the game, and despite having a considerable gamer level, he did not experience any emotion during the game, but he did when he was the first in the Game score list (thus obtaining the only emotion jump of his game).

Highly responsive players had less physiological response in the second game, suggesting that the music changes generated by the action of the game may have acted as a "warning", preparing the player for a more tense action and attenuating the emotional reactions triggered by unexpected situations of the game.

5   Conclusions

The system seems to be successful in generating an adapted gaming experience, responding to the individual emotional characteristics of the player. This could be used as a way to introduce or reduce difficulty according to the objective and interest of the game.

To rule out the effect that player fatigue or the learning curve may have on the results, it is suggested to carry out other experiments by reversing the order of the Game Modalities and the type of game.

The GSR driven IMS seems to have a different effects depending on the type of physiological responsiveness of the player. While in players with low response the system would not help to motivate them, in players with high response it seems to put them in a situation of more physiological reaction. The system could be understood as an added feature in advanced stages of a game (where only devoted gamers can access) or in conjunction with an action-based IMS.

References

1. Schachter, S., Singer, J.: Cognitive, social, and physiological determinants of emotional state. Psychol. Rev. **69**, 379–399 (1962)
2. Juslin, P.N.: Music and emotion. seven questions, seven answers. In: Music and the Mind Essays in honour of John Sloboda, Oxford University Press, New York (2011)
3. Dainow, E.: Physical effects and motor responses to music. J. Res. Music Educ. **25**(3), 211–221 (2010)
4. Khalfa, S., Roy, M., Rainville, P., Dalla Bella, S., Peretz, I.: Role of tempo entrainment in psychophysiological differentiation of happy and sad music. Int. J. Psychophysiol. **68**(1), 17–26 (2008)
5. Watanabe, K., Ooishi, Y., Kashino, M.: Heart rate responses induced by acoustic tempo and its interaction with basal heart rate. Sci. Rep. **7**, 1–12 (2008)
6. Ehrlich, S., Guan, C., Cheng, G.: A closed-loop brain-computer music interface for continuous affective interaction. In: Proceedings of the 2017 International Conference on Orange Technologies, ICOT 2017, pp. 176–179 (2018)
7. Baumgartner, T., Lutz, K., Schmidt, C., Jäncke, L.: The emotional power of music: How music enhances the feeling of affective pictures. Brain Res. **1075**, 151–164 (2006)
8. Thayer, J.F., Levenson, R.W.: Effects of music on psychophysiological responses to a stressful film. Psychomusicology J. Res. Music Cogn. **3**(1), 44–52 (1983)
9. Koriat, A., Melkman, R., Averill, J.R., Lazarus, R.S.: The self-control of emotional reactions to a stressful film 1. J. Personality **40**(4), 601–619 (1972)
10. Hébert, S., Béland, R., Dionne-Fournelle, O., Crête, M., Lupien, S.J.: Physiological stress response to video-game playing: the contribution of built-in music. Life Sci. **76**(20), 2371–2380 (2005)
11. Ravaja, N., et al.: Spatial presence and emotions during video game playing: does it matter with whom you play?. Presence Teleoperators Virtual Environ. **15**(4), 381–392 (2006)
12. Cassidy, G., MacDonald, R.A.: The effect of background music and background noise on the task performance of introverts and extraverts. Psychol. Music **35**(3), 517–537 (2007)
13. Williams, D.: Affectively-Driven Algorithmic Composition (AAC). In: Williams, D., Lee, N. (eds.) Emotion in Video Game Soundtracking. ISCEMT, pp. 27–38. Springer, Cham (2018). https://doi.org/10.1007/978-3-319-72272-6_4
14. Granato, M.: Emotions Recognition in Video Game Players Using Physiological Information (2019)
15. Wallis, I., Ingalls, T., Campana, E., Goodman, J.: A rule-based generative music system controlled by desired valence and arousal. In: Proceedings of 8th international sound and music computing conference (SMC), pp. 156–157 (2011)
16. Brookhart, C.E.: The effects of changes in harmonic tension upon listener response. Bull. Council Res. Music Educ. **6**, 64–70 (1965)

Changing Citizens' Attitude Towards Novel Mobility Measures with a Game: Procedure and Game Concept

Svenja Polst[✉], Jill Tamanini, and Frank Elberzhager

Fraunhofer IESE, Fraunhofer-Platz 1, 67663 Kaiserslautern, Germany
`svenja.polst@iese.fraunhofer.de`

Abstract. Climate change is one of today's big topics, so climate-friendly mobility habits are needed. The digital transformation, another mega-trend, can support changing these habits. One step in the change process is the establishment of a positive attitude towards novel mobility measures such as the reduction of parking spaces. In this paper, we present an unobtrusive way to change citizens' attitude towards new mobility measures: We have developed a game, called 'MiniLautern', that introduces novel mobility measures to the players and lets them explore their effects on a smart city district. The target group are citizens. We present how we developed this game based on a Design Sprint, provide background information about the design decisions, and show examples from our solution.

Keywords: Mobility · Attitude change · Smart city · Innovation design · Game · Gamification

1 Introduction

Currently, cars dominate the streets in many cities. From an economic point of view, cars are inefficient because on average, they are unused most of the day. Moreover, there is often just a single passenger, namely the driver. Cars have even more disadvantages; their emissions pollute the air, their noises might affect the health of residents, and parking spaces compete with spaces for recreation and living. Alternative measures for fulfilling citizens' mobility needs are highly necessary. In the research project

'EnStadt:Pfaff', environment-friendly mobility concepts and measures are being developed for a smart city district in the city of Kaiserslautern, Germany. However, developing and caring about the realization of the measures is only one step. The citizens also need to use them or at least accept them. Thus, it is necessary to support the citizens on their way towards accepting and using these novel mobility measures.

© Springer Nature Switzerland AG 2021
C. Stephanidis et al. (Eds.): HCII 2021, CCIS 1421, pp. 170–178, 2021.
https://doi.org/10.1007/978-3-030-78645-8_22

Our goal is to support citizens on their way to understanding, accepting, and adopting a more climate-friendly behavior with a special focus on mobility measures. We de-fined five milestones that are helpful in this regard:

1. Citizens share the belief that novel mobility measures are desirable
2. Citizens feel able to use novel mobility measures
3. Citizens have the intention to change their mobility habits
4. Citizens try new mobility measures for the first time
5. Citizens establish new mobility habits

We developed measures for all milestones, with a focus on residents who theoretically have the possibility to use novel mobility measures instead of their own car, but do not use these alternatives regularly.

In this paper, we present our work regarding the first milestone. We would like the citizens to share the belief that 'Novel mobility measures can have positive effects for citizens including me'. To support citizens on their journey towards this milestone, we must inform them about novel mobility measures and the positive effects they have on the environment, the people, and the climate.

While elaborating on ideas how to do this, we faced this major challenge: How can we persuade as many citizens of Kaiserslautern as possible that novel mobility measures are desirable?

We identified three sub-challenges to this major challenge:

a. How can we introduce novel mobility measures to them even if they are not interested in dealing with them or even have an aversion to it?
b. How can we change their attitude?
c. How can we reach a large number of citizens?

In this paper, we demonstrate how we addressed these challenges with a game and how we arrived at our solutions. Our goal is to provide inspiration to practitioners and scientists facing similar challenges. We start with a description of our method (Sect. 2), continue with our concrete solution and show our game (Sect. 3), and then give a brief overview of related work (Sect. 4). We conclude this article with a summary and an outlook on future work (Sect. 5).

2   Method

The starting point of our considerations was the previously mentioned central challenge, namely: How can we convince many citizens in Kaiserslautern that novel mobility measures are desirable? Since the challenge is not a technical, but rather a socio-cultural issue, no concrete digital solution or design to address this problem adequately was available. Thus, we needed an approach capable of dealing with this level of abstraction. Another requirement was that we wanted to have a first proto-type quickly in order to communicate the solution idea to the project partners and citizens to get early qualitative feedback.

For these reasons, we decided to conduct a Design Sprint with the design question "FasciNATION Mobility: How can people living in Kaiserslautern be fascinated by novel, environmentally friendly mobility?". The only restriction for the solution was that it had to be digital or digitally supported, as this matches the competences of our institute.

2.1 Design Sprint

A Design Sprint [1] is a method for co-creation and rapid prototyping that is suitable for vague and challenging research questions where fast evaluation is desired. The Design Sprint method requires a team of about seven people to work on a question for five consecutive days. Day 1 is dedicated to understanding the problem, day 2 to creating solution ideas, day 3 to deciding on one story and formulating it by means of a storyboard, day 4 to creating next a prototype, and day 5 to testing it with five potential users. Since 2018, we have conducted Design Sprints to explore complex issues in research projects and are therefore convinced that when accurate adjustments are made, it is also a valuable method for scientific work. As described in the book, we also experienced that this highly distilled work process enables participants to create faster and more creative results.

Fig. 1. The Design Sprint was held in a room equipped with a multitude of materials for creativity sessions and lots of whiteboard walls and tables.

2.2 Project Team and Setting

We included a cross-disciplinary set of people in the Design Sprint. Since our aim was to start the development afterwards, we involved two developers, two designers, two requirements engineers, one digital innovator, one psychologist, and one project manager. The latter two acted as a decision-making tandem who ultimately decided on the desired path. One designer facilitated the Design Sprint and joined the team only later for the prototype design. We conducted the Design Sprint in a room dedicated to creative work with a multitude of whiteboards, post-its, pencils, and inspiring decoration (see Fig. 1). Even the prototype was created in this room.

2.3 After the Design Sprint

The Design Sprint was just the starting point of our game. We continued working on it and still do. We added some tweaks to it, for example, including a citizens' council to clarify the different perspectives on the mobility concepts.

3 Result – Game 'MiniLautern'

In the following, we will describe our game design and explain our design decisions and their rationale in detail.

3.1 Game Concept

The game 'MiniLautern' (short for Tiny Kaiserslautern) is a single-player game currently realized as a web app solution (see Fig. 2). In the game, novel mobility measures are to be established in a smart city district in Kaiserslautern to enhance the quality of life, reduce negative impacts on the environment, and increase the individual happiness level of the citizens. The player's task is to select the mobility measures that have the most positive effect on all of these parameters. By achieving this, the player can rank high on the scoreboard.

We chose a game since the target group includes persons who have low intrinsic motivation to deal with mobility measures and who do not want to be lectured. When confronted with this topic, people often fear that one wants to impose an ecological ideology on them. We assume that having fun playing a game could increase people's motivation to inform themselves about novel mobility measures and could avoid the impression of being lectured (cf. Challenge a). The high score is intended to motivate the players to play the game more often and thereby learn more about the mobility measures and their effects. As a web app, the game can be easily accessed by many people at home as well as on the go (cf. Challenge c).

Fig. 2. Left: Screen depicting mobility concepts categorized into three tabs labeled 'off the road', 'parking', 'from A to B'. Right: Last screen of the game showing the points achieved and the player's rank on the scoreboard.

3.2 Setting and Task

The player is guided through the game by a character called Ellen Mask (see Fig. 3). Ellen is a do-gooder and computer scientist who aims to improve the smart city district in Kaiserslautern with the help of the player. A fictional citizen council supports Ellen and the player in their endeavor by informing them about their needs and providing feedback about the selected mobility measures. We chose a setting that is between fantasy and reality. Ellen Mask is clearly a funny reference to Tesla's Elon Musk.

In each round, the player can first read about the citizens' mobility needs, then the player has a look at the mobility measures and select one which, in the player's opinion, has the most positive effects regarding the environment, quality of life, as well as the individual happiness of the council.

We chose this task since the player must anticipate and elaborate on the effects of the mobility measures. According to the Elaboration Likelihood Model (cf. Related Work), elaborating leads to a strong attitude (cf. Challenge b). Our evaluation con-firmed the assumption that this task appeals to several player types (cf. Related Work, cf. Challenge c). Some players like to 'help' the citizens of the council by fulfilling their needs, other players like to identify the measures resulting in the highest possible number of points, and yet others enjoy learning about the measures and their effects.

Fig. 3. The character 'Ellen Mask' introduces the task to the player.

3.3 Citizens' Council and Mobility Needs

The citizens' council consists of several persons (see Fig. 4). In each round, an-other person is added. After clicking on one, a text bubble appears describing their mobil-ity needs at an abstract level. The player must derive concrete needs from the textual description to match them with the mobility measures.

We created a variety of personas representing a cross-section of society (cf. Challenge c) based on a persona template introduced in the Related Work section. By looking at a wide variety of people and their individual mobility needs, the player's horizon expands. We also assume that the player will identify with a subset of these personas which will contribute to their engagement with the game. Also, the personas who represent a contradictory point of view are useful as they enforce a change in mind and thereafter also in attitude. There are also personas with aversions to novel mobility measures so that the players sharing this view also feel involved in the game (cf. Challenges a, c).

By randomly letting the personas appear in the game, we keep the game interest-ing even if it is played more often. Also, not knowing which person will join when adds an additional challenge.

Fig. 4. Left: Overview of the citizens' council. Right: Description of a person

3.4 Mobility Measures

We offer twelve mobility measures separated into three categories. For each mobility measure, a title, an icon, and a one-line explanation are provided on the overview screen. For instance, the mobility measure 'Company Shower' is shown in the category 'Off the road' with its icon and the one-liner. When clicking onto it, a more detailed description and pros and cons are displayed. The pro and contra arguments are in-tended to trigger the players to consider negative consequences as well.

We follow the rule of least affordance as we want to quickly and easily inform in order to continue the game flow. At the end of the game, additional links are present-ed according to the four previously chosen measures that lead to further information about these mobility measures. The different levels of detail respect the different degrees of interest the players might have towards the topic (cf. Challenge c) (Fig. 5).

Fig. 5. Left: Overview of the mobility measures in the category "Off the road". Right: Details of the measure 'Company shower'.

3.5 Explaining the Effects of Mobility Measures

At the end of each round, the player receives feedback regarding the impact of the chosen measure on the environment, quality of life in the smart city district, and the citizens' satisfaction. Feedback is provided in several ways. Ellen Mask explains the effect of a mobility measure accompanied by before and after images (see Fig. 6). For instance, she explains that measures could impact the air quality and the level of noise caused by cars. Also, Ellen awards a certain number of points for a positive impact on the environment and on the quality of life. The members of the citizen's council award points when they are happy with the measure (see Fig. 6, right side). Points are withdrawn for negative effects. The number of points depends on the degree of the effect. Moreover, the fictional citizens' faces express approval or dislike. Text bubbles add an explanation to the facial expressions.

We added additional points and explanations when specific mobility measures are activated together to reflect positive interaction effects. The three categories of points let the player experience that a tradeoff is often necessary between environment, quality of life, and individual happiness.

Showing unhappy fictional citizens might seem counterproductive when trying to establish a positive attitude towards mobility measures; however, we assume that this reflects reality, enforces the credibility of the game, and allows players who dislike a measure to empathize with the fictional citizens. Thus, the diverse opinions of the citizens add to resolving Challenge c. The player likewise learns that new mobility concepts do not satisfy all types of citizens equally, and they understand the dilemma of change.

Information about the effects, which are nevertheless mainly positive, is the basis for a change in attitude (cf. Challenge b). The explanations are short and visually supported. Therefore, we assume that even players with little interest in the topic will consume the information provided (cf. Challenge a). By displaying combinations of measures, we add more realism to the game, but also an element of surprise. The 'free spirit' player type [4] is especially captivated by being surprised and finding out new aspects of the game.

Fig. 6. Left: Explanation of the measures' impact supported by a before and after picture. Right: Reaction to measure.

4   Related Work and Background

In this section, we present more background information on the project 'EnStadt:Pfaff' and the theories and models we considered while developing the game.

The mentioned persona template [4] was created in the context of the project

'EnStadt:Pfaff' to record a person's characteristics and mobility needs. Characteristics are, for instance, their attitude towards sustainability, their socio-economic status, and their regular travel destinations, as well as personal preferences.

We referred to two theories about attitudes in the previous chapter. According to the Theory of Planned Behavior, a prerequisite to reaching a desired behavior is that a person's attitude is in line with the desired behavior [2]. Attitudes can be changed by persuasion. The Elaboration Likelihood Model states that there are two ways of persuasion, the central route to persuasion and the peripheral route to persuasion [3]. Taking the central route means a person processes arguments, while taking the peripheral route means a person mainly relies on peripheral cues such as the attractive-ness of an expert. The central route leads to stronger attitudes.

As mentioned above, the game should appeal to various people. What kind of game we like depends on what type of player we are. The well-known player type classification by Marczewski [4] distinguishes six types of players; socializers, free spirits, achievers, philanthropists, players, and disruptors. Each type is motivated by something else. For instance, the socializers are motivated by relatedness, the achievers by mastery, and the philanthropists by purpose. Marczewski suggest game elements for each player type.

5 Summary and Future Work

We addressed the challenge 'How can we persuade many citizens in Kaiserslautern that novel mobility measures are desirable?' by creating a game that informs about mobility measures and their positive effects while respecting negative opinions about mobility measures and different levels of interest in the topic.

Currently, the development of the game is still ongoing. Therefore, we have evaluated only the effect of a prototype so far, with promising results. At the end of the Design Sprint, some test users gave initial feedback. This helped us to decide about the further direction. In addition, we had a remote usability test, two test mobs, and several reviews by project partners. An extensive evaluation is planned when the game prototype has achieved a stable and somewhat final version.

When we tested the game, the participants were passionate about the game and empathized with the council. The participants were interested in learning about the mobility measures and their effects.

Besides the web app, we will have the opportunity to implement the game as part of an exhibition where we expect continuous feedback from people representing various player types. We also plan to accompany players after they have played the game and to interview those who are willing in order to investigate whether the game had an influence on their attitude towards novel mobility measures.

Acknowledgments. Parts of this work have been funded by the "EnStadt: Pfaff" project (grants no. 03SBE112D and 03SBE112G) of the German Federal Ministry for Economic Affairs and Energy (BMWi) and the Federal Ministry of Education and Research (BMBF). We thank Sonnhild Namingha for proofreading.

References

1. Knapp, J., Zeratsky, J., Kowitz, B.: Design Sprint (2016)
2. Ajzen, I.: The theory of planned behavior. Organizational Behav. Hum. Decis. Processes **50**(2), 179 (1991)
3. Petty, R.E., Briñol, P.: The elaboration likelihood model. Handb. Theories Soc. Psychol. **1**, 224–245 (2011)
4. Marczewski, A.: User types. In: Even Ninja Monkeys Like to Play: Gamification, Game-Thinking and Motivational Design (2015)
5. Polst S., Stüpfert P.: A comprehensive persona template to understand citizens' mobility needs. In: Krömker H. (ed.) HCI in Mobility, Transport, and Automotive Systems. HCII 2019. LNCS, vol 11596. Springer, Cham (2019). https://doi.org/10.1007/978-3-030-22666-4_22

Gaeta: The Great Adventure - A Cultural Heritage Game about the History of Gaeta

Francesco Sapio[(✉)] [iD], Lauren S. Ferro[iD], and Massimo Mecella[iD]

Sapienza University of Rome, Rome, Italy
{sapio,lsferro,mecella}@diag.uniroma1.it

Abstract. As new historical sites are continuously discovered many existing ones are suffering from deterioration due to age, war, and natural disasters. Given the inability for us to travel due to the COVID-19 pandemic, we must adapt ways to experience the world in a safe and accessible way. One such area that enables us to interact with the world safely is video games. Therefore, the use of games for cultural heritage can allow us to not only preserve a digital "copy" of such places and artifacts thus providing the opportunity to educate and inform current generations as well as promote tourism. Therefore, this paper proposes a game about the Italian city of Gaeta, which adopts principles seen in commercial entertainment games with the intention of educating the user of historical periods leading up to the modern-day Gaeta. Results from empirical testing using focused groups and semi-structured interviews have been positive.

Keywords: Gaeta · Cultural heritage · Game design · Game development · Interactive experience · Mobile gaming · Interactive experience

1 Introduction

It is clear the affordances that games can offer in modern day society. Games are no longer used solely for entertaining us they have the power to engage us in enticing, interesting, and educational experiences. In recent times, we have seen the use of games and gaming technology (e.g. virtual and augmented reality) as a way to enhance museum visits. There have been many entertainment games that contain a historical aspect (including real information) such as Sid Meier's Civilization[1] series and Assassin's Creed Series[2]. In addition, we have also seen commercial games offer stand-alone experiences that allow players to engage with historical periods of time (e.g. Assassin's Creed Discovery Tour) that bring to life periods of time that we have previously only read or watch documentaries about.

---

[1] www.civilization.com/.

[2] https://www.ubisoft.com/en-us/game/assassins-creed.

© Springer Nature Switzerland AG 2021
C. Stephanidis et al. (Eds.): HCII 2021, CCIS 1421, pp. 179–187, 2021.
https://doi.org/10.1007/978-3-030-78645-8_23

Games of cultural heritage exist under the umbrella of *Serious* and *Educational* games. In some cases, they may also employ approaches used in *gamified/gamification*.

We must consider the context that such games are to be played in. For example, unlike traditional *Serious* or *Educational* games, games for cultural heritage are often restricted due to time, budget, and technology [3,5,9]. Moreover, the consideration that such experiences are intended to be engaged with in a context such as a museum or stand lone exhibition and users are considered unlikely to engage in the experience again. However, we argue that this should not necessarily be the case. Therefore, this game proposes a demonstration towards designing and developing games within context of cultural heritage/preservation in such a way that reflects contemporary games.

After introducing current research in *Games and Cultural Heritage* (Sect. 2), this paper describes elements of design (Sect. 3) and development (Sect. 4) of the serious game *Gaeta: Great Adventure*. Conclusions are drawn and future research outlined in Sect. 6.

2   Cultural Heritage and Games

As we move towards a more digitally interactive world, cultural heritage and tourism has also begun to follow suit [6]. Many historical sites have adapted or even created entirely new experiences that connect the digital world to a physical historical location in ways that enhance the experience or provide an added layer of interactivity. To this end, games in the context of cultural heritage are not only preserving what was, but also adapting it towards a modern audience and their expectations. Therefore, to maintain relevancy with digital natives, such approaches are also fundamental.

The use of games towards cultural heritage or cultural preservation has been analyzed in many studies and publications [1,13] that stress the importance of both the preservation and the ability of games to achieve that.

Games in the context of cultural heritage include many different approaches that span museums [6] and various exhibits within it and as well as stand alone experiences like VR [12], some of which the user can download (AR) [4].

In addition, some authors, such as [7] and [8], try to propose different models that can inform designers on how to better include cultural heritage information within the context of commercial games. Other frameworks and models, such as Andreoli et al. [2], try to include the whole process, from the design phase all the way through development and the eventual evaluation of a *Serious Game*.

Liarokapis et al. [10] describes how multimodal serious games can create an immersive experiences that work towards enhancing a visitor's experience.

3   Designing *Gaeta: The Great Adventure*

Gaeta is an Italian town of 20,000 inhabitants located in lower Lazio. It has a remarkable historical relevance, a rich artistic heritage and tourist resources that make it a very popular tourist destination. For this reason, the municipality of Gaeta is supporting the development of a Serious Game aimed at preserving the cultural heritage of the city, named *Gaeta: The Great Adventure*.

3.1 Overview

Gaeta: The Great Adventure is a 3D mobile city building game in which the user has to reconstruct the city of Gaeta through different historical periods. The premise is that the player needs to collect resources, construct buildings, and optimize the city economy to complete the game. Popular mobile commercial games with similar mechanics include *Disney Magic Kingdoms*[3] and *Townsmen*[4].

The aim is not only to provide entertainment, which remains one of the key aspects of the game, but also touristic promotion and the preservation of cultural heritage. In fact, *Gaeta: The Great Adventure* differs from other cultural heritage game, because the focus is still on making the game appealing by its own, while having cultural heritage and touristic promotion as side effects.

3.2 A Co-design Approach

During development of *Gaeta: The Great Adventure*, we adopted a co-design approach, by involving the stakeholders and the development team, along with some expert figures in order to achieve the goals we decided. In particular, we have organised four focus groups and several semi-structured interview, so to gather feedback to better iterate the game. Also, we collected some preliminary quantitative data regarding the game with the use of a small sample of beta testers.

Focus groups are a standard practice in social sciences, allowing interviewers to study people in a more natural setting than a one-to-one interview. They can be used for gaining access to various cultural and social groups and raising issues for exploration [11]. In particular, we organised four focus groups during the development of the game. Two of which have been in presence, and the last two were over distance due to the recent COVID-19 pandemic. At each group there were present: the mayor of the city of Gaeta, the local councilor of cultural heritage, the local minister of cultural heritage, a gamification expert, a UX expert, a psychologist, four inhabitants of the city of Gaeta, and the whole development team. Results of the focus groups are the different iterations of the game, leading to the current one described in Sect. 4.

After a few days from the last two focus groups, all the participants (excluding the development team) were video-called for a semi-structured interview with three sets of questions. The first set of questions regarded the learning, education, promotional, and touristic aspects of the game. The questions in the second set were about the user experience and how enjoyable the game was to play. The last set concerned the usability of the game by different types of people (e.g. young or elderly groups of people).

---

[3] https://www.gameloft.com/game/disney-magic-kingdom.

[4] https://handy-games.com/en/games/townsmen-mobile/.

4   Developing *Gaeta: The Great Adventure*

In *Gaeta: The Great Adventure* we tried to meet the lines of work mentioned in Sects. 2 and 3, aiming at developing a serious game to improve the sensibilitation toward a specific cultural heritage site.

Fig. 1. Overview of the Gaeta in the game, once the player has fully built it.

4.1   Historical Periods

During the game-play the player will rebuild the city of Gaeta, through different Historical Periods:

- *Mythological Era*: the legends associated with the origins of the city.
- *Roman Era*: Gaeta became a popular holiday resort for Roman emperors and a port of considerable importance.
- *Ducal Era*: The Docibili dinasty made Gaeta an independent duchy and a Maritime Republic, with its own laws, naval fleet and currency, the *"Follaro"*.
- *Medieval Era*: a period characterized by the dominion of the Angevins and the Aragonese, and by the spread of religious orders which introduced the Italian Gothic style to Gaeta.
- *Renaissance Era*: renowned artists embellished Gaeta with their creations, while the city grew of strategic importance and was equipped with imposing fortifications.
- *Nineteenth Century*: a century characterized by the exile of Pope Pius IX , and by the siege of 1860-61, which marked the ending of the Bourbon reign in the south of Italy.

In Fig. 1 is possible to observe Gaeta once it has been fully rebuilt by the player.

During gameplay or during certain quests, the player will face some special events that characterized the history of Gaeta. Some of these events, such as the *"Raids by the Saraceni"* or the *"Earthquake"* create an obstacle to the player (e.g. resources get lost, buildings get destroyed or loose some levels). Other events, such as *"The Battle of Lepanto"*, are part of a quest in which the player needs to prepare the fleet for Pope Pious V.

4.2 Resources

In order to build and upgrade new structures and buildings, the player will need to manage four resources (shown in Fig. 2) as well as time, in order to leverage the game economy and to complete all the assigned quests.

Fig. 2. Resources Icons shown in the game. From the left: *Gold*, *Lumber*, *Stone* and *Food*.

In particular, the player can collect (or exchange with trading activities) three resources:

- **Gold**: while the population of the city grows, *Gold* can be accumulated by collecting taxes from the people.
- **Lumber**: with the use of a *Lumber Mill* the player can produce *Lumber*, however its availability is limited, pushing the player to trade more often.
- **Stone**: is an important element to build historical buildings, and it is very rare; in fact, *Stone* can be obtained mainly by trading.

The fourth resource, **"Food"**, provides an upper limit to the number (and levels) of the buildings that the player can have (or reach).

The player can obtain these resources by building **Resources Building**. For instance, *Farms* produce *Food* at a constant rate, whereas *Houses* generate *Gold* from taxes. The *Harbour* provides a way for the player to trade resources.

Most of the buildings of the game can be upgraded by the player (e.g. *Farms*, *Lumber Mills*, *Houses*) will provide more resources, whereas other buildings, like the *Storages*, will provide a better general storage for the player).

4.3 Wonders

Wonders are special buildings the characterize the history of Gaeta and nowadays provide a point of interest for tourism. During the game, the player is asked to build nine wonders in their respective historical period. Differently from the other building type, they have only one level, and it takes a lot of resources to build them (especially *Stone*, which is the rarer among the resources). All of them have been recreated in 3D by keeping their visual aspect, but at the same time they have been stylized.

(a) Bell Tower

(b) Lucio Munazio Planco Mausoleum

Fig. 3. Some examples of the stylized 3D models in the game.

In *Gaeta: The Great Adventure*, some of the wonders that the player can build are: the **Lucio Munazio Planco Mausoleum** (shown in Fig. 3(b)), the best-preserved Roman tomb in all of Italy; the **Castle**, an impressive rectangular fortress with four formidable cylindrical towers, built in different phases by the Angevin and Aragonese rulers; **Cathedral and Belltower** (shown in Fig. 3(a)), built in the 12th century and complemented by a beautifully ornate byzantine bell tower; or even the **Sanctuary of Montagna Spaccata**, built during the 11th century by the Benedictine monks to honor the giant cracks in the mountain said to be produced at the crucifixion of Christ.

4.4 Research

Among the different city management options, the player can perform "*Research*" by spending resources and time. Researches, once they are completed, provide a permanent advantage/effect for the city. Research effect types include *increasing production rates*, *decreasing building time* or *Unlocking features and/or buildings* among others.

The player is limited by a "*Research Tree*" that creates dependencies between researches, making the game more challenging.

5   Preliminary Test Results

In this first phase, we decided to test just some of the learning objective of the game to gather some preliminary results, before finalizing the game and releasing it to the public. We selected $N = 15$ beta testers for the game and administered them a questionnaire about the culture and history of Gaeta, before and after playing the beta version of the game (for at least one hour).

Some of the learning objectives of *Gaeta: The Great Adventure* were validated using a paired *t*-test (with a confidence level set to 95%) in order to evaluate if the beta testes learnt something about the history of Gaeta by playing the game. We intentionally did not have a control group, because our focus was not to compare this game with more traditional methods, but rather understanding and testing whether the game can achieve some of the basic learning aims defined. In fact, the Experimental Hypothesis was about the knowledge retention about the culture and history of Gaeta.

The questionnaire was comprised of 4 parts depending on the historical period. Each question was a culture or historical question, with 5 possible choices, only one correct. For each corrected answer, a single point was awarded. In Table 1 are the p-values for each section of the questionnaire.

Table 1. *p*-values for each scenarios resulted from the paired *t*-test.

Questionnaire section	p-value
Mythological era	0.0251
Roman and ducal era	0.0297
Medieval era	0.0066
Renaissance era and nineteenth century	0.0196

Future tests will be conducted on a larger scale, once the game is published, and results published in a separate work.

6   Conclusions and Future Work

In this paper, we presented a serious game, *Gaeta: The Great Adventure*, aimed at both educating the player and providing a way to preserve the cultural and historical heritage of the Italian town of Gaeta as well as to promote tourism and interest in the town.

Our approach tries to place the content first, and continuing assessing this goal with a co-design approach. In fact, we consider the appeal of popular titles of games for entertainment to find a way to develop a game that aligns with such directions, while at the same time providing educational or promotional material.

In this way, we expect that such approaches might even generate more interest and longer engagement than standalone experiences as the player unfolds the story.

From the preliminary tests, the games has the potential to educate the players; however it is still under development. In fact, more data will be collected after the game has launched to assess the effectiveness of *Gaeta: The Great Adventure* for entertaining, tourism, promotion, and cultural heritage purposes. In-game player data along with player profiling techniques, marketing data, questionnaires and survey are among the methodologies we will adopt to assess the quality of our game.

References

1. Anderson, E.F., McLoughlin, L., Liarokapis, F., Peters, C., Petridis, P., De Freitas, S.: Developing serious games for cultural heritage: a state-of-the-art review. Virtual Reality **14**(4), 255–275 (2010)
2. Andreoli, R., Andreoli, R., et al.: A framework to design, develop, and evaluate immersive and collaborative serious games in cultural heritage. J. Comput. Cult. Herit. (JOCCH) **11**(1), 1–22 (2017)
3. De Freitas, S.: Are games effective learning tools? a review of educational games. J. Educ. Technol. Soc. **21**(2), 74–84 (2018)
4. Ekonomou, T., Vosinakis, S.: Mobile augmented reality games as an engaging tool for cultural heritage dissemination: a case study. Sci. Cult **4**, 97–107 (2018)
5. Fu, F.-L., Yu, S.-C.: Three layered thinking model for designing web-based educational games. In: Li, F., Zhao, J., Shih, T.K., Lau, R., Li, Q., McLeod, D. (eds.) ICWL 2008. LNCS, vol. 5145, pp. 265–274. Springer, Heidelberg (2008). https://doi.org/10.1007/978-3-540-85033-5_26
6. Georgopoulos, A., Kontogianni, G., Koutsaftis, C., Skamantzari, M.: Serious games at the service of cultural heritage and tourism. In: Katsoni, V., Upadhya, A., Stratigea, A. (eds.) Tourism, Culture and Heritage in a Smart Economy. SPBE, pp. 3–17. Springer, Cham (2017). https://doi.org/10.1007/978-3-319-47732-9_1
7. Haddad, N.A.: Multimedia and cultural heritage: a discussion for the community involved in children's heritage edutainment and serious games in the 21st century. Virtual Archaeol. Rev. **7**(14), 61–73 (2016)
8. Hanes, L., Stone, R.: A model of heritage content in serious and commercial games. In: 2017 9th International Conference on Virtual Worlds and Games for Serious Applications (VS-Games), pp. 137–140. IEEE (2017)
9. Ibrahim, R., Jaafar, A.: Educational games (EG) design framework: combination of game design, pedagogy and content modeling. In: 2009 International Conference on Electrical Engineering and Informatics, vol. 1, pp. 293–298. IEEE (2009)
10. Liarokapis, F., Petridis, P., Andrews, D., de Freitas, S.: Multimodal serious games technologies for cultural heritage. Mixed Reality and Gamification for Cultural Heritage, pp. 371–392. Springer, Cham (2017). https://doi.org/10.1007/978-3-319-49607-8_15
11. Marshall, C., Rossman, G.B.: Designing Qualitative Research. Sage Publications, Newbury Park (2014)

12. O'Connor, S., Colreavy-Donnelly, S., Dunwell, I.: Fostering engagement with cultural heritage through immersive VC and gamification. In: Visual Computing for Cultural Heritage, pp. 301–321. Springer (2020)
13. Zeiler, X., Thomas, S.: The relevance of researching video games and cultural heritage. Int. J. Herit. Stud. **27**, 1–3 (2020)

Gothic VR Game Scene Automatic Generation Design

Rui Tian, Jianwen Yang, and Jian Tan[✉]

Beijing University of Posts and Telecommunications, Beijing 100876, China

Abstract. Computer-aided technology and automatic programs are critical to improve the efficiency of game design. The goal of the paper is to research the automated design method of the Gothic architectural scene in VR games as to facilitating the existing design procedure. Firstly, we analyzed the aesthetic and structural characteristics of Gothic architecture, summarized the spatial and topological features of Gothic buildings. Secondly, we discussed the connection probability between Gothic building modules based on the principle of space topology. Then based on the Wave Function Collapse algorithm, an automatic generation model of Gothic VR game scenes was established. Finally, this model was tested on the U3D virtual simulation platform and proved its availability. The contribution of this work is to directly improve the efficiency and scale of Gothic building scene construction in VR games with an automatic generated program, but also present a reference to the design and generation of the other game architectural art scenes.

Keywords: Wave function collapse algorithm · Automated generation · Gothic game scene

1 Introduction

Architecture game scene is an important part of the production of virtual game scenes. The suitable and beautiful VR architectural scene can enhance the aesthetics of the game, strengthen theme when running with characters and other game special effects [1]. Besides, the quality of virtual reality game scenes also affects the competitiveness of the game. Well-made games are more attractive to players and can attract them to dig deeper into the experience value of the games. In order to illustrate realistic, complex and artistically virtual building scenes, game scene designers need to finely build three-dimensional models for each part of the scene building in VR games [2]. This process consumes a lot and has high requirements for the ability of the game scene designers.

And now, Gothic architecture often appears in the existing excellent game scenes. In "Assassin's Creed: Revolution" where the exquisiteness of the game scene can almost simulate the real world, gamers can "return" to Paris during the French Revolution and visit the authentically restored large and small Gothic architecture churches in the city. These Gothic game scenes set the tone of the game and improve the aesthetics of the

© Springer Nature Switzerland AG 2021
C. Stephanidis et al. (Eds.): HCII 2021, CCIS 1421, pp. 188–195, 2021.
https://doi.org/10.1007/978-3-030-78645-8_24

scenes. Therefore, the design and production of Gothic architectural scenes are very essential in VR games.

The scenes of classical architectural style in VR games now have low efficiency and high cost in the production process. Specific to the gothic scenes in VR games, firstly, designers need to collect materials for the first step, determine the story background and style setting of the game scene, and plan the game copy. Secondly, it requires designers to create the original paintings of the scenes, then it needs digital artists to build 3D architectural models. Finally, the game scenes are edited, which mainly includes testing for building connectivity and modification [3]. This method relies heavily on the designers' architectural quality and the level of geometric reconstruction of digital arts. Moreover, the process of developing is one-way, lacking a cancellation and adjustment mechanism. Therefore, if a problem needs to be modified in the game experience test, all the work can only be restarted. Besides, it is difficult to transfer the production of the classical architectural game scenes [4].

2   Related Work

However, the automated generation of architectural scenes for VR games has made some progress. Among these methods, there are mainly include 3 types. First, the city engine developed by ersi company which is based on 2D floor plans, height attributes, and building facade material libraries, can quickly convert 2D digital maps into 3D simple building scenes with materials. The second method is 3D scene generation based on building layout rules with procedure generation. Programmatic modeling software and plug-ins represented by Houdini have been widely used in game development. A third approach is a production tool for building scenes based on the combination of building modules. Ubisoft, which developed the "Assassin's Creed" series, developed a special tool for producing architectural scenes. It adopts modular ideas and uses replaceable 3D building components to assist developers quickly to build a complex [5]. Compared with the traditional method of game scenes, the automatic generation method is lower cost and higher efficiency.

Unfortunately, no current automatic generation method has been applied successfully in Gothic architectural scenes. There have three reasons. First, the method of vertical stretching a plane is only suitable for the generation of 3D architectural scenes with simple 2D plans and no internal structure, while Gothic buildings most have a large amount of 3D decoration and complex internal-space characteristics. Second, the procedural generation method requires the developers to parametrically express the architectural rules, which requires a high level of quantitative thinking for them. For instance, Gothic architecture has various scales, and its artistic characteristics run through different parts such as columns, windows, roofs, etc., which are difficult to quantify and generate. Third, the scene combination method based on the building module library requires manual intervention to ensure the connectivity of the building space and the overall aesthetics of the building scene. Therefore, the innovative exploration of the automated generation of Gothic VR architectural game scenes is of great significance in both technical and artistic aspects.

3   Application of Wave Function Collapse Algorithm in the Automatic Generation of Gothic VR Architecture Game Scenes

3.1   Theory Introduction

Wave Function Collapse (WFC) is a very promising method for generating VR construction game scenes. It is a non-backtracking greedy search algorithm proposed by Maxim Gumin et al. in 2016 [6], named by the concept of "wave function collapse" in quantum mechanics. The working principle of WFC in VR game building scene generation is: First of all, the space area in the game scene is regarded as "microscopic particles" in quantum mechanics. Each "microscopic particle" contains a series of possible building modules corresponding to a different probability of appearance. And the mechanical observations of each "microscopic particle", such as geometric coordinates, colors, angles, are uncertain. Next is "observation", which solidifies the probability of occurrence of a building module. After being "observed", the "microscopic particles" will be filled by a certain building module. In this way, the process of using probability to determine the building modules in the spatial region is called "wave function collapse (WFC)".

The WFC algorithm is very suitable for generating Gothic buildings. To use WFC, it is necessary to split the Gothic building into various building modules, such as roofs and stairs. This is also the idea of modular design in the construction of VR game scenes [7]. For Gothic architecture, building modules such as spires, flower windows, spire arches, and beam-columns undertake different architectural functions, making realistic construction more convenient [8], and they also have a unique and very recognizable artistic style. Using WFC to randomly generate scenes can not only show the artistic characteristics of Gothic architecture but also ensure the diversification of scenes.

In June 2019, marian42 released a 3D infinite city generative model based on WFC [9]. Although the structure of this architectural scene is simple, it provides a research foundation for this topic.

3.2   Design and Implementation

The automated generation of Gothic VR architectural game scenes based on WFC is achieved through the following steps (Fig. 1).

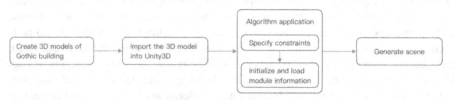

Fig. 1. Design flow.

Create 3D Models of Gothic Building. We divide the Gothic building structure into six parts: walls, columns, floors, stairs, doors, windows, and roofs [10]. These basic components of Gothic architecture have distinct artistic features. Figure 2 respectively show the internal structure and some typical structures of Gothic architecture.

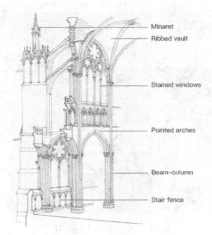

Fig. 2. Gothic building structure.

The unique "beam-column" of Gothic architecture is not a simple circular column, but a combination of multiple columns with prominent vertical lines. The floor cover of the Gothic building is a "ribbed vault", which can distribute the load of the vault to the horizontal piers or columns. The stained windows and arches of Gothic architecture have complex decorations and are very characteristic.

Based on the above analysis of the characteristics of Gothic architecture, we used software to create a Gothic building model. As shown in Table 1, these models are mainly divided into six categories: columns, floors, stairs, doors, windows, and others.

Table 1. Gothic architectural models.

Column	Floor	Stair	Door	Window	Other

Import the 3D Model into Unity3D. Figure 3 shows all the created models had imported into Unity3D.

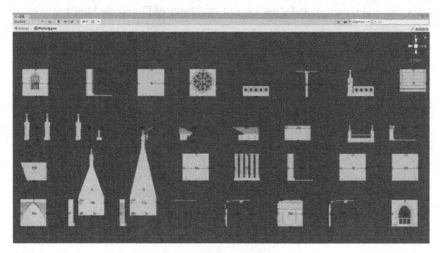

Fig. 3. Models in Unity3D.

Algorithm Application. It is mainly divided into three steps: specifying constraints, initializing, and loading module information and collapsing to generate scenes.

Specify Constraints. The constraint condition is mainly related to the script data of each building model. If the building model whose script data meets the constraint condition can be determined and appear in the generated building space scene. The script data of the building model includes the weight of the model, whether it is inside, and the conditions of neighbors in six directions. The size of the weight affects the number of occurrences of this model in a block. Use a Boolean variable to distinguish whether the model is inside the building. For each model, the program assigns six numbers as the neighbors in the six directions of the model. This neighbor may be an empty model. For

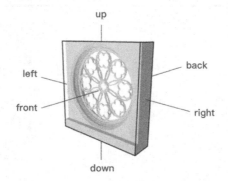

Fig. 4. Model "High Wall Flower Window".

example, the front, rear, left, and right directions of the roof are all empty. Taking the "High Wall Flower Window" as an example, its neighbors in 6 directions are shown in Table 2 (Fig. 4).

Table 2. Neighbors of model "High Wall Flower Window".

Direction	Neighbors		
Left	Wall R3	Wall_Window R3	Railing R2&R3
Down	Empty	Wall R1	Stairs_Top R1
Back	Empty		
Left	Wall_Bench R0	Wall_Corner_Fountain R3	Railing_Corner_2 R2&/R3
Up	Railing_Wall_3 R1	Roof_Corner R1	Pillars R3
Front	Empty		

Initialize and Load Module Information. The initialization function of the mapping behavior runs every time the program starts and initializes the model data, map, boundary constraints, and data removal so that subsequent calls to these contents can be performed normally.

The next step is the collapse process, which is the core of this method. As shown in Fig. 5, its core is a cycle, which is an expansion from the determined architectural space area to the non-determined area, to gradually expand the deterministic space area.

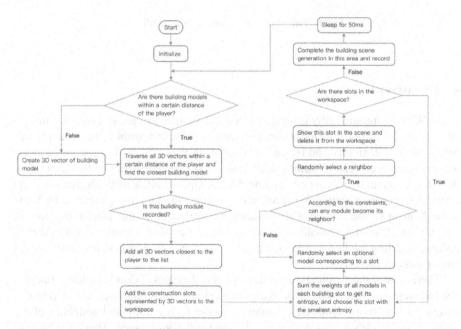

Fig. 5. Collapse process.

Generate Scene. As shown in Fig. 6, the same Gothic architectural model can be combined into different architectural scenes with the WFC, ensuring the diversity of VR architectural game scenes.

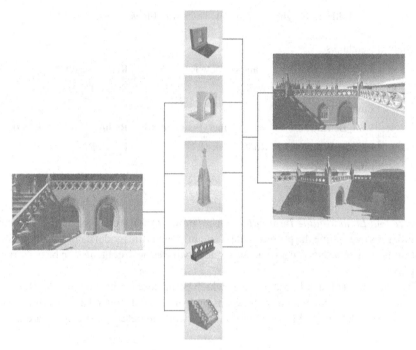

Fig. 6. Different scenes generated with WFC.

4 Discussion

Using WFC to automatically generate Gothic VR architecture game scenes has unique advantages. Compared with the traditional manual production method, this method guarantees random flexibility and is more reversible, easy to modify. The generated architectural space scene can be automatically inspected without relying on the level of the designer. Compared with the city engine, Sketch Up and other methods that use a 2D extruder to generate simple 3D architectural scenes, the building generated by WFC not only includes the surface of the building but also includes the internal structure of the building. It is more suitable to use as a VR game scene. Compared with the procedural modeling method represented by Houdini, this method has more advantages in randomness and artistry.

There are still shortcomings in this design. First, the types of Gothic building modules need to increase. Many typical structures of Gothic architecture were not used in this design, such as flying buttresses. Second, considering the unity and aesthetics of the building, the models in this design are all white and non-textured. Third, the form of the model is relatively simple, and the decoration of the architectural model is less considered. Fourth, the connection method of building modules needs to be further studied to make the scene more realistic.

5 Conclusion

In recent years, the game industry has developed rapidly, and users have increased their requirements for the aesthetics and accuracy of game scenes, which has brought new challenges to the construction of game scenes. This paper uses the wave function collapse algorithm to automate the design practice of generating gothic VR architectural game scenes. In the design process, first, use the modular design concept to extract the characteristics of Gothic architecture and create a model. Then set the adjacent relationship between the building module models. Finally, the wave function collapse algorithm is used to realize the automatic random generation of Gothic infinite architectural game scenes. This design practice not only provides a new way for the design of gothic VR architectural game scenes but also provides new ideas for the design of other architectural styles of VR game scenes. Designers can use this method to generate VR game scenes of more styles such as Roman architecture and Chinese architecture by changing the style of the models.

References

1. Fu, Y.: Research on the Method of 3D Game Scene Design. China Academy of Art, pp. 9–12 (2016)
2. Cui, L.: Development and realization of VR virtual reality technology in 3D game design. Video Eng. **42**(5), 44–48 (2018)
3. Tongtong, X.: Research on the design and production of game scene. Satell. TV IP Multimedia **24**, 114–115 (2019)
4. Zhang, C. E.: Practice of 3D game scene design based on Unity 3D. Hefei University of Technology (2016)
5. GDCVault Assassin's Creed Syndicate. https://www.gdcvault.com/play/1023305/-Assassin-s-Creed-Syndicate. Accessed 24 Mar 2021
6. Sandhu, A., Chen, Z., McCoy, M.: Enhancing wave function collapse with design-level constraints. In: Proceedings of the 14th International Conference on the Foundations of Digital Games 2019, FDG, New York, vol. 17, pp. 1–9. Association for Computing Machinery (2019)
7. Song, B.: Research on the application of modular design in immersive game design. Dazhongwenyi **18**(24), 62–63 (2018)
8. Grodecki, L., Zhou, L.V.: World Architecture History Series–Gothic architecture. China Architecture and Building Press, Beijing (2000). LNCS Homepage, http://www.springer.com/lncs. Accessed 21 Nov 2016
9. Marian42. https://github.com/marian42/wavefunctioncollapse. Accessed 21 Sept 2020
10. Yang, W.: Architectural Design. China Architecture and Building Press, Beijing (2005)

Enticing Spectators into Playing: How to Improve the Spectator Experience in Commercial Games Streaming

Yixi Wang[✉] and Xinwei Chang

Netease, 599 Wangshang Road, Hangzhou 310052, Binjian District, China
wangyixi@corp.netease.com

Abstract. Game streaming has become increasingly popular, making it one of the most important advertising channels for the game developers. However, the most profitable game type, MMORPG, has a bad level of performance in streaming. Thus, the present study investigated the visual factors that may influence spectator experience in MMORPG's streaming. The study employed mixed qualitative research methods (interviews and questionnaires) in the sample consisting of 30 participants from different game backgrounds. Results from interviews revealed positive ratings of improved streaming UI display, as well as complex understandings of all display plans: different gaming environments and individual game experience will affect participants' preferences in terms of UI elements. In addition, participants' sensitivity of character camera angle is lower than expected.

Keywords: Streaming · UI · Experience

1 Introduction

After nearly 10 years of rapid development, video game live streaming has formed a mature market, and has a strong momentum of continued expansion. Initially, game live streaming relied on popular games to bring more viewers, but now streaming has become an effective approach that games are relying on to reach new players (Edge 2013).

The major international game streaming platforms are still dominated by traditional popular games like *League of Legends*, *Fortnite*, *CS:GO*, and *DOTA2* (SullyGnome 2021). Besides these traditional games, there are also some games with a rapid rise in popularity that appear at the top of the list, such as *Fall Guys*, *Among Us* etc. These games have acquired many players due to streaming. Take *Among Us* for example, the increase of PCU (peak concurrent users) has exceeded 350 times through the streaming boom since June 2020 (Fig. 1).

However, some high-revenue online games with a steady DAU cannot benefit much from game live streaming and MMORPGs are the most typical examples. Besides *WoW*, none of MMORPGs move up to the top of the most viewed games list. They have made many efforts, including inviting famous streamers, adding in-game embedded streaming entrance, and giving rewards for streaming. But these approaches did not change the current situation of the low streaming popularity of MMORPGs.

C. Stephanidis et al. (Eds.): HCII 2021, CCIS 1421, pp. 196–204, 2021.
https://doi.org/10.1007/978-3-030-78645-8_25

Fig. 1. The user status of *among us*

Previous streaming-related studies mainly focused on the relationship among streaming platforms, streamers, and spectators. Few researchers paid attention to the games themselves and how games can better attract audiences through streaming and finally transfer audiences into players. Therefore, the following research questions are proposed:

1. What are the visual factors that make a game leading on the live streaming top list?

2. Can different types of games be presented in a certain version to help poor streaming performance games achieve better results?

This study will use mixed qualitative methods to evaluate whether game developers can improve spectators experience through the optimization of streaming visualization.

2   Design

2.1   Experimental Subject: Mobile MMORPG '*Revelation Mobile*'

The high revenue and long-term stable DAU make MMORPGs attractive to game industry investors. Unlike Buy-to-play games, MMORPGs need to keep constantly recruiting new players in order to continue their long-term operation. However, the MMORPGs' performance in streaming is not good, and the effect of redirecting and recruiting is limited as well.

In order to access accurate data, this research uses '*Revelation Mobile*' that was developed by NetEase as our experimental subject. In addition, the operation area will be shown up on the bottom right corner of the main interface of mobile games while PC games usually do not, which makes mobile game UI more complex during streaming.

2.2   Appropriate Game Interface for Streaming

According to the data in Steamstats (2021), we have targeted some online multiplayer games that gained a large number of players through streaming. *PUBG* is one of the most typical games which spread among streamers and then made viewers buy it (Sathyamurthy 2017). Besides, there are some other examples like *Fall Guys* and *Among Us*. These different types of games shared similarities in the game interface. We conducted a questionnaire survey regarding 'better game interface for streaming' and finally we summarized two directions.

Simple and Clear. For *PUBG*, *Fall Guys* and *Among Us*, the main interfaces of all three games are simple and clear (Fig. 2). These games removed all irrelevant non-diegetic UI elements (Carlsson and Pelling 2015) and only displayed specific UI in the edge area of the game interface (Young-In 2006).

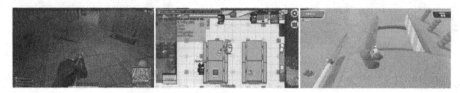

Fig. 2. The main interface of three games

These games made the entrance of other mechanisms outside the core gameplay image. Thus, viewers will pay more attention to gameplay itself in streaming.

Camera Angle of Characters. *PUBG*, compared to *Fall Guys* and *Among Us*, brings the view of character closer to players because its gameplay determines that the camera angle should focus on the surroundings and the field of view ahead of the character, while the other two games emphasize the whole scene. The design of two types of camera angle—long shot and close-up—is aligned with the information required to display by the gameplay, and, as a result, brings a better spectating experience to the audience (Fig. 3).

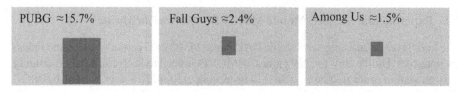

Fig. 3. The proportion of character in main interface

The Existing Interface of '*Revelation Mobile*'

Compared with those top games in streaming platforms, MMORPGs have significant differences in interface design. This is because the game type and gameplay are different among these games. *PUBG*, *Fall Guys* and *Among Us* are round-based games that each round may take 2–30 min. Instead, MMORPG players have continuous experience in a virtual world where all functions spread around the main interface (Fig. 4). Meanwhile, the default camera angle is long-shot which shows more gaming environment.

The complex UI layout and elements make the game hard to understand for viewers. Therefore, we have designed a new streaming mode for '*Revelation Mobile*' in response to UI and camera issues.

Fig. 4. The interface of 'Revelation Mobile'

2.3 The Design of Streaming Mode in *'Revelation Mobile'*

Scene. According to internal data, we learned that the most common activities in 'Revelation Mobile' are Raid, PVP Battle and Free Exploration. Compared with the real time streaming data, the content of streaming basically coincides with internal data. As a result, our streaming mode will be designed based on these three scenes.

UI Design. For the original interface of *'Revelation Mobile'*, we divided it into some different AOIs (Area of Interest) in the eye track test. According to the index of fixation duration and visit count, four levels of AOIs are defined: Most Views (Green) > Often Views (Yellow) > Occasionally Views (Red) > and Hardly Views (Grey).

Referring to many popular games' spectator mode, we extracted some essential UI elements in the design of the streaming mode which made the UI display more simplified. The new UI structure mode is basically consistent with the original game, and it can help reduce the difference which may cause cognitive difficulties (Carlsson and Pelling 2015).

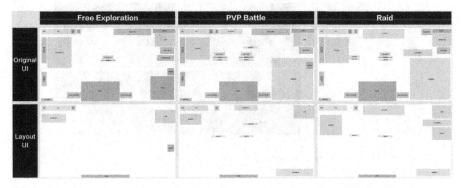

Fig. 5. The original UI layout and streaming UI layout

Figure 5 indicates three designs with different scenes and each of design has different elements.

In addition to the original interface as the control group, we also designed another UI interface which removed all elements for comparison to verify whether the UI is necessary for viewers.

Camera Design. Besides the complexity of in-game UI, the camera angle is another significant factor which will affect viewers' experience. Therefore, we designed two plans, long-shot and close-up, to see the extent of this influence.

UI and Prototypes. In our experiment, we made four sets of UI designs for streaming mode and one default interface as a control group. In total, there will be five plans: (1) Default Interface; (2) Long-shot camera & simplified UI; (3) Close-up camera & simplified UI; (4) Long-shot camera without UI; (5) Close-up camera without UI.

For each different plan, we made three prototype videos which correspond to typical scenes: Riad, PVP, and Free Exploration (Fig. 6).

From top to bottom：
1. Default Interface 2. Long-shot camera with simplified UI
3. Close-up camera with simplified UI 4. Long-shot camera without UI
5. Close-up camera without UI

Fig. 6. Screenshots of prototype videos in three scenes

3   Experiments

3.1   Participants

We have previously placed 67 recruitment questionnaires. Based on the participants' gaming and streaming experience, 30 participants were selected for the experiment. Participants included 19 men and 11 women, and 13 have played *Revelation Mobile* while 17 have not.

3.2   Experiment Design

In the previous recruitment, we summarized the factors that may affect the player's viewing experience while watching streaming. Three dimensions were mentioned the most: immersion, usability, and clarity.

In order to analyze the viewing experience better, mixed methods in this test were conducted with Likert scale questionnaire and in-depth interview, which would be incorporated into this analysis to form a multi-dimensional research.

We showed participants 5 different plans including the control group in random order, and each set of plans contains 3 prototype videos with different scenes. Participants were informed that those videos are replays of certain parts of streaming.

The participant needed to fill in a questionnaire every time after he/she finished watching a plan. The questionnaire consists of 15 items arranged in a Likert scale format, with spaces for specific and general comments.

The level of agreement includes: (1) Strongly disagree; (2) Disagree; (3) Neither agree nor disagree; (4) Agree; (5) Strongly agree.

When participants have filled all five questionnaires, we will have an in-depth interview to help participants share their thoughts regarding previous viewing experience.

3.3   Results

In General, Participants Prefer the Simplified UI Streaming Mode. Participants thought the original UI is too complicated that they can hardly see what the streamer is doing. The data is mainly reflected in the dimensions of clarity and usability (Table 1 and Table 2).

The viewing experience in the default version was considered to be messy and uncomfortable while the comments were more positive for two simplified UI versions.

Zhenyu: "The fourth one (Close-up & simplified UI) is the best. The content of the UI is relatively moderate, discarding some messy information, but retaining some core element. Everything can be easily understood."

On the other hand, streaming plans without UI are unpopular as well. The information presented on the interface is crucial for participants. Otherwise, they cannot know the gameplay or what the streamer is doing.

Shuhan: "I find it more uncomfortable if I cannot get any information."

Table 1. Differences in clarity

Question	Default	Long-shot & simplified UI	Close-up & simplified UI	Long-shot & no UI	Close-up & no UI
The UI layout and information are comfortable and will not affect the viewing scene/battle/character	2.7	4.4	4.3	3.7	3.7
The interface performance in the video makes me feel too complicated and looks very messy	3.7	1.4	1.5	1.1	1.3

Table 2. Differences in usability

Question	Default	Long-shot & simplified UI	Close-up & simplified UI	Long-shot & no UI	Close-up & no UI
I think all the UI elements appearing in the video are related to the gameplay that the streamer is participating	2.3	4.6	4.4	3.6	3.5
After watching the video, I think I can understand the operation of the corresponding gameplay	2.9	3.7	3.5	1.8	1.7

Participants have Different Preferences Among Different Scenes. For example, in free exploration, players will be more accepting of two no UI versions, because there is no learning or operation involved, which means there is no usability problem. But when it comes to Raid or PVP, the audience cannot get any specific information without UI, nor can they learn any operations.

Players are not Sensitive to the Camera Angle of the Character. Regarding the two different camera angles in the same set of UI content, some did not recognize the difference. There is basically no difference in questionnaire rating as well. The biggest rating difference is within 15%. Meanwhile, participants may prefer a more flexible angle adjustment.

Qidan: "I don't think there is any difference between the two plans(Long-shot and Close-up), at least I cannot say any difference."
Wangze: "Rather than defining the solid camera angle, I think it is better to just let the streamer switch the angle of the camera freely."

Participants who have Played *Revelation Mobile* and those who have not will also have Different Preferences. Those who have played this game have significantly higher acceptance of the default version because they are already familiar with *Revelation Mobile*'s existing UI. If some changes are made to the UI during the streaming, it may be confusing to them.

Table 3. Differences for two different game experience groups

Question (For Long-shot & simplified UI)	Have played	Have not played
The interface performance in the video makes me feel too simple and looks very monotonous	2.8	1.5
The UI layout and information are comfortable and will not affect the viewing scene/battle/character	4.0	4.7

Taking the Long-shot & simplified UI version as an example, participants who have played considered the simplified UI to be too simple and monotonous (Table 3).

Dehang: "For me, the original version is absolutely acceptable, and I will still use the original UI plan."

4   Conclusion

As stated at the outset, this research was driven by one main objective: to enhance the experience of watching MMORPG streaming with improved visualization plans. To accomplish this objective, four independent samples were designed—two from UI changes and two from camera angle settings. The findings from this research provide new evidence for the impact of UI on streaming, and it gives rich information about the players' preference in the streaming of MMORPGs.

References

Carlsson, C., Pelling, A.: Designing Spectator Interfaces for Competitive Video Games (Master's thesis) (2015)

Edge, N.: Evolution of the gaming experience: live video streaming and the emergence of a new web community. Elon J. Undergraduate Res. Commun. **4**(2), 22 (2013)

eMarketer. https://www.emarketer.com/content/twitch-on-pace-to-surpass-40-million-viewers-by-2021. Accessed 4 Jan 2021

Sathyamurthy, A.: What is PUBG? Why is it so popular? Is it worth playing? https://medium.com/iqube-kct/what-is-pubg-why-is-it-so-popular-is-it-worth-playing-470c28ed12d1. Accessed 4 Jan 2021

Steamstats. https://steamstats.cn/. Accessed 4 Jan 2021

SullyGnome. https://sullygnome.com/games/365/watched. Accessed 4 Jan 2021

Young-In, Y.: A contents analysis of massively multiplayer online role-playing games' graphic interfaces. In: 한국디지털디자인협의회 Conference, pp. 183–185 (2006)

NEO-WORLD: Enhancing Young People's Experience of Visiting Science Museum Through Gamification and Digital Technology

Ying Wang, Jiong Fu[✉], and Wenxuan Gong[✉]

Shanghai Jiaotong University, Shanghai, China
{WWWangying,redfox78}@sjtu.edu.cn

Abstract. In response to the current situation that the development of Chinese science museums has fallen behind the increasing sightseeing demand of the public in recent years, this study uses interviews, questionnaires and other qualitative and quantitative analysis methods to conduct user insights, and proposes an application called 'neo-world', to help young people aged 18–30 improve the experience of visiting the Science Museum. 'Neo-World' is a gamification app for science museums based on AR technology, with 'Socialization', 'Fun' and 'Big Data' as product highlights. Through the redesign of the exhibition process, the online and offline experience of the exhibition is combined. This research is based on the double diamond model, and this paper introduces the whole design process from user research to usability testing in detail.

Keywords: Science Museum · User experience · AR technology · Gamification · Heuristic evaluation

1 Introduction

Science museum, also known as technology museum, is an important part of public science education. However, research shows that the existing problems of Chinese science museum are obvious: insufficient exhibition and education resources; obsolete exhibition methods; single target audience (youth groups' needs are ignored) [1]. In short, Chinese science museum has been unable to meet the public's multi-level and diversified science needs in the information age [2].

Games are an important way for recreation and informal learning. Jack Ludden believes that games can stimulate learning and promote audience participation, and are a wonderful tool for museum tours [3]. At present, gamification learning is also becoming an important aspect of museum learning [4]. Many innovative museum gamification designs have emerged at home and abroad. At the same time, the development of digital technologies such as AR/VR is also constantly broadening the use context, exhibition mode and the communication and interaction between museum and the public [1]. However, many current museum gamification designs have a series of problems, such as single type, simple content, and not strong integration with museum themes [5]; Some good

© Springer Nature Switzerland AG 2021
C. Stephanidis et al. (Eds.): HCII 2021, CCIS 1421, pp. 205–213, 2021.
https://doi.org/10.1007/978-3-030-78645-8_26

designs mostly require high-tech equipment, have strong dependence on designers, or have poor universality.

Therefore, we designed NEO-WORLD, hoping to address the existing problems of the science museum, combine digital technology and gamification, and design a highly integrated and universal product for the science museum to enhance young people's tour experience.

2   User Research

In order to clarify the problems of science museum and the true demands of young people on museums, researchers conducted a comprehensive and in-depth investigation based on Double Diamond Model.

2.1   Qualitative Research and Data Collection

This survey recruited the main user group for Chinese museum tours -- mainly young people aged 18–30, and have certain museum or other creative exhibition experience. In the end, 11 users were recruited. The survey method intends to use a combination of observation method and diary study, and the research method was determined to be one-on-one semi-structured interviews, and the whole process was recorded by audio recording.

2.2   Data Analysis

The data obtained from the interview were analyzed. Based on Maslow's hierarchical theory of needs, the objective needs behind user behaviors were sorted out (Fig. 2). In general, users have higher expectations for entertainment, sociability and vivid and effective information delivery during museum visits.

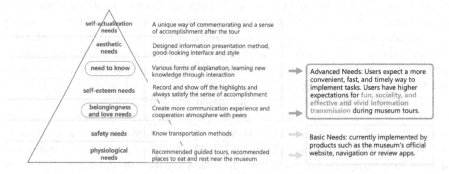

Fig. 2. Maslow's hierarchical theory of needs during visiting the museum

In order to help make more targeted market choices, researchers conducted a more in-depth user segmentation. Combining the mental space analysis of user samples, researchers located and integrated their behavior motivations according to the two dimensions of "experience entertainment - content professionalism" and "individual tour - group tour", and finally came to four types of user groups (Fig. 3): the social-entertainment pays attention to the entertainment and social companionship; the personal recreation tends to enjoy leisurely time alone; the self-consciousness is more concerned about the richness of the exhibition content and the quiet and comfortable atmosphere; the knowledge learner is generally high-skilled people, whose tour purpose is often to learn professional knowledge.

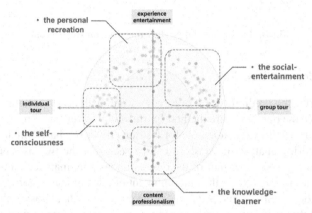

Fig. 3. User clustering in the museum tour experience (The colorful scattered points represent the requirement points of each sample)

Based on the conclusion of lack of fun and group museum experience optimization products, and the summary of user demands and pain points, the target user group is initially defined as the social entertainment and the personal recreation.

The Social Entertainment. Such users value the sense of entertainment and social companionship, and are not very purposeful in learning knowledge. They are more concerned that the interesting content in the museum can be used as a medium for interaction with peers or to generate new social topics. Taking into account their strong social attributes, this group of people can help science museums to effectively attract users.

The Personal Recreation. This type of users' tour is mainly relaxed and leisure, the itinerary is often unplanned, and they value the surprise and pleasure brought by the rich and vivid content in the museum. They enjoy the time alone. Such users often have unique insights that can unearth interesting highlights and are opinion leaders in the crowd. If they are given a unique and unforgettable tour experience, they will be very happy to share and recommend the corresponding venues to the public.

Combining the user journey analysis of the two types of users, researchers finally put forward a science museum tour experience optimization program with the keywords of 'Fun', 'Sociality', and "Big Data". And based on the existing specific pain points during the tour, the targeted product function transformation is proposed (Fig. 4).

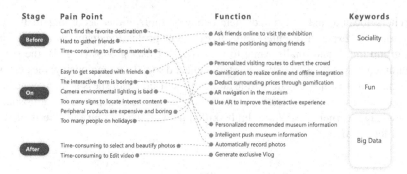

Fig. 4. Pain point and product function transformation

2.3 Verification and Revision

In order to verify the credibility and accuracy of the qualitative research conclusions, this section uses the questionnaire method for quantitative verification [6].

By setting up a self-evaluation scale for visiting propensity based on the two dimensions and clustering analysis in SPSS, it can be seen that the two user groupings are basically the same. The upper half of the entire dimensional map accounts for most of the number of users. Therefore, the entertainment of content is a major trend for users, which proves the rationality and accuracy of the early target user positioning.

In terms of the verification of other product functions, the questionnaire data shows that 42.81% of users who have visited science museums are not satisfied with the visiting experience. And Fig. 5 shows that adding gamification experience and new technologies is accepted by most users, and can greatly improve satisfaction, especially for the target users (the social entertainment, the personal recreation).

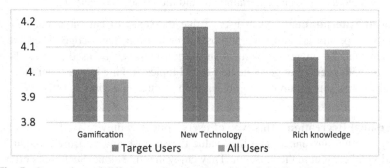

Fig. 5. Comparison of different ways to improve the satisfaction of science museums

Data shows that 49% of users are not satisfied with the museum's information acquisition channels and the process of beautifying photos and editing videos before and after the visiting. Therefore, designers can collect museum information for users and carry out timely, integrated and personalized recommendation, and provide users with photo records and generate exclusive Vlogs.

Through quantitative investigation and verification, researchers can conclude that: at present, the frequency of museum users visiting exhibitions is low, and user viscosity is not high. In terms of user types, those who pursue leisure and social entertainment account for the vast majority. In view of the current situation that users are not satisfied with the visiting experience, diversified exhibition forms, gamified design and application of new technologies all have a good effect on improving the satisfaction of both acquiring knowledge and improving the sense of entertainment.

3   Concept Design

Aiming at issues such as the obsolete and boring display methods of science museums, homogeneous and poor user experience and low user stickiness, this research started with insights into user needs, and discovered the gaps in the group and interesting categories of display experience upgrade products in the current market. The final solution is an AR-based gamification app for science museums – 'NEO-WORLD' (Fig. 6).

Fig. 6. 'NEO-WORLD' product concept map

3.1   Product Positioning

The product is aimed at the social-entertainment users and the personal recreation, and mainly serves young people aged 18–30 who love to travel, like to share, and are willing to accept new things. According to the results of demand insights, the product's characteristic functions include: (1) Intelligent push of museum information based on user preferences and behavior habits; (2) Personalized tour route recommendation based on user preferences and the number of companions, helping the museum to divert the crowd while providing users with a unique experience of multiple tours; (3) Combining the gamification of new technologies, using online and offline integration to extend the knowledge learning and experience of science museums; (4) Learning new knowledge in team games, creating meaningful forms of team interaction to help provide new social topics.

The specific form of the product is a collection and development game, and the user is given a role from the future earth that is about to be destroyed. In order to save the world civilization that is about to be burned, users need to return to the museum where human civilization was concentrated in the past, find and interact with the exhibits to obtain civilization fragments through offline exhibitions, and synthesize a new world containing different types of civilizations. The synthesized new world can be brought back online to continue developing (Fig. 7). Unlocking different worlds with the help of a wealth of offline tour experiences, and realizing world upgrades based on online app usage time are the main gameplay of this product. In the interaction with friends, you can not only use offline teams to start heavyweight tasks; you can also visit each other online, give away supplies, or participate in world cultivation rankings.

Fig. 7. 'NEO-WORLD' game world view

3.2 Product Highlights

According to the results of demand insights, the characteristic functions of the product can be summarized as: Fun, Sociality, Big Data.

Fun. In order to increase the entertainment experience of visiting the exhibition, researchers designed the process of visiting the exhibition into a game process. Each offline exhibition hall is designed as different new worlds (see Fig. 8), and users need to scan different products offline to obtain world fragments in order to obtain the corresponding new world.

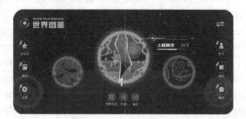

Fig. 8. World Atlas.

Sociality. In order to improve the sociality of the experience, researchers have made corresponding designs during the online and offline experience. Therefore, multiple people visiting mode can get more rewards and excitement during the offline tour. At the same time, the online game app has also set up a social section (see Fig. 9) to encourage users to visit each other and form continuous interaction.

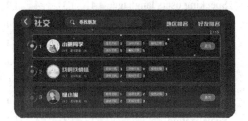

Fig. 9. Social section.

Big Data. When registering, users can fill in their personal information and interest preferences. With the help of the big data platform, the system will personally recommend museums and articles. For example, in the homepage museum Atlas (Fig. 10), a different homepage is personalized for each user, and different museums are integrated on the same page according to the user's preferences, so that users can check the tour progress.

Fig. 10. Museum Atlas.

4   Heuristic Evaluation

Finally, researchers employed a heuristic evaluation [8] from three aspects of User Interface, User experience and Problem Solving. During the evaluation, researchers recruited 5 professional designers to use the application under the record, finish the evaluation form (Table 1) and have a short interview. Finally we found that the evaluators are highly satisfied with the app's UI and user experience, but have doubts about the duration of problem solving. This also requires more long-term field research and panel study to improve.

Table 1. Evaluation form

Evaluation perspective		P1	P2	P3	P4	P5	Average
UI	Color combination	4	4	4	5	4	4.2
	Style consistency	5	4	4	5	5	4.6
Using experience	Specking users language	4	3	4	4	4	3.8
	Feedback	4	4	4	4	4	4.0
	Functions reasonable	4	3	3	4	4	3.6
	Navigation	3	3	3	4	3	3.2
Problem solving	Attractive	3	3	3	5	4	3.6
	Fun	3	3	3	4	3	3.2
	Socialization	2	3	4	3	4	3.2
	Duration	2	2	2	3	3	2.4

5 Conclusion

The product "NEO-WORLD" is an AR-based gamification app for science museums, which is designed to enhance the visiting experience of young people aged 18–30 in science museums. It combines online virtual games with offline physical displays and creates a personalized experience that combines personal leisure/team entertainment and knowledge learning by solutions of fun, socialization, and big data.

In the follow-up research, researchers will consider the promotion of the product in other types of museum usage scenarios, and improve the corresponding product functions. For example, the function of friends giving gifts to each other in different time and space; combine with multi-sensory interaction to form a variety of tourist touch points, and further improve the experience process.

References

1. Wang, K., Li, C.: Research report on science and nature museums in China (in Chinese). Nat. Sci. Mus. Res. 1(02), 5–13 (2016). Author, F., Author, S.: Title of a proceedings paper. In: Editor, F., Editor, S. (eds.) CONFERENCE 2016, LNCS, vol. 9999, pp. 1–13. Springer, Heidelberg (2016)
2. Huang, K., Li, W.: From the analysis of limitations to targeted practice——reflections on breakthrough the predicaments of theme exhibition in science and technology museum (in Chinese). Nat. Sci. Mus. Res. 2, 47–54 (2018)
3. Ludden, J.: Museum education in a technology-driven world – take SWOT analysis of museum game development as an example (in Chinese), Leming Huang, translated. China Mus. 1, 6–11 (2015)
4. Zhang, J., Xia, W., Yanfang, Y.: Museum learning in information age and its research outline (in Chinese). Open Educ. Res. 1, 102–109 (2017)
5. Chai, D.: Design and Implementation of RPG for Museum Education (in Chinese), pp. 2–3. Shandong University, Jinan (2007)

6. Banerjee, P.: About Face 2.0: the essentials of interaction design: Alan Cooper and Robert Reimann published by John Wiley & Sons, 2003, 576 pp, ISBN 0764526413. Inf. Visual. **3**(3), 223 (2004)
7. Zhang, Y.: The application of Censydiam model theory in character construction. Design **11**, 133–134 (2013)
8. Nielsen, J., Molich, R.: Heuristic evaluation of user interfaces. In: Proceedings of the SIGCHI Conference on Human Factors in Computing Systems Empowering People - CHI 1990, Seattle, pp. 249–256 (1990). https://doi.org/10.1145/97243.97281

Interacting and Driving

Comparative Study on Differences in User Reaction by Visual and Auditory Signals for Multimodal eHMI Design

Seonggeun Ahn[1] ⓘ, Dokshin Lim[1](✉) ⓘ, and Byungwoo Kim[2]

[1] Department of Mechanical Engineering, Hongik University, Seoul, Korea
doslim@hongik.ac.kr
[2] Hyundai Motor Group, R&D Division, UX Strategy Team, Hwaseong-si, Gyeonggi-do, Korea

Abstract. Autonomous vehicles (AV) from level 4 to level 5 will drive in traffic in a few years. The interaction between AVs and other road users could be supported by external human-machine interfaces (eHMIs). eHMIs have been suggested in various formats so far. In this study, an experiment was carried out to compare differences between visual and auditory signals. It assumed specific situations in which the AV is close to a pedestrian to assess the types of response, reaction speed, and warning. It was conducted with the Wizard of Oz technique, and individual experimental data from 18 participants were measured and analyzed. Research showed that a combination of a visual and auditory interface is most effective in understanding information. Also, auditory signals are advantageous in cognitive response in most cases, and such warnings were evaluated more highly. Therefore, it is required to consider an appropriate multimodal design when pedestrians need to pay attention.

Keywords: Autonomous vehicle · Multi-modal · Sound · eHMI · Eye tracking · Usability

1 Introduction

Autonomous vehicles (AV) will drive in today's traffic (i.e., manually driven traffic conditions) and so communication with other road users is one of the major challenges associated with the development of AVs [1]. In particular, insufficient communication with pedestrians can cause problems [2]. These problems may include not only safety issues, but also a decrease in confidence [3]. This could also lead to a decrease in social acceptance of AVs.

Under these circumstances, various studies on external human-machine interfaces (eHMIs) have been conducted to support interactions between AVs and other road users [4]. Various ways to convey AV intent are being explored. Most of the eHMI solutions that have been proposed so far mainly use techniques that rely on visuals [5].

However, a combination of auditory signals may also be used as a secondary aid, given situations in which other road users are visually careless, or unable to read or understand icons. Therefore, this study seeks to compare the differences between visual

© Springer Nature Switzerland AG 2021
C. Stephanidis et al. (Eds.): HCII 2021, CCIS 1421, pp. 217–223, 2021.
https://doi.org/10.1007/978-3-030-78645-8_27

and auditory signals in certain situations to determine the effect of auditory signals and to aid in the direction of multimodal design.

Studies that compare or evaluate existing eHMI solutions have mainly been conducted in studios or as VR studies. This study conducted an experiment by directly manufacturing LED display devices and attaching them to real vehicles. The vehicle was stationary in an underground parking lot and mixed naturally with the surrounding vehicles. The data was measured through an eye tracker worn by the subjects.

2 Method

2.1 Participants

A total of 18 participants (nine males, nine females) were recruited for the experiment. They consisted of undergraduate and graduate students (mean age = 24, range = 22 to 34) majoring in either mechanical engineering, industrial design, or smart design engineering, 15 of whom have a driver's license and seven who are actual drivers.

2.2 Experimental Design and Procedure

The experiment was designed to compare the difference in response between the visual and auditory signals sent by an AV in specific situations where pedestrians are close to the AV. Four scenarios were set up to measure and analyze the two responses to visual and auditory signals from the subject vehicle with their respective metrics. Details of each are described in 2.4. Each participant experienced all scenarios, whereas the order of the signals (either visual or auditory) was random to avoid time-based effects. Signals (visual, auditory), tasks, vehicle placement, and test routes were set differently for each scenario. The signals and instructions by scenario are shown in Table 1.

The experiment was conducted in a parking lot at Hongik University. Each session was started immediately after eye tracker calibration. It took approximately 10–15 min for a session including a short duration (of approximately less than one minute) between each experience.

2.3 Equipment

The vehicle used in the experiment was a Kia New Ray (2020 Ray) from a car rental service. For visual signals, a 102.4 cm × 12.8 cm and 256 × 32 pixel display was attached to the front and rear top of the vehicle and controlled by wire using Raspberry Pi. For audible signals, a Bluetooth speaker was attached to the lower left end of the vehicle's front glass. Technicians were in the driver's and rear seats of the vehicle for signal generation control and hid themselves to avoid exposure to the subjects during the experiment (Wizard of Oz technique).

An Ergoneers Dikablis eye tracker was used to measure the response and time of the subjects, and the same company's D-Lab was used as a measurement and analysis tool (Dikablis Professional Wireless DGW18032, D-Lab 3.55).

In Scenario 1, an LED device was used to record the start and end reference points of the experiment in the image, where a user presses a button and lights go out. The device was also used for eye fixation during the eye tracker calibration phase.

Table 1. Signals and tasks by scenario

Scenario No. and Task	Signal
1. Identify signals from parked vehicles and locate the vehicles they thought were called	████████████████████████
	Beep 1
	Display + sound shown above
2. Watch a video on a cell phone and walk straight past the front of the vehicle	████████████████████
	Virtual engine sound
3. Walk to the front of the subject vehicle and look inside through the windshield (read business cards, memos, etc. on the dashboard)	📷 블랙박스촬영중 * black box in operation
	Vehicle warning sound
4. Watch a video on a cell phone and pass the side of the vehicle from behind	주 🦌 의 * caution
	Beep 2

2.4 Measurements

Response actions were recorded for the visual and auditory signals that occur in each scenario. It was recorded differently depending on the scenario, and details are given in Table 2.

Time taken to find the vehicle was measured in Scenario 1. From the time the subject pressed the LED device to the time the vehicle was found was determined, and the LED device was pressed again.

Time taken for the eyes to move to the vehicle after recognition was measured in Scenarios 2 and 4. It was measured only when the signal was responded to, and the time was measured from the last time the eyes were on the cell phone to the time of arrival in the vehicle.

Warning was evaluated by the subjects in Scenario 3. After the Scenario 3 experiment, the subjects chose what they considered to be stronger warnings between the visual and auditory signals, which was recorded by the moderator.

Table 2. Response action by scenario

Scenario no.	Response action	Definition
1	Decide immediately	The decision was made when the subject vehicle was not fully exposed, or within 1.5 s after the subject vehicle was fully exposed
	Decide hesitatingly	Determined 1.5 s after the subject vehicle was fully exposed
	Cannot decide	No decision has been made/Another vehicle has been mistaken for the subject vehicle
2, 4	Stop walking	The subject stopped walking, but it was not observed in this experiment
	Pass by glancing	The eyes looked at the car once and did not stay for more than 1 s
	Pass by hesitatingly	The eyes looked at the car more than twice or stayed for more than 1 s
	Do not see/hear	The eyes are only on the cell phone without any response
3	Flinch and move back	After the signal is recognized, immediately retired/did not fulfill instructions
	See/hear but continue	The signal was recognized (eyes looked at the display/speaker) but the instructions were subsequently followed
	Do not see	Instructions continue to be fulfilled without any response (the eyes remain on the business card/note)

3   Results

3.1   Response Action

In Scenario 1, the rate of *Decide immediately* was slightly higher when auditory signals occurred compared to visual signals, and the rate of *Decide immediately* was the highest at 100% when visual and auditory signals were provided at the same time.

In Scenario 2, the *Do not see* rate (72.2%) when only visual signals occurred was more than twice the *Do not hear* rate (33.3%) when only auditory signals occurred. In addition, when an audible signal occurred, *Pass by hesitatingly* that was not observed when the visual signal occurred was observed.

In Scenario 3, there was an overwhelming percentage of *Flinch and move back* when auditory signals occurred. In addition, there were even cases of *Do not see* when a visual signal occurred.

In Scenario 4, the *Do not see* rate (50%) when only visual signals occurred was more than four times higher than the *Do not hear* rate (11.1%) when only an auditory signal occurred.

3.2 Time Taken to Find the Vehicle

When visual and auditory signals were provided at the same time, *Time taken to find the vehicle* was fastest (refer to Table 3). No significant differences were found between visual and auditory signals (p-value = .401). Refer to Table 4 for comparisons using paired sample t-tests.

Table 3. Simple descriptives for *time taken to find the vehicle*

	Mean	SD
Display	11.62	3.29
Sound	10.94	2.86
Display + Sound	8.48	1.74

Table 4. Paired sample T-test statistics for *time taken to find the vehicle*

		Statistic	p
Display	Sound	0.258	0.401
Display	Display + Sound	2.582	0.014
Sound	Display + Sound	2.371	0.016

Note. H_a Measure 1 > Measure 2

3.3 Time Taken for the Eyes to Move to the Vehicle After Recognition

Time taken for the eyes to move to the vehicle after recognition of a person who responded to both visual and auditory signals was faster when hearing the auditory signal (p-value < .001). Refer to Table 5–Table 6 for the data.

Table 5. Simple descriptives for *time taken for the eyes to move to the vehicle after recognition*

	Mean	SD
Display	0.427	0.207
Sound	0.221	0.102

3.4 Warning

In Scenario 3, only 11 subjects participated in the assessment of warning. Auditory signals were counted as a stronger warning effect by a larger number of participants (Fig. 1).

Table 6. Paired sample T-test statistics for *time taken for the eyes to move to the vehicle after recognition*

		Statistic	p
Display	Sound	4.42	<.001

Note. H_a Measure 1 > Measure 2

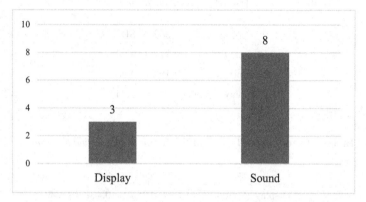

Fig. 1. Warning evaluation for visual and auditory signals

4   Discussion

First of all, it was noteworthy that auditory signals performed very well in cognitive responses compared to visual signals in practice. In Scenario 2, there were more than twice as many *Do not see* as *Do not hear*, and more than four times more in Scenario 4. Even in situations where the display was very close, such as Scenario 3, *Do not see* occurred. In addition, the proportion of *Pass by hesitatingly*, which was relatively more sensitive to signals and vehicles than *Pass by glancing*, was also more common when an auditory signal occurred.

The *response action* form in Scenario 3 shows a very similar appearance to the *warning*. Most of the subjects rated the auditory signal a stronger warning, with a higher rate of *Flinch and move back* when the auditory signal occurred in Scenario 3. In other words, there were overwhelming more cases where the auditory signal was alerted, and the task was not performed normally.

Time taken for the eyes to move to the vehicle after recognition was shorter for the auditory signal. This can be thought of as an analysis of the measured gaze from the flicking of the head that was fixed to look at the cell phone, which means a shorter time is a faster flicking of the head. Therefore, it can be interpreted that the subjects reacted more sensitively when the auditory signal occurred.

5 Conclusion and Limitations

It is regrettable that more experiments were not carried out in this study. Because the LED display had high enough luminosity, it was expected that *Don't see* would have a very small ratio, which in turn was not small. As a result, the number of samples that could be compared and analyzed was smaller than the total number of participants in the experiment because the time of the gaze's movement could not be measured if the subjects failed to respond to the signal. We could have achieved more statistically significant results if we had anticipated these problems and conducted more experiments. In addition, the displays and sounds used as visual and auditory signals in the experiment may have affected the subjects' responses to the signals. For auditory signals in particular, they can have a greater impact depending on the type and volume of the sound, where it occurs, etc. This is another point to study in multimodal design or sound design in the future.

Despite these limitations, the results showed that in situations where the pedestrian is close to the vehicle and visually careless, an auditory signal is advantageous to the cognitive response relative to a visual signal, and is a stronger warning. In particular, the experiment instructed subjects to watch videos on the cell phones to create visually careless situations, which were designed to target "smombies" (smartphone + zombie, people walking on the street with their heads down looking at smartphone screens), who have been cited as the cause of car accidents. These results suggest the need to adequately fuse auditory signals when designing eHMI for pedestrians.

Acknowledgements. This research was supported by the Hyundai Motor Group, and some work is part of research supported by the Basic Science Research Program through the National Research Foundation of Korea (NRF) funded by the Ministry of Education (No. NRF-2018R1D1A1B07045466).

References

1. Müller, L., Risto, M., Emmenegger, C.: The social behavior of autonomous vehicles. In: Proceedings of the 2016 ACM International Joint Conference on Pervasive and Ubiquitous Computing Adjunct - UbiComp 2016 (2016). https://doi.org/10.1145/2968219.2968561
2. Clamann, M., Aubert, M., Cummings, M.L.: Evaluation of vehicle-to-pedestrian communication displays for autonomous vehicles. In: TRB 96th Annual Meeting Compendium of Papers (2017)
3. Lundgren, V.M., et al.: Will there be new communication needs when introducing automated vehicles to the urban context? In: Stanton, N.A., Landry, S., Di. Bucchianico, G., Vallicelli, A. (eds.) Advances in Human Aspects of Transportation, pp. 485–497. Springer, Cham (2017). https://doi.org/10.1007/978-3-319-41682-3_41
4. Bazilinskyy, P., Dodou, D., de Winter, J.: Survey on eHMI concepts: the effect of text, color, and perspective. Transp. Res. F Traffic Psychol. Behav. **67**, 175–194 (2019). https://doi.org/10.1016/j.trf.2019.10.013
5. Benderius, O., Berger, C., Lundgren, V.M.: The best rated human-machine interface design for autonomous vehicles in the 2016 grand cooperative driving challenge. IEEE Trans. Intell. Transp. Syst. **19**(4), 1302–1307 (2018). https://doi.org/10.1109/TITS.2017.2749970

Efficient Communication of Automated Vehicles and Manually Driven Vehicles Through an External Human-Machine Interface (eHMI): Evaluation at T-Junctions

Hüseyin Avsar[✉], Fabian Utesch, Marc Wilbrink, Michael Oehl, and Caroline Schießl

Institute of Transportation Systems, German Aerospace Center (DLR), Braunschweig, Germany
{hueseyin.avsar,fabian.utesch,marc.wilbrink,michael.oehl,
caroline.schiessl}@dlr.de

Abstract. The absence of a human driver in an automated vehicle (AV) raises new challenges in communication and cooperation between road users, especially for ambiguous situations where road users would like to communicate their intention explicitly. This paper investigates the effect of a novel external human-machine interface (eHMI) which was designed to address this issue by signaling the AV's intention through a 360° LED light-band mounted outside of the AV. In a simulator study an eHMI interaction strategy was implemented that should convey the message "I am giving way" to a manually driven vehicle operated by participants waiting at a t-junction. The experimental study incorporated three t-junction scenarios where the AV had always the right of way but may yield to a driver waiting at the intersection. The intention of the AV was communicated either implicitly (braking) or implicitly and explicitly (braking and eHMI). It was analyzed whether participants would understand the AV's intention and accept the gap provided in front of the AV. Through participants' subjective ratings the understandability, the usability and the acceptance of the eHMI solution were evaluated. The results showed that the majority of participants (85%) understood the meaning of the eHMI signal after two interactions. Initial gap acceptance results showed a positive effect of the eHMI solution. The presence of an eHMI improved participants perceived safety and trust. Subjective ratings for usability and acceptance indicated that participants perceived this eHMI interaction strategy as easy to use and were willing to communicate with an AV in this way. The results of the present study will be used to investigate the beneficial impact of this eHMI interaction strategy further in more complex traffic scenarios.

Keywords: Automotive user interfaces · External human-machine interface · Automated vehicles · t-junctions · Gap acceptance · Usability

© Springer Nature Switzerland AG 2021
C. Stephanidis et al. (Eds.): HCII 2021, CCIS 1421, pp. 224–232, 2021.
https://doi.org/10.1007/978-3-030-78645-8_28

1   Introduction

Vehicle automation and advanced driver assistance systems have seen rapid technological development over the past years. This progress will enable the integration of highly and even fully automated vehicles (AV; SAE Level 4 and 5 [1]) on public roads [2]. Initially, AVs will share the road space with other non-automated vehicles and vulnerable road users in mixed traffic, such as cyclists and pedestrians. Road users have to communicate with each other in order to maintain road safety and the efficiency of traffic flow, especially in ambiguous situations. Therefore, road users can communicate their intention implicitly by adapting their speed and trajectories or explicitly by using visual and audible signals [3]. There are existing external human-machine interface (eHMI) designs, aiming to enable communication between AVs and other road users [4]. A study investigating various visual and audible eHMI solutions found a LED light band as a suitable solution to convey certain messages [5]. Especially the information whether an AV is giving way seems to be important for road users communicating with an AV [6]. Recent study results revealed that the presence of an eHMI can improve crossing initiation time, acceptance, perceived trust and safety ratings of AV-pedestrian interaction. Authors stated that the positive effects can only be achieved if the meaning of the eHMI signal is known by other road users and when implicit and explicit signals are consistent [7]. Other studies showed no effect of the eHMI on pedestrians' crossing initiations or their intention recognition times. In these studies, the deceleration strategy of the AV had a significant effect on the crossing initiation time, which suggests that the underlying scenario setting may have a significant effect on the eHMI benefit [8].

The vast majority of research in this area concentrates on AV-pedestrian interactions. In the present study, we transferred interaction strategies into an experimental setting to investigate the potential benefit of an eHMI solution in AV-vehicle interactions. The aim is to explore the understandability, the usability and the acceptance of an eHMI interaction strategy and to identify conditions that need to be fulfilled in order to observe a positive impact of the eHMI on gap acceptance results. The intention is to use the initial results of this explorative study to inform and optimize future studies. The present paper focuses on the final interaction design of the Horizon 2020 EU-Project 'interACT' [9]. The main focus was to convey explicit signals to other road users, using a 360° LED light-band mounted on the outside of the AV [10].

2   Method

The study was conducted in the Virtual Reality Lab of the German Aerospace Centre in Braunschweig (Fig. 1). Participants sat in an actual vehicle which was adapted so that throttle, brake pedal, steering wheel and indicators control the driving simulation (created in Unreal Engine 4). An active force-feedback system was utilized to simulate realistic steering force [11].

Fig. 1. DLR Virtual Reality Lab © DLR

A three factor within-subject design was used (2 signals × 3 gaps × 3 scenarios). Each participant conducted 27 trials interacting with an AV. The AV's signal type represents the first independent variable and varies between implicit (braking) or implicit and explicit (braking plus eHMI) and additional no signal as distracting trials. In order to reduce the predictability of AV behavior during the experiment a no signal condition where the AV is not giving way and continues with constant speed was included. An additional condition where the AV is communicating its intention to give way by sending explicit signal only was excluded because it was assumed that an inconsistency (as stated in [7]) with the vehicle behavior would impede participants understanding of the eHMI signal.

The gap size was considered as the second independent variable. Interaction between road users at t-junctions is only applicable if the approaching vehicle, which has the right of way, is within a certain range. The aim was to select one small gap which would be rejected by the majority of drivers, a medium gap which is large enough where approximately half of the drivers would accept it, and a large gap which would be accepted by the majority of drivers. To achieve this, the gap sizes from [12] were used (small – 4.5 s, medium – 5.5 s, large – 6.5 s).

The third independent variable was the scenario. Three different t-junction scenarios were defined [13] (Fig. 2) and included to increase the diversity of scenarios and identify possible scenario specific effects. Participants were instructed to turn either right into the main road (RTM), left into the main road (LTM) or left into the side road (LTS).

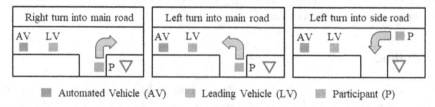

Fig. 2. Pictogram of the scenarios.

In order to provide a natural driving experience three closed test tracks were created, where participants drove from one intersection to another without any interruptions. Each test track featured nine t-junctions. The driving order of the t-junctions per test track was similar for each driver. However, to reduce position effects, the order of all conditions was randomized. Additionally, the order of the three test tracks was controlled by the latin square method for each participant. All t-junctions had similar starting conditions at each trial. The main and side roads were approximately perpendicular to each other. Turn direction and give way signs were placed at each intersection. A leading vehicle in front of the AV was set to create the desired gap and to stop participants at the intersections. Objects (houses, play grounds etc.) were set at positions that blocked the sight at the intersection, so participants could not adjust their speed to avoid a full stop. This ensured that participants would approach the intersection until they see the leading vehicle, stop at the intersection and decide whether to turn in front or behind the AV.

Fig. 3. InterACT VR-model BMW i3 with eHMI (maximum and minimum brightness).

For the implicit signal a specific deceleration profile was created for the AV. The deceleration was initiated one second after the AV decided to yield, which was equal to the point where the leading vehicle left the intersection. At that time the gap between the AV and its leading vehicle was approximately 37 m for the small gap, 45 m for the medium gap and 54 m for the large gap. The AV decelerated linearly to $-0,5$ m/s^2 within two seconds, from 30 km/h to 20 km/h. The AV continued with reduced speed until 25 m before the intersection. If participants did not turn in front of the AV, the eHMI was disabled, the AV accelerated and closed the gap. Otherwise, the AV adjusted its speed to avoid a critical situation. For the eHMI condition a cyan colored, slow pulsing light-band with a frequency of 0.4 Hz was used to convey the message 'I am giving way' to other road users (Fig. 3). Communication was considered as successful, if the AV was signaling that it is giving way and the participant accepts the offer and turns in front of the AV. The number of accepted and not accepted gaps were recorded in order to calculate the gap acceptance rate at each specific trial. After each trial, participants were asked why they had turned in front or behind the AV (open question). If applicable, the meaning of the eHMI signal was asked (open question). Then, participants rated their perceived safety (5-point scale, 'very unsafe' (1) – 'very safe' (5)), perceived support from the AV (supported – yes/no? and an open question – how?), and perceived gap size (5-point scale, 'small' (1) – 'large' (5)).

After completing the study participants were asked to rate the experienced eHMI signal in three questionnaires; System Usability Scale (SUS – 5 point scale) [14], Van der Laan Acceptance Scale (5 Point – Bipolar) [15] and a questionnaire based on the unified theory of acceptance and use of technology model (UTAUT – 5 point scale) [16]. To avoid positional effects, the order of questionnaires given was controlled using the latin square method.

20 (9 female) participants conducted the study. Every participant had a driving license. On average participants were 38 years old (SD = 17.5 years), ranging from 19 to 69 years. All participants drove their car on daily basis with an average of 10,900 km per year. An analyses of the ATI score [17] (M = 4.75, SD = 1.21) showed that the majority of the participants had a positive affinity for technology interaction.

3   Results

3.1   Effects Influencing Decision to Turn

The final data set which was used for further analysis included 337 trials (163 trials with implicit signal, 174 trials with implicit and explicit signals). The following analysis was structured with regard to four main categories:

Effect of gap size - Gap size was stated in 55% of the trials as one of the main reasons that influenced participants' decisions to turn. In 47% of the trials the gap size was perceived as large enough to turn safely in front of the AV. In 8% of the trials, participants decided to turn behind the AV because the gap in front of the AV was not large enough. Perceived gap size results may explain the reason why there were more trials where a gap was perceived large enough to turn safely. The perceived gap size reflected the order of the actual gap size (small – M = 3.42, SD = 0.32, medium – M = 3.91 SD = 0.36, large – M = 4.16, SD = 0.28). However, the gaps were perceived larger than anticipated, with the small gap size being already perceived as medium sized. There were only small differences between the means of perceived gap sizes. The gap acceptance rates at trials with medium gaps (M = 85%) were 1.15 times, and at trials with large gaps (M = 89%) were 1.19 times higher than trials with small gaps (M = 74%). Objective and subjective results show that participants were ready to accept smaller gaps than the smallest gap tested in this study.

Effect of implicit signal - Participants perceived in 56% of the trials that the AV tried to support them during the turn maneuver by braking only. However, only in 38% of the trials, participants stated that this factor influenced their decision to turn. The implicit signal was mentioned in 31% of the trials as a main factor that lead participants to decide to turn in front of the AV. At 7% of the trials, participants stated that they recognized a deceleration but it was too late to turn safely in front of the AV.

Effect of explicit signal - Percentages in this paragraph are based on the trials where the AV communicated its intention through implicit and explicit signal. Participants stated in 89% of trials that the AV tried to support them during the turn maneuver by sending explicit signals. However, only in 75% of the trials participants stated that the eHMI signal influenced their decision to turn. In 71% of trials participants turned in front of the AV indicating that the eHMI signal influenced their decision to turn. In 4% of trials the eHMI signal was seen by the participants but the meaning of the explicit signal was not understood. In these trials, participants preferred to turn behind the AV. This shows that in 96% of trials participants understood the meaning of the eHMI signal indicating that this interaction strategy was easy to learn. This finding is supported by responses to the understandability question. The results showed that 11 participants correctly understood the meaning of the explicit signal after the first trial. Another 6 participants required two interactions and 3 participants required 3 interactions until they had the desired understanding of the eHMI signal. Subjective ratings revealed that the eHMI has the potential to improve perceived safety. Mean perceived safety rating at trials where the AV was sending implicit and explicit signals (M = 4.58, SD = 0.21) were 1.09 times higher than the trials where the AV communicated its intention by using the implicit signal only (M = 4.22, SD = 0.30). The positive effect of the eHMI solution is also reflected in gap acceptance results. The mean gap acceptance rate at trials where the AV communicated its intention by using implicit and explicit signals (M = 91%) was 1.23 times higher than trials where the AV communicated its intention by using implicit signals only (M = 74%).

Effect of scenario - The results show that the scenario design might have an impact on gap acceptance rates (Fig. 4). The gap acceptance rates at LTM scenarios (M = 79%) were 1.04 times and RTM scenarios (M = 92%) were 1.22 times higher than LTS scenarios (M = 76%). The gap acceptance results and participants' responses of the right turn into main road scenario (RTM) show that there might be situations where no implicit and explicit communication is needed. However, trials with implicit signal by small gaps indicate that there might be a potential positive effect achieved through the eHMI. Left turn into main road (LTM) scenarios scored the second highest gap acceptance results. The impact of the explicit signal on top of the implicit signal is especially visible at trials with small and large gaps. Left turn into side road (LTS) scenarios scored the lowest gap acceptance.

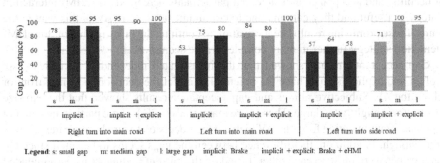

Fig. 4. Gap acceptance in all conditions.

3.2 Subjective Rating of the eHMI

Post-experiment questionnaires showed that the mean SUS score for AV with eHMI is 83.6 (SD = 10.4). Considering that the average SUS score is 68 [18], the results can be graded as excellent where users are more likely to recommend a product, which was in this case an AV communicating its intention using implicit and explicit signals, to others. Learnability (M = 4.23, SD = 1.01) and usability (M = 4.40, SD = 0.80) subscales of the SUS suggest that participants found the interaction with the AV equipped with an eHMI easy to learn and easy to use [19]. The two subscales of the Van der Laan acceptance scale; usefulness (M = 1.44, SD = 0.69) and satisfying scales (M = 1.40, SD = 0.70) showed that participants liked the interaction strategy (implicit and explicit signal) of the AV and found this way of communication useful. The results of the questionnaire, based on the UTAUT model, showed that participants found the eHMI concept useful (M = 4.30, SD = 1.12) and it supported them during the turn maneuver (M = 4.45, SD = 0.49). The visibility of the eHMI was good (M = 4.70, SD = 0.46) and the signal was clear and understandable (M = 4.50. SD = 0.68). Participants indicated that the eHMI did not distract them from driving (M = 1.45, SD = 0.82) and the communication with the eHMI did not require an increased attention (M = 2.35, SD = 1.00). Participants expressed that they have rather no concerns about interacting with the AV in this way (M = 2.00, SD = 1.17). Participants were not afraid that they do not understand (M = 1.65, SD = 1.03) the eHMI signal and they did not fear to have an accident (M = 2.00, SD = 1.17) while interacting with the AV. In future, participants would rather like to communicate with the AV in this way (M = 4.10, SD = 1.10).

4   Discussion and Recommendation for Future Work

Overall the results of this explorative study showed that the eHMI signal used was easy to learn and it was perceived as beneficial once it was understood, and it showed a positive effect on gap acceptance. Perceived safety results showed that participants feel safer when the eHMI was enabled. The majority of participants had the desired understanding of the eHMI message immediately after their first interaction. Questionnaire results for usability and acceptance indicated that participants perceived this eHMI interaction strategy as useful and they can imagine to communicate with an AV in this way in the future. These promising results are motivating to continue the investigation of this eHMI interaction strategy further in more complex traffic scenarios.

Gap acceptance results showed that the investigated independent variables (gap, implicit and explicit signal) have the potential to affect the decision to turn in front or behind the AV. Subjective ratings and gap acceptance results showed that the gap size selection was slightly too large. There were many trials (47%) where participants did not require a communication from the AV to make their decision to turn because the gap was large enough. In addition, the difference between the gaps seems to be small since the mean values were close to each other. Based on the current findings it is recommended to set a difference between gap levels of at least 1 s. For future simulator studies it is recommended to conduct pilot studies to determine suitable gap sizes for a simulator study because they seem to differ from real world traffic observation studies.

Another variable which might impact the effect of the eHMI solution is the implicit signaling. The implicit signal was present in each trial where the AV tried to communicate its intention to give way. The reduced perception of the implicit signal (56%) may depend on the fact that participants made the majority (89% of the trials) of their decision based rather on the gap size and not so much on the vehicle behavior (implicit signaling). Even an adjustment in gap size selection as stated above will not eliminate the fact that some participants will consider only the gap size to make their decision to turn, which should be considered in future studies.

The initial gap acceptance results might be only applicable for the implemented deceleration strategy. The authors assume that the change in gap size and consequently the intention that the AV is giving way can be recognized better with a stronger deceleration (implicit signal). This might diminish the effect of the explicit signal. Various deceleration strategies can be created and tested in order to find the optimal interaction strategy at specific situations.

The gap acceptance results showed that there might be scenario specific effects. The biggest effect of the explicit signal on top of the implicit signal was observed in left turn into side road scenarios. The reason why the explicit signal had a bigger effect at this scenario might be explained with the viewing angle and the location that participants had in these particular trials. Being on the same road as the leading vehicle and the AV makes observing a change in gap size and speed difficult. The viewing angle might be better for scenarios where participants were instructed to turn from a side road into a main road. The difference between right turn into main road and left turn into sideroad might be caused by the fact that drivers have to pay attention to both directions if they want to turn left.

The measures which were taken to ensure similar starting conditions at each trial (e.g., leading vehicle and objects blocking sight) were efficient and should be implemented in future studies. To distinguish the effect of the eHMI from the braking it would be interesting to investigate the effect of the eHMI only in future studies. However, previous research shows that the explicit signals have to be consistent with the implicit signals otherwise this could lead to negative effects (e.g., accidents or near miss situations) [6].

In this study the effect of the eHMI on AV-vehicle communication was only measured through the gap acceptance rate and subjective ratings. For future studies, it can be expected that improved intention recognition time through the eHMI will probably lead to reduced waiting times and reduced acceleration behavior at vehicles waiting at the intersection. This and other objective measures like minimum distance between vehicles, post encroachment time and longitudinal jerks could provide additional information about the quality of communication.

Repeated successful interaction might lead to over trust in the capabilities of the AV. The driver waiting at the intersection has the responsibility for his turn maneuver, even if the AV is giving way. Drivers could get the feeling once they see the eHMI signal it is safe to turn without paying attention to the rest of the traffic. This could lead to critical situations. Applying realistic scenarios with multiple road users could have a trust calibrating effect. The explicit signal is visible to everybody which can cause another critical situation where drivers could think that they are the intended interaction partner of the AV, but the AV is actually communicating to another road user.

References

1. On-Road Automated Driving (ORAD) Committee: Taxonomy and Definitions for Terms Related to Driving Automation Systems for On-Road Motor Vehicles (2021). https://www.sae.org/standards/content/j3016_202104/
2. Bansal, P., Kockelman, K.M.: Forecasting Americans' long-term adoption of connected and autonomous vehicle technologies. Transp. Res. Part A Policy Pract. **95**, 49–63 (2017). https://doi.org/10.1016/j.tra.2016.10.013
3. Fuest, T., Sorokin, L., Bellem, H., Bengler, K.: Taxonomy of traffic situations for the interaction between automated vehicles and human road users. In: Stanton, N.A. (ed.) AHFE

2017. AISC, vol. 597, pp. 708–719. Springer, Cham (2018). https://doi.org/10.1007/978-3-319-60441-1_68

4. Dey, D., Habibovic, A., Löcken, A., et al.: Taming the eHMI jungle: a classification taxonomy to guide, compare, and assess the design principles of automated vehicles' external human-machine interfaces. Transp. Res. Interdisc. Perspect. **7**, 100174 (2020). https://doi.org/10.1016/j.trip.2020.100174

5. Mahadevan, K., Somanath, S., Sharlin, E.: Communicating awareness and intent in autonomous vehicle-pedestrian interaction. In: Mandryk, R., Hancock, M., Perry, M., et al. (eds.) Proceedings of the 2018 CHI Conference on Human Factors in Computing Systems (2018)

6. Merat, N., Louw, T., Madigan, R., et al.: What externally presented information do VRUs require when interacting with fully Automated Road Transport Systems in shared space? Accid. Anal. Prev. **118**, 244–252 (2018). https://doi.org/10.1016/j.aap.2018.03.018

7. Lee, Y.M., Madigan, R., Garcia, J., et al.: Understanding the messages conveyed by automated vehicles. In: Proceedings of the 11th International Conference on Automotive User Interfaces and Interactive Vehicular Applications, pp. 134–143. Association for Computing Machinery, New York (2019)

8. Madigan, R.: interACT D.6.3. Impact assessment of the new interaction strategies on traffic cooperation, traffic flow, infrastructure design and road safety (2020). https://www.interact-roadautomation.eu/wp-content/uploads/interACT D6.3_v1.0_FinalWebsite.pdf

9. Schieben, A.: Designing cooperative interaction of automated vehicles with other road users in mixed traffic environment (2017). https://www.interact-roadautomation.eu/. Accessed 20 Mar 2021

10. Weber, F.: interACT D4.2 Final interaction strategies for the interACT Automated Vehicles (2019)

11. Fischer, M., Richter, A., Schindler, J., et al.: Modular and scalable driving simulator hardware and software for the development of future driver assistence and automation systems. In: New Developments in Driving Simulation Design and Experiments, pp. 223–229 (2014)

12. Fitzpatrick, K.: Gaps accepted at stop-controlled intersections (1991)

13. Wilbrink, M.: interACT D1.1 definition of interACT use cases and scenarios (2018). https://www.interact-roadautomation.eu/wp-content/uploads/interACT_WP1_D1.1_UseCases_Scenarios_1.1_approved_UploadWebsite.pdf

14. Brooke, J.: A "quick and dirty" usability scale. In: Jordan, P.W., Thomas, B., Weerdmeester, B.A, McClelland, A.L. (eds.) Usability Evaluation in Industry. Taylor, London (1996)

15. van der Laan, J.D., Heino, A., de Waard, D.: A simple procedure for the assessment of acceptance of advanced transport telematics. Transp. Res. Part C Emerg. Technol. **5**, 1–10 (1997). https://doi.org/10.1016/S0968-090X(96)00025-3

16. Venkatesh, V., Morris, M.G., Davis, G.B.: User acceptance of information technology: toward a unified view. MIS Q. **27**, 425 (2003). https://doi.org/10.2307/30036540

17. Franke, T., Attig, C., Wessel, D.: A personal resource for technology interaction: development and validation of the affinity for technology interaction (ATI) scale. Int. J. Hum.-Comput. Interact. **35**, 456–467 (2019). https://doi.org/10.1080/10447318.2018.1456150

18. Sauro, J.: Measuring usability with the system usability scale (SUS) (2011). https://measuringu.com/sus/. Accessed 07 Mar 2021

19. Lewis, J.R., Sauro, J.: The factor structure of the system usability scale. In: Kurosu, M. (ed.) HCD 2009. LNCS, vol. 5619, pp. 94–103. Springer, Heidelberg (2009). https://doi.org/10.1007/978-3-642-02806-9_12

User Experience of Connected Services in Cars

Kathrin Ganser[1,2][✉][iD], Tanja Kojic[2][iD], and Jan-Niklas Voigt-Antons[2,3][iD]

[1] P3 Automotive GmbH, Stuttgart, Germany
[2] Quality and Usability Lab, Technische Universität Berlin, Berlin, Germany
[3] German Research Center for Artificial Intelligence (DFKI), Berlin, Germany
`jan-niklas.voigt-antons@tu-berlin.de`

Abstract. Connected Services are innovative, mostly web-based features of state-of-the-art cars that offer the user a broad range of entertainment, communication, or navigation functionalities. The trend towards connectivity and the accompanying customer expectations can be seen as one of the driving forces for the automotive industry's rapid transformation. Car manufacturers can achieve a competitive advantage only through an extensive service portfolio coupled with great user experience, which is expressed through the fulfillment of underlying customer needs. In this paper, a scoring model for evaluating the user experience of Connected Services based on need structures was designed and tested on ten different cars. A general impression of the user experience can be drawn by focusing on need structures. In the future, this can be translated into product requirements which may lead to more satisfied customers.

Keywords: User experience · Need structures · Connected car

1 Introduction

The trend towards connectivity and digitization is approaching our daily lives more and more, and has hugely affected the automotive industry in recent years. Cars have become connected and are now able to interact with each other and the internet. They come with web-based services, which transform them into personal communication-centers and interactive workplaces. At the same time, general product development has shifted from a manufacturer- to a user-centered approach. In today's hyper-connected world, a single recommendation can reach a far greater group of people, which is why the experience of these users has become the center of development processes. Users are being involved from the beginning for iterative evaluation phases and their feedback enables companies to identify flaws in products and services early on.

1.1 Connected Cars and Connected Services

Connected Services are innovative, web-based features offered by state-of-the-art car-models, which have the ability to connect to the Internet and can interact

C. Stephanidis et al. (Eds.): HCII 2021, CCIS 1421, pp. 233–240, 2021.
https://doi.org/10.1007/978-3-030-78645-8_29

with it as well as smart devices [3]. The goal of integrating these services is to enhance the value for drivers by providing a broad range of entertainment and functionalities to transform the car into a personal communication center.

The following shows an exemplary classification of these services: **Personalization Services** enable the user to individualize the car to her desires. **Smartphone Connection Services** enable a seamless integration of Smartphone data into the car. **Navigation Services** enable navigation based on real-time traffic data, the maximum range, and/or proximity to charging or fuel stations. **Entertainment Services** enable a broad range of entertainment (Spotify, InTune Radio, YouTube). **Communication Services** enable the communication between the driver and the outside world (E-Mail, messages, telephone conferences, calendar updates). **Remote App Services** enable the remote control of car features through mobile devices (e.g., Lock/Unlock, sending navigation routes).

Many of these services are either operated through the in-car head unit, a smartphone, or a web portal and can therefore be associated with the field of human-computer-interaction (HCI).

1.2   User Experience

User experience describes the user's impressions and quality perceptions that result from the usage of a system and hence has a strong subjective character. These perceptions can either be from a pragmatic or a hedonic nature [5].

In contrary to the former, the latter are independent of a specific context of usage and address underlying psychological needs [4]. The fulfillment or non-fulfillment of these needs has an impact on user experience and hence can be used as an evaluation method [7].

Research shows that there exist specific sets of needs that are of relevance in certain circumstances. Table 1 lists a set of needs that were identified to be of relevance in the context of human-computer interaction and experience design [6]. Since the interaction with Connected Services can be regarded as such, this set was used as the baseline for all further actions in this study.

Table 1. Relevant needs in the context of experience design

Need	Description
Autonomy	*'Feeling of being the cause of your own actions [...].'*
Competence	*'Feeling of being very capable and effective in your actions [...].'*
Relatedness	*'Feeling of having regular contact with people who care about you [...].'*
Stimulation	*'Feeling of getting plenty of enjoyment [...].'*
Security	*'Feeling of safety and in control of your life [...].'*
Popularity	*'Feeling of being liked, respected and having influence on others [...].'*

Various methods for measuring need-fulfillment, such as interviews, focus groups and questionnaires, have been studied and standardized forms can be found in literature. In the context of Connected Cars, many studies have been conducted (e.g., see [3]), but none of them focused on the interaction of the user with Connected Services.

2 Scoring Model

The conception of a scoring model for the User Experience of Connected Services in cars was the focus of this work. In the first step, a qualitative survey was conducted to identify the relevant underlying needs for each Connected Service category. All findings were afterward tested with a higher sample in a quantitative survey. The final scoring model was then tested on a trial basis to evaluate the user experience of Connected Services in ten different cars.

2.1 Qualitative Survey

The set of candidate user needs that is shown in Table 1 was used together with the Connected Service categories as the theoretical basis for the qualitative survey with one little adjustment.

It was assumed that the need 'relatedness' is not necessarily relevant in this context since Connected Services are generally designed in a way that they can be operated by the driver only. The need was therefore not investigated.

Method. For the study, 12 participants of different genders and ages, all in possession of a driver's license, were selected. They were asked to fulfill two use cases for every Connected Service category in two different test cars (Tesla Model S, VW eGolf). Whereas the first use case served as a short introduction for participants to get to know the system and its functionalities, the second one aimed at creating a specific hypothetical scenario for which they should elaborate their thoughts and feelings. During the survey, they were accompanied and interviewed by an expert following a semi-structured interview-guideline which had been designed by the authors of this study. To get a more in-depth view of their feelings and needs, participants were additionally asked to use the 'Think aloud'-technique while completing their tasks [9].

Data Analysis. All statements were analyzed, interpreted, and categorized based on the underlying needs by the authors of this research. Since a semi-structured interview technique was used, those statements were mostly spontaneous narratives [10].

Results. The aim of the qualitative survey was to identify and allocate the relevant user needs for each Connected Service category based on the real user's experiences and thoughts. Tabular 2 shows how many of the 12 participants indicated the relevance of the fulfillment of the specific need for each service category. The results show that different needs are of the highest relevance for different service categories. Security was thereby mentioned the most and seems to be of high priority in the context of Connected Cars. The aspect of 'Time Saving' had been proactively mentioned by the participants many times and was therefore added for further investigation. All needs that had been mentioned twice or more were used as the baseline for the following quantitative survey. All other needs were not further investigated.

Table 2. Resulting allocation of candidate needs to Connected-Service-categories based on user data

	Autonomy	Competence	Popularity	Stimulation	Security	Time saving
Personalisation	–	1	2	5	4	5
Smartphone C.	2	3	–	–	3	2
Navigation	2	2	–	–	2	1
Entertainment	4	2	2	1	–	–
Communication	3	–	3	1	6	–
Remote App	2	–	4	–	4	1

2.2   Quantitative Survey

A quantitative online-survey was then conducted to validate the findings of the qualitative survey, namely the identified relevant user needs for each service category. Additionally, participants were asked to rank all identified needs within each service category based on their perceived relevance.

Participants. The data of 86 participants, out of which 37,2% were female (F) and 62,7% were male (M), was collected. All of them were in the possession of a driving license, almost 60% owned a car and another 28% were using carsharing solutions. The age distribution showed that 59,3% of them were 20–30 years old (YP) and the remaining 40,7% were older than 30 years (P).

Method. For the quantitative validation of the findings, a questionnaire was designed, which consisted of two sections. In the first section, the participants were given the identical hypothetical scenario used in the qualitative survey for each service category as well as one statement per identified need. They were asked to rate their agreement to this statement with a 5-stage Likert scale ranging from 'I agree' to 'I disagree'. In the second section, all needs should be ranked based on the perceived relevance, thereby forcing participants to make a clear decision as to which need has a higher priority.

Data Analysis. The medium need-rating was determined for every group (F, M, YP, P) and every need in every service category (see (1)). All results were then analyzed using a univariate ANOVA, which enables comparison of the variance of response tendencies (see (2)) between two groups and the variance of response tendencies within a group [8]. This method allows assessing whether the medium need-ratings of the relevant groups can be regarded as differing significantly.

$$\overline{N_{(x,y)}} = \frac{1}{n} \sum_{i=1}^{n} N_{(x,y)_i} \tag{1}$$

with $0 \leq \overline{N_{(x,y)}} \leq 4$ and $x = F; M; YP; P$ and $y = 0; F; M; YP; P$
and $n = number\ of\ participants\ per\ group_{(x,y)}$

$$\sigma = \sqrt{\sigma^2} = \sqrt{\frac{1}{n-1} \sum_{i=1}^{n} (N_{(x,y)_i} - \overline{N_{(x,y)}})^2} \tag{2}$$

Based on the need-rankings from the second section of the questionnaire a medium rank for each need (see (3)) was determined and then transformed into a weight for each need within each service category. Additionally, a Wilcoxon Rank-Sum test was conducted to determine a significant difference in the average rank between two needs within a service category. The null hypothesis for this test states that the ranks of both groups are similar, hence a rejected null hypothesis at a chosen significance level ($\alpha = 0,05$) indicates a significant variance in the average rank and therefore shows if one need is perceived significantly more or less relevant than others. Since only two values can be compared at a time, the test had to be performed with every possible need-combination within each service category. To reduce the risk of identifying significant differences that are non-existing (Type I error), a Bonferroni correction to test each individual hypothesis was performed [1].

$$\overline{MR_{N,C}} = \frac{1}{n} \sum_{i=1}^{n} (n_{N,C} - MR_i) \tag{3}$$

with $0 \leq \overline{MR_{N,C}} \leq (n_{N,C} - 1)$ and $n_{N,C} = 3; 4$ and $n = 86$

$$W_{N,C} = \frac{\overline{MR_{N,C}}}{n_{N,C} - 1} * \frac{1}{\sum_{i=1}^{n_{N,C}} \frac{\overline{MR_{i,K}}}{n_{N,C}-1}} \tag{4}$$

with $0 \leq W_{N,C} \leq 1$ and $\sum_{i=1}^{n_{N,C}} W_{i,K} = 1$

Results. Corresponding to the structure of the questionnaire, the results of the research will be presented in two separate sections with the first one introducing the comparison of the medium need-ratings between the groups and the second one focusing on the ranks of the needs.

Need-Statements: Table 3 shows all needs where a significant variance ($p < 0.05$) between female ($\overline{N_{(F)}}$) and male ($\overline{N_{(M)}}$) participants was identified. In general, male participants showed a significantly higher rating of the needs within a Connected Service category. The two different age groups, young professionals ($\overline{N_{(YP)}}$) and professionals ($\overline{N_{(P)}}$), only showed significance ($p < 0.05$) in rating popularity in the context of communication-services, where professionals showed a higher average rating than young professionals. For all other investigated needs, no significance could be identified.

Need-Ranking: Table 4 shows the average rank for each need within a service category $(\overline{MR_{N,C}})$, the variance (σ) and the calculated weight within each service category $(W_{N,C})$. The weight indicates how important the need is perceived within a service category. Additionally, the results of the Wilcoxon rank rum test indicate if one need is rated significantly more or less important within a

Table 3. Results of the univariate ANOVA comparing the gender- and age-groups

Gender							
Service category	Need	$\overline{N_{(F)}}$	$\overline{N_{(M)}}$	DFn	DFd	F	p
Entertainment	Autonomy	2,563	3,148	1	82	5,314	0,024
	Competence	3,156	3,815	1	82	5,799	0,018
Remote App	Security	3,063	3,611	1	82	4,610	0,035
	Popularity	3,313	3,963	1	82	7,303	0,008
Age							
Service category	Need	$\overline{N_{(YP)}}$	$\overline{N_{(P)}}$	DFn	DFd	F	p
Communication	Popularity	2,490	3,114	1	82	6,475	0,013

Table 4. Relevant needs for each service category and the corresponding weighting

Service category	Need	$\overline{MR_{N,C}}$	σ	$W_{N,C}[\%]$
Personalisation	Security	1,709	0,78	0,285
	Stimulation	1,860	0,82	0,310
	Popularity	1,919	1,06	0,085
	Time saving	0,512	1,12	0,320
Smartphone connection	Security	1,477	1,22	0,246
	Autonomy	0,919	1,00	0,153
	Competence	1,744	1,17	0,291
	Time saving	1,860	0,78	0,310
Navigation	Autonomy	1,058	0,54	0,353
	Security	1,047	0,89	0,349
	Competence	0,895	0,95	0,298
Entertainment	Autonomy	0,883	0,83	0,295
	Popularity	0,930	0,86	0,310
	Competence	1,186	0,72	0,395
Communication	Autonomy	1,035	0,56	0,345
	Security	1,535	0,71	0,512
	Popularity	0,430	0,76	0,143
Remote App	Security	1,314	0,63	0,438
	Autonomy	1,209	0,79	0,403
	Popularity	0,477	0,74	0,159

service category. Popularity for example is rated as significantly less relevant than the other identified needs, Security, Stimulation and Time Saving, within the service category Personalisation. The same applies for Autonomy in the context of Smartphone Connection. With a weight of only 15.3% Autonomy is seen as the least relevant need. The identified relevant needs in the Navigation- and Entertainment-category on the other hand are perceived as equally relevant.

3   Live Test

To show the feasibility of the final scoring model, it was used as the basis for the evaluation of Connected Services of ten different cars on a trial basis during a live event. The online-questionnaire was transformed into an evaluation sheet that was applicable to rate the actual implementation of Connected Services in-car. The resulting average value was then used to compare the implementation of the Connected Services based on the need-fulfillment. As this test is not part of the current publication the results are not described.

4   Discussion

In this paper, a scoring model for evaluating the user experience of Connected Services based on the users' need structures was designed. Since the interaction with Connected Services can generally be regarded as human-computer-interaction, an existing set of needs for this context was used as a baseline. It was hypothesized that some candidate needs are perceived as more relevant in certain categories for Connected Services than others.

The study was conducted in two steps, a qualitative and quantitative survey. In the first part, relevant needs for each service category were identified. The results were then validated in the second part of the study through an online survey with high sample size. Participants were given two different tasks, rating the relevance of certain needs and ranking the relevance of these needs within a service category.

Nevertheless, further research needs to be conducted in this regard. In this study, participants indicated, that it was hard to understand or imagine certain scenarios and statements. Autonomy was named as being the hardest to understand which is why this particular need should be investigated in more depth during future studies. Apart from need-fulfillment, there are additional influencing factors on user experience that have to be taken into account. Brand awareness, for example, can have an impact on the perceived amount and quality of available services in-car and therefore the user experience [2].

Finally, it has to be stated that actual user experience evaluation can only be conducted by users who have used the product over a long period of time and are therefore familiar with all its features and functionalities [11]. We believe that this approach can be used as a baseline for further evaluation of HCI applications especially in the context of Connected Cars. The analysis of such innovative technologies needs to be conducted regularly in order to ensure up-to-date results.

5   Conclusion

User experience includes both, pragmatic and hedonic quality perception of users as well as further influencing factors. Even though this paper focuses on hedonic quality perceptions and the underlying need structures, it has to be made clear that a holistic evaluation of user experience of Connected Services can only be conducted by integrating pragmatic aspects as well. The field of usability testing has been at the center of HCI-research for a long time and there exist many standardized methods to measure the usability of interactive products. An optimal user experience can only be achieved if the interaction also meets usability requirements.

This research has covered a broad range of services and a heterogeneous target group and therefore stays on a low level of detail. By reducing the number of relevant Connected Services or by reducing the diversity of the target group more detailed future work results can be generated even to the extend of receiving specific product requirements.

References

1. Armstrong, R.A.: When to use the Bonferroni correction. Ophthalmic Physiol. Opt. **34**(5), 502–508 (2014)
2. Brakus, J.J., Schmitt, B.H., Zarantonello, L.: Brand experience: what is it? How is it measured? Does it affect loyalty? J. Mark. **73**(3), 52–68 (2009)
3. Coppola, R., Morisio, M.: Connected car: technologies, issues, future trends. ACM Comput. Surv. **49**(3), 46:1–46:36 (2016)
4. Hassenzahl, M.: Experience design: technology for all the right reasons. Synt. Lect. Hum. Center. Inform. **3**(1), 1–95 (2010)
5. Hassenzahl, M., Burmester, M., Koller, F.: Der user experience (ux) auf der spur: Zum einsatz von www. attrakdiff. de. Usability Professionals, pp. 78–82 (2008)
6. Hassenzahl, M., Diefenbach, S., Göritz, A.: Needs, affect, and interactive products-facets of user experience. Interact. Comput. **22**(5), 353–362 (2010)
7. Hassenzahl, M., Eckoldt, K., Diefenbach, S., Laschke, M., Len, E., Kim, J.: Designing moments of meaning and pleasure. Experience design and happiness. Int. J. Des. **7**(3) (2013)
8. Huber, F., Meyer, F., Lenzen, M.: Grundlagen der varianzanalyse (2014)
9. Konrad, K.: Lautes denken. In: Mey, G., Mruck, K. (eds.) Handbuch Qualitative Forschung in der Psychologie, pp. 476–490. Springer (2010). https://doi.org/10.1007/978-3-531-92052-8_34
10. Mayring, P.: Qualitative inhaltsanalyse. In: Baur, N., Blasius, J. (eds.) Handbuch qualitative Forschung in der Psychologie, pp. 601–613. Springer, Wiesbaden (2010). https://doi.org/10.1007/978-3-531-18939-0_38
11. Väänänen-Vainio-Mattila, K., Roto, V., Hassenzahl, M.: Towards practical user experience evaluation methods. In: International Workshop on Meaningful Measures: Valid Useful User Experience Measurement, vol. 11, pp. 19–22 (2008)

In-Vehicle Frustration Mitigation via Voice-User Interfaces – A Simulator Study

Sandra Krüger[(✉)], Esther Bosch[(✉)], Klas Ihme[(✉)], and Michael Oehl[(✉)]

Institute of Transportation Systems, German Aerospace Center (DLR), Braunschweig, Germany
{Sandra.Krueger,Esther.Bosch,Klas.Ihme,Michael.Oehl}@dlr.de

Abstract. Frustration while driving possibly causes accidents. Therefore, frustration-aware in-vehicle systems that help to mitigate frustration have gained increasing attention. Until now, little is known about effective interaction strategies. Recent studies indicate that voice interfaces enable natural human-machine interaction and thus could be valuable for in-vehicle frustration mitigation. Hence, this study investigates the effects of a frustration mitigation assistant via a voice-user interface as well as on its related user experience (UX) and users' acceptance ratings. For this, a voice-user interface was designed that interacted with participants exposed to frustrating traffic situations during simulated driving. Frustration mitigation was adapted to these situations and based on well-established general emotion regulation theories. Participants (N = 13) took four drives in a driving simulator. Three drives served as distraction from the actual study goal while in the experimental drive participants were frustrated by goal-blocking traffic situations integrated in the simulation. In order to compare frustrating drives with and without voice interface, one half of the participants experienced the intervention of the voice-user interface (assisted group) while the other half drove without voice assistant (control group). After each drive the subjective frustration level was assessed via self-report. In addition, participants who experienced the voice interface were asked about their UX and acceptance. The frustration ratings indicate a tendency towards reduced frustration in the assisted compared to the control group. UX and acceptance ratings indicate positive experiences. Thus, this study provides first insights into the feasibility of assistants via voice-user interfaces for in-vehicle frustration mitigation.

Keywords: Voice assistants · Frustration · Driver state · Affect-aware systems · Empathic vehicles · User experience

1 Introduction

Frustration is a negative affective state that may occur when goal-directed behavior is blocked [1]. Recent research has confirmed that drivers often experience frustration in the vehicle due to different goal-blocking factors such as dense traffic, weather conditions or red lights among others [2]. In the car, persistent frustration can be problematic because it may result in more risky and aggressive behavior and can negatively influence cognitive processes relevant for driving, so that performance may deteriorate [3–5]. Therefore

© Springer Nature Switzerland AG 2021
C. Stephanidis et al. (Eds.): HCII 2021, CCIS 1421, pp. 241–248, 2021.
https://doi.org/10.1007/978-3-030-78645-8_30

reducing frustration while driving is an important step towards improving road safety (e.g., zero-vision of the European Commission, as expressed in [6]).

However, many of the sources of frustration in the traffic system revealed by [2] are hard to eliminate by design, so that other solutions to reduce the experienced frustration in the car need to be found. One promising idea is the development of frustration-aware intelligent vehicles that are able to detect and react to the driver's current level of frustration in real time [7–9]. Recent studies have addressed the development of methods for interpreting the frustration level based on video recordings of the face, speech analysis or physiological data (e.g. [9–12]) that can form the basis for the real-time recognition of frustrated driving. Still, on the contrary, little is known about effective human-machine interface (HMI) strategies to counteract frustration and its negative impacts.

The work of Gross [13] provides interesting insights on how humans regulate their emotions in general and hence it can form the theoretical fundament for designing in-vehicle strategies for mitigating frustration. It postulates that humans can alter their emotional responses by choosing strategies out of five emotion regulation families: situation selection, situation modification, attentional deployment, cognitive change and response modification. Earlier studies have already made attempts to implement frustration-reducing HMI interventions in a vehicle context based on this theory. For example, Harris and Nass [14] used speech message to guide the driver to a cognitive change after experiencing frustration. Based on the results of an expert workshop, Löcken et al. [7] generated strategies to support attentional deployment by guiding attention to an optimal fuel consumption instead of frustrating traffic or by supporting response modi-fication through a kind of biofeedback based on an in-vehicle ambient light. In addition, Zepf and colleagues described a driving assistant combining elements from the strate-gies attentional deployment and situation modification indicating its potential to improve the user experience of frustrated drivers [9]. Another study presented on this conference employed a user-centered approach to develop interaction strategies for the mitigation of frustration in the car based on user focus groups [15]. This study revealed that users pre-fer strategies that support situation selection, situation modification as well as cognitive change and that speech-based interaction in a voice-user interface (VUI) is favorized. Interestingly, older users (>65 years) tended to find cognitive change particularly helpful [15].

Based on these considerations, we infer that in-vehicle driving assistants based on VUIs supporting drivers to regulate their frustration through cognitive change bear good prospects for effective frustration mitigation during driving. Hence, we designed and implemented a demonstration of an in-vehicle frustration mitigation assistant interacting with drivers via a VUI. This assistant is triggered in situations of high frustration and addresses the driver with short voice messages that help to change the cognition of the current frustrating situation. Here in this paper we present the set-up of the assistant and its evaluation in a driving simulator study with users.

2 Method

A total of $N = 13$ participants (7 male) aged between 19 and 53 years took part in the study ($M = 29.69$, $SD = 11.66$). On average, participants held their driver's license for 11.77 years (SD = 11.25) and about half of them drove less than 5,000 km per year (53.8%), 30.8% drove 10,000 to 20,000 km, and 15.4% reported to drive 20,000 to 30,000 km per year. To control for participants' affinity for technology, the standardized ATI questionnaire [16] was used with a six-point Likert scale ranging from *completely disagree* (1) to *completely agree* (6). Technology affinity was quite high (M = 4.35, SD = 0.59).

Each participant drove four drives of five minutes length in a driving simulator in a within-subjects block design. Participants could control a virtual car in a driving simulation via a steering wheel and the pedals. Sounds of the driving simulation as well as the voice-user interface (VUI) were presented via loudspeakers.

Fig. 1. Examples of frustrating goal-blocking situations during the experimental drive: slow lead vehicle (left) and short green phases at left-turning traffic light (right).

Before each drive, participants read a user story which described reason and destination of the drive. Three of the drives served as a distraction from the actual study's goal and were driven as the first, second and fourth drives. They were designed without emotion-triggering events and participants reached the destination by a direct route with moderate traffic. During the experimental drive (third drive) with or without frustration mitigation assistant, frustration was triggered by a phone call and high traffic volume integrated in the simulation. This drive's user story told the participants to imagine that they had bought tickets to meet friends at the cinema at 6 p.m. after work but were held up by their boss shortly before closing time, so that they left work only five minutes before 6 p.m. Because frustration can be intensified by additional time pressure [17], a phone call from the friends, who were already waiting at the cinema, was played shortly after the start of the drive. Since frustration is experienced while goal-directed behavior is blocked [1], participants experienced a high traffic volume during the drive. On the highway, two slow-moving transport vehicles turned in one after the other, which could not be overtaken due to oncoming vehicles. The route to the cinema then led into a town with speed limit. Shortly before the destination, the participants were instructed via the VUI to turn left at a traffic light. Five cars were already lined up in front of the traffic light. Due to the short green phases, only one car could turn per phase and the last car missed a green phase, so that the waiting time was extended further. In total, the participants waited about two minutes at the traffic light until they could turn into the target street leading them to the cinema. Figure 1 shows the goal-blocking traffic situations from the driver's point of view.

The design of the experimental drives in terms of event design and induced time pressure was similar to experimental manipulations in previous studies that assessed the subjective experienced frustration of the driver [5, 12, 18, 19]. In order to investigate the frustration mitigating effect of the voice assistant, one half of the participants experienced the intervention of the frustration mitigation assistant via the voice-user interface during the experimental drive (assisted group), while the other half of the participants drove without the intervention (control group). Based on previous research, a female rather human-like sounding voice was artificially generated using speech synthesis. The interface voice was professionally produced by SoundReply GmbH [20] using a text-to-speech system. The content of the sentences was based on the findings of previous research. In focus group studies on the development of frustration-sensitive assistance systems, voice assistants were rated as potentially helpful in a frustrating situation caused by traffic. Addressing individual and situational needs by announcing useful information, i.e., situation modification, for example, about the current traffic situation or information to calculate the fastest route turned out to be particularly helpful [8, 15]. Therefore, in the present experiment, sentences were created to provide participants with useful information about the journey. In addition to situation modification, the sentences were presented in such a way that the drivers could activate an additional emotion regulation strategy also rated in previous research as very helpful for mitigating frustration in such situations, i.e., cognitive change [15]. Cognitive change was used in order to enable change the driver's view on the frustrating situation and consequently facilitate frustration mitigation. Each frustrating event was followed by the interaction with the frustration mitigation assistant (see Table 1).

Table 1. Goal-blocking situations and sentences verbally provided by the assistant (VUI).

Goal-blocking situation	Sentence presented via VUI
First slow lead vehicle	"You still have plenty of time before the targeted arrival."
Second slow lead vehicle	"You're still making it on time."
Car queue at traffic light	"Stay relaxed. Before the movie starts there's also the commercial part." "According to my calculations, you will arrive only 5 min later than planned."
Last car in front misses green phase	"You almost reached the destination. There are only 500 m to go."

After each drive, participants filled in a questionnaire that consisted of an adapted from a German version of the positive and negative affect scale (PANAS, [21]). More specifically, the emotions words: 'active', 'distressed', 'interested', 'excited', 'upset', 'scared', 'proud', 'enthusiastic', 'ashamed', 'awake', 'nervous', 'determined', 'alert', 'confused', 'afraid' (from the original PANAS) and 'insecure', 'frustrated', 'angry', 'sad', 'surprised', 'relaxed', 'inspired' (own addition) were rated on a 5-point Likert scale from 1 = *not at all* to 5 = *extremely*. Additionally, participants in the assisted experimental group (n = 5) filled in the following standardized questionnaires about their user experience (UX) and acceptance of the frustration mitigation assistant presented via the VUI: Modular evaluation of key components of UX (meCUE), i.e., Module 3 (rated on a 7-point scale from 1 = *strongly disagree* to 7 = *strongly agree*) consisting of the subscales 'positive' and 'negative emotions' and additionally Module 5 as an overall evaluation of the assistant in one item rated from −5 = *bad* to + 5 = *good* [22]. The German version of the Van der Laan Acceptance Scale including nine opposite adjectives rated on a bipolar scale from −2 to + 2 consisting of the subscales 'satisfaction' and 'usefulness' [23].

After all drives, participants filled in their sociodemographic data and a German version of the 9-item Affinity for Technology Interaction Scale (ATI) rated on a 6-point scale from 1 = *completely disagree* to 6 = *completely agree* [16].

3   Results

The results of the manipulation check based on frustration levels across all drives showed that the manipulation did not work for three participants as they did not experience frustration during the experimental drives. Therefore, three participants had to be excluded from the following analyses. Thus, N = 10 participants experienced frustration and could be included in the further analyses. Since the data collected did not meet the requirements for parametric tests, non-parametric tests were used to evaluate the data. Effect sizes were interpreted according to Cohen (1992) as follows: r = .10 corresponds to a weak effect, r = .30 corresponds to a medium effect and r = .50 corresponds to a strong effect. All statistical analyses are performed using IBM SPSS Statistics software (version 21) with α-levels of .05.

The frustration-reducing effect of the assistant was tested by comparing the subjective frustration level between the assisted group and the control group. Descriptively, the frustration level was lower in the assisted group than in the control group (M = 3.0, SD = 1.0 vs. M = 3.4, SD = 0.9) (see Fig. 2).

According to the Man-Whitney U-test, the difference was not significant (p > .05, r = .19). The effect size corresponded to a small effect. However, a tendency of the frustration-reducing effect due to the assistant is recognizable.

With regard to acceptance and UX the assistant for frustration mitigation was rated on the Van der Laan subscales usefulness (M = 0.85, SD = 0.89) and satisfaction (M = 0.45, SD = 1.11) as positive, but on a moderate level. The UX subscales of meCUE module 3 on positive and negative emotions showed that the assistant was associated with positive emotions (M = 4.27, SD = 1.41), while negative emotions were activated less (M = 2.67, SD = 1.27). Regarding the item for an overall UX evaluation (meCUE module 5), the assistant was rated as good with a mean of (M) = 2.00 (SD = 2.35). Overall, the results indicated positive experiences with the frustration mitigation assistant via the VUI.

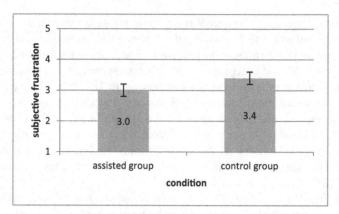

Fig. 2. Mean subjective levels of frustration and standard errors during the experimental drive for the assisted group and the control group. Values 1 = *not at all*, 5 = *extremely*.

4   Discussion

Up to date there has been only little research regarding HMI interaction strategies helping to mitigate the user's frustration level in frustrating driving situations. In this study we designed and implemented a demonstration of an in-vehicle frustration mitigation assistant interacting with drivers via a VUI. This assistant was triggered in a driving simulator in situations of high frustration and addressed the driver with short voice messages that should help to change the cognition of the current frustrating situation, i.e., to reappraise a specific driving situation in order to mitigate the driver's experienced frustration due to this specific driving situation. Here, we presented the set-up of this assistant and its first evaluation in a driving simulator study with users.

The results illustrate that participants in the assisted group (descriptively) showed less frustration than participants in the control group. This clarifies that the intervention of the voice assistant successfully reduced the frustration level of the drivers and could therefore also be applied in a real driving context. Despite the small number of participants and the brevity of the experiment, a small effect size can be seen. The subjective ratings regarding acceptance and UX differ between individuals. While the participants' acceptance of the assistant is moderate, the UX rating is positive.

Future studies need to further evaluate whether the descriptive results reported here can be confirmed with more participants. In this study participants took a short five-minute drive in the driving simulator and could therefore only interact with the voice assistant in a few frustrating situations. A prolonged exposure to frustration and longer interaction times with the assistant in other driving situations or other frustration-triggering events could be valuable to further study the effectiveness of the designed voice assistant. Nevertheless, this study provides valuable insights into the feasibility of in-vehicle frustration assistants via a VUI supporting emotion regulation and hence frustration mitigation based on strategies like situation modification reappraisal through cognitive change.

References

1. Lazarus, R.S.: Progress on a cognitive-motivational-relational theory of emotion. Am. Psychol. **46**, 819–834 (1991). https://doi.org/10.1037/0003-066X.46.8.819
2. Bosch, E., Ihme, K., Drewitz, U., Jipp, M., Oehl, M.: Why drivers are frustrated: results from a diary study and focus groups. Eur. Transp. Res. Rev. **12**(1), 1–13 (2020). https://doi.org/10.1186/s12544-020-00441-7
3. Jeon, M.: Towards affect-integrated driving behaviour research. Theoret. Issues Ergon. Sci. **16**, 553–585 (2015). https://doi.org/10.1080/1463922X.2015.1067934
4. Berkowitz, L.: Frustration-aggression hypothesis: examination and reformulation. Psychol. Bull. **106**, 59–73 (1989). https://doi.org/10.1037/0033-2909.106.1.59
5. Lee, Y.-C.: Measuring drivers' frustration in a driving simulator. Proc. Hum. Factors Ergon. Soc. Ann. Meet. **54**, 1531–1535 (2010). https://doi.org/10.1177/154193121005401937
6. European Commission: White Paper 'Roadmap to a single European Transport Area - Towards a competitive and resource-efficient transport system' (2011)
7. Löcken, A., Ihme, K., Unni, A.: Towards designing affect-aware systems for mitigating the effects of in-vehicle frustration. In: Boll, S., Löcken, A., Schroeter, R., et al. (eds.) Adjunct Proceedings, AutomotiveUI 2017: The 9th International ACM Conference on Automotive User Interfaces and Interactive Vehicular Applications, September 24–27, Oldenburg, Germany. Association for Computing Machinery, New York, pp. 88–93 (2017)
8. Oehl, M., Ihme, K., Drewitz, U., et al.: Towards a frustration-aware assistant for increased in-vehicle UX. In: Janssen, C.P., Donker, S.F., Chuang, L.L., et al. (eds.) Proceedings of the 11th International Conference on Automotive User Interfaces and Interactive Vehicular Applications: Adjunct Proceedings, pp. 260–264. ACM, New York (2019)
9. Zepf, S., Stracke, T., Schmitt, A., et al.: Towards real-time detection and mitigation of driver frustration using SVM. In: Wani, M.A. (ed.) 18th IEEE International Conference on Machine Learning and Applications: ICMLA 2019, Boca Raton, Florida, USA, 16–19 December 2019. Proceedings, pp. 202–209. IEEE, Piscataway (2019)
10. Requardt, A.F., Ihme, K., Wilbrink, M., et al.: Towards affect-aware vehicles for increasing safety and comfort: recognising driver emotions from audio recordings in a realistic driving study. IET Intel. Transport Syst. **14**, 1265–1277 (2020). https://doi.org/10.1049/iet-its.2019.0732
11. Franz, O., Drewitz, U., Ihme, K.: Facing driver frustration: towards real-time in-vehicle frustration estimation based on video streams of the face. In: Stephanidis C., Antona M. (eds.) HCI International 2020 - Posters. HCII 2020. CCIS, vol. 1226, pp. 349–356. Springer, Cham (2020). https://doi.org/10.1007/978-3-030-50732-9_46
12. Ihme, K., Unni, A., Zhang, M., et al.: Recognizing frustration of drivers from face video recordings and brain activation measurements with functional near-infrared spectroscopy. Front. Hum. Neurosci. **12**, 327 (2018). https://doi.org/10.3389/fnhum.2018.00327
13. Gross, J.J.: Emotion regulation: current status and future prospects. Psychol. Inq. **26**, 1–26 (2015). https://doi.org/10.1080/1047840X.2014.940781
14. Harris, H., Nass, C.: Emotion regulation for frustrating driving contexts. In: Tan, D., Fitzpatrick, G., Gutwin, C., et al. (eds.) Conference Proceedings and Extended Abstracts/The 29th Annual CHI Conference on Human Factors in Computing Systems: CHI 2011, Vancouver, BC, May 7–12, 2011, p. 749. ACM, New York (2011)
15. Oehl, M., Lienhop, M., Ihme, K.: Mitigating frustration in the car: which emotion regulation strategies might work for different age groups? Paper in Proceedings of HCII 2021 (accepted)
16. Franke, T., Attig, C., Wessel, D.: A personal resource for technology interaction: development and validation of the affinity for technology interaction (ATI) Scale. Int. J. Hum. Comput. Interac. **35**, 456–467 (2019). https://doi.org/10.1080/10447318.2018.1456150

17. Rendon-Velez, E., van Leeuwen, P.M., Happee, R., et al.: The effects of time pressure on driver performance and physiological activity: a driving simulator study. Transp. Res. Part F Traffic Psychol. Behav. **41**, 150–169 (2016). https://doi.org/10.1016/j.trf.2016.06.013
18. Ihme, K., Dömeland, C., Freese, M., et al.: Frustration in the face of the driver. IS **19**, 487–498 (2018). https://doi.org/10.1075/is.17005.ihm
19. Roidl, E., Frehse, B., Höger, R.: Emotional states of drivers and the impact on speed, acceleration and traffic violations - a simulator study. Accid. Anal. Prev. **70**, 282–292 (2014). https://doi.org/10.1016/j.aap.2014.04.010
20. Homepage how.fm. https://www.how.fm/. Accessed 24 Mar 2021
21. Krohne, H.W., Egloff, B., Kohlmann, C.-W., et al.: Untersuchungen mit einer deutschen Version der 'Positive and Negative Affect Schedule' (PANAS). Diagnostica **42**, 139–156 (1996)
22. Minge, M., Riedel, L., Thüring, M.: meCUE – Ein modularer Fragebogen zur Erfassung des Nutzungserlebens. In: Boll, S., Maaß, S., Malaka, R. (eds.) Mensch und Computer 2013: Interaktive Vielfalt, pp. 89–98. Oldenbourg Verlag, München (2013)
23. van der Laan, J.D., Heino, A., de Waard, D.: A simple procedure for the assessment of acceptance of advanced transport telematics. Transp. Res. Part C Emerg. Technol. **5**, 1–10 (1997). https://doi.org/10.1016/S0968-090X(96)00025-3

Analysis of Driver Judgment and Reaction by Different Levels of Visual Information on eHMI

Yongwhee Kwon[1] , Dokshin Lim[1(✉)] , and Byungwoo Kim[2]

[1] Department of Mechanical Engineering, Hongik University, Seoul, Korea
doslim@hongik.ac.kr
[2] R&D Division, UX Strategy Team, Hyundai Motor Company,
Hwaseong-si, Gyeonggi-do, Korea

Abstract. As autonomous vehicles make their debut on public roads, communicating with other drivers via an external human-machine interface (eHMI) has become crucial for road safety. Our work explores required visual information levels by observing participants' judgment time in the driver's seat and by measuring the ability metrics of eHMI implemented on autonomous vehicles (AVs) passing by. We evaluated about 10 eHMI design alternatives, and measured the time from perceiving the rear-facing eHMI of an AV passing by to the moment the participants decide how to drive using eye tracking glasses. Also, we surveyed subjective evaluations of how participants feel about seeing the eHMIs. The results show that using text reduces the time to drivers' judgment, and fast flashing effects and the color red effectively draw attention and give warning. The results suggest that it is essential for future AVs to use text and practical visual elements when other drivers on the road require quick reactions.

Keywords: Autonomous vehicles · External communication · eHMI · Driver judgment · Eye tracking

1 Introduction

As autonomous vehicles (AVs) appear on the road, the means of communication between AVs and other traffic participants are increasing in importance. The driver expresses intent through eye contact or hand gestures while facing a pedestrian or other driver on the road. Since an AV cannot control the movement of the vehicle, the occupants must express their intentions. Therefore, many AV concepts apply a variety of communication methods (external display, light band, projector, sound). In order to provide information to external human machine interfaces (eHMIs) such as external displays and light bands, it has become important to choose how and in what contexts (text, images, light patterns, colors) to do so. Most concepts focus on yielding when a pedestrian tries to cross the road. However, according to a study conducted by Debargha Dey (2017) [1] with only one implicit eHMI of an AV designed like a safe driver, expression of intention through vehicle movement, most interactions with pedestrians are possible. In addition, a study by

© Springer Nature Switzerland AG 2021
C. Stephanidis et al. (Eds.): HCII 2021, CCIS 1421, pp. 249–256, 2021.
https://doi.org/10.1007/978-3-030-78645-8_31

Michael Clamann [2] showed that even though a 42-cm-high display was attached to the front of the vehicle and a message was provided, pedestrians were more dependent on the existing crossing strategy than the message on the display. Another study by Debargha Dey (2019) [3] also shows that people are more dependent on vehicle movement and implicit information.

We acknowledged that the role of eHMIs is limited and considered how eHMIs can help in reducing accidents, the goal of AV technology. We also explored whether eHMIs could provide a strong warning to the drivers of other vehicles.

2 Method

Although there are various visual elements of eHMIs, they are typically divided into colors and blinking in light bands and text and images in displays. The difference in these visual elements is expected to change the time and subjective assessment made by observers to recognize and judge messages in eHMIs.

2.1 Participants

The experiment was conducted in October 2020. We recruited total 18 subjects (nine males, nine females, mean age: 24). Since it was needed to observe and respond to eHMIs from the perspective of passengers, driver's license holders who are used to looking around and reacting in the road environment were selected.

2.2 Apparatus

Two vehicles were used for the study (Kia Ray, Renault Samsung SM5). The vehicles in which the subjects rode were conventional sedans so that they could be identical to the view of a general driver on the road. The Kia Ray was chosen as the vehicle on which the eHMI was attached because it was easy to install and observe due to vertical rear glass and low overall width, and the eHMI prototype was manufactured according to the width.

The eHMI prototype (shown in Fig. 1) was made by fixing four LED display modules in a row. The dimensions are 1,024 mm × 128 mm (256 mm × 128 mm × 4 modules) and the resolution is 256 × 32. The top four pixel rows were used as light bands and the rest of the pixels at the bottom were used as a display. On the back of the display module, Raspberry Pi was attached to display an eHMI UI image.

A simple clicker (see below on the right in Fig. 1) was made of green, blue, and red 10 mm LEDs and switches. The subjects were asked to press the green button if they thought it was okay to proceed with the vehicle they were in, the blue button if they thought they should slow down and be careful, and the red button if they decided they needed to urgently reduce speed.

Eye tracking was implemented through a head-mounted Dikablis/D-Lab system (Dikablis Professional Wireless DGW18032, D-Lab 3.55, Ergoneers GmbH, Manching).

Fig. 1. eHMI prototype on Kia Ray (Left)/Clicker (Right).

2.3 eHMI Designs

The eHMI consisted of a light band and display. Each scene was designed as dot images to match the pixels of the eHMI protocol (see Table 1). The cyan color suggested by the SAE J3134 standard [4] was used for the light band, along with orange and red, which are used in existing traffic signals. Each design had a different flash, color, text, and graphic arrangement to see each element's effect on perception. Flash refers to the light band, which uniformly and alternately glowed with full brightness and then turned off according to Debargha Dey's classification [5].

Table 1. eHMI designs used in the experiment.

No	Scene	Color	Text	Graphic	Flash	Display
1	(No display) Cyan (Autonomous driving)	Cyan	X	X	X	
2	U-turn	White	X	O	X	
3	(No display) Orange (Caution)	Orange	X	X	X	
4	(No display) Red (Warning)	Red	X	X	X	
5	(No display) Orange (Caution)	Orange	X	X	3 Hz	
6	(No display) Cyan (Autonomous driving)	Cyan	X	X	1 Hz	
7	(No display) Orange (Caution)	Orange	X	X	1 Hz	
8	Kickboard ahead	Orange	O	O	3 Hz	주 ⚠ 의
9	School safety zone	Red	O	O	X	⚠ 어린이보호구역
10	Parking	White	X	O	X	P

2.4 Experimental Design and Procedure

The experiment was conducted simultaneously with the response time assessment and the subjective assessment of eHMI designs. When each subject arrived at the test site, eye tracking glasses were worn and calibration was conducted. After calibration, the subjects got in Car 1 and sat in the driver's seat. The procedure and layout are shown in Fig. 2.

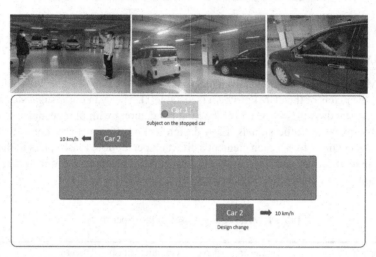

Fig. 2. Procedure and layout of the experiment.

We asked the subjects to assume that the vehicle was driving on the road (momentarily stationary but driving) in a second lane. The clicker was put on the steering wheel of Car 1. The subjects were asked to decide the expected future movement of the Car 1 by pressing buttons on the clicker each time Car 2 overtook Car 1 to the left.

After manipulating the clickers, subjective evaluations of "Draw attention," "Give warning," and "Make a feeling of urgency" of each eHMI design were measured using a five-point Likert scale questionnaire. Car 2 continued circulating around the route where Car 1 was parked and changed the design of the eHMI for the evaluation at each turn.

2.5 Metrics

Subject gaze data was obtained from the Dikablis system. We measured the judgment time by measuring from the time the subject first stared at the eHMI to the time the LED was lit by pressing the clicker button after the decision. Also, the movement of the subject's gaze was visualized with a heatmap. Subjective evaluations of "Draw attention," "Give warning," and "Make a feeling of urgency" were measured using the five-point Likert scale questionnaire.

3 Results

The effect of each eHMI design factor on the driver's judgment and reaction, response time and subjective evaluation, was analyzed by ANOVA using SPSS (version 26.0.0.0).

3.1 Effects of Text

Text was expected to be detrimental to response time because it takes time to read and comprehend. However, Fig. 3 indicates clearly that the decision time was faster when eHMI included text (p-value = .007). Also, subjective evaluation showed that eHMI with text drew more attention (p-value = .000), more warning (p-value = .000), and a more urgent feeling (p-value = .000).

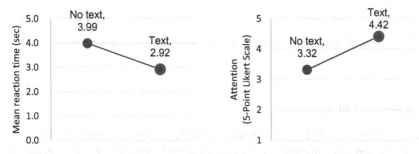

Fig. 3. Decision time and attention level by text.

3.2 Effects of Flash

In terms of reaction time depending on flashing frequency, there was no significant difference (p-value = .136) judging from one-way ANOVA analysis (dependent variable = reaction time, independent variables: frequency of flashing) (see Fig. 4). When the light band flashed slowly (1 Hz), the reaction time was slower than when there was no flash effect (N/A).

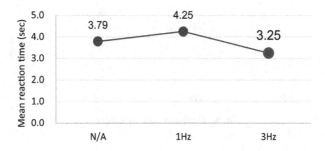

Fig. 4. Decision time depending on flashing frequency.

However, there were clear effects on attention, warning, and urgency depending on the effect of flashing light. Therefore, it is better to have a flashing effect, either slow or fast, when we intend to raise more attention (p-value = .000), warning (p-value = .000), and urgency (p-value = .000) referring to Fig. 5. In all cases, there were no differences between no flash and 1 Hz according to post-hoc ANOVA analysis.

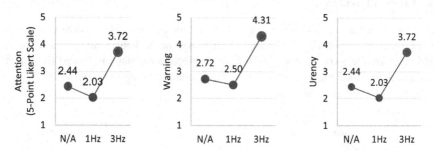

Fig. 5. Attention, warning, and urgency levels by flashing frequency.

3.3 Effects of Color

Three colors were used in the light band (see display samples in Table 1). The reaction time was fastest when the light strip was red (Mean 3.09 s, SD 1.82. On the contrary, the reaction time was slowest when there was no color in the status bar area (Mean 4.43 s, SD 1.12). The difference by color (see Fig. 6) was not significant (p-value = .053) according to ANOVA analysis. Assuming equal variances, Bonferroni post-hoc analysis indicated that only the difference between N/A and red was significant (p-value = .044).

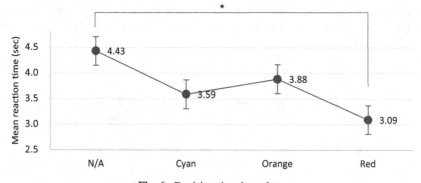

Fig. 6. Decision time by colors.

There were significant differences in attention (p-value = .000), warning (p-value = .000), and urgency (p-value = .000) by color. The results of a Games-Howell non-equal variance multiple comparison test (all have a very small p-value $< .001$) are shown in Fig. 7. Urgency showed similar trends to warning. Cyan showed the lowest warning and urgency effects, which proves it is good as a normal status color for AVs.

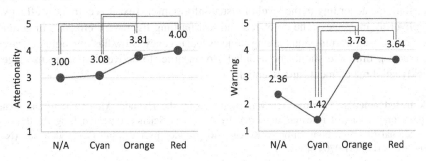

Fig. 7. Attention and warning levels by color.

4 Discussion and Limitations

A light band alone can only convey the feeling of an approximate condition (normal driving condition/something dangerous) but cannot help accurately judge and cope with the situation, so it can only play an auxiliary role. However, most people get information through the movement of the vehicle (Dylan Moore 2019). So, when the eyes need to focus on the vehicle, a flashing light band can be used as an auxiliary.

Slow flashing receives greater attention than the case without flashing, but a faster reaction time is not guaranteed. We recommend using fast flashing for attention and warning, as much as for a quick response.

People first judge the main message from the color. Using a color suitable for the situation of communication is a primary design decision. Even if there is no flashing, the color red has an excellent effect in communicating attention, warning, and urgency.

In the absence of text, it took a surprisingly long time for the driver to judge messages. Orange and red and fast flashing lights can attract people's attention, but it is difficult to deliver a message accurately. According to Aurora Harley [6], users are roughly 37% faster at finding items on a list on a web page when visual indicators vary both in color and icon compared to text alone. These results show that people rely on secondary cues such as color to distinguish and locate relevant information quickly and easily. Therefore, to deliver an important message, it is essential to use visual cues such as unique colors and flashing light, and most importantly, text, to reduce response time.

There were a number of limitations to this study. First, the vehicle in which the test subject was seated was not actually driven. Also, it was not in the same lane as the prototype displaying the eHMI. The environment did not reflect actual driving realism in terms of the complexity of tasks the driver handles in real driving. The subjects commented that another shortcoming was that the tail lamps did not work in synchronization with the eHMI. The vehicle with the eHMI moved very slowly (at a speed of 10 km/h or less), which also lacked the feeling of real driving.

5 Conclusion

We acknowledged that the role of eHMIs is limited and considered how eHMIs can help reduce accidents. Therefore, the experiment was conducted to see the driver's reaction or decision time according to the level of visual information. Text was extremely effective in delivering messages. The color red and fast flashing light were effective in getting attention, giving warning and making subjects feel urgency. Slow flashing light increases the reaction time and should be avoided. So, in order to deliver important messages quickly, all three elements are essential.

Acknowledgements. This research was supported by the Hyundai Motor Group and some of the work is part of research supported by the Basic Science Research Program through the National Research Foundation of Korea (NRF) funded by the Ministry of Education (No. NRF-2018R1D1A1B07045466).

References

1. Dey, D., Terken, J.: Pedestrian interaction with vehicles: roles of explicit and implicit communication vehicles. In: Proceedings of the 9th International Conference on Automotive User Interfaces and Interactive Vehicular Applications, pp. 109–113 (2017). https://doi.org/10.1145/3122986.3123009
2. Clamann, M.A., Cummings, M.L.: Evaluation of Vehicle-to-Pedestrian Communication Displays for Autonomous Vehicles. In: Transportation Research Board 96th Annual Meeting Transportation Research Board (2017). https://trid.trb.org/View/1437891
3. Dey, D., Walker, F., Martens, M., Terken, J.: Gaze patterns in pedestrian interaction with vehicles: towards effective design of external human-machine interfaces for automated vehicles. In: Proceedings of the 11th International Conference on Automotive User Interfaces and Interactive Vehicular Applications, pp. 369–378 (2019). https://doi.org/10.1145/3342197.3344523
4. SAE: Automated Driving System (ADS) Marker Lamp Ground Vehicle Standard (SAE J3134) (2019). https://saemobilus.sae.org/content/J3134_201905/
5. Dey, D., Habibovic, A., Pfleging, B., Martens, M., Terken., J.: Color and animation preferences for a light band eHMI in interactions between automated vehicles and pedestrians. In: CHI 2020: Proceedings of the 2020 CHI Conference on Human Factors in Computing Systems April 2020, pp. 1–13 (2020). https://doi.org/10.1145/3313831.3376325
6. Harley, A.: Visual Indicators to Differentiate Items in a List. Nielsen Norman Group, 7 August 2016. https://www.nngroup.com/articles/visual-indicators-differentiators/

A Comparative Study of In-Car HMI Interaction Modes Based on User Experience

Qiang Li[(⊠)], Jingjing Wang, and Tian Luo

Shenyang Aerospace University, Shenyang, China
qiangli@sau.edu.cn

Abstract. Human Machine Interface (HMI) is the medium of interaction between user and vehicle, and its usability is affected by many factors such as human, automobile and environment. With the development of science and technology, the human-computer interaction mode of automobile has changed. In order to improve the user experience and operational efficiency, this paper compares three modes of human-computer interaction in the vehicle: digital interaction, physical interaction and voice interaction mode, and analyze the characteristics and advantages and disadvantages of the three interactive modes by experiments and interviews. The research found that users need longer time to finish tasks by voice interaction mode, and a short time to use physical interaction mode. From the perspective of user satisfaction, people prefer to use voice interaction mode, but also need the cooperation of digital interaction and physical interaction mode, so as to improve the user's operation efficiency and ensure the safety of driving.

Keywords: User experience · Interface design · Automotive · HMI · Voice interaction

1 Introduction

With the wide application of computer technology in the field of transportation, Human Machine Interface (HMI) has changed greatly, and in-car HMI will be designed and reformed completely [1]. Driving is a complex task, which will be affected by people's behavior and habits to a certain extent. Automotive interaction has become a complex interaction system [2]. Presently, the internal function of automobile is no longer a single mode, but a complex information system. In such a complex situation, the driver should not only complete the main tasks such as vehicle control and road observation, but also perform a lot of secondary tasks. These secondary tasks will be not directly related to driving, and distract the driver's attention, which poses a threat to the driver's safety [3].

In addition to the HMI, interaction mode is also an important aspect of human-computer interface design [4]. The traditional vehicle interface is mainly based on physical buttons. After many years of development, the in-car physical interaction model has been very mature, which is considered to be an efficient interactive model. But with the gradual introduction of intelligent transportation, physical interaction mode is facing great challenges. Digital interaction is more popular, and it uses the screen to display

© Springer Nature Switzerland AG 2021
C. Stephanidis et al. (Eds.): HCII 2021, CCIS 1421, pp. 257–261, 2021.
https://doi.org/10.1007/978-3-030-78645-8_32

a large number of functions. But from the perspective of control, digital interaction is not as direct as physical interaction. Compared with physical and digital interactions, the voice interaction is simpler. Professor Yuanbo Sun studied the different interaction modes of human-computer interface and proposed the principle of hierarchy design of HMI [5]. James Cannan discussed the development of in-car HMI and predicted that the futural human-computer interaction mode would be the mode of multi-technology cooperation [6]. Biometric technology can detect the behavior characteristics of user interaction, and design the interface according to the habits of user behavior [7]. Mathilde François has explored user participatory design and considered the user's suggestions in the design of in-car HMI [8].

2 Experiment Design

2.1 Experiment Content

This experiment is divided into three groups: physical in-car HMI, digital in-car HMI and voice in-car HMI. The experiment content is to test the time when user complete tasks by using three different vehicle interface control modes (Car A digital interaction; B physical interaction; C voice interaction), and make a comparative analysis based on participants' completion time.

2.2 Experiment Subjects

Five experienced drivers for each vehicle type are selected to conduct operation test for the corresponding vehicle type. The participants were between 20–50 years old, the number of men and women is the same as far as possible, and their driving age was limited to more than three years, all the experimental participants have no disabilities, normal color vision, and are familiar with the in-car equipment and operating device.

2.3 Experiment Process

The experiment was carried out in the real environment of the corresponding vehicle (see Fig. 1). There are five tasks in the experiment: (1) playing songs (2) turning on the air conditioner (3) adjusting the temperature of the air conditioner (4) turning on the radio and tune to a channel (5) adjusting the temperature of the seat. The reason for choosing these five tasks is that they are relatively common and simple.

The participants entered the in-car HMI environment in turn, and carry out the operation tests of three different interfaces: digital interaction, physical interaction and voice interaction (see Fig. 2). Participants completed five tasks after entering the corresponding vehicle model, and the researchers recorded the completion time of the tasks respectively.

After the experiment, each participant was interviewed and asked about "what do you feel about this kind of interaction mode and what are the advantages and disadvantages do you think of this interaction mode". The purpose of the interview is to obtain users' views on different interaction modes and the inconveniences. After the interview, we summarize the user feedback.

Fig. 1. The real In-car HMI environment example

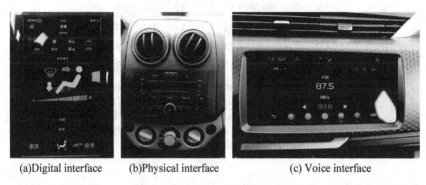

(a)Digital interface   (b)Physical interface   (c) Voice interface

Fig. 2. Three types of In-car HMI

2.4 Data Analysis and Discussion

According to the experimental records, the basic operation mode steps of different types of interaction modes are summarized (see Fig. 3). Participants perform voice interaction in several steps. The first step is to wake up the voice assistant, then give the voice commands, wait for the feedback, and finally complete the operation task. In physical interaction mode, participants only need to find the corresponding buttons to execute the command and complete the task.

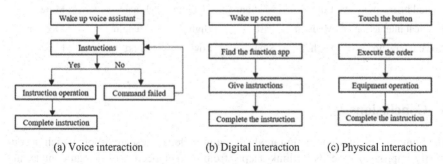

(a) Voice interaction   (b) Digital interaction   (c) Physical interaction

Fig. 3. Analysis of operation steps

According to the data analysis on average task completion time (see Table 1), we can see that there are slight differences in the operation of three different interaction modes. Generally, voice interaction needs longer operation time, because it needs to wait for the feedback information of voice assistant to complete the instruction. However, physical interaction can be simple and fast to complete the task. Usually, the operation can be completed in one or two steps.

Table 1. Average task completion time

Interaction mode	T1	T2	T3	T4	T5
C1	5.32	5.12	5.63	4.97	5.42
C2	4.21	3.28	4.83	3.97	5.16
C3	6.13	5.91	6.05	6.83	6.73

(C1 - digital interaction, C2 - physical interaction, C3 - voice interaction; T1 - playing a song, T2 - turning on the air conditioner, T3 - tuning up the air-conditioning, T4 - turning on a radio, T5 - adjusting the seat temperature).

According to the feedback information of the participants, the operation steps of the three interaction modes are summarized as follows (see Table 2). We can see that the voice interaction is convenient to use and low cost of learning. The interface of digital interaction can carry out both leisure and entertainment functions in addition to the main driving tasks and it is important for drivers. By comparison, physical interaction is more secure.

Table 2. Characteristics of three interaction modes

Interaction type	Security	Feedback speed	Attention required	Learning time	Attention required
Digital interaction	Low	Medium	Medium	Long	More
Physical interaction	Medium	Fast	High	Medium	Medium
Voice interaction	High	Slow	Low	Short	Less

3 Conclusions

The human-computer interaction mode of automobile is a research topic which is constantly improved. It needs to think deeply from the perspective of design content and user experience, and continue to practice. Informatization and networking make great changes in the mode of in-car HMI. In-car interaction forms, mobile interactive devices and user interface make great contributions to a more comfortable driving experience.

Through the comparative analysis of three interaction modes of automobile, this paper evaluates the emotional experience of users in the process of using, concludes that people prefer to use simple and direct voice interaction, and also need the cooperation of physical interaction and digital interaction, so as to meet the physiological and psychological needs of people. The discussion of automobile interaction modes depicts the development status of industry in this field, which will be helpful for designers to think about the future design of in-car HMI and interaction mode.

Acknowledgement. The work was supported by Liaoning Province Education Department (JYT2020098) PhD startup fund of Shenyang Aerospace University (20YB15), Social science development project of Shenyang Federation of Social Sciences (SYSK2020-13-05) and planning fund of Liaoning philosophy and social science (L20BXW011).

References

1. Yan, Y., Zhou, Y., Yu, M.: Study on layout design of intelligent drive vehicle interface. Ind. Eng. **21**(01), 96–102 (2018)
2. Schmidt, A., Dey, A.K., Kun, A.L., et al.: Automotive user interfaces: human computer interaction in the car. In: CHI 2010 Extended Abstracts on Human Factors in Computing Systems (2010)
3. Wang, J.S., Knipling, R.R., Goodman, M.J.: The role of driver inattention in crashes: new statistics from the 1995 Crashworthiness Data System. In: 40th Annual Proceedings of the Association for the Advancement of Automotive Medicine (1996)
4. Tan, H., Zhao, J., Wang, W.: Study on design of human-computer interaction interface. Autom. Eng. J. **2**(05), 315–321 (2012)
5. Sun, B., Yang, J., Sun, Y.: Study on hierarchical design of automotive human-computer interface. Mech. Des. **36**(02), 121–125 (2019)
6. Cannan, J., Hu, H.: Human-machine interaction (HMI): a survey. University of Essex (2011)
7. Gamboa, H., Fred, A.: A behavioral biometric system based on human-computer interaction. In: Biometric Technology for Human Identification. International Society for Optics and Photonics (2014)
8. François, M., Osiurak, F., Fort, A., et al.: Automotive HMI design and participatory user involvement: review and perspectives. Ergonomics **60**(4), 541–552 (2017)

What Will Influence Pregnant Women's Acceptance of Fully Automated Vehicles?

Xinyue Liu[1]([⊠]), Siqi He[2], Xue Zhao[1], and Hao Tan[1]

[1] Hunan University, Changsha, China
htan@hnu.edu.cn
[2] University of Science and Technology Beijing, Beijing, China

Abstract. In the 21st century, with the development of society and the economy, people are paying more and more attention to the special needs of special groups of people, for example, pregnant women's problem of transportation. As we could imagine, FAV (Fully Automated Vehicles) has the potential to become the measurement of this problem, by improving the safety and flexibility of traffic for pregnant women. However, FAV can only help when women can accept FAV while pregnancy.

According to the existed research, Chinese women have less trust in smart driving technology than men. We need to question: why?

This article will study on factors affecting pregnant women's acceptance of fully automated vehicles, by showing the participants fully automated driving videos and playing semi-immersive video simulations.

After our work, these theories can counteract the FAV design for pregnant women groups, so that pregnant women's travel problems can be optimally solved, thereby improving the quality of their life and increasing their employment of FAV and the willingness to buy fully autonomous vehicles. The research in this article aims to explore the relationship between pregnant women's acceptance of fully automated vehicles, individual internal factors, and weather conditions in the driving environment.

Keywords: Self-driving car · Pregnancy · Acceptance of FAV · Analog video

1 Introduction

Thanks to the technological breakthroughs made by humans in the field of fully automated driving, "freedom of mobility" will become a reality for more and more people including pregnant women. Fully automated driving will bring more possibilities and convenience to their individual travel.

Subsequent paragraphs, however, are indented. The pregnancy and postpartum period are the most vulnerable periods for women, accompanied by continuous and complex changes in physiology at the same time, it also faces strong psychological pressure. Some mental health assessments show that pregnant women have a higher proportion of psychological changes in anxiety and depression in early pregnancy, as shown in Table 1.

© Springer Nature Switzerland AG 2021
C. Stephanidis et al. (Eds.): HCII 2021, CCIS 1421, pp. 262–272, 2021.
https://doi.org/10.1007/978-3-030-78645-8_33

Table 1. Anxiety and depression assessment results at different stages of pregnancy.

Pregnancy stage	Total people	Anxiety	Percentage	Depression	Percentage
Early	329	66	20.1%	26	7.9%
Mid-term	356	36	10.1%	16	4.5%
Late	347	61	17.6%	21	6.1%

Common pregnancy psychological problems such as depression, anxiety, worry, tension, etc., emotional instability caused by hormone secretion, low level of self-efficacy during pregnancy, may cause pregnant women to face driving with a negative attitude, directly or indirectly affecting pregnant women's willingness to drive. If driving is restricted, it will adversely affect pregnant women in lots of aspects, such as reduced self-identity, worsening depressive symptoms, increased indirect postpartum depression, increased fetal growth retardation, premature delivery, and abnormal growth and development in childhood, and affect the pregnant women's quality of life, may lead to suicide and other consequences [1].

Also, during the October-long pregnancy, pregnant women's travel is relatively unavoidable. Most pregnant women remain employed during the first and second trimesters of pregnancy because healthy women who choose to continue working during pregnancy can not only help adjust their mood but also bring a positive attitude to the fetus. Besides this, normal shopping and hospital inspections are factors that increase the need to go out during pregnancy. Survey data show that with the gradual increase in car ownership, the number of female home car owners is increasing year by year. Women also tend to drive independently during pregnancy [2]. Besides, research shows that women are more willing to buy higher-priced vehicles. Therefore, car manufacturers can focus on female consumers as the future of smart driving [3]. In conclusion, it is of certain value and significance to investigate the design of fully automated driving vehicles for this special stage of female pregnancy.

However, due to women's concerns about accidents or accidents during driving and low trust in fully automated driving technology, the realization of the desire of pregnant women to benefit from automated vehicles faces certain resistance.

At present, research on car design to help pregnant women travel mainly include: through targeted design, improve the comfort of pregnant women in-car hardware such as seats and seat belts, and create a reasonable pregnant woman model in the car when an accident occurs in the factor of safety testing. However, the technical acceptance and psychological adaptation of pregnant women to FAV have not been studied.

Vehicles on the current market are not designed to meet the human-machine needs of pregnant women as a special group, while research on pregnant women and fully autonomous driving are scarce. Based on existing research [5], it can be known that the many internal factors related to personal characteristics (e.g. cognitive level, sensory abilities, driving experience, emotional state) may affect their acceptance of FAV. Besides, external factors such as environmental conditions while users are driving may also affect the group's acceptance.

To find out how and which of these factors (see Fig. 1) influence pregnant women's acceptance of FAV (excluding AV driving styles, excluding AV driving styles and traffic density), we launch a simulation-based experiment to study the influence of weather conditions, mood, driving experience, cognitive ability and sensory ability on FAV acceptability separately. Participants were evaluated under three different environmental conditions (sunny, rainy, foggy) to participate in fully-automated driving simulation experiments to evaluate the acceptability of FAV.

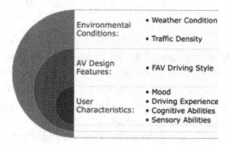

Fig. 1. Factors that may affect FAV acceptance based on Hoff & Bashir's three-tier automated trust framework focusing especially focus on internal factors. User characteristics and weather conditions within environmental conditions are considered in this study.

Confirming the association of these factors with FAV acceptance can provide references for future designs and guidelines to increase the acceptance of FAV by pregnant women, thereby bringing the greatest benefits to pregnant women.

2   Experiment Method

Informed Consent. To get a comprehensive vision of participants personal features, some basic private information (age, driving experience, etc.) concerned is indispensable. Prior informed consent that personal is guaranteed, which is achieved by stating that data collected in the experiment is linked to some individual privacy and will be applied to comparison, analysis and other reasonable use at the head of the questionnaires on demographics (Fig. 2).

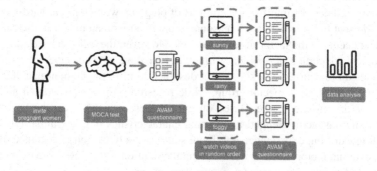

Fig. 2.   User flow chart

Finding Participant. To date, 8 participants have completed the experiment, with the ultimate goal of 10 participants. One participant was excluded from the sample for an unhealthy cognitive level according to MOCA that will be explained later. The sample reported includes 7 healthy pregnant women (age range = 22–33 years, M = 27 years, SD = 3.51), they hold a valid driving license and have not previously contacted a high level of automated driving (see Table 2).

Table 2. Age of participants, years of driving experience, MOCA score range from zero to 30.

M (SD)	
Demographics	
Age (years)	27.00 (3.51)
Driving experience (years)	4.00 (3.38)
Cognition	
MOCA score	27.43 (1.29)

Demographics, Driving Habits, Emotional, and Cognitive Measurements. Participants answered questionnaires on demographics. In order to gauge participants' typical driving behavior, they are asked to offer single or multiple answers to questions from the perspectives of frequency of driving, typical reasons to drive and regularly used means of transport before the experiment, and these questions are based on a previous study.[6] Among 7 qualified participants, their regularly used means of transport are mainly driving or taking a car (see Table 3).

Table 3. Regularly used means of transport of experimental participants

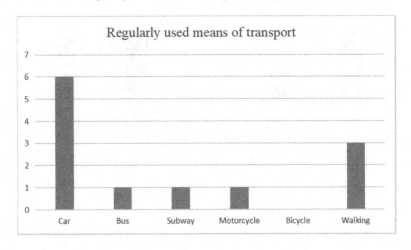

Their purpose of driving is mainly to deal with personal and family affairs and enjoyment (see Table 4). With 33% of participants driving every day (see Table 5).

Table 4. Participants' typical reasons to drive.

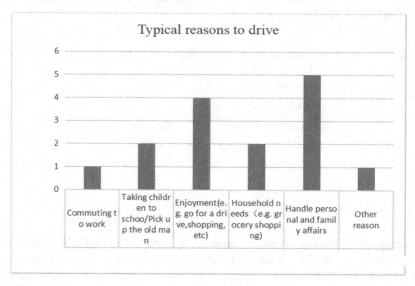

Table 5. Participants' frequency of driving.

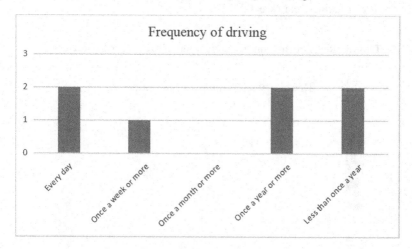

The mood of the day was measured using a simplified version of the emotiona state profile (POMS) [7].

To evaluate the participant's cognitive ability levels, the Montreal Cognitive Assessment Questionnaire (MOCA) [8] is employed.

FAV Acceptance Measurement. According to the automated vehicle acceptance model (AVAM) questionnaire [9] consisting of 26 items, the acceptance of FAV can be assessed through 9 dimensions, which includes: expected performance, effort expectancy, social impacts, attitudes towards technology, convenience, self-efficacy, anxiety, the intention of behavioral, and perceived safety.

Stimulation and Appliances. By displaying pictures of fully-automatic driving application scenarios (see Fig. 3), participants can get a preliminary understanding about FAV. To allow participants to experience fully automated driving, we offer three demonstration videos showing a hypothetical fully-automatic simulated driving environment from the perspective of the driver (see Fig. 3), each of them is undergoing different weather conditions and one-minute in length.

We employ videos as the method of fully automated driving-experience as it mobilizes visual and auditory sense at the same time, offering participants a higher sense of engagement [10].

All three one-minute videos are captured from videos of Tesla.

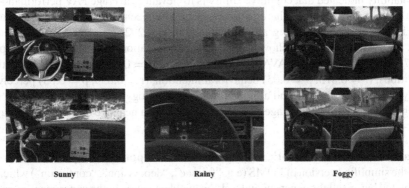

Sunny   Rainy   Foggy

Fig. 3. Screenshot of a fully automated driving demonstration video from the driver's perspective

3   Data Collection

At the beginning of experiments, participants were required to answer the questionnaire based on demographics and driving habits and the MOCA questionnaire. Before the start of the formal experiment, the participants were described the scenario of fully automatic driving so they have sufficient information about the FAV and their role [11] (see Table 6) and shown the pictures of application scenes of fully automatic driving vehicles. During the process of experiment, manual driving sensation test and full-automatic driving video simulation test are both run in one of the following three driving circumstances:

(1) rainy day; (2) sunny day; (3) foggy day.

The orders of driving circumstances and trials (manual vs. FAV) are neutralized to eliminate the impact that different orders may make. POMS was performed at the beginning of the experimental phase, and AVAM was performed both before and after completing the three driving conditions (video playing).

Table 6. Description of fully automatic driving (giving to participants)

> **Full Driving Automation**
> This car is completely autonomous. You can enter the car and indicate where you want to go, and then the car performs the route you want without any further interaction. When driving without any interaction from you, there is no steering or speed control.

4   Preliminary Results

4.1   Source of Internal Differences

Demographic, and Cognitive Effects. Correlation analysis between demographic data (as described in Table 2) collected to represent the characteristics of participants and FAV acceptability indicated that cognitive ability is irrelevant to average FAV performance ($r = -0.388$, $p = 0.390$), and there is no correlation between average FAV performance and driving experience among all participants. ($r = 0.292$, $p = 0.525$). At the same time, the FAV acceptability showed a significant correlation with age ($r = 0.893$, $p = 0.007$). Among all scales of AVAM, social influence, ($r = 0.822$, $p = 0.05$) facilitating conditions, ($r = 0.873$, $p = 0.05$) behavioral intention, ($r = 0.835$, $p = 0.05$) perceived safety ($r = 0.953$, $p = 0.01$ and attitude towards technology ($r = 0.708$, $p = 0.075$) are all significantly correlated to age. While anxiety shows a negative correlation with age. ($r = -0.798$, $p = 0.05$).

Impact of the Driver's Emotional State on FAV Acceptance. Forty adjectives compose the simplified version of POMS (e.g. "fatigue", "depression", "confusion") which is completed before all the experimental tasks to avoid any parts of the experiment's procedure make participants' mood change. Participants evaluated the extent of all adjectives which mostly correlates to their emotions at the moment. POMS produced total mood disturbance scores (TMD) and seven parts scores for tension, anger, fatigue, depression, emotions which are relative to self-esteem, vigor, and confusion. (see Table 7) Correlation analysis between the POMS score and the average AVAM score in all three driving situations shows that there is no correlation between the POMS mood scale and the acceptable scale. ($r = 0.355$, $p = 0.435$).

Table 7. Participant sentiment assessment scale {TMD (total mood disturbance) = [TEN + DEP + ANG + FAT + CON] – [VIG + ERA] + 100}

	Tension	Anger	Fatigue	Depression	Esteem-related Affect	Vigor	Confusion	TMD
1	1	0	0	0	17	6	4	82
2	0	0	1	0	8	0	1	94
3	0	0	0	0	22	12	4	70
4	4	1	3	0	17	12	6	85
5	3	1	0	0	13	5	5	91
6	9	0	6	5	12	5	7	110
7	7	0	6	5	22	16	6	86

4.2 Source of Diverse External Conditions

How environmental conditions influence pregnant women's acceptance of FAV?

Factors in weather conditions were manipulated in this research study and the different environments are shown in the driving videos. And each participant was required to experience each of the three conditions of rainy, sunny, and foggy weather in different orders, and then answered the AVAM questionnaire on their FAV experience.

As shown in Fig. 4 and Fig. 5, under the three environmental conditions, there is no significant difference between the average value of the AVAM scale and the single AVAM scale.

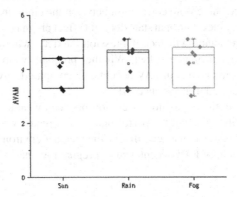

Fig. 4. Average of all AVAM scales across driving conditions.

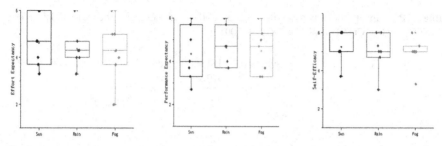

Fig. 5. The average of three selected sub-scales of AVAM under the entire driving conditions.

5   Conclusion

According to the current study of seven pregnant women (normal cognitive ability, driving experienced, no exposure to FAV), the participants mainly use cars for daily travel, but rarely drove themselves in pregnant period. Participants travel for more than one purpose, mainly to deal with family or personal affairs and to shop. Obviously, pregnant women have a lot of car travel needs.

Until now, our research statistics only show relevancy between age of pregnant women and acceptance of FAV. The other possible factors tested in our study such as driving experience, driving environments and drivers' mood before driving has not been proved to be relative with the acceptance yet.

The age of pregnant women was positively correlated with their acceptance of FAV, and the older pregnant women are, the more receptive they were to fully automatic driving. In general, older pregnant women had a higher level of experience, which led to a stronger sense of identity and was associated with greater acceptance of FAV.

At the current stage, there is no correlation between the emotional state and the FAV acceptance data, namely the emotional state does not affect pregnant women's acceptance of FAV. Women in pregnancy will face depression, anxiety, worry, tension, and other unstable emotions, it is an objective fact. Whether pregnant women have differences in anxiety and worry dimensions in FAV acceptance compared to women who are not pregnant, further controlled trials are needed.

At the current stage, there was no correlation between weather and environmental factors and acceptability data, and the performance of pregnant women in rainy, foggy and sunny environments was consistent, that is, the weather environment during driving does not affect the degree of FAV acceptance of pregnant women.

6   Future Work

Based on practical factors, this paper has the following problems:

1. Because the experimental method is limited to questionnaires and simulation videos, the results may be different from the experimental results of the participants using the FAV driving simulator;

2. The potential factors affecting pregnant women's-acceptance of FAV selected in this study were selected based on the previous Hoff & Bashir's three-tier automated trust framework focusing especially focus on internal factors. However, due to the limitations of experimental conditions, the FAV driving style that characterizes the internal factors and the two factors of traffic density that characterize external factors cannot be correspondingly experimentally studied. The two may be potential factors affecting pregnant women's acceptance of fully automated vehicles.
3. The number of samples currently being tested in this article is small, and increasing the sample size may make the final research results different from the current analysis results.

The number of samples will be further expanded in the future, and more participants corresponding to the standards will be searched for fully automated driving simulation experiments. The experimental process will be continuously optimized during the experiment, and new experimental variables will be set according to the experimental feedback.

Future analyses with complete data sets will be the version which includes the full sequence of conditions and clarify a larger measure of the association of established factors with the acceptability of FAV to pregnant women.

The influential factors related to pregnant women's acceptance of fully automatic driving provide a reference for the design of fully automatic driving in the future, so that this new type of transportation can maximize and optimally serve the special group of pregnant women.

Acknowledgement. The paper is supported by Hunan Key Research and Development Project (Grant No. 2020SK2094) and the National Key Technologies R&D Program of China (Grant No. 2015BAH22F01).

References

1. Ma, X.: The design and analysis of pregnant women's transportation. North China Electric Power University (2017)
2. You, F., Chu, X.: Research on investigation of consumer market acceptance for intelligent vehicles in China: case study in Guangzhou. J. Guangxi Univ. (Nat. Sci. Ed.) **44**(02), 534–545 (2019)
3. Yang, W.: Depression status and group mindfulness intervention study of pregnant women. Southern Medical University (2019)
4. Haghzare, S., Bak, K., Campos, J., Mihailidis, A.: Factors influencing older adults' acceptance of fully automated vehicles, pp. 135–139 (2019). https://doi.org/10.1145/3349263.3351520
5. Auriault, F., et al.: Pregnant women in vehicles: driving habits, position and risk of injury. Accid. Anal. Prev. **89**, 57–61 (2016)
6. Politis, I., Langdon, P., Bradley, M., Skrypchuk, L., Alexander Mouzakitis, P., Clarkson, J.: Designing autonomy in cars: a survey and two focus groups on driving habits of an inclusive user group, and group attitudes towards autonomous cars. In: Di Bucchianico, G., Kercher, P.F. (eds.) AHFE 2017. AISC, vol. 587, pp. 161–173. Springer, Cham (2018). https://doi.org/10.1007/978-3-319-60597-5_15

7. Grove, R., Prapavessis, H.: Abbreviated POMS Questionnaire (items and scoring key) (2016)
8. Nasreddine, Z.S., et al.: The Montreal Cognitive Assessment, MoCA: a brief screening tool for mild cognitive impairment. J. Am. Geriatr. Soc. **53**(4), 695–699 (2005)
9. Hewitt, C., Politis, I., Amanatidis, T., Sarkar, A.: Assessing public perception of selfdriving cars: the autonomous vehicle acceptance model. In: Conference on Intelligent User Interfaces (IUI 2019), March 2019
10. Jensen, T., Khan, M.M.H., Albayram, Y., Al Fahim, M.A., Buck, R.: Anticipated emotions in initial trust evaluations of a drone system based on performance and process information. Int. J. Hum.–Comput. Interact. https://doi.org/10.1080/10447318.2019.1642616
11. SAE International: Taxonomy and Definitions for Terms Related to Driving Automation Systems for On-Road Motor Vehicles (2016). https://www.sae.org/standards/content/j3016_201609/

Mitigating Frustration in the Car: Which Emotion Regulation Strategies Might Work for Different Age Groups?

Michael Oehl[1]($\boxtimes$), Martina Lienhop[2], and Klas Ihme[1]

[1] Institute of Transportation Systems, German Aerospace Center (DLR),
Braunschweig, Germany
{Michael.Oehl,Klas.Ihme}@dlr.de
[2] Faculty of Psychology, FernUniversität in Hagen, Hagen, Germany
Martina.Lienhop@studium.fernuni-hagen.de

Abstract. Frustration negatively affects user experience both in manual and automated driving and negatively influences driving performance and system acceptance. Hence, frustration-aware in-vehicle systems that assess the drivers' current level of frustration and help to mitigate it have gained attention. However, while there has been ample of research on the assessment of the user's affective state in the vehicle, little progress has been made on the mitigation of these affective states. Thus, little is known about interaction strategies for automotive user interfaces that successfully mitigate the user's frustration in frustrating situations. To bridge this gap, the aim of this study was the investigation of potential frustration regulation strategies as basis for supporting frustrated vehicle users in frustration-aware systems based on user needs. We conducted focus groups with users of different age groups (below and above 65 years) to explore which different emotion regulation strategies might work for different age groups in a user-centered way. Two representative use cases of today's and future driving were chosen, one for manual and one for automated driving, respectively. Only slight differences for the suggested emotion regulation strategies were observed between the age groups with respect to their rated helpfulness. The results provide a helpful basis to develop future in-vehicle frustration mitigation systems in terms of intelligent automotive user interfaces.

Keywords: Automotive user interfaces · Frustration · Driver state · Affect-aware systems · Empathic vehicles · User experience

1 Introduction

In general frustration is a negative affective state occurring when goal-directed behavior is blocked [1]. Within the context of automotive human-machine interaction (HMI), vehicle users are frequently experiencing frustration when faced for instance with red lights, traffic jams or problems while interacting with their navigation or infotainment system [2, 3]. Frustration does not only lead to negative driving and user experiences,

© Springer Nature Switzerland AG 2021
C. Stephanidis et al. (Eds.): HCII 2021, CCIS 1421, pp. 273–280, 2021.
https://doi.org/10.1007/978-3-030-78645-8_34

but it may also trigger aggression and influences cognitive processes relevant for driving, so that performance may suffer when frustrated [4].

Because it is very challenging to reduce all sources of frustration by design in a complex system like the modern traffic sector, the idea arose to equip vehicles with the ability to individually react to the current frustration level of their users. Such frustration-aware vehicles need the ability to estimate the users' current frustration level in real-time based on intelligent data processing as well as interaction strategies that help to mitigate the frustration or support the user in handling its negative effects [5–7]. In the past years, research on frustration-aware systems has become quite popular and first approaches for the real-time estimation of the driver's frustration level based on video recordings of the face, speech analysis or physiological data exist, e.g., [8, 9]. However, while there has been progress on the assessment of the user's affective state in the vehicle, little advances have been made on the mitigation of those affective states. As basis for the generation of strategies that technical systems can use to support their user in dealing with emotions such as frustration, it could be valuable to consider how humans generally regulate their own emotion. According to the work of Gross [10], a person can alter her or his emotional response by choosing strategies out of five emotion regulation families: situation selection, situation modification, attentional deployment, cognitive change or response modification (see Fig. 1(c)). Gross further differentiates these strategies by their underlying components of emotion generation, i.e., the respective focus of the strategy (b) and the time at which the strategy is implemented (a).

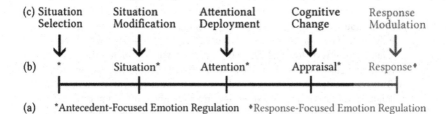

Fig. 1. The process model of emotion regulation adapted from Gross [10]

Interestingly, for reducing frustration, some researchers have already attempted to transfer these strategies to intelligent vehicles. For instance, a study by Harris and Nass [11] found that speech messages guiding the driver to a cognitive change ("Reappraise-Down") after experiencing frustration lead to a significantly better driving behavior and user experience (UX). Löcken et al. [5] generated (but did not evaluate) strategies based on an in-vehicle ambient light that supported attentional deployment by guiding attention to an optimal fuel consumption instead of frustrating traffic or by supporting response modification through a sort of biofeedback. A recent work showed that offering an autonomous driving assistant, which might be seen as a combination of attentional deployment and situation modification, has the potential to improve the user experience of frustrated drivers [9]. However, all these proposed interventions were quite selective and mostly designed top-down without asking users about their specific need for support in frustration-eliciting situations.

Therefore, the goal of this study is the investigation of potential frustration regulation strategies as basis for supporting frustrated vehicle users in frustration-aware systems based on user needs. As approach, we chose user focus groups with different age cohorts (below and above 65 years) in order to explore potential interaction strategies in a user-centered way, while accounting for preference differences related to age. To structure the explorations, we provided the participants with two different use cases eliciting frustration that were selected as relevant for today's and future driving [6].

2 Method

In general focus groups are a qualitative research approach often used to explore peoples' opinions, ways of understanding, or experiences of complex phenomena. Normally, a moderator conducts the group interview for a given topic to guide participants through the process. Hence, focus groups offer an exploratory research approach and the opportunity to enrich the available data by context information and depth, if applicable. In our current study, focus groups were used to explore potential emotion regulation strategies for frustration mitigation in vehicles with users. In total, six focus groups were conducted with $N = 32$ participants (12 female) aged between 19 and 74 years ($M = 47.4$, $SD = 20.9$). Two focus groups consisted of elderly participants over 65 years ($M = 71.2$, $SD = 2.9$). The other four focus groups consisted of participants under 65 years ($M = 35.0$, $SD = 14.6$). All participants held a valid driver's license with a mean mileage per year of $M = 18,016$ km ($SD = 19,447$). To control for participants' technology affinity the standardized ATI questionnaire [12] with a six-point Likert scale from $1 =$ "completely disagree" to $6 =$ "completely agree" was used. Technology affinity was quite high in general ($M = 4.6$, $SD = 0.9$) and similar for both groups, i.e., the younger ($M = 4.7$, $SD = 0.5$) and the elderly ($M = 4.4$, $SD = 0.9$) participants.

Each focus group consisted of five or six participants, a moderator, and a person protocolling the session, and lasted for about three hours including breaks. After an introduction round, participants were presented with a definition of frustration. Then, in a warm-up phase, participants were asked to remember frustrating situations as a car driver in everyday life and to write down their own regulation strategies on a separate card (nominal group brainstorming). In the following, participants presented them to the group on a pin board to discuss with the moderator's help. During this discussion, new strategies that came up were also noted on cards. Following this, the same nominal group brainstorming approach was used to generate ideas on how technical systems could support users in the car (for the results of this warm up phase, see [2]). Finally, after the warm-up phase two use cases (UC) were presented:

UC1 – Frustrating experience with navigation system: Paul is going to a business meeting in another city using a rented automated vehicle (SAE level 4 [13]), when he receives a call from the children day care that his son had an accident and needs to be picked up to see a doctor. As he wants to reprogram the route planner, he struggles with its confusing menu structure and becomes really frustrated because of losing valuable time to get to his son ...

UC2 – Frustrating experience due to traffic: Tina wants to meet friends for a movie's night in the neighboring town. While driving there on rural roads, she cannot overtake a slow truck due to heavy traffic on the opposite lane. Already being late and frustrated, she finally sees the cinema – just one left turn is needed. However, other cars are already cueing up on the left turn lane due to the very short green phases of the traffic light …

Familiarized with the use cases, participants had to reason about possible mitigation strategies helpful for the both use cases (UC1 and UC2) and to write them down on separate cards (again nominal group brainstorming). All mitigation options were rated on a Likert scale from 1 (not so helpful) to 5 (very helpful). In the following, participants presented them to the group on a pin board to discuss with the moderator's help. During this discussion, new strategies that came up were also noted on cards. For both use cases, we were interested in the mentioning frequencies and the different age groups' final group ratings of helpfulness of the frustration mitigation strategies.

3   Results

Since the data collected did not meet the requirements for parametric tests, non-parametric tests such as the Mann-Whitney U-test were used to evaluate the data. All statistical analyses were performed using IBM SPSS Statistics software (version 25) with α-levels of .05.

When asked about specific emotion regulation strategies for the two UCs, participants came up with a total of 54 mentions for UC1 and 47 for UC2. The mentioned regulation options in the two scenarios were categorized after the focus group sessions into the five Gross' emotion regulation families by two independent raters. If an assignment to more than one regulation family was theoretically possible (e.g., if relaxation techniques were mentioned by the groups that could be assigned to both cognitive change and response modulation depending on the focus of the strategy mentioned), the categorization was made according to the context mentioned in the respective focus group. In six cases of discrepancies between the raters (6.0%), disagreements were solved by discussion. Table 1 shows the mean group rating values of helpfulness for the emotion regulation strategies for each of the two use cases as well as for the two age groups 19–64 and 65+. The mean values were calculated as follows: The individually rated strategies were first aggregated on a group level. These group specific means were then averaged across all groups – thus representing weighted means. The right two columns display examples of desired strategy-specific emotion regulation methods with the highest mean values of helpfulness per use case. The following sections describe separately for each of the two use cases how helpful these examples were assessed across the groups and which regulatory families were preferred by the two age groups considered. Furthermore, quantitative and/or qualitative differences between the age groups are reported.

Table 1. Mean group rating values of helpfulness for Gross' emotion regulation strategies for UC1 and UC2 considering the two age groups 19–64 (<65) and 65+.

		UC 1			UC2			UC1	UC2
		M (SD)	M (SD)	M (SD)	M (SD)	M (SD)	M (SD)	Highest ranked examples[1]	Highest ranked examples[1]
		(<65)	(65+)	(all)	(<65)	(65+)	(all)		
	Number of participants[2]	21	11	32	21	11	32		
Emotion Regulation Strategies	Situation selection Number of mentions[3]	- -	- -	- -	4.1 (0.8) 4	- -	4.1 (0.8) 4	-	Navigation system with warnings when parking space is blocked; communication with traffic light
	Situation modification Number of mentions[3]	3.5 (1.1) 31	4.1 (0.8) 7	3.6 (1.1) 38	3.5 (1.0) 17	4.4 (0.5) 3	3.6 (1.0) 20	Switch to manual driving; voice-controlled guidance; contact support	Overtaking assistance; parking space finder; automated SMS to friends
	Attentional deployment Number of mentions[3]	3.2 (1.2) 3	2.7 (-) 1	3.1 (1.0) 4	2.5 (0.5) 5	3.0 (-) 1	2.6 (0.5) 6	Using entertainment system and listening to music after problem solving	Listening to radio, music or podcast; swearing assistant
	Cognitive change Number of mentions[3]	2.2 (-) 1	2.8 (2.0) 2	2.6 (1.5) 3	2.7 (0.8) 7	4.7* (0.7) 4	3.4 (1.2) 11	Reappraisal of the situation; empathic assistant; pray	Acceptance of the situation; change plans; positively re-interpret the situation
	Response modulation Number of mentions[3]	1.7 (0.4) 7	2.1 (0.4) 2	1.8 (0.4) 9	1.7 (0.5) 4	3.8 (1.7) 2	2.4 (1.4) 6	Using meditation or relaxing techniques; take a rest	Take a deep breath; sit comfortably; swear

[1] Examples were suggested and rated per focus group. Some of the examples were suggested by several or all focus groups so that the number of participants here is between 5 and 32. Options were rated on a Likert scale from 1 (not so helpful) to 5 (very helpful). [2] Number of participants across focus groups. [3] Sum of mentioned and rated functionalities across focus groups. * Significant differences between age groups (significance level = .05).

For UC1 seven proposals for helpful emotion regulation strategies in the car mentioned a speech-based solution. Desired functionalities were speech support (M = 4.7, SD = 0.8), a tutor-like assistant helping to reprogram the navigation system (M = 4.2, SD = 0.5) (situation modification) or an empathic agent supporting problem solving (M = 2.2, SD = 1.0) (cognitive change). Ten more participants suggested functionalities like contacting the technical support service (M = 4.2, SD = 1.3), finding a friend or neighbor that could fetch the kid from the kindergarten (M = 3.9, SD = 1.3) or activating an emergency mode via speech that directly changes the current navigation route to a predefined target, e.g., the kindergarten (M = 4.8, SD = 0.8) (situation modification). Switching off the system and continuing driving manually was mentioned six times (M = 4.7, SD = 0.5) and thus this is the strategy that was rated as the most helpful in this use case (situation modification). Strategies from the situation selection family were not mentioned due to the clear specifications of UC1. In UC1, there were no statistically significant differences between the two age groups. On a qualitative level, differences could be observed for desired strategies after problem solving (attentional deployment): While the older age group of 65+ tended to prefer classical entertainment such as radio, younger participants (<65) favored music or films through infotainment systems and podcasts. Response modulation strategies such as using relaxing techniques were rated as more helpful by the age group 65+. As a conclusion for UC1, situation modification seems the most promising emotion regulation family with 38 mentions and a mean helpfulness group rating of 3.6 (SD = 1.1).

Concerning UC2, situation modification strategies were evaluated as promising for this UC as well with 20 mentions and an identical mean for the helpfulness group rating (M = 3.6, SD = 1.0), although most of the strategies came out of the age group <65 (85%). After situation modification, cognitive change was the most frequently mentioned and most helpful evaluated regulation family for UC2 across the two age groups. Acceptance of the situation was here the strategy mentioned most often (M = 3.8, SD = 1.4). On a qualitative level, similar strategies for UC2 were mentioned by both age groups. However, especially in the sixth focus group, the 65+ participants unanimously rated the acceptance of the situation, the positive reinterpretation or the re-evaluation of the situation as a very helpful strategy (M = 5.0, SD = 0.0). A Mann-Whitney U-test for independent samples shows that participants above 65 years rated this strategy in UC2 significantly higher than younger participants (u = 2.7; p = .007). Situation selection strategies were only referred to by the age group <65. The most helpful strategy here was a navigation system with an early warning when parking space is blocked (M = 5.0, SD = 0.0). Qualitative differences could further be observed for response modulation strategies. While the age group <65 more often cited emotional abreactions such as swearing or complaining – however, evaluated as little helpful (M = 1.5, SD = 1.4) – the age group 65+ tended to focus on relaxation techniques such as adopting a comfortable sitting position (M = 2.7, SD = 1.9). In general, emotion regulation strategies that were rated as helpful for UC2 were an overtaking assistant (M = 4.4, SD = 0.8) (situation modification), listening to radio, music or podcasts (M = 2.7, SD = 1.4) (attentional deployment), or taking just a deep breath (M = 5.0, SD = 0.0) (response modulation).

4 Discussion

In this study focus groups with different user groups (<65 vs. 65+ years) were used to explore potential emotion regulation strategies for frustration mitigation in vehicles as basis for the development of future in-vehicle frustration mitigation. For both UCs we were interested in the mentioning frequencies and the different age groups' final ratings of helpfulness of the suggested frustration mitigation strategies by the groups.

For both UCs (automated vs. manual driving) situation modification was most often suggested by both age groups and rated as the most helpful emotion regulation strategy. Across all emotion regulation families, we observed only slight differences between age groups on a quantitative level. Here, cognitive change was the only regulation strategy for UC2 with significantly higher helpfulness ratings for older participants. This effect might be due to age differences in coping strategies when it comes to negative emotions. In general, beyond this study, the elderly were able to better deal with negative emotions compared to the younger. This might be in line with the observed differences for the suggested family of response modulation as emotion regulation strategy. Here, only the elderly rated this emotion regulation family as rather helpful, especially for UC2. Additionally, for UC2 only the younger groups mentioned situation selection as an emotion regulation strategy suggesting examples (e.g., communication with traffic lights, communication with parking space) that might have arisen out of their mobile phone usage – the elderly might not be so familiar with these forms of daily information supply via apps. Moreover, we observed age group differences for attentional deployment. All in all, even though we found only one significant difference between both age groups, the study results provide valuable hints for future research and further in-depth analyses of age group differences when frustration mitigation systems in vehicles will be further explored.

As a conclusion from the mentioned mitigation examples in both UCs, speech interventions seem particularly promising, probably due to the high naturalness and the comparably little cognitive strain imposed by spoken language and auditory interaction on other tasks [14]. To add, with the rise of commercial speech assistants, such as, e.g., Apple's Siri or Amazon's Echo, naturalistic speech interaction with technical systems is of course no science fiction anymore. With an exploratory approach, this study provides first valuable hints for the user-centered design of frustration-aware in-vehicle systems providing tailored adaptive mitigation strategies to their users. More user research is necessary to get deeper insights into the needs of different user groups and more relevant use cases need to be defined and explored [15]. Prototypical mitigation strategies need to be set-up and tested in iterative user tests. Our results provide a helpful basis to develop future in-vehicle frustration mitigation systems in terms of intelligent automotive user interfaces.

References

1. Lazarus, R.S.: Progress on a cognitive-motivational-relational theory of emotion. Am. Psychol. **46**, 819–834 (1991). https://doi.org/10.1037/0003-066X.46.8.819
2. Bosch, E., Ihme, K., Drewitz, U., Jipp, M., Oehl, M.: Why drivers are frustrated: results from a diary study and focus groups. Eur. Transp. Res. Rev. **12**(1), 1–13 (2020). https://doi.org/10.1186/s12544-020-00441-7
3. Zepf, S., Dittrich, M., Hernandez, J., Schmitt, A.: Towards empathetic car interfaces. In: Proceedings of the CHI 2019: CHI Conference on Human Factors in Computing Systems, pp. 1–6 (2019). https://doi.org/10.1145/3290607.3312883
4. Lee, Y.C.: Measuring drivers' frustration in a driving simulator. In: Proceedings of the Human Factors and Ergonomics Society Annual Meeting, vol. 54, pp. 1531–1535 (2010). https://doi.org/10.1177/154193121005401937
5. Löcken, A., Ihme, K., Unni, A.: Towards designing affect-aware systems for mitigating the effects of in-vehicle frustration. In: Proceedings of the 9th International Conference on Automotive User Interfaces and Interactive Vehicular Applications Adjunct, pp. 88–93. ACM, New York (2017). https://doi.org/10.1145/3131726.3131744

6. Oehl, M., Ihme, K., Drewitz, U., Pape, A.A., Cornelsen, S., Schramm, M.: Towards a frustration-aware assistant for increased in-vehicle UX. In: Proceedings of the 11th International Conference on Automotive User Interfaces and Interactive Vehicular Applications: Adjunct Proceedings, pp. 260–264. ACM, New York (2019). https://doi.org/10.1145/334 9263.3351518

7. Bosch, E., et al.: Emotional GaRage: a workshop on in-car emotion recognition and regulation. In: Adjunct Proceedings of the 10th International ACM Conference on Automotive User Interfaces 2018 – AutomotiveUI 2018 Adjunct, pp. 44–49. ACM, New York (2018). https://doi.org/10.1145/3239092.3239098

8. Franz, O., Drewitz, U., Ihme, K.: Facing driver frustration: towards real-time in-vehicle frustration estimation based on video streams of the face. In: Stephanidis, C., Antona, M. (eds.) HCII 2020. CCIS, vol. 1226, pp. 349–356. Springer, Cham (2020). https://doi.org/10.1007/978-3-030-50732-9_46

9. Zepf, S., Stracke, T., Schmitt, A., van de Camp, F., Beyerer, J.: Towards real-time detection and mitigation of driver frustration using SVM. In: Proceedings of the 18th IEEE International Conference on Machine Learning and Applications – ICMLA, pp. 202–209 (2019). https://doi.org/10.1109/ICMLA.2019.00039

10. Gross, J.J.: Emotion regulation: current status and future prospects. Psychol. Inq. **26**, 1–26 (2015). https://doi.org/10.1080/1047840X.2014.940781

11. Harris, H., Nass, C.: Emotion regulation for frustrating driving contexts. In: Proceedings of the SIGCHI Conference on Human Factors in Computing Systems, p. 749 (2011). https://doi.org/10.1145/1978942.1979050

12. Franke, T., Attig, C., Wessel, D.: A personal resource for technology interaction: development and validation of the affinity for technology interaction (ATI) scale. Int. J. Hum.-Comput. Interact. **35**, 456–467 (2018)

13. SAE International: Taxonomy and Definitions for Terms Related to On-Road Motor Vehicle Automated Driving System, J3016 (2014)

14. Large, D.R., Burnett, G., Clark, L.: Lessons from Oz: design guidelines for automotive conversational user interfaces. In: Proceedings of the 11th International Conference on Automotive User Interfaces and Interactive Vehicular Applications: Adjunct Proceedings. AutomotiveUI 2019, pp. 335–340. Association for Computing Machinery, New York (2019). https://doi.org/10.1145/3349263.3351314

15. Oehl, M., Ihme, K., Bosch, E., Pape, A.A., Vukelić, M., Braun, M.: Emotions in the age of automated driving: developing use cases for empathic cars. In: Proceedings of ACM Mensch und Computer conference (Mensch und Computer 2019), 2 p. ACM, New York (2019). https://doi.org/10.18420/muc2019-ws-267

Toward Standardizing Wizard of Oz Driving Behavior: A Decision Ladder Analysis of the Driving Wizard's Task

Andrea Isabell Scheiter[1][✉] [ID], Michael Domes[2] [ID], Uwe Herbst[3] [ID],
and Klaus Bengler[1] [ID]

[1] Chair of Ergonomics, Technical University of Munich, Munich, Germany
{andrea.scheiter,bengler}@tum.de
[2] Technical University of Munich, Munich, Germany
michael.domes@tum.de
[3] AUDI AG, Ingolstadt, Germany
uwe2.herbst@audi.de

Abstract. The Wizard of Oz (WoOz) research paradigm is very versatile in terms of experimental procedure, which is why special attention has to be paid to achieving valid results. In this context, for example, driving wizards must be able to consistently reproduce the driving style of an automated vehicle to ensure reliability and validity of the experiment. Since this is a challenging task for human drivers, it is advisable to provide driving wizards with assistive equipment, such as additional information systems. Before designing these systems, it is important to find out how driving wizards can best be supported. Therefore, we conducted a decision ladder analysis to understand what information driving wizards must perceive, what decisions they must make and what actions they must perform. We discovered that additional information, for example, regarding the longitudinal and lateral acceleration, the distance between ego vehicle and leading vehicle as well as the lateral position of the ego vehicle within the lane could be helpful for driving wizards.

Keywords: Wizard of Oz · Methodology · Driving Wizard Task

1 Introduction

Using the Wizard of Oz (WoOz) technique to prototype automated vehicles (AVs) has become popular in human-vehicle interaction research. While participants in these kinds of experiments are led to believe that they are interacting with a real AV, a hidden driver, the so-called driving wizard, in fact drives the research vehicle [1]. However, since the WoOz methodology is versatile in terms of its application, standardizing the experimental procedure seems necessary to guarantee scientific quality [2]. To ensure validity and reliability of the experiment, for example, driving wizards must be able to consistently reproduce the

We would like to thank the AUDI AG for funding this work.

C. Stephanidis et al. (Eds.): HCII 2021, CCIS 1421, pp. 281–288, 2021.
https://doi.org/10.1007/978-3-030-78645-8_35

driving style of an AV [3]. This seems challenging since the driving style of an AV is often substantially different from the driving wizards' natural driving style [4] and humans are not as capable as machines in repetitively performing uniform actions [5]. Therefore, assistive equipment for driving wizards, such as the information system AUTOAccD developed by Karjanto et al. [6], is advisable [3].

2   Theoretical Background

As a first step toward the development of such additional information systems, we conducted a thorough analysis of driving wizards' tasks. To do so, we performed a decision ladder analysis (see Fig. 1, Fig. 2 and Fig. 3), which is part of the framework of Cognitive Work Analysis and represents one possible approach to evaluate what needs to be achieved within a system regardless of who performs the action and how it is done [7]. Here, processes regarding the situation analysis are mapped on the left leg of the decision ladder, while the top part represents the evaluation of options for action and the right leg is concerned with planning, timing and executing the chosen option of action [7]. The decision ladder template consists of rectangles, which stand for activities of information-processing, as well as ovals, which represent the resulting states of knowledge [7]. Its structure along the perimeter is a model of knowledge-based behavior that is primarily employed by novice users [9] or during rational decision processes [8]. Rule-based behavior, which is typically shown by expert users, as well as during heuristic decision processes [8] can be depicted by adding short-cuts from the right leg of the ladder to the left leg [9].

3   Method

We performed the decision ladder analysis using a template by Jenkins et al. [9] (adapted from [10]). To populate this template we conducted interviews with five human factors experts (3 men, 2 women, 27.40 ± 2.15 years old), who have all previously acted as driving wizards. Participation in the interviews was voluntary and not compensated. Each interview lasted approximately two hours. At the beginning of the interview, we asked the participants to watch a short video explaining the fundamental functionality of an AV, the expected driving style of an AV as well as resulting aspects that driving wizards must consider during the ride. Then, we explained the decision ladder template to them. We asked participants to put themselves in the situation of simulating a SAE Level 4 AV on a highway and provided them with instructions similar to the quantitative-qualitative instruction set used in Scheiter et al. [4]. For our data collection, we chose to create decision ladders for the prevalent maneuvers "follow a lane behind a leading vehicle (LV)", "follow a lane without a LV" and "change lanes". To help facilitate discussion, we presented each maneuver to participants in a randomized order using pictograms. As recommended by Jenkins et al. [9] we divided the interview process in two phases to ensure the development of a prototypical model of the work situation: For every maneuver, we first guided participants through the decision ladder template by asking specific questions for each node. Then participants were encouraged to go through the template by themselves and add any additional information. Since the participants' answers were often inter-related (especially for the nodes "Information" and "System State" as well as "Task" and "Procedure"), we rearranged interview data to fit the template. Since we were interested in the rational decision process of driving wizards, no shortcuts were added to our decision ladders.

4 Results

Based on the work narrative developed by Lintern (2010), the driving wizards' task as analyzed by means of the decision ladder template can be described as follows: Driving wizards are alerted by either detecting another road user within sensor range for the maneuvers "follow a lane behind a LV" (see Fig. 2) or "change lanes" (see Fig. 3) or by detecting no other road user within sensor range for the maneuver "follow a lane without a LV" (see Fig. 1). This first step already offers potential for unwanted variations in driving behaviour. The human perception range in daylight conditions exceeds that of sensors used in AVs [11] and also humans are less capable than machines at measuring or quantifying signals [11]. Therefore, an additional information display regarding whether possible preceding objects are within sensor range or not might be helpful for driving wizards at this stage to prevent acting too early in comparison with AVs.

After being alerted, driving wizards observe the situation around them and subsequently assess the states of their environment and the research vehicle. For all three driving maneuvers, driving wizards can directly read the ego-velocity from the tachometer. Moreover, they have to judge the lateral position of the ego vehicle (EV) within the lane by examining the lane markings. This can, however, be challenging since the seating position of driving wizards in the research vehicle is often different from the normal seating position of drivers. Thus, a visualization of the EV's current position within the lane might be helpful for driving wizards. Also, driving wizards can only judge longitudinal and lateral acceleration values through feeling for vestibular motion cues or listening for engine sounds, which makes an information display regarding acceleration values seem reasonable. In case of a present LV (see Fig. 2 and Fig. 3), driving wizards can only estimate the absolute distance to said LV by monitoring the number of reflector posts between EV and LV, which also makes it a parameter worth visualizing. Alternatively, it might be useful to inform driving wizards about the time headway (THW) or the time to collision (TTC). Combining a visualization of these parameters with an indication of increase or decrease in value possibly could make information about the speed of the LV and the relative velocity between EV and LV, respectively, obsolete. For all examined driving maneuvers (see Fig. 1, Fig. 2 and Fig. 3), the load on driving wizards by constantly having to look out for road signs can be reduced by providing them with a traffic sign recognition system.

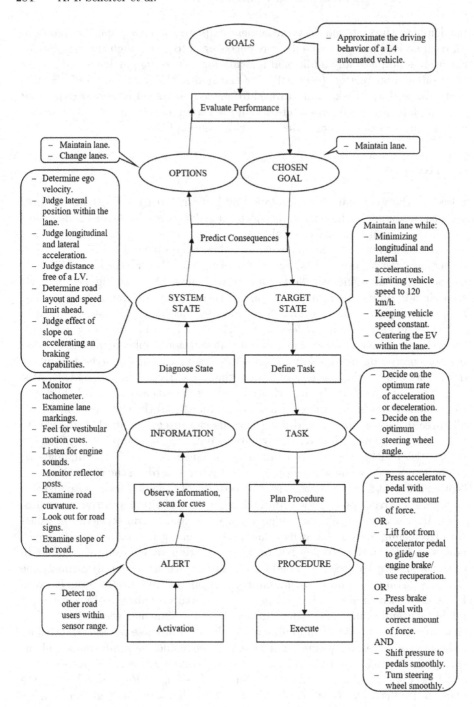

Fig. 1. Decision ladder for following the lane without a leading vehicle

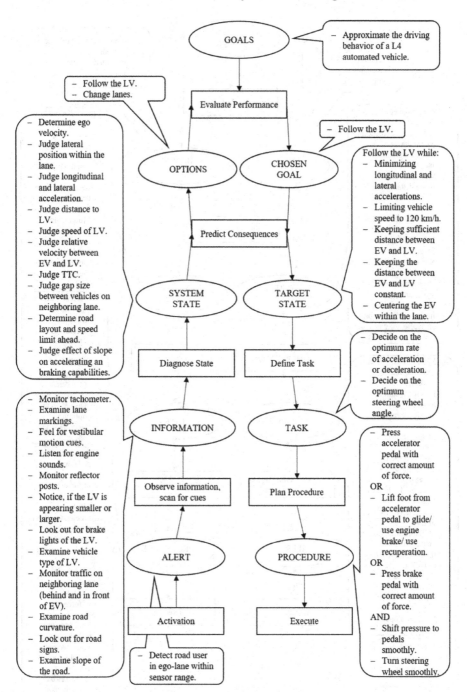

Fig. 2. Decision ladder for following the lane behind a leading vehicle

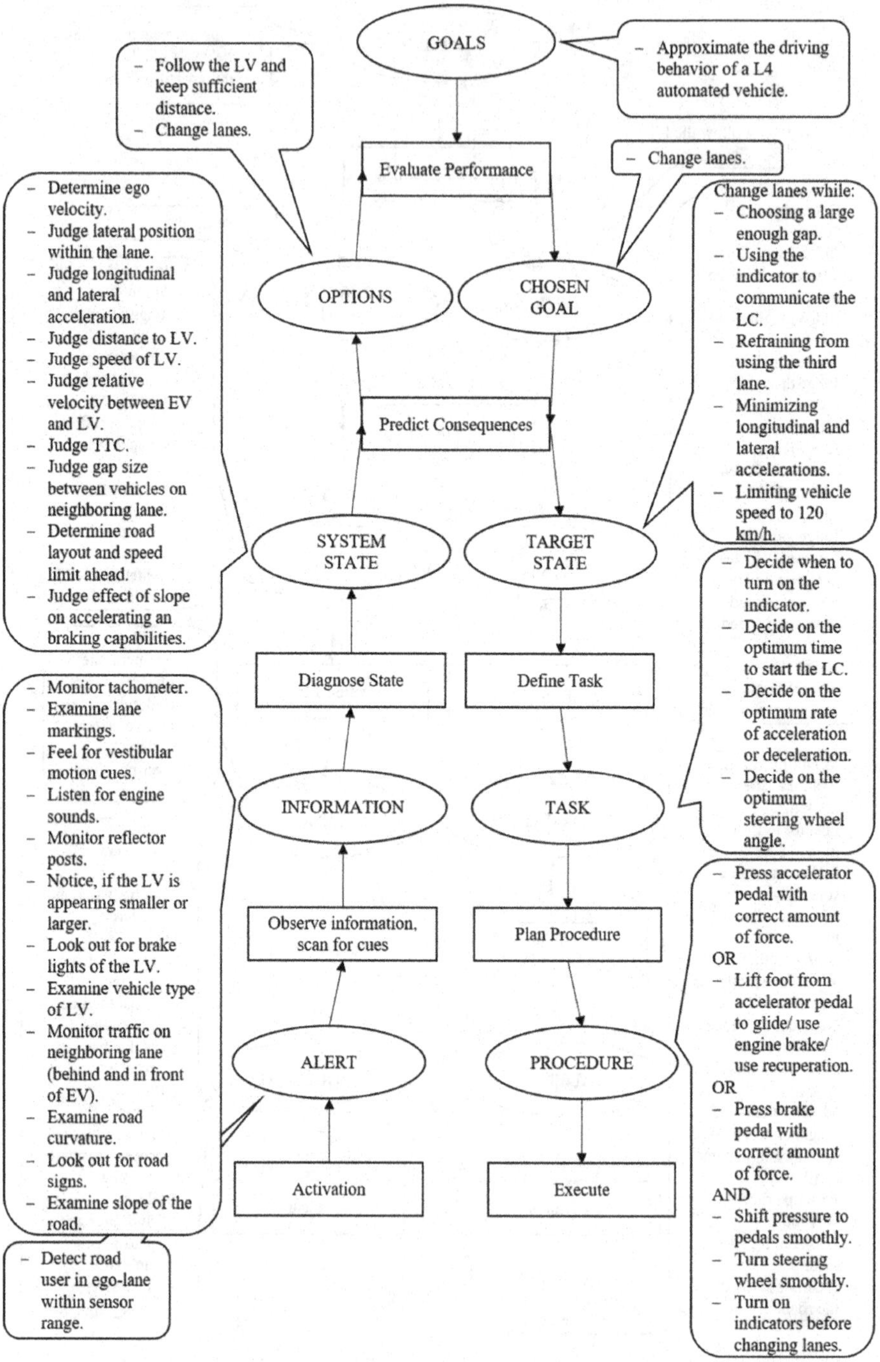

Fig. 3. Decision ladder for changing lanes

Once driving wizards have assessed the environment's and the research vehicle's current state, they determine the implications of the current state for their task. Based on that, driving wizards identify a target state. In case it is hard for them to determine a target state based solely on the current system state, they may use the value-judgement loop to identify and subsequently compare their options before deciding on their final goal. Driving wizards then evaluate the consequences of this so-called chosen goal and thereafter decide on the target state. This state reflects on the instructions provided to driving wizards before the ride which are applicable to the chosen driving maneuver.

After having identified a suitable target state, driving wizards specify the task, that is needed to achieve it. When changing lanes (see Fig. 3), one task is to decide on the appropriate time to start the lane change (LC). If the test vehicle is equipped with all necessary sensors and functional logic, driving wizards could be provided with a cue as soon as an AV would change lanes. Alternatively, a lane change assist may be used to prevent overly dynamic LCs. Then, on the basis of the target state, driving wizards devise a procedure for carrying out the task and eventually perform said procedure. In doing so, driving wizards may use driver assistance systems such as adaptive cruise control (ACC) and Lane Keeping Assist to mitigate the human weakness of not being able to achieve a highly consistent and repeatable behavior compared to machines [5]. However, this bares the risk of accidentally replicating a state-of the art system rather than a novel automated driving function [2]. Practicing the test route with the research vehicle before the experiment starts can help driving wizards mitigate the weakness of not having detailed information on road curvature and slope compared to highly accurate digital cards used in AVs and provide certainty when deciding on a procedure to accelerate or decelerate the vehicle.

5   Discussion and Conclusion

Whereas a standard vehicle display set-up will usually only provide driving wizards with information regarding velocity and motor speed, additional information displays might be helpful for driving wizards as decision-making and driving support. In this paper we examined what kinds of information driving wizards must perceive, what decisions they must make and what actions they must perform to fulfil their task by means of a decision ladder analysis to inform the design of assistive equipment. However, it needs to be kept in mind that the decision ladder does not represent the actual perception, decision-making and action processes, but rather contains a collection of steps [8] that might be used by driving wizards to accomplish their task. Additionally, although the interviewed human factors experts have all previously acted as driving wizards, none of them do so on a regular basis and therefore cannot be considered professional driving wizards. Nevertheless, we are still of the opinion that the presented findings can be useful indications when designing assistive information displays for driving wizards in the future. Design concepts based on our findings should always be verified by means of a heuristic evaluation or user study to ensure suitability of the information and minimal additional load on driving wizards. Moreover, it needs to be evaluated what kind of information can be displayed from a cost-benefit point of view, since there is no use in equipping a WoOz vehicle with the same amount and kind of sensors as well as functional logic compared to automated test vehicles.

References

1. Baltodano, S., Sibi, S., Martelaro, N., Gowda, N., Ju, W.: The RRADS platform. A real road autonomous driving simulator. In: 7th International Conference on Automotive User Interfaces and Interactive Vehicular Applications, Nottingham, UK, 01–03 September 2015, pp. 281–288. ACM, New York (2015)
2. Bengler, K., Omozik, K., Mueller, A.I.: The renaissance of Wizard of Oz (WoOz). Using the WoOz methodology to prototype automated vehicles. In: de Waard, D., et al. (eds.) Proceedings of the Human Factors and Ergonomics Society Europe Chapter 2019 Annual Conference, Nantes, France, 02–04 October 2019, pp. 63–72 (2020)
3. Mueller, A.I., Weinbeer, V., Bengler, K.: Using the wizard of Oz paradigm to prototype automated vehicles. Methodological challenges. In: Adjunct Proceedings of the 11th International Conference on Automotive User Interfaces and Interactive Vehicular Applications, Utrecht, Netherlands, 21–25 September 2019, pp. 181–186 (2019)
4. Scheiter, A.I., Linnemann, J.A., Herbst, U., Bengler, K.: Mental model of driving wizards when simulating an automated drive. In: Proceedings of the 11th Nordic Conference on Human-Computer Interaction: Shaping Experiences, Shaping Society, Tallinn, Estonia, 25–29 October 2020. ACM, New York (2020)
5. Fitts, P.M. et al.: Human engineering for an effective air-navigation and traffic-control system. National Research Council Division of Anthropology and Psychology Committee on Aviation Psychology (1951)
6. Karjanto, J., Yusof, N.M., Terken, J., Delbressine, F., Rauterberg, M., Hassan, M.Z.: Development of on-road automated vehicle simulator for motion sickness studies. Int. J. Driv. Sci. 1, 1–12 (2018)
7. Naikar, N.: A comparison of the decision ladder template and the recognition-primed decision model. Report no. DSTO-TR-2397, Air Operations Division, DSTO Defence Science and Technology Organisation (2010)
8. Lintern, G.: A comparison of the decision ladder and the recognition-primed decision model. J. Cogn. Eng. Decis. Making 4, 304–327 (2010)
9. Jenkins, D.P., Stanton, N.A., Salmon, P.M., Walker, G.H., Rafferty, L.: Using the decision-ladder to add a formative element to naturalistic decision-making research. Int. J. Hum.-Comput. Interact. 26, 132–146 (2010)
10. Rasmussen, J.: The human data processor as a system component. Bits and pieces of a model. Report no. 1722, Riso National Laboratory (1974)
11. Schoettle, B.: Sensor fusion: a comparison of sensing capabilities of human drivers and highly automated vehicles. Report no. SWT-2017-12, The University of Michigan (2017)

Modelling Turning Intention in Unsignalized Intersections with Bayesian Networks

Alexander Trende[1](✉), Anirudh Unni[2], Jochem Rieger[2], and Martin Fraenzle[1,2]

[1] OFFIS e.V., Escherweg 2, 26121 Oldenburg, Germany
alexander.trende@offis.de
[2] University of Oldenburg, Ammerländer Heerstraße 114-118, 26129 Oldenburg, Germany

Abstract. Turning through oncoming traffic at unsignalized intersections can lead to safety-critical situations contributing to 7.4% of all non-severe vehicle crashes. One of the main reasons for these crashes are human errors in the form of incorrect estimation of the gap size with respect to the Principle Other Vehicle (POV). Vehicle-to-vehicle (V2V) technology promises to increase safety in various traffic situations. V2V infrastructure combined with further integration of sensor technology and human intention prediction could help reduce the frequency of these safety-critical situations by predicting dangerous turning manoeuvres in advance, thus, allowing the POV to prepare an appropriate reaction.

We performed a driving simulator study to investigate turning decisions at unsignalized intersections. Over the course of the experiments, we recorded over 5000 turning decisions with respect to different gap sizes. Afterwards, the participants filled out a questionnaire featuring demographic and driving style related items. The behavioural and questionnaire data was then used to fit a Bayesian Network model to predict the turning intention of the subject vehicle. We evaluate the model and present the results of a feature importance analysis. The model is able to correctly predict the turning intention with an accuracy of 74%. Furthermore, the feature importance analysis indicates that user specific information is a valuable contribution to the model. We discuss how a working turning intension prediction could reduce the number of safety-critical situations.

Keywords: Human-computer-interaction · Autonomous driving · Human modelling · Machine learning

1 Introduction

Turning through oncoming traffic at unsignalized intersections can lead to safety-critical situations [1, 2] contributing to 7.4% of all non-severe vehicle crashes [2]. One of the main reasons for these crashes are related to human errors in the form of incorrect estimation of the gap size [3] of the principle other vehicle (POV). Several factors can influence decision-making during turning maneuvers, e.g., gap sizes, waiting time at the intersections [1], gender and age [4].

© Springer Nature Switzerland AG 2021
C. Stephanidis et al. (Eds.): HCII 2021, CCIS 1421, pp. 289–296, 2021.
https://doi.org/10.1007/978-3-030-78645-8_36

Vehicle-to-vehicle (V2V) or vehicle-2-infrastructure technology could help to reduce safety-critical situations [2]. V2V technology describes systems that sends information about a vehicle's state to another vehicle. This concept could also be extended to send information collected via user state assessment within the vehicle. The US National Highway Traffic Safety Administration (NHTSA) estimated that V2V technology could save between 49 to 1083 lives on an annual basis and avoid up to 270000 1-5 MAIS (Maximum Abbreviated Injury Scale) injuries [2].

[5] proposed a general human driver model at intersections, which contains decision-making module that simulates the decision process during both signalized and unsignalized intersections. [6] performed a driving simulator study featuring unsignalized intersections and roundabouts to record manoeuvre data. This data is then used to build a human-like decision-making algorithm for such traffic situations. [7] provided a proof of concept of how the combination of human state estimation, human intention prediction and safety impact analysis could lead to a substantial safety gain based on experimental data reported in [8, 9].

In this study, we first performed a driving simulator experiment to record turning decisions at unsignalized intersections. This data is then used to create a human intention model to predict turning. We discuss how the classification of turning decisions can be improved by synthesizing information from the POV and the turning vehicle.

2   Methods and Materials

2.1   Data Acquisition

Thirteen volunteers (7 females, 54%, mean age $\pm$ SD $= 23.8 \pm 2.61$) participated in the driving simulator study. All participants possessed a valid German driving license and received a financial reimbursement of 10€ per hour. The experiment was implemented in a full-scale fixed-base driving simulator, which offered a 150° field of view. The vehicle mock-up (Subject Vehicle, SV) contained a standard interface consisting of a throttle, brake pedal and steering wheel.

The participants encountered several left-turn manoeuvres with oncoming traffic (Principle Other Vehicle, POV) in an urban environment. Every intersection showed a stop sign, so the SV had to stop before the intersection (s. Fig. 1). A gap between two POVs presented the opportunity to turn before an oncoming POV.

Gap sizes between 1 s and 6 s, corresponding to 13.9 m and 83.4 m respectively, were presented during the experiment. This distribution of gap sizes was based on the findings of [10]. The researchers examined the gap distributions from five different intersections and found that most observed gaps were 4 s or shorter with the highest number of gaps being around 2 s.

To get the participants accustomed to the experimental setting, a short scenario consisting of rural roads and eleven intersections was presented to the participants. The main experiment lasted around 70 min and each participant encountered 100 intersections in total. A block consisted of ten intersections and was followed by a short break of around 90 s. The participants had a time constraint to finish each block. The time constraint was necessary to motivate the participants decide on a gap instead of waiting until all cars

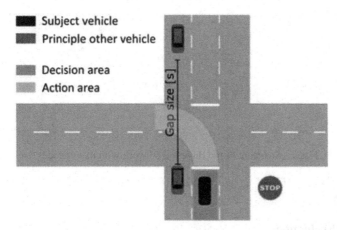

Fig. 1. Sketch of the intersection and the corresponding turning maneuver.

have passed. We designed a head-up display to display the number of intersections the participants had already crossed and the time elapsed since the start of the block.

The participants answered a questionnaire featuring demographic and driving style related items. Driving style related items were taken from [11]. Based on the questionnaires, we calculated a mean score for the driving style items "Angry", "Risky", "Careful" and "Anxious".

2.2 Modelling

We used a Bayesian network (s. Fig. 2) to model the turning intention of the Subject Vehicle (SV) [7]. More than 5000 turning decisions were recorded during the study. All variables were discretized modeled as discrete variables. For each of these decisions, we extracted the gap size for the current POV, and counted the cars that had already passed since the SV stopped at the intersection. Gap size and the corresponding gap acceptance is one of the most crucial factors that influences the turning decision [1]. [1] also suggested that elapsed waiting time is an important parameter that influences gap acceptance. Therefore, we decided to include the number of cars that have passed since the subject waited at the intersection. Additionally, we extracted the driving style and demographic questionnaires to add subject-specific information to the model. [4] suggests that age and gender also influence decision making concerning turning in left-turns through oncoming traffic. Furthermore, we included driving style related factors derived from the questionnaires. Conditional probabilities of the Bayesian network were fitted via maximum likelihood estimation. Inferences shown in the results were calculated via variable elimination. We calculated classification metrics such as the model's accuracy and area under the curve (AUC) with 4-fold cross-validation. The train and test data sets were balanced to include an equal number of positive and negative turning decisions. The training and test data set of each fold consisted of around 1500 and 500 turning decisions.

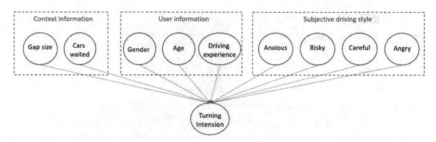

Fig. 2. Structure of the Bayesian network with its ten nodes.

3 Results

3.1 Model Evaluation

As shown in Fig. 2 the model is constructed to classify the turning intension of the SV. The receiver operating characteristic curve and is shown in Fig. 3. Random classifications would lead to an accuracy of 0.5 since the training and test data was balanced w.r.t to turning decisions. Furthermore, binary decisions imply a theoretical guessing level of 0.5. The model is able to predict the turning decision with a mean accuracy of 0.74. Furthermore, the AUC with a value of 0.81 is also far above the AUC of an uninformative classifier (0.5).

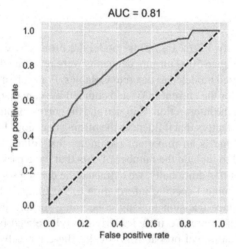

Fig. 3. ROC curve for the model. The model's AUC = 0.81 and the accuracy with a classification output of 0.5 is 74%.

3.2   Feature Importance

We used SHAP (**SHapley Additive exPlanations**) [12] to evaluate the importance of each variable in the model. SHAP is a technique to explain the output of machine learning models using cooperative game theoretic methods. Simply put, model features each contribute to the model's prediction. Some features may contribute more to the model's output (positive SHAP values) and some may reduce the output (negative SHAP values). The mean absolute SHAP values for each feature can be interpreted as an overall importance of said feature. The summary plot of the calculated SHAP values is shown in Fig. 4. As expected, the numbers of cars waited and the gap sizes are the most important variables in the model for predicting the turning decision. Large gap sizes (red) have a high positive SHAP value and thus increase the turning probability in the model and vice versa. Longer waiting times, resulting in high values for "Cars waited" increase the model's predicted turning probability accordingly. The absolute SHAP values (s. Fig. 5) for the user specific variables are not as high as the context variables (Cars waited, Gap size). Nevertheless, the user specific information is also relevant for the decision. For example, the fact that a participant is male (red) seems to lead to higher SHAP values and thus increases the turning intention probability. The results for the other features cannot be interpreted as straightforward.

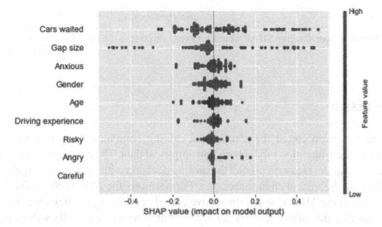

Fig. 4. Summary plot for the SHAP feature importance analysis (Color figure online).

Figure 5 shows the absolute SHAP values for all features. All variables, except for the variable "Careful" driving style, seem to have some impact on the model's prediction. The user specific variables range between 0.02 and 0.03 mean absolute SHAP values, whereas the "Gap size" and "Cars waited" have 0.11 mean absolute SHAP values render them the most important features.

Since inference in large Bayesian networks can be slow, it is useful to just incorporate relevant variables into the model. Results from a feature importance analysis could be used to reduce the number of features in the network, which in turn could increase the inference speed, as relevant for real-time application.

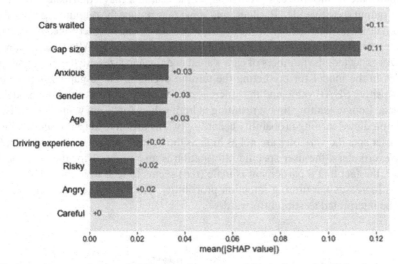

Fig. 5. Overview over absolute SHAP values for every variable in the model (Color figure online).

4 Discussion

In this study, we presented the results of a driving simulator study and proposed a predictive turning-intention model based on empirical data. The evaluation of the model shows that the model is able to predict the turning decision with an accuracy significantly higher than the theoretical chance accuracy. Furthermore, the AUC with a value of 0.81 is also far above the AUC of an uninformative classifier (0.5). A false negative prediction would mean that the model predicts the SV to wait, whereas it actually will turn. Such a prediction of defensive and safe behavior not reflecting actually risky ground truth would be the worst case from a safety-critical viewpoint and should be avoided as much as possible. The classification threshold should be adjusted accordingly.

Using feature importance analysis, we showed how user-specific information could improve the prediction of turning intention in our sample. However, it has to be mentioned that the participants stemmed from a relatively homogeneous study group. The standard deviations of both age and driving experience were moderate. The same is true for the questionnaire results. Furthermore, subjective assessment of driving styles is not always accurate (e.g. [13]). Moreover, a sample size of N = 13 is low for generalization.

User specific information could be acquired via a short questionnaire after the purchase of the vehicle and updated regularly if the user is willing to share his personal data in return for a hypothetical safety increase gained by the turning prediction model. Similar models could be built for other traffic situations like lane-merging. The predictions of such a model could then be used to display warning via a human-machine-interface in the POV, thus helping the driver to prepare an appropriate reaction. Considering the technological progress in the field of advanced driver-assistance systems and autonomous driving, a more direct intervention could be tested. If the model predicts a dangerous turning maneuver, the POV could react automatically by braking without the POV's driver's reaction.

As indicated in [7], a model with an accuracy of 74% and more can lead to a safety improvement when the model is integrated in a traffic controller. Overall, we hypothesize that V2V communication in combination with context information and human intention prediction could reduce safety-critical situations in traffic.

Acknowledgment. This work was supported by the DFG-grants RI 1511/3-1 to JWR and LU 1880/3-1 to AT (both "Learning from Humans – Building for Humans") and FR 2715/4-1 ("Integrated Socio-technical Models for Conflict Resolution and Causal Reasoning") to MF.

References

1. Hamed, M.M., Easa, S.M., Batayneh, R.R.: Disaggregate gap-acceptance model for unsignalized T-intersections. J. Transp. Eng. **123**(1), 36–42 (1997)
2. Harding, J., et al.: Vehicle-to-vehicle communications: readiness of V2V technology for application (No. DOT HS 812 014). National Highway Traffic Safety Administration, United States (2014)
3. Plavšić, M., Klinker, G., Bubb, H.: Situation awareness assessment in critical driving situations at intersections by task and human error analysis. Hum. Factors Ergon. Manuf. Serv. Ind. **20**(3), 177–191 (2010)
4. Yan, X., Radwan, E., Guo, D.: Effects of major-road vehicle speed and driver age and gender on left-turn gap acceptance. Accid. Anal. Prev. **39**(4), 843–852 (2007)
5. Liu, Y., Ozguner, U.: Human driver model and driver decision making for intersection driving. In: 2007 IEEE Intelligent Vehicles Symposium, pp. 642–647. IEEE, June 2007
6. De Beaucorps, P., Streubel, T., Verroust-Blondet, A., Nashashibi, F., Bradai, B., Resende, P.: Decision-making for automated vehicles at intersections adapting human-like behavior. In 2017 IEEE Intelligent Vehicles Symposium (IV), pp. 212–217. IEEE, June 2017
7. Damm, W., Fränzle, M., Lüdtke, A., Rieger, J.W., Trende, A., Unni, A.: Integrating neurophysiological sensors and driver models for safe and performant automated vehicle control in mixed traffic. In: 2019 IEEE Intelligent Vehicles Symposium (IV), pp. 82–89. IEEE. June 2019
8. Trende, A., Unni, A., Weber, L., Rieger, J.W., Luedtke, A.: An investigation into human-autonomous vs. human-human vehicle interaction in time-critical situations. In: Proceedings of the 12th ACM International Conference on Pervasive Technologies Related to Assistive Environments, pp. 303–304, June 2019
9. Ihme, K., Unni, A., Zhang, M., Rieger, J.W., Jipp, M.: Recognizing frustration of drivers from face video recordings and brain activation measurements with functional near-infrared spectroscopy. Front. Hum. Neurosci. **12**, 327 (2018). https://doi.org/10.3389/fnhum.2018.00327

10. Ragland, D.R., Arroyo, S., Shladover, S.E., Misener, J.A., Chan, C.Y.: Gap acceptance for vehicles turning left across on-coming traffic: implications for intersection decision support design (2006)
11. Taubman-Ben-Ari, O., Mikulincer, M., Gillath, O.: The multidimensional driving style inventory—scale construct and validation. Accid. Anal. Prev. **36**(3), 323–332 (2004)
12. Lundberg, S., Lee, S.I.: A unified approach to interpreting model predictions. arXiv preprint arXiv:1705.07874 (2017)
13. McKenna, F.P., Stanier, R.A., Lewis, C.: Factors underlying illusory self-assessment of driving skill in males and females. Accid. Anal. Prev. **23**(1), 45–52 (1991). https://doi.org/10.1016/0001-4575(91)90034-3

Research on Service Design of Balanced Vehicle Based on Kansei Engineering

Yajing Xu[(⊠)], Zhengyu Wang, Meiyu Zhou, Lu Zhong, Hanwen Du, Li Wang, Yibing Wu, and Jinyao Zhang

School of Art Design and Media, East China University of Science and Technology, No. 130, Meilong Road, Xuhui District, Shanghai, People's Republic of China

Abstract. With improvement of people's consumption level and the comprehensive promotion of the concept of low-carbon globalization, people's demand for balanced vehicle has been upgraded from a single transportation function to personalization and service, and meeting people's demand through service innovation is a hot research topic nowadays. Through the collection and analysis of a large number of related literatures, we find that domestic and foreign experts and scholars have done extensive research on the combination of Kansei Engineering and service design, but relatively few studies have been made on balanced vehicle service innovation. Based on this, this research plans to study and optimize the service of the balanced vehicle by combining Kansei Engineering and service design. Firstly, the user's key perceptual images of the balanced vehicle are extracted by Kansei Engineering theory and principal component analysis. Second, according to the user's perceptual demand for the product, sort out the corresponding service blueprint and user journey map. Finally, according to the different service stages of the product, the service design strategy of the product is summarized, and the service system of the product is optimized. Integrating users' emotional demands into the optimization of product service design, it improves the service quality of different service stages of the product while effectively meeting users' emotional demands, thus improving the user experience.

Keywords: Balanced vehicle · Kansei engineering · Service design · User experience

1 Introduction

Balanced vehicle is a new generation of energy saving and environmental protection transportation tool that can allows people to stand on top of the body and walk automatically according to the balance of the body. Because of its small size, it can ride on any narrow road [1], which brings people a more convenient way to travel and is deeply loved by people. With the improvement of consumption level and low-carbon globalization [2], the demand for balanced vehicle has changed from single transportation function to personalized and humanized service [3]. And meeting people's demand through service innovation is a hot research topic nowadays.

© Springer Nature Switzerland AG 2021
C. Stephanidis et al. (Eds.): HCII 2021, CCIS 1421, pp. 297–304, 2021.
https://doi.org/10.1007/978-3-030-78645-8_37

Through holistic, human-centered design thinking method [4], service design is becoming increasingly important as a key capability for companies to survive in a service-oriented economy [5]. The intervention of Kansei Engineering has realized the connection between service design elements and users' emotional perception [6]. Through the collection and analysis of many related literatures, it is found that domestic and foreign experts and scholars have done extensive researches on the combination of Kansei engineering and service design. For example, Yan et al. combine service design with kansei engineering to design an emotional interaction system for driverless food trucks [7]; Hsiao and Chen used Kansei engineering to provide ideas for the development of cross-border logistics services [8]; Cahigas and Prasetyo improve customer service strategies by analyzing the relationship between emotional vocabulary and service characteristics [9]; Hapsari et al. have changed the image of public transportation by putting emotion into service [10]. However, the current research on transportation vehicles only uses one method of kansei engineering or service design, and the number of researches on innovation of balanced vehicle service is relatively small.

Therefore, this study adopts the method of combining Kansei Engineering and service design to optimize the service of balanced vehicle. First, the key perceptual images are extracted by using Kansei engineering theory and principal component analysis, and then the corresponding service blueprint and user journey map are sorted out according to the users' perceptual demand for the products, finally, according to the different service stages of the product, the service design strategy of the product is summarized, and the service system of the product is optimized.

2 Users' Perceptual Demands in Product Service Design of Balanced Vehicle

2.1 Acollection and Selection of Perceptual Images

First, 86 perceptual images were selected from multiple related news, websites, books, magazines and papers. Secondly, by using the card sorting method and focus group method to eliminate the meaningless and semantic fuzzy words, we got 18 perceptual words and made a perceptual vocabulary list to carry out a questionnaire survey, and got 52 valid questionnaires, take the top six words to describe the balanced vehicle service system, and take the antonyms to form six pairs of perceptual words, respectively, safe-dangerous, light-heavy, simple-flowery, comfortable-uncomfortable, personal-boring, intelligent-mechanical.

2.2 Sample Collection of Balanced Vehicle

Based on the research of e-commerce platform and literature, 98 different kinds of balanced vehicle samples were preliminarily sorted out. After analyzing and comparing the characteristics of the balanced vehicle, 18 representative samples were selected.

2.3 Establishment of Fifth-Order Perceptual Image Questionnaire

Likert five-order scale was used to make 6 groups of perceptual images into a five-order perceptual image questionnaire, and 52 questionnaires were sent, 48 valid ones were collected and their results were processed.

2.4 Principal Component Analysis of Perceptual Images Adjectives of Balanced Vehicle

In order to understand the users' perceptual cognition of balanced vehicle product service and grasp the users' perceptual demand in the later design, this paper adopts the principal component analysis to obtain the key perceptual image of the users. The data was first tested by KMO and Bartlett to determine whether it was suitable for principal component analysis. Secondly, the total variance interpretation table (see Fig. 1) is obtained, from which two principal component factors can be extracted. P1 and P2 explained 54.844% and 25.606% of the variance, respectively, and cumulatively explained 80.450%, indicating a high level of recognition of these two principal component factors extracted (Table 1).

Table 1. Total variance explained.

Heading level	Initial eigenvalues			Extraction sums of squared loadings		
	Total	% of variance	Cumulative %	Total	% of variance	Cumulative %
1	3.312	55.194	55.194	3.312	55.194	55.194
2	1.473	24.549	79.743	1.473	24.549	79.743
3	3.312	55.194	55.194	3.312	55.194	
4	.866	14.432	94.175			
5	.188	3.137	97.312			
6	.087	1.451	98.763			

It can be seen from the composition matrix (Table 2) that primary component 1 is mainly related to "safe" and "comfortable", among which the "safe" can best represent principal component 1, so it is called the "trust factor". Principal component 2 is primarily related to "light", "simple", "personality" and "intelligent", and the "intelligent" is more explicable in the case of principal component 2, which can be named the "efficiency factor".

Table 2. Component matrix[a].

	Component	
	1	2
Safe	−.790	.564
Light	.880	.062
Simple	.762	.467
Comfortable	−.696	.689
Intelligent	.692	.672
Personality	.607	.082

2.5 Results Analysis

According to the principal component analysis (see Fig. 1), two main components, trust factor and efficiency factor, are extracted. According to the influence of each factor on the main component, two key perceptual intentions of security and intelligence are obtained. The results show that in the existing balanced vehicle service system, the perception images concerned by users are safe and intelligent, which provides design direction for further perception design work.

3 Product Service Design for Balanced Vehicle

3.1 Service Blueprint and User Journey Map Output

The service flow and service contact points of the existing balanced vehicle are combed with the purchase-process as clues to construct the service blueprint of balanced vehicle (see Fig. 1).

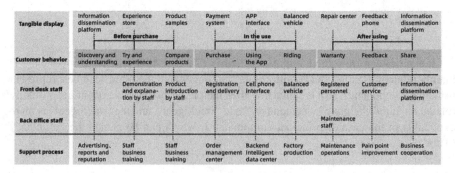

Fig. 1. Service blueprint.

Taking the core users of the balanced vehicle as the specific users of the user journey map (see Fig. 2), it describes the behaviors, attitudes, emotions and ideas of each touch point in a typical user use scenario, so as to help solve the user's pain points and optimize the emotional feelings of the user during the use process, so that the user can get a better overall use experience.

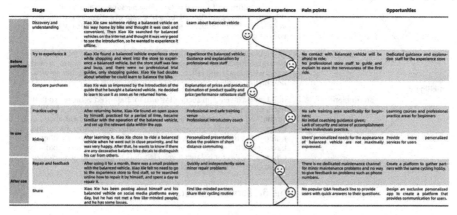

Fig. 2. User journey map.

1. Before buying: the user's goal is to understand what a balanced vehicle is and whether they can learn to drive it.
2. In use: The user's goal is to be more skilled in manipulating the balanced vehicle and keeping themselves safe. At this stage, the key factors affecting the user's mood are the balanced vehicle's own hardware and the use of mobile phone applications.
3. After use: The user's goal is to share their experience and feedback on problems encountered during use.

3.2 Service Content

Through the research of user demand and user perceptual image in the process of balanced vehicle service, it is necessary to focus on improving the user's perception of perceptual image in the design, and further transform and list the service content through user demand that affects the user's perceptual image (see Fig. 3).

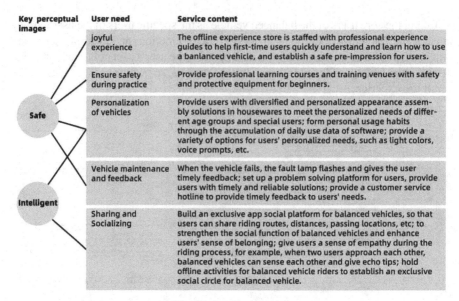

Fig. 3. Service content.

4   Design Strategy

Through the above study, the following design strategies are proposed to address the perceptual needs of users.

4.1   Pay Attention to User Needs and Ensure Vehicle Safety

In the service of balanced vehicle, the safety in the process of learning and using is the problem that the user pays close attention to. In terms of vehicle design, intuitive visual perception and potential interaction details can have an impact on the user's judgment of vehicle safety. The design details and interaction details of the existing balanced vehicle in the process of driving have fully taken into account the user's demand for safety, such as strengthening the security of the vehicle through APP positioning, protecting the user's driving safety by changing the lights in the process of driving, etc. But the need for safety is also very strong in the process of users' preliminary understanding and learning to use the balanced vehicle. If we help users to establish the perception of safety of the balanced vehicle in the preliminary stage of using the vehicle, it will help the company's business operation and image establishment. Therefore, the experience store can be equipped with special guidance and explanation staff, providing beginners with a simple learning process and a safe learning site, etc., to enhance users' sense of security and make them trust in the company.

4.2 Intelligent Optimization of Products and Development of User Habits

From the "intelligent" perceptual image can be seen, smooth, personalized operation process allows users to deepen the dependence on the product. At present, the application of big data and artificial intelligence technology for balanced vehicle can analyze the behavior pattern of users, so as to predict the market trend and scientifically and purposefully adjust and optimize each link in the balanced vehicle service process. In addition, companies should also pay attention to the personalized needs of different age groups and special users, targeted to improve response efficiency, and establish a common emotion with users to make them develop the habit of using it. While meeting the explicit needs of users, the company should also explore the implicit needs of users and give them satisfaction to surprise them, thus enhancing their emotional attachment to the company.

5 Conclusion

In this study, the perceptual intention of user needs was studied and extracted through quantitative statistical methods, and the two most important perceptual words for users were "safe" and "intelligent". Then, through the study of balanced vehicle users and user needs survey, the pain points in the user service process are restored. According to the user's safe and intelligent perceptual needs, it strengthens the user's sense of security in the early stage of understanding and learning as well as in the process of using the vehicle. By analyzing the personalized data of user behavior, it adjusts each link of the balanced vehicle service process in a targeted way, so as to cultivate the user's use habits. In addition, this study proves that the combination of Kansei Engineering and service design can effectively meet users' perceptual needs, and at the same time improve the service quality of products in different service stages, thus improving the overall user experience. However, this study also has some limitations, such as a small sample size and lack of representativeness. This problem can be discussed in more detail in future studies.

References

1. You, G., Zeng, W.: Design of two-wheel balance car based on STM32. In: 2018 9th International Conference on Information Technology in Medicine and Education (ITME). IEEE Computer Society (2018)
2. Li, J., Yang, L., Li, Y.: Research on consumption level upgrading and legal system guarantee. Summit International Marketing Science and Managment Technology Conference. School of Management, Changchun Taxation University, P.R.China (2009)
3. Yong, Q.Y.: The research of service process innovation. In: Fourth International Conference on Multimedia Information Networking & Security. IEEE (2013)
4. Teixeira, J.G., Patrício, L., Tuunanen, T.: Bringing design science research to service design. In: Satzger, G., Patrício, L., Zaki, M., Kühl, N., Hottum, P. (eds.) IESS 2018. LNBIP, vol. 331, pp. 373–384. Springer, Cham (2018). https://doi.org/10.1007/978-3-030-00713-3_28
5. Andreassen, T.W., et al.: Linking service design to value creation and service research. J. Serv. Manag. 27(1), 21–29 (2016)

6. Yan, H.B., Li, M.: An uncertain Kansei Engineering methodology for behavioral service design. IISE Trans. **53**(5), 497–522 (2020)
7. Yan, M., Wang, J., Wang, W.: Emotional interaction design for driverless food truck under campus scenarios. In: Di Bucchianico, G., Shin, C.S., Shim, S., Fukuda, S., Montagna, G., Carvalho, C. (eds.) AHFE 2020. AISC, vol. 1202, pp. 464–471. Springer, Cham (2020). https://doi.org/10.1007/978-3-030-51194-4_61
8. Hsiao, Y.H., Chen, M.C.: Kansei Engineering with online content mining for cross-border logistics service design. In: 2016 5th IIAI International Congress on Advanced Applied Informatics (IIAI-AAI). IEEE (2016)
9. Cahigas, M.M.L., Prasetyo, Y.T.: Kansei Engineering-based model and online content assessment in evaluating service design of Lazada express. In: ICIBE 2020: 2020 The 6th International Conference on Industrial and Business Engineering (2020)
10. Hapsari, S.N., et al. Designing train passenger seat by Kansei Engineering in Indonesia. In: MATEC Web of Conferences, vol. 135, p. 00017 (2017)

Digital Wellbeing, eHealth and mHealth

Intelligent Work: Person Centered Operations, Worker Wellness and the Triple Bottom Line

Joan Cahill[1]([⊠]) [ID], Vivienne Howard[1], Yufei Huang[2], Junchi Ye[1,2,3], Stephen Ralph[3], and Aidan Dillon[3]

[1] School of Psychology, Trinity College Dublin, Dublin, Ireland
cahilljo@tcd.ie
[2] Trinity School of Business, Trinity College Dublin, Dublin, Ireland
[3] Zarion Ltd., Dublin, Ireland

Abstract. Work has an important role in terms of promoting wellbeing. However, it can also have negative effects on our physical and mental wellbeing leading to stress, fatigue, poor teamwork and engagement, and burnout. Many companies treat workers in terms of enterprise resources. Operations management often overlooks the 'human factor' and specifically, the relationship between worker wellbeing and performance, and the design of work management processes and associated technologies to support this. The impact of new work and workforce practices/trends such as the blended and flexible workforce along with new automation and artificial intelligence (AI) technologies enabling business process, performance/work, and workforce management, presents both risks and opportunities. This paper introduces a new work management concept – namely, 'intelligent work'. Intelligent work is defined in relation to work that is smart, health, ethical and safe. Critically, it is underpinned by concepts of workplace health protection and promotion, along with progress in automation and AI technologies. This concept has been advanced a part of a human factors action research program addressing responsible business, sponsored by the Irish government.

Keywords: The future of work · Intelligent work · Healthy work · Triple bottom line · Health promotion · Health protection · Operations management · Human factors · Ethics · Sustainable people centered operations · Financial services

1 Introduction

Operations management practices focus heavily on metrics such as productivity, efficiency, and customer experience. This has consequences for individuals (i.e., employee wellness and health impact) and for society. As stated by Elkington (2019), human activity should not compromise the long-term balance between the economic, social, and environmental pillars [1]. Many Fortune 500 companies have embraced concepts of 'responsible business' [2]. However, as argued by the International Labor Organisation (ILO) [3] and the Tripartite Labor Coalition [4], organizations must act on their responsibilities to their workforce too.

© Springer Nature Switzerland AG 2021
C. Stephanidis et al. (Eds.): HCII 2021, CCIS 1421, pp. 307–314, 2021.
https://doi.org/10.1007/978-3-030-78645-8_38

Financial institutions are utilizing new automation, artificial intelligence (AI) and machine learning (ML) technologies to better manage their business processes, their workforce, and customer relationships. Such technologies are changing how work is managed and delivered, and the human role in the system. Workers have concerns about how these technologies will change their job status, their role, and their experience of work. Further, the movement to remote work arising from the COVID 19 pandemic has highlighted the need to address the human and ethical issues surrounding both remote work and technology mediated work supervision. In addition, worker expectations of 'work' and the home/work interface have changed. Specifically, Millennial and Generation Z employees are looking for more autonomy and flexibility in work.

This paper reports on a new concept for work management and monitoring – Intelligent Work (IW). First, a background to this concept is provided. The methodological approach underpinning the specification of this concept is then introduced. The findings are then presented. A short overview of the emerging IW concept is outlined. The concept is then discussed, and some conclusions drawn.

2 Background

Financial Services (FS) refers to professional services involving the investment, lending, and management of money and assets. Work is serviced and managed by finite teams to provides value to the company and its customers. This work can be classified into two types - transactional work and knowledge work. Transactional work involves the processing of information related to a particular transaction or work item. Knowledge work denotes any activity involving the application of existing knowledge to current problems, the use of knowledge within production processes and the creation of new knowledge.

Operations management refers to the ways in which a business manages the resources (i.e., people, materials, technologies) responsible for delivering work. This spans the production lifecycle including planning, organizing, and supervising work. Lean methods emphasize productivity/efficiency and effectiveness [5]. More recently, people centered operations methods are being deployed. These methods recognize the important contribution of work to a person's wellbeing.

Most financial institutions utilize technology to manage their business processes, their workforce, and customer relationships. These technologies are shaping both work and the role of the human in the system. Increasingly, transactional work is undertaken by robotic agents (i.e., robotic process automation technologies). Other kinds of technologies are deployed for the management of work. This includes business process management (BPM) technologies, digital process automation (DPA) technologies and dynamic case management (DCM) technologies.

As stated by the Centers for Disease Control and Prevention (CDC), the workplace is an important setting for health protection, health promotion and disease prevention programs [6]. The World Health Organisation (WHO) propose a model of 'healthy work' and a 'healthy workplace' in which both physical and psychosocial risks are managed [7]. Critically, a healthy workplace is defined 'as one in which workers and managers collaborate to use a continual improvement process to protect and promote the health, safety and well-being of all workers, and the sustainability of the workplace' [7]. The management of psycho-social risk is also emphasized in the new international standards on psychological health in work [8] and safe work during the COVID 19 Pandemic [9].

As proposed in the 'Job Strain Model' [10], employees whose jobs involve high demands and low decision latitude experience the highest levels of work-related stress (WRS). Studies in the information systems literature have found that individuals who experience technostress have lower productivity and job satisfaction, and decreased organization commitment [11]. A 2015 study by Barber and Santuzzi introduced the construct of workplace 'tele-pressure' [12]. This represents the combination of both preoccupation and urge to immediately respond to work-related messages (for example, emails). Such behavior to be associated with poor physical and psychological employee health.

Workers are not immune from common mental health problems such as anxiety and depression. The prevalence of mental health problems among sickness benefit claimants is increasing with over 40% of sickness claims recording a mental or behavioral disorder as a primary condition [13]. The business case for investing in worker wellbeing is well documented [14]. Poor worker wellbeing has a cost implication. For example, costs associated with reduced productivity/delays, reduced worker motivation and poor-quality work, staff retention, sick leave, errors, and poor customer service/customer retention. Unsurprisingly, many companies have introduced workplace Stress Management Initiatives' (SMI) and 'Workplace Wellbeing Programs' (WWP) programs [15]. Some wellness programs deploy corporate wellness self-tracking technologies (CWST) [16]. However, it has been argued that such technologies conflate work and health [17] and may exacerbate worker stress and/or anxiety [18].

3 Research Project and Methodology

The 'Intelligent Work' project investigates how workers, automation, artificial intelligence technologies can collaborate in an efficient, intelligent, and humane way, to enhance worker wellbeing along with boosting the company's long-term revenue. The human factors approach involves building an evidence map in relation to the requirements for future work practices and the allied specification of new technologies to support this. The stakeholder evaluation approach involves the use of a community of practice [19] comprising both internal stakeholders (IS) and external stakeholders (ES). As defined in Table 1 below, this has involved eight phases of research. As each phase of research has progressed, the progressive findings have been triangulated, to further develop and validate the evidence map. The specific methodology combines traditional human factors action research methods (i.e., interviews and workshops), with participatory foresight activities, participatory co-design and evaluation activities, and data assessment. The study protocol was approved by the Ethics Committee of the School of Psychology, Trinity College Dublin.

Table 1. Overview of research stages

#	Method	Description of research and analysis
1	Existing product review	Product demonstration and review (Workshop 1, IS, N = 4)
2	Preliminary human factors and ethics assessment	HFEC Evaluation/IS (N = 2) Personae & Scenarios Specification/IS (N = 2)
3	New Product Ideation	N/A
4	Mapping the problem space & further specification/validation of Concept & Requirements	Interviews/IS (N = 6) Interview/ES (N = 3) Modelling IW Concept (Workshop 2, IS, N = 7). Survey/ES (N = 47)
5	Prototype Development & Interviews/Codesign	IW Concept Evaluation (Workshop 3, I, N = 7) Interviews & Codesign with External Stakeholders (N = 15)
6	Operations Management – Data Analysis	Analysis of anonymous data set
7	Implementation & Business Analysis. Final Ethics Assessment	Using Data (Workshop 4, IS N = 10) Business Case (Workshop 5, IS N = 10) Implementation, Ethics & Acceptability (Workshop 6, IS, N = 10). Final Specification & Implementation (Workshop 7/IS, N = 10)
8	Final Analysis & Specification	Content Analysis (interviews – IS & ES) Final requirements specification

4 High Level Results and Emerging Concept

4.1 Experience of Work and Concepts of Healthy Work

Survey findings indicate varied sources of WRS. Unclear processes present the biggest challenge (11.65%) followed by long working hours (9.71%). Three factors were rated third. These are pressure to meet deadlines, repetitive work. And the commute to work (all 7.77%). 75% of survey respondents indicated that their company is interested in their wellbeing. All interview participants stated that their company was mostly interested in protecting employee wellbeing. Both survey and interview findings suggest that healthy work is defined in relation to management of workload, supporting positive team relations and communications, and the provision of autonomy and flexibility in work.

4.2 Intelligent Work: Concept and Features

Both survey and interview feedback highlight the requirement to advance a 'people centered operations concept' which prioritizes the human role, in an increasingly technology mediated work environment. The 'intelligent work' (IW) concept is characterized by an information access/availability approach - the ability to work from anywhere at any time. From an operational perspective, IW involves providing support for managing work/workload, the home/work interface, and sources of work-related stress (WRS), but not necessarily health monitoring in work. Both interview and survey feedback indicate that the focus should be on enabling/augmenting people as opposed to either work monitoring and/or health monitoring. Health in work relates to the transparent management of work and workload, being assigned the right work (i.e., matching competency/skills) and good communication across team members. This requires a strong emphasis on supporting teamwork. However, field research indicates that the person should be in control of how they obtain help from team members, team supervisors, and the system (including task assistants and robotic agents). Performance monitoring is a key issue. IW needs to be framed from the perspective of self-regulation. The person controls how information about their work and their work performance (i.e., through-put and work quality) is shared with others. Employees would like to obtain feedback to improve their own performance (self-regulation). Further, employees would like to benchmark their own performance against others.

4.3 Role of Technology

The person is allocated work based on smart allocation technology. This technology is predicated on (1) human factors best practice (i.e., model of relationship between work variety/complexity and engagement/performance), and (2) specific knowledge of the individual (i.e., abilities, experience, preferences, working hours and working styles). Importantly, work allocation follows a real-time model of specific worker competencies and experience levels. Also, it is based on a fair capacity/workload assignment (considering the workload of other team members and the business demand). Further, it is balanced to provide appropriate levels of work variety/diversity and complexity (i.e., the sweet spot for engagement and personal development). In addition to smart allocation, the proposed IW technology should provide task assistance to workers – to minimize the stress of looking for information and/or seeking help. Further, this technology might include robotic agents, who perform certain repetitive tasks and provide supports to human team members (for example, finishing tasks, monitoring team member needs, monitoring quality issues, and providing automated feedback to customers).

The worker provides real-time feedback about their performance both in relation to factors such as work suitability, work performance, worker engagement, and health in work. The system also provides the person with feedback about their own performance, so that the worker can assess themselves and manage their own performance – and alert the supervisor if help/intervention is required. Equally, the supervisor has access to this information, so that they can 'coach' the worker. Participants highlighted that performance information should be carefully protected, with clear rules as to how the supervisor or other managers might use this information. Further it was suggested that the introduction of performance feedback should happen gradually – starting with individual feedback. Once this new approach has been accepted and adopted, it might be possible to provide team level feedback, to support self-regulating teams.

4.4 Structuring Framework and Measuring

As reported by interview participants, 'what gets measured gets done'. Thus, is it necessary to select the right performance targets at different levels (i.e., work, individual, team etc.). To this end, performance assessment and feedback needs to reflect a 'contract concept', informed by concepts of accountability. Data and intelligence can be used to generate leading indicators for business success along with employee health. Figure 1 provides an overview of relevant evaluation metrics linked to this. This contract concept contributes to a 'balance score card', to access organizational performance across the triple bottom line.

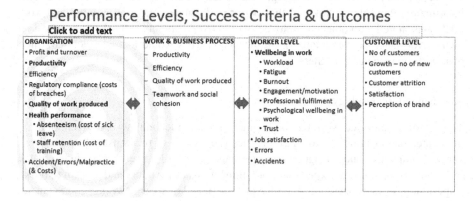

Fig. 1. Performance levels, success criteria & outcomes

5 Discussion

Workplace stress and psychosocial risk is an organizational issue which should be addressed in relation to the introduction of smart work management systems. Automation, AI & ML technologies can be used to capture and analyze data pertaining to the relationship between work, human performance and health, customer outcomes and organizational outcomes. This will ensure that employee health protection and promotion is an outcome of work management. The introduction of these technologies will be underpinned by positive change in relation to supporting wellbeing culture in financial services, and the integration of previously diverse processes and functions pertaining to business process management, customer management, human resources, occupational health and safety/health protection, and health promotion.

Future work technology will enable 'intelligent work' through the application of AI/ML, which enables healthy work allocation and monitoring - balancing different perspectives and needs – the work, the person, the team, the customer, and business value. Intelligent assistants function as supportive team members – augmenting and transforming all roles, including team members, supervisors, operations managers, and the customer. Critically, the system supports 'coaching' of team members and worker self-regulation and self-management.

Healthy work underpins intelligent work. Healthy work can be defined in relation to several features – (1) knowing the person (identity, motivations/goals, skills, preferences, working styles, cases worked on, team experience and achievements), (2) focusing on flow and work performance (i.e., workload balancing, type of work, flexibility, communications, feedback), (3) fostering autonomy and self-management, (4) ensuring the people are part of a team and have a purpose and (5) developing people's strengths. As such, it is more aligned with concepts of workforce monitoring, as opposed to health monitoring.

Intelligent work involves understanding the performance of an organization through the lens of multiple stakeholders. Stakeholders have divergent goals and are rewarded differently. This requires rethinking the organization's mission and purpose and the role of people in supporting this (i.e., focus on human needs and outcomes). For this to happen, there needs to be a shared understanding of the relationship between business objectives and how work is managed, the requirements for healthy work, along with common goals and trust. There are roles and responsibilities on different sides (i.e., individual, team, automation, and organization). The 'contract' is embedded in the 'socio-technical' system and requires elaboration in relation to process definition, training, tools design and culture. Evidently, the implementation of the 'contract' will vary according to the organization's culture and technology capacity.

Some limitations should be noted. Observational research at financial services companies was planned, but not possible during the COVID 19 pandemic. The numbers in each of the three phases of combined interviews and co-design/evaluations were small (N = 5 in each phase, total: N = 15). Further, a small number of participant's completed the survey (N = 47). Limited feedback was obtained from team members. The operations management dataset reflected work activity that was managed without a formal work allocation/process management software. The next phase of research will involve deep human factors research and potential implementation, with an organization, involving the participation of different operational roles, the customer, and the regulator.

5.1 Conclusion

New intelligent work technologies should support enable work that is smart, healthy, and ethical. This involves moving beyond simply process automation and the use of robotic team members. Technologies should augment all human actors, promote teamwork behaviors, and ensure that human actors can self-manage and monitor their own performance. This new concept of 'intelligent work' and 'self-monitoring employees' is underpinned by automation and AI technologies, which deliver on an 'intelligent contract'. There is a strong human/moral imperative along with a business case to move towards 'intelligent work' concepts. Healthy work concepts need to be embedded in how work is planned/allocated, carried out, monitored, and evaluated/assessed, linking to workplace health protection and promotion processes.

References

1. Elkington, J.: Cannibals With Forks: The Triple Bottom Line of 21st Century Business. Capstone, Oxford. ISBN 9780865713925. OCLC 963459936 (1999)

2. Conaway, R.N., Laasch, O.: Communication in Responsible Business: Strategies, Concepts, and Cases. Business Expert Press (2012)
3. Sengenberger, W.: The International Labour Organization: Goals, Functions, and Political Impact. Friedrich Ebert Stiftung, Berlin (2013)
4. International Labour Organisation (ILO): Tripartite Conculation. https://www.ilo.org/global/standards/subjects-covered-by-international-labour-standards/tripartite-consultation/lang--en/index.htm
5. Cooper, R.: Lean enterprises and the confrontation strategy. Acad. Manag. Perspect. **10**(3), 28–39 (1996)
6. Centre for Disease Control and Prevention (CDC). Workplace Health Model. https://www.cdc.gov/workplacehealthpromotion/model/
7. The World Health Organisation (WHO). Healthy workplace model. https://www.who.int/occupational_health/healthy_workplace_framework.pdf
8. International Standards Organisation (ISO): ISO/FDIS 45003. Occupational health and safety management — Psychological health and safety at work — Guidelines for managing psychosocial risks. https://www.iso.org/standard/64283.html
9. International Standards Organisation (ISO). ISO/PAS 45005 (2020)
10. Occupational health and safety management — General guidelines for safe working during the COVID-19 pandemic. https://www.iso.org/standard/64286.html
11. Hackman, J.R., Oldham, G.R.: Motivation through the design of work: test of a theory. Organ. Behav. Hum. Perform. **16**(2), 250–279 (1976)
12. Ragu-Nathan, T.S., Tarafdar, M., Ragu-Nathan, B.S., Tu, Q.: The consequences of technostress for end users in organizations: conceptual development and empirical validation. Inf. Syst. Res. **19**(4), 417–433 (2008)
13. Barber, L.K., Santuzzi, A.M.: Please respond ASAP: workplace telepressure and employee recovery. J. Occup. Health Psychol. **20**(2), 172–189 (2015). https://doi.org/10.1037/a0038278. Epub 2014 Nov 3 PMID: 25365629
14. Brown, J., Hanlon, P., Turok, I., Webster, D., Arnott, J., Macdonald, E.B.: Mental health as a reason for claiming incapacity benefit—a comparison of national and local trends. J. Public Health **31**(1), 74–80 (2009)
15. Bevan, S.: The business case for emplo. http://workfoundation.org/assets/docs/publications/245_iip270410.pdf
16. Tetrick, L., Winslow, C.: Workplace stress management interventions and health promotion. Annu. Rev. Organ. Psych. Organ. Behav. **2**(1), 583–603 (2015)
17. Till, C., Petersen, A., Tanner, C., Munsie, M.: Creating "automatic subjects": corporate wellness and self-tracking. Health Interdisc. J. Soc. Study Health Illness Med. **23**(4), 418 (2019)
18. Hull, G., Pasquale, F.: Toward a critical theory of corporate wellness. BioSocieties **13**(1), 190–212 (2018)
19. Moore, P., Robinson, A.: The quantified self: What counts in the neoliberal workplace. New Media Soc. **18**(11), 2774–2792 (2016)
20. Wenger, E.: Communities of Practice: Learning, Meaning, and Identity. Cambridge University Press, Cambridge (1998)

PatchAi: An e-Health Application Powered by an AI Virtual Assistant to Support Patients in Their Clinical Trials

Luciano Gamberini[1], Patrik Pluchino[1(✉)], Luigi Porto[1], Filippo Zordan[1],
Alessandro Monterosso[2], Kumara Palanivel[2], and Adriano Fontanari[2]

[1] Human Inspired Technologies (HIT) Research Centre, University of Padova, Padua, Italy
patrik.pluchino@unipd.it
[2] PatchAi S.r.L, Padua, PD, Italy

Abstract. In the last decade, there has been a rapid widespread of applications that support different types of patients in self-managing some aspects concerning their health (e.g., drugs assumption) and reporting specific relevant events (e.g., symptoms) daily. Furthermore, these apps turn out to be very important for patients in social isolation and lockdown due to pandemics in which direct contact with their physicians may be hampered and not frequent. Despite the importance of such applications, patients often cease to use them for several reasons increasing the drop-out rate of clinical research. The current paper describes PatchAi, an end-to-end patient engagement solution. The mobile health solution of PatchAi has been designed and developed following a user-centric perspective, intended to support patients and doctors, reduce drop-out rates, while improving patient adherence to protocols and care schedules in clinical trials.

Keywords: Digital health · e-health apps · Virtual assistants · Chatbot · Artificial intelligence · Treatments adherence · Clinical trials

1 Introduction

The increment in life expectancy due to the improvement in health care services underlies some critical issues. Indeed, best health treatments entail an increased incidence and prevalence of chronic non-communicable diseases (CNCD). Nevertheless, CNCDs are associated with complications (comorbidity of multiple pathologies), involving high costs in treatments compromising an individual's productivity and quality of life [1]. The World Health Organization defined as CNCDs the following health conditions: cardiovascular diseases, neoplasms, chronic respiratory diseases, and diabetes mellitus [2].

The adopted lifestyle determines the quality of human aging. Adequate food and time spent in personal, social, and daily activities influence physical and mental functioning [3]. Lifestyle is related to attitudes and behaviors that affect people's health [4].

Health-related mobile applications (viz., m-Health) have been attracting increasing attention [5] because they have great potential to aid in behavior change encouraging

© Springer Nature Switzerland AG 2021
C. Stephanidis et al. (Eds.): HCII 2021, CCIS 1421, pp. 315–322, 2021.
https://doi.org/10.1007/978-3-030-78645-8_39

healthy habits. These applications present various features, including medical information exchange, text messaging, educational content, and web-based video [6]. The
m-Health apps can reduce the disparity in health care, achieving high, medium, and low-
income savings, from delivering integrated information on the management of CNCD
[7]. Besides, these apps enable continuous monitoring of chronic diseases, improve
quality of care and patients feedback, resulting in shorter hospital stays, better health
outcomes [8], and reduce overall healthcare costs [9]. These applications conceived for
the self-management of CNCD aim to support professional caregivers in improving
patients' lifestyle and health conditions [10]. Nevertheless, the assessment (i.e., overall
quality, usability, safety, acceptance) of these digital solutions shows some gaps [11].
Several aspects related to behavioral change have been explored, but further study is
required to identify whose heavily contribute to positively affect the compliance to the
disease treatments [12].

Bashshur and colleagues [13] highlighted how the assessment of e-Health interventions rests on the three pillars of effective healthcare: access, quality, and cost. Access
is a multidimensional concept and it refers to ease or difficulty in obtaining health
services. From the clients perspective, it is defined in terms of the extent to which
they face geographic, economic, architectural, cultural, and/or social barriers to needed
care. The concept of quality refers to the relationship between health care interventions
and/or expenditures and health status. It is possible to conduct different economic analyses. Cost-Effectiveness Analysis (CEA) compares alternative sets of services considering their costs. Differently, Cost-Benefit Analysis (CBA) evaluates various services
measures (i.e., monetary) in terms of costs and benefits. These analyses on e-Health
interventions must be conducted to attain successful outcomes [13].

Within the quality of healthcare category, a positive impact in clinical care appears to
be relevant to the adoption of e-Health. The outcomes are, for instance, improved diagnosis, clinical management, and increased patient-centered healthcare. There is consensus
on the relevant role of cost reduction due to the adoption of e-Health [14].

The concept of using mobile phone messaging for healthcare interventions has been
explored in the scientific literature since 2002 [15]. A series of systematic reviews
on text messaging exploitation in treatments of different health disorders has shown
effectiveness thanks to the ubiquity of smartphones [16, 17].

The conversational agents (CAs) are an additional element that further increases the
efficacy of supporting the treatment's compliance. These solutions originally present in
messaging or other mobile apps, on websites, are increasingly adopted in health care
[18, 19]. Various reviews described the specific types of CAs e.g., virtual coaches [20],
embodied CAs [21], or particular features of the virtual agents for supporting behavioral
change [22]. Other reviews analyzed technical features of CAs, e.g., the back-end system
architecture or the interface's graphical appearance [23].

2 Conversational Agents

2.1 The Role of CAs in the Healthcare Domain

Conversational agents are inserted in software applications that individuals utilize daily.
Users prefer to engage with a CA to complete simple activities (e.g., check the weather)

than through a web page [24]. The most popular conversational agents are those able to use unbounded Natural Language (NL) inputs and that exploit Artificial Intelligence (AI) and Machine Learning [25]. Progress in NL processing and voice recognition has allowed more complex dialogue management and increased conversational flexibility [26]. The essential role of CAs is assisting patients directly in their life contexts or clinicians during the consultations [27]. Several experiments showed the CAs' capability of enhancing patients' access to their online health data, improving their physical activity and diet (i.e., fruits/vegetables consumption, [28]. Besides, in contrast to standard user interfaces, a key feature is the tailored conversations to patients' needs and health literacy that results in better communication, increased satisfaction, and adherence to treatments [29]. Barak and colleagues [30] reported that the CAs' ability to appropriately react to emotions (i.e., empathy) is related to higher compliance with clinical treatments.

Also, regarding shift workers, or people living in rural communities, who may have problems accessing appointments, chatbots (a type of CAs) may be exploited as a potential solution to reduce waiting lists [31]. In response to similar problems (i.e., waiting lists, difficulties in accessing mental health services), Cameron and collaborators [32] developed iHelpr, a chatbot for mental health issues. In this specific healthcare area, chatbots are suggested to be helpful because they offer instant access to support [32].

Kumar and colleagues [33] proposed an app with a conversational agent that allowed users to input their health queries, resulting in a reduced time needed for clinicians' response [33]. When a user's input did not match a set of pre-specified keywords, authors have pointed out that the CA provided the doctor's contact details.

Chatbots are considered an aid for diabetic patients to control their conditions and receive advice [34]. Chatbots' usage has also been assessed in the pharmaceutical industry. A study showed the effectiveness of a chatbot that exploited NL in responding to patients' questions, prescribing, suggesting, and providing information on children's medicines [35]. Besides, a review of AI in healthcare [36] underlined the benefits of CAs: cost reduction, improvement in treatment efficacy, and decrement in time required to reach a correct diagnosis (e.g., avoiding several questions to patients; [36]). Finally, CAs help to abandon the paternalistic concept of "doctor who makes decisions" towards a chatbot-based cooperative model in which the patient-clinician relationship is crucial. The virtual agents are not considered a mere replacement for clinicians [37].

2.2 Personalization of Chatbots

Personalization in chatbots can be achieved implicitly by processing past interactions with users [38, 39], explicitly by user-entered information at the first setup [40], and using ongoing confirmation style input [41]. The messages presented to users [42], or the conversational style [43], can be personalized considering the final user. Personalized and adaptive system behavior in CAs can improve user perception and gratification, task efficiency, and the possibility of behavior change [44]. Besides, studies focused on other elements as dialogue management [45], personalized messages [42], and recommendations [39], and adaptive systems [46].

3   PatchAi

The version of PatchAi that is already on the market presents several exciting features. Patients can report in real-time their symptoms (e.g., nausea; Fig. 1a) through a chat equipped with a chatbot. This CA supports them in inserting all the needed information (e.g., intensity symptoms, drugs assumption). Besides, users complete an eDiary on a daily basis to record information about their disease, symptoms, and other external trigger factors (Fig. 1b) that may have played a role in the symptoms' occurrence. A visual depiction of the symptoms over time is also present, allowing patients to check weekly/monthly their health patterns through the clinical trial. In addition, users can fill out a standardized questionnaire to assess their general quality of life before visiting their physician. A specific menu is devoted to allowing the management of visits with the clinicians (i.e., scheduling, rescheduling). Doctors may access and evaluate real-time clinical trial patient-related information (e.g., protocol adherence) through a web dashboard. Furthermore, friendly therapy reminders are provided to support users in following their regimen. Regarding aspects of health education, PatchAi delivers, through a news section, tailored content related to the specific patient's disease.

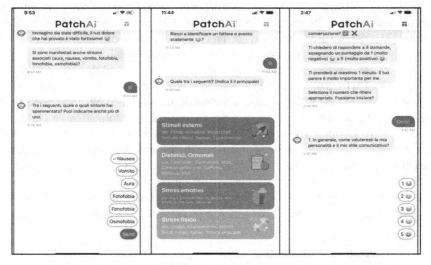

Fig. 1. a) Symptoms; b) External trigger factors; c) Personality style assessment.

The current version of PatchAi follows the basic principles of usability and accessibility [47]. Concerning usability, it is easy to navigate inside and across the different screens, there is a rich and deep tutorial and a help and documentation section, the system status is clear (e.g., changes of colors in selectable items), the utilized icons are easily identified and of everyday use, the menu and chat language are familiar, and the error messages are easy to understand. Finally, the end-users can send direct feedback (e.g., comments, malfunctioning) to designers and developers, shaking their phones and providing the related information.

Regarding accessibility, the app presents easy to select and well-spaced buttons (i.e., avoiding unintentional selection), the possibility of modifying text dimensions (i.e., readability), and a sufficient contrast of icons-background colors (i.e., low-vision individuals).

In the context of persuasion and behavioral change [48–50], the app's key features are two: an AI chatbot [18, 51] and gamification elements (i.e., badges earned by achieving specific goals, e.g., completing an eDiary). The aim of these features is to increase end-users motivation and engagement and support continuous usage of the app throughout clinical trials. Besides, it is possible to customize the AI chatbot by choosing its personality among different ones (i.e., reassuring, comforting, rigorous). Personality selection influences the bot's language and communication style. If the selected personality is not satisfying, patients can change it. The bot sometimes asked users to assess its personality, communicative style (Fig. 1c), notifications, and reminders. Designers and developers might exploit these feedbacks for eventual app re-design highlighting the relevance of the end users' opinions in the design process. Other persuasion strategies for supporting patients' engagement are related to the frequency of bot-initiated interactions, the CA icon's expressions that change based on the patients' regularity in completing their daily activities, and the badges for each achievement.

Further trials will be carried out with re-designed versions of the app adopting a user-centered approach (i.e., involving patients, clinicians) in the assessment (i.e., user experience, usability, etc.) of the prototypes that will be developed. The aim of supporting an effective behavioral change in patients (i.e., increasing the so-called m-Adherence) will be pursued by operating on the bot's personalization to better match the end-users' characteristics. This will result in an improved user experience and engagement which are essential conditions, along with usability, to increase acceptance, intention of usage, and the actual adoption of every technology.

References

1. Bahia, L.R., et al.: The costs of type 2 diabetes mellitus outpatient care in the Brazilian public health system. Value Health **14**, S137e40 (2011). https://doi.org/10.1016/j.jval.2011.05.009
2. World Health Organization: The World Health Report 2003: reducing risks promoting healthy life. World Health Organization, Geneva (2002)
3. de Oliveira, S.F.D., de Duarte, Y.A.O., Lebrão, M.L., Laurenti, R.: Demanda referida e auxílio recebido por idosos com declínio cognitivo no município de São Paulo. Saúde e Sociedade **16**, 81e9 (2007). https://doi.org/10.1590/S0104-12902007000100008
4. Oliveira, L.S., Rabelo, D.F., Caires Queroz, N.: Life style, perceived control and quality of life: a study with the aged population of Patos de Minas-MG. Estudos e Pesquisas em Psicologia **12**, 416e30 (2012)
5. Nahar, P., Kannuri, N.K., Mikkilineni, S., Murthy, G.V.S., Phillimore, P.: mHealth and the management of chronic conditions in rural areas: a note of caution from southern India. Anthropol. Med. **24**, 1e16 (2017). https://doi.org/10.1080/13648470.2016.1263824
6. Isakovic, M., Sedlar, U., Volk, M., Bester, J.: Usability pitfalls of diabetes mHealth apps for the elderly. J. Diabetes Res. **2016**, 1604609 (2016). https://doi.org/10.1155/2016/1604609
7. Slater, H., Campbell, J.M., Stinson, J.N., Burley, M.M., Briggs, A.M.: End user and implementer experiences of mHealth technologies for noncommunicable chronic disease management in young adults: systematic review. J. Med. Internet Res. **19**, e406 (2017). https://doi.org/10.2196/jmir.8888

8. Quaosar, G.M.A.A., Hoque, M.R., Bao, Y.: Investigating factors affecting elderly's intention to use m-health services: an empirical study. Telemed. J. e Health **24**, 309e14 (2018). https://doi.org/10.1089/tmj.2017.0111

9. Eagleson, R., et al.: Implementation of clinical research trials using web-based and mobile devices: challenges and solutions. BMC Med. Res. Methodol. **17**, 43 (2017). https://doi.org/10.1186/s12874-017-0324-6

10. Chen, J., Bauman, A., Allman-Farinelli, M.: A study to determine the most popular lifestyle smartphone applications and willingness of the public to share their personal data for health research. Telemed. J. e Health **22**, 655e65 (2016). https://doi.org/10.1089/tmj.2015.0159

11. Bellei, E.A., Biduski, D., Cechetti, N.P., De Marchi, A.C.B.: Diabetes mellitus m-health applications: a systematic review of features and fundamentals. Telemed. J. e Health **24**, 839e52 (2018). https://doi.org/10.1089/tmj.2017.0230

12. Sudhir, P.M.: Advances in psychological interventions for lifestyle disorders. Curr. Opin. Psychiatr. **30**, 346e51 (2017). https://doi.org/10.1097/YCO.0000000000000348

13. Bashshur, R.L., Shannon, G., Krupinski, E.A., Grigsby, J.: Sustaining and realizing the promise of telemedicine. Telemed. J. E Health **19**(5), 339–345 (2013). https://doi.org/10.1089/tmj.2012.0282. [Medline: 23289907]

14. Granja, C., Janssen, W., Johansen, M.A.: Factors determining the success and failure of eHealth interventions: systematic review of the literature. J. Med. Internet Res. **20**(5), e10235 (2018)

15. Neville, R., Greene, A., McLeod, J., Tracey, A., Tracy, A., Surie, J.: Mobile phone text messaging can help young people manage asthma. Br. Med. J. **325**(7364), 600 (2002). https://doi.org/10.1136/bmj.325.7364.600/a. [Medline: 12228151]

16. Hall, A.K., Cole-Lewis, H., Bernhardt, J.M.: Mobile text messaging for health: a systematic review of reviews. Ann. Rev. Public Health **36**, 393–415 (2015). https://doi.org/10.1146/annurev-publhealth-031914-122855. [Medline: 25785892]

17. Rathbone, A.L., Prescott, J.: The use of mobile apps and SMS messaging as physical and mental health interventions: systematic review. J. Med. Internet Res. **19**(8), e295 (2017). https://doi.org/10.2196/jmir.7740. [Medline: 28838887]

18. Car, L.T., et al.: Conversational agents in health care: scoping review and conceptual analysis. J. Med. Internet Res. **22**(8), e17158 (2020)

19. Hoermann, S., McCabe, K.L., Milne, D.N., Calvo, R.A.: Application of synchronous text-based dialogue systems in mental health interventions: systematic review. J. Med. Internet Res. **19**(8), e267 (2017). https://doi.org/10.2196/jmir.7023. [Medline: 28784594]

20. Tropea, P., et al.: Rehabilitation, the great absentee of virtual coaching in medical care: scoping review. J. Med. Internet Res. **21**(10), e12805 (2019). https://doi.org/10.2196/12805. [Medline: 31573902]

21. Provoost, S., Lau, H.M., Ruwaard, J., Riper, H.: Embodied conversational agents in clinical psychology: a scoping review. J. Med. Internet Res. **19**(5), e151 (2017). https://doi.org/10.2196/jmir.6553. [Medline: 28487267]

22. Pereira, J., Díaz, O.: Using health chatbots for behavior change: a mapping study. J. Med. Syst. **43**(5), 135 (2019). https://doi.org/10.1007/s10916-019-1237-1. [Medline: 30949846]

23. Xing, Z., et al.: Conversational interfaces for health: bibliometric analysis of grants, publications, and patents. J. Med. Internet Res. **21**(11), e14672 (2019). https://doi.org/10.2196/14672. [Medline: 31738171]

24. Følstad, A., Brandtzæg, P.B.: Chatbots and the new world of HCI. Interactions **24**(4), 38–42 (2017)

25. Grosz, A.J., et al.: Artificial Intelligence and Life in 2030: One Hundred Year Study on Artificial Intelligence. Stanford University (2016)

26. Radziwill, N.M., Benton, M.C.: Evaluating Quality of Chatbots and Intelligent Conversational Agents, April 2017

27. Wolters, M.K., Kelly, F., Kilgour, J.: Designing a spoken dialogue interface to an intelligent cognitive assistant for people with dementia. Health Inform. J. **22**(4), 854–866 (2016)
28. Bickmore, T.W., Schulman, D., Sidner, C.: Automated interventions for multiple health behaviors using conversational agents. Patient Educ. Couns. **92**(2), 142–148 (2013)
29. Denecke, K., Tschanz, M., Dorner, T., May, R.: Intelligent conversational agents in healthcare: hype or hope? Stud. Health Technol. Inform. **259**, 77–84 (2019)
30. Barak, A., Klein, B., Proudfoot, J.G.: Defining internet-supported therapeutic interventions. Ann. Behav. Med. **38**(1), 4–17 (2009). https://doi.org/10.1007/s12160-009-9130-7. ID: Barak2009
31. Goldstein, I.M., Lawrence, J., Miner, A.S.: Human-machine collaboration in cancer and beyond: the centaur care model. JAMA Oncol. **3**, 1303–1304 (2017)
32. Cameron, G., et al.: Towards a Chatbot for digital counselling. In: Proceedings of the 31st British Computer Society Human Computer Interaction Conference (HCI 2017). BCS Learning & Development Ltd., Swindon, UK, pp. 24:1–24:7 (2017). https://doi.org/10.14236/ewic/HCI2017.24
33. Kumar, V.M., Keerthana, A., Madhumitha, M., Valliammai, S. Vinithasri, V.:Sanative Chatbot For Health Seekers (2016)
34. Lokman, A.S., Zain, J.M., Komputer, F.S., Perisian, K.: Designing a Chatbot for diabetic patients (2009)
35. Comendador, B.E.V., Francisco, B.M.B., Medenilla, J.S., Mae, S.: Pharmabot: a pediatric generic medicine consultant chatbot. J. Autom. Control Eng. **3**(2) (2015)
36. Ilić, D.T., Marković, B.: Possibilities, Limitations and economic aspects of artificial intelligence applications in healthcare. Ecoforum J. **5**(1) (2016)
37. Bibault, J.E., Chaix, B., Nectoux, P., Pienkowski, A., Guillemasé, A., Brouard, B.: Healthcare ex Machina: are conversational agents ready for prime time in oncology? Clin. Transl. Radiat. Oncol. **16**, 55–59 (2019)
38. Aha, D.W., Breslow, L.A., Muñoz-Avila, H.: Conversational case-based reasoning. J. Appl. Intell. **14**(1), 9–32 (2001). https://doi.org/10.1023/a:1008346807097
39. Thompson, C.A., Goker, M.H., Langley, P.: A personalized system for conversational recommendations. J. Artif. Intell. Res. **21**, 393–428 (2004). https://doi.org/10.1613/jair.1318
40. Rich, E.: User modeling via stereotypes. In: Maybury, M.T., Wahlster, W. (eds.) Readings in Intelligent User Interfaces, pp. 329–342. Morgan Kaufmann Publishers Inc., San Francisco (1998)
41. Chen, L., Pu, P.: Critiquing-based recommenders: survey and emerging trends. User Model. User-Adap. Inter. **22**(1–2), 125–150 (2012). https://doi.org/10.1007/s11257-011-9108-6
42. Kim, Y., Bang, J., Choi, J., Ryu, S., Koo, S., Lee, G.G.: Acquisition and Use of Long-Term Memory for Personalized Dialog Systems. In: Böck, R., Bonin, F., Campbell, N., Poppe, R. (eds.) Multimodal Analyses enabling Artificial Agents in Human-Machine Interaction. MA3HMI 2014. LNCS, vol. 8757, pp. 78–87. Springer, Cham (2015). https://doi.org/10.1007/978-3-319-15557-9_8
43. Levin, E., Levin, A.: Evaluation of spoken dialogue technology for real-time health data collection. J. Med. Internet Res. **8**(4), e30 (2006). https://doi.org/10.2196/jmir.8.4.e30. [Medline: 17213048]
44. Kocaballi, A.B., et al. The personalization of conversational agents in health care: systematic review. J. Med. Internet Res. **21**(11), e15360 (2019). https://doi.org/10.2196/15360. [Medline: 31697237]
45. Pargellis, A., Kuo, H., Lee, C.: An automatic dialogue generation platform for personalized dialogue applications. Speech Commun. **42**(3–4), 329–351 (2004). https://doi.org/10.1016/j.specom.2003.10.003
46. Litman, D.J., Pan, S.: Designing and evaluating an adaptive spoken dialogue system. User Model. User-Adap. Inter. **2–3**, 111–137 (2002). https://doi.org/10.1023/A:1015036910358

47. Sharp, H., Rogers, Y., Preece, J.: Interaction Design: Beyond Human-Computer Interaction, 5th edn. Wiley (2019)
48. Alahäivälä, T., Oinas-Kukkonen, H.: Understanding persuasion contexts in health gamification: a systematic analysis of gamified health behavior change support systems literature. Int. J. Med. Inform. **96**, 62–70 (2016)
49. Sardi, L., Idri, A., Fernández-Alemán, J.L.: A systematic review of gamification in e-Health. J. Biomed. Inform. **71**, 31–48 (2017)
50. Baumeister, H., Kraft, R., Baumel, A., Pryss, R., Messner, E.-M.: Persuasive e-health design for behavior change. In: Baumeister, H., Montag, C. (eds.) Digital Phenotyping and Mobile Sensing. SNPBE, pp. 261–276. Springer, Cham (2019). https://doi.org/10.1007/978-3-030-31620-4_17
51. Abd-Alrazaq, A., Safi, Z., Alajlani, M., Warren, J., Househ, M., Denecke, K.: Technical metrics used to evaluate health care chatbots: scoping review. J. Med. Internet Res. **22**(6), e18301 (2020)

Cloud System for the Management of Neuropsychological Test in Mexico

Erika Hernández-Rubio[1], Amilcar Meneses-Viveros[2]([✉]),
Ariana I. Aguilar-Herrera[3], Oscar Zamora Arévalo[4],
and Yeni L. Hernández-Rubio[5]

[1] Instituto Politécnico Nacional, SEPI-ESCOM, Ciudad de México, Mexico
ehernandezru@ipn.mx
[2] Departamento de Computación, CINVESTAV-IPN, Ciudad de México, Mexico
ameneses@cs.cinvestav.mx
[3] Instituto Politécnico Nacional, ESCOM, Ciudad de México, Mexico
[4] Posgrado - Faculta de Psicología, Universidad Nacional Autónoma de México,
Ciudad de México, Mexico
[5] Instituto Politécnico Nacional, ESCA, Ciudad de México, Mexico

Abstract. In last years, the population growth rate is higher than the growth rate of health personnel in Mexico. This phenomenon has generated a health gap problem. The e-Health systems can help mitigate this problem because rehabilitation can be done from home, and the specialist doctors can review the test results remotely. In particular, for older adults with neuropsychological problems, it is very feasible to use this type of tool and the neuropsychological tests can be programmed on mobile devices such as tablets or smartphones.

Keywords: eHealth · Cloud computing · Neuropsychological tests · Older adults · User experience

1 Introduction

In last years, the population growth rate is higher than the growth rate of health personnel in Mexico. This phenomenon has generated a health gap problem [9]. Another problem that has been observed is that the average age of health specialists is 50 years old. The recent COVID-19 pandemic problem revealed the shortage of personnel and infrastructure in the Mexican health area. As an emergency measure, all the available medical personnel were oriented to attend to COVID patients, leaving aside the follow-up of their usual patients. However, a high percentage of medical personnel belong to vulnerable groups, both due to health problems and age [3,6,7]. Furthermore, with confinement, older adults have not been able to attend hospitals and continue their treatment, because they are a vulnerable group. This represents a risk in patients who require follow-up with specialists [6,19,20].

© Springer Nature Switzerland AG 2021
C. Stephanidis et al. (Eds.): HCII 2021, CCIS 1421, pp. 323–327, 2021.
https://doi.org/10.1007/978-3-030-78645-8_40

The e-Health systems can help mitigate this problem because rehabilitation can be done from home, and the specialist doctor can review the test results remotely. In particular, for older adults with neuropsychological problems, it is very feasible to use this type of tool and the neuropsychological tests can be programmed on mobile devices such as tablets or smartphones [11,16,21]. Thus, the elderly can carry out the tests without having to make appointments with the specialist, and the specialist can schedule the tests that the patient must perform and monitor their progress [14,20]. In this work we present an eHealth system in the cloud to management the Luria's neuropsychological tests in elderly patients. This system has been developed for three types of users: specialist, patients and administrators. The specialist user is responsible for registering, deleting and editing patient records. In addition, specialist can program the neuropsychological tests that a patient must perform, and monitor and evaluate the results of the tests. These actions are carried out through cloud services that the specialist execute in a web browser. The patient user performs the neuropsychological tests assigned by the specialist. Neuropsychological tests are services that the cloud system calls. The user performs the tests on a tablet or smartphone. The admin user has two main tasks: adding new neuropsychological tests to the system and associate them as services; and register, delete and edit specialist user records.

The system is developed in the cloud. For an interaction between users, the system is responsible for sending notifications to users when they have tasks to perform. These tasks can be to perform tests or evaluate test results. Thus, specialists can use the tool from a browser on a computer, tablet or smartphone. Because patients only enhance the tests that the specialist schedules, they use tablets and both the cloud system and the Luria's tests have a user-oriented design so that they are intuitive and easy to use. The usability of each test applied in tablets has been studied in previous works. Finally, an advantage of systems developed in the cloud is that they can be easily scaled. In particular we refer to scaling the system to the possibility of adding new Luria's tests, provided they have been developed as services.

2   Related Work

Cloud computing has been presented as a viable alternative to develop eHealt systems [5,13,18]. The use of Cloud Computing allows systems to be cheaper, easier to maintain, with fast, efficient and secure data distribution [1].

Most of the works in the literature on eHealth systems using Cloud Computing focus on data security [2,4,15,17,18].

Some works have been developed combining mobile devices with cloud computing for eHealth systems, such as [8,10]. The main advantage of combining the mobile computing and cloud computing approaches is that the system includes a user-centered human-computer interaction development [12].

3   Design

The system was designed using middleware patterns and cloud patterns. The middleware approach allows design a distributed system for this eHealth system. Cloud pattern allow include some characteristics such as horizontal scaling and queue-centric workflow [22].

Figure 1 shows the architecture systems based on middleware. Two main users can be identify: patient and specialist. Users patient are older adults. This module run on a mobile device such as smartphone or tablet. Patient would be able to perform the neuropsychological tests. User specialist is a neuropsychologist. This user must manage patient records, view test results, and assign new tests. The data layer is maintained on the servers.

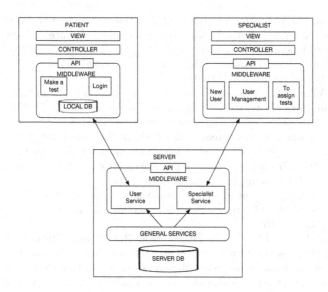

Fig. 1. Design of system based on middleware design

4   Development

Javascript, Angular, Java Spring Framework, and MongoDB were used to develop the system. Javascript and Angular were used for the presentation layer, this include the modules for patients and specialists users. Java Spring Framework was used for business layer. MongoDB was used for the data layer. A non-SQL database manager was chosen because the test results can be documents or multimedia files. The system can be scaled in the neuropsychological test space. Its mean that, each neuropsychological test is a service, so it is enough to include the URL address to access it. The neuropsychological tests have been developed with design centered for older adults in tablets.

5   Conclusions

In this work a cloud system development for Luria's Neuropsychological test have been presented. Cloud computing offers the potential for eHealth systems to reduce maintenance costs, large storage capacity, high availability, and collaboration, to name a few. Combining mobile devices with a Cloud Computing technology allows operating and maintenance costs to be reduced, users can use the system anywhere and at any time as long as they have an internet connection. Also, its allows achieve user centered design for modules for patients and specialist users.

References

1. Al Nuaimi, N., AlShamsi, A., Mohamed, N., Al-Jaroodi, J.: e-health cloud implementation issues and efforts. In: 2015 International Conference on Industrial Engineering and Operations Management (IEOM), pp. 1–10. IEEE (2015)
2. Albuquerque, S.L., Gondim, P.R.: Security in cloud-computing-based mobile health. IT Prof. **18**(3), 37–44 (2016)
3. Antonio-Villa, N.E., et al.: Assessing the burden of COVID-19 amongst healthcare workers in Mexico City: a data-driven call to action. medRxiv (2020)
4. Azeez, N.A., Van der Vyver, C.: Security and privacy issues in e-health cloud-based system: a comprehensive content analysis. Egypt. Inform. J. **20**(2), 97–108 (2019)
5. Bahrami, M., Singhal, M.: A dynamic cloud computing platform for ehealth systems. In: 2015 17th International Conference on e-Health Networking, Application & Services (HealthCom), pp. 435–438. IEEE (2015)
6. Caldera-Villalobos, C., et al.: The Coronavirus Disease (COVID-19) challenge in Mexico: a critical and forced reflection as individuals and society. Front. Public Health **8**, 337 (2020)
7. Delgado-Gallegos, J.L., Montemayor-Garza, R.J., Padilla-Rivas, G.R., Franco-Villareal, H., Islas, J.F.: Prevalence of stress in healthcare professionals during the COVID-19 pandemic in northeast Mexico: a remote, fast survey evaluation, using an adapted COVID-19 stress scales. Int. J. Environ. Res. Public Health **17**(20), 7624 (2020)
8. Fong, E.-M., Chung, W.-Y.: Mobile cloud-computing-based healthcare service by noncontact ECG monitoring. Sensors **13**(12), 16451–16473 (2013)
9. Hernández-Rubio, E., Meneses-Viveros, A., Muñoz Salazar, L.: User experience in older adults using tablets for neuropsicological tests in Mexico City. In: Rau, P.-L.P. (ed.) HCII 2019. LNCS, vol. 11577, pp. 135–149. Springer, Cham (2019). https://doi.org/10.1007/978-3-030-22580-3_11
10. Karaca, Y., Moonis, M., Zhang, Y.-D., Gezgez, C.: Mobile cloud computing based stroke healthcare system. Int. J. Inf. Manag. **45**, 250–261 (2019)
11. Krausz, M., Westenberg, J.N., Vigo, D., Spence, R.T., Ramsey, D.: Emergency response to COVID-19 in Canada: platform development and implementation for ehealth in crisis management. JMIR Public Health Surveill. **6**(2), e18995 (2020)
12. Kulkarni, G., Shelke, R., Patil, P.B.N., Kulkarni, V., Mohite, S.: Optimization in mobile cloud computing for cloud based health application. In: 2014 Fourth International Conference on Communication Systems and Network Technologies, pp. 569–572. IEEE (2014)

13. Kuo, M.-H.: Opportunities and challenges of cloud computing to improve health care services. J. Med. Internet Res. **13**(3), e67 (2011)
14. Lam, K., Lu, A.D., Shi, Y., Covinsky, K.E.: Assessing telemedicine unreadiness among older adults in the United States during the COVID-19 pandemic. JAMA Internal Med. **180**(10), 1389–1391 (2020)
15. Li, M., Yu, S., Zheng, Y., Ren, K., Lou, W.: Scalable and secure sharing of personal health records in cloud computing using attribute-based encryption. IEEE Trans. Parallel Distrib. Syst. **24**(1), 131–143 (2012)
16. Licciardone, J.C., Pandya, V.: Feasibility trial of an ehealth intervention for health-related quality of life: implications for managing patients with chronic pain during the COVID-19 pandemic. In: Healthcare, vol. 8, pp. 381. Multidisciplinary Digital Publishing Institute (2020)
17. Löhr, H., Sadeghi, A.-R., Winandy, M.: Securing the e-health cloud. In: Proceedings of the 1st ACM International Health Informatics Symposium, pp. 220–229 (2010)
18. Michalas, A., Paladi, N., Gehrmann, C.: Security aspects of e-health systems migration to the cloud. In: 2014 IEEE 16th International Conference on e-Health Networking, Applications and Services (Healthcom), pp. 212–218. IEEE (2014)
19. Pelayo-Nieto, M., Linden-Castro, E., Gómez-Alvarado, M.O., Bravo-Castro, E.I., Rodríguez-Covarrubias, F.T.: la pandemia por covid-19 ha impactado a la práctica urológica en méxico. Rev. Mex. Urol. **80**(1), 1–7 (2020)
20. Rivero, J.A.V., Ledezma, J.C.R., Pacheco, I.H., Gurrola, M.R.A., Pontigo, L.L.: La salud de las personas adultas mayores durante la pandemia de COVID-19. J. Negative No Positive Results **5**(7), 726–739 (2020)
21. Timmers, T., Janssen, L., Stohr, J., Murk, J., Berrevoets, M.: Using ehealth to support COVID-19 education, self-assessment, and symptom monitoring in The Netherlands: observational study. JMIR Mhealth Uhealth **8**(6), e19822 (2020)
22. Wilder, B.: Cloud Architecture Patterns: Develop Cloud-Native Applications. O'Reilly, Sebastopol (2012)

Adoption of Smart Hospital Services by Patients: An Empirical Study

Pi-Jung Hsieh[1], Hui-Min Lai[2(✉)], Zhi-Cheng Liu[1], and Shui-Chin Chen[1]

[1] Department of Hospital and Health Care Administration, Chia Nan University of Pharmacy and Science, Tainan, Taiwan, R.O.C.
`beerun@seed.net.tw`, {`3b0505133,b0505106`}`@gm.cnu.edu.tw`
[2] Department of Business Administration, National Taichung University of Science and Technology, Taichung, Taiwan, R.O.C.
`hmin@nutc.edu.tw`

Abstract. With an increasingly aging population and advances in the Internet of Things (IoT), the concept of a "smart hospital" has become an important topic. Although several prior studies have focused on factors that impact the adoption and use of electronic medical records and health information management systems, the literature directly related to patients' adoption behaviors toward smart hospital services is scant. Thus, this study proposed a theoretical model to explain patients' intentions to use smart hospital services as part of the healthcare process. A field survey was conducted in Taiwan to collect data from patients. A total of 213 valid responses were obtained, constituting a response rate of 85.2%. The results show that attitude, perceived usefulness, perceived ease of use, and health literacy had positive effects on usage intention. In contrast, perceived risk had a direct negative effect on the patients' intentions to use smart hospital services. These findings have implications for the development of strategies to improve smart health care acceptance.

Keywords: Self-health management · Health management mobile service · Health belief

1 Introduction

With Taiwan now considered an aging society, its hospitals must meet a growing demand for chronic illness and geriatric care. In order to improve clinical outcomes and operational efficiency, many hospitals are groaning under the pressure to improve their operational efficiencies and quality of care while controlling healthcare costs and doing better resource management. They need innovative solutions and mobile technologies to match their patients' needs to the available physical resources. A "smart hospital" has become an important part of national strategic planning. Smart hospitals are likely to have a critical impact on the quality of care and patient-centered governance issues [1]. A smart hospital is defined as an information-based infrastructure and information and communication technology (ICT) environment that combines the functions of sensing,

© Springer Nature Switzerland AG 2021
C. Stephanidis et al. (Eds.): HCII 2021, CCIS 1421, pp. 328–334, 2021.
https://doi.org/10.1007/978-3-030-78645-8_41

actuation, and control over a traditional hospital [2]. Thus, a smart hospital depends on optimized and automated processes built into an ICT environment of interconnected assets, particularly based on the Internet of Things (IoT), to improve existing health care processes and implement new operational capabilities [1]. For example, outpatient registration and fee payment processes are being expedited by technology in the form of automatic registration machines. Patients can receive a basic health check at a vital sign-measuring station. After they insert their National Health Insurance (NHI) integrated circuit (IC) cards, their height, weight, body temperature, and blood pressure are measured and automatically uploaded into the hospital information system. Further, IoT applications and services enable the monitoring of patients' usage of hospital rooms and can assist in the allocation of medical professionals to these rooms to meet the patients' needs [3]. As accurate patient information becomes more centralized and available, the system could become capable of describing and analyzing certain aspects of disease and making decisions based on the available data in a predictive or adaptive manner, thereby performing smart actions. As a result, smart hospitals are likely to have a significant effect on customer satisfaction and operational efficiency issues. Therefore, patients' acceptance of, and support for, a smart hospital is particularly critical in Taiwan.

Although several prior studies have focused on care outcomes and the practicalities of smart health services [3–5], the literature directly related to patients' adoption behaviors toward smart hospital services is scant. However, a smart hospital is not a simple service but an interactive process between patients and healthcare providers. Thus, the existing variables of technology acceptance models do not fully reflect the motives of its adoption or use. Previous research has suggested the need for incorporating additional health behavior factors to improve the explanatory power of these technology acceptance constructs. To comprehensively understand various factors that are associated with smart hospitals and those factors' effects on patients' adoption behaviors, this study proposed that a patient's intention to use a smart hospital was based on two opposing forces: enabling and inhibiting perceptions. In the case of enabling perceptions, we propose that a user's intention to use a smart hospital is based on four enablers of information system (IS) usage: attitude, perceived usefulness (PU), perceived ease of use (PEOU), and health literacy. In the case of inhibiting perceptions, perceived risk is experienced regarding the possible negative consequences of using smart hospital services.

2   Literature Review

The technology acceptance model (TAM) was introduced by Davis [6] to understand and explain the acceptance and adoption behavior of a new technology. TAM advances that behavior intention is affected by an individual's attitude toward using the new technology. Attitude, in turn, has two critical determinants: perceived usefulness (PU) and perceived ease of use (PEOU). Further, PU is specified to have an independent influence on behavior intention, and PEOU has an influence on PU. Attitude is defined as an individual's positive or negative perception about performing a particular behavior. PU refers to the degree to which an individual perceives that the usage of a new technology will improve his or her job performance, while PEOU is the degree to which an individual perceives that his or her usage will be relatively free of effort [6]. TAM has been the most frequently cited and influential model for explaining the acceptance of new technology and has received extensive support from empirical studies. Numerous past studies have confirmed that the TAM model has good explanatory power for explaining health information technology (IT) acceptance [7–9]. In addition, having a low level of health literacy will make an individual less likely or less willing to seek health information in their everyday life [10]. Thus, health literacy is also a critical factor in most widely explained health-related behaviors [11]. With low-level health literacy, patients have difficulty reading, writing, and using health information through smart hospital services. Thus, we proposed that patients' intention to use a smart hospital was based on four enablers of system usage: attitude, PU, PEOU, and health literacy.

Perceived risk is defined as the possible negative consequences of using a service [12]. From the perspective of the patient, there are several kinds of perceived risk involved with the use of smart hospital services. These include performance, privacy, and psychological risk. Performance risk is the probability of a healthcare provider harming a patient because of an incorrect clinical decision based on inadequate information. Privacy risk for a patient is a lack of control over personal health information. Psychological risk is the potential that using smart hospital services may induce psychological discomfort and tension because it could have a negative effect on the patient's self-perception. Perceived risk has been employed to assist in the explanation of users' adoption of health IT [13]. Thus, perceived risk is a critical factor that can potentially affect a patient's perception of smart hospital services. This study integrates perceived risk into the TAM to obtain a more comprehensive understanding of the behavioral intention of the patient with regard to smart hospital services.

3 Research Model

We propose that a patient's intention to use a smart hospital is based on two opposing forces: enabling and inhibiting perceptions. In the case of enabling perceptions, we propose that a user's intention to use a smart hospital is based on four enablers of IS use: attitude, PU, PEOU, and health literacy. In the case of inhibiting perceptions, perceived risk is an inhibitor that can negatively affect the intention to use smart hospital services. Figure 1 presents the proposed research model.

According to the TAM perspective, behavior intention is positively affected by attitude, PU, and PEOU. Meanwhile, attitude is positively affected by PU and PEOU; PU is directly affected by PEOU. In this study, a patient's perception of the extent to which smart hospital services are easy to use affects the perception of usefulness, attitude toward using the technology, and behavior intention. Attitude is also affected by the technology's usefulness, as perceived by a patient. Further, the patient's intention to use smart hospital services can be explained by attitude (towards using the technology) and its perceived usefulness. Aldosari et al. [8] provide empirical support for these associations within a healthcare context, which led us to hypothesize the following:

H1.   Attitude will be positively related to the intention to use the smart hospital.
H2.   The PU will be positively related to the intention to use the smart hospital.
H3.   The PEOU will be positively related to the intention to use the smart hospital.

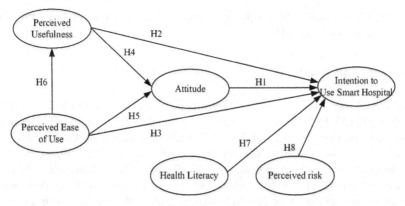

Fig. 1. Research framework

H4. The PU will be positively related to attitude towards using.
H5. The PEOU of a smart hospital will be positively related to attitude towards using.
H6. The PEOU will be positively related to the PU of the smart hospital.

Health literacy represents a person's cognitive skills that determine their competency and motivation to access, understand, and use information about their health in a manner that promotes or solves their health status [11]. Consequently, if the health literacy of individuals is high, they are likely to have greater intentions to adopt a health passbook for self-management. Further, perceived risk enhances the anticipation of negative consequences, thus leading to an unfavorable attitude that typically results in a negative effect on a user's intention to use [14]. In the context of this study, if smart hospital services are perceived to have a large risk (i.e., an incorrect clinical decision or psychological discomfort), the patient may resist using smart hospital services. Therefore, we predicted the following:

H7. Health literacy will be positively related to the intention to use the smart hospital.
H8. Perceived risk will be negatively related to the intention to use the smart hospital.

4 Research Methodology

The target participants consisted of hospital patients in Taiwan. Three hospitals were successfully contacted to secure their collaboration. A total of 250 questionnaires were distributed through an administrator of the hospital, and 213 questionnaires were returned to be used as the sample. We used structural equation modeling with partial least squares (PLS) for the data analysis. We also examined the reliability and validity of the research model. The model was deemed reliable if the construct reliability was greater than 0.8 [15]. Convergent validity was assessed based on the following criteria: (a) statistically significant item loadings greater than 0.7, (b) composite construct reliabilities greater than 0.8, and (c) average variance extracted (AVE) values greater than 0.5 [16]. The discriminant validity of the constructs was assessed based on the criterion that the square root of the AVE for each construct should be greater than the corresponding correlations with all the other constructs [15].

5 Results and Analysis

The 213 valid responses we obtained constituted a response rate of 85.2%. Slightly more than half (55.9%) of the respondents were females. The majority of respondents (50.7%) were between the ages of 20 and 29 years. The education level for 66.3% of the respondents was university. The construct reliabilities were all greater than 0.85. For convergent validity, the item loadings were all greater than 0.7, and the AVE values ranged from 0.60 to 0.81. For discriminant validity, the square root of the AVE for each construct was greater than its corresponding correlations with the other constructs. These results indicated acceptable reliability and validity. Figure 2 presents the test results for the structural model. The results indicated that attitude, PU, PEOU, and health literacy had positive effects on behavior intention, while perceived risk had a negative effect on behavior intention. Further, PU and PEOU have positive effects on attitude, while PEOU has a positive effect on PU. The explained variance (R^2) for intention to use, attitude, and PU was 0.46, 0.27, and 0.10, respectively.

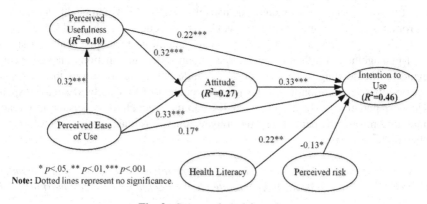

Fig. 2. Structural model results.

6 Conclusion and Discussion

The effects of these usage intention variables were important in understanding patients' usage behavior because they are consistent with Aldosari et al. [8] and Nunes et al. [9], who maintained the relative importance of attitude, PU, and PEOU in explaining that usage intention varies across behaviors and situations. Thus, individuals who perceive a higher degree of attitude, PU, and PU are more likely to use smart hospital services so that they can facilitate their care efficiency and care quality in the hospital. Further, our results also highlight the critical role of attitude in smart hospital acceptance decision-making by patients and, therefore, single out the importance of attitude cultivation and management for successful smart hospital implementation. Thus, it indicates that a positive attitude toward smart hospital services can be fostered by focusing on patients' care needs, as well as design simplicity. In addition, a smart hospital service that requires less effort and is easier to use will be perceived as more useful. Furthermore, the results showed that health literacy had the strongest effect on behavioral intention. This result coincides with the findings of previous studies on health IT adoption [17]. Thus, high-level health literacy enhances an individual's intention to use the smart hospital. In contrast, perceived risk had a direct negative effect on patients' use intentions, meaning that higher levels of perceived risk resulted in lower intention to use the smart hospital services. This result coincided with the findings of a previous study on health technology adoption [13].

In summary, the main contribution of this study was that it was the first to explore patients' usage with technology acceptance theory. The integration approach adopted as the basis of the proposed model provides a more complete set of antecedents that offers a better explanation of patients' intentions to adopt smart hospital services, thus enhancing the practical contributions of this study. For example, as attitude had a significant impact on continued use intention, system managers and healthcare providers should develop health management strategies that promote activities among patients and visitors and ensure that they have a positive attitude toward the smart hospital. Further, our results show that health literacy is an important factor that influences patients' intentions to use a smart hospital. Thus, to attract more potential users, system managers should strive to improve the function and quality of their services. Furthermore, they should employ user-friendly designs and ensure not only that people can easily learn how to use the smart hospital, but also that the medical professionals offer education to patients. The results indicate that this provides a good initial look at some of these factors. Although this study produced useful results, the findings and implications drawn from this study cannot be generalized to other groups. Since our sample was highly educated and young. There might see a greater effect if a greater percentage of less educated individuals and more older individuals were included. Future research could focus on accumulating empirical evidence and data to address the limitations of this study. We offer implications regarding medical practice and academic research that are based on our findings. We hope that this study will stimulate future interest in the big health data acceptance phenomena and motivate researchers to examine in greater depth this unexplored yet potentially fertile area of research.

References

1. Visconti, R.M., Martiniello, L.: Smart hospitals and patient-centered governance. Corp. Ownersh. Control. **16**, 83–96 (2019)
2. Guo, J., Chen, Z., Ban, Y.L., Kang, Y.: Precise enumeration of circulating tumor cells using support vector machine algorithm on a microfluidic sensor. IEEE Trans. Emerg. Top. Comput. **5**, 518–525 (2017)
3. Fischer, G.S., Righi, R.D.R., Costa, C.A.D., Galante, G., Griebler, D.: ElHealth: using Internet of Things and data prediction for elastic management of human resources in smart hospitals. Eng. App.l Artif. Intell. **87**, 103255 (2020)
4. Riahi, I., Moussa, F.: A formal approach for modeling context-aware Human-Computer System. Comput. Electr. Eng. **44**, 241–261 (2015)

5. Yoo, S., et al.: A personalized mobile patient guide system for a patient-centered smart hospital: lessons learned from a usability test and satisfaction survey in a tertiary university hospital. Int. J. Med. Inform. **91**, 20–30 (2016)
6. Davis, F.D.: Perceived usefulness, perceived ease of use, and user acceptance of information technology. MIS Q. **13**(3), 319–340 (1989)
7. Holden, R.J., Karsh, B.T.: The technology acceptance model: its past and its future in health care. J. Biomed. Inform. **43**, 159–172 (2010)
8. Aldosari, B., Al-Mansour, S., Aldosari, H., Alanazi, A.: Assessment of factors influencing nurses acceptance of electronic medical record in a Saudi Arabia hospital. Inform. Med. Unlocked. **10**, 82–88 (2018)
9. Nunes, A., Portela, F., Santos, M.F.: Improving pervasive decision support system in critical care by using technology acceptance model. Procedia Comput. Sci. **141**, 513–518 (2018)
10. Kim, Y.C., Lim, J.Y., Park, K.: Effects of health literacy and social capital on health information behavior. J. Health. Commun. **20**, 1084–1094 (2015)
11. Aydın, G.Ö., Kaya, N., Turan, N.: The role of health literacy in access to online health information. Technol. Forecast. Soc. Change. **195**, 1683–1687 (2015)
12. Featherman, M.S., Pavlou, P.A.: Predicting e-services adoption: a perceived risk facets perspective. Int. J. Hum. Comput. Stud. **59**(4), 451–474 (2003)
13. Hsieh, P.J.: Physicians' acceptance of electronic medical records exchange: an extension of the decomposed TPB model with institutional trust and perceived risk. Int. J. Med. Inf. **84**(1), 1–14 (2015)
14. Benlian, A., Hess, T.: Opportunities and risk of software-as-a-service: findings from a survey of IT executives. Decis. Support Syst. **52**(1), 232–246 (2011)
15. Chin, W.W.: Issues and opinion on structural equation modelling. MIS Q. **22**(1), 7–16 (1998)
16. Fornell, C., Larcker, D.: Structural equation models with unobservable variables and measurement error: algebra and statistics. J. Mark. Res. **18**(3), 382–388 (1981)
17. Hsieh, P.J., Lai, H.M.: Exploring people's intentions to use the health passbook in self-management: an extension of the technology acceptance and health behavior theoretical perspectives in health literacy. Technol. Forecast. Soc. Change. **161**, 120328 (2020)

PixE: Home Fitness Method Using Machine Learning with Smartphone

Jimin Kim and Yang Kyu Lim[(✉)]

Duksung Women's University, 33, Samyang-ro 144-gil, Dobong-gu, Seoul, Republic of Korea
Trumpetyk09@duksung.ac.kr

Abstract. The COVID-19 outbreak has caused worldwide confusion. However, in the Republic of Korea, it has overcome the situation by using a variety of communication infrastructures. Especially in Korea, a new word Homt appeared. Home fitness is referred to as 'home training' in Korea and is called Homt for short. It is a word for a new method of home fitness which has emerged based on Internet infrastructure. This is a service made possible on a fast network in Korea, where a great deal of data is transmitted at high speed. Our research goal is to create fitness game, *PixE*, using a smartphone camera that everybody has. Basically, it is a game of strength exercises such as squats and lunges. It uses machine learning technology to exchange information over a fast network in Korea while minimizing the burden of poor smartphone resources. It is based on the detection of human movements by getting images from a smartphone in real time on the server. Motion recognition and a variety of effects are created using extracted images. The final image is pixelated and sent back to the smartphone. With the edited image by using ML, the user himself becomes a main character in the fitness game. It is a fitness game for Homt that can be easily used anytime, anywhere. If the user only has a smartphone, that's all! In particular, it has a user focus and be immersed in it by becoming the main character that appears directly into the game. Before the official release, we demonstrated with two groups, exercise experts and laymen. We found that the effects of the exercise were no different than the existing effects. We hope to create an environment where you can easily home fitness anytime, anywhere, not in a special situation such as COVID-19.

Keywords: Home fitness · Homt · Machine learning · Fitness game

1 Background

In 2020, a sudden COVID-19 brought about a social shutdown. In Korea, one of the Asian countries, nightlife and street culture are very famous. This culture disappeared instantly. Korean society, which has the fastest Internet in the world, has become an era of Avant-Garde. All school conferences were delivered online. Homeworking has become the norm, and many people have only begun to live at home because of COVID-19. Since people spend most of their time at home, their movements have decreased significantly, which has made them worry about their health. People began to feel that it is difficult to maintain health due to two circumstances: the restrictions on exit and COVID-19.

© Springer Nature Switzerland AG 2021
C. Stephanidis et al. (Eds.): HCII 2021, CCIS 1421, pp. 335–340, 2021.
https://doi.org/10.1007/978-3-030-78645-8_42

In Korea, where 5G communication has been commercialized, realistic exercise programs using VR and AR technologies are successfully published [1]. Various content using K-pop stars were sufficient to attract interest at first, but usage is decreasing greatly due to various reasons. Firstly, people need to purchase additional and expensive VR equipment, and secondly, they have difficulty in using unfamiliar equipment. In addition, there is no guarantee that everyone has the most current equipment.

The topic of our research this time is to do home fitness with easy-to-use equipment that everybody already has. The concept of home fitness regularly progresses with aerobics in Western countries since the development of television. In conservative Asian countries focused on Korea, home fitness for television has not developed well because the design of sportswear and other apparel has become an issue.

The Korean gaming market is growing around mobile based on a rapid network. Especially, competition between humans is a phenomenon in Korea which is appreciated as a culture rather than stress. The most important feature is to add elements of play that can be enjoyed by the competition instead of home fitness, which is a personal activity. The home fitness program developed by this study is intended to be a game that everyone can appreciate while reflecting this national reality. In particular, it will be a form that can be enjoyed simply without the addition of equipment and an increase in cost by using machine learning technology that has been attracting attention recently.

2 Related Works

Kinect is the console gaming interface for Microsoft [3]. It recognizes the body and movement of the user through an infrared camera without a special handheld controller. *Kinect* receives depth information, RGB values and joint tracking information in real time using image information. In particular, the picture captured by the RGB camera and the image depth information is combined to express the user's skeleton. It has attracted the attention of interactive artists because it is a great product for posture recognition. In other words, it is being actively used in the media art field in addition to the original purpose of game control. There have been attempts to use *Kinect* in a greater variety of fields while officially supporting the connection between *Kinect* and PC in version 2. A fitness program created through the acquisition of correct posture information with *Kinect* and the accumulation of this data has also been released to the market. From 2021, *Kinect* was reportedly discontinued and is looking for new developments. The cause of *Kinect*'s failure is the failure of the *Xbox*, a home gaming console. We are more interested in motion recognition using the latest technology rather than devices that are difficult to get right now.

The portable sensor is literally measuring the degree of motion by wearing a separate sensor over the body. Portable also means that it is a small size. However, these sensors do not recognize motion with 1 or 2 installations. A number of sensors are necessary for each part of the body. In this case, the actions may be more precise, but the feeling is very different from when you do the exercise. Several dancers and athletes have already mentioned this. We do not use portable sensors. The movement is monitored with images from the camera. This was made possible by advances in machine learning technology. It was an important development that could solve the inconvenience of having to reset the settings each time according to the size of a person's body.

The *Densepose* of Facebook is a technology that uses deep learning to map all human images in a 3D structure [2]. The coordinates of each part of the human body are regressed all the different frames. In addition, it uses a region-based model and fullyconvolutional networks and improves its accuracy through cascading. It is connected to the realm of posture estimation and object detection.

Google *PoseNet* is a real-time human posture estimation method in a browser developed by Google with the help of TensorFlow.js [3]. We can develop our program easier with *PoseNet* than through direct learning by adding a library [4, 5]. By using this advantage, many individuals in different areas can easily perform tasks through motion recognition. We selected a single pose algorithm that recognizes only one object and takes a shorter time to recognize the pose. This is because home fitness typically targets individuals. By estimating a person's posture in real time like that, it can be used gently in low-performance devices such as smartphones.

3   Game, *PixE*

3.1   Scenario

The story of the game is simple. Users explore the planets of the solar system in spacecraft. The power of that spacecraft is our kinetic energy. The more you repeat the exercise, the higher the rocket will fly. It also acts as a distraction or help, according to the precision of the exercise. Each step will aim to fly to a planet or space station.

Fig. 1. *PixE* is a Retro Space Game for Homt.

3.2   Program Design

As the first step in game production, movement learning was conducted with advice from persons specializing in exercise. The data was obtained from the work of tracking more accurate movements. Posture data are important to correct people who exercise in poor posture. The function of the game is to compare and fix the user's movement data with the existing expert's movement data. For example, non-professionals are not always in line with the direction of the toes and knees when squatting. With this silly posture, the center of the body collapses and puts a lot of stress on the knees. It compares the shoulder and knee points of the general and the exercise professional and warns you when you move incorrectly. The program helps to keep the knees from gathering in the internal direction of the body. In the case of the lunge, it works in a similar way. The lunge is a good workout when the hip joint, knee and foot are in a straight line. It is difficult for the average person to maintain that position. This is also made to be done correctly by referring to expert motion data.

We used *PoseNet* for gesture recognition. *PoseNet* is an algorithm that recognizes a person through a small camera of a smartphone and a computer. Special motion learning can be applied to fitness programs. Based on the movement information saved by an expert earlier, it was compared with the user's input data. In other words, it is a program that can determine whether it is right or wrong when each person carries out a specific action.

The main character in the game is created by transforming the camera picture. By increasing the pixels you will maintain the 80's graphic style. This is enough to make this program look like a retro game. This is also the reason that the name of this game, in which the pixelized self appears, has become *PixE*.

We have also added a social media function, and by adding your own *facebook* record, you can feel the competition with your friends. On social networks, you can record the training you have completed and the number of times. Depending on the scenario, the score is displayed in height shown in Fig. 2.

Fig. 2. Result screen after finishing *PixE*.

4   Experiment

The experiment was divided into two sections. The subjects of the experiment were 20 males and 20 females in their 20s and 30s who are not interested in sport. Each group of 10 males and females were allowed to exercise freely using the existing home fitness method. It is difficult to tell what kind of product it is, but it is a way to follow the exercise by watching a video. The rest of the group has used *PixE*. What we had initially intended was to measure the health of the two methods of exercise. However, something came up during the experiment. As I mentioned earlier, home fitness based on video viewing, which is unfamiliar in Korea, has been dropped one after the other. 8 people dropped out after 3 days or less and 6 people attempted only about 5 days. Of course, the other 6 people completed the exercise well. On the other hand, in the group that used our program, all except 3 defectors finished the experiment until the end.

Looking at the reason for quitting in the existing method, as in Fig. 1 5 people were "not interested", 4 people "did not like the original exercise", "doubt about the effect of exercise", and the last one was "lack of time" as shown in Fig. 3. Those who finished to the end had reasons such as "duty to experiment", "fun", and "no reason".

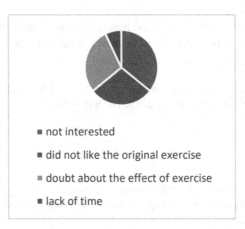

Fig. 3. The reason for quiting in the existing method.

Then, among those who conducted the experiment in our way, the answers of the three givers are as shown.

On the contrary, the reasons that the people who used our method of exercise completed the experiment to the end were: first, a sense of obligation to be recorded on social media, second, a feeling that there is an exercise effect, and third, a sense of reward (gaming) (Fig. 4).

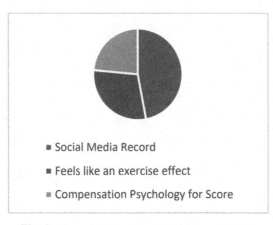

Fig. 4. The reason that the people who used *PixE*.

5   Conclusion

First of all, this experiment had many limitations. As a result of the COVID-19 attack, it was difficult to find and support the experimenter. And because the experimentalists gave up on the experiment, it was also very unfortunate. Even so, we were able to extract significant data. It is a fact that many people in Korea have a reluctance to home fitness. In Korea, where mobile games are popular, it looks good to approach home fitness with games using smartphones.

In particular, the demand for in-home fitness increases during this time of difficult outdoor activities. We hope that this will become a long-term phenomenon, rather than a temporary one.

Acknowledgement. This work was supported by the National Research Foundation of Korea Grant funded by the Korean Government (2019S1A5B5A07110229).

References

1. Lee, J.: 'Home Training' and 'Homemade' are popular... The phenomenon changed by COVID-19 re-proliferation. https://www.newspim.com/news/view/20200901000472. Accessed 25 Feb 2021
2. densepose. http://densepose.org/. Accessed 25 Mar 2021
3. Kinect. https://en.wikipedia.org/wiki/Kinect. Accessed 25 Mar 2021
4. Medium. https://medium.com/tensorflow/real-time-human-pose-estimation-in-the-browser-with-tensorflow-js-7dd0bc881cd5. Accessed 25 Mar 2021
5. Yoon, S.-W., Oh, J.-M., Jung, C.-H., Lee, K.-C.: A research of action recognition based on Kinect for constructing a smart home system. The Korean Institute of Information Scientists and Engineers Proceedings of Academic Presentation, pp. 610–612, 12 2017
6. Tensorflow. https://www.tensorflow.org. Accessed 25 Mar 2021

Causality: A Portable Protocol for Rapid Development of Applications for Social Interactions

Taein Kim, Taeyong Kim, and Bowon Lee[✉]

Department of Electrical and Computer Engineering, Inha University, Incheon, South Korea
{tikim,taeyong.kim,bowon.lee}@dsp.inha.ac.kr

Abstract. This paper proposes Causality, a portable protocol for quickly developing HCI applications for social interactions based on the context through cause and effect, and a Windows application assisting social and emotional behavior targeted to help people with autism spectrum disorder. For application's interactivity and convenient post-analysis, we added some enhancements to our protocol. For example, we implemented speech synthesis and recognition modules to promote users' participation and natural interactions. Our application generates a summary when the user finishes the application for the post-analysis of the user's interactions for further refinement. We expect our Causality protocol can help future researchers as a starting point to make their own social and sentimental assistance application without requiring extensive programming skills.

Keywords: Human computer interaction · Autism spectrum disorder · Object-oriented programming

1 Introduction

There are several things to consider for creating an application that simulates social interactions. For example, program developers need to decide how to express the flow of time in a social interaction scenario. Each flow needs to present various types of media such as text, image, and video, and it is important to consider how they are presented to users within the flow. In addition, the sequence of flow may change little once designed while dynamic change of flow may be required based on the selected actions by the users. Thus, it will significantly reduce the time and efforts needed for development with the help of a protocol that can manage various media types and handle information flow in an application separately from the program source code.

Autism spectrum disorder (ASD) is a broad term for a developmental disability that can cause significant social skill deficits [6]. Especially since ASD has been closely related to racial, ethnic, and socioeconomic aspects [3], improving the social interaction skills of people with ASD is an important problem.

© Springer Nature Switzerland AG 2021
C. Stephanidis et al. (Eds.): HCII 2021, CCIS 1421, pp. 341–347, 2021.
https://doi.org/10.1007/978-3-030-78645-8_43

Due to the complexity of research on interaction systems for people with ASD, HCI-oriented studies in this area have relatively not been well explored [5,11]. In recent years, an iPad-based application to help ASD students enhance social or academic skills [1,10] and robot-based social-emotional intervention have been suggested. However, the target ages were 4–8, which is too young and narrow in scope, and the study only emphasized behavioral outcomes, not the feedback on user interaction [9].

There can be two aspects to consider when developing social interaction applications. The first is to design methods to write and manage contents used in the program, and the second is design the UI/UX to provide better accessibility for people with ASD. To effectively improve the social interaction ability of people with ASD, we have focused on two parts when designing our suggested interaction protocol, *Causality*. First, since they have difficulties in understanding social interaction, our system is conceived to improve their ability to understand the program's contents. Also, for easy interaction with the content, our UI/UX system is implemented to provide better accessibility and ease-of-use.

In summary, we introduce a handy protocol to conveniently create and utilize the contents, which helps people with ASD to enhance their social interaction skills. The paper then presents a Windows demo application to guide the direction to design UI/UX with our protocol. We expect our work on the protocol and UI/UX design can serve as starting point for people who need to develop their social interaction application for research.

2   Proposed Approach

2.1   Protocol Design: Causality

The protocol design of our interface is based on the motivation for efficient design of the program in order to simulate social interaction for people with ASD. For example, it is relatively simple to make the environment that the flow of the context is fixed and the actions that the user chooses from the available options do not affect the flow. However, there exist numerous cases to consider when the user's selection dynamically affects the flow of the context. From the perspective of object-oriented design [2], we can design such a structure by abstracting essential classes based on cause and effect.

The whole scenario of our interface comprises small scenes where each scene is connected to the next scene in the flow of the scenario. The choice and behavior information of the users are described in *Action* class and the current state information of the scenario is saved in *Context* class. One scene can contain action options that the users can choose from. By performing one of the actions, a user creates a causal entry by marking a flag to show whether the user has previously acted specific action in other scenes.

If it contains a decision-making process that tells the ongoing context, an interactive story can be created. For example, it can be implemented as a simple condition check if the user has to perform actions 1, 3, and, 4 to move from scenario A to C by skipping B. However, there can be questions like what if it requires to assign importance to each action or how the scenario can switch to C if the user did not do actions 1 and 3 but did action 4.

In such cases, it may be better to implement branching in the form of *Perceptron* [12] rather than the condition test in the form of Boolean Algebra (AND, OR, NOT). Setting the weights of actions 1 and 3 to 0.3 and the weights of action 4 to 0.6 makes the conditions mentioned above easy to implement with a *Perceptron* operation. It will be possible to develop an interactive application that is not a one-way story like open-world games.

It is expected that separation of roles between content creators and programmers will be difficult if scenarios, options, and actions are designed to be programmer-friendly, such as subroutines and conditional statements. Thus, the protocol is designed based on XML (eXtensive Markup Language) [4] and perceptron-based conditional operations, enabling scenarios to be constructed without the need for programming knowledge.

2.2 Protocol Classes

This section introduces three types of classes used in Causality protocol. Only essential logic or relationships among classes will be explained.

Classes Related to Behavior. *Action*, *CustomAction*, *Option*, and *Role* classes belong to this category (see Fig. 1).

An *Action* class represents one of the behaviors that the user can execute while running the scenario. Generally, an *Option* class provides actions as choices. *CustomAction*, which inherits from the *Action* class, is suitable for saving an answer for a short-answer question since it can store a string message.

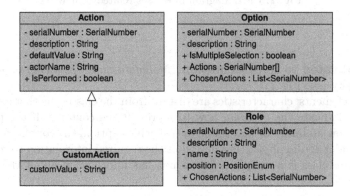

Fig. 1. UML diagram of classes related to behaviour

Classes Related to Flow. *Perceptron, Cause, Caption, Scene,* and *Scenario* classes belong to this category (see Fig. 2). The smallest unit of flow is the *Caption* class. Each *Caption* object contains the dialogue and speaker's name to be seen in the flow and contains the serial number of the *Caption* corresponding to the following flow. If a user is required to choose action or answer the question, the *Caption* object will also have a serial number for the corresponding *Option* object.

If it is required to make a conditional breakpoint, the *Cause* object's serial number will be added. To illustrate the process how a conditional branch operates, at first the program calculates the value of *Perceptron,* to which the *Cause* object points, and compare it with the *Cause* object's threshold values. The result of comparison determines what is the next *Caption* object to be shown.

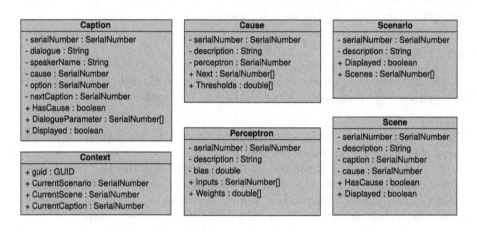

Fig. 2. UML diagram of classes related to flow

Classes Related to Representation. *Metadata* and *Media* classes belong to this category (see Fig. 3).

Those elements' characteristics are distant from the classes in other categories since they indicate the program how to represent the contents. If the program needs to show an image or play audio at a specific caption, the content developer can just add a *Media* object that describes the required information to represent it. *Metadata* class is a unique object which has information about the current scenario.

2.3   Implementation

This section will present the code that implements some of the essential classes introduced in Sect. 2.2. The source code of the program is written in C#. Each content to be retrieved from the program is written in XML. The following

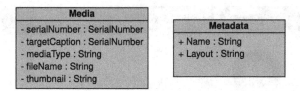

Fig. 3. UML diagram of classes related to representation

Code 1 shows the fragment of *Perceptron* content data. To simplify the representation of references between each class, we assign each object a serial number.

```
<Perceptrons>
  ...
  <Perceptron>
  <SerialNumber>PER002</SerialNumber>
  <Description>Have the player been feeling nervous and anxious
      lately?</Description>
  <Inputs>
    <Input>ACT011</Input> <!-- Have not felt anxious lately -->
    <Input>ACT010</Input> <!-- Had felt anxious lately -->
  </Inputs>
  <Weights>
    <Weight>0.6</Weight>
    <Weight>0.0</Weight>
  </Weights>
  <Bias>0</Bias>
  </Perceptron>
</Perceptrons>
```

Code 1. XML implementation of *Perceptron* data

3   Application Design: ASDryRunner

To improve the social interaction skills of people with ASD, we conceive our application, ASDryRunner. This program helps them have better understanding of cause and its presumed effect by letting them interact with contents rendered via a windows application.

3.1   Implementation

When considering UI and UX of the application, those elements should be as intuitive and straightforward as possible since people with ASD have difficulties in handling the situation when many choices or exceptions exist. Since the experiment is being prepared for people with ASD, we have designed and enhanced UI/UX expecting how they will use the program. This application provides three screens: the main screen, the scenario selection screen, and the content progress

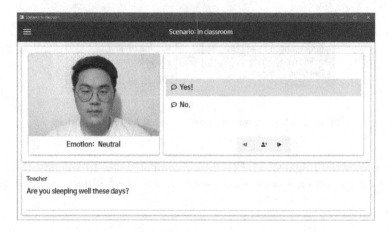

Fig. 4. Screenshot of ASDryRunner

screen. We have used WPF (Windows Presentation Foundation) framework to provide a GUI screen (Fig. 4).

For the application's interactivity and convenient post-analysis, we added some enhancements to our protocol. To collect crucial information about participation, we have implemented speech recognition and facial expression recognition to promote users' participation and natural interactions. To this end, we extended the structure to exchange information with a server providing voice recognition and emotion recognition functions using REST (Representational State Transfer) API [7]. Our application generates a summary when the user finishes the application for the post-analysis of the user's interactions for further refinement of the scenario.

4   Discussion

In this paper, we proposed a protocol to write applications and their contents that enhance social interaction capabilities, and presented a Windows GUI application. For further improvements, we plan to conduct both quantitative and qualitative experiments to see how much benefit that the proposed protocol provides. Our further objective is to perform user studies with people with ASD and collect user feedback on the UI/UX perspective.

We also plan to create and use Android apps for experiments because the ASD adults who participated in our internal survey use mobile devices such as smartphones more often than computers. Furthermore, additional UI/UX considerations for touchscreen interface will be explored. Our Causality protocol has been released on Github for researchers to use and we will continue to update its capabilities [8].

Acknowledgements. This work was supported by the Ministry of Education of the Republic of Korea and the National Research Foundation of Korea (NRF-

2018S1A5A2A03037308), the Industrial Technology Innovation Program funded by the Ministry of Trade, Industry & Energy (10073154), and the Institute of Information & communications Technology Planning & Evaluation (IITP) grant funded by the Korea government (MSIT) (2020-0-01389, Artificial Intelligence Convergence Research Center (Inha University)).

References

1. Almutlaq, H., Martella, R.C.: Teaching elementary-aged students with autism spectrum disorder to give compliments using a social story delivered through an iPad application. Int. J. Spec. Educ. **33**(2), 482–492 (2018)
2. Booch, G.: Object Oriented Design with Applications. Benjamin-Cummings Publishing Co., Inc., San Francisco (1990)
3. Centers for Disease Control and Prevention: Data & statistics on autism spectrum disorder, September 2020. https://www.cdc.gov/ncbddd/autism/data.html. Accessed 25 Mar 2021
4. World Wide Web Consortium, et al.: Extensible markup language (XML) 1.1 (2006)
5. DiPietro, J., Kelemen, A., Liang, Y., Sik-Lanyi, C.: Computer- and robot-assisted therapies to aid social and intellectual functioning of children with autism spectrum disorder. Medicina **55**(8), 440 (2019)
6. Diagnostic and Statistical Manual of Mental Disorders, 5th edn, vol. 21. American Psychiatric Association (2013)
7. Fielding, R.T., Taylor, R.N.: Principled design of the modern web architecture. ACM Trans. Internet Technol. **2**(2), 115–150 (2002). https://doi.org/10.1145/514183.514185
8. InhaDSP: InhaDSP/Causality (2021). https://github.com/InhaDSP/Causality. Accessed 24 Mar 2021
9. Marino, F., et al.: Outcomes of a robot-assisted social-emotional understanding intervention for young children with autism spectrum disorders. J. Autism Dev. Disord. **50**(6), 1973–1987 (2020). https://doi.org/10.1007/s10803-019-03953-x
10. Van der Meer, L., et al.: An iPad-based intervention for teaching picture and word matching to a student with ASD and severe communication impairment. J. Dev. Phys. Disabil. **27**(1), 67–78 (2015). https://doi.org/10.1007/s10882-014-9401-5
11. Odom, S.L., et al.: Technology-aided interventions and instruction for adolescents with autism spectrum disorder. J. Autism Dev. Disord. **45**(12), 3805–3819 (2015). https://doi.org/10.1007/s10803-014-2320-6
12. Rosenblatt, F.: The perceptron: a probabilistic model for information storage and organization in the brain. Psychol. Rev. **65**(6), 386–408 (1958). https://doi.org/10.1037/h0042519

Habit Formation Dynamics: Finding Factors Associated with Building Strong Mindfulness Habits

Robert Lewis[✉] [ID], Yuanbo Liu[ID], Matthew Groh[ID], and Rosalind Picard[ID]

MIT Media Lab, Massachusetts Institute of Technology, Cambridge, MA, USA
{roblewis,picard}@media.mit.edu, {yuanbo,groh}@mit.edu

Abstract. Mindfulness is widely recognized as an effective technique for managing mental and physical health. However, a significant challenge remains when attempting to transform its practice into a habit. To understand the individual characteristics and contexts that correlate with habit formation experiences, we conducted a six-week observational study involving 62 participants who planned to adopt a new mindful breathing habit. Overall, 47.4% (N = 1,234) of daily surveys were completed and 41 participants completed the post-study survey. Using a growth curve modeling framework, we confirm the presence of significant overall change in habit automaticity across participants in the first 21 days of habit practice. Furthermore, we identify four factors that are significantly correlated with the gradient of participant habit formation trajectories: how committed a participant is to building the habit before starting the practice period, their prior mindfulness experience, and two dimensions of personality – agreeableness and emotional stability.

Keywords: Habit formation · Health behavior change · Well-being · Mindfulness · Growth curve modeling · Observational study

1 Introduction

The practice of mindfulness has wide-ranging health benefits [4,9,15]. While even a single session can be advantageous, many of its benefits require regular practice over extended periods of time. *Habit formation* is an effective mechanism through which to achieve such behavioral regularity and is associated with improving long-term health outcomes [7]. Building a habit allows one to transition a behavior from a deliberation that requires motivation into an automatic impulse [8]. By doing so, habit serves as a form of self-control [6], enabling consistent performance of health behaviors even with inevitable motivation lapses.

However, habit formation is not straightforward and attempts to develop new habits often end up unsuccessful. While past work identifies the archetypal shape of successful habit formation and the importance of consistent repetition in the forming process [11,13], little is known about the individual characteristics and contexts that correlate with different outcomes during habit formation attempts.

© Springer Nature Switzerland AG 2021
C. Stephanidis et al. (Eds.): HCII 2021, CCIS 1421, pp. 348–356, 2021.
https://doi.org/10.1007/978-3-030-78645-8_44

Our ongoing work addresses this gap by applying an interpretable quantitative framework to data collected from our observational study on forming mindful breathing habits. We report results on significant factors associated with the observed heterogeneity in participant outcomes, and outline how we will extend this analysis. More broadly, our investigation relates to established challenges in the HCI community, including personalized and context-dependent user modeling, as well as the role technology can play in supporting human well-being and *eudaimonia* [16]. An eventual goal of our work is to design a digital health behavior change system that helps users to form new healthy habits.

2   Related Work

Lally et al. [11] analyzed the process of habit formation by fitting nonlinear regression models to self-reported habit strength on a per-individual basis. Their study participants selected a target behavior from categories of healthy eating, drinking or exercise. Items from the Self-Report Habit Index (SRHI [19]), reported by participants daily, were then used to quantify the concept of habit *automaticity* – the extent to which an individual is aware of, intentional about, in control of, or efficient with their practice of the target behavior [1]. The authors regressed automaticity against time using an asymptotic function, and concluded that it took between 18 to 254 days for an individual to reach 95% of the asymptote in their automaticity trajectory, emphasizing the heterogeneity in habit formation experiences. Furthermore, they observed that consistent target behavior repetitions were associated with better model fits.

Our work extends this quantitative understanding of habit formation by using a growth curve modeling framework [2,5]. Growth curve models are used in *repeated measures* data scenarios – such as those that occur in disease progression [3] and developmental psychology [10] – to model the between-person differences in within-person change processes. More specifically, they provide an interpretable lens through which we can scrutinize how both time-invariant factors (such as demographics and personalities) and time-varying factors (such as daily mood and context) correlate with the shape of participant growth trajectories, and thus serve as a way to categorise the observed heterogeneity in habit formation journeys and outcomes.

3   The Forming Healthy Habits Study

We conducted a six-week observational study, from November 2020 to January 2021, that involved 62 participants who planned to develop a new daily mindful breathing habit. At study initiation, participants received an overview of the study protocol and the concept of a habit, and were guided to choose a daily cue on which to anchor their mindful breathing practice. They then completed the Self-Report Habit Index (SRHI [19]) for mindful breathing to baseline the strength of any existing habit. Information on personality [12], mindfulness experience, commitment to forming the habit, and well-being [17] was also collected.

Table 1. Data collected from our six-week observational study in which 62 participants attempted to develop a new daily mindful breathing habit.

A. Daily survey items	
1. Completion	Whether or not the participant did the mindful breathing exercise
2. SRHI habit automaticity	3 questions from the SRHI [19] scale related to habit automaticity. On a 7-point scale from "Extremely Inaccurate" to "Extremely Accurate", participants rate the extent mindful breathing is something that: i) I do automatically, ii) I do without having to consciously remember, iii) I would find hard not to do. Note: on every seventh day, participants complete the full 12-item SRHI
3. Other habit reflections	Participants rate (7-point scale) their i) motivation and ii) confidence for the building the habit. Additionally, if they did the breathing exercise they rate how iii) rewarding and iv) how challenging it felt
4. Mood	For the past 24 h, participants rate (7-point scale) how often they felt in i) a good mood and ii) a bad mood; the extent they felt iii) calm or stressed and iv) lethargic or energetic; and v) their overall rating of mood from extremely unpleasant to extremely pleasant
5. Daily context	Participants rate (7-point scale) i) how busy their day was, ii) how well they slept, iii) how physically active they have been, iv) how well they ate, v) how much they interacted with other people, vi) how much they enjoyed the weather, and vii) how much time they spent away from their home residence.
B. Pre-survey items	
1. Demographics	Various items of information on how participants identify (for example age, gender and ethnicity)
2. Past experience	Participants rate (7-point scale) how experienced they are at mindfulness
3. Commitment	Participants rate (7-point scale) how committed they are to forming the daily mindful breathing habit during the study
4. Habit strength	Participants complete the 12-item SRHI [19] to survey the strength of their mindful breathing habit at study initiation
5. Well-being	Participants complete The Warwick-Edinburgh Mental Well-being Scale survey (WEMWBS [17])
6. Personality	Participants complete the Five Factor Personality Model survey [12].
C. Mid- and post-survey items	
1. Well-being	Participants complete the WEMWBS survey again [17]
2. Habit formation reflections	Participants are prompted to rate (7-point scale) how i) rewarding, ii) challenging, and iii) frustrating their habit formation experience has been. There is also space for participants to provide open-ended reflections on their experiences.
D. Passive smartphone usage data	
1. Smartphone usage	The Beiwe *digital phenotyping* platform [18] was also used to passively collect data on participant daily smartphone usage for the duration of the study period. Data includes location, accelerometer, and screen lock/unlock time

Every day for the next six weeks, participants completed daily surveys, including whether they did the breathing exercise; how rewarding and challenging it felt; their confidence and motivation for building the habit; three SRHI items on perceived habit automaticity; and questions about mood and daily activities. Participants also installed Beiwe [18] on their smartphones for passive smartphone data collection, including streams for location, activity and screen-time. Finally, participants completed a mid- and post-study survey (after 3 and 6 weeks, respectively), that resurveyed their well-being and habit strength. Overall, 47.4% (N = 1,234) of daily surveys were completed and 41 participants completed the post-study survey. Table 1 presents details of the data collected.

4   Habit Formation Insights Using Growth Curve Models

4.1   Data, Methods and Assumptions

Our initial analysis focuses on the association of *time-invariant covariates* with the shape of habit formation trajectories. To this end, we use a simple average of the three SRHI items collected daily from participants (A2 in Table 1) to define a measure of habit automaticity to use as the target variable in our model. Habit automaticity is a component of habit strength, though it is worth noting that it does not encompass the full concept[1]. We use items B2-B6 from Table 1 as our time-invariant independent variables. Our future work will incorporate further variables from Table 1 as *time-varying covariates* [5].

We use the multilevel modeling paradigm to define the linear growth curve model in Eqs. 1–3. The self-reported automaticity score for participant i on day t of the study is represented by $y_{ti}^{SRHI\text{-}A}$. Equation 1 is a *level-1 equation* (i.e. time-varying and within-person): b_{1i} and b_{2i} are the fitted intercept and gradient for participant i, respectively, and u_{ti} is a time-specific residual score. Equations 2–3 are *level-2 equations* (i.e. time-invariant and between-person): β_{01}-β_{C1} and β_{02}-β_{C2} are level-2 regression parameters that represent relations between time-invariant covariates values X_{1i}-X_{Ci} for participant i and their individual-level intercept (b_{1i}) and gradient (b_{2i}), respectively, and d_{1i} and d_{2i} are residual scores that capture the variance at the between-person level not explained by X_{Ci}.

$$y_{ti}^{SRHI\text{-}A} = b_{1i} + b_{2i} \cdot t + u_{ti} \tag{1}$$

$$b_{1i} = \beta_{01} + \beta_{11} \cdot X_{1i} + \beta_{21} \cdot X_{2i} + ... + \beta_{C1} \cdot X_{Ci} + d_{1i} \tag{2}$$

$$b_{2i} = \beta_{02} + \beta_{12} \cdot X_{1i} + \beta_{22} \cdot X_{2i} + ... + \beta_{C2} \cdot X_{Ci} + d_{2i} \tag{3}$$

The following further assumptions apply to our analysis:

1. Only participants with 3 or more observations are included in the analysis, which ensures the linear growth curve model is over-identified [2,5]. We also exclude 1 participant who is the only participant to report high well-being in the pre-survey, thus avoiding the use of a covariate value with very low representation in our models
2. Only the first 21 consecutive observation days for each participant are used (including days where surveys were not completed). While participants may have up to 42 days each of data, we make this simplifying assumption as a) a large number of participants reported in the post-survey that the end of

---

[1] *Behavioral frequency* and *identity* also relate to the notion of habit strength. However, we do not assess these concepts given: i) our study introduces bias on behavioral frequency by asking participants to practice the habit daily, and ii) related work cites disagreements in using identity as a measure of habit strength [11,19].

semester (which occurred after 3 weeks for all participants) disrupted their practice of the habit, thus presenting a bias that may need to be explicitly accounted for, and b) data incompleteness is less severe in our first 3 weeks of observation (58.9% in first 3 weeks vs 38.0% in last 3 weeks). Combined, assumptions (1–2) reduce the observations to 713 days from 52 participants

3. Finally, a participant may be missing a full observation (dependent and all independent variables) at any given time point, however partial observations are not possible. We assume that these full observations are missing at random [2,5], and we do not explicitly handle them when fitting our model[2]

4.2   Results

We first assess different growth curve models for how well they fit the empirical data in Table 2. First, we compare an unconditional linear growth model (M2) to a no-growth model (M1). Using a likelihood ratio test, $\chi^2(3) = 169.14$ ($p \ll 0.01$), we conclude that a linear growth process is a significantly better representation of the data than a model in which the dependent variable does not vary with time. Thus, on average, participants' habit automaticity is changing with practice over time.

Table 2. Model fit statistics for unconditional (M1 and M2) and conditional (M3) growth curve models.

	No growth (M1)	Linear (M2)	Linear with TICs (M3)
Observations	713	713	713
Participants	52	52	52
Degrees of Freedom (DF)	3	6	26
Log Likelihood	−880.86	−796.29	−764.41
Akaike Inf. Crit	1,767.71	1,604.57	1,580.83
Bayesian Inf. Crit	1,781.42	1,631.99	1,699.64
Model Comparison	–	M2 vs. M1	M3 vs. M2
Likelihood Ratio	–	169.14	63.75
ΔDF	–	3	20
p-value	–	≪0.01	≪0.01

No growth model: $y_{ti}^{SRHI\text{-}A} = (\beta_{01} + d_{1i}) + u_{ti}$
Linear model: $y_{ti}^{SRHI\text{-}A} = (\beta_{01} + d_{1i}) + (\beta_{02} + d_{2i}) \cdot t + u_{ti}$
Linear with time-invariant covariates (TICs): Eqs. 1–3.
Data and modeling assumptions are detailed in Sect. 4.1

---

[2] We use the maximum likelihood (ML) estimation algorithm in R's *nlme* package [14].

Table 3. Fixed effect intercept and gradient parameters for conditional linear model with time-invariant covariates.

Parameters	Intercept	Gradient
Grand mean	2.71 (2.44, 2.97)	0.01 (−0.01, 0.03)
Medium Experience	−0.03 (−0.35, 0.28)	0.03*** (0.01, 0.05)
Low Experience	0.10 (−0.34, 0.55)	−0.03 (−0.06, 0.01)
Medium Commitment	0.12 (−0.14, 0.37)	−0.03*** (−0.04, −0.01)
Low Wellbeing	0.30** (0.03, 0.57)	0.00 (−0.02, 0.02)
Pre-Study SRHI Automaticity	0.61*** (0.37, 0.84)	−0.01 (−0.02, 0.01)
Lower Extraversion	−0.01 (−0.27, 0.25)	−0.00 (−0.02, 0.01)
Lower Agreeableness	0.16 (−0.10, 0.42)	−0.02** (−0.04, −0.01)
Lower Conscientiousness	−0.07 (−0.31, 0.18)	0.01 (−0.01, 0.03)
Lower Emotional Stability	−0.11 (−0.38, 0.16)	0.02* (−0.00, 0.04)
Lower Openness	-0.09 (−0.37, 0.19)	0.00 (−0.02, 0.02)

Parameter values are relative to grand mean with confidence intervals (lower, upper). Categorical variables are effect coded using the highest bucket of each variable as the reference category and continuous variables (only Pre-Study SRHI Automaticity) are group mean centered. Equations 1-3 define the model. Significance: $^*p < 0.1$; $^{**}p < 0.05$; $^{***}p < 0.01$.

We subsequently introduce time-invariant covariates into our linear model (Eqs. 1–3) to begin to associate differences in between-person habit automaticity trajectories with observed participant characteristics. From Table 2, we confirm that this conditional linear model (M3) fits the empirical data significantly better than the unconditional linear model (M2) using a likelihood ratio test, $\chi^2(20) = 63.75$ ($p \ll 0.01$). That this difference is significant suggests that at least some of the variance in habit formation trajectories between participants can be associated with characteristics we know about them before they commence habit building practice.

Having established its superior fit, we then report the coefficients for the time-invariant covariates of the conditional linear model in Table 3, where, as a result of the choice of variable coding, all differences implied by the coefficients are relative to a hypothetical participant with an average value for all covariates (the *grand mean* row). Our first conclusion from these coefficients matches intuition: how strong a participant's mindful breathing habit is before they begin practice - quantified by the pre-study SRHI automaticity score - is significantly correlated with the intercept of their growth trajectory. We also note that participants who report lower initial well-being have, on average, higher intercept values.

More noteworthy from Table 3 are the four significant correlations between participant characteristics and the gradient of their habit strength trajectories during the first 21 days of practice. Pre-study commitment to forming the habit, pre-study mindfulness experience, and two dimensions of personality–agreeableness and emotional stability – all have significant associations with this

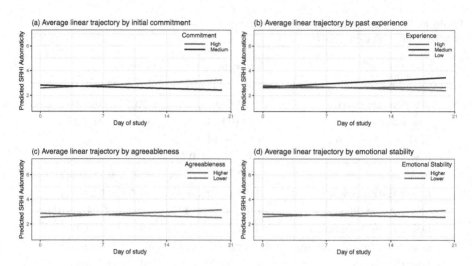

Fig. 1. Model-implied average automaticity trajectories for different participant sub-groups identified by time-invariant covariates with significant gradient parameters in Table 3. Sub-group sizes: a) $N_{High} = 27$, $N_{Medium} = 25$; b) $N_{High} = 14$, $N_{Medium} = 27$, $N_{Low} = 11$; c) $N_{Higher} = 26$, $N_{Lower} = 26$; d) $N_{Higher} = 25$, $N_{Lower} = 27$.

parameter. Figure 1 displays the model-implied trajectories for participant sub-groups defined by these significant factors. By discovering the *a priori* covariates that correlate with different habit formation experiences, a system designer – for example, a care professional or behavioral health app developer – might be able to personalize their services to help their clients form stronger habits.

5   Conclusion

In this work, we have identified individual characteristics that correlate with significantly different habit formation trajectories. However, there are several limitations to our approach. Firstly, we only assess the fit of linear growth curve models to habit automaticity, which may be an oversimplification of the true dependence of habit strength on days practiced. For example, habit development may be better described by nonlinear trajectories, such as quadratic or piecewise linear. Secondly, our models do not yet incorporate the time-varying covariates collected – practice frequency, mood, daily context, and smartphone usage data – which may enable the explanation of more variance between participants.

Beyond these immediate limitations, future work will also consider participant sub-groupings. For example, we will fit separate models for participants with different outcomes at the mid- and post-study checkpoints (such as those that have significantly increased their habit strength versus those that have not or who have dropped out by this stage). Separate models by sub-group will grant us more flexibility to categorise between participant heterogeneity, for example by varying the functional form (linear or nonlinear) and variance/covariance structures between sub-groups and assessing the impact this has on model fit statistics. Finally, our current framework does not allow us to comment on causality, which is an important area for future investigation.

References

1. Bargh, J.: The four horsemen of automaticity: awareness, intention, efficiency, and control in social cognition (1994)
2. Bollen, K., Curran, P.: Latent Curve Models: A Structural Equation Perspective. Social Forces 467 (2006). https://doi.org/10.1002/0471746096
3. Clapp, J., et al.: Modeling trajectory of depressive symptoms among psychiatric inpatients: a latent growth curve approach. J. Clin. Psychiatry **74**, 492–499 (2013). https://doi.org/10.4088/JCP.12m07842
4. Creswell, J.D.: Mindfulness interventions. Ann. Rev. Psychol. **68**, 491–516 (2017). https://doi.org/10.1146/annurev-psych-042716-051139
5. Curran, P., Obeidat, K., Losardo, D.: Twelve frequently asked questions about growth curve modeling. J. Cogn. Dev. **11**, 121–136 (2010). https://doi.org/10.1080/15248371003699969
6. Galla, B., Duckworth, A.: More than resisting temptation: beneficial habits mediate the relationship between self-control and positive life outcomes. J. Pers. Soc. Psychol. **109** (2015). https://doi.org/10.1037/pspp0000026
7. Gardner, B.: A review and analysis of the use of 'habit' in understanding, predicting and influencing health-related behaviour. Health Psychol. Rev. **9**(3), 277–295 (2015). https://doi.org/10.1080/17437199.2013.876238, pMID: 25207647
8. Gardner, B., Rebar, A.L.: Habit formation and behavior change (2019). https://doi.org/10.1093/acrefore/9780190236557.013.129
9. Hofmann, S.G., Sawyer, A.T., Witt, A.A., Oh, D.: The effect of mindfulness-based therapy on anxiety and depression: a meta-analytic review. J. Consult. Clin. Psychol. **78**(2), 169–183 (2010). https://doi.org/10.1037/a0018555
10. King, K.M., Littlefield, A.K., McCabe, C.J., Mills, K.L., Flournoy, J., Chassin, L.: Longitudinal modeling in developmental neuroimaging research: common challenges, and solutions from developmental psychology. Dev. Cogn. Neurosci. **33**, 54–72 (2018). https://doi.org/10.1016/j.dcn.2017.11.009
11. Lally, P., van Jaarsveld, C.H.M., Potts, H.W.W., Wardle, J.: How are habits formed: modelling habit formation in the real world. Eur. J. Soc. Psychol. **40**(6), 998–1009 (2010). https://doi.org/10.1002/ejsp.674
12. McCrae, R.R., Costa Jr., P.T.: The five-factor theory of personality. In: Handbook of personality: theory and research. 3rd ed., pp. 159–181. The Guilford Press, New York (2008)
13. Neal, D.T., Wood, W., Quinn, J.M.: Habits - a repeat performance. Curr. Dir. Psychol. Sci. **15**(4), 198–202 (2006). https://doi.org/10.1111/j.1467-8721.2006.00435.x
14. Pinheiro, J., Team, R.C.: nlme: linear and nonlinear mixed effects models. R Package Version **3**(4), 109 (2006)
15. Schöne, B., Gruber, T., Graetz, S., Bernhof, M., Malinowski, P.: Mindful breath awareness meditation facilitates efficiency gains in brain networks: a steady-state visually evoked potentials study. Sci. Reports **8**(1), 13687 (2018). https://doi.org/10.1038/s41598-018-32046-5

16. Stephanidis, C., et al.: Seven HCI grand challenges. Int. J. Human-Comput. Interac. **35**(14), 1229–1269 (2019). https://doi.org/10.1080/10447318.2019.1619259
17. Tennant, R., et al.: The Warwick-Edinburgh Mental Well-being Scale (WEMWBS): development and UK validation (2007). https://doi.org/10.1186/1477-7525-5-63
18. Torous, J., Kiang, M.V., Lorme, J., Onnela, J.P.: New tools for new research in psychiatry: a scalable and customizable platform to empower data driven smartphone research. JMIR Mental Health **3**(2), e16 (2016). https://doi.org/10.2196/mental.5165
19. Verplanken, B., Orbell, S.: Reflections on past behavior: a self-report index of habit strength. J. Appl. Soc. Psychol. **33**, 1313–1330 (2003). https://doi.org/10.1111/j.1559-1816.2003.tb01951.x

Mental Stress Evaluation Method Using Photoplethysmographic Amplitudes Obtained from a Smartwatch

Yu Matsumoto[✉], Tota Mizuno, Kazuyuki Mito, and Naoaki Itakura

The University of Electro-Communications, 1-5-1 Chofugaoka, Chofu, Tokyo, Japan
m2040008@edu.cc.uec.ac.jp

Abstract. In recent years, the number of patients with mental illness due to mental stress has steadily increased. Hence, the evaluation of mental stress in daily life is necessary to prevent mental illness. The conventional method for mental stress evaluation adopts biological information such as respiration, heart rate, saliva composition, and photoplethysmograms (PPGs). Among them, PPGs can be measured daily by a smartwatch. Therefore, we examined the feasibility of evaluating mental stress using PPG obtained by a smartwatch. In the mental stress evaluation, we focused on the photoplethysmographic amplitude (PPGA), which is a characteristic point of PPG. This amplitude can evaluate mental stress even with intermittent data, which makes it suitable for evaluating smartwatches when the obtained data are limited owing to body movements. In contrast, the accuracy of obtaining PPGA from a smartwatch might be low owing to various factors such as changes in blood flow or skin temperature. Hence, in this research, we proposed a method for obtaining a highly accurate PPGA. This method adopts PPGA via fast Fourier transform (FFT). In addition, matching the changes in PPGA for a short period of time is considered a challenge. Consequently, PPGA was calculated at regular time intervals. In the experiment, measurements from a photoplethysmograph and smartwatch were taken simultaneously. The measurement positions of the photoplethysmograph and smartwatch were at the left fingertip and left arm, respectively. After the measurements, the correlation coefficient between the photoplethysmograph and the PPGA of the smartwatch, to which this method was applied, was obtained. Accordingly, it was confirmed that PPGA can be obtained via the proposed method with high accuracy.

Keywords: Photoplethysmogram · Photoplethysmographic amplitude · Smartwatch

1 Introduction

Mental illness due to stress is being regarded as a crucial societal challenge. To prevent the occurrence of mental illnesses, a simple mental stress evaluation system that can be used in different places, such as offices, is required. Furthermore, it is essential for the evaluation system to possess a lifelog function, such that it can measure excessive or chronic psychological stress, which are known to cause depression.

© Springer Nature Switzerland AG 2021
C. Stephanidis et al. (Eds.): HCII 2021, CCIS 1421, pp. 357–362, 2021.
https://doi.org/10.1007/978-3-030-78645-8_45

The conventional method for evaluating mental stress is primarily subjective and involves a psychological questionnaire, which is unsuitable for lifelogging because it requires multiple questions to be answered each time. Other assessment methods include the collection of biometric information, such as respiratory rate, heart rate, blood pressure, saliva composition, thermal images, and photoplethysmograms (PPGs). Among these, PPGs are considerably beneficial because they contain information such as blood vessel status, blood pressure, and heart rate. Furthermore, because it is non-invasive and can be obtained upon contact with the skin, it can be estimated using a lifelogging device, such as a smartwatch. Therefore, in this study, we obtained PPGs from a smartwatch.

PPGs exhibit a waveform, as illustrated in Fig. 1, and we can obtain some features from the shape of this waveform. The points "a" and "b" depict the starting points of systole and diastole, respectively. To assess mental stress, the interval between points "a" and "b," which is significantly correlated with the heart rate's peak, is adopted. Frequency analysis of this interval is performed to determine the low frequency (LF) and high frequency (HF) components, which are influenced by the sympathetic and parasympathetic nervous systems, respectively, where LF/HF is adopted as an index of mental stress [1]. However, this index is influenced by respiration, which in turn is influenced by physical movements; hence, the accurate determination of the mental stress index requires frequency analyses conducted over extensive periods of time.

Another method for evaluating mental stress using a PPG is the photoplethysmographic amplitude (PPGA), which is measured from the minimum point to the maximum point of the PPG (Fig. 1). This amplitude primarily reflects changes in blood vessels and blood pressure, which provide the basis for obtaining an estimate of mental stress [2, 3]. Because a PPGA can be acquired for each PPG, PPGA provides a detailed picture of changes in blood pressure, as well as the advantage of using fragmented data. Furthermore, the effect of physical movement on the value of PPGA is negligible. In contrast, because the sampling frequency of a PPG with a smartwatch is lower than that of a generic biometric measuring system, it may be impossible to accurately acquire measurement figures that change rapidly, such as the PPGA.

Therefore, we examined a method for improving the accuracy of the PPGA obtained from smart watches and reported the effectiveness of the proposed method.

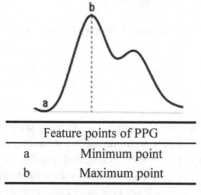

Feature points of PPG	
a	Minimum point
b	Maximum point

Fig. 1. PPG example

2 Experiment

2.1 Experimental Conditions

Seven healthy adults in their twenties (six males, one female) participated in the study. PPGs were measured simultaneously using a smartwatch (Galaxy watch Gear S2, Samsung) and a medical device called a plethysmograph (MPP-3U, NIHON KOHDEN). With an analog filter of 0.08–100 Hz, the sampling frequencies of the smartwatch and plethysmograph were 25 Hz and 1 kHz, respectively. After applying the finite impulse response (FIR) filter (0.8–5.0 Hz) to the PPG data obtained from each measuring device, comparisons and examinations were performed.

2.2 Experimental Conditions

A computational task was applied to alter the PPGA. The task involved four questions each of addition, subtraction, multiplication, and division, and each question had a time limit of 20 s.

As illustrated in Fig. 2, the experimental protocol was performed in the order: rest (1 min), calculation task (10 min), and rest (1 min). In addition, the measurement position of the photoelectric pulse wave meter was the left fingertip, while that of the smartwatch was the left arm, and an instruction was given not to move the left arm during the experiment.

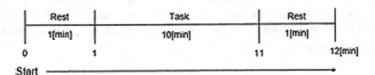

Fig. 2. Experimental protocol

3 Proposed Method

A schematic of the proposed method is presented in Fig. 3.

In this method, overlap FFT was first performed on the PPG data divided at regular time intervals. Next, to obtain the PPGA, we considered the square root of the power spectral density obtained by the overlap FFT as the amplitude. In addition, the frequency component of PPGA was considered to appear in the frequency component of the heartbeat. Therefore, the square root of the peak value in the frequency band (0.7 to 3.0 Hz), where the heart rate appears, was evaluated as PPGA.

Because this method calculates the average of PPGA at regular time intervals by overlapping FFT, we considered the possibility of obtaining the change in PPGA with less influence owing to the difference in measurement positions. Furthermore, this approach tends to be an effective method because it does not require the minimum and maximum points of PPG to be tracked by peak detection for each beat.

Finally, the effectiveness of proposed method was verified by correlating the photoelectric pulse wave meter and PPGA of the smartwatch when the PPG was divided into sections every 30 s or 60 s, with 80% overlap and 256 FFT data.

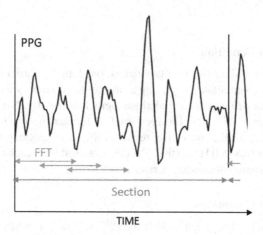

Fig. 3. Schematic of the proposed method

4 Results and Discussion

4.1 Comparison of PPG

Figure 4 presents standardized PPG data for the plethysmograph and smartwatch.

The figure shows that the waveforms of the plethysmograph and smartwatch are different. Furthermore, because the maximum point required to obtain the amplitude value is delayed, it is necessary to make comparisons with changes over a certain period of time as in the proposed method.

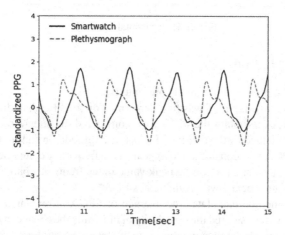

Fig. 4. PPGs of plethysmograph and smartwatch

4.2 Comparison of PPGA

Table 1 presents the correlation coefficient between PPGAs of plethysmograph and smartwatch. The right column of the subject presents the data collected by obtaining the PPGA from the minimum and maximum points of the PPG data and correlating the obtained results with the PPGA for each beat.

From the mean of the correlations in Table 1, the proposed method was used at 60-s intervals to improve the correlation, thereby indicating its effectiveness. It was also demonstrated that the amplitude of FFT may be the PPGA value.

However, correlation did not improve in all data samples, as some of them actually decreased. This is probably because the FFT overlap is an amplitude value that includes components different from the heart rate, such as body movement and skin surface condition, as the results of each FFT are averaged at the end. Therefore, in the future, we will consider addressing this limitation by excluding FFT results containing many components other than PPGA, which we will achieve by setting a threshold value for the FFT data before overlap.

Table 1. Correlation coefficient between PPGAs of plethysmograph and smartwatch

Subject	–	Proposed method	
		30 s	60 s
A	0.29	0.68	0.72
B	0.24	0.25	0.11
C	0.25	0.03	0.24
D	0.13	0	0.39
E	0.49	0.43	0.67
F	0.3	0.50	0.42
G	0.11	0.03	0.30
Mean	0.26 ± 0.12	0.27 ± 0.25	0.41 ± 0.21

5 Conclusion

The proposed method was suggested as a feasible technique for obtaining PPGA from the amplitude value of FFT. In addition, by obtaining PPGA at regular time intervals, it may be possible to reduce the influence of the differences in measurement positions.

In the future, we will investigate a method to exclude FFT results containing many components other than PPGA by setting threshold values for FFT data before overlap.

References

1. Hayano, J., Okada, A., Yasuma, F.: Biological significance of heart rate variability. Jpn. J. Artif. Organs **25**(5), 870–880 (1996). Japan

2. Yoshida, N., Asakawa, T., Hayashi, T., Mizuno-Matsumoto, Y.: Evaluation of the autonomic nervous function with plethysmography under the emotional stress stimuli. Jpn. J. Med. Biol. Eng. **49**(1), 91–99 (2011). Japan
3. Miyagawa, D., et al.: Evaluation of autonomic nervous function using photoplethysmography under emotional stress stimuli on a cellular phone. Jpn. J. Clin. Neurophysiol. **40**(6), 540–546 (2012). Japan

The Mediating Effect of Smartphone Addiction on the Relationship Between Social Skills and Psychological Well-Being

Rageshwari Munderia[✉] and Rajbala Singh

The LNM Institute of Information Technology, Jaipur, India
{y14pg933,rajbala}@lnmiit.ac.in

Abstract. Social skills play a pivotal role in fabricating and consolidating social relationships. Presently, smartphones have completely changed the mode of social communication. Individuals equipped with adequate social skills may use smartphones for diverse purposes ranging from social needs and hedonic needs to cognitive needs. Despite having many advantages, smartphones also serve as a source of immediate gratification and may make individuals vulnerable to addiction to their smartphones with several consequences for their well-being. The study attempts to establish a model for analyzing the mediating effect that smartphone addiction may have on the relationship between social skills and psychological well-being. A sample of 509 adult participants from the capital and national capital region, India, responded to questionnaires related to social skills, smartphone addiction, and psychological well-being. Data retrieved from this phase was analyzed using PROCESS macro [7]. The mediation analysis yielded the following results: (I) Two dimensions of social skills, namely social expressivity, and emotional control, significantly predicted dimensions of smartphone addiction and psychological well-being. (II) Two dimensions of smartphone addiction- uncontrolled usage and cyberspace orientation, showed the full mediating effect on the relationship between social skills and psychological well-being. (III) Social expressivity positively influenced smartphone addiction (uncontrolled usage and cyberspace orientation), leading to diminished psychological well-being. (IV) On the contrary, emotional control curbed the tendency for smartphone addiction, resulting in better psychological well-being. The present study has many important implications for both researchers as well as to common masses. An effective intervention program based on emotional regulation and emotional control will help control the disadvantages of smartphone addiction, which will also help achieve greater psychological well-being levels.

Keywords: Social skills · Smartphone addiction · Psychological well-being · Emotional control · Cyberspace orientation

ⓒ Springer Nature Switzerland AG 2021
C. Stephanidis et al. (Eds.): HCII 2021, CCIS 1421, pp. 363–370, 2021.
https://doi.org/10.1007/978-3-030-78645-8_46

1 Introduction

Human beings are social animals, and communication is the primary source for maintaining an interpersonal relationship. Social skills play a crucial role in the formulation and consolidation of social bonds for every individual in society. Presently, smartphone proliferation is increasing by leaps and bounds and has changed the world of social communication. Smartphone provides a plethora of opportunities to individuals for a virtual social environment that enables them to initiate and maintain social connections with significant others. Despite having many advantages, smartphones also act as a source of immediate gratification, leading to various consequences for their well-being.

2 Literature Review and Hypothesis

2.1 Social Skills

Scholars have defined social skills from various perspectives. Social skills can be described in terms of receiving, predicting, and interpreting social cues and consolidating these social cues to exercise control over social interaction situations [16]. According to [6] "cooperation, collaborating with others, helping, and initiating a relationship, request for help and appreciating others are some of the common examples of social skill behavior (p. 513)." Scholars [15] utilized the operant conditioning approach to explain the functional aspect of social skills. Social cues that are instrumental in eliciting positive feedback get reinforced and are likely to be repeated and vice versa is true for negative feedback.

2.2 Smartphone Addiction

Smartphone addiction falls under the category of behavioral addiction as it involves some of the standard components of behavioral addictions such as salience (behavioral and cognitive), tolerance, withdrawal, relapse, conflict, and mood disturbances [3]. Smartphone addiction refers to individuals' compulsive use of smartphones to a level that they tend to abstain from other activities [2].

As stated earlier, smartphones are great sources of immediate gratification and can make individuals addicted to their smartphones. The immediate gratification acts as a source of reinforcement (both positive and negative) that may bring individuals in a state of flow [5], leading to cognitive absorption [1]. Moreover, over gratification of these tendencies may make individuals vulnerable for smartphone habit formation to the point that it becomes a 'bad habit' [22] with several psycho-social consequences such as, uncontrolled usage, problematic behaviors, fear of missing out, sleeplessness, and dependency etc.

2.3 Psychological Well-Being

Well-being is broadly classified under two disparate paradigms-hedonic and eudaimonic. The concept of subjective well-being relies on hedonism, whereas psychological well-being comes from a eudaimonic perspective. Eudaimonia emphasizes the highest of all the goods that an individual can achieve through his/her action [18]. Psychological well-being can be defined in terms of having meaningful goals in life, evolving as an individual, and maintaining close bonds with significant others. In [19], the authors provided a comprehensive view of psychological well-being and suggested six core dimensions; (i) positive relations with others (ii) personal growth (iii) purpose in life (iv) environmental mastery (v) self-acceptance (vi) autonomy.

2.4 Smartphone Addiction as a Mediator Between Social Skills and Psychological Well-Being

There is evidence in the literature regarding the relationship between social skills and smartphone addiction [4,13], between social skills and various psychological well-being dimensions [14,20]; and between smartphone addiction and psychological well-being [9]. Past literature has demonstrated that smartphone addiction can be a potential mediator between various psychological characteristics and other variables [8,24]. The present study attempts to explore the mediating role of smartphone usage between social skills and psychological well-being. There is no study to date that has examined this relationship.

H1. Smartphone addiction will have a mediating effect on the relationship between social skills and psychological well-being.

3 Method

3.1 Participants

The survey method was employed to collect the data from adult participants ($n = 509$; $n = 313$ males and $n = 196$ females; mean age = 23.9 years, SD = 6.30) residing in India's capital and the national capital region.

3.2 Measures

The measured variables were social skills, smartphone addiction, and psychological well-being. The data was collected through self-administered questionnaires on a seven point Likert scale.

Social Skills: A brief version of social skills inventory (SSI) was employed [17]. It is a thirty item scale. The items of the scale were subjected to factor analysis. The KMO measure of sampling adequacy was .71 and Bartlett's test of sphericity was $\chi^2(171) = 16.83, (p < .50)$. The factor analysis resulted in a five-factor structure. Two factors were discarded due to Chronbach's $\alpha > .50$. Finally, three factors namely social expressivity (Chronbach's $\alpha = .74$, overt deception (Chronbach's $\alpha = .53$) and emotional control (Chronbach's $\alpha = .58$) were included in the final analysis. The overall reliability of the scale was good, Chronbach's $\alpha = .65$.

Smartphone Addiction: The study employed smartphone addiction inventory (SPAI) [12]. The SPAI comprised of 26 items and measures four dimensions: (i) tolerance (ii) withdrawal behavior (iii) compulsive behavior, and (iv) functional impairment. Seven items of the cyberspace orientation were also adopted from smartphone addiction scale [11] as these items deemed fit to measure smartphone addiction thoroughly. Thus, the final questionnaire consists of thirty-three items. The items of the scale were subjected to factor analysis. The KMO measure of sampling adequacy was .73 and Bartlett's test of sphericity was $\chi^2(171) = 18.04, (p < .00)$. Five factors emerged from factor analysis; cyberspace orientation (Cronbach's $\alpha = .85$), problematic smartphone behavior (Cronbach's $\alpha = .87$), personal & social consequences (Cronbach's $\alpha = .81$), physical & psychological impairment (Cronbach's $\alpha = .83$) and uncontrolled usage (Cronbach's $\alpha = .82$). The Cronbach's $\alpha = .82$ for overall scale was excellent.

Psychological Well-Being: The short version of the psychological well-being inventory was employed [19]. The scale consists of eighteen items. The KMO measure of sampling adequacy was .74, and the Bartlett's test of sphericity yielded $\chi^2(120) = 14.0, (p < .00)$. Four dimensions were identified; personal growth & autonomy (Cronbach's $\alpha = .75$), purpose in life & interpersonal relationship (Cronbach's $\alpha = .55$), affective well-being (Cronbach's $\alpha = .75$) and self-acceptance (Cronbach's $\alpha = .60$). The internal consistency of all the items was good, Chronbach's $\alpha = .65$.

4   Results

The data were analyzed with a statistical package for social sciences (SPSS, version 23.0) software. PROCESS macro [7] was employed to investigate whether smartphone addiction mediates the relationship between social skills and psychological well-being. The dimensions of social skills were treated independent variables, dimensions of smartphone addiction were treated as mediating variables, and dimensions of psychological well-being were treated as dependent variables.

The results presented in Fig. 1 depict two significant models of mediation. Model I describes that the direct effect of social expressivity on personal growth & autonomy (path c), and the direct effect of social expressivity on cyberspace orientation (path a) was statistically different from zero. After controlling for social expressivity, the mediator (cyberspace orientation) significantly predicted personal growth & autonomy (path b). The coefficient for the association between social expressivity and personal growth & autonomy was increased after accounting for cyberspace orientation as a mediator (c') indicating that cyberspace orientation fully mediates this relationship.

Similarly, Model II depicts that after controlling for social expressivity, the mediator (uncontrolled usage) significantly predicted personal growth & autonomy (path b). The coefficient for the association between social expressivity and personal growth & autonomy was increased after accounting for uncontrolled

Model I → Direct effect: c′ = .184**, Indirect effect: ab = −.028**

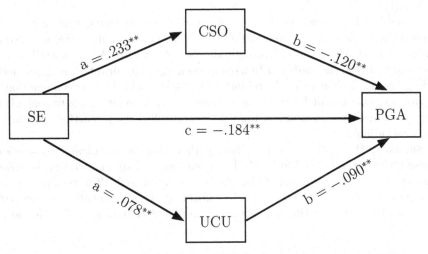

Model II → Direct effect: c′ = .163**, Indirect effect: ab = −.007**

Fig. 1. Mediation model of indirect relationship between Social Expressivity (SE) and Personal growth and autonomy (PGA) through Cyberspace orientation (CSO; Model I) and through Uncontrolled usage (UCU; Model II). *p < .01, **p < .05.

Model I → Direct effect: c′ = .017**, Indirect effect: ab = −.090**

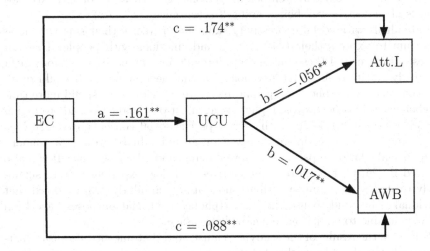

Model II → Direct effect: c′ = .088**, Indirect effect: ab = −.002**

Fig. 2. Mediation model of indirect relationship between Emotional control (EC) and Attitude towards life (Att.L) through uncontrolled usage (UCU; Model I) and between Emotional control (EC) and Affective well-being (AWB) through uncontrolled usage (UCU; Model II). *p < .01, **p < .05.

usage as a mediator (c') indicating that uncontrolled usage fully mediates this relationship.

Model I of Fig. 2 depicts that the direct effect of emotional control on attitudes towards life (path c), and the direct effect of emotional control on uncontrolled usage (path a) was statistically different from zero. After controlling for emotional control, the mediator (uncontrolled usage) significantly predicted attitudes towards life (path b). The coefficient for the association between emotional control and uncontrolled usage was increased after accounting for uncontrolled usage as a mediator (c'); indicating that uncontrolled usage partially mediates this relationship.

Similarly, the path a, path b, and path c show a significant association between the variables in Model II. The coefficient for the association between emotional control and uncontrolled usage was increased after accounting for uncontrolled usage as a mediator (c'); indicating that uncontrolled usage partially mediates the relationship between emotional control and affective well-being.

5 Discussion

The present study results confirmed that smartphone addiction mediates the relationship between social skills and psychological well-being. Cyberspace orientation and uncontrolled usage; two dimensions of smartphone addiction emerged as a potential mediator between social skills (social expressivity and emotional control) and psychological well-being (personal growth & autonomy, attitude towards life, affective well-being, and self-acceptance).

Individuals with social expressivity skills may perceive their smartphone as a medium to express their true feelings and emotions with people of similar interest. However, all these factors may provide instant positive reinforcement and overly gratify their social, psychological, and hedonic needs. It could result in uncontrolled smartphone usage and motivate individuals to spend more time in cyberspace. In other words, higher engagement on the device leads to higher dependence on smartphones with several psycho-social consequences [22]. Further, it may cause a detrimental impact on an individuals' growth, autonomy, interpersonal relationships, emotional well-being, and self-acceptance. It was also reported in [26] that reinforcement motives and flow experiences were significantly related with compulsive smartphone usage. Similarly, [23] reported that individuals who tend to use their smartphones for social purposes have been more vulnerable to addiction to smartphone usage.

Secondly, the results of the study also illustrated that uncontrolled usage partially mediated the relationship between emotional control and two dimensions of psychological well-being; attitude towards life and affective well-being. The present study results may imply that individuals who can regulate their emotions efficiently in various social situations tend to use their smartphones competently to facilitate their actions towards goal achievement and foster their interpersonal relationships with others. Thus, emotional control help individuals to use their smartphones in a controlled manner. Past research has also demonstrated that difficulties in regulating one's emotions are associated with addictive behavior of substance abuse [10]. Similar results were also found in the case of problematic internet use [21,25]. The results of the study confirmed that social skills play a significant role in the appropriate usage of the smartphone leading to higher levels of well-being.

References

1. Agarwal, R., Karahanna, E.: Time flies when you're having fun: cognitive absorption and beliefs about information technology usage. MIS quarterly 665–694 (2000)
2. Al-Barashdi, H.S., Bouazza, A., Jabur, N.H.: Smartphone addiction among university undergraduates: a literature review. J. Sci. Res. Reports 210–225 (2015)
3. Billieux, J., Maurage, P., Lopez-Fernandez, O., Kuss, D.J., Griffiths, M.D.: Can disordered mobile phone use be considered a behavioral addiction? An update on current evidence and a comprehensive model for future research. Curr. Addic. Reports **2**(2), 156–162 (2015)
4. Chan, M.: Mobile-mediated multimodal communications, relationship quality and subjective well-being: an analysis of smartphone use from a life course perspective. Comput. Hum. Behav. **87**, 254–262 (2018)
5. Csikszentmihalyi, M.: Beyond boredom and anxiety. Jossey-Bass (2000)
6. Daraee, M., Salehi, K., Fakhr, M.: Comparison of social skills between students in ordinary and talented schools. In: Selection & Peer-review under responsibility of the Conference Organization Committee, pp. 513–521. European: ICEEPSY. vol. 2016, p. 7th (2016)
7. Hayes, A.F.: PROCESS: A versatile computational tool for observed variable mediation, moderation, and conditional process modeling (2012)
8. Hong, F.Y., Chiu, S.I., Huang, D.H.: A model of the relationship between psychological characteristics, mobile phone addiction and use of mobile phones by Taiwanese university female students. Comput. Hum. Behav. **28**(6), 2152–2159 (2012)
9. Horwood, S., Anglim, J.: Problematic smartphone usage and subjective and psychological well-being. Comput. Hum. Behav. **97**, 44–50 (2019)
10. Kelly, T.H., Bardo, M.T.: Emotion regulation and drug abuse: implications for prevention and treatment (2016)
11. Kwon, M., et al.: Development and validation of a smartphone addiction scale (SAS). PloS one **8**(2), e56936 (2013)
12. Lin, Y.H., Chang, L.R., Lee, Y.H., Tseng, H.W., Kuo, T.B., Chen, S.H.: Development and validation of the smartphone addiction inventory (spai). PloS one **9**(6), e98312 (2014)
13. Munderia, R., Singh, R.: The relationship between social skills and percived smartphone usage. J. Psychosocial Res. **14**(1) (2019)
14. Munderia, R., Singh, R.: Mobile phone dependence and psychological well-being among young adults. Indian J. Community Psychol. **14**(2), 321 (2018)
15. Nangle, D.W., Hansen, D.J., Erdley, C.A., Norton, P.J.: Practitioner's Guide to Empirically based Measures of Social Skills. Springer Science & Business Media (2009)
16. Norton, P.J., Hope, D.A.: Analogue observational methods in the assessment of social functioning in adults. Psychol. Assess. **13**(1), 59 (2001)

17. Riggio, R.E.: Assessment of basic social skills. J. Pers. Soc. Psychol. **51**(3), 649 (1986)
18. Ryan, R.M., Deci, E.L.: On happiness and human potentials: a review of research on hedonic and eudaimonic well-being. Ann. Rev. Psychol. **52**(1), 141–166 (2001)
19. Ryff, C.D., Singer, B.: The contours of positive human health. Psychol. Inquiry **9**(1), 1–28 (1998)
20. Segrin, C., Hanzal, A., Donnerstein, C., Taylor, M., Domschke, T.J.: Social skills, psychological well-being, and the mediating role of perceived stress. Anxiety, Stress, Coping **20**(3), 321–329 (2007)
21. Spada, M.M., Marino, C.: Metacognitions and emotion regulation as predictors of problematic internet use in adolescents. Clin. Neuropsychiatry **14**(1), 59–63 (2017)
22. Turel, O., Serenko, A.: The benefits and dangers of enjoyment with social networking websites. Eur. J. Inf. Syst. **21**(5), 512–528 (2012)
23. Van Deursen, A.J., Bolle, C.L., Hegner, S.M., Kommers, P.A.: Modeling habitual and addictive smartphone behavior: the role of smartphone usage types, emotional intelligence, social stress, self-regulation, age, and gender. Comput. Human Behav. **45**, 411–420 (2015)
24. Yang, Z., Asbury, K., Griffiths, M.D.: An exploration of problematic smartphone use among Chinese university students: associations with academic anxiety, academic procrastination, self-regulation and subjective wellbeing. Int. J. Mental Health Addict. **17**(3), 596–614 (2019)
25. Yu, J.J., Kim, H., Hay, I.: Understanding adolescents' problematic Internet use from a social/cognitive and addiction research framework. Comput. Human Behav. **29**(6), 2682–2689 (2013)
26. Zhang, K., Chen, C., Zhao, S., Lee, M.: Compulsive smartphone use: the roles of flow, reinforcement motives, and convenience. In: 35th International Conference on Information Systems: Building a Better World Through Information Systems, (ICIS) (2014)

Nutritional Data Accuracy of West Africa Foods in mHealth Applications

Eric Owusu[1]([⊠]), Nana Afari[2]([⊠]), and Emmanuel Saka[3]([⊠])

[1] Department of Computing Sciences, State University of New York, Brockport,
350 New Campus Drive, Brockport, NY 14420, USA
eowusu@brockport.edu

[2] Department of Health Informatics, Rutgers University, 65 Bergen Street, Suite 120,
Newark, NJ 07107, USA
nka23@shp.rutgers.edu

[3] Department of Art and Design, Belmont University, 1900 Belmont Boulevard, Nashville,
TN 37212, USA
emmanuel.saka@belmont.edu

Abstract. A plethora of mobile health applications have been developed globally to promote self-management behaviors and improve the quality of healthcare delivery services. To realize this potential there is the need for data accuracy and information integrity in Mobile health tools. The delivery of accurate data by Mobile health tools enhances adherence to optimum self-care goals. Self-care is an essential component in the management of health conditions which includes the provision of accurate diet and nutritional information to enable users make informed lifestyle decisions. The provision of inconsistent or inaccurate nutritional data misinforms users and affects the usability of Mobile health interventions. The purpose of this study is to investigate the nutritional data accuracy of several mHealth applications in the market and measure their perceived usefulness and effectiveness. Specifically, this study compares the caloric information of certain West African foods provided by several mHealth applications.

Keywords: Data accuracy · mHealth · Nutritional · Self-care · User satisfaction

1 Introduction

Mobile health (mHealth) interventions have become effective tools in promoting patient self-care. Empirical research has confirmed the effectiveness of mHealth interventions in modifying health lifestyles, especially those related to dietary behaviors and physical activity [1]. mHealth applications such as "fitness apps and diet apps" are well accepted among West Africans in the diaspora in relation to healthcare adherence [2], however little is known about the consistency of the nutritional information of the west African foods provided by these health applications.

To optimize the hypothetical data accuracy of mHealth applications, there is a need to investigate data accuracy of some West African foods in mobile health applications.

© Springer Nature Switzerland AG 2021
C. Stephanidis et al. (Eds.): HCII 2021, CCIS 1421, pp. 371–375, 2021.
https://doi.org/10.1007/978-3-030-78645-8_47

Griffiths et al. [3] recommend further research on the accuracy of data on crowd sourced information found on nutritional tracking applications as the nutritional values of food on popular applications are generally lower as compared to the Nutrition Data System for Research (NDSR) calculations. This is important in determining the user's choice of measurement for appropriate consumption. This in effect will have an impact on how users perceive the needed steps or precautions in managing their dietary plan. In light of the above this paper aims to provide an overview by examining the data inconsistency of West African foods using five popular fitness and diet applications. Specifically, we aim to evaluate the accuracy of caloric intake calculations of West African foods from five nutritional and fitness applications.

2   Research Background

Nutrition is an important part of adopting a healthy style. Physical activity and diet management can reduce risk of chronic diseases [4], however perceived nutritional values and caloric intake of West African foods are hard to predict and not readily available [3]. Culturally, the West African diet consists of an expansive repertoire of carbohydrate rich foods. To maintain a cultural identity and satisfy their acquired taste preferences, West African migrants continue to consume carbohydrate-rich diets. A few of the most popular foods include jollof rice made from white rice, banku made from corn meal and cassava (yuka), kenkey made from corn meal, and fufu. Fufu can be made from, yam, plantain, cocoyam or cassava.

With the advancement in technology and the subsequent increase in eHealth interventions, migrants have access to mHealth tools that provide real time data on health conditions and deliver appropriate behavior change information targeted at promoting positive lifestyle resolutions. Having access to accurate and consistent nutritional data information will help migrants make informed decisions about their diets and promote adherence to positive behavior change regimens.

In the proliferation of mobile health technology, there is no accurate data on the measurement of West African foods on mobile applications in the consumer market. Data accuracy can be defined as the closeness of values in a database to the true values of the entities that the data in the database represents, when the true values are not known [5]. Data accuracy is essential toward an effective user experience in mobile application design. It helps to promote integrity and trustworthiness among users seeking to attain and establish healthy lifestyle goals. The level of data accuracy determines users perceived usefulness, ease of use and attitude toward mHealth applications [6, 7].

3   Methodology

The study prioritized accuracy checking in caloric intake values for four traditional West African foods - Jollof rice, Kenkey, Banku and Fufu (plantain), in five existing mobile health applications namely, MyfitnessPal, LoseIt calorie counter, MyPlate, CarbManager, and MyNetDiary. For the purpose of this study plantain fufu was chosen because West African migrants have easier access to the plantain powder. The mHealth applications contained relevant information about the identified foods for the study. In order to establish consistency in data across the selected mHealth applications, and for the purpose of conformity, a serving size of 100g for each of the foods was utilized to analyze the data to help establish a uniform serving size as the basis for the study.

Each food item was entered into the mHealth application to identify the nutritional value, specifically, caloric value. Using SAS Studio, the populated data was analyzed, and descriptive statistics was utilized to examine the inconsistency patterns in caloric values of the four selected West African foods.

4 Results and Discussions

All five applications selected were rated as most popular and frequently used by users from West Africa. As indicated in Table 1, there was a wide dispersion in the results recorded from the five selected mHealth applications. For 100 g of jollof rice, one application (Loselt) indicated a low caloric value of 88 cal, while the MyNetDiary application indicated a very high caloric value of 362 cal. Two of the applications (MyPlate and MyNetDiary) had no data on the caloric value of kenkey. From the 3 applications that had data on Kenkey, Loselt indicated a value of 158 cal, while a high value of 400 cal was indicated by MyfitnessPal. Caloric values for fufu ranged from a low value of 44 cal (Loselt) to a high value of 340 cal (MyfitnessPal) per 100 g. Of all the data collected, banku was the only food item that recorded the same caloric values of 333 cal in two applications (MyNetDiary and CarbManager). However, banku had a low caloric value of 94 cal (MyfitnessPal) and a high value of 353 cal (MyPlate) (Fig. 1).

Table 1. Caloric values per 100 g of selected West African foods in mHealth applications.

APPS	Jollof (cal)	Kenkey (cal)	Fufu (cal)	Banku (cal)
MyfitnessPal	102	400	340	94
LoseIt	88	158	44	130
MyPlate	172	–	289	353
MyNetDiary	362	–	156	333
CarbManager	137	168	264	333
Coeff variation	**64.4**	**56.5**	**54.2**	**50.5**

As indicated in the results above, with the exception of banku which recorded the same caloric value per 100 g in two of the fitness applications, there was no consistency in the data recorded for the other applications. The values obtained for the same measure (100 g) of food varied widely with an example being fufu which recorded a low value of 44 cal by one application (Loselt) and an extremely high value of 340 cal by another (MyfitnessPal) for the same amount of food. To further examine the recorded values, coefficient of variation (CV) was used to measure the degree of variability. Distributions with a CV less than 1, are considered low-variance, whereas distributions with a CV

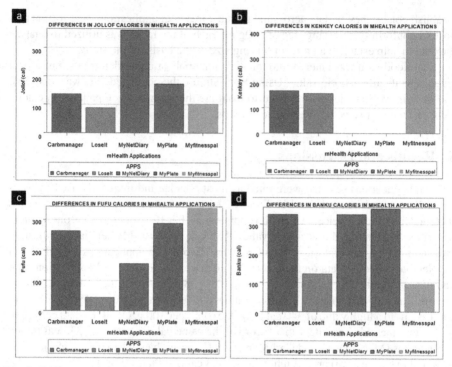

Fig. 1. Differences in (a) Jollof rice (b) Kenkey (c) Fufu (d) Banku in mHealth application per 100 g

greater than 1 are considered high variance. The high CV obtained by the data analysis for all the foods signifies a high degree of data dispersion. This finding is very alarming as it undermines the integrity of the data being provided by these health applications. One factor that adds to the data inconsistencies is the crowdsourcing nature of the health applications. The crowdsourcing feature enables users to directly enter data on nutritional values without source verification.

Lack of data accuracy on dietary or nutritional information could be potentially harmful to users in circumstances where adherence to strict nutritional protocols is mandatory in their health care management. The benefits of mHealth technology are also limited by lack of data accuracy. To realize the potential benefits of mHealth solutions, data accuracy and information integrity is a necessity.

Research shows that hypertension and diabetes are highly prevalent among West African populations [8]. West African migrants stand to benefit by taking advantage of the influx of mHealth interventions for informed decisions on self-care. The West African dietary repertoire is composed mainly of carbohydrate rich foods and having access to accurate nutritional information will help users make the right decisions on their food choices for optimum healthy lifestyles.

The lack of data accuracy and information integrity undermines the usefulness of mHealth applications and presents a hindrance to the adoption of these health applications by users who stand to benefit the most [8–10].

5 Conclusion

mHealth technology provides a viable platform for the delivery of timely and accurate dietary and healthcare information to empower people from all walks of life with the necessary data to make ideal decisions about their diet and lifestyle. However, findings from this study indicates a major deficiency in data accuracy for the four West African foods utilized in the study. The crowdsourcing nature of the applications contributes to the inconsistencies observed. This lack of accuracy compromises data integrity affects the adoption of mHealth applications and limits the potential benefits of the applications to users. To remedy this finding mHealth application developers should be mandated to adhere to Nutrition Data System for Research (NDSR) calculations for the provision of accurate and consistent data across platforms. Crowdsourced data also needs to be validated before acceptance. In future research this study would be extended to investigate the impact of the lack of data accuracy on user experience by exploring the following questions:

- Does nutritional data accuracy improve user satisfaction?
- Does nutritional data accuracy influence design rationale?

References

1. Free, C., et al.: The effectiveness of mobile-health technologies to improve health care service delivery processes: a systematic review and meta-analysis. PLoS Med. **10**(1), e1001363 (2013)
2. Galbete, C., et al.: Food consumption, nutrient intake, and dietary patterns in Ghanaian migrants in Europe and their compatriots in Ghana. Food Nutr. Res. **61**(1), 1341809 (2017)
3. Griffiths, C., Harnack, L., Pereira, M.A.: Assessment of the accuracy of nutrient calculations of five popular nutrition tracking applications. Public Health Nutr. **21**(8), 1495–1502 (2018)
4. Gibson, R., et al.: Comparing dietary macronutrient composition and food sources between native and diasporic Ghanaian adults. Food Nutr. Res. **59**, 27790 (2015). https://doi.org/10. 3402/fnr.v59.27790
5. Fan, W.: Data quality: from theory to practice. ACM SIGMOD Rec. **44**(3), 7–18 (2015)
6. Davis, D.: Perceived usefulness, perceived ease of use, and user acceptance of information technology. MIS Q. **13**(3), 319 (1989). https://doi.org/10.2307/249008
7. Davis, F.D., Bagozzi, R.P., Warshaw, P.R.: User acceptance of computer technology: a comparison of two theoretical models. Manage. Sci. **35**(8), 982–1003 (1989). https://doi.org/10. 1287/mnsc.35.8.982
8. Agyemang, C., Owusu-Dabo, E., de Jonge, A., Martins, D., Ogedegbe, G., Stronks, K.: Overweight and obesity among Ghanaian residents in The Netherlands: how do they weigh against their urban and rural counterparts in Ghana? Public Health Nutr. **12**(7), 909–916 (2009)
9. O'Keefe, S.J., et al.: Why do African Americans get more colon cancer than Native Africans? J. Nutr. **137**(1 Suppl), 175S–182S (2007)
10. Anderson, S.G., et al.: Nutrient intakes and dysglycaemia in populations of West African origin. Br. J. Nutr. **105**(2), 297–306 (2011)

User Experience and Usability Comparison of Mental Health Intervention Websites

Chelsea Roberts and Jennifer Palilonis^(✉)

Ball State University, Muncie, IN 47304, USA
{clroberts3,jageorge2}@bsu.edu

Abstract. This paper presents an evaluation of usability and user experience perceptions of two suicide prevention websites to explore ways these critical resources may be improved. Suicide is one of the leading causes of death in the world and is most prevalent in teen and young adult populations. Studies have provided evidence that the Internet can influence behavior related to suicide. Therefore, this paper explores usability and user experience to better understand how the language, design, and ease of navigation contribute to user perceptions.

Keywords: Usability · User experience · Health website

1 Introduction

Usability and user experience (UI/UX) are exceptionally important for websites that provide critical information and/or services to vulnerable populations. For example, suicide is one of the leading causes of death around the world and is most prevalent in teens and young adults. UI/UX evaluation of suicide prevention websites is important in determining whether these critical resources may be improved to more effectively help at-risk individuals. Studies show that the Internet can influence behavior related to suicide. Research has also demonstrated that technology can play a predominantly pro-suicide role in the journey of a suicidal user, providing more information about *how* to commit suicide than how to *prevent* it [1]. At the same time, technology manufacturers have attempted to make service and care more convenient by providing users additional ways to receive help [2]. For example, studies have identified areas of improvement for personal assistance devices that include more empathetic responses to suicidal users. Previous research has also explored prediction of suicide through artificial intelligence, as well as building additional resources through applications like conversational chatbots. However, privacy and usability problems have been a roadblock.

Published research comparing existing suicide prevention websites has not been conducted. To pilot this type of research, this paper presents a focused UI/UX study of two suicide prevention websites, one hosted in a state with a high suicide rate (New Mexico) and one hosted in a state with a low suicide rate (New Jersey). The intention is to identify usability and user experience differences. New Mexico has the second-highest suicide rate in the U.S. and sponsors the Agora Cares Crisis Center (agoracares.org) website; New Jersey has the lowest suicide rate in the U.S. and supports the Caring Contact

C. Stephanidis et al. (Eds.): HCII 2021, CCIS 1421, pp. 376–383, 2021.
https://doi.org/10.1007/978-3-030-78645-8_48

(caringcontact.org) website. Identifying opportunities for website improvement is a step toward ensuring that individuals at risk for self-harm have better access to resources meant to provide positive direction and assistance [3]. This paper compares these sites on the following dimensions of user perception: 1) helpfulness and satisfaction, 2) trust among users, and 3) design and layout quality. A task-based usability survey addresses the following research questions: **RQ 1:** How do users' perceptions of helpfulness and satisfaction for two different suicide prevention websites affect overall perceptions of usability? **RQ 2:** How do users' perceptions of trust, engagement, and interest for two different suicide prevention websites affect overall perceptions of credibility? **RQ 3:** How do users' opinions about the design and layout of two different suicide prevention websites affect overall perceptions of desirability?

This paper explores three interaction goals to measure user experience: 1) how language and ease of navigation contribute to perceptions of the helpfulness; 2) how much visceral and cognitive judgments affect users' perceptions of the trustworthiness of each site; and 3) how perceptions of attractiveness affect perceptions of usability. Combining these principals provides a mechanism for assessing the quality of each site [4]. People who struggle with mental health often seek information online due to the stigma associated with seeking in-person help [1]. This paper attempts to contribute to literature related to improving online resources often used by at-risk populations. Intervention delivered via the Internet has the ability to positively change at-risk behaviors, but studies have found that more than half of the target audience leaves this type of site after 30 s, without resource engagement [5]. Therefore, suicide prevention sites must provide satisfying and valuable user experiences.

2   Literature Review

2.1   Risk Factors and Suicide Prevention

Research indicates that individuals at risk for suicidal behavior "would probably benefit the most from receiving anonymous treatment online, wherein they can openly discuss their feelings without being exposed to the stigma and taboo of discussing mental health issues and suicidality" [11]. Individuals seeking help online provide researchers a space to define possible website improvements. When communication primarily takes place online, an individual is likely to feel lonelier and could be more prone to depression or suicidal behavior [12]. Likewise, when social interaction is primarily performed online, the number of users a person communicates with could expose them to risks they would not typically face in an in-person setting [13]. Heavy online usage has also been linked to an increasing number of mental health disorders [14].

In 2015, the World Health Organization (WHO) reported the suicide rate had increased 60% worldwide over the past 45 years. The CDC has found family and community support, connectedness, and easy-to-access health care helps decrease the risk of suicide [6]. Suicide prevention resources exist in many forms, including websites with call lines and chat features. In 2014, the Department of Mental Health and WHO conducted a global survey to better understand how audiences viewed the importance of suicide reduction. Sixty-one percent of responding countries perceived suicide as a significant public health concern [7]. However, only 31% of countries had an action plan in place to decrease the suicide rate [8]. The most difficult obstacles for suicide prevention are accuracy and reliability of information [9]. Likewise, the most important factors to reduce risk of suicide attempts are perceived connectivity, appropriate language, and the ability to connect to a person via phone or text [10].

2.2 Previous UI and UX Studies

Suicide prevention websites are commonly used in 49 states in the U.S. Research has shown that predictive analytics have been perceived as invasive; chatbots can be powerful but take a lot of time to perfect due to continuous data collection; and forcing site navigation can cause negative user perceptions [15]. It is now more common for technology to facilitate a heathy conversation with users that appear to be considering suicide [2]. Stanford identified a usability gap in intelligence for personal assistance devices, which encouraged manufacturers like Siri, Google Assistant, and Alexa to edit scripts with more appropriate responses [1]. Researchers found that when a user asked a personal assistance device a mental health question, the device often did not flag the question as concerning. Performance of personal assistance devices leaves room for improvement, as they rely heavily on "a clear verbal indication of suicidal thoughts" [2]. The researchers compared pre- and post-surveys after users spent two weeks communicating with a Cognitive Behavior Therapy chatbot (CBT), Woebot. This application can be found on Facebook and through anonymous applications for iOS and Android. Woebot was "designed to deliver CBT in the format of brief, daily conversations and mood tracking" [16]. The chatbot features empathic responses that are tailored to user moods, goal setting, accountability, motivation, engagement, and reflection. Results indicated that the chatbot significantly reduced users' measured depression, and users found the system convenient enough to use frequently.

A Vanderbilt University research group conducted a study that complements the Stanford work by attempting to predict suicide attempts through machine learning. Early forms of predictive analytics focused on isolation and depression; but machine learning would allow for higher complexity [17]. Increasing suicide rates have led to the creation of new platforms instead of exploring the efficacy of what is already available. Since no one can identify when a suicide attempt is near, all available resources must provide positive usability and user experience.

3   Methodology

This study employed a mixed-methods approach that included quantitative and qualitative research methods. Instruments included online survey questionnaires that compared user perceptions of two suicide prevention websites. Results were collected in Loop11, a remote user testing tool.

3.1   Websites

Two suicide prevention websites–Agora Cares (agoracares.org) and Caring Contact (caringcontact.org)–are publicly accessible online resources. The Agora Cares site includes multiple ways for individuals to seek help, including through phone calls, online chats, email, and text messaging. The site also provides information about how to volunteer for the crisis center, upcoming events, local resources, and community education. According to the site, Agora Cares was founded by the University of New Mexico and is one of the first free, confidential, compassionate crisis centers in the U.S. The Caring Contact site encourages visitors to use a call or text support line for services. The site also provides information about how to get support, how to give support, and applied suicide intervention skills training. Caring Contact is a non-profit organization and receives funding through public donations. Founded in 1975, the organization receives more than 13,000 calls each year in support of the New Jersey population.

3.2 Survey, Participants, Data Collection and Analysis

A user testing survey was designed to explore participant perceptions of each website. The survey explores whether perceptions of the language and navigation, content, and attractiveness of each site affects how users judge usability and user experience. The survey asked participants to complete eight tasks that required them to interact with various areas of each site and then answer 12 UI/UX questions. The survey also included an adjective list to better understand the desirability of the website. The adjective options were generated from the Microsoft Desirability Toolkit that allows for a mix of positive and negative terms [20]. An optional, open-ended question was included for participants to document what they liked and/or disliked most about each website. Both male and female participants over the age of 18 were recruited through social media and email.

Post-task questions were reviewed through a comparison analysis, and responses to survey questions were compared according to the following dimensions: usability, credibility, and desirability. Usability was measured for tasks related to site use and value, navigation, and action. Credibility was measured for tasks that focused on up-front disclosure, comprehension, and connection. Desirability was measured for tasks focused on perceptions of the design and layout. An analysis of an adjective list allowed for a better understanding of desirability. Terms were grouped by frequency, and a comparison was conducted to determine differences. Responses to open-ended questions were also coded and grouped by topic to capture common themes.

4 Results

Participants were first introduced to the homepage of the website for five seconds and then asked to rate the design and layout by attractiveness. The average attractiveness rating for Agora Cares was 3.43, falling between attractive and neutral. The average attractiveness rating for Caring Contact was 4.52, falling between attractive and very attractive. Participants were then asked to rate their level of agreement with a statement related to how easy it is to locate the purpose of the site. Agora Cares participant responses averaged 3.73, falling between neutral and agree that the purpose of the site was easy to discern. The average level of agreement recorded for Caring Contact was 3.98. Participants were also asked to rate their level of agreement with how easy it is to locate information about how to help a friend. Agora Cares participant responses averaged 3.9, falling close to agree that it was easy to find information about how to help a friend. The average level of agreement recorded for Caring Contact was 3.83.

Participants were also asked to identify how many ways the website offers support. Forms of support participants could identify included: 1) intangible social support (i.e., phone number, chat/text, email, social media links); 2) informational social support (i.e., website text, resource guide); and 3) companionship social support (i.e., community education, events). Agora Cares participants indicated an average of 3.85 ways they perceived the site offers support, while Caring Contact participants indicated an average of 3.24 perceived support features. Both Agora Cares and Caring Contact provide more than six methods of support. Participants were also asked to rate their level of agreement with a statement related to how easy it is to locate a call to action on the site. Agora Cares participant responses averaged 4.1 (falling between agree and strongly agree that a call to action is easy to find), while Caring Contact participant responses averaged 4.26.

Participants were also asked to evaluate the language used on each website based on a five-point scale that ranged from *excellent* (5) to *very poor* (1). Agora Cares participant responses averaged 4.18. The average level of language perception recorded for Caring Contact was 4.07. Participants were also asked to rate their level of agreement with a statement related to how easy it is to locate who runs the website. Agora Care participant responses averaged 3.78 (falling between neutral and agree that it is easy to locate who runs the website). The average level of agreement recorded for Caring Contact was 4.29. This result was statistically significantly, with Caring Contact website scoring much higher (2.23 ± 1.25) than Agora Cares ($1.71 \pm .995$), $t(80) = 2.052$, $p = 0.043$. There were no other individual items in the survey that yielded statistically significant results, likely due to the relatively small participant sample size. Participants were also asked to rate their level of agreement with a statement related to how easy it is to locate testimonials on the websites. Average responses to both sites were 1.93, falling between strongly disagree and disagree that it is easy to find testimonials.

Tasks related to site use and value, navigation, and action were indicative of participants' assessment of site usability. There was not a statistically significant difference in perceptions of usability. Tasks that focused on up-front disclosure, comprehension, and connection were indicative of participants' perceptions of website credibility. Compared to Agora Cares, participants found Caring Contact more credible than Agora Cares $t(80) = 1.795$, $p = .076$, a marginally significant difference. Finally, tasks focused on perceptions of the design and layout were indicative of users' perceptions of desirability. Compared to Agora Cares, participants found Caring Contact had a significantly higher desirability, $t(80) = 2.425$, $p = .018$.

The final task asked participants to select five adjectives that describe the website. The most common adjective recorded for Agora Cares was *professional*. Participants who identified as male frequently defined the site as *boring* and *old*, while women recorded *calm* and *trustworthy* at the highest rate. The most common term to describe the Caring Contact site was *trustworthy*. Participants who identified as male most frequently defined the site as *calm, familiar,* and *trustworthy,* while women most commonly recorded *professional* and *trustworthy*.

5   Discussion

This research compared two suicide prevention websites on perceived usability and user experience differences. Overall, participants found the Caring Contact website to be more aesthetically pleasing than the Agora Cares site. However, on all dimensions, there were no statistically significant differences for how participants rated either site. Following is a brief analysis of how the sites fared according to each research question.

Regarding RQ1 – *How do users' perceptions of helpfulness and satisfaction for two different suicide prevention websites affect overall perceptions of usability?* – Participants did not rate either site as significantly better than the other on helpfulness or satisfaction. On all related usability dimensions, both sites were rated slightly above average. Additionally, for both sites, a prominent display of call to action and contact information seemed to contribute to a positive user experience. While Caring Contact often averaged stronger ease of use scores than the Agora Cares site, the difference between the two sites did not result in significant statistical data. Qualitative responses to open-ended questions indicated that participants were most concerned about how effectively the sites presented contact information and ease of navigation. Participants often focused on the ease of getting help and ease of use. Because both sites provided clear and easy-to-find information about resources for at-risk individuals, participants generally responded positively, which also improved overall usability scores.

Regarding RQ2 – *How do users' perceptions of trust, engagement, and interest for two different suicide prevention websites affect overall perceptions of credibility?* – participants rated Caring Contact significantly better than Agora Cares on trust. Responses indicated difficulty finding testimonials; however, this did not negatively affect the perception of overall trustworthiness. On engagement and satisfaction, both sites were rated slightly above average. Additionally, for both sites, the purpose and content of the site seemed to contribute to a positive user experience. Qualitative responses to open-ended questions indicated that participants were most concerned about the topic of the website and the need for the resource. In addition, the responses from the adjective collection indicated that participants' level of trust was not affected by the elements of either website. Participants often focused on the subject of the website and information available. Because both sites provided clear purpose and content on how they can help at-risk individuals, participants generally responded positively, which also likely improved overall credibility scores.

Regarding RQ3 – *How do users' opinions about the design and layout of two different suicide prevention websites affect overall perceptions of desirability?* – participants rated the first impression of Caring Contact significantly better than Agora Cares on design and layout. Responses indicated the design and layout of Agora Cares was more attractive. However, on all related desirability dimensions, both sites were rated slightly above average. Additionally, for both sites, the calm design and familiar layout seemed to contribute to a positive user experience. While the first impression of Caring Contact averaged stronger attractiveness than the Agora Cares site, the difference between the two sites did not result in significant statistical data. Qualitative responses to open-ended questions indicated that participants enjoyed the colors used on Agora Cares due to the simplicity and participants enjoyed the use of color on Caring Contact due to the emotion it evoked. In addition to the qualitative responses, the adjectives selected indicated the design and layout did not affect the overall desirability. Because both sites used color and a familiar layout, participants generally responded positively, which also improved overall desirability scores.

In spite of the fact that participants rated both websites as usable, desirable, and credible, there is still room for improvement. Sites that serve such a critical need among a high-risk demographic should always be looking for ways to improve usability and user experience. For both the Caring Contact and Agora Cares websites, participants were generally pleased that resources like this exist at all. They recognized the importance of such resources, and as a result were less critical than expected about the nature and quality of the content and presentation. However, possible options to improve each site should not be ignored. For example, it's possible that adding a bit of color could increase user satisfaction and increase the users' perception of the homepage during first impressions. In addition, Agora Cares could implement language on the donation page that allows users to understand how much their donations benefit the organization. This research determined that participants noticed and appreciated the statement, "$1,000-Volunteer training materials for 1 year." By outlining the effect of donations, the organization could increase funds and generate more tools to support the community. Additionally, for Caring Contact, the first impression that the site is attractive may help draw in users; however, it is also important to account for resource findability. By prominently laying out all the methods of support, users may consider the site to be more helpful. Finally, the colors used on the donation page could be improved to simplify the visual appeal. While vibrant colors can be attractive, the overuse of color can deter users from engaging with the content on the page.

5.1 Conclusion

Positive user experiences encourage users to engage with the site and explore more content. The stigma that exists around psychological issues has made it difficult for individuals to recover. Identifying opportunities to improve a website would be a significant step towards providing better access to resources. The research analyzed what elements of a website contributed to a positive user experience and attempted to find differences between the two websites. The results of this research indicate that the use of color is appealing but does not affect the overall user experience. Overall, participants felt the most important elements within a health intervention site are usability and credibility, but additional research would be needed to validate those dimensions.

References

1. Miner, A.S., Milstein, A., Schueller, S., Hegde, R., Mangurian, C., Linos, E.: Smartphone-based conversational agents and responses to questions about mental health, interpersonal violence, and physical health. JAMA Int. Med. **176**(5), 619–625 (2012)
2. Andrade, N., Pawson, D., Muriello, D., Donahue, L., Guadagno, J.: Ethics & artificial intelligence: suicide prevention on Facebook. Philos. Technol. **31**(4), 669–684 (2018)
3. Hartmann, J., Sutcliffe, A., Angeli, A.: Towards a theory of user judgment of aesthetics and user interface quality. ACM Trans. Comput. Hum. Interact. **15**(4), 1–30 (2008)

4. Preece, J., Rogers, Y.: Interaction Design: Beyond Human-Computer Interaction. Wiley, Chichester (2015)

5. Crutzen, R., Goeritz, A.S.: Social desirability and self-reported health risk behaviors in web-based research: Three longitudinal studies. BMC Public Health **10**(1), 720 (2010)

6. CDC Suicide Prevention Homepage. https://www.cdc.gov/suicide/factors/index.html, last accessed 2020/3/1.

7. World Health Organization Suicide Homepage. https://www.who.int/news-room/fact-sheets/detail/suicide. Accessed 1 Mar 2020

8. Arensman, E., Scott, V., De Leo, D., Pirkis, J.: Suicide and suicide prevention from a global perspective. J. Crisis Interv. Suicide Prev. **41**(Suppl 1), S3–S7 (2020)

9. Tøllefsen, I.M., Hem, E., Ekeberg, Ø.: The reliability of suicide statistics: a systematic review. BMC Psychiatry **12**(1), 1–11 (2012)

10. Reger, M.A., et al.: Implementation methods for the caring contacts suicide prevention intervention. Prof. Psychol. Res. Pract. **48**(5), 369–377 (2017)

11. Durkee, T., Hadlaczky, G., Westerlund, M., Carli, V.: Internet pathways in suicidality: a review of the evidence. Int. J. Environ. Res. Public Health **8**(10), 3938–3952 (2011)

12. Masuda, N., Kurahashi, I., Onari, H. Suicide ideation of individuals in online social networks. PLoS ONE **8**(4), e62262 (2013)

13. Luxton, D.D., June, J.D., Fairall, J.M.: Social media and suicide: a public health perspective. Am. J. Public Health Res. **102**(2), 195–200 (2012)

14. Tripathi, A.: Impact of internet addiction on mental health: an integrative therapy is needed. Integr. Med. Int. **4**(3–4), 215–222 (2017)

15. O'Brien, K.H. McManama, R.T. Liu, J.M. Putney, Burke, T.A., Aguinaldo, L.D.: Suicide and self-injury in gender and sexual minority populations (2018)

16. Fitzpatrick, K.K., Darcy, A., Vierhile, M.: Delivering cognitive behavior therapy to young adults with symptoms of depression and anxiety using a fully automated conversational agent (Woebot): a randomized controlled trial. JMIR Mental Health **4**(2) (2017)

17. Walsh, C.G., Ribeiro, J.D., Franklin, J.C.: Predicting risk of suicide attempts over time through machine learning. Clin. Psychol. Sci. **5**(3), 457–469 (2017)

18. Walker, D. M., Johnson, T., Ford, E.W., Huerta, T.R. Trust me, I'm a doctor: examining changes in how privacy concerns affect patient withholding behavior. J. Med. Internet Res. **19**(1), e2 (2017)

19. Abdelhamid, M., Gaia, J., Sanders, G.L.: Putting the focus back on the patient: how privacy concerns affect personal health information sharing intentions. J. Med. Internet Res. **19**(9) (2017)

20. Benedek, J., Miner, T.: Measuring desirability: new methods for evaluating desirability in a usability lab setting. In: Proceedings of Usability Professionals Association, vol. 57, pp. 8–12 (2002)

Designing BookClub: Technologically Mediated Reading and Distant Interactions to Promote Well-Being

Evan Sobetski[1][✉], Sylvia Sinsabaugh[1], Gowri Balasubramaniam[1], and Omar Sosa-Tzec[2]

[1] University of Michigan, Ann Arbor, MI 48109, USA
sobetski@umich.edu
[2] San Francisco State University, San Francisco, CA 94132, USA

Abstract. This poster introduces *BookClub*, a design proposal of technology to promote well-being through reading and social interaction. Here we describe the early stages of our process, including our initial ideas and graphic documentation of our prototyping process. We also discuss a preliminary qualitative study with potential users that helped us identify the areas of opportunity in this design and future research work.

Keywords: Well-being · Delightful design · Human-computer interaction · User experience · Reading · Healthy habits · Social interaction · Home devices

1 Introduction

Many individuals have suffered from negative effects to their well-being due to poor mental health, caused by social isolation and insignificant cognitive activity [1, p. 167, 473], [2]. Affected groups include the elderly population, college students, and immigrants [3–5]. One can promote an active and healthy mind by comprehending new information [6, p. 298]. By reading a book, a reader is challenged to constantly comprehend and interpret new information [7, p. 194]. Because of this, reading has been shown to enhance one's mental health significantly because it is an intellectual activity [6, p. 371]. Turning the intellectual activity of reading into a social activity as well is crucial to not only maintaining social well-being, but to also motivating the user to read more through social proof [11]. Based on this, we propose *BookClub,* an interactive technological reading companion that seeks to combat the detrimental effects that cognitive inactivity and isolation can cause.

2 Related Work

Well-being has been a topic of interest for researchers and scholars for centuries [12]. As technology has become pervasive in modern society, it is no surprise that researchers of

© Springer Nature Switzerland AG 2021
C. Stephanidis et al. (Eds.): HCII 2021, CCIS 1421, pp. 384–391, 2021.
https://doi.org/10.1007/978-3-030-78645-8_49

human-computer interaction (HCI) and design have engaged in studying how designed products support or undermine people's well-being. We identified that significant contributions towards well-being appear in the form of models or frameworks. *Positive computing* appears as a robust framework to design technology that focuses on well-being [13]. This framework defined by Calvo and Peters comprises three dimensions, namely, self, social, and transcendent. The dimensions comprise in turn a series of factors by which human psychological well-being can be targeted and measured. Such factors include positive emotions, motivation & engagement, self-awareness, mindfulness, resilience, gratitude, empathy, compassion, and altruism [13, p. 85].

Peters, Calvo, and Ryan have developed the model *Motivation, Engagement, and Thriving in User Experience* (METUX) for HCI researchers to define design strategies for technology that boost a user's motivation and engagement by addressing their basic psychological needs, including autonomy, competence, and relatedness [14]. According to this model, an HCI researcher can frame such strategies by paying attention to a set of six spheres: adoption, interface, tasks, behavior, life, and society [14, p. 9]. On the realm of design, there is another framework that represents a robust research agenda concerning design for well-being. Desmet and Pohlmeyer formulate Positive Design as a framework to support the creation of artifacts that enable or stimulate human flourishing [12]. Positive Design comprises three ingredients, namely, virtue, pleasure, and personal significance. Designers utilizing this framework should aim at finding a balance between these three ingredients though the success of a design will be in the end a function of how it fits to the user's life, supports agency, and attains a long-term impact [12].

We also identified cases of object-led work in our exploratory secondary research. Pichlmair et al. investigate how to induce relaxation to travelers through *Pen Pen,* a combination of a technologically-intervened neck cushion and a mobile app [15]. Desmet and Sääksjärvi have designed a series of key ring coins indented to develop intrinsic motivation [16]. Ludden and Meekhof designed and evaluated *Break Trigger,* a system comprising of a personal pebble and an interactive table intended to lower the stress of office workers by promoting breaks and guided interactions [17]. Finally, Höök, Jonsson, Ståhl, and Mercurio prototyped the *Soma Carpet* and the *Breathing Light,* which focus on bodily sensations and aims at directing a person's attention inwards [18]. Through the combination of these designed objects and our understanding of the above mentioned frameworks we recognize the potential in designing objects that support reading and social interactions as a viable way to tackle the problem we have identified.

3   Approach

3.1   Secondary Research, Ideation, and Design Critique

We have informed our work through a literature review on well-being and several design-oriented activities, including sketching, design critique and form explorations. Literature review led our team to encapsulate a combination of the six domains of self-care [19] and five dimensions of design delight [20] in our design to therefore promote well-being. Through individual sketching sessions, our team ideated with the framework of self-care and design delight in mind. These sketches were then presented in multiple team design critique sessions where we uncovered that the combination of reading and social interaction could effectively promote well-being (Fig. 1). After completing our several design-oriented activities we went forward with material and form exploration of the design idea shown in Fig. 2.

Fig. 1. Design critique session with input from an expert.

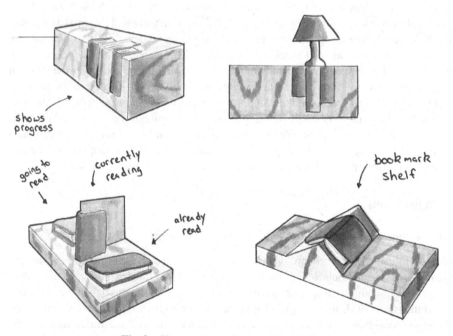

Fig. 2. Chosen proposal to promote reading.

3.2 Material and Form Exploration

The prototyping phase revealed areas of concern with the originally sketched concepts (Fig. 2) such as adaptability and ease of use. Instead of designing an entire bookshelf, we developed a product that could be implemented with preexisting infrastructure and in multiple user environments. The first prototype of *BookClub* (Fig. 3) gave the user the ability to track their reading progress and view when their reading partner was actively reading. These features were communicated to the user through light gestures that illuminated the surface below *BookClub*. In this prototype we explored different material selections, forms (Fig. 4) and light panel configurations (Fig. 5).

Fig. 3. The first generation prototype of *BookClub*.

Fig. 4. Designers discussing form exploration of *BookClub*.

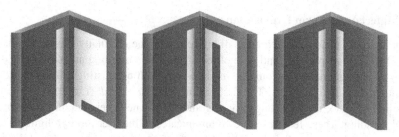

Fig. 5. The multiple light panel configurations considered during the design process.

We then engaged in design critique of the first generation prototype (Fig. 3). This evaluation exposed opportunities for improvement such as larger space necessary to integrate electronics. After the completion of our design critique we engaged in an iterative process to create the second generation prototype of *BookClub* (Fig. 6, 7). An accelerometer provided the user the ability to communicate whether they were actively reading by setting the device down in a certain orientation. The new translucent encasement (Fig. 7) of electrical components allowed for more advanced light gestures to interface with users through light color, movement and brightness.

Fig. 6. The second generation prototype of *BookClub*.

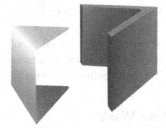

Fig. 7. The addition of a translucent encasement cover.

3.3 Exploratory Evaluation

Six students from various schools of the University of Michigan were interviewed about the user experience and delightfulness of *BookClub*. The interviewees were shown a user scenario storyboard of two reading partners using the product (Fig. 8). After conducting the interviews, several themes emerged from the interviewees' responses.

Fig. 8. Sample of storyboard presented to interviewees.

The first theme is how synchronous activities provide social connection even when the activity is a distant interaction. Through the communication of two *BookClub* devices, users are able to synchronously read which is juxtaposition of a traditional book club which has participants typically read asynchronously. Interviewees expressed that they would feel more socially connected to their reading partner if they read synchronously.

Another theme is how a non-screen centered device does not hinder or limit delightful interactions. Many people socially connect with one another through screen centered applications such as social media which has led to screen addiction and negative health consequences. *BookClub* communicates with the user solely through the usage of light.

This provides a more subtle, less distracting interaction with the device and allows the user to focus on the activity of reading.

Finally, another significant theme is how social proof can motivate users to form healthy habits. *BookClub* brings attention to when a reading partner is actively reading. This awareness will therefore motivate both users to read more frequently.

4 Conclusion and Future Work

This research shows that the combination of technologically-mediated distant interactions and the intellectual activity of reading can be useful to improve a person's mental health and well-being. However, limitations in the form and functionality of *BookClub* and other unforeseen considerations emerged from the conducted interviews. Based on the feedback and knowledge gained from these initial stages, future work will consist of a redesign of *BookClub*. This work will include modifications to form and further exploration of the user experience in regards to the interactive light panel.

References

1. David, S.A., Boniwell, I., Ayers, A.C. (eds.): The Oxford Handbook of Happiness. Oxford University Press, Oxford (2014)
2. Wang, J., et al.: Social isolation in mental health: a conceptual and methodological review. Soc. Psychiatry Psychiatr. Epidemiol. **52**(12), 1451–1461 (2017). https://doi.org/10.1007/s00 127-017-1446-1
3. Golden, J., et al.: Loneliness, social support networks, mood and wellbeing in community-dwelling elderly. Int. J. Geriat. Psychiatry **24**(7), 694–700 (2009). https://doi.org/10.1002/gps.2181
4. Thomas, L., Orme, E., Kerrigan, F.: Student loneliness: the role of social media through life transitions. Comput. Educ. **146**, 103754 (2020). https://doi.org/10.1016/j.compedu.2019.103754
5. De Jong Gierveld, J., Van der Pas, S., Keating, N.: Loneliness of older immigrant groups in canada: effects of ethnic-cultural background. J. Cross Cult. Gerontol. **30**(3), 251–268 (2015). https://doi.org/10.1007/s10823-015-9265-x
6. Billington, J.: Reading and Mental Health. Springer, Cham (2019). https://doi.org/10.1007/978-3-030-21762-4
7. Thorburn, M., (ed.): Wellbeing, Education and Contemporary Schooling. Routledge, Taylor & Francis Group, London (2018)
8. Buxton, B.: Sketching User Experiences: Getting the Design Right and the Right Design, Nachdr. Morgan Kaufmann, Amsterdam (2011)
9. Connor, A., Irizarry, A.: Discussing Design: Improving Communication and Collaboration Through Critique, 1st edn. O'Reilly, Bejing (2015)
10. Hanington, B., Martin, B.: Universal Methods of Design Expanded and Revised. Rockport Publishers, Beverly (2019)
11. Cialdini, R.: Influence the Psychology of Persuasion. First Collins Business Essentials edn. HarperCollins Publishers, 195 Broadway, New York (2007)
12. Peters, D., Calvo, R.A., Ryan, R.M.: Designing for motivation, engagement and wellbeing in digital experience. Front. Psychol. **9** (2018). https://doi.org/10.3389/fpsyg.2018.00797

13. Maddux, J.E. (ed.): Subjective Well-Being and Life Satisfaction. Routledge/Taylor & Francis Group, New York (2018)
14. Calvo, R.A., Peters, D.: Positive Computing: Technology for Wellbeing and Human Potential. The MIT Press, Cambridge (2014)
15. Pohlmeyer, A.E.: Positive design: new challenges, opportunities, and responsibilities for design. In: Marcus, A. (ed.) Design, User Experience, and Usability. User Experience in Novel Technological Environments. LNCS, vol. 8014, pp. 540–547. Springer, Heidelberg (2013). https://doi.org/10.1007/978-3-642-39238-2_59
16. Pichlmair, M., et al.: Pen-Pen: a wellbeing design to help commuters rest and relax. In: Proceedings of the Workshop on Human-Habitat for Health (H3): Human-Habitat Multimodal Interaction for Promoting Health and Well-Being in the Internet of Things Era, New York, NY, USA, October 2018, pp. 1–9 (2018). https://doi.org/10.1145/3279963.3279966
17. Desmet, P.M.A., Sääksjärvi, M.C.: Form matters: design creativity in positive psychological interventions. Psychol. Well-Being **6**(1), 1–17 (2016). https://doi.org/10.1186/s13612-016-0043-5
18. Ludden, G.D.S., Meekhof, L.: Slowing down: introducing calm persuasive technology to increase wellbeing at work. In: Proceedings of the 28th Australian Conference on Computer-Human Interaction, New York, NY, USA, November 2016, pp. 435–441 (2016). https://doi.org/10.1145/3010915.3010938
19. Höök, K., Jonsson, M.P., Ståhl, A., Mercurio, J.: Somaesthetic appreciation design. In: Proceedings of the 2016 CHI Conference on Human Factors in Computing Systems, New York, NY, USA, pp. 3131–3142 (2016). https://doi.org/10.1145/2858036.2858583
20. Butler, L.D., Mercer, K.A., McClain-Meeder, K., Horne, D.M., Dudley, M.: Six domains of self-care: attending to the whole person. J. Hum. Behav. Soc. Environ. **29**(1), 107–124 (2019). https://doi.org/10.1080/10911359.2018.1482483
21. Sosa-Tzec, O.: Design delight: an experiential quality framework. In: Selected Papers of Senses & Sensibility 2019, Lost in (G)locatization, Portugal, November 2019, in Press

Leveraging Virtual Reality and Exergames to Promote Physical Activity

Thomas Stranick[1] and Christian E. Lopez[2($\boxtimes$)]

[1] Department of Electrical and Computer Engineering, Lafayette College, Easton,
PA 18042, USA
[2] Department of Computer Science, Lafayette College, Easton, PA 18042, USA
lopebec@lafayette.edu

Abstract. This work introduces a Virtual Reality Exergame application to promote physical activity. With obesity on the rise, it is more important than ever to encourage and motivate people to be active. Exercise helps with the expenditure of energy via body movements, which is key to living a healthy life. However, exercise by itself is not an engaging activity for most people. The objective of the exergame introduced in this work is to encourage users to perform full-body movements to pass through a series of obstacles and achieve higher scores, unlock content, and complete a series of achievements. The application implements a variety of game elements to help motivate users to play the game and perform physical activity. Each of the game elements can be toggled on or off depending on whether the player feels they are benefitting or hindering the experience. This feature allows users to customize the application. Moreover, this exergame application leverages Virtual Reality and Depth-sensor technology to help provide users with an immersive first-person experience. While in the game, users can visualize their motions. This is because the users can control their virtual avatar with their body movements with the use of the depth-sensor. It is expected that this immersivity will motivate and encourage the users even more. The objective of this work is to introduce this Virtual Reality Exergame application as well as the hardware and software development aspects of it.

Keywords: Virtual reality · Exergame · Physical activity · Obesity

1 Introduction

Obesity within the United States and the world is on the rise. Obesity is defined as abnormal or excessive fat accumulation that may impair health [1]. Within the United States, 42.4% of adults are obese as well as 13% of the world adult population [1, 2]. This is an important issue as obesity and being overweight can lead to major health issues including heart disease, stroke, type 2 diabetes, and some types of cancer [2]. Each of these are detrimental to a person's health and can lead to premature death.

One method for the prevention of obesity is regular physical activity and healthier eating habits [1]. Obesity is caused when a person consumes more calories than they burn or use up. This causes an imbalance in the energy that is stored in fat and the energy

© Springer Nature Switzerland AG 2021
C. Stephanidis et al. (Eds.): HCII 2021, CCIS 1421, pp. 392–399, 2021.
https://doi.org/10.1007/978-3-030-78645-8_50

that is used to perform physical activity. When somebody exercises they can burn those stored calories from the food that was eaten. However, one limitation to the exercise method is individual motivation to exercise. Even in those who are obese, some might not feel motivated enough to exercise and improve their condition [3]. One potential solution would be to promote physical activities through Exergames.

Exergames are active video games that can help in promoting exercise for users. These exercise games are beneficial for adapting sedentary games into ones that can make the user physically active [4]. Exergames can also help make standard physical activity more fun and enjoyable. One study examined that exergames, compared to traditional machine exercise, promoted better self-efficacy, positive engagement, enjoyment, stress management, and reduction in depressive symptoms [5]. Unfortunately, most existing exergames lack immersivity and engagement to motivate the user to continue using the application and exercising [6]. Leveraging Virtual Reality (VR) and body tracking technology could help improve the engagement and immersive factor of exergames that would then promote healthy exercising habits.

VR provides a first-person experience for the user and immerses them within the game world. Two key elements, interactivity and telepresence, contribute to immersion within VR. The immersion created from these two VR elements contributes to the satisfaction of the user when playing the VR exergame [7]. The satisfaction from the immersion in turn creates enjoyment for the user when playing the exergame. Studies comparing VR headsets to traditional screens have determined that VR is more beneficial for immersivity and motivation of exercising [8]. The motivation and enjoyment of the user from the exergame are demonstrated through these studies [7, 8]. However, many of the existing exergame studies do not leverage VR technologies and focus on basic exercise or rehabilitation. Standard exergames also lack the immersivity that VR can provide for motivation. VR could play an important role in helping promote exercise through exergames to burn extra calories.

This study presents an application that leverages VR, Exergames, Depth-sensor technology, and full-body movement for the promotion of physical activities. Each of these elements will be presented through the developed exergame as a means for the promotion of exercise and engaging activities. The application presented also has the potential for more adaptations and changes to allow for more user engagement and increase self-willingness to play the exergame, thus exercising. The engagement through this exergame and its attributes could help motivate people to participate in daily exercise and move their whole body, thus helping prevent obesity through physical activity.

2   Literature Review

Participating in physical activity and regulating the consumption of unhealthy foods are the two basic ways of preventing obesity or overweight [1]. WHO promotes ways to prevent obesity at the individual level; limiting energy intake from fats and sugars, eating more fruits and vegetables, and engaging in regular physical activity. These methods rely on the individual to be proactive in exercising. In a survey about obesity prevention, 26% of the participants cited motivation as a blocking attribute to starting regular physical activity [9]. Many participants stated that they need to find "the right ways to do it [exercise]" or thinking that they just do not need to. Machines at the gym might also not be suitable for obese people and thus making it less effective [10]. One way to motivate individuals to perform physical activities could be through the use of exergames and Virtual Reality.

2.1 Exergames

Exergames are an alternative to traditional exercise; they allow the user to perform the exercise while also engaging with a video game. Through this method, those that may not normally perform typical exercise can be motivated through exergames. These can come in the form of specialized gym equipment or a home-based commercial video game [11, 12]. One of the most popular Nintendo Switch™ titles is an exergame; Ring Fit Adventure™ is rank 12 in Switch sales at 5.84 million units sold [13].

Many of the exergame studies related to obesity focus on the effectiveness of exergames on children or young adults [14–16]. Two of these studies focused on the use of commercial exergames in children's exercise and if it provided any significant difference in obesity levels compared to regular exercise. One study reported that after 24 weeks of exergaming utilizing the Microsoft Kinect, participants recorded a reduced BMI z-score, systolic and diastolic blood pressure, cholesterol levels, and moderate to vigorous physical activity levels [14]. Another study reported that after 6 weeks of exergaming, the participants reported a better waist to hip ratio as well as resting heart rate [15].

Exergames utilize different game design elements to promote users to perform physical activities through enjoyment and engagement. However, studies have shown that individuals' preferences for game elements differ [17]. Thus, different elements might provide different individual results depending on individual characteristics, like player type or game element preferences [18]. The complexity of the physical tasks itself has also been shown to influence user performance; the more complex the task is, the more motivated the individual needs to be in order to perform it [19].

There is a potential that exergames might not motivate its users, given individual differences and task complexity. For example, one study examining older adults' response to a full-body motion exergame demonstrated negative effects on engagement [20]. It was not obvious for participants the direction they should move in order to move the in-game avatar when played on a flat-screen TV. Participants also reported a disconnect with the avatar, stating that the avatar did not move with their body. Utilizing leveraging VR and Depth-sensor technology, exergames could overcome issues of lack of engagement and immersivity to provide a more motivating and enjoyable experience.

2.2 Virtual Reality and Exergames

Virtual Reality could benefit exergames by improving user's motivation for exercise as well as their heart rate when completing VR exergame-induced exercise [8, 21]. One study examining different exercises through exergames observed an increase in heart rate while playing the immersive VR version of the game compared to a regular screen. A volleyball full-body exergame increased the user's average heart rate by 3 beats-per-minute (bpm) more than the flat-screen version of the same exergame.

When comparing the volleyball full-body exergame versus an archery game that only works the upper body, users experience an increase of 10 bpm on their average heart rate [21]. This increase in heart rate could have come from the participant utilizing their whole body while immersed within the game world. Participants stated that it felt like the VR exergame was better at immersion and visualization of motion when completing tasks. Another study focusing on a running exergame came to the same conclusion that utilizing VR in exergames can benefit a user's exercising experience [8]. These studies demonstrate how VR could be used for exercise promotion, however, it is not necessarily beneficial for those with obesity. An exergame based around running might be beneficial for exercise purposes, but the participant might not be able to complete the tasks asked by the exergame due to being obese or overweight. An exergame that takes the condition of the user in mind would be ideal for obesity prevention.

Observing the benefits that exergames and VR could bring to obesity prevention, this work presents a VR exergame that could be utilized as a method of physical activity. An immersive VR exergame could benefit the user in engagement and motivation to continue utilizing the exergame for extended use. An exergame that could be used at various difficulties and promotes physical activity, however, utilizes full-body exercise could be beneficial for the prevention of obesity.

3 Application

3.1 Gameplay

The focus of the gameplay is to encourage exercise through full-body movements. The VR aspect introduced through the headset allows for greater immersivity and engagement with the user and could help motivate players to exercise. Users must stretch and move to pass a series of 14 obstacles that come towards them. These obstacles are made in different shapes and orientations such that the player is required to maneuver their body to fit the shape. Figure 1 demonstrates some of these diverse shapes and a player crouching through a low wall. The player is scored based on how much of their player avatar interacts with the walls as they pass the user. If the player does not hit any of the walls they score higher points compared to the one who hit the wall. This scoring method encourages the player to continue playing to achieve a higher score The Unity3D game engine (www.unity3d.com) was utilized to create the VR exergame and integrate the hardware components (see Sect. 3.2).

The use of the depth sensor technology allowed for a more immersive "pressing" of the menu buttons. This removed the need for any external controllers which could break the immersion. Unity's voice recognition package was also utilized to alleviate the need for a keyboard when entering the user's player name.

Many elements of the exergame are gamified such as the coin collection system, the achievement system, and the leaderboard. These elements could benefit the user in the promotion of physical activity [22]. The coin collection system allows the user to pick up coins while moving through the obstacles utilizing the collision boxes. These coins are placed where the player needs to reach or stretch their hand to reach them. Having the user move more when playing the game adds an element of challenge as well as encourages more exercising to be done while playing. The coins also can unlock a new tropical map

Fig. 1. Example obstacles

when enough are collected, giving the player something to work towards. Achievements are given to the player when they meet a certain requirement while playing the exergame. Player competition may also contribute to a user's experience, the leaderboard allows scores to be recorded and matched against set values or previous players. Each of these menus can be seen in Fig. 2, this indicates how one would navigate to each of these menus as well.

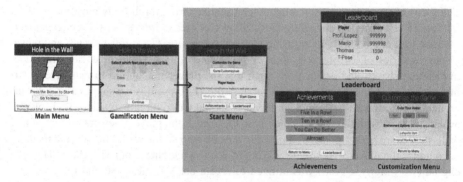

Fig. 2. Menu navigation

3.2 Hardware

To provide a full-body immersive VR experience, the Microsoft Kinect™ and the Oculus Rift™ were chosen. The hardware could be integrated with the game through the Unity game engine where specific features of the game could be tailored for each of these devices. The Microsoft Kinect™ was used to track user motion and translate it to the in-game avatar. This allows the in-game avatar to mimic the user's body motion and encourage exercise through the full-body motion that comes with dodging the obstacles.

The immersion aspect of the VR exergame could be brought by the Oculus Rift™ headset. This immersion brought about by the VR headset and Kinect is shown in Fig. 3. When the user moves their arms, they can watch the in-game avatar's arms move in the same way. The user's vision is strategically placed within the avatar's head to make the in-game avatar feel like the player's own body. Each of these hardware combinations helps bring about the immersion and feeling of presence within the game. This immersion provides engagement and thus user satisfaction, encouraging the user to proactively engage in physical activities [8, 21]. Figure 3 also shows the relations between the hardware, software, and user immersion. The Kinect allows for full-body motion to be translated into the game world. The Oculus Rift brings the user into the game world through an immersive lens. To combine the two, Unity can provide the full exergame VR full-body experience that the user can utilize to prevent obesity and practice healthy physical activity habits.

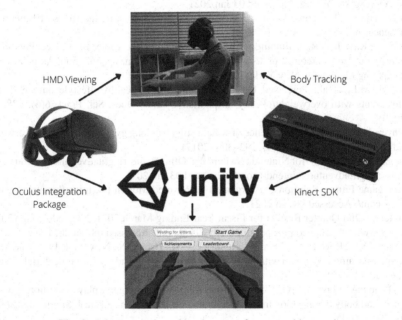

Fig. 3. Interconnection of hardware, software, and immersion

4 Conclusion

Future work regarding the exergame would look at the comparison of the added immersivity that VR could bring to a non-VR version of the same exergame. The game could also be tuned more towards obesity prevention if it is found that some obstacles are not exercised or obesity friendly. Lastly, one limitation of utilizing the VR headset comes from a smaller field of view. Although VR presents a first-person view, the field of view can take away from that immersivity. Future work could look at mitigating this issue and designing the game to accommodate the lack of peripheral vision.

References

1. Obesity and Overweight. https://www.who.int/news-room/fact-sheets/detail/obesity-and-ove rweight. Accessed 06 Mar 2021
2. CDC: "Adult Obesity Facts," Cent. Dis. Control Prev. (2021). https://www.cdc.gov/obesity/ data/adult.html. Accessed 06 Mar 2021
3. Hoare, E., Stavreski, B., Jennings, G.L., Kingwell, B.A.: Exploring motivation and barriers to physical activity among active and inactive Australian adults. Sports 5(3), 47 (2017)
4. "What Is Exergaming?," HealthySD.gov. https://healthysd.gov/what-is-exergaming-5/. Accessed 03 Jan 2021
5. Bock, B.C., et al.: Mediators of physical activity between standard exercise and exercise video games. Health Psychol. 38(12), 1107–1115 (2019)
6. Whitehead, A., Johnston, H.: Exergame Effectiveness: What the Numbers Can Tell Us. ACM.org. https://dl.acm.org/doi/abs/10.1145/1836135.1836144?casa_token=IIGIp8PBY YMAAAAA:i43zKNls2RypoEyRoSJIXLwrRCLdM_8toXSFdBvk1sJYChVeqsFZaeMbt 41EYviK8grk4TWhhc8. Accessed 03 Jan 2021
7. Mütterlein, J.: The Three Pillars of Virtual Reality? Investigating the Roles of Immersion, Presence, and Interactivity, p. 9
8. Yoo, S., Kay, J.: VRun: running-in-place virtual reality exergame. In: Proceedings of the 28th Australian Conference on Computer-Human Interaction, pp. 562–566. Association for Computing Machinery, New York (2016)
9. Cardel, M.I., et al.: Perceived barriers/facilitators to a healthy lifestyle among diverse adolescents with overweight/obesity: a qualitative study. Obes. Sci. Pract. 6(6), 638–648 (2020)
10. Schvey, N.A., et al.: The experience of weight stigma among gym members with overweight and obesity. Stigma Health 2(4), 292–306 (2017)
11. Ring Fit Adventure™ for Nintendo Switch™ – Official Site. ringfitadventure.nintendo.com. https://ringfitadventure.nintendo.com/. Accessed 03 Jan 2021
12. "Exergame Fitness Solutions," Exergame Fit. Powered Motion Fit. https://www.exergamef itness.com/. Accessed 08 Jan 2021
13. Nintendo: 2nd Quarter Results for Fiscal Year Ending March 2021. Nintendo.co.jp (2020). https://www.nintendo.co.jp/ir/pdf/2020/201105_4e.pdf. Accessed 08 Jan 2021
14. Staiano, A.E., Beyl, R.A., Guan, W., Hendrick, C.A., Hsia, D.S., Newton, R.L.: Home-based exergaming among children with overweight and obesity: a randomized clinical trial. Pediatr. Obes. 13(11), 724–733 (2018)
15. van Biljon, A., Longhurst, G., Shaw, I., Shaw, B.S.: Role of exergame play on cardiorespiratory fitness and body composition in overweight and obese children. Asian J. Sports Med. 12(1), e106782 (2021)
16. González-González, C.S., Gómez del Río, N., Toledo-Delgado, P.A., García-Peñalvo, F.J.: Active game-based solutions for the treatment of childhood obesity. Sensors 21(4), 1266 (2021)
17. Orji, R., Mandryk, R.L., Vassileva, J.: Improving the efficacy of games for change using personalization models. ACM Trans. Comput.-Hum. Interact. 24(5), 32:1–32:22 (2017)
18. Lopez, C.E., Tucker, C.S.: The effects of player type on performance: a gamification case study. Comput. Hum. Behav. 91, 333–345 (2019)
19. Lopez, C.E., Tucker, C.S.: A quantitative method for evaluating the complexity of implementing and performing game features in physically-interactive gamified applications. Comput. Hum. Behav. 71, 42–58 (2017)
20. Subramanian, S., Dahl, Y., Skjæret Maroni, N., Vereijken, B., Svanæs, D.: Assessing motivational differences between young and older adults when playing an exergame. Games Health J. 9(1), 24–30 (2020)

21. Cao, L., Peng, C., Dong, Y.: Ellic's exercise class: promoting physical activities during exergaming with immersive virtual reality. Virtual Real. (2020)
22. Mazéas, A., Duclos, M., Pereira, B., Chalabaev, A.: Does gamification improve physical activity? a systematic review and meta-analysis (2020)

Research on Emotional Design of Sleep Aid Products Based on the Theory of Design for Sustainable Behavior

Huizi Wu and Junnan Ye[✉]

East China University of Science and Technology, Shanghai 200237, People's Republic of China

Abstract. Staying up late has become an increasingly common bad habit among young people, and it can cause great harm. Based on the promotion of human sustainable development, this research introduces the theory of sustainable behavior design. Through literature review, it is known that the effectiveness of sustainable behavior design strategies is positively related to product dominance, and there is a relationship between product dominance and user acceptance contradiction. In order to improve user acceptance, this research introduces emotional design theory, and builds a product emotional design model based on sustainable behavior theory by analyzing the combination of sustainable behavior design theory and emotional design theory in the Fogg behavior model. Finally, based on this model, the design practice of desk lamps is used to improve the behavior of staying up late, while verifying the logic of the theory.

Keywords: Emotional design · Sleep aid products · Design for sustainable behavior · FOGG behavior model

1 Introduction

Modern people's life is full of many bad habits, and in these bad life style, staying up late is the most common. The age of those who stay up late is mainly distributed between 18 and 30 years old, that is, the post-90s and some post-00s. Taking college students as an example, only 49.56% go to bed before 12 am, while 17.76% go to bed after 1 am [1]. At the same time, experimental studies show that sleep deprivation caused by staying up late will cause damage to the body including nervous system, endocrine system, immune system, stress system and so on [2]. Therefore, for the sustainable and healthy development of the human world, it is necessary to intervene and improve the bad habit of staying up late by some strategies.

2 Research Method Analysis of Product Emotional Design Based on Sustainable Behavior Design Theory

2.1 Design for Sustainable Behavior

Staying up late is a kind of social unsustainable behavior, which belongs to the research category of sustainable behavior design. In the research field of sustainable design,

© Springer Nature Switzerland AG 2021
C. Stephanidis et al. (Eds.): HCII 2021, CCIS 1421, pp. 400–407, 2021.
https://doi.org/10.1007/978-3-030-78645-8_51

people pay more attention to the product itself, the material, process, assembly and recycling of the product, but less attention to the human factor, that is, the relationship between people and the product in the use process. For products that consume energy or resources in the use stage, such as automobiles, home appliances and other products, the environmental impact is mainly at the use end [3]. It is therefore equally important to discuss the environmental impact of the product's use. Sustainable behavior design focuses on exploring ways to achieve sustainability from the perspective of human behavior. Compared with other sustainable design theories, it focuses more on people's psychology, behavior, emotion and thinking.

The research on sustainable behavior design has made some achievements at home and abroad. Wever (2008) believes that sustainable behavior design strategies can be divided into two categories. One is "functionality matching", such as automatic detection and regulation of intelligent products. The second is "behavior adaption", which includes "eco-feedback", "scripting" and "forced functionality" [4]. Tang and Bhamra (2008) analyzed the theory of social psychology in some specific behavior model and six obstacle of sustainable energy consumption, puts forward seven design intervention strategy, namely "eco-information", "eco-choice", "eco-feedback" and "eco-spur", "eco-steer", "eco-technical intervention" and "clever design" [5]. Zeng Zhen et al. summarized three strategies according to the cases: "attraction", "limitation", and "comfort" [6]. Lilley (2009) conducted a study and found that in different sustainable behavior design strategies, the dominant power of products and users is different. The "eco-feedback" strategy only provides information, and whether sustainability can be truly achieved is determined by users. while products using "persuasive technology" strategy are largely led by product; "behavior guide" strategy lies between the two [7]. In this research, on the basis of Bhamra (2011) discussed the seven design such as the leading factor in the intervention strategy, think the above seven design intervention strategy, from the "ecological information" to the "clever", the user behavior change way from the dominance of the "user" gradually transition to the dominance of "products", "product dominance" stronger, behavior change is more likely to happen, that the higher the effectiveness "design strategy", and "user acceptance" is the lower, [8] this view has been widely spread and accepted. Therefore, to solve the contradictions between the effectiveness of design strategy, product dominance and user acceptance should be paid more attention to when the sustainable behavior design theory is applied to solve problems (Fig. 1).

2.2 FOGG Behavior Model

Stanford University psychologist B.J. Fogg has come up with a new Model for understanding human Behavior, called the Fogg Behavior Model (FBM). According to this model, when an individual has a certain behavior, he/she must have three elements: sufficient Motivation, Ability to implement the behavior, and Trigger to implement the behavior [9] (Fig. 2).

Sustainable behavior design focuses on changing human behavior to make it develop towards sustainable direction. Essentially, it is a kind of behavioral intervention with predetermined goals, which is in line with the explanatory scope of Fogg's behavior model. Therefore, in the sustainable behavior design strategy, in order to make the

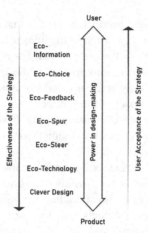

Fig. 1. Difference between user and product dominance in sustainable behavior design strategies.

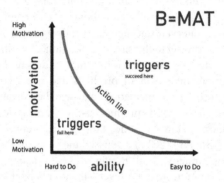

Fig. 2. Fogg's user behavior model.

behavior more likely to happen, there are three feasible methods, as shown in the figure below. After evaluation, method three is the most effective, but the required conditions are difficult to achieve: on the one hand, the sustainable behavior design strategy with high product dominance makes sustainable behaviors more likely to occur; on the other hand, the product dominance and the User acceptance always presents a negative correlation. Strong product dominance corresponds to weak user acceptance, so the key point is how to improve user acceptance of the product, that is, enhance the stickiness between users and products, and make Users have a stronger willingness to use the product, thereby enhancing the motivation for behavior change. Therefore, it is necessary to introduce emotional design theory to solve this problem; when the above two conditions are met, and then the trigger point is added to induce, sustainable behavior is easier to occur (Fig. 3).

	Ways to make sustainable behavior easier to happen	Essence	Assessment
Method one	Increase capability (or lower the threshold for users to achieve goals) without increasing motivation	Strong product dominance - weak user acceptance	Products tend to be automated and require less effort from users, but their goal of changing users' habits is often repulsed and resisted by users' instincts
Method two	Increase motivation without increasing ability (or lowering the barrier to user achievement)	Weak product dominance - strong user acceptance	Users have a strong sense of control over the product, but the realization of the sustainable goal largely depends on the establishment of the user's own sustainable consciousness. For a user who has no strong sense of sustainability, it
Method three	Both increase capability (or lower the threshold for users to achieve their goals) and increase motivation	Strong product dominance - strong user acceptance	Behavioral change is easy to happen and acceptable to users

Fig. 3. Methods of achieving sustainable behavior.

2.3 Emotional Design Theory

Emotional design theory was originally developed by psychologist Donald. Norman, in his book "Psychology of Design: Emotional Design", defined it as a design designed to capture the user's attention and induce an emotional response in order to improve the likelihood of performing a particular behavior [10]. Norman explained the three characteristic levels of human nature from the perspective of cognitive psychology, that is, visceral, behavioral and reflective. The basic principle of visceral level design comes from human instinct. The main physical characteristics of this level are the five senses of vision, hearing, smell, taste and touch, which are the dominant factors. Behavioral level design focuses on utility. Items are functional, easy to understand, and easy to operate. The highest level is the level of reflection, which is the complex emotion generated by deeper feelings, consciousness, understanding, personal experience, cultural background and other factors in the hearts of consumers due to the role of the first two levels [11].

3   The Construction of Product Emotion Model Based on the Theory of Sustainable Behavior Design

In the theory of sustainable behavior design, the "effectiveness of design strategy" and "user acceptance" always present a negative correlation, which brings challenges to sustainable behavior design. When designing products, it is always necessary to a balance point is achieved between the participants, and such a balance point may not necessarily promote the occurrence of sustainable behaviors. In order to make the behavior more likely to happen, we choose a design strategy with high product dominance. At this time, user acceptance is low, that is, lack of motivation. Combine the emotional design theory with the sustainable behavior design theory, through the emotional link established between the user and the product, to "soften" the discomfort caused by the strong dominance of the product to the user, so as to improve user acceptance In order to meet the requirements of behavior occurrence, considering the design of trigger points at this time, the goal of transforming unsustainable behaviors into sustainable behaviors can be achieved.

As shown in the figure, in the course of a certain behavior, the probability of the occurrence of an behavior is expressed as region A; When we introduce the emotional design theory to enhance the acceptance, that is, to improve the motivation, then the probability of the behavior will also increase. The area is expressed as region A + B. To sum up, the sustainable behavior design strategy has some shortcomings, and the analysis based on the Fogg user behavior model shows that the emotional design theory has a complementary role for the sustainable behavior design strategy (Fig. 4).

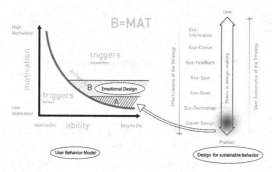

Fig. 4. The relationship between the three theories.

4 Design Practice

4.1 Design Process Construction

This research combines the Fogg behavior model to clarify the sustainable behavior design strategy that is highly effective and within the range of user acceptance from the theoretical level, that is, the introduction of emotional design theory, from the level of visceral, behavior, and reflection. And "soften" the user discomfort caused by the compulsory strategy. Based on this concept, we built the design process, as shown in Fig. 5.

From a practical point of view, in view of the phenomenon of staying up late, considering that the role that accompanies people to stay up late is usually a desk lamp, so we use the "desk lamp" as the carrier of design. From the perspective of sustainable behavior design strategies, among the seven interventions proposed by Tang and Bhamra, the "eco-technology" strategy and the "smart design" strategy have high product dominance, and their strategy effectiveness is also high. The method it points to is to enhance the dominance of the product through technology, design, and mandatory methods. Corresponding to the design of the table lamp, we conceived a table lamp design that will automatically turn off at a specific time, thereby prompting users to go to sleep. From the perspective of emotional design, emotional design includes three levels of visceral, behavior, and reflection. The methods they point to are to design attractive appearances, design reasonable human-computer interaction methods, and arouse users to reflect on their own behavior. Corresponding to the design of the desk lamp, the visceral level corresponds to the anthropomorphic form of the desk lamp, while imitating the behavior of people during sleep; the behavior level corresponds to the desk lamp is easy to operate and the light is appropriate; the reflection level corresponds to the desk lamp and the The behavior mapping between users triggers the user's emotional resonance.

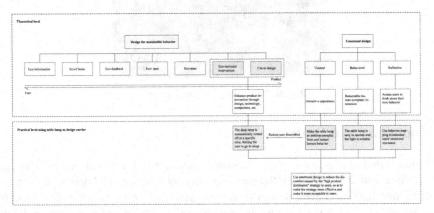

Fig. 5. Design process construction.

4.2 Design Process Construction

Through the construction of the design process, we carried out design practice. The designed carrier table lamp was given an anthropomorphic form. When it was a certain time at night, the table lamp began to "sleepy" and showed a "sleepy" posture. "The behavior of" enhance people's motivation to go to sleep; as the time gradually gets late, the light of the desk lamp will gradually dim, and suddenly turn off at the time when you should sleep. This is the application of the mandatory function strategy in the sustainable behavior design theory, To make the product independent of users, perform functions in an automated manner, and force users to go to bed at that point in time to change their behavioral habits of going to bed late. At the same time, turning off the light can also provide a trigger point for sleeping behavior.

As mentioned above, under the mandatory function strategy, the product dominance is strong, the design strategy is more effective, but the user acceptance is low. Therefore, on the basis of "mandatory function", we combine the design method of "reflection layer" in the emotional design theory to give the table lamp an anthropomorphic form to enhance the emotional resonance between the user and the product. At a certain time, the desk lamp starts to be "sleepy" and shows a "sleepy" posture-frequently lowering and raising the head, and dark circles appear. After a period of time, the lamp gradually dims until it goes out. This is based on the behavior between the product and the user. Through the behavioral mapping between the product and the user, the emotional link between the two is deepened, and the user can think about his own behavior, thereby guiding the user to sleep. This change is unconscious (Fig. 6).

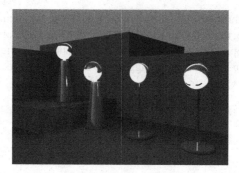

Fig. 6. The lamp that can "sleepy".

5 Summary and Outlook

This study is based on promoting the sustainable development of human beings. Through literature review, it is found that there are certain contradictions and deficiencies in the existing sustainable behavior design strategies. After analyzing from the dimension of user behavior model, it is found that in order to make sustainable behavior more likely to happen, we should improve the acceptance of the product by users, so as to improve the motivation of behavior. Therefore, the emotional design theory can be introduced to achieve this goal, and the sustainable behavior design strategy can be supplemented. Finally, the logic of the theory is verified through design practice.

There are still some problems to be discussed in the conclusion of "using emotional design to enhance users' acceptance, so as to supplement the sustainable behavior design strategy" proposed in this study. For example, how to grasp the balance between "emotional design" and "product dominance"; To what extent "emotional design" should be achieved, and whether it is obvious to improve "user acceptance"; How should the acceptance level of users be measured? This also provides a direction worth discussing for future research on sustainable behavior design.

References

1. Zhang, Y., Wang, H., Wang, Z.: An investigation on the correlation between late night and college students' self-control and time management ability. Shanghai Bus. **10**, 122–125 (2020)
2. Ding, L., Hu, X.: Effects of sleep deprivation on the body. Trace Elements Health Res. **27**(06), 45–48 (2010)
3. Rodriguez, E., Boks, C.: How design of products affects user behaviour and vice versa: the environmental implications. In: Yamamoto, R., Furukawa, Y., Hoshibu, H., Eagan, P., Griese, H., Umeda, Y., Aoyama, K. (eds.) 4th International Symposium on Environmentally Conscious Design and Inverse Manufacturing, pp. 54–61, Tokyo, Japan (2005)
4. Wever, R., van Kuijk, J., Boks, C.: User-centred design for sustainable behaviour. Int. J. Sustain. Eng. **1**(1), 9–20 (2008)
5. Tang, T., Bhamra, T.A.: Changing energy consumption behavior through sustainable product design. In: 10th International Design Conference, pp. 1359-+. Univ Zagreb, Faculty Mechanical Engineering & Naval Architecture, Ivanalucica 5, 10000 Zagreb, CROATIA, Dubrovnik, CROATIA (2008)

6. Zhen, Z.: How visual elements guide sustainable lifestyle in behavioral design. Ecol. Econ. **02**, 257–260 (2014)
7. Lilley, D.: Design for sustainable behaviour: strategies and perceptions. Des. Stud. **30**(6), 704–720 (2009)
8. Bhamra, T., Lilley, D., Tang, T.: Design for sustainable behaviour: using products to change consumer behaviour. Des. J. **14**(4), 427–445 (2011)
9. Fogg, B.J.: A behavior model for persuasive design. Pers. Technol. 1–7 (2009)
10. Noman, D.A.: The Emotional Design. Electronic Industry Press, China (2005)
11. Ding, J., Yang, D., Cao, Y., Wang, L.: Main theories, methods and research trends of emotional design. Chinese J. Eng. Des. **17**(01), 12–18+29 (2010)

Application of 5G Technology in the Construction of Intelligent Health Management System

Shuang Ying and Wei Yu[✉]

School of Art Design and Media, East China University of Science and Technology,
Shanghai 200237, China
weiyu@ecust.edu.cn

Abstract. At the beginning of 2020, COVID-19 was wreaking havoc around the world, exposing a serious imbalance in the distribution of healthcare resources. In addition, the proportion of people with sub-health and chronic diseases is increasing, the population aging is serious, and the low utilization rate of public medical resources is also a topic of increasing attention in recent years. Most countries and regions have realized the importance of disease prevention. Smart medical system relies on artificial intelligence, Internet of Things, cloud computing, virtual reality and many other modern technologies. The development of 5G technology has laid a foundation for the rapid development of these technologies. As part of smart medicine based on 5G technology, smart health management emphasizes helping people build a healthy lifestyle before they get sick. This kind of health management is based on a variety of modern science and technology, the collection of user information, the establishment of information database, data mining and analysis, the establishment of the user's personal health file, and for different users to provide thousands of health advice.

Keywords: 5G technology · Intelligent health management · Information security · Big data · The Internet of Things

1 The Introduction

In recent years, along with the unbalanced level of economic development, the imbalance between supply and demand of medical resources, the aggravation of population aging, the growth of chronic diseases and other problems are increasingly exposed and need to be solved urgently. The outbreak of the epidemic highlights the uneven distribution of medical resources in some regions, and the unbalanced medical situation highlights the importance of developing smart medical treatment. With the deepening of the aging of the population, China's aging population will further increase in the future, and the aggravation of the aging of the population will bring about a sharp increase in the medical and health care needs of the elderly group. With the improvement of people's attention to health, people gradually shift from the previous passive medical treatment after the occurrence of problems to the active and early preventive health care.

© Springer Nature Switzerland AG 2021
C. Stephanidis et al. (Eds.): HCII 2021, CCIS 1421, pp. 408–413, 2021.
https://doi.org/10.1007/978-3-030-78645-8_52

In the past two years, 5G technology has been deployed at an accelerated pace, and its applications in various fields are also developing and advancing rapidly. The characteristics of 5G technology with high speed, low delay and large amount of information have laid a solid foundation for its rapid development in various industries. The practice of 5G technology in the Internet of Things, big data and other fields also lets people see the huge development potential behind it. There is no doubt that the application of this new technology holds great promise, which can dramatically change people's existing life patterns and ultimately bring about great changes in society.

2 Overview of 5G Technology

5G, the fifth-generation communication technology. The first generation realized analog voice communication. The second generation realized the digitization of voice communication. The third generation realizes multimedia communication of pictures other than voice. The fourth generation realized local high-speed Internet access. The fifth-generation communication technology will realize the interconnection of everything at any time, anywhere.

5G technology is characterized by the following aspects: first, the amount of data is large. 5G communication technology has changed the status quo and promoted the transmission of large traffic data. Compared with the previous generation network technology, be is more than 1000 times higher. Even in the case of network overload, the amount of information transmitted is far more than 4G. Second, the number of networking devices has increased. The increase of the number of networking devices realized by 5G is not only based on the powerful data transmission function of 5G itself, but also the rapid development of intelligent terminal equipment and Internet of things to achieve large coverage of 5G network units. Third, the data transmission rate is increased. The rapid increase of data transmission rate is usually applied in special social needs, such as automatic driving, emergency rescue and rescue, emergency, etc. need instant HD information transmission activities. Fourth, the improvement of security. 5G powerful information transmission ability can effectively reduce network delay, which is 5–10 times shorter than 4G in time, which ensures the timeliness and reliability of 5G mobile signal when transmitting key data.

5G will build a comprehensive economic and social critical infrastructure of the digital transformation, 5G and the integration of vertical industry applications will emerging information products and services, changing people's way of life, promote the information consumption, and gradually penetrated into social and economic industry in various fields, remaking traditional industry development pattern, and expand creative space.

3 Intelligent Medical Treatment and Intelligent Health Management System

Smart medical aims to realize the interaction among patients and medical personnel, medical institutions and medical equipment by building a regional medical information platform for health records and utilizing the most advanced Internet of Things technology, and gradually achieve informatization. Smart medicine consists of three parts, namely smart hospital system, regional health system, and family health system, which need to integrate multiple technologies such as the Internet of Things, cloud computing, big data processing, and blockchain. With further development, smart medicine has penetrated into People's Daily life, including the use of daily data for health management, the prevention and pre-control of diseases through artificial intelligence technology, and the application of technology to biomedicine.

As a part of smart medicine, intelligent health management emphasizes helping people build a healthy lifestyle before they get sick. Intelligent health management system combines medical and computer related technologies to establish a set of efficient and quality health monitoring, disease prevention and disease reminder system for the population, which can effectively implement personalized health evaluation for the population and develop personalized health plans.

4 Development and Problems of Intelligent Health Management System

The intelligent health management system is mainly divided into three steps: real-time collection of health information, establishment of multi-dimensional health model and establishment of healthy lifestyle.

Collect health information in real time. Upload disease and health information to the cloud through mobile terminals, such as outpatient and hospitalization related information, physical disease symptoms, allergy history, associated diseases, relevant examination and laboratory results, medication status and disease incidence degree, etc. Vital signs information such as heart rate, blood pressure, etc.

Build a multi-dimensional health model. The system transfers the collected data to the server of the medical cloud for cleaning, removing dirty data, cloud computing, data mining and knowledge discovery, and classifies these health data through calculation, modeling and analysis to establish an association rule base between vital signs and health conditions. The user health data is compared with the health standard value, and the abnormality of the user health data is analyzed. Based on the association rule base, early diseases and health risks can be detected reliably, quickly and efficiently.

Build a healthy lifestyle. According to the above health data analysis score, it automatically generates health suggestion report, and gives health advice for projects with low scores to remind users to pay attention to their own health; The collected user basic information and health information can also be matched with the corresponding content of health knowledge to provide accessible health and keeping in good health guidance (including diet, exercise and medication guidance) for individual health prevention and management services, so as to achieve the purpose of personalized health management.

However, 5G health management system has not yet formed a mature mode, mainly reflected in the following aspects: intelligent health management system needs the coordination and cooperation of the communication industry, intelligent terminal equipment manufacturing industry and industry organizations; In this system, both health information collection and data collection and processing are only in the exploratory stage, and only stay in the small-scale experiment. The integration application of 5G and intelligent health management has many normative problems, such as the security boundary of information collection, data transmission and processing, unified data format, etc. Information security is an urgent problem to be solved in the era of big data and the Internet of Things. As soon as the user's information is leaked, there will be serious security risks. Protecting database stability and data security is the top priority.

5   Application of 5G Technology in Building Intelligent Health Management System

In recent years, as cloud computing, big data, Internet of Things, mobile Internet, artificial intelligence and other emerging technologies continue to mature, the rapid development and popularization of 5G technology has taken it to a new level, accelerating the integration of the traditional medical industry and emerging technologies.

5G network technology can improve system efficiency, reduce energy consumption, further reduce part of the cost, realize the rapid deployment of new services in the Internet of Things, fully meet the needs of the Internet of Things management, provide security guarantee for the Internet of Things system, and strengthen the mobility and intelligence. With the development of communication technology, the Internet of Things is developing rapidly. The Internet of Things is integrating with all fields, and its application is also reflected in the medical field. It is mainly manifested in the following aspects: First, the application demonstration of electronic health records and other links in the Internet of Things; Second, promotes the hierarchical diagnosis and treatment model of community medical care + Grade A hospitals; Third, the establishment of clinical data centers to carry out precision medical applications based on the Internet of Things and big data; Fourth, we will develop smart wearable devices for remote health management, elderly care and other health service applications, and promote the development of innovative applications and services of big data on health.

At present, big data, as a national strategic emerging industry and key technology innovation project, is mainly developed in the field of medical technology. On the one hand, it is necessary to carry out the collection and analysis of health big data information; on the other hand, it is necessary to build a big data center and knowledge base to build the foundation of health management system. Using big data technology, aiming at different health data sources, wireless network, Bluetooth and other transmission technologies are adopted to achieve stable and accurate data transmission. Establish a public health management system based on database integration and big data analysis technology.

5G technology is good for protecting information security. First, strengthen the security management of the "client" network equipment. For client devices, one is to strengthen physical protection to prevent criminals from directly operating the device to steal information or through the terminal device to invade the network; The second is to strengthen the physical main machine anti-virus, anti-invasion function. Second, strengthen the meaning of network information security laws and regulations. When collecting, storing, analyzing, transmitting and processing data using 5G technology and big data technology, laws and regulations on network information security must be observed. Third, store data scientifically and safely. 5G network is a high-bandwidth network. Data can be uploaded to the "cloud" for storage anytime and anywhere, and important and sensitive data can be protected with the help of the security protection capability of cloud storage.

In recent years, various government departments actively promote the development of intelligent medical treatment. Support the development of smart medical industry from the policy level. Under the common drive of national policies and technologies, a personal smart medical system based on national health informatization and health care big data is taking shape, and the embryonic application of cross-space and cross-sector medical data fusion is beginning to form. In order to further promote and regulate the development and application of the smart medical industry, the country has accelerated the introduction of the development and regulation policies of the smart medical industry and established the pilot areas successively. Under the guidance of the national level and pilot areas, various regions have also accelerated the introduction of the development and regulation policies of the industry.

6 Intelligent Medical Treatment and Intelligent Health Management System

The outbreak of COVID-19 has promoted the development of smart medicine. The construction of a smart medical system based on 5G network can realize the interconnection and real-time information sharing among patients, medical personnel, medical institutions and medical equipment, and promote the efficient allocation of medical resources. The future blue ocean is just around the corner. Medical wisdom is still in the exploratory stage in our country, but in the rapid development in recent years, both the market demand, is the inevitable result of the scientific and technological progress and the fusion, how in disease surveillance and auxiliary decision-making, health management, and other fields play an important role, is one of the concerns of the medical wisdom, to solve these problems to make medical services to better meet the demand of people's health. With the application of 5G network, the personal health management system based on cloud computing, big data and the Internet of Things will have a more extensive application prospect.

References

1. Bin, Y., Zexi, H.: Personal intelligent health management system based on cloud computing. Southwest Jiaotong University, School of Electrical Engineering (2013)
2. Chen, K., Qi, X.: Analysis and research on monitoring data of intelligent wearable devices. Internet Things Technol. (2016)
3. Application of 5G Communication Technology under the Situation of Internet of Things, Chen Xianyuan, Gansu Branch of China Iron Tower Co., Ltd (2015)
4. Jia, S.: Prospects of internet of things and big data in medical industry. China New Commun. (2017)
5. Fan, C., Zheng, T.: Discussion on whole-process health management service mode based on big data. China Med. Equip. (2018)
6. Grobelnik, M.: Big Data Tutorial [EB/OL] (2012)
7. Chen, P., Jin, G., Lin, C., et al.: Design of intelligent health service platform system. Chinese J. Med. (2018)

8. Qu, J., Peng, L.: Design of personal health management platform. Commun. Power Res. (2019)
9. Manyika, J., Chui, M., Brown, B., et al.: Big Data: The next frontier for innovation, competition, and productivity [R/OL] (2012)
10. Barwick, H.: The "Four Vs" of Big Data, Implementing Information Infrastructure Symposium [EB/0L] (2012)
11. IBM: What is big data? [EB/OL] (2012)
12. Erhuan, Yan, Z., Yan, J.: Research on the application of intelligent health management system at home and abroad. Nurs. Manage. China (2017)

Interacting and Shopping

Investigating the Relationship Among Ease-of-Use, NPS, and Customers' Sequent Spending of Cloud Computing Products

Ease-of-Use Research in Cloud Computing Field

Xinyu Gao[✉], Shang Zhi, and Xiaoming Wang

Alibaba Cloud Design, Alibaba Group, Hangzhou, People's Republic of China
{ningxi.gxy,zhishang.zs,xiaoming.wxm}@alibaba-inc.com

Abstract. Ease of use is one of the crucial principals when evaluating the experience of interacting with the product consoles, and NPS measures the customers' brand loyalty. This study aimed to investigate the possible relationship between the two metrics in the cloud computing field, and explore whether the customers' attitude influence their actual consuming behavior, which has been rarely discussed in the enterprise service industries. Researchers collected data though questionnaires and background databases, then correlation analysis, regression and ANOVA were conducted to test the hypotheses. One of the main procedures was to compare the sequent monthly spending of customers from different groups, and samples were grouped by their ease-of-use rating and NPS identities (promoters/passives/detractors). The final results indicated a positive correlation between the ease-of-use scores and NPS of a cloud computing product, especially when their usage experience lays emphasis on operating consoles. Furthermore, a notable finding showed that, promoters' monthly spending increase were significantly higher than those of detractors and even reached 8 times in 9 months after the NPS survey, with the sample roles controlled as the purchase decision-makers rather than merely users. However, no difference was detected between the retention of promoters and detractors, which might due to the ambiguity in precisely defining the churn/retention. This is the first scientific research that investigated the relationship between ease-of-use and NPS, and the impact of attitudes towards products on sequent spending at the micro (customer) level, with the innovative perspective from the cloud computing industry.

Keywords: Human-centered computing · HCI design and evaluation methods · Human-centered computing · Empirical studies in HCI ease-of-use · NPS · Actual consuming behavior · Cloud computing product

1 Introduction

With the development of the internet, various studies have examined the influence of users' attitudes on their consuming purchasing behaviors in the online and computer-mediated environment [1, 2]. However, most of them investigated those topics in business scenarios with customers rather than enterprises as the target groups. If we change

© Springer Nature Switzerland AG 2021
C. Stephanidis et al. (Eds.): HCII 2021, CCIS 1421, pp. 417–422, 2021.
https://doi.org/10.1007/978-3-030-78645-8_53

the angle of view to the cloud computing industry, more complex variables should be considered: first, the targets of cloud offerings involve different roles; second, for those technical products, it is not easy to find suitable metrics to measure audiences' attitudes and usage experience.

In the technology acceptance model (TAM), systems use (actual behavior) is determined by perceived usefulness and perceived ease of use [3]. According to the theory, users' motivation can be explained by three factors: perceived ease of use, perceived usefulness and attitude towards the system. It is reasonable to infer that concepts from TAM can explain the acceptance and use of technical products, and we are inspired to choose the ease-of-use as one of the metrics to evaluate the user experience of cloud offerings. Subsequently, a scale about the ease-of-use was developed with reference of other related scales such as QUIS (Questionnaire for User Interaction Satisfaction) [4], SUS (Software Usability Scale) [5] and PSSUQ (Post-Study System Usability Questionnaire) [6, 7]. After years of cloud-computing design practices, ease-of-use becomes one of the crucial principals when evaluating the experience of interacting with the product consoles.

Another metric we adopted to evaluate the user experience is NPS, which has been regarded as the classic method to measure customers' brand loyalty [8]. Many companies such as Amazon, Apple and Microsoft use NPS as the core metric to reflect reputation and feedback status from the market. The NPS is based on a single question as "How likely you are to recommend the product to other people with similar demand?" and the respondents are classified as promoter, passives or detractors. Researches showed, the detractors might complain to their colleagues or friends, which had high risk to drift away and it undermined sales and growth of the brand [9, 10].

In light of the previous literature, this study aimed to explore the following topics in a certain context of the cloud computing products: the positive correlation between ease-of-use and NPS, the effects of the intention to recommend the product on the follow-up consuming behavior, and the indirect effects of the ease-of-use on users' consumption.

2   Method

Questionnaires and background databases analysis were mainly adopted in the research, and the former of which aimed to collect the key metrics and the latter focused on tracing the expenditure of different customer groups. The Elastic Computing Server (ECS) is one of the most fundamental and important cloud offerings, and we chose it as the subject product to fulfill the affiliated measurements. The questionnaires were sent to all the actual product users by UONE system (an in-house survey platform) and the background databases of our enterprise stored large amounts of business data.

2.1 Metric Measurements

The two main metrics collected by questionnaires were ease-of-use score and NPS. It is worth noting that, Alibaba Cloud Design center adjusted the concept ease-of-use of cloud offerings through work practices in 2019. According to the theory framework, the ease-of-use contained three sub-concepts: learnability, clarity and operational ease.

To directly quantify the ease-of-use, we set the 10-point scale "Is the product generally easy to use?" for respondents' opinions, ranging from 1 (very difficult to use) to 10 (very easy to use). As for NPS, the classic rating method was adopted. We asked respondents how likely they were to recommend the product to other people with similar demand, ranging from 0 (Not at all likely) to 10 (Extremely likely). Respondents who scored 9 or 10 were tagged as promoters and those who score 0 to 6 as detractors. The NPS was calculated by the percentage of promoters subtracted by the percentage of detractors. Both the ease-of-use and NPS were measured in the same questionnaire through the Elastic Computing Server user survey, which tried to avoid the possible error caused by the differences among respondents (Table 1).

Table 1. Scales and question descriptions

	Scale	Question description
Ease-of-use	1–10	Is the product generally easy to use
NPS	0–10	How likely are you to recommend the product to other people with similar demand

To verify whether users with different ease-of-use scores have various attitudes towards recommendation, we divided the respondents into three groups according to his/her ease-of-use score. The grouping rules were listed as the following table (Table 2).

Table 2. Different levels of Ease-of-Use scores

	Score	Level	Interpretation
Ease-of-Use	1–6	Low	The product is very difficult to use
	7–8	Medium	The product is fairly easy to use
	9–10	High	The product is very easy to use

2.2 Customers' Sequent Spending Tracing

Based on NPS ratings, we tagged respondents as their identities (Promoter/Passive/Detractor) and there formed three groups. Before tracing each respondent's spending data, we balanced the initial purchasing capacity among the three groups to ensure no significant difference in the variable. Each respondent has a unique ID in the background databases, which offered a clue to track the detailed spending data from various dimensions. For example, the ID of a promoter was 123456, then we used the unique numeric string to identify this customer in databases and extracted his monthly spending data after the survey. We set the time span in 12 months, which was also frequently used as enterprises' financial reporting period.

3 Results

After the data cleansing procedure, we collected 2677 effective samples in total. All the respondents' spending data were extracted from background databases and AVOVA was conducted to test our hypotheses.

3.1 The Relationship Between Ease-of-Use and NPS

The relationship between ease-of-use and NPS was investigated from two aspects, the one of which was to analyze the relevance of the two metrics, and the other was to detect the possible differences in NPS scores among respondents of different ease-of-use levels. Results showed a significant positive correlation, $r = 0.593$ ($p < 0.01$), which indicated if the respondent rated the ease-of-use with a high score, he/she probably had high intention to recommend the product.

Furthermore, we compared the NPS ratings among the three groups with different ease-of-use score levels (low/medium/high) on a total sample of 2157. The findings also dovetailed with the aforementioned correlation results (Fig. 1).

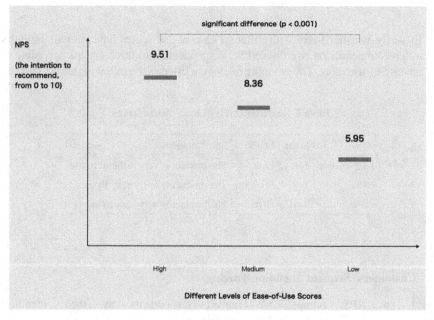

Fig. 1. Comparing the NPS ratings

3.2 The Sequent Spending of Customers with Different NPS Identities

Respondents were divided in three groups based on their NPS identities (Promoter/Passive/Detractor). After balancing the initial purchasing capacity across the groups, we traced the sequent monthly spending of every respondent by his/her user-id and compared the spending increase. A notable finding showed that, promoters' monthly spending increase were significantly higher than those of detractors, and the maximum gap was observed in 9 months after answering the questionnaire. According to the survey, 85% of the respondents indicated their participation in the purchase-decision of cloud offerings, which might explain why the attitudes pf those people had such a significant effect on the follow-up consuming behaviors (Fig. 2).

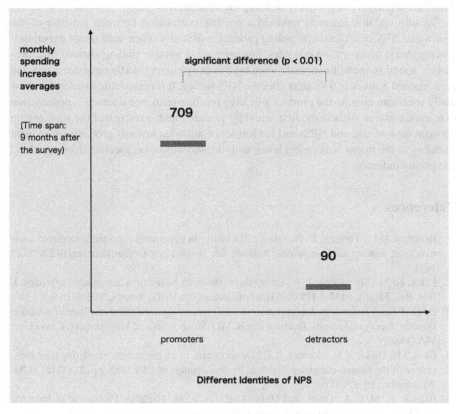

Fig. 2. Comparing the spending increase

4   Discussion and Conclusion

The purpose of this study was to detect i) the positive correlation between ease-of-use and NPS; ii) the effects of the intention to recommend the product on the follow-up consuming behavior, and we inferred the indirect effects of the ease-of-use on users' consumption if the previous two hypotheses were proved true. However, the establishment of those conclusions had preconditions. First, operating the console should play a crucial part through the overall usage experience. For example, those conclusions cannot apply to cloud offerings with the focus on API usage. Second, the sample roles were controlled as the purchase decision-makers rather than merely users, and it can be inferred that the effect lessened when the samples had little participation in purchase decision. Third, when tracing the follow-up spending data of those respondents, we found the time span mattered: if it was set too short or too long, effects would be unobserved, which might due to the very point-in-time when the consumers' attitudes impacted on their purchase intentions and those intentions turned to actual behaviors. However, no difference was detected between the retention of promoters and detractors, which might due to the ambiguity in precisely defining the churn/retention.

To sum up, this research reported a positive correlation between the ease-of-use scores and NPS of a cloud computing product, especially when their usage experience lays emphasis on operating consoles. Furthermore, a notable finding showed that, promoters' monthly spending increase were significantly higher than those of detractors and even reached 8 times in 9 months after the NPS survey. It is reasonable to infer that, how easily users can operate the product will have positive influence on users' consumption to a certain extent. This is the first scientific research that investigated the relationship between ease-of-use and NPS, and the impact of attitudes towards products on sequent spending at the micro (customer) level, with the innovative perspective from the cloud computing industry.

References

1. Hoffman, D.L., Thomas, P., Novak, T.: Marketing in hypermedia computer-mediated environments: conceptual foundations. J. Mark. **60**, 50–68 (1996). https://doi.org/10.2307/1251841
2. Laros, F.J.M., Steenkamp, J.-B.: Emotions in consumer behavior: a hierarchical approach. J. Bus. Res. **58**(10), 1437–1445 (2005). https://doi.org/10.1016/j.jbusres.2003.09.013
3. Davis, F.D.: A technology acceptance model for empirically testing new end-user information systems: theory and results. Doctoral thesis, MIT Sloan School of Management, Cambridge, MA (1985)
4. Chin, J.P., Diehl, V.A., Norman, K.L.: Development of an instrument measuring user satisfaction of the human-computer interface. In: Proceedings of CHI 1988, pp. 213–218. ACM, Washington, DC (1988)
5. Brooke, J.: SUS: A "Quick and Dirty" Usability Scale. Usability Evaluation in Industry, pp. 189–194. Taylor & Francis, London (1996)
6. Lewis, J.R.: Psychometric evaluation of a post-study system usability questionnaire: the PSSUQ (Technical report 54.535). International Business Machines Corp, Boca Raton, FL (1990)
7. Lewis, J.R.: Psychometric evaluation of the post-study system usability questionnaire: the PSSUQ. In: Proceedings of the Human Factors Society 36th Annual Meeting. Human Factor Society, Santa Monica, CA, pp. 1259–1263 (1992)
8. Reichheld, F.F.: The one number you need to grow. Harv. Bus. Rev. **81**(12), 46–54 (2003)
9. Reichheld, F.F.: The microeconomics of customer relationships. MIT Sloan Manag. Rev. **47**(2), 73–78 (2006). https://doi.org/10.1007/978-3-642-03243-1_3
10. Reichheld, F.F., Markey, R.: The Ultimate Question 2.0: How Net Promoter Companies Thrive in a Customer-Driven World. Harvard Business Review Press, Boston (2011)

Service Innovation of Physical Bookstores: Applying Service Design Perspectives to Develop Service Innovation to Enhance Customer Loyalty

Yu-Hsuan Hung and Hsien-Hui Tang[✉]

National Taiwan University of Science and Technology, Taipei, Taiwan
{10710204,drhhtang}@gapps.ntust.edu.tw

Abstract. The diversified applications of the Internet have caused the knowledge economy to flourish. Physical bookstores must not only meet the changing needs of readers in the digital age, but also compete with the convenience and low price discounts of online shopping.

This research is based on the theory of service innovation thinking and customer loyalty. Through the service design methods, it explores the customer journey in the bookstore and after purchasing the goods, proposes the possibility of improving the service design through multi-channels, and examines whether service innovation can help increase customer loyalty.

The objectives of this research are (1) understand bookstore customers' satisfaction with membership and the challenges they face through questionnaires and interviews; (2) analyze the needs and pain points of stakeholders in their respective journeys; (3) through service design thinking, examine whether the design concepts help increase customer loyalty.

The research results are (1) through service design thinking, the design concepts proposed according to persona help to improve two of the indicators of customer loyalty, namely personal attitude and repurchase behavior; (2) providing services to meet the individual needs of stakeholders in the bookstore retail scenario, that is, improving the work efficiency for bookstore clerks, while increasing the convenience of buying books for customers. The results of this research put forward the service direction and suggestions of future bookstores, and look forward to creating an innovative book retail experience.

Keywords: Service design · Service innovation · Customer loyalty

1 Introduction

The diversified application of the Internet has enabled the knowledge economy to flourish. Physical bookstores not only have to face changing needs of modern readers but also the convenience of online shopping and low-price competition. The total number of bookstores in Taiwan is declining year by year, 2020 is the lowest in 30 years.

© Springer Nature Switzerland AG 2021
C. Stephanidis et al. (Eds.): HCII 2021, CCIS 1421, pp. 423–430, 2021.
https://doi.org/10.1007/978-3-030-78645-8_54

The success of new services lies in the fact that customers pay attention to the product itself or service benefits in the consumption process and concern whether they can get fresh and pleasant feelings from the consumption process. Therefore, it will be the future trend to attract consumers by perceptual, experience marketing (Li 2008). Customer satisfaction has an essential impact on the enterprise management (Kotler 1997). Satisfying consumer needs is the most central principle of business operation. Through marketing strategy, customer satisfaction can be improved, and maximum profit can be obtained. The higher the customers' satisfaction can lead to higher follow-up behavior, better competitive advantage, and higher market rate (Bearden and teel 1983; Cornell 1992; Fornell et al. 1996).

This study hopes to understand the service status and consumer demand of bookstores through service design thinking, explore the opportunities, design innovative services that are compatible with business, and put forward the optimization direction of future reading services through concept test, as a reference for the development of innovative services of bookstores in the future.

2 Literature Review and Related Work

2.1 Customer Loyalty

Customer loyalty is the basis of achieving sustainable competitive advantage (Dick and Basu 1994; Bagram and Khan 2012) and has become an important strategic goal of the service industry (Oliver 1999); it refers to a sense of belonging or identity of customers to the company's personnel, services or products, which will directly affect customer behavior (Jones and Sasser 1995). Behavioral loyalty refers to the behavior that customers purchase products or receive services many times. Attitude loyalty means that the customer continues to maintain a relationship with the service provider. Therefore, it is defined as evaluating customers' behavior in the bookstore to understand the impact of service innovation on customer loyalty.

Measuring Customer Loyalty
Griffin (1997) pointed out that customer loyalty is related to purchase behavior, which is defined as follows: (1) Repeat purchases; (2) Patronize various products or service series provided by the company; (3) Build reputation; (4) Customers are not influenced by other companies' promotional activities. In summary, this study defines customer loyalty as "customers' attitudes and performance of repurchase behavior" and proposes three measurement aspects of customer loyalty: (1) Repurchase willingness: revisit the physical bookstore; (2) Cross-buying: Re-use other physical bookstore services; (3) Recommend others: Recommend others to patronize the physical bookstore.

2.2 Service Design

Service can be regarded as a system, including multiple channels. According to the definition of Nielsen Norman Group, service design is mainly composed of people, assets, and processes. Through planning and integration of the three elements, the experience of users and employees can be improved (Gibbons 2017). Service process is the result and structure of service design, and its application elements are divided into six channels, including physical and virtual personnel, machines, and environment. The application of service design can be summarized and innovated and integrated in the six channels to influence the user experience (Tang 2019).

2.3 Service Innovation

Whether an enterprise is engaged in products or services or innovative activities, it is to enhance business value and service quality. Rogers (1995) defined innovation as "the process of spreading a new idea from the source of innovation or creation to the end-user or user." It divides customer's psychology of "innovation" into five stages: knowledge, perception, decision, implementation, and confirmation. Lovelock (2009) classified service innovation into seven types: style change, service improvement, subsidiary service innovation, process line extension, product line extension, main process innovation, and main service innovation.

3   A Discussion on User Experience of Physical Bookstores

3.1 Service Discussion on the Issues in the Customer Experience of Physical Bookstore

This study interviewed and analyzed 16 stakeholders in the bookstore consumption scene, and counted out the "key goals" and "key pain points" of each stage, as shown in the table:

Table 1. .

Stakeholder	Objective	Pain
Customer	Trial read evaluation product search efficiency	1. Fragmented assessment information 2. Insufficient product introduction information
Staff	1. Customized recommended 2. Assist in finding books	1. The goods cannot be temporarily transferred 2. The goods cannot be temporarily transferred
Commodity provider issuer editor	1. Demand transformation 2. To understand the needs of readers	Reach out to customers

Our analysis found that customers think that the current information is fragmented in the consumption process, and the physical and digital services lack personalization. They want to find the products efficiently and provide relevant assistance services when trying them out. Service providers often need to help customers find books and recommendations, and the current software and hardware service system are not enough to share the human resources. The editor-in-chief of the publishing house is concerned that it is crucial to raise the demand of a new generation of people to read printed books and improve the book content and physical store.

3.2 Customer Journey Map (CJM)

CJM presents the interaction among users, products, and services by stages visually, showing the characteristics, emotions, and problem points of the interaction between users and services. It is convenient for researchers to study and analyze various stages and improve their user experience (Song 2014). Collect data through interviews, photographs, etc., to understand users' thoughts on the service (Yang et al. 2017). Based on field observations and questionnaire surveys, we summarized the customer journey map, as shown in Table 1.

Table 2. Customer journey

Stage	Journey	Objective	Goal
Before going to the bookstore	Get information	Personalized product promotion, Rather than a regular digital publication	Get personal recommended information
Shopping	In-store browsing	Feel the book display method is complicated	Get trending information
	Find specific goods	The hardware service information is insufficient to find the book clearly	Find products efficiently
	Evaluate	Consider commodity demand Value the opinions of other consumers	Aggregate information evaluation
	1. Checkout 2. Member accumulation	Low willingness to download the app, because the above functions are not used Accumulate points by phone, check out more efficiently	Cumulative membership efficient checkout
After shopping	Read and record	Feel trouble with copying and typing records	Records to support learn and absorb
	Share	Curious about what other people think of the same book	Express feelings after reading

4   Optimization Design Concept Developing

4.1   Co-creation Workshop

We invited stakeholders (8 designers, two shop assistants, and three-member customers) to participate in the workshop aimed to brainstorm the design objectives to make the design closer to users' needs. Participants are shown in Table 2 (Fig. 1 and Table 3).

Table 3. .

Occupation	Role in co-creation workshop	Session
Service designer	Designer with UX design experience	A.B
Clerk	Have two years of service experience	A
Clerk	Three years of service experience	B
Member customer	Premium member customers	A
Member customer	Medium member customers	A
Member customer	Junior member customers	A
Non-member customers	Non-member customers	B
Non-member customers	Non-member customers	B
Service designer/customer	Medium member customers	A
Service designer/customer	Designer with UX design experience	A
Service designer/customer	Designer with UX design experience	B
Service designer	Designer with UX design experience	B
Service designer	Designer with UX design experience	B

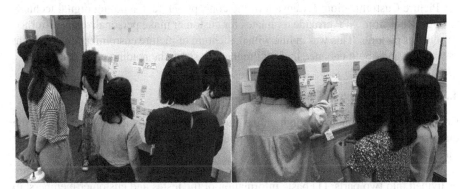

Fig. 1. Co-creation workshop, participants are discussing ideas.

4.2 Design Concept

Based on design workshop and preliminary conceptual solutions, innovative service concepts are proposed through integration and adjustment, which are described as follows:

1. Well-turned Quotes Widgets: Added the Widgets function of the Bookstore app (IOS system). The APP selects Well-turned Quotes from the customer's favorite book to the mobile desktop every day to strengthen resonance between readers and books.
2. Book Stories: The existing banner advertising is adjusted to an interactive way in line with the user's habits. Customers can browse much information and recommend books they may be interested in by sliding their fingers.

3. Author's narration: Provide audio/video of the book author's storytelling in the store to help readers understand the book.
4. Book fans sharing with friends: Together with bookstore service providers and readers to create a personal preference map of reading field, which can make both more sympathetic, and through the discussion activities of the fans, we could improve the professional and cordial service together.
5. Advertising book packaging: Bookstore service providers use different themes and styles to allow advertisements to be delivered to consumers more directly, thereby enhancing the uniqueness of physical store sales and protecting readers' shopping privacy.
6. Digitization of book search: After customers select books on the book store APP, which can provide a dynamic map and book location on the mobile phone to improve the efficiency of customer search for books; Increase online shopping entry to extend consumers' consideration time and improve sales opportunities.
7. Text note album: extend the reading service of the bookstore. Readers who buy books in the store can automatically open the note-taking function after purchase. Customers can click the words they are interested in and quickly convert them into digital notes after taking pictures of books with their mobile phones. The classification of books helps customers quickly write down short sentences of interest, replacing the original handwritten note-taking method and improving efficiency.
8. Picture Customization: Extension of the concept (7) Text shooting digital technology. Bookstore APP provide templates for customer make personalized well-turned Quotes pictures. This was in line with the feature of picture customization of current readers and could enhance their willingness to share the reading experience.

4.3 Questionnaires and Quantitative Analysis Results

Collecting users' opinions through online questionnaires, statistics, and analysis of the questionnaire data's data distribution is conducive to grasping the target users' relevant information (Wang 2010).

To understand the current status of service satisfaction and loyalty, the questionnaire is divided into two parts: (1) basic information of the testes and customer membership levels; (2) differences in customer loyalty to bookstores. The pre-test is "for the current status of the service"; the post-test is "if this service is provided" as the questionnaire item's premise and compare the differences before and after. A total of 40 questionnaires were returned in the previous test, with an average value of 3.48 for the five indicators; 30 questionnaires for new service design were returned, with an average value of 4.2 (Table 4).

The results show that in the new service, all five indicators have been improved. In order to evaluate the customer loyalty of new bookstores, this study uses Net Promoter Score to measure the value of question "the possibility that I will introduce bookstores to my relatives and friends ?" in the questionnaire. The volunteers were divided into three groups according to the score (1–10 points): detractors, passives and promoters. The detractors' statistical score of the former Bookstore service volunteers was −28 (including 6 promoters, 17 passives and 17 detractors). After optimizing the service, the

Table 4. Loyalty indicators for new service design

Measure	Before N = 40		After N = 30	
	N	Average	N	Average
I think it's the right decision to spend in this bookstore	40	3.7	30	4.46
I am very satisfied with the current status of the services provided by the company	40	4	30	4.43
I will continue to spend at the bookstore	40	3.8	30	4.4
I think I am loyal to the bookstore brand	40	3.2	30	4.33
When products from other stores are cheaper, I am still willing to buy products from this bookstore	40	2.7	30	3.7
Average		3.48		4.2

detractors' statistical score was 10 points (including 11 promoters, 11 passives and 8 detractors) (Table 5).

Table 5. The net recommendation value

Measure	Before N = 40		After N = 30	
	N	NPS	N	NPS
How likely would I recommend a purchase to my friends and family in this bookstore?	40	−28	30	10

Overall, the new service design showed significant improvement in all aspects, and the average score in attitude and behavior was higher than the current service status.

5 Conclusion

Exploring and analyzing stakeholders through the service design thinking, clarifying the service process and service gap, and sorting out the stage design objectives according to their essential needs, make the solution closer to the actual situation. Based on the principle of service innovation, concept development is focused on solving the design goal. The research finds that through the service design thinking, the design concept proposed by Persona is helpful to improve the two indicators of customer loyalty, namely personal attitude and repurchase behavior.

References

Yin, R.K.: Case Study Research: Design and Methods, 4th edn. Sage, Thousand Oaks (2009)

Stake, R.E.: Case Studies. Handbook of Qualitative Research. Sage Publications, London (1995)

Dick, A.S., Basu, K.: Customer loyalty: toward an integrated conceptual framework. J. Acad. Mark. Sci. 22(2), 99–113 (1994)

Bagram, M.M.M., Khan, S.: Attaining customer loyalty! The role of consumer attitude and consumer behavior. Int. Rev. Manage. Bus. Res. 1(1), 1 (2012)

Estimation of Consumer Needs Using Review Data in Hotel Industry

Shin Miyake[1](✉), Kohei Otake[2], Tomofumi Uetake[3], and Takashi Namatame[4]

[1] Graduate School of Science and Engineering, Chuo University, 1-13-27, Kasuga, Bunkyo-ku, Tokyo 112-8551, Japan
a15.66cc@g.chuo-u.ac.jp

[2] Faculty of Science and Engineering, Tokai University, 2-3-23, Takanawa, Minato-ku, Tokyo 108-8619, Japan
otake@tsc.u-tokai.ac.jp

[3] School of Business Administration, Senshu University, 2-1-1, Higashimita, Tama-ku, Kawasaki 214-8580, Kanagawa, Japan
uetake@isc.senshu-u.ac.jp

[4] Faculty of Science and Engineering, Chuo University, 1-13-27, Kasuga, Bunkyo-ku, Tokyo 112-8551, Japan
nama@indsys.chuo-u.ac.jp

1 Introduction

With the digitalization of product sales channels in business, consumers who use each service can reserve, use, and evaluate them through the platforms such as websites.

Especially from the voices of consumers such as word-of-mouth data, companies can grasp the actual evaluation of customers. The utilization of word-of-mouth data for business is one of important issues for all companies, and it is necessary to consider a marketing approach using mathematical technology [1].

2 Purpose of This Study

In this study, we focus on hotel industry in Japan and attempt to clarify the relationship between services provided by companies and the consumer needs for each service in hotel industry. Currently, various bookings are done via the Internet, but these sites have not only bookings but also the function of displaying the reviews of actual users [2]. Word-of-mouth information is known to have a significant impact on the booking behavior of other customers. Specifically, we separate the 623 hotels into two groups according to the services provided such as for tourists or for business, and using 150,622 review texts and evaluation points, we clarify the difference of relationship between customer needs for services and evaluations.

3 Data and Analysis Method

3.1 Flagging of Review Data

In this study, we analyze the relationship between service providers and customer needs using hotel reviews (Word-of-mouth) and rating scores. These reviews and rating scores

© Springer Nature Switzerland AG 2021
C. Stephanidis et al. (Eds.): HCII 2021, CCIS 1421, pp. 431–438, 2021.
https://doi.org/10.1007/978-3-030-78645-8_55

were posted on the reservation sites by customers who had previously used the hotel (Table 1). In this study, we targeted data submitted during the period from January 1, 2016 to January 1, 2020.

Table 1. Data description

Data type	Data details
Master data in the hotels (total of 623)	623 hotels offering services at reservation sites For business: 178 hotels For tourists: 210 hotels ・Average evaluation score in the hotels
Review data (total of 150,622)	Data about customer who posted the revies ・Review texts ・Evaluation Score in the hotels

First, we extracted 1000 reviews from all reviews by random sampling and divided them into sentences. Using these parts of sentences, we flagged them for each label of the services provided by the hotel as categories. In particular, we set 11 categories (Interior design of room, Structure of building, Environment around the hotel, Landscape, Policy, Hotel staff, Toiletries in room, Access to hotel, lodging charge, Other Guests). Table 2 shows the actual sentences in part of category. In Table 2, the upper part shows the original Japanese text, and the lower part shows the English translation.

Table 2. Examples of sentences of category

Category	Examples of Review
Meals	朝食時の長蛇の列が残念 (It's a pity that there was a long queue at breakfast.) 夕食のバイキングが豪華で良い (It was nice that the dinner buffet was gorgeous.) 朝食は品数も多く美味しかった (Breakfast was delicious and many items.)
Lodging charge	宿泊代は高すぎると感じた (I felt that the accommodation fee was too expensive.) 価格に対し充実したホテル (Contrary to the price, it was a hotel with a lot of contents.) 部屋は古いが値段は適切 (I felt the room was old, but the price was reasonable.)
Hotel staff	スタッフの方の対応もよく快適でした (The correspondence of the staff was good.) 客の動作を見て考えてほしい (I want staff should think the behavior of customers.) フロントの電話対応に感謝 (I'm very thankful for the telephone correspondence of front.)

Next, Table 3 shows the number of sentences corresponding to each category.

Table 3. Number of sentences in each category

Category	Number of sentences
Meals	1141
Interior design of room	1412
Structure of building	789
Environment around the hotel	478
Landscape	223
Policy	281
Hotel staff	1012
Toiletries in room	133
Access to hotel	410
lodging charge	312
Other Guests	62

From the results of Table 3, it can be seen that there are many sentences about "Meals," "Interior design of room" and "Hotel staff". On the other hand, there are few sentences about Other Guests. Using these results, we calculate the feature words of each category.

3.2 Feature Extract by Natural Language Processing

Using sentences divided by category in the previous subsection, we create the documents about service using each label and calculate the feature words in each document by TF-IDF methods from Eqs. (1) to (3). In this study, we analyzed using Mecab, a Japanese morphological analysis engine [3]. Moreover, we focused on nouns whose meanings can be understood by themselves.

$$\text{TFIDF}_{i,j} = tf_{i,j} \times idf_i \tag{1}$$

$$tf_{i,j} = \frac{n_{i,j}}{\sum_s n_{s,j}} \tag{2}$$

$$idf_i = log\frac{|D|}{|\{d : d \in t_i\}|} \tag{3}$$

$n_{i,j}$ The number of appearing frequency about word i in the sentence j.
$\sum_s n_{s,j}$ The number of appearing frequency of all words in the sentence j.
$|D|$ The total number of all sentences.
$|\{d : d \in t_i\}|$ The number of sentences containing word i.

Table 4 show the results of characteristic noun words in each category. In Table 4, the upper part of each category shows the original Japanese word, and the lower part shows the English translation.

Table 4. Characteristic noun words in each category

Category	Characteristic noun words (Categorical Top 5 words)				
Meals	食	朝	朝食	バイキング	食事
	Meal	Morning	Breakfast	Buffet	Meal
Interior design of room	広い	お部屋	風呂	泊	ベッド
	Large	Room	Bath	Stay days	Bed
Structure of building	風呂	大	ホテル	浴場	温泉
	Bath	Big	Hotel	Bathhouse	Hot spring
Environment around the hotel	立地	駅	コンビニ	便利	ホテル
	Location	Station	Store	Convenient	Hotel
Landscape	眺め	景色	夜景	窓	高
	View	Landscape	Night View	Window	High
Policy	サービス	ホテル	チェック	イン	朝
	Service	Hotel	Check	In	Morning
Hotel staff	対応	スタッフ	フロント	ホテル	親切
	Correspondence	Staff	Front	Hotel	Kindness
Toiletries in room	アメニティ	充実	アメニティー	歯ブラシ	設備
	Amenity	Enrichment	Amenity	Toothbrush	Equipment
Access to hotel	駅	便	便利	ホテル	立地
	Station	Flight	Convenient	Hotel	Location
Lodging charge	泊	高	段	料	ホテル
	Stay days	Heigh	Price	Price	Hotel
Other guests	マナー	国	人	多い	アジア
	Manners	Country	People	Many	Asia

In Meal category, not only the words for meal like "Meal" and "Buffet", but also there are many words representing time zones such as "Morning". In Interior design of room category, almost words are related to the room, and in Structure of building category, many words related to the facilities such as the "bath". In addition, although Environment around the hotel category and Access to hotel category are similar in that there are words about "location", but there are some words such as means of transportation in Access to hotel category. At the results of other categories, they contain the many words that describe each service that hotel provides. In addition, we calculated the evaluation value for each category of each text by multiplying the TF-IDF values of characteristic noun words and the scores of the adjective emotion value in the polar phrase dictionary (Table 5) [4].

Table 5. Emotion value of word in Polar phrase dictionary

Word		Part of speech	Emotion value	Box-Cox transformation ($\lambda = -0.22$)
優れる	(Excellent)	Verb	1	17.45354
すぐれる	(Surpass)	Verb	1	17.45354
良い	(Good)	Adjective	0.999995	17.453405
よい	(Nice)	Adjective	0.999995	17.453405
よろこぶ	(Be delighted)	Verb	0.999979	17.452973
...		...	...	...
死ぬ	(Die)	Verb	−0.999999	−2.546459
しぬ	(Perish)	Verb	−0.999999	−2.546459
わるい	(Bad)	Adjective	−1	−2.54646
悪い	(Wrong)	Adjective	−1	−2.54646

Using the results of characteristic words and emotion value, we calculate the evaluation value for the service corresponding to the category in each review. We obtained the score by multiplying the TF-IDF value and the emotion value when there is a relationship between the target words about each category, using the dependency relationship between the feature words and emotion words in each review.

In particular, in order to calculate the score for each category of each review, when multiple words of the same category are included in the review, we use the sum of the results of multiplying the TF-IDF value and the polarity value. From this result, we obtained the emotion evaluation of consumers for each service by each review.

Next, using the evaluation of each service, we clarify that how the evaluation of each service affects the entire facility evaluation.

3.3 Classification by Random Forest

Using the evaluation about the category of each text, we constructed a c model based on the Random Forest [5] to determine the rating score for each review is higher or lower than the average rating of each company. Table 6 shows the outline of the discriminant model.

Here, the number of reviews for resort hotel is 55,382, and the number of reviews for business hotel is 95,240. Table 7 show the outline of each review depending on the purpose of use. Using data in each model divided into model learning data (70%) and evaluation data (30%).

The data to be handled is treated as model training data and model evaluation data.

Furthermore, when training each model, the imbalance of learning data adjusts by SMOTE method [6].

Table 6. Objective and explanatory variables used in the discriminant model

Objective variable	Whether the evaluation score of each review is high compared to the average evaluation of the target hotel
Explanatory variable	Scores of each category based on the content of the review

Table 7. Outline of each review depending on how to use

For business model (95,240 data)	Learning data 66,668 data {0: 54%, 1: 46%}
	Evaluation data 28,572 data {0: 53%, 1: 47%}
For Resorts model (55,382 data)	Learning data 38,766 data {0: 41%, 1: 59%}
	Evaluation data 16,616 data {0: 41%, 1: 58%}

4   Results

The accuracy result of the model learned in each data represents at Table 8.

Table 8. Confusion-Matrix of each model (using evaluation data)

For Business model results				For Resorts model results			
	Predicted Negative	Predicted Positive			Predicted Negative	Predicted Positive	
Actual Negative	10331	4812	15143	Actual Negative	4841	2031	6872
Actual Positive	4298	9131	13429	Actual Positive	2854	6890	9744
Accuracy	0.681				0.706		

From the results of Table 8, it can be seen that both models can make predictions with an accuracy of about 70%. Both models use data with the number of labels adjusted by the SMOTE method, but when evaluating the model, each model discriminates in unbalanced data.

In addition, Fig. 1 and Fig. 2 show the feature variables that important for discrimination in each model.

From Fig. 1 which is the results for resorts reviews, it can be seen that customers are high interest in quality of each service in the order of Structure of building, Hotel staff and Meals. In addition, it found that Policy, Lodging charge, Landscape and Interior design room are important in order in the 4th place or below.

Furthermore, from the Fig. 2 which is about the results for business reviews, it can be seen that customers are high interest in quality of each service in the order of

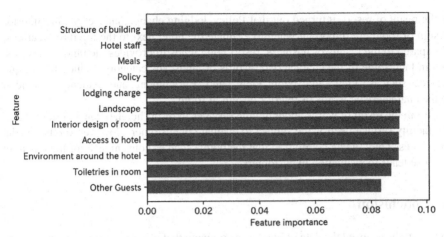

Fig. 1. Results of variable importance of Random Forest in Resorts reviews

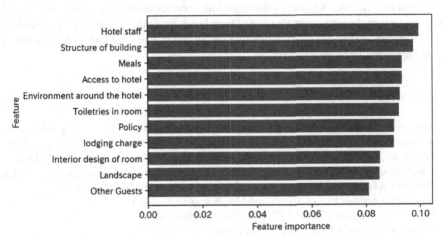

Fig. 2. Results of variable importance of Random Forest in Business reviews

Hotel staff, Structure of building and Meals. The upper level of the variable is similar to the result of resort results, but it can be seen that services related to staff are more important. Furthermore, it become clear that Access to hotel, Environment around the hotel, Toiletries in room and Policy are important in order in the 4th place or below.

5 Discussion

From the results of the above two models, it can be seen that the customer evaluates the facility from different needs. Especially for business use other than tourism, it can be predicted that access and environment around hotel will be important. From the results of feature importance, it can be seen that Access to hotel and Environment around the hotel are more important when to evaluate than the results of resort. On the other hand, in the result of resort, it turned out that Policy, lodging change, landscape, and Interior design of room are important when to evaluate the hotel next to the top three features. Compared to the results of business, resort hotel tends to provides the unique services, and in fact, some of the characteristic words of landscape category include the unique services such as "View" and "Night View", and "Enrichment" and "Amenity" included in the characteristic words of Interior design of room.

From the result of words about unique services in resort hotel, it can be inferred that the facility service itself is the subject to evaluate in customer. However, on the results of business hotel, it can be inferred that the points such as convenience for the business purpose leads to evaluation in customers.

6   Conclusion

In this study, we used the data of hotel as a company that provides services to customers and clarified what kind of needs exist in customers by words in reviews. In addition, we compared the differences between the important services in customers who gave higher evaluations than the average evaluation of each hotel. From these results, it became clear that the evaluation criteria differ depending on the needs, and what factors are important when each hotel improve the services.

References

1. Manes, E., Tchetchik, A.: The role of electronic word of mouth in reducing information asymmetry: an empirical investigation of online hotel booking. J. Bus. Res. **85**, 185–196 (2018)
2. Nishikawa, T., Okada, M., Hashimoto, K.: Verification of text preprocessing method in automatic classification of review sentences. In: Proceedings of the 18th Annual meeting of the Association for Natural Language Processing, pp. 246–251 (2012). (in Japanese)
3. MeCab: Yet Another Part-of-Speech and Morphological Analyzer
4. http://taku910.github.io/mecab/. (2021/3/25 author checked)
5. J Japanese Sentiment Polarity Dictionary (Noun)
6. https://www.nlp.ecei.tohoku.ac.jp/research/open-resources/. (2021/3/25 author checked)
7. Breiman, L.: Random forests. Mach. Learn. **45**(1), 5–32 (2001)
8. Fernandez, A., Garcia, S., Herrera, F., Chawla, N.V.: SMOTE: synthetic minority over-sampling technique. J. Artif. Intell. Res. **16**, 321–357 (2002)

The Influence of Interactive Form on Advertisement Design Creativity

Hao Shan, Peng Liu[✉], and Wei Yu[✉]

School of Art Design and Media, East China University of Science and Technology,
No. 130, Meilong Road, M. BOX 286, Xuhui District, Shanghai 200237, China
{liupeng,weiyu}@ecust.edu.cn

Abstract. The traditional media model has not been able to fully meet the needs of the public and media. Driven by the concept of interaction, design performance and creativity have turned to diversified development, and the communication mode has also developed from the original one-way communication to today's all-round interactive communication. The advent of interactive advertising has made advertising smarter and more interesting. Interactive advertising design is a new creative way of advertising. Of course, the so-called "new" can be understood as a change. Such "new" is also a concept derived from the "traditional", which will also change based on the future development of science and technology and the progress of society. "New" is rather than a fixed concept, but a dynamic and progressive existence. Driven by the concept of interactive design, the expression means and concept of design have turned to diversified development, the communication mode has also developed from the original one-way communication to today's all-round interactive communication, and the creative dimension has also changed from single to multi-dimensional.

Keywords: Interactive advertising · Creative advertising · Interactive form

1 The Change of Interactive Form to Traditional Advertising

1.1 Understanding of New Media Advertising

Advertisement design with interactive forms is a new creative way of advertising. Of course, the so-called "new" can be understood as a change. The so-called new is also a concept derived from traditional advertising creative forms. Changes will also occur with the development of science and technology and the progress of society in the future. "New" does not seem to represent a fixed concept, but a dynamic existence that advances with the times.

Today, all forms of communication media that are different from traditional media concepts and supported by new technologies and new concepts with features such as interaction and innovation can be included in the category of new media. However, simply defining new media as a form of composite digital media with interactive functions does not seem so precise. New $\neq$ digitization. Digitization is one aspect. In the final

© Springer Nature Switzerland AG 2021
C. Stephanidis et al. (Eds.): HCII 2021, CCIS 1421, pp. 439–446, 2021.
https://doi.org/10.1007/978-3-030-78645-8_56

analysis, the development of any technology: people are fundamental, and communication between people is fundamental. Therefore, non-digital advertising forms that reflect the characteristics of interactive innovation can also be considered as new forms of interactive advertising. In our era, there are many new things emerging in an endless stream, and there are many new things that integrate the old and the new. We are changing. At the same time, the four traditional media are also changing. More and more traditional media are also combining interactive forms. Combination methods are becoming more and more common.

For advertising, the emergence of new media has had a huge impact on the traditional advertising industry, and the advertising industry is also undergoing an unprecedented change in blood. The past media model or a single form of communication can no longer fully meet the needs of the public and the media. Driven by the new interactive design concepts, the means of design expression and concepts have turned to diversified development. The communication method has also developed from the original one-way communication to today's all-round interactive communication, and the creative dimension has also changed from single to multidimensional. The concept of interaction is rapidly changing the face of the advertising industry and the rules of the game. In the past, many things that we thought were necessary for creativity may not be regarded as the key points in many interactive advertisements. For example, we always believed that the content of the screen must be creative, and the layout must have a sense of design, etc. But today, we see many excellent interactive advertisements are not outstanding in these two aspects, and some are even mediocre. However, we are stunned by the idea of these works. What is the reason? The dimension of advertising creative points has changed. It may reflect creativity in interactive form, or it may reflect creativity in a virtual space. However, the flat form has fallen to the next level. Therefore, the concept of communication and the way of communication have changed. The dimensions have also changed.

1.2   Interaction Changes to Traditional Advertising

For creative advertising design, the impact of interaction is both a challenge and a good opportunity. Our consumer vision is more and more high, the choice of space is more and more large, the acceptance degree of hard advertising is gradually reduced; Our clients are increasingly looking for innovative, communicable, targeted advertising that can be fully integrated into all media platforms, such as brand elements embedded in games, or brand image communication in videos, micro films, and mobile applications. To make advertising to achieve good results, in the creation and performance communication form must constantly innovation, all of these are directed to a could be called "creative" multi-dimensional, and here refers to the creative images can be content, form, street performances, or just a simple actions to cooperate with you. Anything we can be integrated into the creative according to the needs, as long as you have a good creative, in today's means of realization and creative expression is a variety of forms. For the creative departments of advertising companies, such "multi-dimensional creativity" also challenges the classic mode of traditional art directors combining advertising copywriting. In the era of interactive media, you will find that multi-arms or cross-industry joint operations such as digital technical experts, planners and design creatives are a common form.

Interactive advertising will occupy a larger and larger market in the future advertising market. In order to adapt to this change, advertising agencies should take the initiative to compete with rivals such as Internet search and social media, and also have to change their talent concepts and creative concepts.

We're seeing more and more ads that seem to have nothing to do with branding, less and less like advertising, and more and more hidden (and certainly more and more human) in their ways. Erik Vervroegen, the former global creative director of Publicis, is right when he says, "No one really likes advertising, but the vast majority of people like something new, interesting, exciting, or completely unexpected." Because we don't like them, good advertisements always approach us in a more intelligent way. The emergence of interaction makes advertisements smarter and more interesting. Never before has advertising been so close to people as it is today through interactive advertising supported by new technologies and ideas.

2   The Manifestation Form of New Media Interactive Advertising

The creative development of interactive advertising in new media is a creative break-through brought by mobile media. The popularity of smartphones and tablets has opened up a whole new platform for advertising. The intelligent and strong interactive functions of mobile terminals provide more possibilities for advertising performance, which is also not available in previous TV media, outdoor media or network media. The terminal with the mobile Internet will print, web, film and television media, APP software application, interactivity, virtual reality, image intake and scanning, online offline capabilities, and so on all can be included, it is because this kind of comprehensive qualities, advertising creative forms in the intelligent mobile terminal media obtained the very big breakthrough.

2.1   New Media Interactive Advertising Combined with Traditional Media

This interactive form is a combination of traditional media and mobile terminal media to do an integration, resulting in a new mode of communication.

In the days of smartphones, this kind of integration was mostly in a single form, such as scanning a QR code in a magazine or newspaper to connect to a website. Today, the boring way is not as exciting as a quick scan. Traditional ways of generating interest, creating suspense, or sharing profits are still effective for interactive advertising, but the dimensions of presentation are much bigger than before, and new technologies are changing the face of advertising in incredible and rapid ways. Although the media used in this kind of advertising is not entirely new, this mode of communication has its unique market. First, it is a combination of "new + old", which is also a very interesting mode of communication. Secondly, in terms of media, paper, TV, radio and network have their own advantages. In terms of future development, the integration of advantages of traditional media and new media is also an inevitable trend. The advantages of integrating the two new media have not been limited. On the contrary, the possibilities of creativity and expression have actually been expanded.

The most representative work of this approach is the Lexus advertisement in the Sports Illustrated magazine, which has overturned many people's views on print advertising. Team One spent several months developing CinePrint technology on the Lexus, which combines print ads with iPad interactions. The static print ads are instantly visually, audibly, and tactile, creating the most "interactive" print AD in history.

When you place the iPad under the page of a magazine advertisement, you can activate a section of light and shadow on the iPad that combines with the picture of the magazine and produces rich changes. The gorgeous light and shadow of the new Lexus will appear on the paper, and the original static advertisement on the page of the magazine will instantly produce vivid and dazzling dynamic effect, which is unforgettable. This is a milestone in the combination of print and media tablets, a creation that fully reflects the innovative and enterprising spirit of the Lexus brand.

Another well-known example is the Toyota PSA by Y&R in Lima, Peru, which uses mobile phones in conjunction with traditional magazine media. In the print AD, there is no text or brand except for the children and cows with QR codes in the middle of the road. Manufacturing suspense is a very common one kind of gimmick in advertising creative, when readers see QR code, and would like to know what the implication, the subconscious will pick up the smartphone scan to find out, when the mobile phone on the QR code, mystery solved: the road in the center of the child and cows were gone, slogan: "when you use a smart phone, you can't really see what's on the road." Just think, if these two advertisements are simply released on the traditional paper media, will they have the same communication effect? Therefore, the integration advantage of new media greatly expands the space and dimension of traditional advertising design creativity in creative expression.

2.2 Augmented Reality (AR) and Virtual Reality (VR) Technology Under the New Media Interactive Advertising

Augmented Reality (Augmented Reality) is a kind of technology that can combine virtual objects or information with the real environment in real time, so as to enhance people's understanding and experience of virtual things in the real environment.

In recent years, with the popularization of intelligent mobile terminals, the application of augmented reality in advertising has been more widely used, which is also a form of new media advertising that attracts the most attention.

Augmented reality can bring everything in the advertisement into your world, showing the advertisement scene, product features and message in a very vivid, intuitive and three-dimensional form of expression. A fashion magazine, for example, when you through the phone or the scan a you like clothes, suitable model between fleshed out, introduce the suit for you, then all angles to show you the dress of dress effect, and through a flat screen you feel no longer exists, but it is a vivid the three-dimensional or standing in the magazine is to film.

For example, Haagen-Dazs launched an augmented reality interactive advertisement, a small creative let people feel its meticulous and considerate service to consumers. Haagen-Dazs ice cream needs 2 min to soften to achieve the best taste, but how to arrange the two minutes? Just open the APP, point your smartphone at the cup, and a virtual violinist will play a 2-min piece of music for you. The waiting time will not be long. After the music is finished, it is the perfect time to enjoy Haagen-Dazs ice cream.

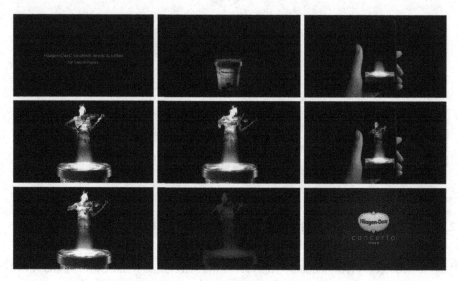

Through augmented reality technology, any object in the world can become a carrier of information transmission, which greatly expands the space for the realization of advertising, and augmented reality technology has a great space for development in the future. As far as current technology is concerned, augmented reality is a technology in development, and most of its applications are still in the stage of superficial display. Its interactive control is difficult to reach an ideal state at present. I believe that in the future, all of these will be solved perfectly with the development of technology.

Virtual Reality technology is a kind of three-dimensional simulated Reality that makes people immerse themselves in through VR glasses. This Virtual world has a certain nature of interactive control and has the characteristics of relatively real three-dimensional vision, hearing, touch and even smell. VR technology can realize virtual scenes, have interactive characteristics and bring people intuitive panoramic immersive sense of the sensory experience, all kinds of corporate brands in the actual advertising design creativity, a large number of integration of VR technology, advertising in the way of communication and effect of a step forward. VR interactive advertising can be more realistic in terms of product experience. Compared with traditional film and television advertising, it is also more vivid and intuitive. The immersive experience of "reality" and "presence" brought by VR technology is incomparable with that of other media, and game-like manipulation also greatly enhances the experience of advertising.

3   Interactive Forms of Advertising Other Than Digital Technology

The reason I included this type of advertising is because it is "new", although the "new" is not necessarily related to digital, but is mainly reflected in its creative integration and new forms of communication, such as the current popular environmental media advertising. It is precisely because of the novel and interesting ideas of this kind of advertising that many excellent works spread throughout the world through digital network media.

As for brand image communication, many changes have taken place in the way of expression. This change is reflected in advertising, which is not so direct and forceful in its narrative, as opposed to pure branding, which has become diversified. The form may be a short narrative, is likely to be a street performance, can also be an art exhibition but its purpose is not to an audience interested in or have use value, in the form of forming propagation effect, achieve the goal of brand promotion, in the osmosis advertising at this time is no longer a medium between product and content, its itself has become a popular content, share reproduced by tens of thousands of people, reproduction.

Ogilvy & Mather Paris launched a series of ads for IBM in 2012 that were nothing new in terms of graphic content or format, where the traditional standard of print advertising was overthrown and visual creativity was less important, but it emerged in a more interesting creative form. Relative to the traditional outdoor billboard, focus on the picture to move people? To be more practical, IBM's outdoor advertising has done this. There are many disadvantages in urban life, such as no chair when walking tired, no place to take shelter from the rain when it rains, and stairs when dragging heavy luggage.... Who pays attention to these details? IBM is working to create solutions that help cities around the world become smarter and make life better for them.

This a series of outdoor billboards, start from details, breaking the traditional outdoor advertising form, into the practical caring functional elements, the print advertising combined with urban public facilities, the simple plane advertisement becomes a bench, shelter tent and barrier-free ramp, make a cold billboards form is full of the milk of human kindness will follow IBM smart idea for smarter city "concept cleverly combined with one of them.

This series of ads did not use any new technological means, but this innovative form narrowed the distance between IBM and the audience, and the related pictures and videos were also widely circulated on the Internet all over the world, which completely broke the communication distance and strength of outdoor advertising.

4   Conclusion

New media advertising is a relatively broad concept, involving a wide range of classic cases are also very many, due to the length of the article, can only talk about some personal relatively shallow understanding in a limited range.

Whether it is correspond to what kind of art form, technique and how to develop, how rich performance means, we can define these in the scope of the form is still, so the definition of new media is WIRED magazine "the spread of all the people for all the people." In this sense, it's a back-to-basics definition that goes way beyond any technical definition.

New media age we got great development in the form of creativity, traditional media advertising design a lot of rules in today is completely overturned, but we are fighting for, for the creative hadn't changed: both the traditional media advertising and new media advertising, attract law did not change, form in the service of creativity, and creativity are attracted to a more powerful, the purpose of only interested in "people", can obtain the effective information transmission, thus achieve the purpose of the brand, product, or idea promotion. Compared with traditional media advertising, new media advertising makes the distance between people and advertising closer, and the way of advertising has become more intelligent and interesting, and the dissemination is more extensive and effective, which is also the key factor for new media advertising to become the development trend of advertising in the future.

A Benefit-Cost Perspective on Consumers' Purchase of Online Content

Qianru Tao, Xintong Wang, Yanyu Zhao, Mingzhu Li, and LiLi Liu[✉]

College of Economics and Management, Nanjing University of Aeronautics and Astronautics, Nanjing, China
{taoqianru,wangxintong09,zhaoyanyu,limingzhu99,
llili85}@nuaa.edu.cn

Abstract. In recent years, Chinese netizens have to pay predetermined fees before consuming various online content (e.g., videos and music), implying that the "free content" mode has been gradually replaced by the subscription fee-based mode. However, limited research has explored what motivates consumers to pay for online content, especially those who have already been used to the "free content" mode. To fill this gap, drawing on Perceived Value Theory (PVT), this article seeks to investigate consumers' purchase of online content from a benefit-cost perspective. Contextual benefits (entertainment, information) and costs (perceived price and perceived risk) have been identified as determinants of consumers' perceived value and purchase behavior. A survey was conducted and 227 valid samples were collected. Smart PLS 2.0 was employed to analyze data. Results show that entertainment and information positively affect perceived value, while perceived price and risk negatively influence perceived value, which in turn positively impacts purchase behavior. Finally, theoretical and practical implications are discussed.

Keywords: Online content · Purchase behavior · Benefits · Costs · Perceived value · Perceived Value Theory

1 Introduction

Online content covers information ranging from texts (e.g., The New York Times), pictures (e.g., Getty Images), videos (e.g., Netflix), to audios (e.g., iTunes) [1]. Some online content providers filter and aggregate high-quality information and then sell them to consumers. For instance, in U.S., New York Times and Wall Street Journal are operated under pay-walls mode, which restricts the access to online reports via a subscription [2]. Accumulated evidence indicates that the "free content" mode has been gradually replaced by the subscription fee-based mode [3]. In order to consume various scarce and high-quality content, consumers have to pay for predetermined subscription fees. China's paid content market is growing rapidly. For instance, Baidu Library, a document sharing platform, charges the users membership fee to download majority documents. Besides, Chinese video websites (iQiYi, Tencent video, etc.) also charge VIP membership fee before providing elevated service, including content privilege (watching more videos)

© Springer Nature Switzerland AG 2021
C. Stephanidis et al. (Eds.): HCII 2021, CCIS 1421, pp. 447–455, 2021.
https://doi.org/10.1007/978-3-030-78645-8_57

and advertising privilege (skipping ads). Taking the Chinese digital music industry as an example, the market size has reached 7.63 billion CNY in 2018. A report pointed out that content subscription fee and copyright operation will become two vital factors that drives the growth of Chinese digital music market in the future [4]. While consumers' purchase behavior has been widely studied in the economics and marketing scope, limited research was conducted to explore what motivates consumers to pay for online content [5].

As a type of product, online content has presented many new features, such as bountiful supply of alternatives which are accessible elsewhere, homogeneous quality perception and so on. Hence, contextual variables should be carefully identified and evaluated in the paid-content context, rather than directly transplant theories under the traditional economic circumstance. Drawing on Perceived Value Theory (PVT), this article aims to understand consumers' purchase of online content from a benefit-cost perspective, focusing on promoting and hindering factors. More specifically, determinants have been identified and classified into two categories: benefits (entertainment, information) and costs (perceived price and perceived risk), which affect consumers' perceived value and purchase behavior. The study thus not only provides insights into subscription-based online content consumption, but also help online content providers to effectively attract paying users who may have been used to consuming free content.

2 Theoretical Background

Perceived Value Theory (PVT) defines perceived value as "the overall assessment of the utility of a product or service based on the perceptions of what is received and what is given" [6], which has been widely adopted to explain consumers' purchase behavior [7, 8]. Perceived value can be increased by enhancing the benefits (what is received) and reducing the costs (what is given) [9]. Derived from previous works on the multidimensional nature of perceived value, we harbour the assumption that benefits and costs dimensions should have positive and negative effects on the perceived value respectively. More particularly, Kim et al. [10] argue that consumers are able to obtain useful information and entertainment by consuming online content, which enhances their perception of content value. Besides, Kwon and Schumann [11] indicate that while price of online content (subscription fee) increases, consumers' perception of value declines accordingly. Moreover, Pires et al. [12] state that perceived risk of pre-paid subscription-fees is a key factor, which may decrease our perceived value, as the paid content may not fulfill consumers' expectations.

In conclusion, based on the benefit-cost perspective, we classify independent variables into two categories: benefits (entertainment and information) and costs (perceived price and perceived risk), which affect purchase behavior via the mediation of perceived value.

3 Research Model and Hypotheses

The research model is presented below in Fig. 1. Additionally, corresponding hypotheses are discussed in the following section.

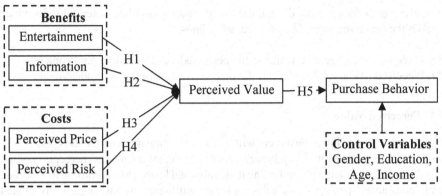

Fig. 1. Research model

3.1 Benefits

Entertainment refers to the relief from daily frustration and exhaustion brought by consuming paid content, especially for introvert consumers [13]. The happiness and satisfaction generated will further lead to a positive attitude towards consumers' perception of content value, which in turn may motivate their purchase behavior [14].

Information is defined as the overall usefulness audiences acquire from consuming the paid content [10]. Audiences are able to obtain superior information by accessing paid content, compared with employing free content. Sharing the information obtained from paid content also helps audiences to improve their authority and social status, which is of considerable benefit to them. According to Osatuyi, customers always seek for useful information while surfing online, which significantly affects their satisfaction [15]. When a customer obtains more useful information from online content, they are more satisfied, thus perceive the online content as more valuable. We therefore hypothesize:

H1. Entertainment positively affects the perceived value of online paid content.
H2. Information positively affects the perceived value of online paid content.

3.2 Costs

Perceived price is described as consumers' evaluation of the absolute online content price based on their affordability, which varies person by person [5]. For instance, despite the absolute price of certain content is fixed (i.e., one dollar), consumers who has a monthly income of 10,000$ will perceive it as cheap while consumers who have a monthly income of 1000$ may consider it as expensive. If consumers perceive that the monetary sacrifice (price need to pay) far outweighs the potential informational and entertaining value that paid content contains, their perceived value will be low [5].

According to Mitchell [16], perceived risk refers to consumers' subjective perception of the possibility to loss and the coming consequences which may not be able to meet their expectations or goals set before. For example, consumers are required to pay before they access the full version of online content, yet the paid content may not be as useful or interesting as they expected, then the dissatisfaction could be potential risks which weaken the perceived value [12]. Hence, we propose:

H3. Perceived price negatively affects the perceived value of online paid content.
H4. Perceived risk negatively affects the perceived value of online paid content.

3.3 Perceived Value

To maximize their utility, consumers will assess and compare benefits and costs before making purchase decisions [10]. Perceived value indicates audiences' perception of the overall paid content value by evaluating their gains and losses [6]. According to Sweeney et al., consumers' perception of value and their willingness to buy are closely related [17]. For example, online practitioners offered quality and satisfactory paid content, and if this was the experience, chances are high that the consumer would return to the online practitioners to purchase the item. We therefore assume:

H5. Perceived value positively affects consumers' purchase behavior.

4 Research Methodology

4.1 Data Collection

An online survey was designed and distributed via WenJuanXing platform (http://www. sojump.com/) to collect data in mainland China. We mainly target at college students and employees from all walks of life since both students and people from all walks of life have a strong receptivity and show respect for copyright, which is the basis of knowledge sharing. Moreover, students and social people choose to pay for online contents to obtain knowledge and resources they need in their study and work, which enables them to filter the information and improve work efficiently. The questionnaire consists of two parts: demographic information and measurement items of variables in the research model, including 26 questions. All measurement items were adapted from relevant previous studies and had been modified to match our research context. Items of entertainment were derived from Hsiao and Chen [5]. Information was assessed with items adapted from Agarwal and Karahanna [18]. Items of perceived price were adapted and adjusted from Voss et al. [19] while items of perceived risk were adapted from the research of Pires et al. [12]. In addition, items of perceived value were adapted from Hsiao's research [20].

Measurement items of purchase behavior were adapted from Richa and Samrat [21]. All the items were measured with Likert seven-point scale, ranging from "strongly disagree" (1) to "strongly agree" (7). The survey was conducted from March 10, 2020 to March 15, 2020. 227 valid responses were received. Among them, 48.46% of the respondents were male and 51.54% were female. Majority of the respondents were between 16 and 35 years old. Respondents' monthly income ranged from 2000 to 8000 CNY. Approximately 93% of the respondents had associate degree or above. Detailed demographic information was shown in Table 1.

Table 1. Demographic information.

Profile of respondents

| Measure | Item | N=227 | |
		Frequency	Percentage(%)
Gender	Male	110	48.46
	Female	117	51.54
Age	16-25	113	49.78
	26-35	71	31.28
	36-45	28	12.33
	46-55	13	5.73
	≥56	2	0.88
Income(CNY)	≤2000	58	25.55
	2001-4000	85	37.44
	4001-6000	54	23.79
	6001-8000	25	11.01
	≥8000	5	2.20
Education	High school or below	16	7.05
	College	60	26.43
	Bachelor	140	61.67
	Master and above	11	4.85

4.2 Analyses and Results

This study utilized a two-step approach to analyze the research model [22]. SmartPLS 3.2.9 was used to analyze the data [23]. First, we tested the reliability and validity of the measurement model. Reliability is evaluated by checking composite reliability and Cronbach's α values. Table 2 showed that composite reliability values of this study ranged between 0.851 and 0.936, all of which are higher than the suggested value of 0.70 [24]. Besides, internal consistency was verified by Cronbach's α values, which were all greater than 0.739, thus exceeding the threshold of 0.70 recommended by Fornell and Larcker [25].

Convergence validity of the measurement model was evaluated via following criteria: (1) the loading values of all index factors should exceed 0.7 [24]; (2) the average variance extracted (AVE) of each constructs should exceed 0.5 [25]. As shown in Table 2, all constructs revealed acceptable factor loadings (greater than 0.7). AVE value of each construct ranged between 0.656 and 0.762, greater than the acceptable value of 0.5. Therefore, convergent validity of this research was verified.

According to Fornell and Larcker [25], discriminant validity of the measurement model can be evaluated by comparing the square root of AVE with the correlation between the measurement items. The results in Table 3 showed that the AVE square root of each structure is greater than the correlation between any pair of corresponding structures, indicating sufficient validity. In summary, our measurement model has sufficient reliability, convergence validity and discriminant validity.

We then tested the structural model and hypotheses. As shown in Fig. 2, perceived value was positively influenced by entertainment and information ($\beta = 0.262$, $t = 3.077$; $\beta = 0.187$, $t = 2.119$). Hence, H1 and H2 were supported. In the measurement costs

Table 2. Individual item reliability.

Measures	Item	Loading	Mean	Composite reliability	Cronbach's α	AVE
Entertainment	ET1	0.903	4.523	0.906	0.844	0.762
	ET2	0.873				
	ET3	0.842				
Information	IF1	0.859	4.765	0.936	0.917	0.708
	IF2	0.851				
	IF3	0.829				
	IF4	0.807				
	IF5	0.859				
	IF6	0.842				
Perceived Price	PP1	0.823	3.570	0.851	0.739	0.656
	PP2	0.793				
	PP3	0.814				
Perceived Risk	PR1	0.814	3.258	0.866	0.769	0.683
	PR2	0.842				
	PR3	0.823				
Perceived Value	PV1	0.809	4.612	0.851	0.739	0.656
	PV2	0.826				
	PV3	0.796				
Purchase Behaviour	PB1	0.841	4.803	0.886	0.806	0.721
	PB2	0.839				
	PB3	0.867				

Table 3. Discriminant validity.

Variables	Entertainment	Information	Perceived Price	Perceived Risk	Perceived Value	Purchase Behaviour
Entertainment	0.873					
Information	0.823	0.841				
Perceived Price	-0.692	-0.614	0.81			
Perceived Risk	-0.616	-0.621	0.419	0.826		
Perceived Value	0.682	0.647	-0.625	-0.512	0.81	
Purchase Behaviour	0.734	0.691	-0.584	-0.601	0.674	0.849

Notes: The diagonal elements show the square root of the AVE; the off diagonal elements show the correlations among constructs.

module, perceived price and perceived risk had significant negative impacts on perceived value ($\beta = -0.279$, t = 3.674; $\beta = -0.117$, t = 1.970), thus hypothesis H3 and H4 were also verified. In addition, this study demonstrated that perceived value was an important antecedent of purchase behavior, which was positively affected by perceived value. Therefore, H5 hypothesis was supported ($\beta = 0.664$, t = 17.474). Finally, 53.4% variance of perceived value while 48.8% variance of purchase behavior were explained respectively, higher than Falk and Miller's recommendation of 10% [26], which implied that the model had high degree of fit and strong prediction ability.

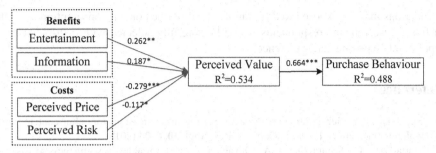

Fig. 2. Structural model

5   Conclusions

As a fast growing market, the scale of China's knowledge payment industry is expected to reach CNY 23.5 billion by the end of 2020, yet limited effort has been made to investigate the purchase of online contents. Drawing on Perceived Value Theory (PVT), this study identifies and verifies particular contextual determinants of consumers' online content purchase behavior. As displayed in Fig. 2, all of the proposed hypotheses are statistically supported. In light of a benefit-cost perspective, our research recognizes four factors affecting perceived value, representing benefits (entertainment and information) and costs (perceived price and perceived risk). On one hand, consumers expect to obtain entertainment and information from online content, which positively contributing to their perception of content value. On the other hand, consumers are worried that pre-paid online content may not be cost-effective and fail to fulfill their expectations. Therefore, perceived price and perceived risk negatively affect consumers' perceived value, thus discouraging them to pay for online content. Moreover, positive relationship between perceived value and consumers' purchase behavior is also in line with Kim et al.'s research which proves that perceived value is a significant predictor of consumers' purchase intention [10].

Theoretically, we verify the applicability of perceived value theory in explaining consumers' purchase behavior in online paid content context. In addition, we examine the impacts of contextual variables in terms of benefits (entertainment and information) and costs (perceived price and perceived risk), thus extends our knowledge on consumers' purchase behavior. Findings of this study also provide important implications for online content market in China. The benefit-cost perspective can be applied to explain consumer behavior in various service industries. Website managers not only have to improve the entertainment and information value of the online content, but also need to reduce consumers' concerns regarding the content price and potential risk. In order to achieve these objectives and maximize the revenue, website operators should learn consumer behavior trends, then develop dynamic and rational pricing strategy by customer segmentation. At the same time, managers should also improve the online content quality and website brand publicity, develop user-friendly and easy-to-operate interface to attract new users as well as retain existing consumers.

There are some limitations in this study. For instance, data collection was confined to Mainland China. Besides, respondents age was not evenly distributed. People in different occupations may be exposed to different levels of online content consumption as well. In future research, the respondents would be carefully selected with distributive and representative profile and preference.

References

1. Xu, J., Duan, Y.: Subscription price and advertising space decisions for online content firms with reference effect. Electron. Commer. Res. Appl. **30**, 8–24 (2018)
2. Marta-Lazo, C., Segura-Anaya, A., Oliván, N.M.: Key variables in willingness to pay for online news content: the professionals' perspective. Rev. Lat. Comun. Soc. **72**, 165 (2017)
3. Kammer, A., Boeck, M., Hansen, J.V., Hauschildt, L.J.H.: The free-to-fee transition: audiences' attitudes toward paying for online news. J. Media Bus. Stud. **12**(2), 107–120 (2015)
4. Research report on the development of digital music content payment in China in 2019. Research report of iresearch series (7th issue of 2019): Shanghai iResearch Market Consulting co. Ltd., 2019-332-365 (2019)
5. Hsiao, K.L., Chen, C.C.: What drives in-app purchase intention for mobile games? An examination of perceived values and loyalty. Electron. Commer. Res. Appl. **16**, 18–29 (2016)
6. Zeithaml, V.A.: Consumer perceptions of price, quality, and value: a means-end model and synthesis of evidence. J. Mark. **52**(3), 2–22 (1988)
7. Dodds, W.B., Monroe, K.B.: The effect of brand and price information on subjective product evaluations. In: ACR North American Advances (1985)
8. Nilson, T.H.: Value-added marketing: marketing management for superior results. McGraw-Hill Book Company, New York (1992)
9. Lovelock, C., Wirtz, J.: Services Marketing: People, Technology. Strategy. Prentice Hall, Upper Saddle River, NJ (2011)
10. Kim, H.W., Chan, H.C., Gupta, S.: Value-based adoption of mobile internet: an empirical investigation. Decis. Support Syst. **43**(1), 111–126 (2007)
11. Kwon, K.N., Schumann, D.W.: The influence of consumers' price expectations on value perception and purchase intention. Adv. Consum. Res. **28**, 316–322 (2010)
12. Pires, G., Stanton, J., Eckford, A.: Influences on the perceived risk of purchasing online. J. Consum. Behav. Int. Res. Rev. **4**(2), 118–131 (2004)
13. Lu, H.P., Hsiao, K.L.: The influence of extro/introversion on the intention to pay for social networking sites. Inf. Manag. **47**(3), 150–157 (2010)
14. Colwell, J.: Needs met through computer game play among adolescents. Personality Individ. Differ. **43**(8), 2072–2082 (2007)
15. Babajide Osatuyi, A., et al.: When it comes to satisfaction ... it depends: an empirical examination of social commerce users. Comput. Hum. Behav. **111**, 106413 (2020)
16. Mitchell, V.: Consumer perceived risk: conceptualisation and models. Eur. J. Mark. **33**(1/2), 163–195 (1999)
17. Sweeney, J.C., Soutar, G.N., Johnson, L.W.: Retail service quality and perceived value. J. Retail. Consum. Serv. **4**(1), 39–48 (1997)
18. Agarwal, R., Karahanna, E.: Time flies when you're having fun: cognitive absorption and beliefs about information technology usage 1. MIS Q. **24**(4), 665–694 (2000)
19. Voss, G.B., Parasuraman, A., Grewal, D.: The roles of price, performance, and expectations in determining satisfaction in service exchanges. J. Mark. **62**(4), 46–61 (1998)
20. Hsiao, K.L.: Android smartphone adoption and intention to pay for mobile internet: perspectives from software, hardware, design, and value. Libr. HiTech **31**(2), 216–235 (2013)

21. Richa, C., Samrat, B.: Factors influencing green purchase behavior of millennials in India. Manag. Environ. Qual. Int. J. MEQ-02–2018–0023 (2018)
22. Chin, W.W., Marcolin, B.L., Newsted, P.R.: A partial least squares latent variable modeling approach for measuring interaction effects: results from a Monte Carlo simulation study and an electronic-mail emotion/adoption study. Inf. Syst. Res. **14**(2), 189–217 (2003)
23. Ringle, C.M., Wende, S., Will, A.: SmartPLS 2.0 (beta). Hamburg (2005)
24. Hair, J.F., Black, W.C., Babin, B.J., Anderson, R.E., Tatham, R.L.: Multivariate 936 Data Analysis. Pearson University Press, London (2006)
25. Fornell, C.R., Larcker, D.F.: Evaluating structural equation models with unobservable variables and measurement error. J. Mark. Res. **18**(3), 375–381 (1981)
26. Falk, R.F., Miller, N.B.: A Primer for Soft Modeling. University of Akron Press, Akron, Ohio (1992)

Research on Smart Shopping Cart Modeling Design Based on Kansei Engineering

Junnan Ye[✉], Menglan Wang, Siyao Zhu, Jingyang Wang, and Xu Liu

East China University of Science and Technology, Shanghai 200237, People's Republic of China

Abstract. With the continuous development of intelligent technologies such as the Internet of Things, traditional supermarkets are also constantly exploring new ways of retailing. The smart shopping cart is a corresponding innovation. Through market and literature research, it is found that the existing design research of smart shopping cart focuses too much on the integration and implementation of technology, without fully considering the aesthetic and emotional needs of users for modeling. In this paper, the modeling design of the smart shopping cart is mainly based on the design method of Kansei Engineering. Firstly, the design positioning of the smart shopping cart is determined, that is, consumers aged 18–35 in large supermarkets are taken as the target users. Secondly, related product databases and perceptual vocabulary databases were established. After screening 40 groups of perceptual vocabulary by KJ method, 6 groups of vocabulary were obtained. Then the SD method is used to conduct a questionnaire survey on users. Finally, by drawing the intention scale map and analyzing the data, the three design elements of "simple and simple", "light and large capacity" and "friendly streamline" were summarized. Combined with the functional requirements and ergonomics, the shape design was carried out. Finally, the design practice was recognized by design experts and the public through the survey of satisfaction. This study is an effective practice and exploration of Kansei Engineering design methods, providing new design ideas for the development of the smart shopping cart industry, and further improving the competitiveness and user experience of supermarkets.

Keywords: Kansei Engineering · Smart shopping cart · Modeling design · Semantic scaling method

1 The Introduction

With the rapid development of Internet technology and mobile Internet terminals, people are more and more inclined to consume online shopping APP. Although the e-commerce market has tended to be saturated, it still poses a huge threat to offline supermarkets and other retail industries. In addition to the impact of the COVID-19, supermarkets urgently need to find countermeasures to improve profitability. Smart shopping cart is the medium between the supermarket and the customers. It is a service platform based on consumption data, user trajectory and geographical location that can set up the supermarket scene. Self-service can reduce the cost of enterprises to a certain extent, and send the data to the

© Springer Nature Switzerland AG 2021
C. Stephanidis et al. (Eds.): HCII 2021, CCIS 1421, pp. 456–463, 2021.
https://doi.org/10.1007/978-3-030-78645-8_58

background for processing, making the results more accurate and faster [1, 2]. Therefore, the innovative design of smart shopping cart will improve the shopping experience of users and promote the economic benefits of offline physical supermarkets, which has a certain design significance. Through the research of market research literature, it is found that the existing smart shopping cart pays more attention to the integration of emerging technologies to improve the intelligent experience, but ignores the users' personalized needs for product modeling. Therefore, this study adopts the semantic difference method to collect users' semantic preferences, conducts data analysis through the intention scale method and extracts design elements, thus concluding the innovative design scheme of the smart shopping cart, which is conducive to further promoting the development of the real economy of supermarkets.

2 Kansei Engineering and Smart Shopping Cart Modeling Design

2.1 Kansei Engineering

Kansei Engineering, originally known as "emotional engineering", is an emerging discipline that combines ergonomics, humanized design concepts and emotional design concepts [3]. Traditional ergonomics focuses on the interaction of product size and function, whether it meets the user's man-machine size and usage habits, etc., and more belongs to the research on physical characteristics. Kansei Engineering, on the other hand, pays more attention to the emotional experience of products on consumers' psychology and more to the study of spiritual experience. Researchers describe the image of products through the combination of adjectives, and consumers make choices according to their own emotional preferences, so that the unquantifiable and irrational emotional demands can finally be studied and discussed through data analysis [4]. Designers can make a comprehensive analysis from the dimensions of color, texture, shape and so on, so as to provide guidance for product shape design.

2.2 Smart Shopping Cart

However, smart shopping cart products still belong to the blue ocean market, and the design of this market is rarely implemented. The outstanding products at home and abroad mainly include "Eli" from South Korea and 7Fresh from Jingdong. Most of them use cameras, infrared sensing technology and advanced obstacle avoidance system, which can take corresponding measures immediately in case of emergency. When the customer no longer needs it, the cart can be automatically returned to the charging point for the next customer to use; Customers can use credit cards or other mobile payment terminals to check out; The shopping cart determines whether the items in the cart have been fully paid for by comparing the total weight of the items in the cart to the weight of the items actually paid for. Smart shopping cart design features not only intelligent shopping experience, but also needs to fully consider the fashion attributes. The appearance of the domestic supermarket shopping cart the same already unable to meet the demand of consumers personalized trend, therefore using the method of perceptual technology to explore the perceptual demand of consumer groups to the shopping cart, will contribute to the innovation of the smart shopping cart design, but in the intelligent design also need to balance the sense of scale and the reasonable rendering function.

2.3 Research Process and Method

The value of a product can be divided into material value and spiritual value. When a product satisfies the material function value such as function, structure and operation mode, it should also enable users to obtain internal satisfaction and well-being such as culture, emotion, happiness and happiness in the process of use, and deliver positive use experience and emotions to consumers [5]. Quantitative analysis of perceptual preferences through SD questionnaire helps designers intuitively explore users' preferences, so as to introduce emotional elements into the design and enable users to have a positive emotional experience when using the product [6]. In this paper, the method of Kansei Engineering is introduced into the design of smart shopping cart. The following is the specific research route, as shown in Fig. 1.

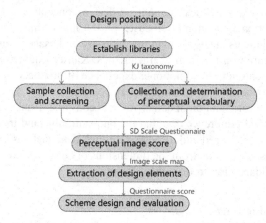

Fig. 1. Research steps of smart shopping cart of Kansei Engineering

The research procedure is divided into six steps. Step 1: The design and positioning of smart shopping cart. Step 2: Build libraries, including product libraries and semantic libraries. Collect the existing smart shopping cart on the market and select more beautiful and fashionable product pictures through KJ classification method, so as to improve the accuracy of subsequent design element extraction. Use brainstorming to build a vocabulary of anti-sense words. Step 3: SD questionnaire survey was used to score perceptual intention. After determining the attributes of the products, words were placed on the left and right ends of the scale, scores were divided into five to nine levels, and appropriate products were selected to form a questionnaire. Step 4: Design elements extraction. Data software is used to quantitatively analyze the results of the above questionnaire, obtain the weight of perceptual words and extract the design elements, so as to guide the design of subsequent programs. Step 5: Plan design and evaluation. Combined with ergonomics and design elements to design the shape. Finally, a questionnaire survey on program satisfaction was conducted. A good score indicated that the program was of high usability.

3 Research on Perceptual Intention of Smart Shopping Cart Shape Design

3.1 Sample Collection and Screening

A total of 15 pictures of the smart shopping cart were collected through various channels. The pictures were screened according to the appearance features of the products, such as color, shape and material, and the products with similar properties were classified. Finally, five representative pictures were selected, as shown in Fig. 2.

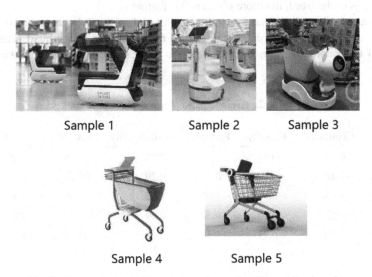

Sample 1   Sample 2   Sample 3

Sample 4   Sample 5

Fig. 2. Research steps of smart shopping cart of Kansei Engineering

3.2 Perceptual Intention Vocabulary Collection

In this paper, a total of nearly 40 pairs of antisense words were collected. After multi-layer screening by designers, the following six pairs of words were finally determined, as shown in Table 1. "Contracted – complex" reflect the characteristics of the product form, "affinity – cool" reflect product to the user's emotional colors, "light, heavy" consider the tolerance of users using psychological, "large capacity, small capacity" reflect the user demand for function, "- a rough texture" measure of texture and color characteristics of products, "streamline – hale" reflect product design language of refining.

Table 1. Determination of perceptual words

The serial number	The perceptual words	The serial number	The perceptual words
1	Minimalist – complex	4	High capacity – low capacity
2	Friendly – cool	5	Textured – rough
3	Light – heavy	6	Streamlined – tough

3.3 Research and Analysis of Smart Shopping Cart Based on SD Method

Each sample image corresponds to six groups of perceptual word pairs. A seven-level scale with scores of $-3, -2, -1, 0, 1$ and 3 is set to form a complete survey questionnaire. Users will rate the product pictures in turn according to their true feelings. The closer the choice is to the word, the more obvious this feature is.

A total of 125 questionnaires were sent out and 121 valid questionnaires were received, among which 31 were young designers with design background. The mean values of the 6 antonym pairs corresponding to the 5 samples are listed, as shown in Table 2.

Table 2. Average score of perceptual words

	Contracted	Friendly	Portable	High capacity	Textured	Streamlined
Sample1	−0.33	−0.14	1.1	0.05	−1.14	−1.29
Sample2	−0.48	−0.67	0.1	0.29	−0.76	−0.67
Sample3	−1.14	−0.71	−1.05	−1.52	0.95	1.1
Sample4	0.33	−0.95	0.52	−0.29	−1.24	−1.62
Sample5	−1.76	−0.71	−1.38	−2	−0.05	1.29

4   Smart Shopping Cart Modeling Design Practice

4.1 Design Elements Extraction Based on Perceptual Image Research

According to the mean value of perceptual words in Table 2, a quadrant graph is drawn. Put "minimalist – complex" at both ends of the X axis and "streamline – tough" at both ends of the Y axis. $(-0.33, -1.29)$ represents the mean value of minimalist and streamline corresponding to sample 1. Similarly, the remaining four adjectives are labeled in the quadrant using this method. Black circles represent "simple – complex" and "streamlined – tough", pink circles represent "textural – rough" and "intimate – cool", and green circles represent "light – bulky" and "large – small", as shown in Fig. 3.

According to Fig. 3, it can be concluded that the third quadrant has the highest sample mean ratio. Therefore, the priority of the design elements of the smart shopping cart is as follows: the first is simple and streamlined; the second is textured and friendly material; the third is portable and large-capacity.

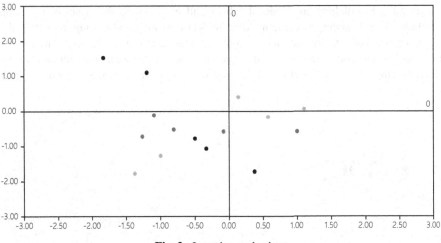

Fig. 3. Intention scale chart

4.2 Scheme Design and Evaluation

According to the perceptual intention screened out in Fig. 4 and the corresponding sample pictures, the reference of design elements is extracted and the final innovative design practice is carried out, including sketch design, three-dimensional modeling and intelligent terminal design, etc.

Streamlined side brackets serve as the main body of the smart shopping cart, including an intelligent terminal and a code scanning port. Intelligent terminal for the 9.7 in. screen size, tilted 45°, is suitable for people look down at reading, considering the stability of the element, directly to the screen fixed on the bracket, no longer can adjust any Angle, and code directly on the right side, customer finish cleaning a commodity, can immediately swept to the information on the screen, in line with people's behavior habits. The bracket connecting plate is engraved with the brand logo, which connects the letter "T" with the straight line, making the whole harmonious and smooth. The hole basket that uses crisscrosive among, break depressing feeling, but also with before stainless steel bar type shopping cart basket differs somewhat, appear more light and fashionable. The wheels are universal wheels, which can rotate freely in 360°. No longer the previous shopping wheel, this design is more plump shape, especially the base and the wheel connected part, increased the stability layer, considering the use of different materials and colors, so that the chromatography is more clear, more stable.

The selection of the right materials can increase the attractiveness of the product and enhance the user's interactive experience with the shopping cart. Different materials, due to their different colors and textures, will give people different visual feelings, tactile feelings and psychological feelings.

Through the research and summary of the current supermarket shopping cart, most of the shopping cart are made of stainless steel, although stainless steel material corrosion resistance, formability is very excellent, but too much stainless steel material will cause a cold hard visual psychology. Therefore, change to ABS plastic material, not only the physical and chemical properties are stable, but also in the sense of more warm and friendly. Handlebars are made of rubber and plastic with the effect of imitation aluminum wire drawing, reducing the discomfort of pushing and pulling, reflecting the people-oriented design concept and strengthening the user's tactile feeling. The bottom frame and bearing pipe are made of stainless steel, which are wear-resistant and strong. The following is the display effect of the specific innovative design, as shown in Fig. 4.

Fig. 4. Smart shopping cart design display

Finally combining the particle scale to satisfaction survey design, seven points represent very satisfied, 6 points represent relatively satisfied, five points represent satisfaction, four points on behalf of the state of compromise, three representative are not satisfied, two points represent more dissatisfied, 1 points represent very dissatisfied, said the average user satisfaction of design scheme evaluation [7]. Eighty-six questionnaires were sent out and 80 were received. The assessors ranged in age from 18 to 35. According to the data, the final satisfaction is estimated to be 5.88 points, which indicates that the subjects are generally satisfied with the design scheme.

5   Conclusion

Research methods in this article, through the perceptual engineering, SD for younger users survey questionnaire, collecting and quantify the sensibility of smart shopping cart vocabulary, through further analysis it is concluded that target users, the perceptual demand for smart shopping cart, finally established have qualitative feeling "contracted", "portable large capacity", "affinity streamline of the" three design elements. At the same time, users' functional needs and scene characteristics should also be taken into account, so as to meet users' expected emotional experience in appearance, and to be intelligent and convenient in operation, in line with consumers' usage habits and meet offline supermarket scenes. Finally combining the basic principles of ergonomics in the final smart shopping cart innovative design practice, also passes through the design experts and public recognition, this suggests that the design method based on perceptual technology, not only provides a new design idea for smart shopping cart direction, also for emotional intention of such products increased worthy of reference and the method.

References

1. Asch Inshi, W., Heuer, H.: A procedure to determine the individually comfortable position of visual displays relative to the eyes. Ergonomics **42**(4), 535–549 (1999)
2. Dillon, T.W.: Some factors affecting reports of visual fatigue resulting from use of a VDT. Comput. Hum. Behav. **12**(1), 49–59 (1996)
3. Zhang, X.: Research on Lamp Design Based on Kansei Engineering. North China University of Technology, Beijing (2019)
4. Song, D., Gu, J., Hou, H.: Modeling design of elderly electric bicycle based on Kansei engineering AHP. Packag. Eng. **40**(8), 130–135 (2019)
5. Jitender, P.S.: Understanding the relationship between aesthetics and product design. Int. J. Eng. Technol. Sci. Res. **5**(3), 6 (2018)
6. Dongjiu, Y., Xianqin, Y., Xiang, W.: Research on shopping cart design for the elderly based on user experience. Packag. Eng. **38**(12), 99–103 (2017)
7. Zhao, X., Wei, F., Hu, Z.: Research on office wireless mouse shape design based on Kansei engineering. J. Fujian Inst. Technol. **18**(04), 403–408 (2020)

New Experience of Maternal and Infant Shopping APP Under VR+AR Technology

Tianyue Zhang(✉), Ren Long, and Fowad Ahmad

School of Mechanical Science and Engineering, Huazhong University of Science and Technology, Wuhan 430074, People's Republic of China

Abstract. In recent years, maternal and child e-commerce has become one of the valuable marketing vehicles for the expansion of the maternal and child market. However, the current maternal and child shopping apps on the market still have some problems such as homogenization of styles, poor icon recognition, and cumbersome operations. To cope up the shopping needs of the parenting user group, the APP will be designed in combination with VR and AR technology. The virtual reality technology will make online flat shopping three-dimensional, and the realistic scenes and real-time interaction will increase the fun of shopping for users. In the design process, the childcare user group used as the research object, and the mother and baby e-commerce platform were researched. Through semi-structured interviews, users' cognition, emotion, behavior, psychology, etc. were explored, observe the pain points faced by the users and shopping needs were analyzed deeply and then summarized. Combining user behavior and interaction design help us to construct an interactive model, and propose design strategies for maternal and infant APP i.e. design styles, interface colors, page layouts, etc. Through VR+AR technology, the difference between photos and physical objects can be solved, and users' safety requirements for maternal and infant products can be followed, whereas psychological expectations are higher and other issues while reducing the experience difference between online shopping and offline shopping through the "people-oriented" interface design method to improve the user's shopping experience. Introducing a new shopping experience without leaving home and immersively, while improving user stickiness, it can also bring us to a new direction of thinking for maternal and child shopping APP design.

Keywords: VR · AR · Maternal and infant online shopping · User experience · Interface design

1 Introduction

1.1 Research Background

With the gradual increase in the level and standards of childcare, the proportion of maternal and child-related expenditures in total household expenditures have rapidly increased. The continuous expansion in the maternal and infant industry will center on the needs and experience of users [1], drive the bottom-up transformation of the supply

C. Stephanidis et al. (Eds.): HCII 2021, CCIS 1421, pp. 464–472, 2021.
https://doi.org/10.1007/978-3-030-78645-8_59

chain, and bring more in-depth online and offline borderless integration. At present, the post-'80s and 90 births are at the peak of their age. Due to the rapid development of the Internet, these young parents are very keen to use mobile smartphones to purchase products in fragmented time through maternal and child apps. Such parenting users need a more comfortable, efficient, and reliable shopping experience. A good shopping experience has gradually become the essence of consumption [2]. Therefore, building a mobile APP can meet the shopping needs of parenting users will definitely have a positive impact on the construction and development of the maternal and infant industry.

1.2 Research Significance

Mostly the childcare users are still having concerns about the difference between photos and the actual product while shopping for maternal and child products online and even about incomplete product information. So we designed a shopping app designed specifically for parenting groups. According to the emotional experience [2], interactive experience, and visual experience of the parenting user group, explore the needs of users [1, 3, 4], realize AR try-on through the motion capture system [5], and view mobile phone screen shopping in VR [6]. These help parenting users to purchase suitable and reliable products in a secure way. But at the same time allowing users to have a fresh and interesting shopping experience during the purchase process [7, 8], help them optimize the shopping process, and to reduce the problems encountered by users found during online shopping.

2 Analysis of Target Users

2.1 User Research

This user survey is aimed at users who are childcare users. The research is conducted through semi-structured interviews to understand the functional and psychological needs of users for the APP. In this interview, there are two parenting users who are preparing for pregnancy, pregnant, and already have a baby, a total of six. In order to protect user privacy, the numbers of A1–A6 are used to replace six users. The interview questions are as follows:

Question

(I)   What needs do you typically use for mother-to-child shopping apps?
(II) When do you generally use the Mother and Child Shopping APP?
(III) What are your satisfactory situations when shopping for APP with mother and child, please specify?
(IV) Have you ever downloaded a mother-to-child shopping APP and then uninstalled it, please specify?
(V)   What do you expect from the Mother and Child Shopping APP?
(VI) Would you like to use a mother-to-child shopping APP that combines VR and AR technology? (Table 1).

Table 1. Interviewed user information.

Name	Age	Profession	Status	Needs	Common functions
A1	23	White-collar workers	Preparing for pregnancy	Diversity, safety	Recommendation purchase experience
A2	25	Teacher	Preparing for pregnancy	Service, price	Experience exchange, preferential benefits
A3	27	Housewife	5 months pregnant	Picture, physical consistency	Experience exchange, purchase experience
A4	31	Sales	8 months pregnant	Safety, price	Product details purchase recommendations
A5	32	Designer	Raising a baby (2 years old)	Comfortable shopping experience, excellent after-sales service	Product details, experience exchange
A6	28	Merchant	Raising a baby (3 months)	Safety, image, consistency	Product classification, preferential benefits

2.2 Result Analysis

(I) At this stage, the age of parenting users is mainly between 25–35 years old, and female users have strong purchasing power and pay more attention to product quality, price, shopping methods, and experience.

(II) The main reasons why parenting users are not satisfied with the existing maternal and infant shopping apps available in the market are: the gap between the product picture and the actual product, the product information is not perfect, the APP interface is not user friendly or not beautiful enough, and the shopping experience is weak.

2.3 Create a Character

Through the above analysis, the main portrait of the character is established (Fig. 1).

2.4 User Needs Analysis

See Table 2.

Ms. Wang, a 32-year-old designer, currently working in Shanghai, has a 6-month-old baby

"It is difficult to have a very comfortable online shopping experience, especially buying clothes for my baby"

Status

1. She is busy at work and tend to shop online.

2. She hopes the shopping process is simple and fun.

3. She often hesitates in the process of shopping.

Behavior

1. She browses shopping apps in her free time.

2. She is not good at choosing products that suit her in shopping apps.

3. She likes to exchange parenting experiences with other parenting users.

Goals

1. She hopes to experience a fun and comfortable shopping experience.

2. She hopes to buy the most cost-effective and desirable products.

3. Higher efficiency

Motivation

1. Advocating scientific economy

2. Pay more attention to the quality and price of goods

3. Browse and shop through fragmented time

Pain points

1. Little parenting experience, hoping to buy easy-to-use and cost-effective products

2. When shopping online, it often happens that the product is inconsistent with the real product, or the upper body effect of clothing is not good, etc.

Fig. 1. The user portrait

Table 2. User needs table based on user interviews

Demand type	Demand
Emotional experience	As a mother-to-child shopping APP, it needs to establish the product brand style, improve the user's awareness of the product. While using these products, the users can really feel the warmth of mother and child software, fresh tone, establish the link between the APP and the user
Interactive experience	APP should give full consideration to the use habits of such special user groups as child-rearing users, be easy to operate, and strengthen the user's operational guidance. Maintain consistency of interaction, optimize the level of information between products, and present information more clearly to users
Visual experience	Users have certain aesthetic requirements for products, the use of warm tones, design elements tend and emotional, so that users from the psychological sense of trust get strong convincement. Streamline the layout of the interface, the interface style warm and warm, so that users more focused on information content. Maintain visual style consistency and improve the user experience
Functionality	In order to meet the user's needs for APP, streamline the shopping process, classify the information, so that users can find the content they need more quickly and accurately. Introduce a new form of shopping ways in existing VR and AR technology based shopping and social features

After digging into the needs of users, the following design principles are proposed for the design of APP:

(I)   Clear: Clear structure, Clear style, and layout, increase user's operational fluency.
(II) Efficient: Let users better understand product information functions through a simple and beautiful interface design.
(III) Quality: Reflect product quality through user's interaction and feedback.

3   Design Practice

3.1   Software Architecture Design and Low-Fidelity Flow Chart

Through the way of information architecture, the APP design ideas are visually presented. Through the previous user analysis theory research, the information architecture diagram and flow chart of the Baby APP is designed, so that the parenting users can have the best in the process of using Use experience, as shown in the Fig. 2:

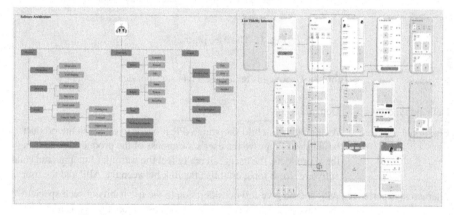

Fig. 2. Software architecture design and low-fidelity flow chart

4   Main Functions

4.1   VR Shopping

A virtual space is created through VR technology. Users can manipulate virtual objects through APP and immerse themselves in the created vivid environment. VR constitutes a traditional flat online shopping platform that is three-dimensional, interactive, and similar to real store shopping. VR vividly fills a three-dimensional space in the experience space, and the user forms a vivid interaction by manipulating the mobile phone. The whole scene is also divided into a special area for nursing products, a special area for clothing products, a special area for food products, and a special area for digital and electronic products, corresponding to the categories on the APP. Here, the VR scene improves the user's immersive shopping experience, increases the user's sense of security during shopping, and effectively combines online shopping with offline shopping. In the interface, a lot of IP images are designed, which can guide users who have just used it (Fig. 3).

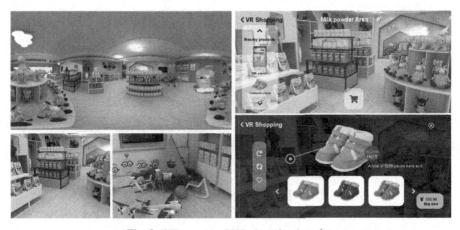

Fig. 3. VR scene and VR shopping interface

4.2 AR Try On

When most people buy clothing online, they imagine the actual state they are wearing. However, the upper body effect of the clothing is very different from the imagined state and it is difficult for users to know whether the clothing is really suitable for them. Therefore, we have enhanced the clothing model through AR technology. When a childcare user buys clothes for a baby, the childcare user turns on the camera of the mobile phone, and the software captures the image of the user through a motion capture system such as *Ryuzo Okada* [2], so that the user can see the baby wearing the clothes on the mobile phone.

Person Recognition. The image information of the baby is input through the depth camera scan, and then the position and dynamics of the baby in reality are captured. This allows the parenting user to directly "dress up" the baby. Choose the clothing type in the clothing category on the left, such as clothes, pants, shoes, hats, etc.; on the right are the specific styles of each clothing type. Parenting users choose clothing styles and drag them to the baby, and the clothing automatically captures the baby's body dynamics, and the user can directly see the baby's upper body effect on the mobile phone (Fig. 4).

4.3 Community Discussion

In the process of desktop surveys and semi-structured user interviews, we found that parenting users have an exciting need for the exchange of parenting-related experiences. Therefore, the two functions of community discussion and parenting encyclopedia are added to the APP. Community discussions are used to post updates, comments, discussions, etc., and parenting encyclopedia is used to publish parenting-related knowledge and parenting experience sharing. These two functions can effectively attract user experience and improve user stickiness (Fig. 5).

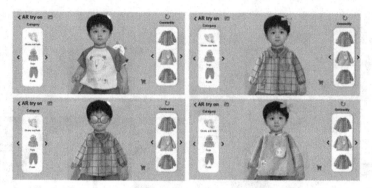

Fig. 4. AR try-on interface

Fig. 5. Community discussion and parenting experience interface

4.4 Immersive Shopping Experience

When the user clicks on the product, he will enter into an immersive page where he can gain a more comprehensive and in-depth understanding of the product's appearance, performance, etc., and present the product as a whole in the most intuitive way (Fig. 6).

4.5 Other Important Functions Display

We have unified the overall style of the APP, applied warm tones and soft curves to the functional components of the APP, and also standardized the icons. The following is a display of other important interfaces (Fig. 7).

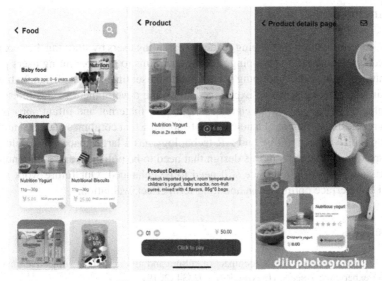

Fig. 6. Immersive page display

Fig. 7. Other important interface display

5 Heuristic Evaluation of the Evaluation Prototype

After completing the interactive prototyping of the APP, we recruited six graduate design students as evaluation experts, focusing on exploring the fun, functionality, usability, and aesthetics of the application. We provided each evaluator with a 0–4 rating table and prototype, and asked the evaluator for their opinions. The evaluation results show that the feedback situation is generally positive, and the VR scene shopping and AR try-on functions of the APP are both exciting. Evaluation experts believe that these two functions can indeed bring users a brand-new shopping experience, which can give users a sense of psychological security to a certain extent, and at the same time stimulate users' desire to buy. Evaluation experts are willing to try this APP.

6 Conclusion

This product simulates the shopping scenes of parenting users by studying the core points and needs in the parenting shopping process, and aims to help parenting users provide more intuitive and natural shopping scenes, while presenting users with a more branded, interesting and strong sense of experience. With the development of the Internet, the development in shopping experience of potential of maternal and infant apps is huge. Therefore, the development of a new form of shopping that combines maternal and child shopping with VR technology and AR technology has a large space for development. There are still some details in this design that need to be polished, and some indication functions under the VR interface still need to be enhanced. Our future work is more focused on interface optimization and long-term effect evaluation.

References

1. Santoso, H.B., Schrepp, M.: The impact of culture and product on the subjective importance of user experience aspects. Heliyon **5**(9), e02434 (2019)
2. Jia, J., Dong, X.: User experience classification based on emotional satisfaction mechanism. In: Marcus, A., Wang, W. (eds.) Design, User Experience, and Usability. Design Philosophy and Theory: 8th International Conference, DUXU 2019, Held as Part of the 21st HCI International Conference, HCII 2019, Orlando, FL, USA, July 26–31, 2019, Proceedings, Part I, pp. 450–459. Springer, Cham (2019). https://doi.org/10.1007/978-3-030-23570-3_33
3. Schmitt, B.: Experiential marketing. J. Mark. Manag. **15**(1–3), 53–67 (1999)
4. Verhoef, P.C., Lemon, K.N., Parasuraman, A., et al.: Customer experience creation: determinants, dynamics and management strategies. J. Retail. **85**(1), 31–41 (2009)
5. Xu, S., et al.: Augmented reality fashion show using personalized 3D human models. In: Yamamoto, S., Mori, H. (eds.) Human Interface and the Management of Information. Designing Information: Thematic Area, HIMI 2020, Held as Part of the 22nd International Conference, HCII 2020, Copenhagen, Denmark, July 19–24, 2020, Proceedings, Part I, pp. 435–450. Springer, Cham (2020). https://doi.org/10.1007/978-3-030-50020-7_31
6. Apostolakis, K.C., Margetis, G., Stephanidis, C.: 'Bring your own device' in VR: intuitive second-screen experiences in VR isolation. In: Stephanidis, C., Antona, M., Ntoa, S. (eds.) HCI International 2020 – Late Breaking Posters: 22nd International Conference, HCII 2020, Copenhagen, Denmark, July 19–24, 2020, Proceedings, Part II, pp. 137–144. Springer, Cham (2020). https://doi.org/10.1007/978-3-030-60703-6_17
7. Pine, B.J., Pine, J., Gilmore, J.H.: The Experience Economy: Work is Theatre & Every Business a Stage. Harvard Business Press, Boston (1999)
8. Veilleux, M., et al.: Visualizing a user's cognitive and emotional journeys: a fintech case. In: Marcus, A., Rosenzweig, E. (eds.) Design, User Experience, and Usability. Interaction Design: 9th International Conference, DUXU 2020, Held as Part of the 22nd HCI International Conference, HCII 2020, Copenhagen, Denmark, July 19–24, 2020, Proceedings, Part I, pp. 549–566. Springer, Cham (2020). https://doi.org/10.1007/978-3-030-49713-2_38

HCI, Safety and Sustainability

Designing Data Visualization Assistance for a Bioacoustics Labeling Software

Carlos Arce-Lopera(✉) (iD), Paula García-Muñoz, Sebastián Restrepo-Quiceno,
Daniel Gómez-Marín, and Gustavo A. Londoño

Universidad Icesi, 760046 Cali, Colombia
caarce@icesi.edu.co

Abstract. Biodiversity monitoring through bioacoustics is gaining momentum as a way to promote conservation in highly biodiverse countries. However, in these regions, bioacoustic analysis is a complex task due to the diversity of overlapping sound sources coming to the recording microphones at the same time. Moreover, commonly, this highly subjective classification is performed manually by expert biologists trained for identifying different species by their particular sound. This cumbersome task is performed with non-specialized software. Here, we propose a visualization interface based on an interaction design process through a user-centered design philosophy.

Keywords: Human-centered computing · Visualization design and evaluation methods · Bioacoustics · Audio labelling

1 Introduction

Bioacoustic monitoring is an increasingly important activity promoting nature conservation. For example, by measuring the impact of human activity on the wild animal population, conservation strategies can be implemented on time [1]. Moreover, current remote monitoring technologies seek not only to register the number of species but also to identify them. Indeed, technology has been a fundamental way to complete the task of monitoring nature, and specifically birds' populations [1]. Birds are one of the most popular animals studied by bioacoustics monitoring due to their sparse distribution over a wide range of landscapes.

Traditionally, to survey animal populations the most common technique is to use manual methods that involve capturing samples. These techniques require considerable amounts of time and energy from biology and ornithology experts. However, the use of digital technology has gained popularity in bioacoustics research projects, as novel remote monitoring techniques facilitate counting and decrease errors when gathering and labeling the data. Moreover, experts do not need to be in the field all the time to obtain data. Also, sound recordings can be reviewed multiple times in laboratories.

Typically, in the field, data is gathered through an Autonomous Recording Unit (ARU). However, ARUs generate a large number of sound files, making difficult the task of archiving, querying, analyzing, and recovering them [2]. Additionally, gathered

© Springer Nature Switzerland AG 2021
C. Stephanidis et al. (Eds.): HCII 2021, CCIS 1421, pp. 475–482, 2021.
https://doi.org/10.1007/978-3-030-78645-8_60

bioacoustics data usually requires to be labeled to identify species present in a determined soundscape [3]. Traditional ARU's are usually made up of a single microphone. However, to enable sound source localization, arrays of microphones have been developed for 360° degree recording.

Biologists use sound data visualizations to aid the labeling task. For example, birds' vocalizations are usually shown as spectrograms. This visualization allows users to see the frequency, energy, and time information of a sound file, which are essential for the identification task. As a result, visualization of bioacoustics data is essential in the data labeling process and presents the main challenges for product designers that develop this kind of visualization software.

Despite their crucial role, bioacoustics researchers have found very few software alternatives that allow simple and straightforward visualization and labeling for their research purpose. Most of them use general-purpose sound labeling software designed for musicians or sound engineers, such as Audacity. In those types of products, the data visualization and annotation are poorly integrated making the task difficult and time-consuming for researchers.

Here, a user-centered design approach was performed to improve the user experience for bioacoustic researchers. A web prototype was built and tested to evaluate several proposals for a graphical user interface separated by functionalities following the Atomic Design framework. The testing of the design proposals was done using quantitative metrics and qualitative feedback to find the best design options for several of the necessities of bioacoustic labeling software users.

2 Methods

The project was divided into two phases following a Research through Design [4] approach. First, a contextual research was performed aiming at the understanding of the people and the context around the problem. Then, a prototype as a possible solution to the problem was tested.

2.1 Contextual Research

As an initial study to define the project scope, users of bioacoustic monitoring systems were approached, mainly researchers in charge of audio-based bird identification. A series of qualitative methods were applied to understand the user's main needs and requirements to visualize this type and amount of data. Eleven expert professionals participated in the study. All of them had previously worked with bioacoustics data analysis. Four of them were ornithologists and the rest were herpetologists who had participated in bioacoustics data reviews for listing species.

All subjects were interviewed using a semi-structured format about their work experience, their needs, and experiences of bioacoustics labeling. In the second stage, an observational method was applied to subjects while labeling to identify possible needs that were overlooked during the interviews. Finally, having an insight into their work, an immersion method was performed to review the scientific software used by the different subjects. Using this method, their most-used scientific software was reviewed. As a result, a usability and design perspective was described and analyzed through an affinity diagram, converging into the main needs and requirements.

2.2 Prototype Testing Phase

A high-fidelity and functional prototype was built in a web environment to test the functionalities. The prototype collected automatically quantitative data useful to analyze the usability performance. The evaluation of the prototype consisted of two measures: the user experience and the usability. The User Engagement Scale was used to measure the quality of the user experience [5]. Usability was measured using two variables: time and number of clicks.

3   Contextual Research Results

Contextual research revealed the following issues in current methodologies used for bioacoustics labeling:

1. A single software is not enough to do all the different tasks.
2. Identifying multiple species recorded singing simultaneously is a very difficult task.
3. Spectrograms are the most important aspect. However, most of the current used software had limited spectrogram interaction.
4. Most interfaces convey an overwhelming sensation of complexity.
5. Users feel the need to speed up the labeling process.

These issues were clustered into three main categories:

Intuitive Information Architecture. To avoid the complexity sensation caused by presenting all possible functionalities, the user interface must prioritize users' main features, which are related to interacting with spectrograms.

Enhanced User Interface Usability. The lack of a friendly and easy-to-learn labeling software is a barrier to having an engaging bioacoustics data labeling experience. To enhance the experience, the software interface should be designed taking a user-centric approach to allow the users to work efficiently.

Multiple Correlated Data Visualization. The bioacoustics data gathered when using microphone arrays is correlated in time and space in which it was recorded. Users should be able to review these arrays and compare records made with different entries at the same time.

4   Design Rationale

According to the contextual research results, a new bioacoustics data visualization and labeling interface was implemented. For this user interface, six different functionalities were the focus of the design. The functionalities were created using the Atomic Design.

This methodology is based on a mental model where the interface is viewed as a system where the most elemental or basic parts are classified as atoms.

For each functionality, two proposals were designed. The proposals were embedded in a web application (see Fig. 1) that randomly presented the functionalities to users in pairs so that they could compare both proposals for each functionality. The web application had three buttons: start/end, save, and next. When the user pressed "start", it began to count the time and number of clicks until the user pressed again to indicate that he had finished interacting. Then, the user could press "next" to see the interaction with another proposal. Finally, pressing the "save" button generated a file with the time and number of clicks for that particular user.

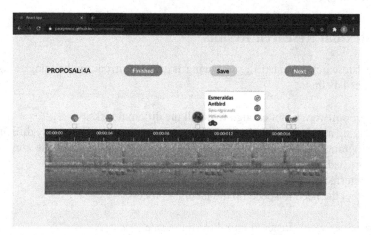

Fig. 1. Web application for testing the design proposals based on functionalities. Note: This figure was translated to English from Spanish.

Based on the insights found in the contextual research, the six most important functionalities for the labelling software are as follows:

1. Spectrogram Adjustments
Proposal 1A displayed default color palettes for the user to choose from along with 2 sliders to change brightness and contrast. Proposal 1B allowed the user to choose their own color palette through a color wheel. In addition, the brightness and contrast were modified through a circular slider.

2. Comparison of Multiple Correlated Data Registers
Proposal 2A was designed using a hexagonal shape from a bird-eye view. In Proposal 2B, the audio channels were placed as vertically stacked layers.

3. Species Labeling of an Identified Fragment of Sound
In Proposal 3A, a labeling form was designed with drop-down menus in the text fields. In Proposal 3B, a "species under study" section was implemented where images of

the species being identified appeared; and by clicking on the image all text fields were auto-completed.

4. System Recommendations in Full Spectrogram
Proposal 4A is based on markers with images of the bird to be suggested above the time when the bird begins to sing. Proposal 4B had colored markers according to the probability of success of the suggestion covering the whole range of time from when the bird starts and finishes singing.

5. System Recommendations in a Selected Section of Spectrogram
Proposal 5A had markers with images and focused only on one suggestion (the one most likely to succeed). Proposal 5B had the classification by color according to the probability of success of the proposal and had more than one suggestion for each stretch where an audio can be found.

6. System Recommendations for a Specific Fragment of Sound Ready for Labeling
The two proposals (6A and 6B) had suggestions from several audios conducted by other researchers of the same suggested species. However, Proposal 6B hid the suggestions with a drop-down menu and implemented the color classification according to probability.

5   Experimental Design

For the evaluation of the designed proposals, a total of 36 participants interacted with the prototype. They were asked to complete a task with both designed proposals for each functionality. Each functionality was evaluated 20 times. After the interaction with each designed proposal, participants filled a user engagement scale survey [5]. When participants interacted with both proposals testing a functionality, they gave their opinion about which proposal was preferred and what aspects were the most interesting. To avoid any bias for a particular designed proposal, the web prototype randomized the order in which functionalities and designed proposals were presented to the participants.

The data obtained for each design was normalized to an expected ideal value. That is, for each designed proposal a pilot test was carried out to obtain the ideal times and numbers of clicks to perform each of the proposed tasks. The data were normalized to compare it with a scale (from 0 to 1) directly proportional to each other. Therefore, all results are normalized to ideal measures controlled by the experimenter.

6   Prototype Results

6.1   Simpler Interactions Should Be Proposed to Save Time

Users sought for the faster way to achieve their tasks in the software, mainly to avoid distractions during the labor. They preferred the proposals where the interaction was standard and limited, rather than the ones where they could have greater freedom manipulating data.

When interacting with the first functionality (spectrogram adjustments) the proposal 1A performed with better results than 1B (see Fig. 2) in general engagement, number of clicks, and time. In general, users expressed that proposal 1B was interesting because it allowed many possibilities and gave them the freedom to select their own color on the wheel. However, their preferred proposal was 1A because it was punctual and saved them from having to think with the default color palettes it offered.

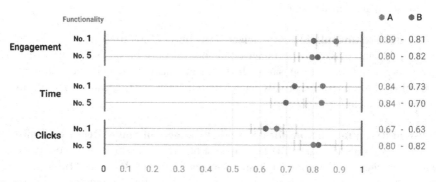

Fig. 2. First and fifth functionality. Engagement and usability metrics performance according to the ideal for each proposal.

In addition, users claimed that it felt easier to interact with proposals where the display of information was limited to the most important aspects. In the 5th functionality, where all engagement and clicks metrics performed similarly (see Fig. 2.), the preferred proposal was 5A on which the time the users spent was slightly more accurate to the ideal. Users felt confused with proposal 5B, and 5A felt easier because not all information was displayed at once. This highlighted the need of providing the least interaction required at first, and leave hints for users to start exploring deep if needed.

6.2   The Spatial Representation of the Data is Important

Users appreciated the visualizations that helped them locate data in space and time accurately. In the second functionality (comparison of multiple correlated data registers), proposal 2A simulated a hexagonal shape using a bird's eye view as if the user were in the field listening to the audios. This proposal had better results than proposal 2B in all the dimensions evaluated. Users expressed that proposal 2B was difficult for spatial location, which rendered it unintuitively. Particularly, proposal A had a higher result in terms of time, which supported the positive perception of usability expressed by the subjects (see Fig. 3).

Something similar happened in the evaluation of the 4th functionality on which users preferred proposal 4A for the use of explicit markers on spectrograms. Markers saved time for completing the task (see Fig. 3.) The interaction let them identify faster when a bird was singing and which species was the system suggesting them. Future visual interface interactions should be designed considering spatial representation as a key for locating and guiding the users through the software.

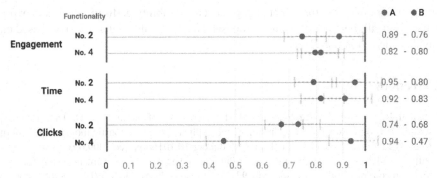

Fig. 3. Second and fourth functionality. Engagement and usability metrics performance according to the ideal for each proposal.

6.3 Good Use of Colors Generates Engagement and Usability Performance

Visual engagement is highly enforced by the use of colors. Multiple participants mentioned they are more likely to enjoy working with software whose visual interfaces are not limited to grayscale colors, such as the software they had used before. When interacting with the 6th functionality, users preferred proposal 6A, mainly because elements were more visually salient than proposal 6B. The clicks performance for proposal 6B was significantly different than the ideal (see Fig. 4). In this case, users couldn't find a specific element to complete the task, it was completely unnoticed by the users. Moreover, after the interaction with both proposals of each functionality, users always highlighted visual interactions from one proposal that they would like to have in their preferred proposal as a complement.

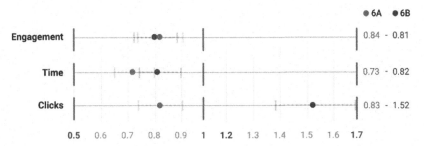

Fig. 4. Sixth functionality. Engagement and usability metrics performance according to the ideal for each proposal.

7 Conclusion

For designing the user interface of a bioacoustics labeling software that seeks an intuitive information architecture and enhanced usability, the use of the Atomic Design approach was applied. The evaluation of the user interface by parts revealed three main guidelines to implement: simpler interactions to save time, spatial representations of the data, and appropriate use of colors for higher engagement and usability performance. Future work should group all the aforementioned proposals in a single user interface (UI), based on insights collected in this phase.

References

1. Bardeli, R., Wolff, D., Kurth, F., Koch, M., Tauchert, K.-H., Frommolt, K.-H.: Detecting bird sounds in a complex acoustic environment and application to bioacoustic monitoring. Pattern Recogn. Lett. **31**, 1524–1534 (2010). https://doi.org/10.1016/j.patrec.2009.09.014
2. Villanueva-Rivera, L.J., Pijanowski, B.C.: Pumilio: a web-based management system for ecological recordings. Bull. Ecol. Soc. Am. **93**, 71–81 (2012). https://doi.org/10.1890/0012-9623-93.1.71
3. Vallee, M.: The science of listening in bioacoustics research: sensing the animals' sounds. Theory Cult. Soc. **35**, 47–65 (2018). https://doi.org/10.1177/0263276417727059
4. Olson, J.S., Kellogg, W.A. (eds.): Ways of Knowing in HCI. Springer, New York (2014). https://doi.org/10.1007/978-1-4939-0378-8
5. O'Brien, H.L., Cairns, P., Hall, M.: A practical approach to measuring user engagement with the refined user engagement scale (UES) and new UES short form. Int. J. Hum. Comput. Stud. **112**, 28–39 (2018). https://doi.org/10.1016/j.ijhcs.2018.01.004

Vulnerability Turning into a Key Design Criterion for Smart Mobility Concepts

Barbara Flügge[✉]

digital value creators (DVC) Ltd., and #MobilityMovesMinds Initiative Lead,
Bottighofen, Switzerland
barbara.fluegge@dvcconsult.com

Abstract. What is the impact of mobility on vulnerable groups? Vice versa we ask about the impact of vulnerable groups on the innovation design process. The poster will be practitioner oriented reflecting the #MobilityMovesMinds movement that converges digital, physical, and mental mobility. It looks into the building yet learning patterns of resilience. The exploration of resilience build is a two years' effort of Barbara Flügge, experts around the globe, vulnerable groups, and the homeless community. We chose the poster format to have an engaging element that the audience can carry on. As a carry-on tool the poster will be presented in audio and video format accessible in onsite and offline modes.

Keywords: Resilience · Inclusive mobility · Vulnerability · Mobility · Mindshift · Homelessness · Empowerment · Smart mobility · Mobility Moves Minds · MMM

1 The State of Play

COVID-19 provoked a massive demand shock. Unemployment and home losses far exceed the last recession. World-wide are more than 100 million people homeless, 1 billion live in inadequate housing, in some countries a 14% to 20% of the population is facing homeless or severe poverty. The vulnerability of many is increasing as the wealth of a few is increasing. How are we contributing to improving the quality of life? The G7 and EU are no exception because their most innovative approaches, housing first and basic universal income, do not aim to solve the real issue at hand: people need to be accountable, to work and have a purpose in life. That relates ultimately to the vision that Mobility Moves Minds is driving when targeting businesses that are able to grow again and herein transform into social business entities who ultimately give back purpose and means to the vulnerable society. In the Mobility Moves Minds research we have been investigating the correlation of individual and organizational resilience. There are several events that, when accumulated, can lead to a critical event, an incident, and herein turn into a barrier that individuals hit hard. What hits us and who is receptive to it is part of a formula we have been identifying throughout a three phased approach: 1) the openness that we apply to capture past experience that individuals acknowledged, 2) the relevance of complexity that steers our systems of thinking and acting, 3) the capacity that fosters

© Springer Nature Switzerland AG 2021
C. Stephanidis et al. (Eds.): HCII 2021, CCIS 1421, pp. 483–488, 2021.
https://doi.org/10.1007/978-3-030-78645-8_61

resilience capabilities, so that individuals nurture to overcome obstacles. The probability of facing a hit and run is increasing in the absence of reception, singular processing, and decreased mobility. Incidents we observed are of distinct nature for example being of geopolitical, pandemic, economic, and for societal nature. The mobility patterns of vulnerable groups were subject of assessing the daily living conditions. One of the personas we created is Geraldine. Here is her story.

1.1 Geraldine's Story

Geraldine could think of a better reason to get up at 4.30 AM in the morning. Walking over 15 min from where she stayed to the central station and catch the train to the airport. She recalls the comment from her boss in the last performance review meeting: "reach is just as important as the business itself". He recommended that she scaled up her project management and self-marketing skills. He handed over the registration documents for the project management certification class. Having already checked the budget and her availability it is better than perfect, Geraldine replied with a smile. She already pictured the next step: the certification will lift my skills up. She carries on: I will meet new peers and connect better with others on the same career level. Then, I am eligible for the program management roles and do not have to fight for being heard anymore. The truth is that it is Geraldine's mind that paints these pictures. After the first certification module, her boss called her in. Project proposals got rejected and the income stream was already in trouble. She got laid off within four weeks. Getting up this morning is hard. Without a future and no train to be caught, no airplane crew to be greeted, desperation wipes off her fighting spirit to get up at 4.30. A bitter tone sneaks in. Getting ready is so easy now. No business dress to choose, no suitcase to be packed and no business brief to be collected. She easily could have slept till lunch time. A pain travels through her body. The homeless shelter where she stays is literally hurting her and her back. Her moves at 4.35 AM carry her to the street around the corner where the supermarket is. Hoping to find PET bottles to collect and trade in. The distance Geraldine is capable to manage by feet with a hungry stomach and desperate thoughts is micro. Drawing our attention to mobility concepts, what does it take to Geraldine's movement radius? Will a better free of charge mobility raise her chances to get back to the working society? We rarely imagine what it takes to slow down moving until the ultimate stop pushes us back from leaning forward - unless an incident or emergency comes in. Following the viewpoint of Geraldine, how is Conrad feeling? Conrad is waiting at the bus stop. We are facing in our communities an increasing number of homelessness due to several reasons. In our daily rush we overlook those that are stuck. The longer it takes to get back into the working and moving society, the harder it gets to break the boundaries. And ultimately morph limits into chances. Geraldine recalls a nice summer break she took one year ago: spontaneously and out of the blue she chose an airline solely by destination and the highly recommended 5* hotels. Times when flexibility was her greatest asset. Her peer Conrad was less demanding. His family and he invested a new home when the call from his boss came in. Swamped by mortgage payments and loosing creditability at his home bank, he moved out and chose to share an Airbnb shelter with two other families. On a Monday morning he is waiting at the bus stop for the 7.38 AM bus to bring him to the unemployment center. At 7.45 AM he is still standing there.

2 Resilience is a Matter of Overcoming Obstacles and Negative Events and Having the Means to Move

There is wide research on the topic of individual, psychological resistance. How do Geraldine's and Conrad's needs are being resolved? What we know is that the resolution is not done with short-term accessibility to shelters and donated food. What we know is that the resolution lies within the amplitude of turning free – free to move and free to get any job, choose the place, and the distance. In the meantime, it is the obligation of the community to offer the public good of mobility to everyone else. One of the resolutions we have been investigating is the active inclusion. This involves homeless individuals without serious mental health and substance abuse issues, and are willing and able to be an active, working citizens. Effectively, the inclusion model called Homeless Entrepreneur provides holistic support during the first year, has a specific target audience, which is aimed at uplifting 20% of the homeless population in the G7 (423,852 homeless people) & EU (820,000 homeless people). Raising the bar high, smart mobility has gained global attendance from the rise of mega cities down to medium sized municipalities, networks of communities, and the rural area. And yet there, where public transportation operators, bus and railway operators focusing on profitability driven competition, these two stakeholder groups were amongst the ones that diminished the access to mobility, cut off urban connectivity and left vulnerable groups alone.

2.1 What is Smart Mobility at All?

The public sector and enterprises are confronted with infrastructure and investment decisions that steer these days the maneuverable mass of tomorrow. Two key prerequisites are apparent for success: 1) the intelligent and creative use of information and communications technologies as well as 2) the conscious alignment of organizational and project-based matters of the respective ecosystem. This is how we postulated it in our series of Smart Mobility. Even without the pandemic, geopolitical incidents or threatening attacks from intruders, the general public is struggling in offering smartness and mobility to everyone. Let's recap what smart mobility means. According to Flügge B. (2017): "Mobility is smart as soon as projects are implemented according to the following criteria: (1) beneficial for all stakeholders, (2) manageable for public and private infrastructures, and (3) for the benefit of the ecosystem. It is not without reason that the successful implementation of smart mobility concepts is one of the most important success factors for those responsible for smart cities, smart nations and smart regions". The cornerstones of proofing the three commandments cannot be less challenging: a functioning infrastructure, zero digital and physical divide, and the right to access mobility means.

2.2 Smart Mobility Solutions Ask for Accepting the Existence of Resilience and the Capacity of Cognitive Flexibility

With respect to vulnerable groups, resilience targets everyone being manager, organization, family, child in any living condition with can think of. Homelessness for example is on the raise in the EU and around the world. Any EU country is subject to homelessness, being it male, female, gender neutral entities or children, families, and singles. Homelessness is directly linked to (1) the maturity of social infrastructure and (2) existence and access to mental, digital, and physical assets. These assets are subject to an effective or ineffective deployment and furthermore operation, not to say automatism of a social infrastructure. Resilience is multi-structural and multi-diverse from reach to accessibility and individual to organizations and furthermore short term and long-term engagements. Pitrenaite-Zileniene, B., Torresi, F. (2014) identified about 30 elements that influence individuals, families and groups, organizations and institutions and communities. The infrastructural element of resilience is measured by silent success factors e.g. do zero incidents indicate the existence of resilience. Another example is the quality of impact measured by speed and performance – a normal performance is less qualitative than advanced performance. The element of systems acting is subject to impact generating resilience frameworks once interdependencies between projects, networks, and systems are recognized and optimized. Mobility Moves Minds by Flügge, B. (2021): we detected over the course of 2 years the resilience element of more than 20 individuals from 4 continents and more than 10 distinct industry segments. We have been focusing on businesspeople by intention. Throughout a specific resilience based semi-structured interview guide, we encountered that the interviewees too had occurrences and past events, showing signs of vulnerability. We turned our observations into more than 40 key takeaways, exercise and the R-Tool® with the so-called Resilience ABC, the Resilience Scouts and the Resilience Membrane. These tools and methods will now be used in the second phase of the project throughout the year 2021 to analyze the impact of resilience driven solution designs on the adoption of digital tools and means. A critical element is the one of the physical and digital mobility infrastructures of urban spaces.

2.3 Resilience and Vulnerability are Associated

Up to the point where resilience eliminates vulnerability and where vulnerability diminishes resilience. Challenges concerning resilience are manifold – a broad body of knowledge is being developed on resilience matters for decades and centuries, the so-called genealogy of the concept of resilience. Points of view are ranging from resilient natural ecosystems to economic stability, from human beings to organizations, ranging from structural recovery to mental health. Humanmade disasters, waste and energy excess are expected to be diminished in a stringent and systematic manner by human society. The Mobility Moves Minds project focused on a transformational framework that helps institutions, policy makers, individuals like experts and organizations to share and apply a human-centric approach that fosters an intrinsic, resilience driven motif to diminish obstacles and grow into a resilient mode from within!

3 Applied Method

We started with the assessment of daily resilience needs and its impact on distinct layers: social and organizational, local and cross-regional. We looked into social and daily living environments, in ecosystems of distinct sizes. Being small cells like a family-friend community, a district, a topic driven community and a larger cell like a region. The life stories we captured through Persona Profiling and the Resilience ABC. The Persona Profiling we have been applying in distinct scenarios over the last two years. The Resilience ABC is a novel method to score the resilience level of organizations and individuals in the urge to amplify the physical, digital, and mental capacity. Our implementation methodology was of active research layer driven, onsite and virtual observations of layers, interviews of layer-relevant associations, interest groups, and social infrastructure relevant policy makers. We dedicated our efforts on life stage assessments as for example of the City of Dresden from 2008 – one of the rare holistic reports that dedicated its focus to the jobless community from a resilience perspective and the element of collapsing into the state of homelessness. Applied project steps included the build of Checklists, Interaction Diagram and Communication Enabler for Stakeholder Communities, Status Tracking, Resilience Structures and Elements Mosaic. We looked into resilience facilitators - mental, physical, and digital means being of human and non-human nature. Results that have been revealed covered the first round of resilience factor determination by structural layers and pre- and post-pandemic elements with an implementation methodology of scene build, graphical and textual outline. Impact has been generated by capturing the impact of resilience with respect to the individual target groups and their influence on decision takers in public and private organizations. The specific of the Implementation Methodology included among scene build and data driven outline, the so-called silent dissemination. Silent dissemination refers to the active and direct involvement of constituents, passive and influential actors and our knowledge transfer and learnings from inside-out.

4   Designing Smart Mobility Solutions

The most challenging incidents are the ones that help vulnerable groups to be seen. The most challenging incidents are the ones that help the stakeholders and solution engineers what is needed. In a pandemic crisis, fulfilling official and appropriate countermeasures to flatten the pandemic curve and diminish the risk of re-vitalization of a virus spread is a huge challenge. In the current state of the Corona pandemic the European wide-spread occurred to very recent sources due to unrecognizable and because of that exponentially growing movements of individuals and groups. Herein, traceability, communicating, maintaining, and ensuring secure accommodation and medical housing are a complex and multi-stakeholder effort. The effort encompasses governmental, non-governmental, inter-governmental, non-profit, commercial, pop-up communities and individual entities. The burden of administrative cross-organizational business processing clashes with the identification and traceability of people that are hard to identify and capture. Herein, the holistic encountering of every facet of a vulnerable individual's living, working, moving, caring, and learning conditions turns into the prerequisite to design smart mobility solutions. Capturing holistically in a 360° manner the empathy, the fear, the movements in a perimeter of 1 to 1000 m maximum should become the first criteria to be addressed. Every vulnerable group has a persona characteristic and a personality of their own. The identity of any society member deserves to be taken into full consideration. That is the critical point where we raise our criticism to the Venture Capital market and the

Investors' Lounges and Large Events to overlook the ones that are in the vicinity, and rather aiming for helicopter driven perspectives – and herein acting superficial.

5   The Element of the Perimeter

So called smart mobility startups these days look into sharing and ride hailing, turn their focus on the ones with money and jobs to freely move around. Smart Mobility in our definition flips the imbalance and takes small steps first within a vicinity or a district. Micro Mobility turns into a whole novel meaning and (!) concept to offer mobility to everyone in every square meter.

References

1. Flügge, B. (ed.): Smart Mobility – Connecting Everyone. Springer, Wiesbaden (2017). https://doi.org/10.1007/978-3-658-15622-0
2. Flügge, B.: Mobility Moves Minds – Build and Grow again as a Business. Dean Publishing, Macedon (2021)
3. Pitrenaite-Zileniene, B., Torresi, F.: Integrated approach to a resilient city: associating social, environmental and infrastructure resilience in its whole. Eur. J. Interdisciplinary Stud. **6**, 1 (2014)

Using Service Design Thinking to Improve the Transportation Service of Shared Electric Scooters in Tourism Scenario

Shao-Yu Lee[ID] and Hsien-Hui Tang[(⊠)] [ID]

Department of Design, National Taiwan University of Science and Technology,
Taipei City 106335, Taiwan
drhhtang@gapps.ntust.edu.tw

Abstract. Taiwan's shared electric scooters suppliers enjoy a bigger market share by offering tourism service to boost the number of users and rental rate. However, they are concerned about maintaining service differentiation and sustainable development to enhance customer loyalty and satisfaction. This study aims to explore the possibility of excellent service. First, we take GoShare, a provider of shared electric scooters in Taiwan, as the research object, and use the regression analysis method to determine the key driving forces affecting NPS, and then use the interview method to determine the problem. Finally, we propose and verify the concept of optimized shared electric scooters tourism service. This study provides a case study on developing new service experience by transportation companies based on service design thinking. It helps companies find the key factors affecting customer loyalty and satisfaction through quantitative and qualitative methods to reference companies' strategy formulation and implementation.

Keywords: Service design · NPS · Driving force · Shared electric scooters · Tourism experience design

1 Introduction

Scooters are one of the most commonly used transportation modes for tourists in Taiwan, which has attracted several shared electric scooters suppliers to offer their services at tourist attractions. Service design thinking and tools can be used to study tourists' journey from a new perspective and provide special and satisfying services for tourists (Stickdorn and Zehrer 2009). However, maintaining service differentiation and sustainable development to improve customer loyalty and satisfaction has always been a problem faced by many companies. Many studies have pointed out a positive correlation between customer satisfaction and loyalty (Fornell et al. 1996; Bolton 1998). The limited resources, providing users with high-quality service, and effectively improving customer loyalty and satisfaction become very important.

Net Promoter Score (NPS) is an indicator for companies to measure and manage customer Loyalty, which is used to replace the lengthy traditional customer satisfaction survey (Reichheld 2003). NPS loyalty management, developed by BeBit, help companies

© Springer Nature Switzerland AG 2021
C. Stephanidis et al. (Eds.): HCII 2021, CCIS 1421, pp. 489–497, 2021.
https://doi.org/10.1007/978-3-030-78645-8_62

make long-term and short-term plans and use statistical analysis to clarify the influence between driving forces, experience scenarios and NPS. The key process and core driving forces are defined, and the crux of the problem is further identified through the qualitative method. The purpose of this case study is to provide potential service for transportation companies to improve user experience, number of users and scooter rental rate.

2   Methods

According to the triple-diamond model's design process, the research is divided into three phases: service design research, service design iteration, and service design validation. The research users are those who have travel experience with GoShare. Referring to the NPS loyalty management, this study analyzes the tourism service of Goshare through three levels: The top-level detects customer loyalty through NPS, and the middle-level measures customers' feelings on the service processes by satisfaction and the bottom-level measures customers' feelings on the service driving forces by satisfaction. The structure is shown in Fig. 1.

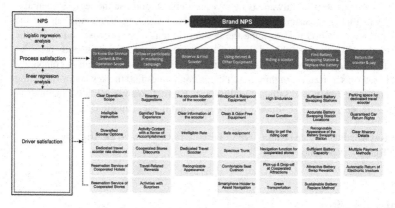

Fig. 1. NPS loyalty management structure

Service Design Research Stage. This study used observation and interview methods to sort out the seven stages of passengers using shared electric scooters and 37 driving forces. Then, we collected 249 valid questionnaires through the questionnaire survey method, including the NPS scores of the separate process and the satisfaction of driving forces. SPSS software is used to perform quantitative analysis for our study, logistic regression analysis to ensure the various processes that affect NPS, and linear regression analysis to determine the driving forces that affect process satisfaction. Finally, we summarize the core issues that affect the experience.

Service Design Iteration Stage. Based on the service concept of the customer journey map, discuss and evaluate the service concept with the product manager and user experience designer of GoShare. Finally, we put forward a feasible service concept.

Service Design Verification Stage. Forty-two volunteers from the service design research stage joined the service concept testing. We used contextual videos to present the service and collected each process's NPS scores and the satisfaction of driving forces through a questionnaire survey. After linear regression analysis of driving forces and satisfaction degree with SPSS software, the execution priority is compared according to the beta and satisfaction degree of driving forces. Finally, we put forward service optimization suggestions.

3 Results

3.1 Factors Influencing Customer Loyalty and Satisfaction of Shared Electric Scooters Tourism Service

NPS is used to measure customers' loyalty to Goshare. According to the score, the volunteers were divided into three categories: detractors (32%), passives (47%) and promoters (19%). The detractors' statistical score is -13, which means that most customers are unwilling to recommend services to relatives and friends, and customer loyalty still needs to be improved.

This study uses logistic regression analysis to test the influence of process satisfaction on NPS, with Passives as the benchmark category. There is a significant difference in the satisfaction of "riding a scooter" between detractors and passives. We also find comparing with the promoters, the passives' satisfaction with "follow or participate in marketing campaigns" and "return the scooter and pay" is statistically significant (Table 1). Therefore, this study speculates that improving the satisfaction of these three processes can turn detractors into passives and passives into promoters.

Table 1. Logistic regression analysis of process satisfaction of original service survey on NPS

Process	Detractors than passives	Promoters than passives
	p	p
To know the service content & the operation scope	0.112	0.261
Follow or participate in marketing campaigns	0.724	0.014*
Reserve & find scooter	0.795	0.422
Using helmet & other equipment	0.579	0.542
Riding a scooter	0.024*	0.050
Find battery swapping station & replace the battery	1.000	0.200
Return the scooter & pay	0.999	0.027*

*$p < 0.05$

According to the above three stages, linear regression analysis is used to test the influence of driving forces on process satisfaction. There are nine driving forces reach a significant level, and the standardization coefficient β is positive (Table 2). It is speculated that improving the satisfaction of these driving forces will have an opportunity to improve the corresponding process's satisfaction and then enhance the NPS.

Table 2. Linear regression analysis of the driving forces of the original service survey on the process satisfaction

Process	Driving force		β	p	Satisfaction
Follow or participate in marketing campaigns	S2-01	Itinerary suggestions	0.177	0.110	4.00
	S2-02	Activity content with a sense of accomplishment	0.274	0.064	3.79
	S2-03	Cooperated stores discounts	−0.118	0.370	3.46
	S2-04	Travel-related rewards	0.479	0.001*	3.83
	S2-05	Activities with surprises	0.234	0.126	3.72
Riding a scooter	S5-01	High endurance	0.175	0.002*	3.77
	S5-02	Great condition	0.361	0.000*	4.07
	S5-03	Easy to get the riding cost	0.281	0.000*	3.13
	S5-04	Navigation function for the APP	0.133	0.016*	3.85
	S5-05	Temporarily leave rate discount	0.039	0.472	2.85
	S5-06	Green transportation	0.146	0.009*	4.22
Return the scooter & pay	S7-01	Parking space for dedicated travel scooter	0.123	0.051	3.01
	S7-02	Guaranteed car return rights	0.222	0.001*	3.74
	S7-03	Clear itinerary details	0.246	0.000*	3.91
	S7-04	Multiple payment methods	0.219	0.001*	3.88
	S7-05	Automatic return of electronic invoices	0.059	0.349	4.07

$^{*}p < 0.05$

Combining the results of qualitative and quantitative research, this study summarizes the core problems of experience and puts forward the following suggestions:

Before Tourism. Link marketing and local tourism activities to avoid boredom and keep the diversity and freshness of activities to attract tourists.

In Tourism. Problems such as hard to find location-based service, few parking spots and unexpected expenses will reduce tourists' experience quality. Company should explain travel expenses clearly to tourists, set up rent-return stations and exclusive parking spaces in popular scenic spots and stations to improve the convenience of tourists' mobility and improve travel satisfaction.

After Tourism. Tourists' perception of the brand needs to be improved. Company can strengthen environmental awareness in their services and encourage tourists to share their experiences on social media to increase customer loyalty.

3.2 Development of Service Concept for Shared Electric Scooters Tourism Experience

Based on the needs and expectations of both users and company for tourism service, this study puts forward four service concepts, while information content, vehicle type specifications, and Internet of vehicles technology maintain the original services. Four service concepts are as follows:

GoShare Vacations. Shared electric scooter company partners with hotels to offer a service that allows users to pre-purchase ride times and book a room at a discounted price. Once they arrive at the hotel, they can travel on their exclusive electric scooter, and at the end of the trip, the remaining ride hours will be converted into coupons.

Worry-Free Travel. Shared electric scooter company cooperates with the government to set up rent-return stations and exclusive parking Spaces at stations and scenic spots and optimizes the navigation function of the APP to improve the convenience of traffic movement.

Industry Alliances. Shared electric scooter company connects the entire tourism ecosystem through cooperation with the store owners, such as restaurants and scenic spots. In addition to booking and paying through the APP, users can also get coupons when they complete specified tasks.

Eco-friendly Travel. Shared electric scooter company actively calculates users' cycling time and carbon emission reduction information during travel, and provides riding discounts and badges to encourage users to share their carbon reduction achievements and promote eco-friendly travel together.

3.3 Service Design Validation for Shared Electric Scooters Travel Experience

After optimizing the service, promoters accounted for 42%, and detractors accounted for 4% among volunteers. The NPS statistical result was 38, with a significant increase

Table 3. Comparison of NPS before and after service optimization

	Original service survey	New service testing	Difference
NPS	−13	38	51
Proportion of promoters	19%	42%	23%
Proportion of passives	47%	52%	5%
Proportion of detractors	32%	4%	−28%

Table 4. Comparison of process satisfaction before and after service optimization

Process	Original service survey	New service testing	Difference
To know the service content & the operation scope	3.77	4.24	0.47
Follow or participate in marketing campaigns	3.78	3.95	0.17
Reserve & find scooter	3.69	4.24	0.55
Using helmet & other equipment	3.40	4.24	0.84
Riding a scooter	3.93	4.31	0.38
Find battery swapping station & replace the battery	3.77	3.95	0.18
Return the scooter & pay	3.80	4.19	0.39

of 51 points than the original service (Table 3). Satisfaction increased in each process (Table 4), indicating that the service concept helps to improve customer loyalty and satisfaction.

A linear regression analysis was conducted on driver satisfaction and process satisfaction after service optimization in this study. There are seven driving forces reached a significant level, and the beta was positive, representing a positive impact on process satisfaction (Table 5). Further chart analysis shows that projects located in the first quadrant can positively influence users' satisfaction with the process and meet their needs and expectations, so they have a higher priority, followed by the fourth quadrant. The results are shown in Fig. 2. Due to the accurate location of the scooter (J3-01), clear information of the scooter (J3-02), safe equipment (J4-03) belong to the original service, no further discussion, so the priority order of execution is parking space for dedicated travel scooter (J7-01), easy to get the riding cost (J5-03), dedicated travel scooter rate discount (J1-04), Navigation function for cooperated stores (J5-04) cooperation businesses.

3.4   Implementation Suggestions on Shared Electric Scooters Travel Experience

Based on the above research, the implementation plan and suggestions of Shared electric scooter company tourism service design are as follows:

Table 5. Linear regression analysis of the driver satisfaction of new service testing on process satisfaction

Process	Driving force		β	p	Satisfaction
To know the service content & the operation scope	J1-04	Dedicated travel scooter rate discount	0.430	0.009*	4.07
Reserve & find scooter	J3-01	The accurate location of the scooter	0.524	0.000*	4.15
	J3-02	Clear information of the scooter	0.270	0.048*	4.32
Using helmet & other equipment	J4-03	Safe equipment	0.436	0.009*	3.75
Riding a scooter	J5-03	Easy to get the riding cost	0.355	0.023*	4.32
	J5-04	Navigation function for cooperated stores	0.383	0.025*	4.07
Return the scooter & pay	J7-01	Parking space for dedicated travel scooter	0.359	0.033*	4.54

$^*p < 0.05$

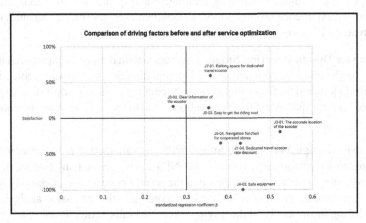

Fig. 2. Comparison of driving forces before and after service optimization

Offering Tourist-Specific Parking. Tourists always can't find parking spaces in popular tourist areas, causing the ride to exceed their budget, resulting in a poor tourist experience. Therefore, shared electric scooter company should cooperate with the government to set exclusive parking Spaces in scenic spots and stations, which can solve users' parking problem and improve the satisfaction of the "return the scooter and pay" process.

Assisting Users to Master Ride Costs. Due to the complex and unfamiliar travel environment, and the shared electric scooter is charged separately, it is difficult for users to estimate the cost, so the operator launched a travel plan of purchasing hours in advance, which can help users effectively grasp the cost of riding, and will improve the satisfaction of "to know the service content and operation scope" process.

Providing Preferential Rental Price. Ride price will affect the travel cost of users, so the cooperation with well-known hotels to provide ride and accommodation discount, to provide users with higher accommodation quality and lower transportation cost, can improve the satisfaction of "riding a scooter" process.

Improving the Navigation Function of Cooperative Stores. Users expect APP map to improve riding efficiency, so improving the navigation function will not only help users to find cooperative stores quickly but also increase the exposure rate of stores, which will improve the satisfaction of "riding a scooter" process.

4 Conclusion

In the Service Design Research Stage. Referring to the management method of NPS, the key process and driving forces affecting NPS are quickly determined by regression analysis. In addition, user interviews are combined to gain an in-depth understanding of users' experience feelings. Combining qualitative and quantitative research, this study can summarize experience problems more comprehensively and help companies to make long-term and short-term plans.

In the Service Design Iteration Stage. Discussion with the case company can not only effectively understand the company's development direction and business objectives but also deeply understand the feasibility of the service concept, helping designers to propose the service concept that meets the expectations of both parties based on the company's views and user needs.

In the Service Design Verification Stage. NPS and satisfaction are used as indicators to measure service performance results. Both NPS and process satisfaction are improved after service optimization, which means that the service concept can effectively improve customer loyalty and satisfaction. Moreover, according to the regression analysis results after comparing the influence of the driving forces and satisfaction. Finally, according to the priority of the driving forces, helps shared electric scooter company put the resource in the right place.

Based on the results of the case study, we noted that NPS loyalty management can help companies find the key factors affecting customer loyalty and satisfaction to reference companies' strategy formulation and implementation. Therefore, this study suggests that service designers can use NPS loyalty management to analyze the effectiveness of the original services, and focus on the processes and touch points that may affect NPS, in order to provide valuable design concepts.

In addition, this study provides four suggestions for tourism services, including offering tourist-specific parking, assisting users to master ride costs, providing preferential rental price, and improving the navigation function of cooperative stores. Expect to help shared electric scooter companies improve user experience, number of users and scooter rental rate.

References

Bolton, R.N.: A dynamic model of the duration of the customer's relationship with a continuous service provider: the role of satisfaction. Mark. Sci. **17**(1), 45–65 (1998)

Fornell, C., Ittner, C.D., Larcker, D.F.: The Valuation Consequences of Customer Satisfaction. National Quality Research Center, The University of Michigan Business School, Michigan, Ann Arbor (1996)

Reichheld, F.F.: The one number you need to grow. Harv. Bus. Rev. **81**(12), 46–55 (2003)

Stickdorn, M., Zehrer, A.: Service design in tourism: customer experience driven destination management. In: First Nordic Conference on Service Design and Service Innovation, pp. 7–23 (2009)

Landmark Training Based on Augmented Reality for People with Intellectual Disabilities

Tom Lorenz, Merle Leopold, Funda Ertas, Sandra Verena Müller,
and Ina Schiering[✉]

Faculty of Computer Science, Faculty of Social Work,
Ostfalia University of Applied Sciences, Wolfenbüttel, Germany
{tom.lorenz1,me.leopold,f.ertas,s-v.mueller,i.schiering}@ostfalia.de

Abstract. People with intellectual disabilities often experience difficulties in wayfinding tasks which obstructs active participation. They typically rely on landmarks but have difficulties in identifying appropriate landmarks on their own. To this aim a concept for an augmented reality application is presented which allows people with intellectual disabilities to train landmark-based navigation based on routes selected together with a guiding person. To enhance training motivation gamification elements are incorporated.

Keywords: Wayfinding · Intellectual disability · Landmark · Augmented reality

1 Introduction

Orientation in a city and wayfinding in general are important skills for participation and autonomy in everyday life. Especially people with intellectual disabilities often experience difficulties in this area which results in the fear of "getting lost" and avoidance of getting around on their own [21]. According to Harniss et al. [9] different types of knowledge for navigation exist ranging from basic landmark-based navigation, to route knowledge up to a survey-level navigation. People with intellectual disabilities tend to rely on landmark knowledge [9] and often have even difficulties in identifying appropriate landmarks. Nakamura and Ooie [20] investigated the potential of training programs to improve the ability of people with intellectual disabilities using public transport. Based on a series of interviews Delgrange et al. [4] point out specific difficulties and problem-solving strategies in wayfinding.

Since digital technologies as smart phones are in widespread use by people with disabilities [19], there is a huge potential for smartphone based trainings programs to enhance wayfinding skills of people with intellectual disabilities. To this aim a concept for a serious game addressing landmark-based navigation using augmented reality on smartphones is proposed.

© Springer Nature Switzerland AG 2021
C. Stephanidis et al. (Eds.): HCII 2021, CCIS 1421, pp. 498–505, 2021.
https://doi.org/10.1007/978-3-030-78645-8_63

As a basis for the use case suitable landmarks for individual routes are identified by people with intellectual disabilities accompanied by a person for guidance. Augmented reality enhances intuitive usage, guidance and movement through the environment. Further the technique allows displaying additional visual information embedded into the real world encouraging users to examine their environment while reducing usage barriers and avoiding problems of extrapolating distances and routes from classic navigation applications, e.g. displayed maps. Further on gamification elements are introduced to enhance training motivation [13].

2 Background

Since landmark knowledge is a central element of navigation for people with intellectual disabilities, while having difficulties in identifying appropriate landmarks [9,21], a differentiation between good and bad landmarks is an essential basis.

(a)   (b)

Fig. 1. Advertisement as bad landmark due to interchangeability and high fluctuation

A lot of elements in the street that gain a lot of attraction are not suitable as landmarks. Advertisement in general classifies as bad landmarks. While they tend to be very eye-catching, ads are replaced regularly. Further one could conclude by remembering an ad at an advertising column (see Fig. 1(a)) that the certain object itself was passed, but people with intellectual disabilities tend to remember content. Confusions may arise due to similarity or due to no present recognition value at all (see Fig. 1), reinforcing insecurities. Therefore prominent ads or ads in general classify as bad landmarks. Alike are construction sites that change appearances over time, even completed and thus might lead to a missing landmark at all. Same applies for post boxes in front of small businesses. While in general these qualify as a good landmark, companies might change and appearances are changed. Sufficient trigger for being lost even might be a different painted house on an important intersection.

Good landmarks are distinctive and consistent. Historical buildings (see Fig. 2(a)), museums or churches mostly meets these criteria and qualify as good landmarks. Old buildings are often maintained well or resistant to visual change due to cultural heritage. Further monuments and sculptures can be used as well. While having a unique design, they often tend to stay at the same spot, will not be changed in appearance and might even be placed at prestigious places (see Fig. 2(b)). If necessary long-established companies, universities normally maintain there original destination, but should only be used if none of the above mentioned, better landmarks are present. To assist people with intellectual disabilities even further, landmarks should be close and visible in the walking direction of the route. Global landmarks or landmarks behind a person could still be used if a participant feels lost at certain point.

(a) Old buildings often stagnate in appreance due to cultural heritage

(b) Sculpture with unique shape and striking color

Fig. 2. Good landmarks due to uniqueness and longevity

Concluding good landmarks qualify by a long-living and distinctive appearance (see Fig. 2). Whereas ads are mostly prominent, objects with a high interchangeability, generally a short life span or not being distinguishable are considered bad landmarks (see Fig. 1). Additionally being guided or rather having a passive spatial learning while being accompanied a lot can influence learning progresses [3]. Therefore independence is developed even more diversified and assistive technologies for self-guided training provide a huge potential for people with intellectual disabilities.

3 Related Work

While multiple papers for people with visual impairment [1,5,8,15] exists there is only little focus on intellectual disabilities. Computer vision approaches exist mostly for indoor navigation. While either using markers (e.g. QR codes, or similar approaches) for positioning [8], or working with concrete instructions [1, 15] these approaches are developed for people with visual impairments. Therefore a camera is mostly used to provide input and guide persons via audio feedback. Similar results can be achieved via beacon technology [5].

Augmented reality as navigational aid was successfully used by Smith et al. [23] for people with intellectual disabilities. While not being able to navigate independently to a novel destination, the technology was usable for persons with intellectual disabilities and provided an improvement in performance. In addition results of previous studies indicate that cues for wayfinding with smartphones in general [18] and augmented reality approaches [17] have potential to increase wayfinding abilities.

Augmented reality solutions are employed for indoor environment as well in the context of visual disabilities but are heavily relying on an unmodified environment [25]. Landmark navigation with augmented reality in general was used in a study by people without disabilities in contrast to classical turn-by-turn navigation and showed an improvement in surrounding perception [2]. Further global landmarks (a very prominent, high building, e.g. eiffel tower, or burj khalifa) were introduced and showed an improvement in navigational tasks [24].

4 Landmark Training

People with intellectual disabilities tend to feel lost fast and there is a high risk that they focus on impractical landmarks. An application is developed to support people with intellectual disabilities to navigate between landmarks on their own. To provide landmark-based route in the application a setup stage is needed. To this aim a guiding person has to navigate through the designated path and spot reasonable landmarks. Preferably, this route and the accompanying landmarks are developed together with the disabled person to train also landmark choice. A photo of each landmark has to be taken and the current position of the landmark will be estimated via global navigation satellite system (GNSS)[1]. A complete route consisting of multiple landmarks or internal waypoints will be saved. Internal waypoints can be used, if a landmark might not be directly visual due to a curved road or similar circumstances to still provide a correct route. Typically it is intended that the next landmark can be directly seen anyway.

---

[1] e.g. GPS (USA), Galileo (EU), ...

If additional waypoints are needed, an adequate visualization needs to be provided. Pictures, names and positions can be altered as well as rearranged in order. If necessary GNSS positions can be adapted.

The central aim is that people with intellectual disabilities are able to master this route on their own. But besides supporting the navigational task the focus is to train landmark-based orientation by guiding and calling peoples attention to reasonable landmarks, e.g. historical buildings, monuments. This is achieved via augmented reality markers that are linked to landmarks via positional information. If close enough participants will receive audiovisual feedback that a landmark is reached and a picture will highlight important parts of the landmark. While a prominent advertisement at a wall tends to be eye-catching but is frequently changed, e.g. a certain door with the producers name above will be long-lasting. Furthermore those eye-catching elements are being remembered by participants.

While augmented reality outperform other methods in immersion and simplicity regarding the mental transfer, a marker might seem lost and won't be visible in the current view port due to the object being behind the person. To tackle such situations arrows pointing left or right on the device are introduced, to support participants view and rotation. Furthermore the need of searching through the environment for arbitrary placed markers is reduced. Another notification is used to inform participants leaving the designated path, while small deviations are used to measure the certainty of participants or the training success along multiple usages (see Sect. 5). The distance for the notification that participants have lost their way has to be evaluated. Therefore multiple factors like GNSS accuracy, as well as the behavior of participants have to be taken into account. In general the design process is agile and incorporated participatory design to address problems of participants in a helpful way and build an easily accessible user interface for people with intellectual disabilities.

As some participants tend to stop if they feel lost optional notifications might be needed after a couple of minutes asking if participants are feeling stuck, or an easily accessible help button could be shown. Latter has to be well thought out since the applications aims to support independence and autonomy, a big help button might lead to over-utilization and an increased tendency of error avoidance. Lastly there will be feedback if a route is successfully completed. Additionally multiple safety aspects are available and have to be evaluated regarding effectiveness while minimizing disruptive or refusing behavior of the application itself. Possibilities range from notifications at app start up to locking behavior completely while moving.

5   Gamification

Gamification is achieved by translating elements usually known from games-design into a non-game context [6,22]. It allows a broad usage e.g. in user engagement [11,12], learning [14] and knowledge retention [7], while positive effects exist [10] but differ from individual and context [16].

The application is designed with gamification elements in mind. For each route participants collect points based on their accuracy or other measurements of training success to support a regular training of certain routes.

Since we want to create a safe learning environment we excluded time needed for a certain route as scoring factor. Since participants train landmark-based routes in a real world environment we want to embrace safety as one of our main priorities. Therefore time saving, risky behavior, e.g. crossing a road without checking even red traffic lights shouldn't be rewarded in any way. Further difficulty of training can increased by fading out elements e.g. reducing the number of landmarks after a certain amount of successful training.

Small adding up features like points, levels and progress per level are adding up over time and provide the possibility to visualize training time. Performance graphs can be used to demonstrate the progress of a participant over time while comparing the score over session/day/week or a different time span. While gamification elements are highly individually absorbed, comprehension and acceptance of performance graphs have to be critically assessed. Highscores could be used to reinforce competitive behavior, but depends on participants interests and are able to motivate, as well as discourage due to pressure and scoring low in contrast to others, while having a really good run in self comparison. Augmented reality allows for even more fancy elements and take story telling to a next level, e.g. participants could taking a walk with a virtual dog, being guided from landmark to landmark.

6 Discussion and Conclusion

While participants struggle with classical navigational devices and maps due to difficulties with mental transferal, augmented reality adds virtual elements to the potential busy environment. Distractions might be taking over, neglecting the application itself or focusing to much on the device. Further safety measures and precautions have to be evaluated and implemented. Usage has to evaluated and a method to measure learning effect needs to be developed. Besides learning a route questions arise, if a general improvement in landmark perception or at least a difference could be achieved. Otherwise the application could be used as a compensational tool. Further methods to distinguish between good and bad landmarks could be structured and included into the application to achieve more transparency and reasoning regarding participants.

Based on the landmark training for following an unknown new route, or being assisted in a daily navigational task, extensions of the basic use case could be developed, if participants have a better understanding of their location and surroundings. This area might differ from a bigger institution site up to a district or similar based on confidence and abilities. Multiple Routes can be combined to a scavenger hunt manually or randomly chosen by the application. An even more complex task might be a number of landmarks that needs to be visited and participants have to choose an appropriate order to minimize distance in the overall route. Questions in such a setting arise if participants pick an optimized path in a round trip or start to navigate back and forth.

Important next steps are user studies to gain insight in usability of the augmented reality approach for people with intellectual disabilities and also their challenges with identifying appropriate landmarks while heavily relying on landmark knowledge. The aim is to foster participation and autonomy.

Acknowledgment. This work was supported by the Federal Ministry of Education and Research (BMBF) as part of SmarteInklusion (01PE18011C).

References

1. Al-Khalifa, S., Al-Razgan, M.: Ebsar: indoor guidance for the visually impaired. Comput. Electr. Eng. **54**, 26–39 (2016)
2. Amirian, P., Basiri, A.: Landmark-based pedestrian navigation using augmented reality and machine learning. In: Gartner, G., Jobst, M., Huang, H. (eds.) Progress in Cartography. LNGC, pp. 451–465. Springer, Cham (2016). https://doi.org/10.1007/978-3-319-19602-2_27
3. Chrastil, E.R., Warren, W.H.: Active and passive spatial learning in human navigation: acquisition of survey knowledge. J. Exp. Psychol. Learn. Mem. Cogn. **39**(5), 1520–1537 (2013)
4. Delgrange, R., Burkhardt, J.M., Gyselinck, V.: Difficulties and problem-solving strategies in wayfinding among adults with cognitive disabilities: a look at the bigger picture. Front. Hum. Neurosci. **14**, 46 (2020)
5. Delnevo, G., Monti, L., Vignola, F., Salomoni, P., Mirri, S.: AlmaWhere: a prototype of accessible indoor wayfinding and navigation system. In: 2018 15th IEEE Annual Consumer Communications Networking Conference (CCNC), pp. 1–6, January 2018
6. Deterding, S., Dixon, D., Khaled, R., Nacke, L.: From game design elements to gamefulness: defining "gamification". In: Proceedings of the 15th International Academic MindTrek Conference: Envisioning Future Media Environments, MindTrek 2011, pp. 9–15. Association for Computing Machinery, New York, September 2011
7. Dincelli, E., Chengalur-Smith, I.: Choose your own training adventure: designing a gamified SETA artefact for improving information security and privacy through interactive storytelling. Eur. J. Inf. Syst. **29**(6), 669–687 (2020)
8. Elgendy, M., Guzsvinecz, T., Sik-Lanyi, C.: Identification of markers in challenging conditions for people with visual impairment using convolutional neural network. Appl. Sci. **9**(23), 5110 (2019)
9. Gupta, M., et al.: Towards more universal wayfinding technologies: navigation preferences across disabilities. In: Proceedings of the 2020 CHI Conference on Human Factors in Computing Systems, pp. 1–13. ACM, Honolulu, April 2020
10. Hamari, J., Koivisto, J., Sarsa, H.: Does gamification work? – a literature review of empirical studies on gamification. In: 2014 47th Hawaii International Conference on System Sciences, pp. 3025–3034, January 2014
11. Hamari, J.: Transforming homo economicus into homo ludens: a field experiment on gamification in a utilitarian peer-to-peer trading service. Electron. Commer. Res. Appl. **12**(4), 236–245 (2013)
12. Hamari, J.: Do badges increase user activity? A field experiment on the effects of gamification. Comput. Hum. Behav. **71**, 469–478 (2017)

13. Hamari, J.: Gamification. In: The Blackwell Encyclopedia of Sociology, pp. 1–3. American Cancer Society (2019)
14. Hamari, J., Shernoff, D.J., Rowe, E., Coller, B., Asbell-Clarke, J., Edwards, T.: Challenging games help students learn: an empirical study on engagement, flow and immersion in game-based learning. Comput. Hum. Behav. **54**, 170–179 (2016)
15. Ko, E., Kim, E.Y.: A vision-based wayfinding system for visually impaired people using situation awareness and activity-based instructions. Sensors **17**(8), 1882 (2017)
16. Koivisto, J., Hamari, J.: Demographic differences in perceived benefits from gamification. Comput. Hum. Behav. **35**, 179–188 (2014)
17. McMahon, D., Cihak, D.F., Wright, R.: Augmented reality as a navigation tool to employment opportunities for postsecondary education students with intellectual disabilities and autism. J. Res. Technol. Educ. **47**(3), 157–172 (2015)
18. McMahon, D.D., Smith, C.C., Cihak, D.F., Wright, R., Gibbons, M.M.: Effects of digital navigation aids on adults with intellectual disabilities: comparison of paper map, google maps, and augmented reality. J. Spec. Educ. Technol. **30**(3), 157–165 (2015)
19. Morris, J.T., Sweatman, W.M., Jones, M.L.: Smartphone use and activities by people with disabilities: user survey 2016, p. 18 (2017)
20. Nakamura, F., Ooie, K.: A study on mobility improvement for intellectually disabled student commuters. IATSS Res. **41**(2), 74–81 (2017)
21. Professor, M.M.S.A., Todis, B., Fickas, S., Hung, P.F., Lemoncello, R.: A profile of community navigation in adults with chronic cognitive impairments. Brain Inj. **19**(14), 1249–1259 (2005)
22. Robson, K., Plangger, K., Kietzmann, J.H., McCarthy, I., Pitt, L.: Is it all a game? Understanding the principles of gamification. Bus. Horiz. **58**(4), 411–420 (2015)
23. Smith, C.C., Cihak, D.F., Kim, B., McMahon, D.D., Wright, R.: Examining augmented reality to improve navigation skills in postsecondary students with intellectual disability. J. Spec. Educ. Technol. **32**(1), 3–11 (2017)
24. Wenig, N., Wenig, D., Ernst, S., Malaka, R., Hecht, B., Schöning, J.: Pharos: improving navigation instructions on smartwatches by including global landmarks. In: Proceedings of the 19th International Conference on Human-Computer Interaction with Mobile Devices and Services, pp. 1–13. ACM, Vienna, September 2017
25. Yoon, C., et al.: Leveraging augmented reality to create apps for people with visual disabilities: a case study in indoor navigation. In: The 21st International ACM SIGACCESS Conference on Computers and Accessibility, pp. 210–221. ACM, Pittsburgh, October 2019

Decision Support Systems in Disaster Risk Management Policies for Adaptation to Climate Change

Jose Ricardo Mondragon Regalado[✉] [iD]
and Carmen Graciela Arbulú Pérez Várgas[✉] [iD]

Universidad César Vallejo, Lambayeque, Peru
{jmondragonr,carbulu}@ucvvirtual.edu.pe

Abstract. Adaptation to climate change requires better decisions in risk management policies, therefore, the objective of this research was to validate a model called "SISDECC" that is based on the Micmac program in prospective scenarios. Through, the expert judgment of various Latin-American countries who evaluated the designed model and the usability of the Mimac program. Which input parameters and the information of the variables show the program is suitable for integration into the new SISDECC model and its application in government prospective investigations.

Keywords: Support systems · Decision making · Climate change

1 Introduction

The world lives in constant challenge due to the complex climatic phenomena that are threaten the survival of the planet. As a result, governments unify efforts to mitigate their impact. The challenge is to innovate in public policies that provide security to humanity (Roth 2019). For Yun et al. (2021) and Silva et al. (2015), Human Computer Interaction (HCI) plays a fundamental role, managing to integrate "brain" - "machine", with the recognition of managing information by part of the human being.

Along these lines, smart technologies have recently generated greater demand in the management of social and investment projects, fostering a positive impact; as a support for decisions of different multidimensional approaches, monitoring and distributed "man-machine" systems. For the administration of complex projects providing sustainability and functionality in operational management in the different work modes (Patsyuk et al. 2021; Perederyi et al. 2021; Ludwig and Mattedi 2018).

Because of this, in prospective scenarios, the decision-making from the public and private spheres generates greater proximity of the reality towards an important future, preparing the path for something that could happen; access to information to possible challenges prepares human and material resources in advance (Baena 2015; Moniz 2006; Torres Fernández et al. 2017).

© Springer Nature Switzerland AG 2021
C. Stephanidis et al. (Eds.): HCII 2021, CCIS 1421, pp. 506–512, 2021.
https://doi.org/10.1007/978-3-030-78645-8_64

The risks in the face of disasters due to the climate change demand urgency to be addressed; According to the United Nations (2018), these will cause an increase in temperature, an imbalance in the sea level, an increase in natural phenomena such as: droughts, hurricanes, landslide and other effects that threaten the subsistence of life on the planet. However, there are factors of pollution, lack of education, corruption among others (Barrera-Hernández et al. 2020).

Possible challenges prepare human and material resources in advance (Baena 2015; Moniz 2006; Torres Fernández et al. 2017). The climate change causes loss of human and material life and threatens global economic sustainability. As evidence, in Peru, the National Institute of Statistics and Informatics INEI (2018), shows data regarding the number of people affected and deceased due to natural disasters during 2016 and 2017, the numbers were 2 million 243 thousand and 2 million 77 thousand respectively.

In the words of Persson (2019), it is necessary for leaders to invest in research issues and adaptation methodologies. Along these lines, Bellamy (2019), Orsato et al. (2019), Fedele et al. (2019), Solecki et al. (2019) and Losada et al. (2019) sustains that governments must adopt new paradigms, social and technological techniques that allow the development of strategies, and address corporate challenges in the face of the climate change, establishing strategic planning frameworks for adaptability. On this lines, is proposed that will the interaction model "SISDECC" improve decision-making by governments to design risk management policies in adaptation to climate change?

The purpose of this study is to put forward the "SISDECC" interaction model that allows process, analyze and decide on the basis of theoretical and expert information in such a way that government authorities made decisions at any level of government, implement policies in order of priorities under a model according to geographic reality, in order to minimize the impact of climate change.

The main objective of the research was to validate the SISDECC theoretical model based on the Micmac method through prospective analysis that allows decision-making in planning risk management policies for adaptation to the climate change.

The most relevant causes that lead to the problem constituted within public management are: few innovative technological management tools for decision-making, poor planning and human actions such as selfishness, consumerism culture, capitalism, over-population, public policies for the prevention of disaster risk according each countries' reality, inability to respond to disasters, inefficient distribution of economic resources to mitigate risks, improvisation in decision-making in the face of disaster risk management. This results in the loss of human and material life, ungovernability, corruption, misappropriation of funds and collateral damage that increases the rates of poverty, hunger, epidemics, migration among others.

2 Methodology

To validate the SISDECC theoretical model, the Micmac method and prospective analysis were used as a basis for decision-making in the formulation of risk management policies in the face of the climate change scenario.

The type of study corresponds to a basic investigation, in which the theoretical interaction model "SISDECC" is endorsed by expert judges from the countries of Ecuador,

Chile, Argentina, Cuba and Peru. Furthermore, the design was holistic predictive, not experimental.

The procedures for the design of the "SISDECC" model took into account theoretical contributions from the Prospectiva and the Micmac program, the research variables were proposed by the researchers and the work variables are the product of the diversification of them.

3   Results

See Fig. 1

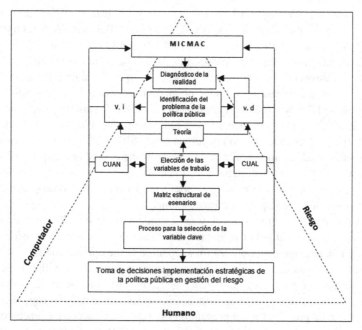

Fig. 1. The interaction model called the climate change decision support system SISDECC is designed to address prospective research, specifically from public management; for making correct decisions about the design of efficient public policies by the authorities.

From this ecosystem, the technological environment represented by the computer and the Micmac program shows a structural ergonomics adaptation to the needs, which it facilitates the operation and the interaction with the human being. It has an ordered and visible semiotic interface, so that the user can graphically identify certain processes. The functions are easily accessed, it is adapted to process ordinal data in prospective research and various lines such as risk management, health, etc. Thanks to its use, a good learning interaction on the input, process and output of information also allows to validate and obtain information of inconsistencies instantly.

From the cognitive perspective, the human being interacts applying logic, performing analysis, understanding, operating the system properly, feeding with real data, processing information and assimilates the results that are key variables, also in based on perception and intuition that transform them into priority alternatives for decision making for new prospective strategic knowledge from any level of government in disaster risk management facing of climate change.

The context shows risks that caused by the climate change that we remain vulnerable. The record is much higher on the loss of human life and economic damage.

Description of the model, the model states the human-computer interaction, so that the government authorities supported by the proposed method and the use of the program allowing to process data and obtaining the key variables in order of priorities and coming from them; make immediate decisions in implementing policies and strategic plans to manage risk efficiently and save lives in the face of an eminent natural disaster.

(1) The model proposes that those who are responsible for national, regional, or local government should identify problems at the national or local level. (2) Identification of the independent variable (i.v.) relating to the issue of public policies (3) Identification of the dependent variable (d.v.) susceptible to diversification to be able to measure it through indicators, it is related to the absence, deficiency, lack and poor policies. (4) The accomplishment of the diagnosis of reality, correspondence, analyze with critical judgment the object of study from a holistic, national, regional, and local perspective, to support, locate and contextualize the research. (5) Determine the theoretical bases that support the research. (6) The choice of the work variables is the dimensioning of the dependent variable, to classify and determine which sub variables should be considered in the research this variable. It is determined based on the preliminary information obtained, which can be qualitative and quantitative. (7) The design of the structural matrix of scenarios corresponds to representing the variables selected by the researcher in a matrix of n * n, the working variables must have a single representative word in the matrix. (8) The analysis for the selection of the key variables and decision-making must take into account the expert opinion. Later, once the matrix or technical sheet is structured, it intervenes to evaluate the dependence of the work variables individually. The evaluation according to the Godet model will be carried out qualitatively to an ordinal degree. 0: Has no influence; 1: Weak influence ratio; 2: Medium influence ratio and 3: Strong influence ratio.

Interaction and usability of the program, for the information processing has been used the Micmac program in its free version because it meets the technical conditions both in the interface, adaptability, and usability. The program can be found on different platforms of strategic planning organizations and universities, it is installed on a computer with the minimum necessary conditions and it is accessed through the icon located on the desktop. The interface is friendly, aesthetic and minimalist with easy interaction and navigation, as well as presenting the option to validate that allows the user to recognize inconsistencies instantly.

To create the project and the database; first, it must carry out a real systematic analysis of the information to be processed, according to the context of the research object. Secondly, the project is created, and the custom database is structured, which allows the information to be stored and managed. Then, the user can assign names to the work variables, adding a complete description of the variables to facilitate their identification and understanding, in addition, the user takes control of them, so they can change, edit, delete or insert other variables to the database. Fourth, after the database is created, its consistency is checked by entering the consolidated data from the technical sheet of experts, the database will only allow the entry of quantitative data. The system will process all the information entered, which was the result of the evaluation of the expert judges. Furthermore, the system shows flexibility and efficiency of use, allows to enter and/or edit and make changes or continue adding data or save progress.

Fifth, the system generates user-friendly reports with processed information that shows the key motor/dependency variable in order of priorities. Based on them, the authorities must make decisions in order to formulate public policies and strategic risk management plans, proposing a desirable future that gives public value to the citizen. In addition, the program allows the results to be exported to a word processor, image, or output to a printer.

The evaluation of the SISDECC model was carried out in two phases, the first throughout the integral evaluation of content, with the participation of nine research professionals from the universities of Camaguey in Cuba, National University of Guayaquil in Ecuador, National Intercultural University of the Amazon in Peru and other professionals specialized in strategic planning and decision making from the countries of Argentina and Chile.

In Table 1, results of the content evaluation of the SISDECC model through indicators of clarity, objectivity, innovation, organization, sufficiency, intentionality, consistency, and coherence. The nine experts after carrying out an exhaustive analysis of the proposed scheme, they gave the evaluation of excellent to the proposed model to address prospective investigations at the government level.

Table 1. Content evaluation of the "SISDECC" model

Indicator	N	Poor	Acceptable	Good	Very good	Excellent
Clarity	9	-	-	-	-	x
Objetivity	9	-	-	-	-	x
Innovation	9	-	-	-	-	x
Organization	9	-	-	-	-	x
Sufficiency	9	-	-	-	-	x
Intentionality	9	-	-	-	-	x
Consistency	9	-	-	-	-	x
Coherence	9	-	-	-	-	x

In the second phase, usability evaluation of the Micmac program, in which the judges who evaluated the content participated; the measurement was carried out using the model based on Nielsen heuristics. Values were assigned 1. Does not comply; 2. If it complies, the results are presented in Table 2.

Table 2 shows the result of the expert evaluation of the model on usability, interface and adaptability, the experts maintain that the dimensions evaluated with respect to the Micmac program are adapted and optimized so that users interact appropriately and maintain control, system in the input, process and output of information.

Table 2. Evaluation of the Micmac program based on Nielsen heuristics

N°	Heuristics	N	Comply	Not comply
1	System state visibility	9	100	0
2	Matching between the system and the real world	9	100	0
3	Control and user freedom	9	100	0
4	Consistency and standards	9	100	0
5	Error prevention	9	100	0
6	More recognition than reminders	9	100	0
7	Flexibility and efficiency of use	9	100	0
8	Aesthetic and minimalist design	9	100	0
9	Support the user to recognize, diagnose and recover from errors	9	100	0
10	Help and documentation	9	100	0

4   Conclusions

The model called the decision support system for climate change - SISDECC was developed to address prospective research that allows improving decision-making in the implementation of efficient strategic public policy at the government level.

Two types of evaluation were carried out on the model; based on the content where the experts gave an excellent evaluation to the proposed model and based on the usability of the Micmac support program. The Nielsen heuristic methodology was applied, the result of the evaluation shows that the program is suitable for its integration into the new SISDECC model, and for its application in government prospective investigations.

References

Alvarado, L., García, M.: Características más relevantes del paradigma socio-crítico: su aplicación en investigaciones de educación ambiental y de enseñanza de las ciencias realizadas en el Doctorado de Educación del Instituto Pedagógico de Caracas. Sapiens. Rev. Univ. Invest. **9**(2), 187–202 (2008). [Fecha de Consulta 10 de Febrero de 2021]. ISSN: 1317–5815. https://www.redalyc.org/articulo.oa?id=410/41011837011

Barrera-Hernández, L.F., Murillo-Parra, L.D., Ocaña-Zúñiga, J., Cabrera-Méndez, M., Echeverría-Castro, S.B., Sotelo-Castillo, M.A.: Causas, consecuencias y quÉ hacer frente al cambio climÁtico análisis de grupos focales con estudiantes y profesores universitarios. Rev. Mexicana Invest. Educ., **25**(87), 1103–1122 (2020). www.scopus.com

Bellamy, R.: Disponibilidad social de las tecnologías de adaptación. ALAMBRES Clim. Change **10**, e623 (2019). https://doi.org/10.1002/wcc.623

Fedele, G., Donatti, C.I., Harvey, C.A., Hannah, L., y Hole , D.G.: Adaptación transformadora al cambio climático para sistemas socioecológicos sostenibles. Ciencias y políticas ambientales **101**, 116–125 (2019). https://doi.org/10.1016/j.envsci.2019.07.001

INEI.: Lineas de Base de los Principales Indicadores Disponibles de los Objetivos de Desarrollo Sostenible (ODS), 454 (2018)

Godet, M.: Creating Futures Scenario Planning as a Strategic Management Tool. Económica, London (2001)

Losada, I.J., Toimil, A., Muñoz, A., Garcia-Fletcher, A.P., Diaz-Simal, P.: A planning strategy for the adaptation of coastal areas to climate change: the Spanish case. Ocean Coastal Manage. **182** (2019). https://doi.org/10.1016/j.ocecoaman.2019.104983

Ludwig, L., Mattedi, M.A.: The Information and communication technologies in the risk management of social and environmental disasters. Ambiente e Sociedade **21** (2018). https://doi.org/10.1590/1809-4422asoc0103r4vu18l1ao

Orsato, R.J., Ferraz de Campos, J.G., Barakat, S.R.: Social learning for anticipatory adaptation to climate change: evidence from a community of practice. Organ. Environ. **32**(4), 416–440 (2019). https://doi.org/10.1177/1086026618775325

Patsyuk, E.V., Krutilin, A.A., Kiseleva, M.N., Lisina, L.M., Liberovskaya, A.N.: "Smart technologies" in project management: rationalization of decision making or a source of new risks for information security. In: Popkova, E.G., Sergi, B.S. (eds.) ISC 2020. LNNS, vol. 155, pp. 77–84. Springer, Cham (2021). https://doi.org/10.1007/978-3-030-59126-7_9

Perederyi, V., Borchik, E., Ohnieva, O.: Information technology for decision making support and monitoring in man-machine systems for managing complex technical objects of critical application. In: Babichev, S., Lytvynenko, V., Wójcik, W., Vyshemyrskaya, S. (eds.) ISDMCI 2020. AISC, vol. 1246, pp. 448–466. Springer, Cham (2021). https://doi.org/10.1007/978-3-030-54215-3_29

Persson, Å.: Global adaptation governance: an emerging but contested domain. Wiley Interdiscip. Rev. Clim. Change **10**(6) (2019).https://doi.org/10.1002/wcc.618

Roth, A.: Climate change and public policies: an approach from the theory of risk society . Prometeica **18**, 36–46 (2019). https://doi.org/10.24316/prometeica.v0i18.250

Silva, K.L., Évora, Y.D.M., Cintra, C.S.J.: Software development to support decision making in the selection of nursing diagnoses and interventions for children and adolescents. Rev. Lat. Am. Enfermagem **23**(5), 927–935 (2015). https://doi.org/10.1590/0104-1169.0302.2633

Solecki, W., et al.: Extreme events and climate adaptation-mitigation linkages: understanding low-carbon transitions in the era of global urbanization. Wiley Interdiscip. Rev.Clim. Change **10**(6) (2019). https://doi.org/10.1002/wcc.616

Torres Fernández, J.P., Gallo Mendoza, J. G., Hallo Alvear, R.F., Jaraiseh Abcarius, J., Muriel Páez, M.H., Fernández Lorenzo, A.: Information management as a decision-making tool in health: Most probable scenarios. Rev. Cubana Invest. Biomed. **36**(3) (2017). https://www.scopus.com/inward/record.uri?eid=2-s2.0-85052651956&partnerID=40&md5=7831c88ef9d956c1c7fd2dba5859a20b

United Nations: Informe de los Objetivos de Desarrollo Sostenible 2018 (2018). https://unstats.un.org/sdgs/files/report/2018/TheSustainableDevelopmentGoalsReport2018-es.pdf

Yun, Y., Ma, D., Yang, M.: Human–computer interaction-based decision support system with applications in data mining. Future Gener. Comput. Syst. **114**, 285–289 (2021). https://doi.org/10.1016/j.future.2020.07.048

Using PLR Syntax to Map Experience-Based Digital/Physical Ecosystems for Strategic Systemic Change

Andrea Resmini[1]([⊠]) [iD], Bertil Lindenfalk[2] [iD], Luca Simeone[3] [iD],
and David Drabble[4] [iD]

[1] Halmstad University, Halmstad, Sweden
`andrea.resmini@hh.se`
[2] Jönköping Academy for the Improvement of Health and Welfare, School of health and
welfare, Jönköping University, Jönköping, Sweden
`bertil.lindenfalk@ju.se`
[3] Aalborg University, Copenhagen, Denmark
`lsi@create.aau.dk`
[4] The Tavistock Institute, London, UK
`d.drabble@tavinstitute.org`

Abstract. PLR (Personal-Local-Remote) is a spatially-oriented syntax for mapping digital/physical experiences as a system of relationships structuring an actor-centered information architecture that is surveyed, explored, and described by means of a set of simple rules. These rules represent the cognitive load, the relationships, and the relative importance of any element in the experience through spatial primitives such as position, proximity, and size. We here present and discuss a case centering on the mobility system in the city of Augsburg, Germany, where the PLR syntax was applied to gain a strategic understanding of Mobil-Flat, a transport service offered by Stadtwerke Augsburg, to map the local mobility experience ecosystem and identify possible leverage points for change.

Keywords: Shared mobility · PLR · Spatial syntax · Experience ecosystems

1 Introduction

HCI has traditionally been interested in the theorization and application of design methods to study affordances of digital objects [7, 13]. Stephanidis et al. [19] identify seven challenges for HCI emerging from the changing socio-technological landscape. Two of these, "human-technology symbiosis" and "human-environment interactions", address the blending of digital/physical environments and the design of seamful transitions between different objects and contexts.

Previous research has investigated the concept of seams [21] and identified seamfulness [5] as a core component of a successful user experience. More recent research originating from user experience and information architecture has examined the in-context exploration of seamfully connected information environments, objects, and locations as

© Springer Nature Switzerland AG 2021
C. Stephanidis et al. (Eds.): HCII 2021, CCIS 1421, pp. 513–520, 2021.
https://doi.org/10.1007/978-3-030-78645-8_65

blended spaces [1, 2] or ecosystems [3, 14–16]. These later contributions center on a more systemic approach that considers as the primary object of design the structural space of relationships of the information architecture rather than the point-to-point interactions provided by the individual elements existing within the blended space [3].

General systems thinking theory stipulates that to affect change in a system, the system must first be surveyed [11] to unearth the "implicit cultural codes responsible for regenerating the existing 'second-order-machine'" [8], so that maps can be produced that identify the leverage points. Leverage points can then be acted upon in order to "produce a change in the behavioral patterns" [8] by challenging underlying assumptions.

The structure of relationships of a system constitutes the purpose of the system and directly determines its behavior and its current outputs [11]. It also influences the behavior of actors within the system by affording certain possibilities of action and impeding others. Relationships between elements in the system create an architecture of feedback loops, often codified through archetypes [20] and represented as either 'causal loop' or 'stocks and flows' diagrams [11]. The identification of existing archetypes and leverage points within the system makes second-order interventions possible, for example by changing the way a specific feedback loop works or what role a leverage point plays. The structure of relationships of a system constitutes its base information architecture [14, 15].

PLR (Personal-Local-Remote, pronounced "pillar") is a spatially-oriented syntax for mapping digital/physical experiences as a system of relationships forming an actor-centered information architecture [10, 15]. It allows designers to survey, explore, and describe the emergent structures of experience-based digital/physical ecosystems [3, 14, 15] by means of a set of simple rules that represent the cognitive load, relationships, and relative importance of any element in the experience through spatial primitives [12] such as position, proximity, and size.

Conceived as part of a hands-on methodology meant to be carried out through low-fidelity, embodied co-design activities, PLR allows to: quickly visualize an individual actor's personal experience as a series of steps on a path whose geometry intuitively represents that experience's duration, structural make-up, and cognitive load; compound many individual actors' experiences into the overall map of the digital/physical ecosystem in which these experiences take place [3, 15].

PLR has been applied to a number of projects in domains such as healthcare and education [10, 15], where it has been used to successfully provide designers with a bird's eye understanding of the ecosystem and to validate design choices. It has not however been empirically explored from a systemic perspective: to document the role PLR can play in large-scale design efforts, we present and discuss a case investigating Mobil-Flat, a shared mobility service offered by the city of Augsburg, Germany. The case focuses on the application of the PLR syntax to gain a strategic understanding of the patterns of behavior of travelers, map the shared mobility experience ecosystem, and identify possible leverage points for change.

2 Shared Mobility in Augsburg

Augsburg is a university city of 300.000 inhabitants in the southwest of Germany. Stadtwerke Augsburg (swa) runs a number of public transportation and shared mobility services, including bike sharing and car sharing. Public transportation comprises tram lines, city and night bus lines, and sees an average of sixty million passengers per year using a number of different subscription plans.

Bike sharing in Augsburg is offered by swa through the nextbike company. While the bikes and their online and offline presence are branded "swa", all services are provided by nextbike: this means that swa has indirect insights into the bike sharing system data and only a measure of control. As a consequence, bike sharing differs greatly from the car sharing system, created and run by swa since 2014, and now offering both station-based and "point-to-point" sharing [9].

In 2019, swa launched Mobil-Flat, a currently suspended city-wide flat rate that could be used across all of swa's mobility services, including bike and car sharing, for a fixed monthly fee and offered in two tiers providing different allowances of kilometers and hours. Mobil-Flat was intended to make sharing more interesting to urban travelers, thus helping reduce the impact of single-occupancy private traffic and pivoting behavior towards more sustainable collective transport solutions. Mobil-Flat was not particularly successful, averaging slightly more than 300 users in 2020, a number too low to sustain service, but was kept running as a subsidized service to the far more popular car sharing option [9]. All of the mobility services offered by swa and part of the Mobil-Flat plan required a registration and centered on the use of one or multiple apps, on phone support, and swa's own service points. Mobil-Flat was also conceived and developed as a closed mobility chain, with all present and future modalities being controlled by swa Augsburg.

Because of these reasons, the benefits resulting from an increase in the number of people using the system, such as more cars and destinations becoming available, did not manifest [9] and network effects did not come into play. This posed a problem to swa in terms of long-term sustainability and value creation that ultimately led swa to rethink the service.

The study, conducted in German, was carried out in 2020 as part of graduate research work under the supervision of two of the authors [9]. Primary data was acquired through semi-structured interviews with swa employees working with Mobil-Flat and with residents of Augsburg who either had a subscription to Mobil-Flat or were using the sharing mobility services offered by swa. Coding and clustering were performed on the transcripts of the interview and customer journeys were created from an analysis of the transcripts. The interview pool had to be reduced as data collection happened during the early stages of the COVID 19 pandemic, but a satisfying level of data saturation was achieved in respect to the base elements that constitute the mobility ecosystems in accordance with Resmini and Lacerda [14]. Secondary sources and in-person observation were also used to complement primary data.

Data from the study was then used to create a view of the Augsburg mobility system as an experience ecosystem. PLR was used to first spatially represent the individual experiences detailed in the interviews and then subsequently compound these into a map of the emergent mobility ecosystem in Augsburg. This map was in turn used to identify leverage points within the ecosystem that could be acted upon to achieve swa's goals, first and foremost that of increasing the number of people adopting shared mobility strategies through the Mobil-Flat offer.

3 Applying PLR

PLR adopts a straightforward syntax to initially represent touchpoints as elements in an individual path in a standardized, spatially-oriented way [10, 15]. Colored hexagonal tiles are used as stand-ins for touchpoints, and gray tiles for the seams between them. Seams identify steps in the path and an information flow that allows a person to move from a touchpoint "a" to a touchpoint "b". The colors and reciprocal position of two subsequent touchpoint tiles identify a partitioned space that discriminates between "personal" (green, straight on), "local" (yellow, right), and "remote" (red, left) touchpoints. Local and remote touchpoints are further divided into weaker (−, backward) and stronger (+, forward) touchpoints "based on the degree of effort their usage requires" [10].

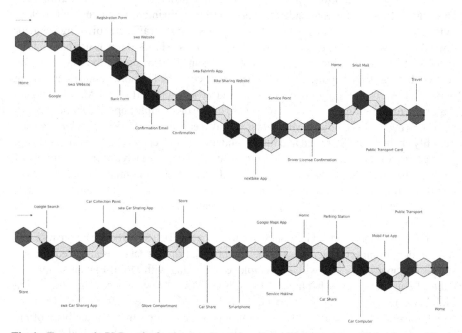

Fig. 1. Two sample PLR paths for the Augsburg shared mobility ecosystem (Color figure online)

A personal touchpoint is something in the person's possession: for example a ticket, or a smartphone, or information they already acquired. A local touchpoint is something in the person's immediate environment: for example "a real-time display that can be checked for information" or "a bystander who can be asked" [10]. It requires a little more effort or time than a personal touchpoint. A remote touchpoint is a touchpoint that requires sizable movement, time, or resources: it could for example be "a rarely used or previously unknown online source" or "a public office when the actor is home" [10].

Figure 1 illustrates how PLR syntax was used to represent mobility customer journeys identified during data collection as individual paths. The image shows the registration path for Mobil-Flat (top), and a car sharing experience (bottom), turned ninety degrees for readability: the arrows on the left mark the start points and the direction of the experience.

The two paths both include a large number of steps, and spatially veer towards the right (downward), signaling that they "rely more on local touchpoints and environmental clues" (yellow hexes), but include a non trivial number of left-going (upward) steps (red hexes), "requir(ing) the most effort" and relying on "remote touchpoints not readily available to actors and (that) usually require movement between locations or (introduce) temporal delays" [15]. Especially for registering, a process entirely under the control of swa and built to maximize onboarding, this is problematic.

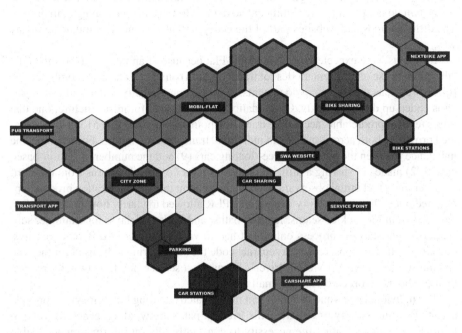

Fig. 2. Simplified PLR map of the Augsburg shared mobility ecosystem

After initial application of the PLR syntax and analysis, paths are compounded into one or more ecosystem maps. PLR maps discard any idea of directionality and only consider flow, integration [4], and relative importance of touchpoints within the ecosystem, manifesting these again as simple spatial relationships. Flow is represented by the presence or absence of seams (gray tiles) between any two touchpoints: the presence of a seam acknowledges that at least once an actor moved between the touchpoints; integration is represented by the number of seamful connections any single touchpoint has with other touchpoints: high levels of integration are an indicator of the system's resilience; importance is represented by the number of tiles used for a touchpoint: these are in turn based on the number of times that touchpoint has been accessed and subsequently accounted for during data analysis. Figure 2 shows a rendition of the emergent PLR map of the Mobil-Flat-centered shared mobility system as it is instantiated by travelers.

The map shows that the car sharing and public transportation clusters do not share a seam, which means there are no information flows of any kind that allow travelers to seamlessly move from one to the other. Co-modality transportation involving these was observed to be problematic. It is worth noting that "Car sharing" is the most integrated element (7) in the ecosystem, but this integration is entirely car-centric.

This absence of seams between transport clusters characterizes the Mobil-Flat ecosystems all throughout, and is also found locally within transport clusters. For example, the car sharing app does not have a seam towards the parking system, meaning that renting a car and finding where to park it are two separate tasks. The Mobil-Flat service plays a central role as it bridges between all shared mobility services, but since it does not provide an actionable single point of access, its importance and weight inside the ecosystem do not provide any significant advantage to travelers, becoming a hindrance. The different apps and websites part of the ecosystem also do not communicate in any way.

Residents were expected to adopt Mobil-Flat because of an interest in co-modality, "the efficient use of different modes (of transportation) on their own and in combination" [6]. However, as the PLR map documents, expected functionality and actual usage patterns ended up differing vastly. Co-modality requires a seamful infrastructure, one that offers regular, predictable, accessible transition points, something that Mobil-Flat struggled providing both across and within individual transportation modes. For example, the unbalance between the number of free-floating cars (9) and the number of station-based cars (192) made car sharing a difficult proposition for co-modal patterns from the start.

Interviews and initial observations made it apparent that the registration process represented a less than satisfactory experience. PLR allowed to clarify how dissatisfaction emerged from the lack of seams, lengthy paths, and built-in delays: for example, subscribers could start the process online but had to visit a number of different websites, download different apps, receive a separate code for bike sharing to be used for the bike sharing service only, verify their driver's license at a service point, and finally receive their public transport card via snail mail at home.

The individual paths and the emergent map created adopting the PLR syntax provide a spatially intuitive way to visualize this friction: paths are winding, generally veering to the right, thus indicating the necessity to constantly rely on information accessible in the local environment, but do also contain steps that indicate delays, the necessity of movement, or cognitive load for the acquisition of new information; the map shows low levels of integration and disconnected clusters that clearly identify bottlenecks and possible leverage points that might be the object of a redesign intervention.

4 Conclusions and Future Work

The PLR map points to a fragmented, cognitively difficult experience for travelers at crucial moments, including when opting in or when engaging the mobility system to support co-modality behavior. Leverage points can be identified in the need to simplify access, payment, and administration of shared mobility as a service from the actors' point of view; in the absence of working seams between a number of different services part of the ecosystem; in the impact that the current environment, comprising both the spatial surroundings and the information available, has on travelers within the city, as it affects their understanding of the offer and their ability to seamlessly move between co-modal transportation options when necessary.

Future work is poised to explore the connection between leverage points, goals and expected outcomes using Theory of Change, a framework that originated in the 1990s to better plan, drive and evaluate community initiatives and philanthropic projects [18, 22] and that has since been used more widely to uncover the underlying logic of complex and systemic interventions [17]. When used in conjunction with PLR syntax, Theory of Change could offer a structured approach to better evaluate the critical factors at play in the identification of what leverage points could produce the type of change to the "second-order machine" [8] required within a given experience ecosystem, such as that of shared mobility Augsburg, to support the desired behavior patterns, thus supporting design choices.

References

1. Benyon, D.: Spaces of Interaction, Places for Experience. Morgan & Claypool (2014)
2. Benyon, D., Mival, O., Ayan, S.: Designing Blended Spaces (2012). https://doi.org/10.14236/ewic/hci2012.1.
3. Benyon, D., Resmini, A.: User experience in cross-channel ecosystems. In: Proceedings of the British HCI 2017 (2017). https://doi.org/10.14236/ewic/hci2017.38.
4. Chalmers, M.: Informatics, architecture and language. In: Munro, A., Höök, K., Benyon, D. (eds.) Designing Information Spaces: The Social Navigation in Information Space, pp. 315–341. Springer, London (2003). https://doi.org/10.1007/978-1-4471-0035-5_14
5. Chalmers, M., Dieberger, A., Höök, K., Rudström, Å.: Social navigation and seamful design. Cogn. Stud. **11**(3), 171–181 (2004)
6. COM: 314 Final. Communication from the Commission to the Council and the European Parliament. Keep Europe moving - Sustainable mobility for our continent. Mid-term review of the European Commission's 2001 Transport White Paper (2006). https://eur-lex.europa.eu/LexUriServ/LexUriServ.do?uri=COM:2006:0314:FIN:EN:PDF
7. Cooper, A., Reimann, R., Dubberly, H.: About Face 2.0: The Essentials of Interaction Design, 1st edn. Wiley, Hoboken (2003)
8. Gharajedaghi, J.: Systems Thinking: Managing Chaos and Complexity: A Platform for Designing Business Architecture, 3rd edn. Butterworth-Heinemann (2011)
9. Hanke, W.: Shared Mobility as a Socio-technical System. Jönköping International Business School. Center for Information Technology and Information Systems (2020)
10. Lindenfalk, B., Resmini, A.: Mapping an ambient assisted living service as a seamful cross-channel ecosystem. In: Pfannstiel, M.A., Rasche, C. (eds.) Service Design and Service Thinking in Healthcare and Hospital Management, pp. 289–314. Springer, Cham (2019). https://doi.org/10.1007/978-3-030-00749-2_17
11. Meadows, D.H.: Thinking in Systems: A Primer. Chelsea Green Publishing (2008)
12. Norberg-Schulz, C.: Existence, Space, and Architecture. Praeger Publishers (1974)
13. Preece, J., Rogers, Y., Sharp, H., Benyon, D., Holland, S., Carey, T.: Human-Computer Interaction. Addison-Wesley, Boston (1994)
14. Resmini, A., Lacerda, F.: The architecture of cross-channel ecosystems. In: Proceedings of the 8th International Conference on Management of Digital EcoSystems – MEDES (2016). https://doi.org/10.1145/3012071.3012087
15. Resmini, A., Lindenfalk, B.: Mapping experience ecosystems as emergent actor-created spaces. In: Hameurlain, A., Tjoa, A.M., Chbeir, R. (eds.) Transactions on Large-Scale Data- and Knowledge-Centered Systems XLVII. LNCS, vol. 12630, pp. 1–28. Springer, Heidelberg (2021). https://doi.org/10.1007/978-3-662-62919-2_1

16. Resmini, A., Rosati, L.: Information architecture for ubiquitous ecologies. In: Proceedings of the International Conference on Management of Digital Ecosystems – MEDES (2009). https://doi.org/10.1145/1643823.1643859

17. Simeone, L., et al.: Articulating a strategic approach to face complexity in design projects: the role of theory of change. In: Proceedings of the Academy for Design Innovation Management Conference, London, UK (2019). https://doi.org/10.33114/adim.2019.01.188

18. Stein, D., Valters, C.: Understanding 'Theory of change' in international development: a review of existing knowledge. The Asia Foundation and the Justice and Security Research Programme at the London School of Economics and Political Science (2012)

19. Stephanidis, C., et al.: Seven HCI grand challenges. Int. J. Hum. Comput. Interact. **35**(14), 1229–1269 (2019). https://doi.org/10.1080/10447318.2019.1619259

20. Stroh, D.P.: Systems Thinking for Social Change. Chelsea Green Publishing (2015)

21. Weiser, M.: Ubiquitous computing. In: Proceedings of the USENIX Conference 1995 (1995)

22. Weiss, C.H.: Nothing as practical as good theory: exploring theory-based evaluation for comprehensive community initiatives for children and families. In: Connell, J.P., Kubisch, A.C., Schorr, L.B., Weiss, C.H. (eds.) New Approaches to Evaluating Community Initiatives: Concepts, Methods and Contexts, pp. 65–92. Aspen Institute, New York (1995)

Design of Sustainable Food Management System Based on User's Whole Behavior Process

Li Wang[✉], Zhengyu Wang, Meiyu Zhou, Yibing Wu, Jinyao Zhang, Yajing Xu, Lu Zhong, and Hanwen Du

School of Art Design and Media, East China University of Science and Technology, No. 130, Meilong Road, Xuhui District, Shanghai, People's Republic of China

Abstract. Food waste is a persistent global problem with negative economic, environmental, and social impacts. Consumers are one of the main sources of food waste. Many scholars have studied consumer behavior, but relatively little research has been conducted on the design and practice of consumer waste behavior intervention strategies, and the construction of a sustainable system is comparatively lacking.

From the perspective of a sustainable system, the article takes human behavior as the key element in the system and promotes sustainable food consumption by intervening in user behaviors. First, user behaviors are integrated according to the processes of food planning, purchasing, storage, cooking, consumption, and disposition, and we analyze the causes of food waste based on the theory of planned behavior using observation and semi-structured interviews. Second, behavioral intervention strategies are formulated, including information, modeling, education, and feedback. Finally, a food management system is constructed, based on which the application that interfere with user behavior are developed.

The research explores the complex relationship between consumer behavior and food waste phenomena, proposes design-led intervention strategies, and provides users with feasible food management processes, thus reducing food waste and providing a reference for future research.

Keywords: The theory of planned behavior · Behavioral intervention · Food management · System development

1 Introduction

The Food and Agriculture Organization of the United Nations estimates that one-third of all food produced for human consumption is lost and wasted, amounting to 1.3 billion tons per year [1]. In addition to causing economic losses, food waste leads to resource waste, climate change and is associated with inequality in social distribution.

Consumers are one of the major sources of food waste. The literature related to consumer food waste mainly focuses on the following aspects: (1) analysis on the causes and motivations of consumers' food waste. Graham-Rowe et al. [2] use the extended theory of planned behavior to predict motivations and behaviors of reducing food waste; (2) the impact of consumer food waste. Jeswani et al. [3] have measured the life-cycle

© Springer Nature Switzerland AG 2021
C. Stephanidis et al. (Eds.): HCII 2021, CCIS 1421, pp. 521–527, 2021.
https://doi.org/10.1007/978-3-030-78645-8_66

environmental influence of food waste; (3) strategies to reduce consumer food waste. Preventive actions [4], demand control [5], food storage, and management strategies [6] have been proposed. At present, many works of literature focus on the theoretical aspects of consumer behavior, however, relatively little research has been conducted on the design and practice of consumer waste behavior intervention strategies. Meanwhile, research of consumer behavior intervention strategies at the system level is comparatively lacking.

Based on the whole behavioral process of consumers from food purchase to disposal, the study uses the theory of planned behavior to analyze the causes of food waste, develops behavioral intervention strategies, and applies them to design practice, thus helping consumers improve their motivations and abilities to reduce waste.

2   Theoretical Background

2.1   The Theory of Planned Behavior

The theory of planned behavior [7] is one of the models for predicting human behavior. According to the theory, behavioral intention affects human behavior, while the intention is influenced by attitude, subjective norm, and perceived behavior control. The theory of planned behavior is currently widely used in the research of consumers' food waste behavior. For example, Stefan et al. [8] explore the core cognitive structure stipulated by the theory of planned behavior in the context of food waste, and Abdelradi et al. [9] use the extended theory of planned behavior to explain consumer food waste behavior in restaurants.

The theory of planned behavior effectively explains the causes of consumer food waste behavior, predicts motivations and barriers to food waste reduction, and provides a reference basis for the formulation of behavioral intervention strategies.

2.2   Behavioral Intervention Strategies

Behavioral intervention is how human beings affect or change specific behaviors through intervention. Tang [10] establishes a design behavioral intervention model, which has applied the social-psychological theories of behavior to user behavior intervention. De Young [11] classifies intervention methods into information intervention, motivational intervention, and compulsory intervention based on different persuasive techniques. Geller et al. [12] divide intervention strategies into pre-action (e.g., information, education, and behavioral commitment) and post-action (e.g., feedback, rewards, and punishment).

This article uses the theory of planned behavior to analyze the specific causes of household food waste and puts forward corresponding design intervention strategies. However, influencing or changing consumer attitude, subjective norm, and perceived behavior control belong to pre-action intervention methods and lack post-action intervention strategies. At the same time, the theory of planned behavior is oriented towards a specific target, action, context, and time, lacking long-term dimension considerations, and it is not clear whether consumers can maintain behavioral changes. Therefore, we should not only formulate intervention strategies according to the theory of planned behavior but also consider the whole behavioral process of users and long-term intervention strategy development.

3 Methods

3.1 Design and Procedure

This research adopts observation and semi-structured interview methods to collect research data.

Observation. Researchers conduct field trips to supermarkets and shopping malls to obtain data on consumer behavior. Besides, the researchers follow the daily dietary habits of three families, thus obtaining more accurate data on food preparation, consumption, and disposition.

Semi-structured interview. Before the interview, participants should complete an informed consent form, confidential information, and a short personal information questionnaire. Based on the interview outline, researchers would ask the participants some questions flexibly, which are recorded with their permission. The interview content mainly includes the following aspects: (1) planning and purchasing. For example, please describe your preparation before buying food; (2) storage. For instance, understanding of the food shelf-life; (3) cooking and consumption; (4) disposal. For example, willingness to donate; (5) attitudes and feelings toward food waste.

3.2 Participants

Sampling criteria for semi-structured interviews are: (1) 18–50 years old; (2) Chinese consumers; (3) provider for the household food independently, with relatively rich cooking experience. The specific sample selection mainly takes into account the differences in age, gender, family structure, educational background, and income. The sample demographics are shown in Fig. 1.

Sample number	Age	Gender	Education	Family Structure	Income
01	25	F	Postgraduate Student	Couples	None
02	22	M	Bachelor Degree	2 Parents /1 Child	None
03	46	F	High school Degree	2 Parents /2 Childs	4-5K RMB
04	33	F	PhD student	Couples	9-10K RMB
05	23	F	Bachelor Degree	2 Parents /3 Childs	None
06	28	F	Bachelor Degree	2 Parents /1 Child	6-8K RMB
07	26	M	Bachelor Degree	Alone	9-10K RMB
08	31	M	Bachelor Degree	2 Parents /1 Child	6-8K RMB
09	20	F	Undergraduate	2 Parents /2 Childs	None
10	27	F	Bachelor Degree	2 Parents /1 Child	6-8k RMB

Fig. 1. Demographics of interview samples

3.3 Analysis of the Causes of Food Waste in Consumers' Households

Based on the observation method and semi-structured interview, this research analyzes the whole behavior process of consumers' food waste from the perspective of planned behavior theory. Barriers to food waste reduction at every stage of the diet, and according to the theory of planned behavior, these unsustainable behaviors are closely related to psychosocial factors such as consumer attitude, subjective norm, and perceived behavioral control. Attitude refers to consumers' positive or negative evaluations of food waste. Subjective norm refers to the social pressure consumers feel when they waste food. Perceived behavior control means that consumers feel relaxed or difficult when reducing food waste [13].

The study has analyzed the behaviors, influencing factors, and specific reflections that led to waste in each diet stage, and mapped household food waste journey, as shown in Fig. 2. It should be noted that Fig. 2 only lists the factors contributing to food waste and not those that contribute to its reduction.

HOUSEHOLD FOOD WASTE JOURNEY					
Planning	**Purchase**	**Storage**	**Cooking**	**Consumption**	**Disposition**
Lack of planning	Impulse consumption	Sub-optimal storage	Waste ingredients	Food preferences	Throw away directly
Attitude -Not very useful Perceived Behavioral Control -Difficult -High time cost	Attitude -Discount Perceived Behavioral Control -Can't resist temptation	Perceived Behavioral Control -Lack of storage knowledge	Attitude -Normal consumption Perceived Behavioral Control -Sub-optimal culinary skills	Attitude -Eating favorite food can bring pleasure -Not want to force themselves to eat food they don't like	Attitude -It is a normal phenomenon Perceived Behavioral Control -Garbage sorting is troublesome -Lack of knowledge about handling leftovers
Lack of communication among household members	Buying too much food	Not eaten within the expiration date	Cooking too much food	Perceived Behavioral Control	
Attitude -No good results -The conflict between favorite foods and healthy eating	Attitude -Worry about not enough to eat -Large package is cheaper Subjective Norm -Want to be a good provider Perceived Behavioral Control -Lack of assessment of food portions -Save time cost	Attitude -Not want to eat Perceived Behavioral Control -Forget -No understanding of food shelf life	Attitude -Not enough to eat -Trying to get family members to eat a little more for nutrition Subjective Norm -Good Provider Perceived Behavioral Control -Hard to control the amount of food -Lack of flexible coping style	-Easier to eat favorite food -Eating unpleasant food is relatively difficult	
Lacking of fridge checking		Lack of food management			
Attitude -Don't want to eat what they have at home Perceived Behavioral Control -Lack of food management skills -High time cost	Choose foods that look good Attitude -Mean better quality and fresh	Attitude -Not necessary Perceived Behavioral Control -High time cost -High cost of learning	No longer cooking leftovers Attitude -No need to be too economical style Perceived Behavioral Control -Inability to cook leftovers into new meals		

Fig. 2. Household food waste journey

4 Results

4.1 Intervention Strategies Formulation

Based on the theory of planned behavior, the research proposes behavioral intervention strategies and takes into account the limitations of the theory, thus complementing intervention strategies after actions. This paper incorporates previous research to classify behavioral intervention strategies into (1) pre-action, including commitment, goal setting, information, modeling (examples of recommended behaviors), education, simplification, and environmental design, and (2) post-action, including feedback (continuous feedback, weekly or monthly feedback, and comparative feedback), rewards, and punishment (Fig. 3).

Intervention Strategies for Household Food Waste Behavior					
Planning	**Purchase**	**Storage**	**Cooking**	**Consumption**	**Disposition**
Lack of planning	Impulse consumption	Sub-optimal storage	Waste ingredients	Food preferences	Throw away directly
① Education. Publicize the importance of food planning. ② Modeling. Provide excellent examples. ③ Simplification. Provide only essential information. ④ Awards. Offer points, coupons and other rewards.	Feedback. Offer information of un-planned food (type, amount, etc.)	① Information. Provide basic information of food storage. ② Feedback. Information on food waste caused by improper storage.	Information. Provide proper cooking methods.	① Education. The importance of balanced nutrition. ② Modeling. Techniques for improving the taste, shape, etc of the unpleasant food.	① Environmental Design. Easier ways of sorting or disposing of waste. ② Modeling. Knowledge sharing on dealing with leftovers.
Lack of communication among household members Information. Provide tailored family diet information, for example, making recipe recommendations based on family members' health information and dietary preferences.	**Buying too much food** ① Simplification. A more convenient way to buy food. ② Information. The balance between the "good provider" role and moderate purchases. ③ Environmental Design. Visualize the amount of food they need.	**Not eaten within the expiration date** ① Feedback. Economic value of loss and environmental impact. ② Information. Remind to eat. ③ Education. Popularization of expiration date knowledge. ④ Awards. Users can get bonus points, coupons, etc. after eating within a specified period of time.	**Cooking too much food** ① Education. The importance of proper diet. ② Modeling. Good examples of balancing the "good provider" role with waste reduction. ③ Awards. Help consumers gain social recognition on the platform. ④ Information. Tailored cooking volume information.		
Lacking of fridge checking ① Goal Setting. Help users consume food within a specified time. ② Awards. Users can get bonus points or coupons after the goal is completed. ③ Simplification. Simplify the method of food management and visualize family food.	**Choose foods that look good** Education. Advocating the value of ugly fruits and vegetables.	**Lack of food management** ① Simplification. Simplify the method of food management and improve the learning ability of users. ② Modeling. Provide excellent cases of food management. ③ Awards. Guide users to share feasible food management methods on the platform and give some rewards.	**No longer cooking leftovers** ① Modeling. Provide tips for rational use of leftovers. ② Awards. Users can gain social recognition by uploading their leftovers using skills.		

Fig. 3. Intervention strategies for household food waste behavior

4.2 Food Management System

Based on the above intervention strategies, we have constructed a food management system and developed an related application to help Chinese consumers improve food utilization and reduce food waste. Data on food storage, consumption, and disposition can provide feedback for the next dietary plan. In the food disposal part, leftovers can be cooked into a new meal, and unwanted food can be donated or resold. Besides, household food storage information can remind consumers to eat as soon as possible (Fig. 4).

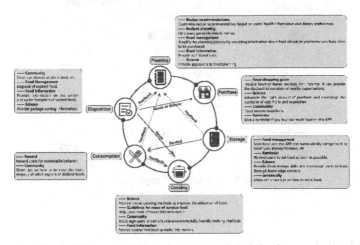

Fig. 4. System model based on user's whole behavior process

The application has the following main functions: (1) Food management. Visualization of the user's household food information; (2) Consumption reminder. Prevent food from being unusable due to expiration and deterioration; (3) Popularization of food science. Provision food planning, storage, cooking, nutrition matching methods, etc.; (4) Recipe recommendation. Customize recipes based on users' health information and dietary preferences; (5) Surplus food utilization guide; (6) Food buying guidelines. Provision of location-based services; (7) Food information analysis. It includes water footprint, carbon footprint, nutritional information, etc.; (8) Community. A platform to provide information on food management, cooking, donations, etc.; (9) Feedback and reward mechanism. It can motivate users to change their behaviors in the long run.

4.3 APP Display —— "FoodSpace"

The "FoodSpace"' application is planned and designed based on the user's whole behavioral process. The picture on the left displays the user's household food information. The user scans the barcode or manually enters the product information, sets the shelf life or freshness date, and the app automatically sorts the food and reminds the user to consume it in time. The right figure shows data on expired food, including the impact of weekly food waste and cumulative effects. The economic loss, water footprint, and carbon footprint impact caused by food waste are described in a visual form (Fig. 5).

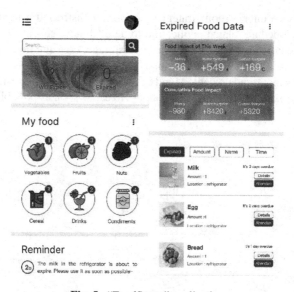

Fig. 5. "FoodSpace" application

5   Conclusion

Based on the whole process of consumer behavior from food purchase to disposition, the research explores the influence of attitude, subjective norm, and perceived behavior control on consumer's family food waste, proposes the intervention strategies before and after food waste. At last, we construct the food management system and develop the "Food Space" application, which aims to apply the design behavior intervention strategies in practice.

However, the study still has some limitations. The influence of attitude, subjective norm, and perceived behavior control on food waste behavior vary from stage to stage, while other psychosocial factors such as negative emotions and social norms are not discussed. In future research, we will discuss the effectiveness of intervention strategies and explore whether these strategies can help consumers maintain long-term behavioral changes.

References

1. Fao, G.: Global food losses and food waste–Extent, causes and prevention. SAVE FOOD: An Initiative on Food Loss and Waste Reduction (2011)
2. Graham-Rowe, E., Jessop, D.C., Sparks, P.: Predicting household food waste reduction using an extended theory of planned behaviour. Resour. Conserv. Recycl. **101**, 194–202 (2015). https://doi.org/10.1016/j.resconrec.2015.05.020
3. Jeswani, H.K., Figueroa-Torres, G., Azapagic, A.: The extent of food waste generation in the UK and its environmental impacts. Sustain. Prod. Consumption **26**, 532–547 (2021)
4. Thyberg, K., Tonjes, D.: A management framework for municipal solid waste systems and its application to food waste prevention. Systems **3**(3), 133–151 (2015). https://doi.org/10.3390/systems3030133
5. Konstadinos, A., Lasaridi, K., Chroni, C.: Food waste prevention in Athens, Greece: the effect of family characteristics. Waste Manag. Res. **34**(12), 1210–1216 (2016)
6. Messner, R., Johnson, H., Richards, C.: From surplus-to-waste: a study of systemic overproduction, surplus and food waste in horticultural supply chains. J. Cleaner Prod. **278**, 123952 (2021). https://doi.org/10.1016/j.jclepro.2020.123952
7. Ajzen, I.: The theory of planned behavior. Organ. Behav. Human Decis. Process. **50**(2), 179–211 (1991). https://doi.org/10.1016/0749-5978(91)90020-T
8. Stefan, V., van Herpen, E., Tudoran, A.A., Lähteenmäki, L.: Avoiding food waste by Romanian consumers: the importance of planning and shopping routines. Food Quality Prefer. **28**(1), 375–381 (2013). https://doi.org/10.1016/j.foodqual.2012.11.001
9. Fadi, A.: Food waste behaviour at the household level: a conceptual framework. Waste Manag. **71**, 485–493 (2018)
10. Tang, T.: Towards sustainable use: design behaviour intervention to reduce household environment impact. Diss. Loughborough University (2010)
11. Raymond, D.Y.: Changing behavior and making it stick: The conceptualization and management of conservation behavior. Environ. Behav. **25**(3), 485505 (1993)
12. Scott, G.E., Winett, R.A., Everett, P.B.: Preserving the environment: New strategies for behavior change. No. 102. Pergamon (1982)
13. Coşkun, A., Özbük, R.M.Y.: What influences consumer food waste behavior in restaurants? An application of the extended theory of planned behavior. Waste Manag. **117**, 170–178 (2020)

Applying Hierarchical Task Analysis to Improve the Safety of High-Speed Railway: How Dispatchers Can Better Handle the Breakdown of Rail-Switch

Ziyue Wang[1,2], Jingyu Zhang[1,2(✉)], Xianghong Sun[1,2(✉)], and Zizheng Guo[3]

[1] Institute of Psychology, Chinese Academy of Sciences, Beijing, China
{zhangjingyu,sunxh}@psych.ac.cn
[2] Department of Psychology, University of Chinese Academy of Sciences, Beijing, China
[3] School of Transportation and Logistics, Southwest Jiaotong University, Chengdu, China

Abstract. The train dispatchers of high speed railways (HSR) play an important role in guarantee the safety and efficiency of railway traffic. However, the task properties and potential human errors lied in the dispatching work is not fully understood. In this study, we intended to make a task analysis and examine the possible human errors in HSR dispatchers' handling of the rail-switch breakdown, a relatively common equipment failure with a serious impact.

To achieve these goals, we conducted semi-structured interviews with five experienced train dispatchers working on the newest centralized traffic control system of China's HSR. We used the hierarchical task analysis (HTA) to understand their critical operations during the handling of rail-switch breakdown. Then we used the systematic human error reduction and prediction approach (SHERPA) to analyze possible human errors throughout the entire process.

We found that this process include detecting the failure, notifying the train drivers to stop or slow down, attempting reinitiation, rescheduling to slow down the traffic, coordinating the repairment, and resuming the normal traffic. The most common human errors include: forget certain operations, conduct wrong operations, and failure to communicate specific information.

We further discussed how these errors should be prevented.

Keywords: China's high-speed railway · Dispatcher · Hierarchical task analysis · Human errors · Breakdown of rail-switch

1 Introduction

During the rapid development of China's high-speed railway (HSR), the core function played by HSR dispatchers has begun to draw the attention of human factor researchers. To ensure a safe and efficient operation of the complex socio-technical system, HSR train dispatchers (hereinafter referred to as "dispatchers") need to monitor the traffic flow and resolve the potential conflicts using the advanced centralized traffic control system. Past studies on normal speed railways have found that human errors made by

© Springer Nature Switzerland AG 2021
C. Stephanidis et al. (Eds.): HCII 2021, CCIS 1421, pp. 528–536, 2021.
https://doi.org/10.1007/978-3-030-78645-8_67

dispatchers can result in severe consequences. For example, based on the analysis of 215 train accidents, dispatching errors were found to be the second most common cause of train's fatal collisions and derailments [1].

In order to effectively reduce the human errors of dispatchers, understanding their tasks is vital. Several attempts have been made by using certain task analyses methods to draw a detailed task diagrams to represent dispatchers' core work elements [2–4]. However, the findings of these studies cannot be directly used for the China's HSR system because they were based on normal speed railway systems or an organizational system very different from the China's. To the best of our knowledge, only one study has examined the general tasks of China' HSR dispatchers [5]. In this study, they have found that each section was managed by a dispatching station run by two dispatchers: the main dispatcher (MD) and the assistant dispatcher (AD). Generally speaking, the main dispatchers take primary responsibility to monitor and manage the trains. In contrast, the assistant dispatchers manage the signals and equipment (taking the role of signalers and on-site operators in traditional railway systems). The dispatchers work in a rotation manner between the two positions. However, the approach used by that study was too broad so it is hardly to understand how a certain work was carried out and how can relevant human errors be prevented.

In order to improve our understanding of the HSR dispatcher's working process, we planned to conduct a detailed hierarchical task analysis (HTA) on dispatchers' handling of a relatively common equipment failure with a large impact, the breakdown of railway-switch. We also attempted to use the Systematic Human Error Reduction and Prediction Approach (SHERPA) to further analyze their possible human errors.

2 Method

2.1 Subjects

Five male licensed HSR dispatchers from Chengdu Railway Bureau participated in this study. The average age was 32.6 (SD = 3.90). Their direct HSR dispatching experience was ranging from six months to four years. To note, all of them had worked as signalers and normal-speed railway dispatchers before becoming an HSR dispatcher. Given the HSR system was very new, those with 3 or 4 years of experience are among the most experienced group when they were interviewed (January 2021) [5].

2.2 Hierarchical Task Analysis (HTA)

HTA is the most popular task analysis technique and has become perhaps the most widely used of all available human factor techniques. HTA involves describing the activity under analysis in terms of a hierarchy of goals, sub-goals, operations and plans. The end result is an exhaustive description of task activity [6].

2.3 The Systematic Human Error Reduction and Prediction Approach (SHERPA)

SHERPA uses a behavioural classification linked to an external error mode taxonomy (action, retrieval, check, selection and information communication errors) to identify potential errors associated with human activity. The SHERPA technique works by indicating which error modes are credible for each bottom-level task step in an HTA. The analyst classifies a task step into a behaviour and then determines whether any of the associated error modes are credible. For each credible error, the analyst describes the error and determines the consequences, error recovery, probability and criticality. Finally, design remedies are proposed for each error identified. In this study, we put the "remedies" in the "Conclusion and Discussion" part to talk about together. And the error modes are listed as follows [6].

Action Errors

A1 – Operation too long/short

A2 – Operation mistimed

A3 – Operation in wrong direction

A4 – Operation too little/much

A5 – Misalign

A6 – Right operation on wrong object

A7 – Wrong operation on right object

A8 – Operation omitted

A9 – Operation incomplete

A10 – Wrong operaon on wrong object

Checking Errors

C1 – Check omitted

C2 – Check incomplete

C3 – Right check on wrong object

C4 – Wrong check on right object

C5 – Check mistimed

C6 – Wrong check on wrong object

Retrieval Errors

R1 – Information not obtained

R2 – Wrong information obtained

R3 – Information retrieval incomplete

Communication Errors

I1 – Information not communicated

I2 – Wrong information communicated

I3 – Information communication incomplete

Selection Errors

S1 – Selection omitted

S2 – Wrong selection made

2.4 Procedure

To conduct the HTA, we first collected and reviewed relevant literature including previous task analyses studies on train dispatchers, the organization description of Chinese HSR system, the job description of Chinese HSR dispatcher's and the handbook of their daily operations. Then we invited five experienced HSR dispatchers to examine the critical operations during the handling of rail-switch breakdown. We transcribed the interviews and we defined the goals and the sub-goals throughout the entire process. Then we extracted the trigger conditions of each goal. By integrating this information, we drew an initial task diagram. Using plans established by the HTA, we conducted the SHERPA analysis and the draw the table in which the error type, error consequence, way of recovery, probability, criticality, and possible remedies were included. Next, we invited a SME to help revise the results of HTA and SHERPA. According to the SME's advice, we refined the results of HTA and SHERPA (Fig. 1).

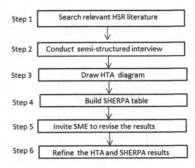

Fig. 1. The procedure of the research

3 Results

3.1 The Breakdown of Rail-Switch Hierarchical Task Analysis

The two dispatchers working on one section would handle the rail-switch breakdown in the following major steps. Firstly, the warning signals would be detected by either MD or AD. Upon that, an initial judgment will be made jointly to determine the use of the standard operation procedure of switch breakdown. Then, they have to quickly notify the nearest train driver to stop and the following drivers to slow down. Next, the MD will reschedule the traffic on the time - distance graph and the AD will readjust the track to be used and place the block sign. Next, the AD will attempt to reinitiate the switch by using a standard reboot operation (maximumly to three times). If the switch can be successfully restarted, the MD and the AD will coordinate to resume the normal traffic. The MD will reschedule the traffic on the time - distance graph and the AD will readjust the track to be used and remove the block sign. Then they will inform train drivers to resume. If the switch cannot be restarted after three attempts, the MD and the AD will coordinate the repairment by contacting many other departments. After the repairment has been finished, MD and AD will coordinate to resume the normal traffic (Fig. 2).

3.2 The SHERPA Analysis of the Breakdown of Rail-Switch

The analysis of SHERPA revealed that most common human errors include: forget certain operations, conduct wrong operations, and failure to communicate specific information. In addition, the mutual check and reminding between MD and AD is very important (Table 1).

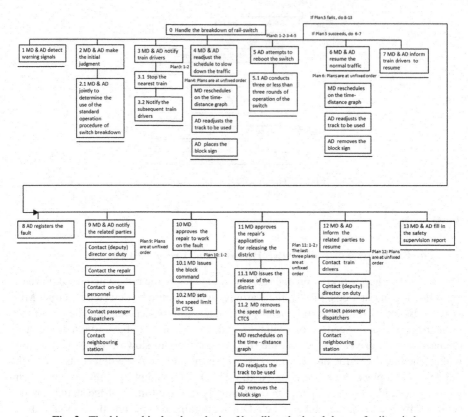

Fig. 2. The hierarchical task analysis of handling the breakdown of rail-switch

Table 1. SHERPA output

Task step	Error mode	Error description	Consequence	Recovery	P	C
1	C1	Omit critical alarms	Train driver passively park	Train drivers contact the main dispatcher	L	M
2	R2	Breakdown diagnosis error	The breakdown doesn't responded correctly	Immediately	L	L
3.1	A8/I1	Omit to notify the train driver	Traffic congestion	AD reminds MD or the train driver contact MD	H	L

(continued)

Table 1. (*continued*)

Task step	Error mode	Error description	Consequence	Recovery	P	C
3.2	A8/I1	Omit one or more certain drivers	Traffic congestion	AD reminds MD or the train driver contact MD	H	H
4 MD reschedules on the time - distance graph	A7/A8	Omit/incorrect operation	Traffic congestion	AD reminds MD or system alarms	M	H
4 AD readjusts the track to be used	A7/A8	Omit/incorrect operation	Traffic congestion	MD reminds AD or system alarms	M	L
4 AD places the block sign	A7/A8	Omit/incorrect operation	Traffic congestion	MD reminds AD	M	M
5.1	A4	Operation too little/much	Train derailment; Waste human and resources; Trains' delay	MD and AD remind and supervise each other	L	H
6 MD reschedules on the time - distance graph	A7/A8	Omit/incorrect operation	Trains' delay	AD reminds MD or system alarms	L	L
6 AD readjusts the track to be used	A7/A8	Omit/incorrect operation	Trains' delay	MD reminds AD or system alarms	L	L
6 AD removes the block sign	A7/A8	Omit/incorrect operation	Trains' delay	MD reminds AD	L	L
7	A8/I1	Omit related staff	The information isn't delivered in time	AD reminds MD or the related parties ask the MD	L	L
8	A8/I2	Forget to register/the content of registration is lack of standardization	The fault isn't recorded in time; Nonstandard content is recorded	Immediately	L	L
9	A8/I1	Forget to contact related staff as required;	Related parties won' t carry out the task; Repairment time delayed	AD or (deputy) director on duty) reminds MD	L	M

(*continued*)

Table 1. (*continued*)

Task step	Error mode	Error description	Consequence	Recovery	P	C
10.1	A7/I1	Issue wrong command; Omit related stations	Block the wrong district; The neighbouring station doesn't know the state of the train	AD, on-site personnel or the neighbouring station reminds MD	L	H
10.2	A2/A7	Wrong time/distance	Train emergency braking; Endangering the safety of the repair	AD or on-site personnel reminds MD	L	H
11.1	A8/I1	Issue wrong command; Omit related stations	Release the wrong district; The neighboring station doesn't know the progress of fault repair	AD or on-site personnel reminds MD	L	L
11.2	A2/A7	Wrong time/distance	Trains' delay	Immediately	L	M
11.3 MD reschedules on the time - distance graph	A7/A8	Omit/incorrect operation	Trains' delay	AD reminds MD or system alarms	L	L
11.3 AD readjusts the track to be used	A7/A8	Omit/incorrect operation	Trains' delay	MD reminds AD or system alarms	L	L
11.3 AD removes the block sign	A7/A8	Omit/incorrect operation	Trains' delay	MD reminds AD	L	L
12	A8/I1	Omit related staff	The information isn't delivered in time	AD reminds MD or the related parties ask the MD	L	L
13	A8	Error in filling	The fault isn't recorded correctly	AD or (deputy) director on duty reminds MD	M	L

4 Conclusion and Discussion

In this study, we aimed to systematically decompose one of the most critical tasks of HSR dispatchers: handling the rail-switch breakdown. In doing so, we used the hierarchical task analysis (HTA). Based on the HTA results, we further conducted the systematic human error reduction and prediction approach (SHERPA) to understand the possible human errors throughout the whole process.

We found that the HSR dispatchers would handle the rail-switch breakdown in the following major steps: detecting the failure, notifying the train drivers to stop or slow down, attempting reinitiation, rescheduling to slow down the traffic, coordinating the repairment, and resuming the normal traffic. The SHERPA analyses further revealed that the most common human errors include: forget certain operations, conduct wrong operations, and failure to communicate specific information. The findings were consistent with a previous study that found that skill-based errors were among the top categories of human errors in dispatchers' work [7].

According to the analyses, we made the following suggestions to improve safety and reduce HSR dispatching operation errors. First, the HSR dispatchers need to have strong safety attitudes and motivation. Whereas slowing down the whole schedule or fulfill mutual checks may result in burdensome operations, it is the best way to guarantee safety. The HSR dispatchers cannot take an opportunistic view and sacrificing safety for efficiency and convenience. Second, coordination is essential. Since most errors can be prevented if the main dispatcher and the assistant dispatcher always check others' operations according to the safety regulations, building a harmonious relationship may help their voluntary mutual monitoring. For procedures that involve many other parties, the HSR dispatchers must have a clear mental picture of all other staff members' working process dynamically. It is possible to add specific visualizing tools to enhance their situational awareness in future systems. Finally, skill training and maintenance are very crucial. Since the equipment failure only occurs infrequently, it is hard for the HSR dispatchers to have an authentic experience. So it is vital to use the high fidelity simulator to improve HSR dispatchers' handling capacity. For this purpose, the present study can help design useful scenarios for HSR dispatchers to learn.

References

1. Evans, A.W.: Fatal train accidents on Europe's railways: 1980–2009. Acc. Anal. Prev. **43**(1), 391–401 (2011)
2. Farrington Darby, T., Wilson, J.R., Norris, B.J., et al.: A naturalistic study of railway controllers. Ergonomics **49**(12/13), 1370–1394 (2006)
3. Roth, E.M., Malsch, N., Multer, J.: Understanding how train dispatchers manage and control trains: results of a cognitive task analysis. No. DOT-VNTSC-FRA-98-3. United States. Federal Railroad Administration (2001)
4. Roth, E.M., et al.: Analyzing railroad dispatchers' strategies: a cognitive task analysis of a distributed team planning task. In: SMC 1998 Conference Proceedings 1998 IEEE International Conference on Systems, Man, and Cybernetics (Cat. No. 98CH36218), vol. 3. IEEE (1998)
5. Chen, Z., Guo, Z., Guo, F., Zhang, J.: A qualitative study on the workload of high-speed railway dispatchers. In: International Conference on Human-Computer Interaction. Springer, Cham (accepted)

6. Stanton, N., Salmon, P.M., Rafferty, L.A.: Human Factors Methods: A Practical Guide for Engineering and Design. Ashgate Publishing, Ltd., Brookfield (2013)
7. Zhou, J.L., Lei, Y.: Paths between latent and active errors: analysis of 407 railway accidents/incidents' causes in China. Safety Sci. (2017)

HCI in the Time of Pandemic

A User-Centered Mobile Interface Design, Promoting Physical Activity in the Covid 19 Pandemic's Sedentary Lifestyle

Zahra Alizadeh Elizei[✉] [iD]

Student of Master of Industrial Design at Georgia Institute of Technology, Atlanta, GA, USA

Abstract. The outbreak of coronavirus disease 2019 (COVID-19) caused by Severe Acute Respiratory Syndrome Coronavirus 2 (SARS-CoV-2), has become a global public health threat [1]. As the number of Covid 19 cases have been increasing worldwide, the governments have tried to control the disease by enforcing severe measures such as the closure of schools, and recreational centers. Under this necessary self-isolating conditions, many people have faced unhealthy behaviors, such as sedentary lifestyle. Physical inactivity raises the risk of many chronic diseases namely coronary heart disease, diabetes, depression, and stroke. Mobile applications as the most engaging medium of interaction can be used to promote physical activity through this condition. The purpose of this research is to design a health and running app based on user-centered research. A systematic review of the functional features of the related "Health & Running" mobile apps is conducted in the first phase. The user-centered research investigating the needs assessment is carried out through the user survey, and focus group. Behavioral Change Techniques (BCTs) and gamification are elements added into design to enhance the efficiency of the app. Passive and active notifications, training screens, goal setting, and action planning are BCT components incorporated into the design. The app would provide the users with active interventions and customizable features in order to help them stay motivated and follow the app. The model-driven development of the user interface from the storyboards to high-fidelity prototypes are produced to create a better perception of the design.

Keywords: User-center · Health & physical activity interface · Behavioral Change Technique · Gamification

1 Introduction

The outbreak of coronavirus disease 2019 (COVID-19) caused by Severe Acute Respiratory Syndrome Coronavirus 2 (SARS-CoV-2), has become a global public health threat [1]. As the number of Covid 19 cases have been increasing worldwide, the governments have tried to control the disease by enforcing severe measures such as the closure of schools, and recreational centers. Under this necessary self-isolating conditions, many people have faced unhealthy behaviors, such as sedentary lifestyle. Physical inactivity raises the risk of many chronic diseases namely coronary heart disease, diabetes, depression, and stroke.

© Springer Nature Switzerland AG 2021
C. Stephanidis et al. (Eds.): HCII 2021, CCIS 1421, pp. 539–550, 2021.
https://doi.org/10.1007/978-3-030-78645-8_68

Regular physical exercise not only helps maintain a healthy weight, but also strengthens the immune system [2]. In addition, it improves mental health. Smart phones as the pervasive devices are an ideal means to promote physical activities in people [7, 8]. In fact, mobile phone interventions can be effectively used to increase physical activity levels and lead to healthy lifestyle.

The importance of a healthy lifestyle and the fact that mobile phones are the most engaging medium of interaction have led to numerous health, and wellbeing related apps in the recent past [4]. However, none of the mobile applications present the holistic and integrative app that promote better adherence to physical activities. The purpose of this research is to design a health and running app based on user-centered research. Behavioral Change Techniques (BCTs) and gamification have been used in the structure and the contents of the designed app in order to effectively change the sedentary behavior of the users.

2   Methodology

In the first phase of the research, the related "Health & Running" apps are analyzed and their functional features are investigated. Second, the user-centered research is conducted through users' survey and focus group to collect more information about the needs of individuals. Behavioral Change Techniques (BCTs) and gamification are elements added into design to enhance the efficiency of the app.

2.1   A Systematic Review of the Functional Features in Related "Health & Running" Mobile Apps

Technological advancements have led to increased digitization within healthcare and sports [3]. There are the number of mobile applications designed for health, fitness, and running. First, the commercially available apps targeting physical activity and health are identified. Seven popular applications are selected, downloaded, and assessed through the next steps. Finally, the apps' main functional features are specified (Table 1).

The list of common features of the health, fitness activity, and running apps consists of the below items to name but a few.

1. Track activity, heart rate, blood pressure, and weight through the App
2. Possible to Customize the App
3. Help user reach his/her health goals
4. Sync data to Apple Health App
5. Help user to stay motivated
6. Connect with other Apps & devices
7. Based on Science
8. Simple & Easy to Use
9. Real-time Tracking
10. Interval Training
11. Live Cheering

12. Audio Cues
13. Assist user discover the best routes for running
14. Support turn-by-turn voice navigation

Table 1. A list of commercially health, fitness, & running apps with their functional features

Application Name	App Features
1. Google Fit App	*- Health and Activity Tracking App* *- Monitor Goals* *- Count Movements*
2. Runkeeper App	*- Track Workouts* *- Set Goals* *- Stay Motivated* *- Blood Pressure Monitor* *- Heart-Rate Measurement* *- Sleep Monitor* *- Calorie-Burn Counter*
3. Runtastic App (Adidas App)	*- Track Runs* *- GPS* *- Motivational App* *- Interval training* *- Customizable*
4. Pacer App	*- Set Goals* *- Personalized Fitness Plans* *- Record Activities* *- Discover Routs* *- Fun Challenges* *- Syncs data to Apple Health App*
5. Steps – Activity Tracker	*- Clear, Uncluttered Design* *- Set Goals* *- Calorie Tracking* *- Customized Activity* *- Activity History* *- Integrates with Apple Health*
6. StepsApp Pedometer	*- Automatic Step Counting* *- Stunning Charts & Animations* *- Apple Health Integration* *- Workouts with GPS Tracking* *- Active calories* *- Daily Goals & Notifications* *- Social Media sharing* *- Wheelchair Support* *- Export Data*
7. RunGo App	- Discover the Best Routs - Voice Navigation - Real-time Tracking - Using HealthKit

The data collected from the investigated apps, their functional features, and the users' ratings are analyzed. Considering the task description, important features are collected to assist a user with sedentary lifestyle to conduct a healthy, active life. Below, the chart represents the mentioned features (Fig. 1).

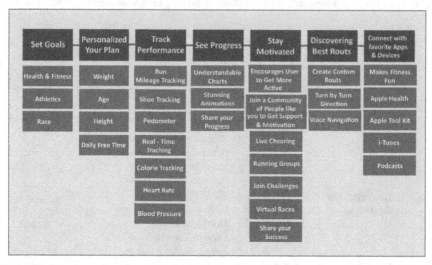

Fig. 1. The flowchart of important app features to assist user with the sedentary lifestyle to conduct a healthy, active life.

2.2 Needs Assessment Study

The needs assessment research is comprised of: 1) a survey, content analysis, and quality appraisal of mobile phone apps used in "Health & Fitness" activities. 2) focus group, a self-contained research method for gathering qualitative data from the users [10].

2.2.1 Survey

A survey containing questions related to "Health & Physical Activity" mobile apps is designed and conducted online. A total of 25 participants, from the age of (18 to 65) takes part in the survey.

2.2.1.1. Survey Analysis

The first question investigates the users' background in using "Health & Physical Activity" mobile apps. Based on the survey results, 80% of the participants have used the "Health & Physical Activity" mobile apps before, while 20% have not used such apps (see Graph 1).

The participants also are asked about the required features for "Health & Physical Activity" mobile app. According to the survey results, the three top features are "Track Performance", "Showing Progress", and "Help the User Stay Motivated". The other related features are represented through the following Graph 2.

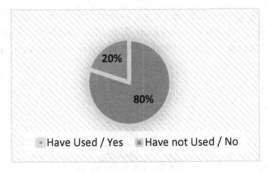

Graph 1. Using "health & physical activity" app

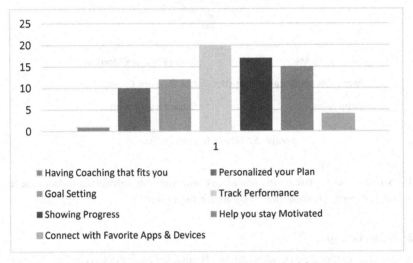

Graph 2. "Health & physical activity" required features

The preferable means for demonstrating the data for the users are considered graphs and charts. Moreover, Most participants, 68% prefer the combination of static and dynamic contents for the app, while 24% only like to face dynamic interface. The Graph 3 and 4 indicates the participants' opinions on the design of the interface of the app.

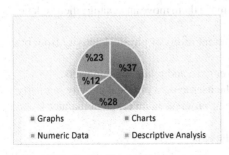

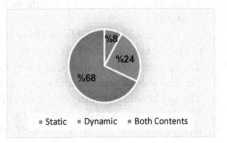

Graph 3. Preferable data demonstration   **Graph 4.** Preferable contents for the app

In addition, the users' ideas about the effective health features for the app are explored. The most important ones are Heart-Rate Measurement, Calorie-Burn Counter, and Blood Pressure Monitor. The related information is represented in the Graph 5.

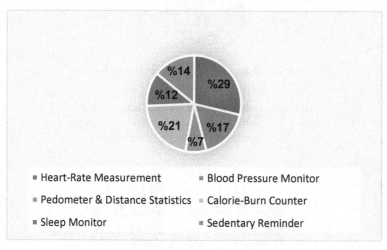

Graph 5. Health features in the app

The survey results provide the researcher with valuable information about the users' needs and demands, creating new insights for the design.

2.2.2 Focus Group

To more deeply explore users' ideas about "Health & Physical Activity" mobile app, an online focus group discussion session for one hour is set up with 9 participants. The session is recorded and transcribed verbatim. Then the qualitative data is analyzed through data grouping, information labels, and implications. The important themes obtained from the focus group are as below:

1. The users need creative, but easy to follow interface for "Health & Physical Activity" mobile app.
2. The users want effective interventions to make them move and change their sedentary lifestyle.
3. The app should be flexible and have different levels of physical activity from basic physical exercises to running.
4. The app should be designed in a way to engage and retain the app users.
5. The app should promote and persuade the user to do a physical activity regularly.
6. The app should demonstrate the users their progress in an efficient manner.
7. The design should avoid complexity.
8. Design of efficient user experience for the app.

2.3 Behavior Change Techniques

A behavior change technique (BCT) is a systematic procedure included as an active component of an intervention designed to change behavior [11]. Many elements of behavior change technique derive from those of health behavior theories, including the theory of reasoned action, the theory of planned behavior, social cognitive theory, the control theory, and the theories of social comparison [12]. The list of behavior change techniques associated with physical activity change are as below (Table 2).

Table 2. The list of behavior change techniques associated with physical activity change [6, 13].

BCT #	Behavior change technique
1	Prompt practice
2	Prompt self-monitoring of behavior
3	Goal-setting/intention formation
4	Barrier identification/problem solving
5	Provide feedback on performance
6	Prompt review of behavioral goals
7	Provide information on consequences of behavior in general
8	Action planning
9	Prompt rewards contingent on effort or progress towards behavior
10	Facilitate social comparison
11	Provide instruction
12	Self-reward
13	Social support
14	Teach to use prompts/cues

2.4 Gamification

Gamification as a technique to insert gameplay elements into design of the app, along with utilizing principles of behavior change technique can enhance user engagement with the app [5, 15]. The central idea is to take the 'building blocks' of games, and to implement these in real-world situations, often with the goal of motivating specific behaviors within the gamified situation [14].

A series of varied exercise in different levels is designed for users in the app, accompanied with game components such as a scoreboard, competition between friends, and awards and achievements to motivate users to achieve their personal goals.

2.5 Storyboard

User's experience with the app can be visually demonstrated through a storyboard. It can help string together personas, user stories and various research findings to develop requirements for the app [9]. In fact, it is a powerful human-centered approach for visualization, empathy and engagement of the user (Fig. 2).

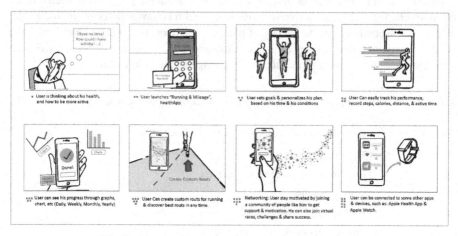

Fig. 2. The "health, fitness & running app" storyboard

3   Design Process

Based on the mentioned user-centered research, user survey and focus group along with the applied techniques such as behavior change techniques, gamification, and user storyboard, the design process begins. The interface design criteria is comprised of below steps:

1. Tailoring Variables
2. Decision Points and Rules
3. Intervention Options
4. Goal Setting
5. Types of Messages
6. Factors Affecting Adherence
7. Feedback, Motivation and Reinforcement
8. User Experience Designs
9. App Usage Patterns
10. App Evaluation Metrics

Considering the design criteria [17, 18], the low-fidelity prototypes of the interface are designed. The user journey map as a path, a user may take to obtain his or her goals in using the app is also provided (Fig. 3).

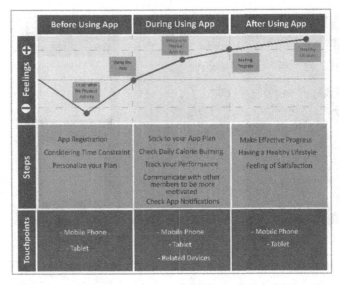

Fig. 3. The user journey map, "health & physical activity app"

3.1 Design of Mobile App Wireframes

Through the next steps, the design is developed and high-fidelity wireframes are produced (Figs. 4 and 5).

Fig. 4. App wireframes, user personalized plan

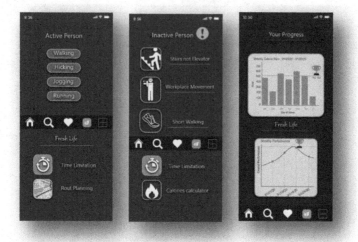

Fig. 5. App wireframes, goal setting – awards & achievements [19, 20]

4 Discussion

There are a number of fitness and running apps available in the market [16]. However, an app is required to increase users' engagement and help them enhance their physical activities regularly, especially during the pandemic sedentary lifestyle. The performed user-centered research and the employed design techniques such as behavioral change techniques (BCTs) and gamification take into account users' needs and their demands securely in the design process. Passive and active notifications, training screens, goal setting, action planning, self-monitoring are items designed in the app to encourage more physical activity in the users. Moreover, active interventions and customizable features of the app can enhance the efficiency.

5 Conclusion

The app is designed effectively in order to motivate the users to increase their physical activity through the app features. The employed design strategies, namely behavioral change techniques (BCTs) and gamification not only promote activeness in the users but also enhance their engagement. In fact, the users will stick to their action plan and finally achieve a healthy lifestyle. The high-fidelity wireframes of the app is produced successfully, which can provide detailed feedback on the certain elements of the design. Through the next steps of the research, the design would be developed; the comprehensive app would be created and evaluated by the users.

References

1. Rahman, E., et al.: Physical inactivity and sedentary behaviors in the Bangladeshi population during the COVID-19 pandemic: an online cross-sectional survey. Heliyon **6**, e05392 (2020)
2. Reiner, M., Niermann, C., et al.: Long-term health benefits of physical activity - a systematic review of longitudinal studies. BMC Public Health J. **13**, 813 (2013)
3. Muntaner-Mas, A., et al.: A systematic review of fitness apps and their potential clinical and sports utility for objective and remote assessment of cardiorespiratory fitness. Sports Med. **49**(4), 587–600 (2019). https://doi.org/10.1007/s40279-019-01084-y
4. Kranz, M., Möller, A., et al.: The mobile fitness coach: Towards individualized skill assessment using personalized mobile devices. Pervasive Mob. Comput. J. **9**(2), 203 (2013)
5. Dunn, E., Gainforth, H., Robertson-Wilson, J.: Behavior change techniques in mobile applications for sedentary behaviour. Digi. Health J. **4**, 2–5 (2018)
6. Brunstein, A., Brunstein, J., Martin, M.K.: Implementing behavior change: evaluation criteria and recommendations for mHealth applications based on the health action process approach and the quality of life technology framework in a systematic review. In: mHealth Multidisciplinary Verticals (2015)
7. Gram-Hansen, S., Jonasen, T., et al.: Persuasive technology designing for future change. In: Proceedings of the 15th International Conference on Persuasive Technology (2020)
8. Gonul, S., Namli, T., et al.: An expandable approach for design and personalization of digital, just-in-time adaptive interventions. J. Am. Med. Inform. Assoc. **26**(3), 198–210 (2019)
9. Haesen, M., Van den Bergh, J., Meskens, J., Luyten, K., Degrandsart, S., Demeyer, S., Coninx, K.: Using storyboards to integrate models and informal design knowledge. In: Hussmann, H., Meixner, G., Zuehlke, D. (eds.) Model-Driven Development of Advanced User Interfaces, pp. 87–106. Springer, Heidelberg (2011). https://doi.org/10.1007/978-3-642-14562-9_5
10. Ruzic, L., Sanford, J.A.: Needs assessment—mHealth applications for people aging with multiple sclerosis. J. Healthc. Inform. Res. **2**(1–2), 71–98 (2018). https://doi.org/10.1007/s41666-018-0023-z
11. Michie, S., Johnston, M.: Encyclopedia of Behavioral Medicine. Springer, New York (2013)
12. Davis, R., Campbell, R., Hildon, Z., et al.: Theories of behaviour and behaviour change across the social and behavioural sciences: a scoping review. Health Psychol. Rev. **9**(3), 323–344 (2015)
13. Lyons, E., Lewis, Z., et al.: Behavior change techniques implemented in electronic lifestyle activity monitors: a systematic content analysis. J. Med. Internet Res. **16**(8), e192 (2014)
14. Sailer, M., Hense, J., Mayr, S., Mandl, H.: How gamification motivates: an experimental study of the effects of specific game design elements on psychological need satisfaction. J. Comput. Hum. Behav. **69**, 371–380 (2017)
15. Cai, F., Dai, G., Han, T.: Gamification design based research on fitness mobile application for university students. In: Marcus, A. (ed.) Design, User Experience, and Usability: Novel User Experiences: 5th International Conference, DUXU 2016, Held as Part of HCI International 2016, Toronto, Canada, 17–22 July 2016, Proceedings, Part II, pp. 240–251. Springer, Cham (2016). https://doi.org/10.1007/978-3-319-40355-7_23
16. Romeo, A., Ther, B., Edney, S., et al.: Can smartphone apps increase physical activity? Systematic review and meta-analysis. J. Med. Internet Res. **21**(3), e12053 (2019)
17. Kim, H., Seo, K.: Smartphone-based health program for improving physical activity and tackling obesity for young adults: a systematic review and meta-analysis. Int. J. Environ. Res. Public Health **17**(1), 15 (2019)
18. Mora, A., Riera, D., González, C., Arnedo-Moreno, J.: Gamification: a systematic review of design frameworks. J. Comput. High. Educ. **29**(3), 516–548 (2017). https://doi.org/10.1007/s12528-017-9150-4

19. Munson, S., Consolvo, S.: Exploring goal-setting, rewards, self-monitoring, and sharing to motivate physical activity. In: International Conference on Pervasive Computing Technologies for Healthcare (PervasiveHealth) and Workshops, May 2012
20. Harries, T., Eslambolchila, P., Rettie, R., et al.: Effectiveness of a smartphone app in increasing physical activity amongst male adults: a randomized controlled trial. J. BMC Public Health, **16**, 5–8 (2016)

Smart 3D Simulation of Covid-19 for Evaluating the Social Distance Measures

Abdulrahman Al-Khayarin$^{(\boxtimes)}$ and Osama Halabi

Qatar University, Doha, Qatar
{aa084038,ohalabi}@qu.edu.qa

Abstract. The aim of this research is to model and simulate the recent and ongoing COVID19 pandemic in terms of virus contagiousness among mixed groups of patients, carriers and unaffected individuals when taking into consideration closed environments (such as malls or schools) which are ideal environments for the spread of COVID19. Machine learning techniques are utilized to model, analysis and predicate the behavior of COVID virus when spreading among human clusters. This prediction model will be used to develop a simulation environment for viewing the propagation of the COVID19 virus under different circumstances related to the type and size of the human gatherings while taking into consideration the spatiotemporal aspects of the crowd. Reinforcement learning techniques is used to train and deploy intelligent human agents that mimic the behavior of humans in real-world setting. By using 3D graphics technology, we are hoping to add a visualization aspect to the simulation to further enhance the usability and engagement level of the simulation, and to provide authorities and non-specialist people with a beneficial experience that aids them in terms of decision-making regarding future spreading of the virus under customizable lockdown scenarios.

Keywords: Agent-based simulation · 3D simulation · Covid19 simulation

1 Introduction

The SARS-COV-2 virus or the more commonly known "Covid19" virus has been continuously spreading globally in a violent manner all over the world with no signs of slowing down in the upcoming future. As of the time of writing this paper, it affected over 124 million people with over 2 million confirmed deaths [1].

Consequently, government entities all over the world have attempted several measures to restrain the propagation of the epidemic. Social control measures are the most commonly deployed countermeasures that achieved varying rates of success depending on a number of environmental and human factors. Such factors may include imposed physical distances, enforcing of safety measures (such as using masks) and rates of compliance among the human population.

Thus, when implementing social and safety control measures, it is of utmost importance to assess a priory the impacts of such measures before deploying those control measures.

© Springer Nature Switzerland AG 2021
C. Stephanidis et al. (Eds.): HCII 2021, CCIS 1421, pp. 551–557, 2021.
https://doi.org/10.1007/978-3-030-78645-8_69

In this paper our aim is support government entities and stakeholders in executing such safety plans by providing them with a 3D-based environment for simulating the propagation of the Covdi19 virus. This environment can be used to analyze and predict the spreading of the pandemic among sample of human populations when applying different safety and control measures.

The paper will be organized as follows: Sect. 2 will demonstrate our preliminary literature survey regarding relevant and recent works on the subject. In Sect. 3 we will explain the methodology that we will follow in this work. In Sect. 4 we will present the preliminary results that we managed to obtain so far. Section 5 will conclude our work.

2   Related Works

In their work [2], Maziarz et al. discussed extensively the merit of using ABM for modeling the spreading of COVID19 from a theoretical and practical point of view. The authors presented an extensive argument in favor of ABM approaches (in comparison to other differential equation models) and advocate for the consideration of ABM as potential reasoning in the standard medical evidence hierarchies. Maziarz et al. argue that while ABM does simplify certain real-world behavioral aspects while discarding certain other features, the overall simulation still captures the core mechanisms of the phenomena (COVID19 epidemic in this case), provided that the model assumptions (incubation period, infection probabilities, reproductive number.etc.) are calibrated based on empirical studies. A modified version of AceMod tailored to the characteristics of the COVID19 virus (which was used to model the viral infection in Australia) was used as a baseline scenario to demonstrate the benefits of using ABM simulations.

Silva et al. [3] attempted to assess the economic effects of lockdown measures on the propagation of COVID19 in Brazil using an agent-based model. To model the spread of the pandemic among the agents, Silva et al. argued that the SEIR model (Susceptible, exposed, infected and recovered) is superior to the traditional SIR model due to the presence of incubation period in COVID19. In this experiment the agents represented real-world entities (humans, households, business, governments) interacting together in the presence of a contagious diseases. The human's agents were divided into different categories (employed, unemployed and homeless) and their movements behaviors was adjusted accordingly. The virus spreads when the distance between two human agents exceed a certain minimum threshold based on an experimental contagion probability. Regarding the economic impacts, the economic environment is modeled as the transfer of wealth between the different agents involved in the simulation. People transfer wealth to business entities and business use this wealth to pay employees' salaries and government taxes. Government then spends part of those taxes on health care institutes as part of the required expenses to run these hospitalization entities. Therefore, people spending patterns are directly related to their mobility which is affected by the lockdown measures resulting in lower number of transactions. The authors simulated several lockdown scenarios ranging from partial lockdown measures to complete lockdown measures.

Chang et al. [4] used a highly modified version of AceMod [20], calibrated with empirical COVID19 parameters to assess different outbreak mitigation strategies across Australia including home quarantine, school closures and forcible social distancing measures. AceMod (Australian Census-Based Epidemic Model) is a discrete-time and stochastic agent-based modeling system originally deployed in Australia in 2016 to simulate complex outbreak scenarios. AceMod consists of 24 million humas agents each with varying characteristics (age, gender, medical history) and social interactions behaviors within different contexts (households, schools, workplaces). Each scenario runs on a 12-h cycle (representing day/night) where the infection spread based on proximity and infection rates parameters.

Cue vas [5] explored the relation between the mobility of humans and the probability of catching COVID19 infection using ABS methodology within the context of indoor facilities. In this work, the probability of movement and infection rate are not set sectionally (by dividing the population into distinct homogeneous groups based on age for example), rather, these probabilities are completely controlled individually per agent in order to provide a detailed picture regarding the spreading of COVID19.

Based on relevant works we analyzed so far, our main contributions can be summarized as:

1. Extended SIER Model: We argue that the traditionally used SIER model is not sufficient enough to capture the main characteristics of the Covid19 pandemics. For this, we will try in our research to propose a derivative of the SIER model that will properly model the virus lifecycle and states.
2. Smart Agent-Based Modelling: Based on our findings, many of the existing agent-based simulations depend on some sort of pre-define paths or static waypoints system in determining the traverse points of their agents. One on our goal in this project is to incorporate reinforcement learning in training out agents in such a way that the agents' behavior could emerge intelligently at runtime in a similar manner to their humans' counterparts.

3 Methodology

3.1 Infection Model

In this paper, the SEIRDV model which is an extension of the well-known SEIR infection model [5] is used. Table 1 demonstrates the different states comprising our infection model.

SEIR models divides the population into different categories (susceptible, exposed, infected and resistant/recovered) and calculates the probability of an individual moving between different categories in the presence of an epidemic. We extend the standard model with two extra states D & V representing dead and vaccinated, respectively. Figure 1 demonstrates the state diagram of our model.

3.2 Crowds Behavior

To simulate human behavior in real-scenario, Agent-based modeling ABM [6] will be used. ABM is a type of simulation modeling that represents the simulated systems as a set of intelligent agents. Those agents are with equipped with decisions-making capabilities in order to communicate with other agents and with the surrounding environment.

Table 1. SEIRDV infection states

Abbreviation	Description
S	**Suspectable**
E	**Exposed**
I	**Infected**
R	**Recovered**
D	**Dead**
V	**Vaccinated**

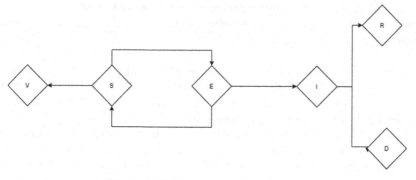

Fig. 1. SEIRDV states transition diagram.

Most of the related works in pandemic simulation such as the works discussed previously in the literature review, use some sort of agent-based modeling approaches.

3.3 Simulation Setup

We use Unity Grocery Store Simulation [7] as starting point of our simulation. Grocery store simulation is an open-source project developed by the Unity team as a demonstration of Unity platform capabilities in modeling pandemics spreading. We extend this simulation to implement our proposed infection model and crown behavior simulations. The next few sections discuss some of the customizations we are currently trying to apply to this work.

Virus Spreading Model: The default project uses a simplified sei model. we aim to extend this simulation to support realistic infection spreading cycle by incorporating extra states (R, D and V). Additionally, we also aim to calibrate the provide model using empirical Covid19 parameters.

Shopper Behavior Model: One of main goals is to support realistic human behavior model where the agents navigate, shop and checkout in a realistic manner resembling real-life shopping scenarios. The provided experiment uses simple and rectilinear movement patterns. To achieve our goal, we have been experimenting with two unity packages:

Navmesh [8] and ML-agents [9]. Navmesh is a path finding API supported out-of-the-box that that provides programming capabilities for ai agents to traverse complex game environments using different random paths based on configurable environment costs. ML-Agents [9] toolkits that allow game scenes to be used as simulation environments for training intelligent AI using reinforcement learning techniques.

4   Preliminary Results

As we are presenting an ongoing work, most of the preliminary results so far are based on initial experiments with various levels of success.

As shown in Fig. 2 we start our implementation by extending the grocery store simulation to add extra state R (recovered) representing individuals who received the infection then recovered over time.

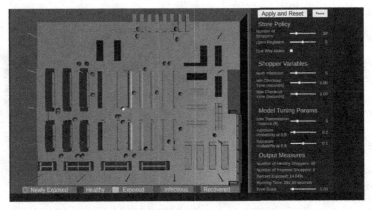

Fig. 2. Sample running of a simulation instance. Blue = health shopper, Red = infectious, Yellow = Exposed and Purple = Recovered. (Color figure online)

We are working on comparing different infection models in order to arrive at most probable and suitable one. We started with conducting two experiments: an experiment using the SEI model (which is already provided as part of the grocery store simulation) and second experiment which uses our implementation of the SEIR model. Each experiment consists of running the simulation over different infection distances values to find possible correlation with the infection rate. The output of simulation is the infection rate I% which is defined as:

$$I\% = I/(I * H) * 100 \tag{1}$$

Where I and H are total number of infected and healthy shoppers, respectively.

In Table. 2 we show the basic calibrated parameters in our experiment.

Table 2. Initial Simulation Parameters

Parameter	Description	Initial Value
P_0	**Initial number of shoppers**	**30**
I_0	**Initial number of infected**	**5**
S_c	**Store max capacity**	**30**
D	**Infection distance in ft**	**d (set differently in each experiment)**

At any point in time, the total number of shoppers should not exceed S_c We ran the simulation using different infection distances (4, 6, 8, 10, 12 ft). For each instance, the simulation is conducted 3 times and the average infection rate is calculated. Figure 3 demonstrates a comparison between two experiments.

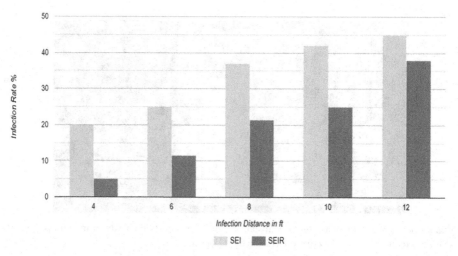

Fig. 3. Infection rates between SEI and SEIR models.

Using SEIR yielded lower infection rates. Based on our analysis, we assume that is a logical observation as recovered people can no longer infect other people nor they can get infected. Therefore, the overall infections rates should get lower in comparison to the SEI model where no such immunity exists (due to the lack of recovered state).

5   Conclusion

In this work we aim to provide an intelligent agent-based environment for simulating the spreading of Covid19 among human populations. In order to model the spread of infection realistically, we extended the model SEIR with extra states relevant to Covid19 in order to capture a more realistic picture of the pandemic. In terms of agent modeling, we follow an agent-based approach in stimulating the crowd behavior within an indoor shopping mall using Unity platform API. Most of the progress so far have been experimental work with different Unity API focused on fine-tuning our shopping agent's behavior to mimic real-life crowds' behavior. Additionally, we are also simultaneously researching recent Covid19 discoveries to arrive at a more realistic and proper picture of the different parameters that control the pandemic.

References

1. https://www.worldometers.info/coronavirus/. Accessed 24 Mar 2021
2. Maziarz, M., Zach, M.: Agent-based modelling for SARS-CoV -2 epidemic prediction and intervention assessment: a methodological appraisal. J. Eval. Clin. Pract. **26**(5), 1352–1360 (2020)
3. Silva, P., Batista, P., Lima, H., Alves, M., Guimarães, F., Silva, R.: COVID-ABS: an agent-based model of COVID-19 epidemic to simulate health and economic effects of social distancing interventions. Chaos, Solitons Fractals, **139** (2020)
4. Cuevas, E.: An agent-based model to evaluate the COVID-19 transmission risks in facilities. Comput. Biol. Med. **121**, 103827 (2020). https://doi.org/10.1016/j.compbiomed.2020.103827
5. José, C., Juan, S., Claudio B., Jing, B.: A simulation of a COVID-19 epidemic based on a deterministic SEIR model. Front. Public Health **8**, 230 (2020)
6. Bonabeau, E.: Agent-based modeling: methods and techniques for simulating human systems. Proc. Nat. Acad. Sci. **99**, 7280–7287 (2002)
7. Unity Coronavirus Simulation. https://github.com/Unity-Technologies/unitysimulation-coronavirus-example. Accessed 04 Mar 2021
8. Unity NavMesh API. https://docs.unity3d.com/Manual/nav-BuildingNavMesh.html. Accessed 04 Mar 2021
9. Unity ML-Agents Package. https://docs.unity3d.com/Packages/com.unity.ml-agents@1.0/manual/index.html. Accessed 04 Mar 2021

ABLE Family: Remote, Intergenerational Play in the Age of COVID-19

Paula Gardner[1]([⊠]), Stephen Surlin[1], Caitlin McArthur[2], Adekunle Akinyema[1], Jessica Rauchberg[1], Rong Zheng[1], Jenny Hao[1], and Alexandra Papaioannou[2]

[1] McMaster University, Hamilton, ON, Canada
gardnerp@mcmaster.ca

[2] GERAS Centre for Aging Research, McMaster University, Hamilton, ON, Canada

Abstract. ABLE Family is a co-located play platform that engages older adults and their family members in intergenerational play and creation, meeting needs during the COVID-19 crisis. Physical distancing is required to ensure the safety of older adults, though, isolation and loneliness contributes to worsening mood, physical and cognitive health. The platform is designed to provide these benefits, by attending to the distinct needs of older adults who are frail and live with dementia. It allows for easy gesture-based engagement for older adults and more sophisticated play for children who, together, draw or paint a picture. The platform encourages low intensity, short duration activity proven to enhance cognitive health in older adults with cognitive impairment and to enhance well-being and mood. ABLE Family also aims to relieve the proven strain experienced by caregivers caring for older adults across private homes, adult residences and care facilities. The platform will operate as an elevated zoom-type platform, allowing multiple players to talk and see each other in real time as they paint and draw together. The final artistic creations can be saved, downloaded and used as screensavers, digital photos or printed.

Keywords: Co-design · Art Based Experience · Dementia

1 Introduction to the ABLE Family Platform

This paper reviews our design of ABLE Family, our new movement and arts-based platform designed for older adults with dementia and loved ones. Distinct to our team are our efforts to adapt standard design thinking methods that ensure a rigorous, lateral relationship between researchers and older adult stakeholders. With the advent of COVID-19 and physical distancing, our design and testing protocols now shift to remote co-design practices. In this paper, we present our efforts to create remote co-design research practices with older adults and stakeholders (families, older adult companions, and physical therapists) and to develop the ABLE Family platform to create artful collaborative interactions via remote participation for all players – older adults and their family members that can endure during and beyond the COVID-19 pandemic. We take on this challenge as an interdisciplinary team equipped with expertise in critical art/design, critical user interaction design, aging studies, gerontology, physical therapy, and computational science.

C. Stephanidis et al. (Eds.): HCII 2021, CCIS 1421, pp. 558–565, 2021.
https://doi.org/10.1007/978-3-030-78645-8_70

1.1 Research Background

Dementia is widely experienced and undermanaged in Canada and around the world. Seven percent (or 500,000) of Canadians over the age of 65 live with dementia (PHAC 2019), which tends to: reduce mobility and social engagement, thus increasing risk of physiological illness, depression and other mood disorders and produce loneliness, boredom, restlessness, and agitation. Also burdened are the 6% (or 486,000 individuals) of Canadians over the age of 65 in caretaking roles (CIHI 2019), 80% of whom express severe stress and feel that they 'can't go on. Affordable and culturally sensitive services are lacking, while surging care costs lead to operationalized and often medicalized treatment to address older adults' loneliness, boredom, agitation and mood ailments (Ducak et al. 2017; Martin & McCarthy 2010). During the COVID-19 pandemic, with requirements for physical distancing and sheltering in place, older adults are more isolated, less mobile and thus more prone to these ailments.

1.2 Combating Isolation and Immobility During the COVID-19 Pandemic

Older adults' mobility is significantly impaired during the pandemic particularly among those with frailty and/or dementia. Mobility is reduced in older adults with frailty and dementia due to increased physical impairment and limitations, and cognitive impairment; this results in loneliness, despair and agitation, and enhanced physical and cognitive impairment (Rockwood et al. 2010). Due to the need to prioritize physical care needs, fewer staff are available to support the emotional, mobility and recreational needs of older adults (Stone and Keller 2020). As well, older adults physically isolating at home have reduced mobility, social interaction, and cognitive engagement, which negatively impacts physical, cognitive and mood health.

A recent Stats Canada study shows 58% of people over the age of 75 were very or extremely concerned about their own health as a result of the pandemic (CTV 2020). Increased stress has been shown to depress the immune system, potentially increasing the risk of acquiring COVID-19. Untreated stress increases risk of physical illness; chronic stressors produce reliable decreases in almost all functional immune measures (Segerstrom et al. 2004) and situational stress increases levels of pro-inflammatory cytokines in blood), dysregulating the immune system (Morey et al. 2015).

On a promising note, research shows making art creates more dramatic outcomes than simply viewing (Stewart 2004), enhancing agency, and lessening social withdrawal and poor communication (Bar-Sela et al. 2007). A 2015 found that participation in intergenerational interaction and meaningful cross-age relationships may have multiple benefits; these include: decreasing social isolation, increasing older adults' sense of belonging, self-esteem, and well-being; improved physical health; and also improved social and emotional skills of children and youth participants. Finally, much research demonstrates that older adults are enthusiastic to try out new technologies and 53% report they would prefer to have their health care needs managed by a mix of medical staff and health care technology (Kakulla 2020). This research suggests ABLE Family could be an effective digital technology intervention aiding older adults and caregivers.

2   The ABLE Family Platform Co-design Process

2.1   ABLE Family Intergenerational Gaming and Co-art Creation

The ABLE Family platform seeks to encourage movement and meaningful interaction among older adults and family members to tackle immobility and isolation, and prevent physical, cognitive and emotional decline during the COVID-19 pandemic. We are designing the ABLE Family as an interactive co-located game designed for ease of use by older adults, and to encourage gesture and walking in low level short duration activities of game play or co-art creation. Our plan is to design ABLE Family to allow for ease of use by older adults, and to encourage gesture and walking in low level short duration activities of game play or co-art creation. We invite grandchildren and children to engage via their computer or mobile phone interface, offering diverse and scaled engagement appropriate to the needs of different family members.

We aim for ABLE Family to encourage intergenerational engagement, art/design and creative play to contribute to enhancing cognitive, physical and mood health of older adults, by fending off loneliness, and engaging them in meaningful, restorative interactions with multiple generations of family members. Finally, ABLE Family aims to relieve the proven emotional strains that have increased with the COVID-19 pandemic. Caregivers can set up ABLE Family and allow older adults to play with little or no assistance; this well offer relief from care and enhance mood and calm loneliness and agitation for an extended period of time following the interaction.

2.2   Disability and Crip-Informed Co-design and Platform Design in the COVID-19 Age

We are adapting design thinking with techniques recognizing the needs of frail older adults; these include time limited sessions, multiple forms of participation, offering examples and inviting recall (rather than memory), and inviting companions to assist older adults' participation. Distinct to our team is our (We build empathy and consent across the research process and share vulnerabilities, interest and objectives to create trust among the team). Emerging from disability justice organizing and critical disability studies, crip theory refers to the study of disability and neurodiversity as fluid and ever-changing political and cultural identities (Kafer 2013). Unlike other models or perspectives that view disability as something that must be cured, rehabilitated, or erased, crip theory calls on able-bodied and neurotypical people to bend toward disability (Clare 2017). Our methods of co-design and our interface design are informed by disability and crip theory and methods to ensure our remote design process is accessible by all stakeholders (e.g. older adults, intergenerational family members and caregivers).

2.3   Planned Co-design Strategy with Older Adults and Stakeholders

In this first stage of remote design and testing, we plan to work with key stakeholders – family and caregivers, who routinely work with older adults with frailty and dementia. Our testing seeks to design two types of methods both informed by disability and crip studies – methods for effective remote co-design and game interactions that employ laptop and/or tablet and sensor affordances to ensure that ABLE Family is: pleasurable, accessible for multi-generational users, and enhances mood and family relations, and finally, decreases boredom and despair among isolated older adults.

Our stakeholders include physical therapists, caregivers and physical therapists serving this older adult population. We plan to meet weekly with each group to demo and obtain feedback on design iterations, which will then be integrated and retested. To facilitate co-design, we will test the efficacy of the Zoom Pro platform in comparison to the MURAL platform – an accessible video conferencing platform allowing us to 'demo' versions of iterations designed, and for participations to add feedback via voice, drawing or voting with digital 'sticky notes' on the interface. Outcome testing will be conducted in the final four weeks designated to testing, we will ask stakeholders to use ABLE Family with their own family members a number of times across a three-week period. Week four, we will conduct focus group interviews with small teams of these stakeholder participants, asking them to report regarding their family, and older adult experiences. We will inquire too about their impressions of the platforms impact on mood, mobility, restored sense of self, and enhanced family relationships and to report on other impacts noted.

2.4 ABLE Family Intergenerational Game Play

ABLE Family will be an easy to use game platform that can be accessed on a website. Multiple family members can visit a private online family room, where up to four members can all draw on the same page/canvas, using a different colour. All members watching can see drawings appear as players draw in real-time in the Internet browser. Users will be assigned a user number that provides them unique access to particular colours, drawing tools and images; as such, family members will be able to distinguish their drawing contributions from others. A chat window and audio/visual live stream will be present in the browser that includes all of the present users; this allows family members to see and hear each user simultaneously. As explained below, interactions are scaled to be accessible to the abilities of different family members. The game provides options for interactive play, ranging from active (gesture-based) engagement, to more passive computer laptop engagement. As well, families can engage in cooperative play (drawing together) or game-based scenarios involving solving a puzzle including competing in teams to win the most points.

Our team has recently conducted proof of concept experiments with a web-based drawing platform; they have successfully created a first prototype allowing multiple users to drawing simultaneously, using distinguished (different) colours, using both mouse and touch pad options on computers and mobile devices. The interface design makes it easy to distinguish one's own play from others. User's contributions to drawings show up in a different colour on the remote users' screen. The contrast between the user's drawing and lines drawn offers a potent opportunity for ABLE Family to trigger emergent and playful behaviour – for example turn-taking, creative family or team collaboration, or competitive game opportunities. According to user interest and ability, users can draw/paint/interact using either a mouse, touch pad or via gesture, using the MbientLabs MetaMotion R+ wearable sensor.

The MetaMotion sensor sends wireless gestural motion data that creates drawings and triggers animations and sounds that correlate with larger/light exercise type gestures, like outward ripples of circles or ribbons that appear like flowing lines from the users' rough position on screen when a hand wave or push motion is done. Older adults particularly may choose this wearable sensor which captures movement and gestures. Worn in a comfortable wristband or clip-on form, and the size of a quarter, the MetaMotion is easy to wear and use, and encourages beneficial low-level activity. Older adults with lesser interest or ability can use a mouse or touch pad to fully engage in the family drawing activity. The sensor option offers older adults a low barrier to entry, and the responsive feedback engages them in sustained engagement with family.

The platform will operate as an elevated zoom-type platform, allowing multiple players to talk and see each other in real time as they create together. The experience will feel responsive, emergent and artful, producing multiple forms of sensory feedback. Sound effects and music will be generated in response to players drawing via their mouse, touch screen or by triggering animations via gestures (captured by with the wireless MetaMotion sensor). For family members sensitive to this added layer of sound, there will be an option to mute the sound feedback.

Because family members can distinguish their contributions from others, various play scenarios are possible. Families can engage in collaborative or cooperative play, seeking to create a beautiful drawing or painting together. Families can engage in the playful drawing game, "Exquisite Creature," where each player contributes a body part to an emerging creature. Families can play charades, guessing the figure being drawn or play a competitive Pictionary-type game strategy. The final artistic creations can be saved, downloaded and used as digital photos or printed.

Grandchildren and children are invited to engage via their computer or mobile phone interface, offering diverse and scaled entry (more or less sophisticated); Older adults, and those who wish, can participate via gesture captured via sensors (MetaMotion). The platform positions grandchildren to 'teach' the use of the platform, allowing grandparents to regain a sense of purpose, encouraging and affirming their grandchildren's skills and abilities. Research shows that intergenerational artful play can positively alleviate feelings of aggression and isolation that many persons with dementia face (Camic et al. 2014). A semi-remote study on developing custom games (e.g.: card games and board games) that revolve around memories, favourite music, hobbies, or a family activity revealed that such personalized interventions strengthened relationships between stakeholder families (Maldonado Branco et al. 2017). These interventions emphasize gaming approaches to maintain social relationships. For instance, tailoring a game or activity around a weekly routine helped persons with dementia maintain or regain a sense of independence. This approach also benefits intergenerational stakeholders (e.g. caregivers) many of whom themselves experience stress due to the pandemic.

3   ABLE Family Hardware and Software Design

3.1   Interactive and Accessible Software Design

When developing the ABLE Family platform, we consider various factors to ensure the interface supports game play that accommodates older adults' abilities when using technology. We implement recommendations outlined by the Web Content Accessibility Guidelines 2.1 (WCAG) to address the accessibility needs of older adult web users and to ensure the creation of an adaptable, user friendly interface meets diverse needs of older adults. We implement guidelines that address users' needs such as text size, text style and layout and use of color. In our design process we gain a comprehensive understanding of user needs, designing and testing the interface with an older adult population in an iterative process. We use Front-end development frameworks for interface design, including React JS framework and Bootstrap to ensure the platform is responsive and adaptable to various devices that it is operated on. The application features allow users to create a private room where only people with the room ID can join and interact. While engaging in their selected activity, users have the option to make a video or audio call with their family members or friends to create a more interactive environment. This feature is implemented using Jitsi API.

3.2 Machine Learning Based Gesture Recognition for Intuitive Interaction

The ABLE Family platform will use machine learning algorithms to identify specific gestures performed by the participants. For instance, to recognize patterns painted in the air by a user wearing an inertial measurement unit (IMU) sensor at the wrist, we propose a 2-step approach. In the first step, a motion trajectory of the user's wrist is reconstructed with data collected from a wrist mounted IMU sensor by the method proposed in (Shen et al. 2016). It imposes kinematic constraints on predicting wrist position with a modified hidden Markov model (HMM) to achieve an around 9.2 cm of median error for free-form postures in real-time. The basic idea behind this approach is, given the orientation of the sensor, the possible space of the wrist and elbow locations are quite limited. Thus, with orientation estimated by a magnetometer in a static pose during calibration, we can track the motion trajectory of the wrist with an accelerometer, a gyroscope, and the known length of limbs (both forearm and upper arm). In the second step, a deep neural network is trained upon the reconstructed motion trajectories to perform classification on predefined shapes (circle, triangle, rectangle, star and etc.). The network consists of 2 convolutional neural network (Lawrence et al. 1997) layers as feature extractor and a fully connected layer with softmax activation function as the output layer. With the recognized pattern from the second step, we can further refine the trajectory predicted in previous steps to make it smoother, and better shaped.

To take advantage of these classified gestures that can be recognized by the platform, a calibration activity is added to a starting sequence for a user who would like to use the MetaMotion sensor to control their activity for the day. This calibration could include holding the users arm on the arm rest of the chair they are sitting in for a few seconds. Afterwards, they will be able to more accurately control the ABLE Family interactions in the browser.

References

Andrews, J., Laura, B., Mark, H., Arlene, A.: Older adults' perspectives on using digital technology to maintain good mental health: interactive group study. J. Med. Internet Res. **21**(2).(2019)

Bar-Sela, G., Atid, L., Danos, S., Gabay, N., Epelbaum, R.: Art therapy improved depression and influenced fatigue levels in cancer patients on chemotherapy. Psychooncology **16**(11), 980–984 (2007)

Berne, P.: "Disability justice- a working draft." Sins Invalids. https://www.sinsinvalid.org/blog/disability-justice-a-working-draft-by-patty-berne. Accessed 14 June 2020

Bosch, L., Bernadina, J., Marije, K.: Design opportunities for supporting informal caregivers. In: CHI 2016 Extended Abstracts, pp. 2790–2797 (2016)

Camic, M., Victoria, T., Chantal, P.: Viewing and making art together: a multi-session art-gallery-based intervention for people with dementia and their carers. Aging Ment. Health **18**(2), 161–168 (2014)

Canada Public Health Service. https://www.canada.ca/en/public-health/services/publications/diseasesconditions/dementia-strategy.html. Accessed 9 Apr 2020

Chen, Y., Victor, N., Sun Young, P.: Caring for caregivers: designing for integrity. ACM CSCW **2013**, 91–102 (2013)

Clare, E.: Brilliant Imperfection: Grappling with Cure. Duke UP (2017)

Cridland, E., Philipson, L., Brennan-Horley, C., Swaffer, K.: Reflections and recommendations for conducting in-depth interviews with people with dementia. Qual. Health Res. **26**(13), 1774–1786 (2016)

CTV staff. COVID-19 sparks health concerns for older people, financial fears for youth: StatsCan (2020). https://www.ctvnews.ca/canada/covid-19-sparks-health-concerns-for-older-peoplefinancial-fears-for-youth-statscan-1.4908472

Dove, E., Arlene, S.: The kinect project: group motion-based gaming for people living with dementia. Dementia **18**(6), 2189–2205 (2019)

Ducak, K., Denton, M., Elliot, G.: Implementing montessori methods for dementia™ in ontario long-term care homes: recreation staff and multidisciplinary consultants' perceptions of policy and practice issues. Dementia **17**(1), 5–33 (2018)

Franz, R.., Munteanu, C., Barbosa Neves, B., Baecker, R.: Time to retire old methodologies?: Reflecting on conducting usability evaluations for older adults. In: MobileCHI 2015 Adjunct, pp. 912–15 (2015)

Gerling, K., Regan, L., Mandryk Linehan, C.: Long-term use of motion-based video games in care home settings. In: CHI 2015: Crossings, pp. 1573–1582 (2015)

Hsieh, C., et al.: The effectiveness of a virtual reality-based Tai Chi exercise on cognitive and physical function in older adults with cognitive impairment. Dementia Geriatric Cogn. Diso. **46**(5–6), 358370 (2018)

Johnson, M.-L., McRuer, R.: Cripistemologies: introduction. J. Literary Cult. Disabil. Stud. **8**(2), 127–148 (2014)

Kafer, A.: Feminist, Queer, Crip. IU Press (2013)

Kakulla, N.B.: 2020 Tech Trends of the 50+. Washington, DC: AARP Research (2020) https://doi.org/10.26419/res.00329.001

Kaufman, D., Louise, S., Alice, I.: Playful aging: digital games for older adults. AGE-WELL 4.2 Project White Paper, pp. 2–36 (2020)

Maldonado, B., Rita, J.Q., Óscar, R.: Personalised participation: an approach to involve people with dementia and their families in a participatory design project. CoDesign **13**(2), 127–143 (2017)

Morey, J.N., et al.: Current directions in stress. Curr. Opin. Psychol. **5**, 13–17 (2015)

Nimrod, G.: Technophobia among older internet users. Educ. Gerontol. **44**(2–3), 148–162 (2018)

O'Connell, M.E., et al.: Anticipated needs and worries about maintaining independence of rural/remote older adults: opportunities for technology development in the context of the double digital divide. Gerontechnology **17**(3), 126–138 (2018)

Lawrence, S., Giles, C.L., Tsoi, A.C., et al.: Face recognition: a convolutional neural-network approach. IEEE Trans. Neural Netw. **8**(1), 98–113 (1997)

Perissinotto, C.M., Cenzer, I.S., Covinsky, K.E.: Loneliness in older persons: a predictor of functional decline and death. Arch. Internal Med. **172**(14), 1078–1084 (2012)

Piepzna-Samarasinha, L.L.: Care Work: Dreaming Disability Justice. Arsenal Pulp Press, Vancouver (2018)

Rendon, A.A., Everett, B.L., Donna, T., Eric, G., Johnson, E.M., Bruce, B.: The effect of virtual reality gaming on dynamic balance in older adults. Age Aging **41**(4), 549–552 (2012)

Rockwood, K., et al.: A global clinical measure of fitness and frailty in elderly people. CMAJ **173**, 489–495 (2005)

Schiphorst, T.: Merce cunningham: making dances with the computer. Merce Cunningham: Creative Elements **4**, 79 (2013)

Segerstrom, S., Miller, G.: Psychological stress and the human immune system: a meta-analytic study of 30 years of inquiry. Psychol. Bull. **130**(4), 601–630 (2004)

Shen, S., Wang, H., Roy Choudhury, R.: I am a smartwatch and I can track my user's arm. In: Proceedings of the 14th Annual International Conference on Mobile Systems, Applications, and Services, pp. 85–96 (2016)

Spina, C.: WCAG 2.1 and the current state of web accessibility in libraries. Weave J. Libr. User Experience **2**(2) (2019)

Sungkarat, S., Boripuntakul, S., Chattipakorn, N., Watcharasaksilp, K., Lord, S.R.: Effects of Tai Chi on cognition and fall risk in older adults with mild cognitive impairment: a randomized controlled trial. J. Am. Geriatr. Soc. **65**(4), 721–727 (2017)

Tse, A.C.Y., Wong, T.W.L., Lee, P.H.: Effect of low-intensity exercise on physical and cognitive health in older adults: a systematic review. Sports Med. **37**, 1–13 (2015)

Tyack, C., Camic, P.M., Heron, M.J., Hulbert, S.: Viewing art on a tablet computer: a well-being intervention for people with dementia and their caregivers. J. Appl. Gerontol. **36**(7), 864–894 (2017)

A Study of Sound Presentation Effects on Silence During Video Conferencing

Arata Higashiguchi and Yu Shibuya(✉)

Kyoto Institute of Technology, Kyoto 6068585, Japan
higashiguchi@hi.is.kit.ac.jp, shibuya@kit.ac.jp
https://www.hi.is.kit.ac.jp

Abstract. We aim to detect unintentional silence during the video conferencing and reduce participants' stress. In this study, as a first step to achieve our aim, we focus on the effects of sound presentation on the silence during video conferencing. Six participants were recruited from our university in our experiment. The Stress Response Scale-18 (SRS-18) is used to measure the participants' psychological stress. Each participant answers to the SRS-18 before and after watching movie. The sum of SRS-18 score is higher, the stress is higher. So, we subtract the sum of SRS-18 score before watching movie from that of after watching movie. We call this value stress value in this paper. If the participants reduce the stress by watching movie and listening sound, the stress value is negative and the absolute value of it increase. Talking about the experimental result, there were too few participants at this moment so we did not do any statistical test. However, the there is a possibility that the chirping of cricket is the lowest stress value, i.e., it is most effective to reduce the stress. Furthermore, in no sound condition, the stress value is highest. This means that it is better to play a sound or music to reduce the stress than to play nothing.

Keywords: Sound presentation effect · Video conferencing · Stress value

1 Introduction

Recently, because of the COVID-19, we have a lot of video conferencing instead of face-to-face meeting. However, in video conferencing, we feel stress about the silence several times. In face-to-face meeting at the same place, we can aware other participants with non-verbal information and we do not feel stress so much because we can easily know why there is a silence. In video conferencing, we can not aware enough about others because there is not enough information of others through the video.

We aim to detect unintentional silence during the video conferencing and reduce participants' stress. In this study, as a first step to achieve our aim, we focus on the effects of sound presentation on the silence during video conferencing.

© Springer Nature Switzerland AG 2021
C. Stephanidis et al. (Eds.): HCII 2021, CCIS 1421, pp. 566–570, 2021.
https://doi.org/10.1007/978-3-030-78645-8_71

2   Proposed Method

We propose that play sound when there is a silence during the video conferencing. We focus on auditory sense not others because there are some demerits of others senses as shown in followings.

Vision: Participants are looking other people so additional image view is obstacle.

Smell: Controlling of the amount of scent is difficult.

Taste: During the talking, it is difficult to eat or drink something.

Touch/Force: A sense of touch or force might be usable, we will try to investigate at next phase.

Furthermore, Labbe et al. found that listening the classical music reduced the stress [1]. However, it is not clear that such stress reducing is still working during conversation. What kind of classic music is effective to reduce the stress? In this paper, we are going to invent what kind of sound reduce the stress during the silence.

3   Experiment

3.1   Procedure

Six participants were recruited from our university. In this experiment, the Stress Response Scale-18 (SRS-18) [2] is used to measure the participants' psychological stress. Figure 1 shows an experimental procedure. As shown in Fig. 1, each participant answers to the SRS-18 before and after watching movie. The sum of SRS-18 score is higher, the stress is higher. So, we subtract the sum of SRS-18 score before watching movie from that of after watching movie. We call this value stress value in this paper. If the participants reduce the stress by watching movie and listening sound, the stress value is negative and the absolute value of it increase. Figure 2 shows an example of movie which each participant watched. There was a speaker with mask, because of simulating COVID-19 state, and background color was white. He looked at the camera in front of him, i.e. his gaze matched with the participant's one. He asked a question to the participants in about 5 s and kept silent for about 10 s. Followings are examples of question.

1. What is your favorite food?
2. What is your favorite color?
3. Where is your favorite place?
4. Could you tell me your job experience?

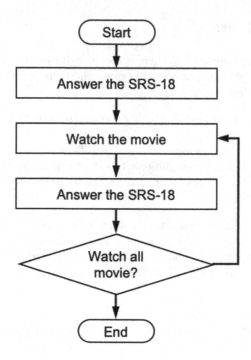

Fig. 1. Experimental procedure.

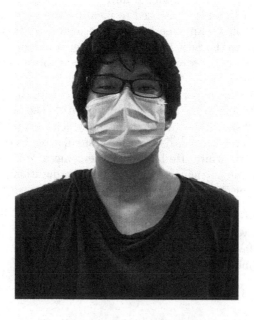

Fig. 2. A speaker on the display.

Above experimental procedure was done in four conditions. While he kept silence there were four kinds of sound condition as shown in following.

1. No sound
2. Chirping of cricket
3. Happy classical music
4. Sad classical music.

Figure 3 shows a snapshot of the experiment. A participant sits down the chair and wear a headphone. He is watching a movie played on the display in front of him.

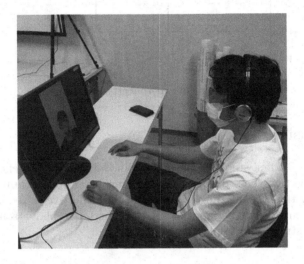

Fig. 3. A snapshot of experiment.

3.2   Result and Discussion

The result of experiment is shown in Fig. 4. It was too few participants at this moment so we did not do any statistical test. However, Fig. 4 shows the possibility that the chirping of cricket is the lowest stress value, i.e., it might be most effective to reduce the stress. Furthermore, in no sound condition, the stress value was highest. This means that it is better to play a sound or music to reduce the stress than to play nothing.

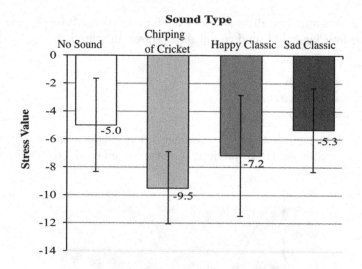

Fig. 4. Result of experiment: stress value.

4   Conclusion

In this study, as a first step to achieve our aim, we focus on the effects of sound presentation on the silence during video conferencing. Experimental result shows the possibility that the chirping of cricket is more effective to reduce the stress than classical music. Furthermore, it might be better to play a sound or music to reduce the stress than to play nothing.

References

1. Labbe, E., Schmit, N., Babin, J., Pharru, M.: Coping with stress: the effectiveness of different types of music. Appl. Psychophysiol. Biofeedback **32**(3), 163–168 (2007)
2. Suzuki, S., Shimada, H., Miura, M., Katayanagi, K., Umano, R., Sakano, Y.: Development of a new psychological stress response scale (SRS-18) and investigation of the reliability and the validity. Jpn. J. Behav. Med. **4**(1), 22–29 (1997). In Japanese

The Impact of Digital Divide on Education in USA Amid COVID-19 Pandemic

Sean Li[1]([envelope]) and Erin Li[2]

[1] Cherry Hill High School East, Cherry Hill, NJ 08003, USA
[2] Rosa International Middle School, Cherry Hill, NJ 08003, USA

Abstract. The goal of this study is to analyze the digital divide among students in various communities and households. This long-term issue has become considerably more pronounced since the lockdown in March of 2020 that was caused by the COVID-19 Pandemic. Due to the shutdown, schools have been forced to go online in order to continue educating their students; however, it has not been as easy as it sounds. Students experiencing a lack of technology and internet connection have had difficulties participating in school and growing education-wise. Furthermore, the long-term goal of this project is to hopefully provide present and future researchers with an adequate understanding of the digital divide among students so that they may more easily find solutions to this dilemma that is impacting many households throughout the country. In order to receive a more comprehensive understanding of digital divide among communities, we also analyze the factors impacting digital divide, the issues caused by digital divide on online learning, and how a lack of technology has negatively impacted students' learning and teachers' educating. This study raises awareness and proposes possible solutions to the digital divide among students. The dilemma of digital divide, if left alone and overlooked, may lead to greater problems in the future.

Keywords: Digital divide · Online learning · Technology use · COVID-19 Pandemic

1 Introduction

Digital divide has many definitions, but it is most commonly referred to as the "systematic inequality in access to technology" [3]. In an online environment, digital divide has negative impacts on students' education, as those who are without internet or technology access is not likely to submit the assignments or participate in class. Households that face difficulties in accessing the internet, have only one device that must be shared with all of the members of the house, or use cellphones to participate in class experience the negative influences of digital divide the most. However, students from households that possess broadband and multiple devices, such as laptops, desktops, or tablets, throughout the house are not negatively impacted by digital divide. This separation, which is commonly called digital divide, is between those "with and those without access to high-speed internet and computing devices at home" [1].

© Springer Nature Switzerland AG 2021
C. Stephanidis et al. (Eds.): HCII 2021, CCIS 1421, pp. 571–576, 2021.
https://doi.org/10.1007/978-3-030-78645-8_72

By researching and understanding the impacts of digital divide on certain communities and households, we are able to form solutions for this long-lasting problem. "Because of the COVID-19 crisis, the distance learning digital divide is no longer a matter of a homework gap but of whether or not a child can access education" [1]. During the pandemic, digital divide among students is no longer a problem of whether or not students can complete homework assignments if they lack internet access; it has become a matter of whether or not students who lack broadband and devices can access their classes and education. With the findings of [1], it is possible to troubleshoot the problems and assist those who experience the negative influences of digital divide the most.

Digital divide was a challenge even before the pandemic. Because the problem has been left untouched, and no one has attempted to solve it, it continues to be an even bigger challenge during the pandemic, when all students are learning from their homes and need technology in order to participate in online school. If once again left untouched, this already problematic issue could go on to negatively impact even more families.

Due to the pandemic, schools have been forced to implement online and distance learning into their education in order for students to continue learning during these unprecedented times. Our school district, the Chery Hill Public School District, has been assisting in providing devices, more specifically Chromebooks, for students who do not have one at home. These computers are meant for students to take home, and if a student is doing the hybrid school model, they are also allowed to borrow Chromebooks from the Chromebook cart to use for the day in school. Furthermore, our schools have also been supplying internet hotspots for families who request them.

In this paper, we first introduce digital divide before and during the COVID-19 pandemic. Afterward, we analyze the technology use of online learning among students and teachers. From then, we view the various factors influencing digital divide and provide statistics for each of these different elements. To end, we include issues that must be addressed, a discussion, and a conclusion, respectively.

2 Digital Divide in the USA

2.1 Before and During the COVID-19 Pandemic

Digital divide is not new. According to the most recent 2018 research from the National Center for Education Statistics and the U.S. Census Bureau, before the COVID-19 pandemic, "an estimated 15 million to 16 million K-12 public school students lived in households without an internet connection or a device adequate for distance learning, representing 30% of all public K-12 students. Of these students, approximately 9 million live in households that have neither an adequate connection nor an adequate device for distance learning" [1]. Based on a report by the Pew Research Center, "85% of suburban residents, 85% of urban residents, and 75% of rural residents have access to the Internet" [4].

Before the pandemic, some families relied on public areas, such as libraries and cafés, for internet connection. However, due to the infectious nature of the virus, these areas have been forced to close or limit the number of people allowed in each time, leaving some families without connection to the internet.

The proportion of digital divide varied in different states. [1] reports that "The top 10 states with the largest absolute number of disconnected students comprise approximately 50% of the overall need, with Texas, California and Florida having the largest populations of students without internet connectivity" (p. 61).

The issues of digital divide have been exacerbated by the COVID-19 Pandemic. Due to infections among teachers and students, schools have been forced to shut down in order to maintain everyone's health. The closure of schools has brought back digital barriers in learning for disadvantaged households. During the pandemic, schools are providing their students with computers to take home for online learning, and governments are thinking about offering internet plans for no charge. Schools have also been asking private business to supply students in need with devices and broadband [2].

2.2 Technology Use for Education

The vast majority of Americans have internet connection; however, not all of their services are robust enough to support virtual and distance learning [1]. For online learning, students need devices, such as desktops, laptops, or tablets. Cellphones are not fit to submit assignments, as educational apps are not effective on them. [1] reports that "Approximately 300,000 to 400,000 public school teachers (8%) lack access to adequate connectivity, and 100,000 (3%) lack devices" (p. 62). This limits the quality of online learning for students. Students and teachers need assistance in implementing a successful and friendly virtual learning environment in their schools. One solution to this would be if stakeholders consider supporting the internet, device replacement, and upgrade costs. During the pandemic, private organizations, schools, governments, and philanthropists have worked hard and seen great success in trying to provide every student with adequate internet connection and devices for virtual learning. Small school districts have faced great challenges in accessing technology, as they have small revenue and are competing with larger districts and even other small districts for supplies [2].

When schools begin to make decisions as to which devices and internet services they will use, the availability of the products may limit their options. For instance, some schools "prioritized procurement of Chromebooks because of simplicity, cost effectiveness and compatibility with Google Classroom and Google Docs. However, the supply of Chromebooks and low-end Windows PCs has quickly become constrained during the pandemic" [1].

According to [1], the costs of internet services and functional devices for all students "[range] from $6 billion to $11 billion in the first year and up to an additional $1 billion for teachers" (p. 62). In a survey that was taken by 105 tenth and twelfth graders, "90.7% said they used their laptops on a daily and weekly basis to search for information, 80.9% to complete homework, 69.8% to organize information, and 67.4% to communicate using e-mail or instant messaging" [4]. In 2020, Ong [3] conducted a study of the low-income households, and found that "over two-in-five households [had] limited access to a computer or the internet for their children. This is well over 2.5 times as high as affluent households" (p. 13). Out of 46 teachers who participated in a survey of which devices they implemented into their classes, 27 teachers used laptops, 3 adopted tablets, and 16 used Chromebooks [4].

In terms of [4], "teachers' demographic characteristics (years of teaching and age) may negatively affect their computer proficiency while other variables (teachers' beliefs and readiness, availability of computers, and availability of technical support) positively affected technology integration" (p. 65).

3 Factors Affecting Digital Divide

The negative impacts of digital divide are most pronounced among "communities of color, rural communities, and those in lower socio-economic groups" [2]. Besides color, rural communities, and socio-economic groups, education level and age also have an impact on the digital divide [3]. Table 1 lists detailed examples and relevant citations for each factor.

Table 1. Factors affecting digital divide

Factors	Examples	Citations
Race/Ethnicity	"Black and Hispanic households are significantly more likely (1.3 to 1.4 times) to experience limited access to technology as compared to non-Hispanic Whites (NHWs). Asians fared better than NHWs."	[3]
	"18% of white households lack broadband, but 26% of Latinx, 30% of Black and 35% of Native American student households lack adequate home internet access."	[1]
Household income	"Higher income is negatively correlated with experiencing limited access to technology. Low-income households fared the worst, with over two-in-five households having limited access to a computer or the internet for their children. This is well over 2.5 times as high as affluent households."	[4]
Education level	"The lack of access to technology is tied to parents' educational attainment, affecting nearly two-in five households where the respondents have no more than a high school education."	[3]
Age	Students in younger households, where the adults' age ranges from 18 to 35, "are between one and three-quarter as likely not to have full access to a computer than students in households with older adults (46–55 years old)."	[3]
Rural area	"In rural communities, 37% of students are without a home broadband connection compared with 25% in suburban households and 21% in urban areas."	[1]

4 Issues Caused by Digital Divide in Online Learning

As discussed earlier, digital divide is dependent upon the socioeconomic and demographic status of households. This problem is most pronounced in rural communities,

Black, Latinx, and Native American households, families with low incomes, households with low educational experiences, as well as young families, meaning those whose parents or guardians are of a young age. Students of Latinx, Black, and Native American households experience the digital divide more than those of white households.

Issues caused by digital divide in online learning of students include lacking technology and internet access/broadband, as well as incapable of receiving a comprehensive education.

According to [1], 30% of Black households, 26% of Latinx households, and 35% of Native Americans households lack broadband. This is compared with 18% of White households lacking adequate technology and internet access (p. 61). Furthermore, in low-income families, meaning those who have an income of less than $50,000 each year, approximately two-in-five households lack broadband, which is over 2.5 times as high as families who have an income of more than $100,000 [4]. In this research, low educational experiences are defined as having no more than a high school degree, and high educational experiences is interpreted as having a bachelor's degree or higher. Around 1/3 of students from low education households have limited access to the internet or technology, which is two times the number of students from high educated families who lack broadband [3]. In addition, if young households have adults between the ages 18 and 35 and old households have adults between the ages 46 and 55, then students in young households are between one and three-quarter less likely to have complete access to technology than those in old families [3].

Digital divide between communities has influenced students' ability to receive a comprehensive education. Children of less advantageous households than their counterparts are also less likely to have full technology access, making keeping up with students from affluent households in the sense of education very challenging. Although solving this problem would take a lot of effort, it is possible. For one, it would take a lot of money, which could be supplied by "school districts, governments, the private sector and philanthropists across the United States" [1]. In addition, stakeholders may "consider [supporting] the recurring costs of home connectivity as well as device replacement and upgrade costs that occur several years after initial purchase" [1]. This money would be used to buy full internet connection and complete computer or technology access for all students. If everyone aforementioned were to work together to solve this long-lasting dilemma, then getting rid of digital divide would be achievable.

5 Conclusion

This paper examined the impact of digital divide on Education in USA and discussed the factors that may have contributed to the digital divide, and the issues caused by digital divide in online learning. The issue of digital divide has been existed before the COVID-19 pandemic and exacerbated during the pandemic, and probably continue to be worsen after the pandemic. One of the goals of this research project is to identify solutions that can improve the technology adoption of the disadvantaged groups. In the near future, we will conduct a survey in our public school district to collect opinions from students and teachers on the impact of digital divide in online learning.

References

1. Chandra, S., et al.: Closing the K-12 digital divide in the age of distance learning. In: Common Sense and Boston Consulting Group: Boston, MA, USA (2020)
2. Clausen, J.M., Bunte, B., Robertson, E.T.: Professional development to improve communication and reduce the homework gap in grades 7–12 during COVID-19 transition to remote learning. J. Technol. Teach. Educ. **28**(2), 443–451 (2020)
3. Ong, P.: COVID-19 and the digital divide in virtual learning (2020)
4. Power, J.R., Musgrove, A.T., Nichols, B.H.: Teachers bridging the digital divide in rural schools with 1:1 computing. Rural. Educ. **41**(1), 61–76 (2020)

Building 5G Network in Bulgaria During COVID-19 Pandemic: National Specifics and Challenges

Nadezhda Miteva^(✉)

The St. Kliment Okhridsky Sofia University, Sofia, Bulgaria
nmiteva1@uni-sofia.bg

Abstract. Coronavirus pandemic makes evident the crucial importance of providing reliable and high-speed connectivity, not only to modernizing Bulgarian economy and society, but also to ensuring the proper functioning of every person and of every system in a lockdown state. The need to mitigate the consequences of the current crisis and to prepare the country for a possible new one, lead to change in the way telecommunications industry, government and regulatory authorities interact. As a result, Bulgaria has its first 5G networks before the end of 2020. They are launched under the exceptional conditions, such as spectrum auctions postponed and temporary frequency usage permits allocated. The intention of the regulatory body to only provide free radio spectrum to operating companies does not allow for new participants to enter the market of telecommunications services in Bulgaria. There is a risk that tenders will be appealed to the national judicial system or the European Commission.

Keywords: 5G · Telecommunications · COVID-19 · Bulgaria · Spectrum assignment

1 Introduction

Leading mobile operators in Bulgaria successfully overcome the challenges and the hardships during the lockdown (13 March–13 May 2020), imposed with a decision of the National Assembly[1], taken in order to limit the spread of the coronavirus. After the end of the state of emergency, telecommunications companies enjoy (in the short term) higher revenues and an improved image. The sudden crisis necessitates changes in the technological renewal and investment plans of both the telecommunications industry and the electronic communications regulatory body – Communications Regulation Commission. A new approach of interaction and cooperation between business, state and regulator is needed to prepare the country for a new crisis of a similar nature. Part of this preparation is the strengthening of existing networks and the creation of fifth generation (5G) transmission networks. Despite the postponed tenders for spectrum allocation, the partial deployment of the first 5G networks takes place by the end of 2020.

---

[1] Parliament of the Republic of Bulgaria. State Gazette (Official Issue of the Republic of Bulgaria), Issue #22/ 13/03/2020. Available at: https://dv.parliament.bg/DVWeb/showMaterialDV.jsp;jsessionid=B61F6F106FBC8D333DC8AFA9155E92A2?idMat=146931 (in Bulgarian).

© Springer Nature Switzerland AG 2021
C. Stephanidis et al. (Eds.): HCII 2021, CCIS 1421, pp. 577–582, 2021.
https://doi.org/10.1007/978-3-030-78645-8_73

2 Research Design

This paper examines the preparation and the first steps in the process of building 5G telecommunications networks in Bulgaria, against the background of the unfolding global COVID-19 pandemic. The aim is to trace the process in its entirety and to highlight its features and challenges at the national level. The research itself is a case study. The methodology used is a mix of descriptive and analytical techniques, such as observation, historical overview, secondary data analysis. Main sources for gathering information are normative and regulatory databases at national and European level, corporate information, websites of non-governmental and professional organizations. The subject of this article is the entire process of deployment of 5G in Bulgaria including the period of preparation. In this regard, the full scope of the research lies between the years 2013–2020.

3 Results

3.1 European Regulatory and Diachronic Framework

Preparations for the building of fifth generation networks can be traced back to 2013, when the analogue terrestrial television switch off in Bulgaria is completed. Within the European Union, the analogue to digital switch-over is a harmonized process aimed at providing a radio frequency resource for the development of the Digital Single market (European Commission 2010). In EU countries, this process ends in 2015. The European Commission coordinates the phasing out of frequencies in the UHF band with a special focus on the 800 MHz band (790–862 MHz) and the 700 MHz band (694–790 MHz), the so-called First and Second digital dividends. The sub-1 GHz band is considered to be a valuable asset for the cost-efficient deployment of wireless networks with universal indoor and outdoor coverage. Currently in Europe, this band includes television broadcasting in 470–694 MHz, and mobile services in 800 MHz and 900 MHz. The 700 MHz band is in the process of being cleared across Europe in line with agreements made in the run up to World Radiocommunication Conference-2015.

In 2015 the European Commission promotes the forthcoming 5G mobile technology, which is supposed to become "the backbone of our digital future and the foundation of a trillion euro EU market in the Internet of Things" (European Commission 2015). According to ITU, the pioneer bands for Region 1 (Europe, Africa and Middle East west of the Persian Gulf) are 700 MHz (universal coverage) and 3,6 GHz (urban and wider coverage). Studies are ongoing on 24–86 GHz spectrum ranges for 5G use (hot spot coverage, e.g. railway stations, sport events, smart factories etc.) (International Telecommunications Union 2018). By decision of the European Parliament, by 30 June 2020 at the latest, Member States should allow the use of band 694–790 MHz (700 MHz band) for terrestrial systems allowing the provision of wireless broadband electronic communications services for the purpose of deploying a new generation of network technologies - 5G, which reveal prospects for new economic and business models (European Parliament and Council 2017). The cited decision provides for a two-year delay when the country has a valid reason.

A typical feature of the European media model is the still strong presence of terrestrial radio and television broadcasting, which takes place primarily in the 700 MHz band. For 29% of European households, digital terrestrial television is the main source to receive a TV signal (European Broadcasting Union 2018). 42% of European households receive TV signal on at least one TV set via digital terrestrial broadcasting (Faisan 2019). This is one of the reasons for the slow process of 700 MHz band releasing in Europe. At the same time, the sub-700 MHz (470–694 MHz) remains reserved for digital terrestrial television (DTT) broadcasting until at least 2030 (European Commission 2016). Thus European legislators protect the interests of DTT consumers and suppliers. However, the sub-1 GHz band usage globally will be among the main topics in the World Radiocommunication Conference-2023 agenda.

3.2 The Bulgarian Case

Bulgaria is among the countries in the EU that are experiencing significant difficulties in providing radio frequency resources for the needs of electronic communications services and the telecommunications sector. The digitalization of television broadcasting has failed to make a significant contribution to the release of frequencies in the scope of the First and Second Digital Dividends. The country is among the last in the European Union to release small portions of 700 and 800 MHz bands. In this way, it barely manages to meet the deadlines set for this purpose by the European Commission and the European Parliament.

One of the main reasons for this delay is the priority use of the two bands for the needs of the national defense, more precisely - for the navigation systems of the Bulgaria's Air Forces. By the mid 2020, digital terrestrial TV broadcasting is located in the 700 MHz band. Therefore, from the very beginning of mobile technologies, the transmission networks in Bulgaria have been developed in 900 MHz, 1800 MHz, 2.1 GHz 2.6 GHz bands (Communications Regulation Commission n.d.)

Another obstacle for mobile operators to improve the existing 4G LTE and the deployment of 5G networks in Bulgaria are the high fees for using the scarce radio frequency resource. The tariffs were formed in the 1990s, when only one frequency band (900 MHz band) was used. In addition, telecommunications companies face cumbersome and expensive administrative procedures to build and upgrade technological equipment (between 6 and 24 months per base station) (Zapryanov 2020).

With the complication of the COVID-19 epidemic situation, a state of emergency was introduced for the period March 13–May 13, 2020. Telecommunications companies have been put under unprecedented strain, bearing the brunt of the remote operation of public administration, business, education and other national systems facing lockdown. Fifth generation (5G) mobile networks are proving to be a key component in the transfer of more and more companies, services and products online and the transition towards a digital society. Bulgaria traditionally ranks among the last in the European Commission's annual ranking of countries' progress towards digital economy and digital society (Digital Economy and Society Index/DESI) (European Commission 2020). The likelihood that Bulgaria will further lag behind technologically and economically forces the government to take urgent measures to remove obstacles to 5G networks deployment.

First, small portions in the 700 MHz (2 × 20 MHz) band have been freed-up by moving digital terrestrial television broadcasting to other frequencies (Communications Regulation Commission 2020a). The released resource is insufficient for the deployment of three mobile 5G networks (there are three leading mobile operators in the country). According to the operators' estimates, the distribution of less than 10 MHz per company makes it technologically impossible and economically unjustified to upgrade the existing 4G technologies. As for the 800 MHz band, in 2016 the Minister of Information Technology Valery Borissov announced that 2 × 10 MHz have been released in this band ("The Government Decided to Free-Up Frequencies in 800 MHz Band" 2016). Following a public consultation and probably for the above mentioned reasons, the free portions remain not allocated. The full release of the First and Second Digital Dividends can be said after the replacement of the Soviet planes based Air Forces with American F16 aircraft, which is not expected before 2024.

The tenders planned for the middle of 2020 for provision of radio spectrum for development of the existing and deployment of new transmission networks are postponed for 2021. CRC grants to the three leading mobile companies temporary licenses for use additional portions in 3.6 GHz band, until an auction is held in March 2021.

From the previously published intentions of CRC it becomes evident that the regulator is preparing to provide the released frequencies in the 700 MHz band for a period of 20 years to telecommunications companies that already have licenses to use national frequency and built transmission networks with coverage of at least 80% of the population. The conditions, as they are set and phrased, in fact exclude the entry of new participants in the market of mobile services in Bulgaria. The Commission's reasoning is that this ensures a smooth transition from one technology to another i.e. from 4G to 5G (Communications Regulation Commission 2020b).

Second, after two years of negotiations with the state and the regulatory body, charges for frequencies used by mobile operators have been reduced by more than 50% since the beginning of 2021 (Communications Regulation Commission 2020c). However, the insistence of the telecoms on extending the term of the licenses for the used radio frequency resource from 10 to 20 years is left without effect.

Finally, legislative changes were adopted so that the procedures for technological upgrades of telecommunications equipment to be eased. Shorter deadlines and lower prices for upgrading and deploying new base stations pave the way for the deployment of next generation networks.

The first announcement for the launch of a 5G network in Bulgaria comes in September 2020. It was made by Vivacom ("5G Now in Bulgaria by Vivacom" 2020). Dynamic Spectrum Sharing (DSS) technology is applied which enables the parallel use of LTE and 5G in the same frequency band. The network is limited to the route of the Trakia highway in the southern part of the country and the central parts of the regional cities. In November 2020, A1 announced that it was launching its own 5G network in parts of the capital Sofia, and later in the Black Sea city of Burgas. Both telecoms offer free tests of their new networks for their users as well as expanding variety of 5G devices. The third mobile operator with national coverage in Bulgaria - Telenor, so far announces only 5G tests.

4 Conclusion and Discussion

The first 5G mobile networks in Bulgaria start operating earlier than planned. Their early launch is in response to the challenges the Bulgarian society facing due to the coronavirus pandemic. The need to mitigate the consequences of the current crisis and to prepare the country for a possible new one lead to a change in the way business, state and regulatory authorities interact. Ensuring reliable and high-speed connectivity is becoming of crucial importance, not only to modernizing the economy and society, but also to ensuring the proper functioning of every person and of every system in a lockdown state.

The first 5G networks are built without effective financial incentives for mobile operators, without spectrum auctions and through temporary permits for the use of frequencies in the 3.6 GHz band, which becomes the 5G pioneer band in Bulgaria. This explains their limited scope and consumption, as well as their slow deployment nationwide. The provision of additional frequency spectrum by conducting tenders and by the reduction of tariffs for its usage as of January 2021 can accelerate the process of innovative technologies to enter the Bulgarian telecommunications market.

The Communications Regulation Commission faces the difficult task of allocating scarce portions of frequencies in the 700 MHz band. Alongside with 26 GHz, both bands can contribute the most for ensuring transmission networks' full national coverage. The intention of the regulatory body to only provide free radio spectrum to operating companies does not allow for new participants to enter the market of telecommunications services in Bulgaria. It can intensify competition between existing telecoms, but does not provide equal opportunities for business participation in this market and its overall development. There is a risk that tenders will be appealed to the national judicial system or the European Commission.

Acknowledgments. This research has been developed within the framework of the Programme "Young Scientists and Postdocs" of the Ministry of Edication of the Republic of Bulgaria.

References

Faisan, J.-P.: The DTT Roadmap. ITU workshop on the future of television for Europe. Itu.int, June 2019. https://www.itu.int/en/ITU-T/Workshops-and-Seminars/20190607/Documents/Jean-Pie rre%20Faisan.pdf

European Broadcasting Union: Looking Beyond the Headlines on DTT (2018). https://tech.ebu. ch/news/2018/12/looking-beyond-the-headlines-on-dtt

European Commission: Decision on harmonised technical conditions of use in the 790–862 MHz frequency band for terrestrial systems capable of providing electronic communications services in the European Union. Europa.eu (2010)

https://eur-lex.europa.eu/legal-content/EN/ALL/?uri=CELEX%3A32010D0267

European Commission: The EU and China signed a key partnership on 5G, our tomorrow's communication networks [Press Release]. Europa.eu (2015)

https://ec.europa.eu/commission/presscorner/detail/en/IP_15_5715

European Commission: Commission welcomes political agreement to boost mobile internet services with high-quality radio frequencies [Press Release]. Europa.eu (2016) https://ec.europa.eu/commission/presscorner/detail/en/IP_16_4405

European Commission: The Digital Economy and Society (DESI) 2020. Europa.eu (2020). https://ec.europa.eu/digital-single-market/en/digital-economy-and-society-index-desi

European Parliament and Council: Decision on the use of the 470–790 MHz frequency band in the Union [Decision 2017/899]. Europa.eu (2017)

https://eur-lex.europa.eu/legal-content/BGALL/?uri=uriserv%3AOJ.L_.2017.138.01.0131.01.ENG

International Telecommunications Union: DigitalEurope: 5G Spectrum Recommendations. Itu.int (2018). https://www.itu.int/en/ITU-D/Regional-Presence/Europe/Documents/Events/2018/5G%20Greece/Session%205%20DIGITALEUROPE%205G%20Spectrum%20Policy%20Recommendations%20(October%202018).pdf

Zapryanov, Y.: The Government Mitigates Procedures for Telecoms' Technological Renovation. Capital.bg, 9 March 2020.

in Bulgarian. https://www.capital.bg/biznes/telekomi/2020/03/09/4038524_durjavata_smekchava_rejima_za_obnoviavane_na_telekom/

Communications Regulation Commission (n.d.): Radiospectrun Assignment in 900 MHz, 1800 MHz, 2100 MHz, 2.6 GHz и 3.6 GHz. Crc.bg. (in Bulgarian). https://crc.bg/bg/statii/840/razpredelenie-na-radiochestoten-spektyr-v-obhvati-900-m-hz-1800-m-hz-2100-m-hz-2-6-g-hz-i-3-6-g-hz

Communications Regulation Commission: DTT Channels' Shift with Effect from June the 1st 2020. Crc.bg. (in Bulgarian) (2020a). https://crc.bg/bg/novini/1317/promqna-na-televizionnite-kanali-za-priemane-na-cifrova-efirna-televiziq-ot-01-06-2020-g

Communications Regulation Commission: Position on the Perspectives and Conditions of the 700 MHz Band's Usage. Crc.bg. (in Bulgarian) (2020b). https://crc.bg/files/URChS/ObstObsazhdane/20200709_Pozicia_700MHz.pdf

Communications Regulation Commission: Fee Tariff 2020. Crc.bg. (in Bulgarian) (2020c). https://crc.bg/files/Tarifa%20taksi%202020.pdf

MobileBulgaria: The Government Decided to Free-Up Frequencies in 800 MHz Band. Mobile-bulgaria.com (2016). (in Bulgarian). https://mobilebulgaria.com/news/darzhavata-reshi-da-osvobodi-chestoti-v-spektar-800-mhz

VIVACOM. 5G Now in Bulgaria by Vivacom. Vivacom.bg (2020). (in Bulgarian). https://www.vivacom.bg/bg/5g

Remote Working Pre- and Post-COVID-19: An Analysis of New Threats and Risks to Security and Privacy

Jason R. C. Nurse[1]([⊠]), Nikki Williams[2], Emily Collins[3], Niki Panteli[4], John Blythe[5], and Ben Koppelman[6]

[1] University of Kent, Canterbury, UK
J.R.C.Nurse@kent.ac.uk
[2] Cranfield University, Cranfield, UK
[3] Cardiff University, Cardiff, UK
[4] Royal Holloway, University of London, Egham, UK
[5] CybSafe, London, UK
[6] CyberSmart, London, UK

Abstract. COVID-19 has radically changed society as we know it. To reduce the spread of the virus, millions across the globe have been forced to work remotely, often in make-shift home offices, and using a plethora of new, unfamiliar digital technologies. In this article, we critically analyse cyber security and privacy concerns arising due to remote working during the coronavirus pandemic. Through our work, we discover a series of security risks emerging because of the realities of this period. For instance, lack of remote-working security training, heightened stress and anxiety, rushed technology deployment, and the presence of untrusted individuals in a remote-working environment (e.g., in flatshares), can result in new cyber-risk. Simultaneously, we find that as organisations look to manage these and other risks posed by their remote workforces, employee's privacy (including personal information and activities) is often compromised. This is apparent in the significant adoption of remote workplace monitoring, management and surveillance technologies. Such technologies raise several privacy and ethical questions, and further highlight the tension between security and privacy going forward.

Keywords: Remote working · Working from home · Coronavirus · Cyber security · Privacy · Human factors · Workplace surveillance · Ethics · Human computer interaction

1 Introduction

The impact that COVID-19 has had on society is undeniable. Countries, companies and individuals have had to drastically change the way they engage and operate to preserve life and prioritise safety [20]. Technology-enabled remote

© Springer Nature Switzerland AG 2021
C. Stephanidis et al. (Eds.): HCII 2021, CCIS 1421, pp. 583–590, 2021.
https://doi.org/10.1007/978-3-030-78645-8_74

working, in particular, has seen a substantial increase with millions across the globe being forced to work from at home. While remote working is not novel, the extent and speed at which it has been implemented over the last year is noteworthy as there are several compounded HCI, security and privacy implications for individuals and their employers. For instance, new forms of cybercrime and misinformation have emerged during the pandemic—both at the point of the initial spread (with online fraud and scams exploiting increased anxiety and poor mental health), and now as vaccines are being administered (with online anti-vax campaigns) [10,11].

In this paper, we report on a critical analysis of the technology-related security and privacy issues arising due to the large-scale move to remote working as a result of COVID-19. This is based on openly available reports, media and academic articles. We consider risks that have arisen due to the increase in makeshift offices at home, the extent of distractions accompanying remote-working environments, and the abrupt adoption of various forms of new technology/apps to interact (e.g., Zoom, Microsoft Teams, Clubhouse, Houseparty). Of particular interest is how cyber security concerns and solutions have shifted before and after COVID-19. This incorporates the upsurge in attacks targeting remote work forces and challenges companies have had securing remote workforces (some of which pertain to difficulties in human use of new technology) [4,8]. Finally, we discuss security implications for the future as remote working and the technologies that support it are likely to become further embedded into society, including workplaces, education institutions and business.

2   Research Methodology

The methodology that we adopt for this research is based on a critical review of current literature, particularly reports from industry over the last year. To direct our study into the actual security and privacy risks to remote working pre- and post-COVID-19, we conduct an online search for current reports and articles around three core areas. The first area seeks to consider the characteristics and features of work-from-home scenarios, and the impact of COVID-19 on employees. The second area examines the security risks that emerge due to characteristics and features of remote working scenarios and COVID-19. The last area pays attention to the privacy risks emerging and the tensions with organisations aiming to secure remote systems, and employees seeking to maintain some privacy in their home environments. Once these articles were identified, they were then assessed to extract key issues, especially ones that have surfaced due to the pandemic. The sections below report the key findings and results from these analyses.

3   Remote Working Since COVID-19

Remote working, and working from home, have become the norm for many due to the pandemic. Such working has been required by governments due to various national and regional lockdowns, and many companies have encouraged this practice even after governmental mandates. Remote working is, of course, not new and has existed for a long time due to its many advantages including flexible working, increased time with family, and better work-life balance [19]. From our research we found that many of these advantages were upheld during the pandemic. There were also some new additions such as an increased feeling of safety, due to lack of the need to commute to work or enter an office or public space, which may put one's health at risk.

The reported concerns accompanying remote working vastly outweighed the benefits in literature. The most commonly appearing were distractions from home life (e.g., family members, pets, chores) and friends, feelings of isolation, difficulties in communicating and team working with colleagues, overworking due to the desire to prove that one is working, technology problems, lack of visibility of staff, and difficulty finding an appropriate work-life balance [6,9,16]; all of which can impact productivity.

Assessing the influence of COVID-19 on remote working, we found that the pandemic exacerbated many of the existing challenges with this type of work. Isolation, burnout, and difficulties managing and supporting remote teams were high on the list of organisational and employee issues. There were some key differences in remote working due to COVID-19 however. For instance, COVID-19 forced employees to work from home, instead of it being a voluntary decision; this led to a completely new working experience for millions who had never worked remotely before [7,17]. Also, employers and employees had little time to prepare for the mass need for remote working [17]. This meant that technology facilities (e.g., laptops, home offices or teleworking software) were often not in place, some technologies had to be rapidly adopted without proper testing (therefore increasing demands on technical support staff as well), and that other important concerns such as family commitments (e.g., new childcare or elderly-care demands) and well-being (both mental and physical) were neglected. These issues were particularly salient given the overall increased negative impact on mental health, job security and finances due to the pandemic [18].

4   Security Risks

Cyber security has been a key concern during the pandemic as companies have been rushed into migrating to new technology platforms and services to communicate, allow remote working (and remote access to corporate systems) and for business engagement. Cyber criminals have kept track of the various issues caused by remote working, as well as the general pandemic, to increase their variety and number of attacks [10]. We examined the challenges to remote working in the context of security vulnerabilities and threats to identify a set of noteworthy risks emerging specifically due to, or greatly exacerbated by, the COVID-19 pandemic. These are arranged into two main areas, security risks associated with employees working remotely, and those related to the technologies that have been in use during the pandemic.

Employee-related security risks are focused on those issues that may target or be caused (intentionally or unintentionally) by an employee. We list exemplars of the key risks below.

- *Increased likelihood of falling victim to cyber-attacks (e.g., phishing) because of a lack of concentration or distractions caused by a home-working space.* This may link to family responsibilities or household needs that are new because of the pandemic (e.g., home schooling, entire families or flatmates at home for extended periods).
- *Lack of remote-working security training resulting in poor security practices* that increase the potential of a compromising cyber-attack. Many organisations were not able to train employees adequately before they were forced to work from home, which compounds this risk.
- *De-prioritisation of security as a key concern because of heightened anxiety, stress, depression, burnout and poor mental health generally motivated by the pandemic.* As individual employees focus more on basic needs (e.g., safety, health, job security), they may be less cognisant of workplace security concerns.
- *Reduced access to information/knowledge that causes poor security practices*, for instance, difficulty in quickly speaking with a work colleague about appropriate security behaviours when faced with a security-related decision. This issue is exacerbated by the length of time at which employees have had to work remotely, and the psychological differences of 'popping by' a colleague's desk or 'disrupting their work' by requesting a video call.
- *Trusted/untrusted individuals in the remote-working environment (or household)* may exploit new access to corporate data or services (e.g., using an unlocked laptop or phone, or listening to a confidential phone call). The reality is that these environments may be shared with unknown flatmates or others that may use this extended home-working period for malevolent purposes.
- *Employees now experiencing minimal management monitoring or oversight may use that opportunity to steal confidential information from their employer or misuse corporate services.* This may be further motivated by perceived job insecurity due to the pandemic; a period where many have been laid off, made redundant or furloughed.

Technology-related security risks are also a noteworthy concern. Exemplars are presented below.

- *Rushed technology adoption due to national lockdowns leading to the deployment of untested or unreliable technologies.* Such technologies may not work well and therefore give rise to employees adopting potentially dangerous shadow IT practices, e.g., not using Virtual Private Network (VPN) adequately, poor connection resulting in preferring insecure WiFi networks with better connection speeds, use of third-party services such as Dropbox, Google Drive for confidential work files.

- *Unfamiliarity (or lack of proficiency) with new remote-working technology (e.g., Microsoft Teams, Zoom, etc.) leading to mistakes in the use and management of security features.* The speed at which these technologies have been implemented because of the pandemic places a technical burden on individuals, at a time when they are already in stressful and tense situations.
- *Security issues with remote-working and remote communication technologies can expose an organisation to increased risk.* As highlighted above, the rush in adoption of new platforms to operate during COVID-19 also exposed enterprises to a range of new threats accompanying such technologies. For instance, we have seen several attacks targeting Zoom and Microsoft over the last year.
- *Intentional or inadvertent use of work devices for personal matters, therefore opening work devices to additional risk.* For instance, using work devices to watch films on illegitimate websites or download malicious attachments from personal emails, social media or gaming websites.
- *Work devices may be stolen from the home or remote-working environment.* If these devices are not appropriately encrypted, they pose a risk to corporate data and services. This risk is increased during the pandemic because criminals are aware that most individuals are working remotely and therefore are likely to have more mobile technology at home.
- *Employees returning to work after a long period of remote working may bring infected devices in to the corporate network.* Home networks are much more likely to be compromised than corporate networks, and therefore the extended period of remote working caused due to lockdowns, can increase the possibility of this risk.

As can be seen from the examples above, security risks can originate from various areas. A primary difference with these risks in a post-COVID world is that they are exacerbated by the physical and mental impact that COVID-19 has had on people's lives.

5   Privacy Risks and Workplace Surveillance

While security risks and discussions dominated business concerns during the pandemic, privacy was a salient factor for employees. We analysed a series of current reports and articles exploring this issue, and noted an increasing prominence of discussions pertaining to workplace surveillance in remote-working setups. This was driven largely by employers and their worries about employee productivity, and secondly in an attempt to secure corporate data and systems. Below, we present exemplars of the primary risks to privacy emerging from our review.

- *The potential infringement of employee's privacy caused by a dramatic surge in employer usage of (remote) workplace surveillance/monitoring technologies.* This could include monitoring of keystrokes, screens and websites visited (e.g., [3]). A significant reality is that in some cases, employees may be using their own technologies (smartphones, iPads, laptops) for remote working, thereby giving employers—or the companies they outsource to—access to vast amounts of personal employees data.

– *New forms of technology emerging during the pandemic that are able to monitor employee emotional state (e.g., as smart technologies* [1]*) could also violate privacy.* For example, such emotional and psychological data, if not properly protected, may be used to profile employees according to their well-being, and thus impact employment or future career prospects.
– *Exposure of personal information as a result of how remote working and communication technologies are used.* For instance, exposing home (living room, bedroom, office) backgrounds in video calls, or posting photos online of home offices can leak personal data (e.g., interest, hobbies) [15] which can be further used as the basis for cybercrime. This touches on the common issue of oversharing online and its link to cyber risk [12]; an issue overlooked in the pandemic as individuals focus primary on staying connected through online services.

6   Discussion and Conclusion

A number of salient risks were identified in our reflection above, and it is important that organisations now reflect on the choices made during an emergency to keep the business going, and ensure they match their business as usual security posture and risk tolerance. Where new software has been adopted there is now an opportunity to update training to remedy lack of proficiency issues, and review configurations to ensure any risks introduced during the pandemic are minimised. Most organisations have cyber security training for employees and it is important for this to include how to minimise security risks whilst working remotely. The training should cover taking sensible precautions to protect privacy, how to protect devices in public spaces (the home is not a public space but it may have untrusted people in it, so can, on occasion, be considered from this perspective), use of non-corporate networks, and the importance of using company sanctioned options for file transfer and access of company resources.

Looking forward, another key risk is related to bringing infected devices back to the corporate network. Prior to COVID-19 many organisations will have assumed that employee devices, which predominantly connect to the corporate network, are trusted devices and unlikely to be bringing infections into the network. A separate guest network may also be available for external visitors. It seems likely that in the future the default will be a Zero Trust architecture (where there is no trust in devices by default) [14]. Therefore, so long as this remains usable for employees, this would eliminate the need to run multiple networks with different levels of trust, and would result in a greater level of security.

Many organisations have indicated they do not expect employees to return to the office full time [2]. There is now time to reflect on how to best support this way of working in the future. To facilitate remote working, more employees will be issued with laptops, to avoid the need for them to use personal devices for work; though this does not address the issue of using work devices for personal activities. Whilst remote working is not new to most organisations, the move to more extensive home working also means employees need to be able to access a wide range of corporate systems and resources remotely in the long term. Now organisations should evaluate whether existing solutions meet future needs, and to identify alternatives if not. Once a solution has been chosen it is also vital to configure it correctly and ensure appropriate employee training is in place.

Some risks are universal, including an increase in COVID-19-related phishing attacks and the need to keep software up to date, and everyone should be taking proactive steps to address them. Some of these steps may also include exploring the utility of cyber insurance, which can offer some level of protection and support after incidents [13]. Other risks, for example the likelihood of confidential conversations being overheard, are context specific, and this highlights the importance of asking people to consider the nature of their work and new work environment. Some jobs require a substantial number of video calls with external contacts, and for these workers the privacy related recommendations are more important than for someone only communicating with other employees.

In terms of privacy, there is a clear tension between an employee's wish for privacy in their own home, and the employer's goal to be able to monitor productivity while workers are not co-located with them. Sometimes monitoring is introduced as a preventative measure, without there being any evidence to indicate it is needed. There is limited evidence to show employees are doing less work whilst at home, in fact some research shows the opposite [5], and the introduction of additional monitoring adds to the perception that employees are not trusted. A perception of a lack of trust coupled with intrusive monitoring may weaken the relationship between the organisation and such individuals.

The pandemic has increased acceptance of flexible work schedules, and this has been a substantial advancement in terms of inclusivity, particularly for those with caring responsibilities who might wish to complete their work according to their own schedule. In order to maintain trust between employers and employees it is important to identify the minimum level of monitoring that could be used to give adequate assurance, and this will vary depending on the roles being undertaken. It is likely that cultural norms around levels of monitoring will develop, similar to expectations around realities such as time recording, which is commonplace in some sectors.

Acknowledgment. Funding for this research was received by SPRITE+: The Security, Privacy, Identity, and Trust Engagement NetworkPlus (EPSRC Grant reference EP/S035869/1).

References

1. BBC: A wristband that tells your boss if you are unhappy (2020). https://www.bbc.co.uk/news/business-55637328. Accessed 14 Mar 2021
2. BBC: No plan for a return to the office for millions of staff (2020). https://www.bbc.co.uk/news/business-53901310. Accessed 14 Mar 2021
3. Bloomberg: Bosses Panic-Buy Spy Software to Keep Tabs on Remote Workers (2020). https://www.bloomberg.com/news/features/2020-03-27/bosses-panic-buy-spy-software-to-keep-tabs-on-remote-workers. Accessed 14 Mar 2021

4. Buil-Gil, D., Miró-Llinares, F., Moneva, A., Kemp, S., Díaz-Castaño, N.: Cybercrime and shifts in opportunities during COVID-19: a preliminary analysis in the UK. Eur. Soc. **23**(sup1), 47–59 (2021)

5. Business Wire: Productivity Has Increased, Led By Remote Workers (2020). https://www.businesswire.com/news/home/20200519005295/en/

6. Green, N., Tappin, D., Bentley, T.: Working from home before, during and after the Covid-19 pandemic: implications for workers and organisations. N. Z. J. Employ. Relat. **45**(2), 5–16 (2020)

7. IBM: IBM Security Work From Home Study (2020). https://newsroom.ibm.com/2020-06-22-IBM-Security-Study-Finds-Employees-New-to-Working-from-Home-Pose-Security-Risk. Accessed 14 Mar 2021

8. Infosecurity Magazine: 21% of UK Workers Feel More Vulnerable to Cybercrime During COVID-19 (2020). https://www.infosecurity-magazine.com/news/uk-workers-vulnerable-cybercrime/. Accessed 14 Mar 2021

9. Insider: 9 of the most challenging things about working remotely, according to people who do it (2019). https://www.businessinsider.com/working-remote-challenges-work-from-home-2019-10. Accessed 14 Mar 2021

10. Lallie, H.S., et al.: Cyber security in the age of COVID-19: a timeline and analysis of cyber-crime and cyber-attacks during the pandemic. Comput. Secur. **105**, 102248 (2021)

11. Naidoo, R.: A multi-level influence model of COVID-19 themed cybercrime. Eur. J. Inf. Syst. **29**(3), 306–321 (2020)

12. Nurse, J.R.C.: Cybercrime and you: how criminals attack and the human factors that they seek to exploit. In: The Oxford Handbook of Cyberpsychology (2019)

13. Sullivan, J., Nurse, J.R.C.: Cyber Security Incentives and the Role of Cyber Insurance (Royal United Services Institute (RUSI) Emerging Insights Paper) (2020). https://rusi.org/publication/emerging-insights/cyber-security-incentives-and-role-cyber-insurance. Accessed 14 Mar 2021

14. ThreatPost: Work-for-Home Shift: What We Learned (2020). https://threatpost.com/2020-work-for-home-shift-learned/162595/

15. ThreatPost: Home-Office Photos: A Ripe Cyberattack Vector (2021). https://threatpost.com/home-office-photos-cyberattack-vector/164460/. Accessed 14 Mar 2021

16. Tremblay, D.G., Thomsin, L.: Telework and mobile working: analysis of its benefits and drawbacks. Int. J. Work Innov. **1**(1), 100–113 (2012)

17. Waizenegger, L., McKenna, B., Cai, W., Bendz, T.: An affordance perspective of team collaboration and enforced working from home during COVID-19. Eur. J. Inf. Syst. **29**(4), 429–442 (2020)

18. Wilson, J.M., Lee, J., Fitzgerald, H.N., Oosterhoff, B., Sevi, B., Shook, N.J.: Job insecurity and financial concern during the COVID-19 pandemic are associated with worse mental health. J. Occup. Environ. Med. **62**(9), 686–691 (2020)

19. World Economic Forum: 6 charts that show what employers and employees really think about remote working (2020). https://www.weforum.org/agenda/2020/06/coronavirus-covid19-remote-working-office-employees-employers. Accessed 14 Mar 2021

20. World Health Organisation (WHO): Impact of COVID-19 on people's livelihoods, their health and our food systems (2020). https://www.who.int/news/item/13-10-2020-impact-of-covid-19-on-people's-livelihoods-their-health-and-our-food-systems. Accessed 14 Mar 2021

A Review of Covid-19 Symptom Checker Mobile Applications

Susan Quinn[1]([✉]), Raymond R. Bond[2], Mark P. Donnelly[2], Shirley Davey[3], James McLaughlin[1], and Dewar Finlay[1]

[1] School of Engineering, Ulster University, Shore Road, Jordanstown, Northern Ireland, UK
{s.quinn1,jad.mclaughlin,d.finlay}@ulster.ac.uk
[2] School of Computing, Ulster University, Shore Road, Jordanstown, Northern Ireland, UK
{rb.bond,mp.donnelly}@ulster.ac.uk
[3] Ulster University Business School, Ulster University, Shore Road, Jordanstown, Northern Ireland, UK
s.davey@ulster.ac.uk

Abstract. Digital technologies have been widely utilized to assist with disease detection and management throughout the Covid-19 pandemic. The prevalence of smartphone usage amongst populations has assisted the provision of mobile applications that citizens can use to manage their health. Covid-19 symptom checker smartphone apps enable users to enter their health characteristics and receive validated advice related to self-isolation, testing and whether to seek clinical care. Moreover, the collection of symptom data can assist healthcare providers with disease surveillance and resource allocation. However, the adoption of symptom checker apps can be influenced by several factors including the functionality of the app, and data privacy and protection policies. In this study, we reviewed nine symptom checker apps that were available on the Android and iOS platforms. We analyzed characteristics related to the functionality and accessibility of the apps, and factors that related to privacy, transparency and trust. We found that most of the apps were multifunctional and several (n = 4) combined contact tracing and symptom checking functionalities. Moreover, there was variation in the quantity of personal data collected and symptom checking questions. For all the apps reviewed information related to privacy and data protection was available, however, there was variability in the content and readability of this material. Information regarding the technical profile of the apps was also inconsistent. For several of the apps, access to the symptom checking functionality was restricted by location. This review suggests that symptom checker apps provide an effective tool for public health management during the Covid-19 pandemic.

Keywords: Covid-19 · Symptom checker · Digital health

1 Introduction and Background

The Covid-19 pandemic has been characterized by the widespread use of digital health tools to help manage public health. Digital solutions have been utilized for public health

© Springer Nature Switzerland AG 2021
C. Stephanidis et al. (Eds.): HCII 2021, CCIS 1421, pp. 591–598, 2021.
https://doi.org/10.1007/978-3-030-78645-8_75

messaging, and disease diagnosis, treatment and management. A Covid-19 symptom checker smartphone app can enable a user to carry out a health assessment and immediately receive clinically validated advice. For health organizations, self-assessment tools can provide a cost-effective method of triaging a proportion of the population outside of healthcare facilities, thereby reducing the burden on health resources, whilst also collecting valuable data to assist with disease surveillance and risk prediction. Governments in the United Kingdom (UK) and the European Union (EU) are encouraging citizens to use these *mHealth* applications as a means of managing their health and reducing virus transmission [1, 2]. However, while these tools are accessible to smartphone users, technology adoption can be impacted by multiple factors including perceived usefulness of the app, and concerns related to privacy and trust. This paper presents a study that reviewed nine symptom checker smartphone apps, available for UK and EU countries. During the study we investigated the functionality, technical features and privacy aspects of each app towards gaining insight to possible barriers to adoption.

A literature search identified several publications that appraised Covid-19 mHealth applications, however we did not find any technology reviews that focused solely on Covid-19 smartphone symptom checkers. For example, [3] provides an evaluation of diverse mobile apps that were launched earlier in the pandemic, and focuses on characteristics such as app function, size, cost and ownership. This review included an earlier version of the Northern Ireland symptom assessment app, *COVID-19 NI*. The authors of [4] used a typology to assess application and context specific risks of mobile apps, which integrated the actors involved, types of data collected, consent model and ethical concerns. An analysis of the *CoronaMadrid* symptom checking app was included. A quality assessment of Covid-19 smartphone applications using the Mobile Application Rating Scale (MARS) is described by the authors of [5]. This included several symptom assessment apps with a country context in Asia, Northern America and Europe. Our study is distinct from those reviewed as we aimed to evaluate the functional, technical and privacy features of Covid-19 symptom checker smartphone apps that were available for UK and EU countries. This resulted in the assessment of nine apps that were available for both the Android and iOS platforms. The remainder of the paper is structured as follows. Section 2 describes the methodology for the review and Sect. 3 provides the results. Section 4 discusses the results prior to discussing the conclusions drawn from the research.

2 Methods

This study involved a review of nine Covid-19 symptom assessment apps that were available in the Google Play Store and the Apple App Store. The inclusion criteria specified that the apps had to be provided by a government agency within the UK or EU, and had to be available for both platforms at no cost. Moreover, to support testing, the app had to be available in the English language. The search was conducted for apps released prior to February 8th, 2021.

There was a two-stage search strategy for identifying suitable apps. Firstly, both online app stores were searched using combinations of the keywords "Covid-19", "Coronavirus", "Symptom Checker" and "Self-Assessment". This identified three UK based apps that incorporated a Covid-19 symptom checking process. In the second stage we completed a web search using the Google search engine and combined the same search terms and the name of each EU country. Subsequently we found the official websites of several EU based apps and used these to link to the apps in the online stores. Depending on the platform requirements the Android apps were tested either on a Samsung Galaxy A40 smartphone with an Android 10 operating system, or an Acer Iconia B3-A40 tablet with Android 7. The iOS apps were tested using an iPhone 12 Pro smartphone running iOS 14. Each app was critiqued with relation to the type of data collected and the symptom assessment process. We also completed an evaluation of any privacy and support materials. This included content that appeared within the app, or on an official website, GitHub repository, or online app store.

3   Results

Nine smartphone apps were installed for evaluation. Table 1 provides an overview of the technical characteristics of each app. As indicated, four of the Android apps required version 6.0 while the others could execute on a device with an earlier version of the operating system. For the iOS apps the minimum platform requirement was 9.0. At the time of review the *NHS COVID-19* app had been installed more often than any of the other apps.

Table 1. Technical profile of apps

App name	Primary usage location	Play store installs	Compatibility android	Compatibility iOS
Asistencia COVID-19 [6]	Spain	100,000+	6.0 and up	11.0 or later
COVIDCare NI [7]	Northern Ireland	100,000+	4.2 and up	9.0 or later
COVID Tracker Ireland [8]	Ireland	500,000+	6.0 and up	11.0 or later
Karantinas [9]	Vilnius, Lithuania	10,000+	5.0 and up	9.0 or later
NHS COVID-19 [10]	England & Wales	5,000,000+	6.0 and up	13.5 or later
NHS 24: Covid-19 and flu information [11]	Scotland	10,000+	4.2 and up	12.0 or later
Stopp Corona [12]	Austria	100,000+	6.0 and up	13.5 or later
STOP COVID19 CAT [13]	Catalunya, Spain	500,000+	5.0 and up	11.0 or later
STOP COVID – ProteGO Safe [14]	Poland	1,000,000+	5.0 and up	12.1 or later

During the study we were able to fully evaluate six of the apps. For two of the apps we were unable to proceed to the symptom checking operation due to a lack of required identification credentials. For *Asistencia COVID-19* a Spanish phone number was needed, and for *STOP COVID19 CAT* the user was required to enter either a Personal Identification Code, National Identification Document, Foreigners' Identity Number or passport number. However, as far as possible the available functionality was tested. At the time of testing the *Karantinas* app had been suspended by the Lithuanian Data Protection Inspectorate [15].

Table 2. Symptom checking characteristics of apps

App name	No. of available languages	No. of personal data	No. of health questions	Symptom checking functionality
Asistencia COVID-19	4	_a	_a	_a
COVID Care NI	1	4	>4	Internet Required
COVID Tracker Ireland	8	4	4	Works Offline
Karantinas	2	_a	_a	_a
NHS COVID-19	12	1	4	Internet Required
NHS 24: Covid-19 and flu information	1	0	4	Internet Required
Stopp Corona	2	0	3	Works Offline
Stop COVID19 CAT	5	_a	_a	_a
STOP COVID - ProteGO Safe	4	2	>4	Works Offline

[a]Due to access issues, we were unable to scrutinize these items for this app.

Most of the apps were multifunctional and in additional to symptom logging and assessment also provided Covid-19 public health information [7, 8, 10, 11], self-isolation timers [7, 10] and contact tracing capabilities [8, 10, 12, 14]. The *NHS24* app also provided information related to Flu symptoms and vaccination. Table 2 provides information related to the symptom checking process. As noted, seven of the apps were available with more than one language. There was variation in the quantity of personal data needed for the symptom checking process, and the most frequently required data item was age or age range [7, 8, 14]. Two of the apps [11, 12] did not request any personal information, and all personal data entry was optional for *COVID Tracker Ireland*. Two of the apps [7, 10] prohibited the user from continuing to the symptom checking operation until they entered a valid UK postcode. The health questions related to symptoms of Covid-19, co-morbidities such as Asthma or Diabetes [7, 14], and health risks such as living with a person that has Covid-19 symptoms [7] or having previously received a shielding letter [11]. The most common symptoms checked were fever, onset of cough, loss of taste or smell and breathing difficulties. For three of the apps the symptom assessment could operate while the app was offline.

Table 3 provides information related to the privacy and transparency features of each app. As indicated, the majority of apps had an opt-in consent model, however, we could not find a consent option within the *NHS24* app. Opt-in consent was available for *Asistencia COVID-19*, however, we were unable to test this. Moreover, we were unable to ascertain whether in-app consent was provided for *Karantinas*.

Privacy information was available for all of the apps. For three of the apps [8, 12, 14] the privacy policy was available as a component of the app and could also be viewed if the app was offline. For most of the apps the privacy information comprised the purpose of data collection, categories of data collected and how these were stored, processed, and shared with third parties. The data controller and data protection officer were also listed. [10] had an easy read privacy policy and a summary for younger users available online, and easy read privacy information and terms of use were also provided for [7].

In some cases the online privacy information was bilingual as, for example, the privacy notice for [10] was published in English and Welsh, and for [14] the privacy policy, and terms and conditions, were available in English and Polish. Other available privacy related documentation included a Data Protection Impact Assessment (DPIA) which was available for [8, 10, 12, 14]. For eight of the apps additional material was available on an official website. However, content provision varied between the apps and could include background information, download instructions, technical help and FAQs.

Table 3. Privacy and transparency features of apps.

App name	Model of consent	Privacy information	Terms of use	Source code available
Asistencia COVID-19	Opt-in[a]	Online	Online	No
COVIDCare NI	Opt-in	In-app[b], Online	In-app[b], Online	No
COVID Tracker Ireland	Opt-in	In-app[c], Online	In-app[c], Online	Yes
Karantinas	_[d]	Online	_[d]	No
NHS COVID-19	Opt-in	In-app[b], Online	In-app[b], Online	Yes
NHS 24: Covid-19 and flu information	None	Online	In-app[b]	No
Stopp Corona	Opt-in	In-app[c], Online	In-app[c]	Yes
STOP COVID19 CAT	Opt-in	In-app[b], Online	In-app[b]	No
STOP COVID - ProteGO Safe	Opt-in	In-app[c], Online	In-app[c], Online	Yes

[a]We were unable to determine whether the consent process was functional.
[b]In-app content requires Internet connection.
[c]In-app content does not require Internet connection.
[d]We were unable to determine whether this content was present in the app.

As a further measure of transparency, a GitHub repository had been provided for four of the apps [8, 10, 12, 14]. These provided source code for the Android and iOS clients and the backend, and associated build instructions for the projects. Technical documentation and specifications included descriptions of the system architecture, data models, data flows and functionalities.

4 Discussion

During this study we evaluated the technical, functional and privacy features of nine government endorsed Covid-19 symptom checker apps. Installation totals varied between the Android apps, however for several symptom checkers installs had reached over half a million. This suggests that there was interest in using these tools amongst smartphone users. Comparable information was not available for the iOS apps. Market share statistics indicate that the nine Android apps would be compatible with over 80% of Android devices [16]. Moreover, as 80% of iPhone devices use iOS14 [17] this suggests that these iOS apps would be accessible to many iPhone users.

Most of the apps required that personal data be entered to assist the symptom checking algorithm. The most common attribute was age, however, this was to be expected as age is a significant risk factor for severe illness with Covid-19 [18]. For two of the apps the user had to enter a postcode to proceed to the symptom assessment. Collecting this information is useful for symptom surveillance and disease incident prediction, however some users may be uncomfortable entering information that, if combined with other information, could be personally identifiable. There is a risk that requesting multiple personal data may dissuade some citizens from using the app. There was variation in relation to the volume and granularity of the health questions and several apps contained only four questions. However, all the apps contained queries focused on the main symptomatic indicators of a Covid-19 infection including cough, fever and loss of smell or taste [19]. Our investigation also found that only three of the apps could provide advice when offline. This may limit the usefulness of the app for those without access to a reliable or secure Internet connection.

The General Data Protection Regulation (GDPR) [20] and the UK implementation, the Data Protection Act 2018 [21], both indicate that data processing procedures must be transparent to the data subject. This includes informing the subject of the purpose of the data processing before data is collected. It is also helpful for users to have clarity surrounding the data collection and sharing procedures, including any third parties involved, in order to determine whether they are willing to let their data be shared. Disclosing accurate privacy information can assist users with making an informed decision about whether to use a digital health tool. Analysis of the privacy documentation suggested that for most of the apps comprehensive information was provided which listed the purpose of data collection, and processing, storage, and data sharing procedures. Contact information was also provided which enhanced the accountability of the app providers. For several of the apps this information was available in an easy read format to enhance readability and accessibility to all citizens, and also some documents were available in two languages. Transparency was also enhanced by the availability of a DPIA for some of the apps. For the six apps assessed only one did not appear to have an in-app consent option, however this app did not collect any personal data from the user. For many of the apps there was additional background information and technical support available online. Four of the apps had a GitHub repository which enabled members of the public to view, download and test the code. For some users this open source licensing may also increase trust in these digital solutions.

5   Conclusion

Covid-19 self-assessment mobile apps can enable the delivery of effective healthcare support at the user's point of need. Furthermore, for healthcare providers these solutions can be a valuable indicator of disease incident and growth. However, several factors may influence the adoption of these technologies including the purpose and usefulness of the tool, as well as consideration of privacy and trust. We aimed to investigate these characteristics for symptom checker apps that were available for citizens in the UK and EU countries. The main limitation of our study related to the quantity of apps reviewed. Play Store content is limited by country therefore we were unable to install all the available apps such as the *CoronaMadrid* app. Future research could involve expanding the search for Covid-19 symptom assessment apps outside the UK and EU, and also exploring the usability of symptom checker apps for citizens within different age groups, considering user preferences and user experience.

We were able to fully test six self-assessment apps and found that they provided useful healthcare advice for the user. Moreover, we found that privacy information had been supplied for all nine apps, and in many cases transparency was supported by the provision of online documentation and source code repositories. Our investigation suggests that symptom checking mobile apps are becoming widely available for use and therefore offer useful support for managing public health concerns, and healthcare delivery throughout the Covid-19 pandemic.

Acknowledgments. This work was supported by the SHAPES project. SHAPES - Smart and Healthy Ageing through People Engaging in Supportive Systems - is funded by the Horizon 2020 Framework Programme of the European Union for Research Innovation. Grant agreement number: 857159-SHAPES-H2020-SC1-FA-DTS-2018–2020.

References

1. European Commission: How tracing and warning apps can help during the pandemic. https://ec.europa.eu/info/live-work-travel-eu/coronavirus-response/travel-during-coronavirus-pandemic/how-tracing-and-warning-apps-can-help-during-pandemic_en (2020). Accessed 20 Mar 2021
2. Crown Copyright: NHS COVID-19 app has been downloaded over 10 million times. https://www.gov.uk/government/news/nhs-covid-19-app-has-been-downloaded-over-10-million-times (2020). Accessed 21 Mar 2021
3. Ming, L.C., et al.: Mobile health apps on COVID-19 launched in the early days of the pandemic: content analysis and review. JMIR Mhealth Uhealth 8(9), e19796 (2020)
4. Gasser, U., Ienca, M., Scheibner, J., Sleigh, J., Vayena, E.: Digital tools against COVID-19: taxonomy, ethical challenges, and navigation aid. Lancet Digit. Health 2(8), e425–e434 (2020)
5. Davalbhakta, S., et al.: A systematic review of smartphone applications available for corona virus disease 2019 (COVID19) and the assessment of their quality using the mobile application rating scale (MARS). J. Med. Syst. 44(9), 1–15 (2020). https://doi.org/10.1007/s10916-020-01633-3
6. Government of Spain: Take your self-assessment of COVID-19. https://asistencia.covid19.gob.es/(2020). Accessed 20 Mar 2021
7. COVID-19 NI: COVIDCare NI Mobile App. https://covid-19.hscni.net/ (2021). Accessed 20 Mar 2021
8. Health Service Executive: COVID Tracker app. https://covidtracker.gov.ie/ (2020). Accessed 20 Mar 2021
9. Useful and meaningful self-isolation with a mobile app Quarantine. https://lietuva.lt/en/naujienos/useful-and-meaningful-self-isolation-with-a-mobile-app-quarantine/ (2021). Accessed 20 Mar 2021
10. Crown Copyright: NHS COVID-19 app support. https://www.covid19.nhs.uk (2021). Accessed 20 Mar 2021
11. NHS 24: NHS 24 Coronavirus (COVID-19) and flu information app. https://www.nhsinform.scot/care-support-and-rights/tools-and-apps/nhs-24-coronavirus-covid-19-and-flu-information-app (2021). Accessed 20 Mar 2021

12. Austrian Red Cross: Stopp Corona App. Now. Always. The app in the fight against the Coronavirus. https://www.stopp-corona.at/ (2020). Accessed 20 Mar 2021

13. Fundació Tic Salut Social: STOP COVID19 CAT. https://stopcovid19.cat/en/stop-covid19-cat/ (2021). Accessed 20 Mar 2021

14. Ministry of Digitization: STOP COVID. https://www.gov.pl/web/protegosafe (2021). Accessed 20 Mar 2021

15. Council of Europe: Digital solutions to combat Covid-19. https://rm.coe.int/prems-120820-gbr-2051-digital-solutions-to-fight-covid-19-text-a4-web-/16809fe49c (2020). Accessed 20 Mar 2021

16. Rahman, M.: Android Version Distribution statistics will now only be available in Android Studio. https://www.xda-developers.com/android-version-distribution-statistics-android-stu dio/ (2020). Accessed 20 Mar 2021

17. Apple Inc: App Store. https://developer.apple.com/support/app-store/ (2021). Accessed 20 Mar 2021

18. Mahase, E.: Covid-19: Why are age and obesity risk factors for serious disease? BMJ **371**, m4130 (2020)

19. Crown Copyright: Symptoms of coronavirus. https://www.nhs.uk/conditions/coronavirus-covid-19/symptoms/ (2021). Accessed 22 Mar 2021

20. Proton Technologies AG: What is GDPR, the EU's new data protection law? https://gdpr.eu/what-is-gdpr/(2021). Accessed 20 Mar 2021

21. Crown Copyright: Data protection. https://www.gov.uk/data-protection (2021). Accessed 20 Mar 2021

Impact of the COVID-19 Pandemic on User Experience (UX) Research

Shibani Shah[1]([⊠]) and Abhishek Jain[2]([⊠])

[1] ServiceNow, Santa Clara, USA
shibani.shah@servicenow.com
[2] ServiceNow, Hyderabad, India
abhishek.jain@servicenow.com

Abstract. The COVID-19 pandemic has globally impacted the world with both near-term and long-term damage. At an individual level the impacts were financially, mentally, physically, etc. which resulted in drastic behavior shifts. The majority of working professionals were permitted by the government, local authorities & the employers continue working from home (remote work) to avoid mass gatherings & maintain social distancing. Considering the user research professionals, conducting in-person user research and other qualitative studies became challenging, which has also impacted the working methodology of a user researcher. The primary goals of the study were to understand the impact of the pandemic on user research activities and identifying the challenges faced in various research stages by a user researcher. In this study, 57 user researchers (work experience ranging from 0 to 10+ years) participated by responding an online survey.

Key themes emerged from the study such as 'increase in effort to co-ordinate', 'exploration & usage of digital tools', 'scope & time-lines', 'virtual cross team collaboration', and 'challenges with participant recruitment' [1]. The current context of a global pandemic presents challenges to the continuation of longitudinal studies [2]. Approximately 67% participants reported facing challenges in working remotely & conducting research. 'Running & Execution (57.89%)', 'Planning (55.26%)' and 'Preparation (47.37%) were identified as the most challenging stages of research.

1 Introduction

The outbreak of COVID-19 has caused disruption to almost every sector right across the globe. The way we live our lives has changed markedly but new opportunities are starting to emerge from this shift in consumer and work behavior. We are also seeing this in the field of user experience research. The primary goal of this study was to understand the impact of the pandemic on user research activities and identify the challenges faced in different research stages by a user experience researcher. UX (user experience) research is the systematic study of target users and their requirements, to add realistic contexts and insights to design processes. UX researchers adopt various methods to uncover problems and design opportunities. Doing so, they reveal valuable information which can be fed into the design process [3]. User research focuses on understanding

C. Stephanidis et al. (Eds.): HCII 2021, CCIS 1421, pp. 599–607, 2021.
https://doi.org/10.1007/978-3-030-78645-8_76

user behaviors, needs, and motivations through observation techniques, task analysis, and other feedback methodologies. Mike Kuniavsky further notes that it is "the process of understanding the impact of design on an audience" [4]. User experience (UX) design is the process to create products that provide meaningful and relevant experiences to users. This involves the design of the entire process of acquiring and integrating the product, including aspects of branding, design, usability and function. UX Research and UX Design work hand in hand to learn about the core user needs, problems to be solved and how to solve them. In fact, research is most impactful when it is conducted collaboratively with all stakeholders including design, product management and engineering. Collaboration was always somewhat of a challenge, but teams learned how to get around these challenges in a variety of ways like physically sitting closer together in the office, having in-person brainstorming sessions, accompanying researchers on in-field research trips, having usability labs set up with hardware, software or physical products to be evaluated such that teams can jointly observe and discuss participant feedback, having physical war rooms set up so everyone could immerse themselves in the research artifacts, and many other workarounds to bring the full team into the research journey. However, with most people working from home due to the pandemic, it has made collaboration even more difficult and some of these things entirely impossible to do. Google and its parent company, Alphabet, will allow its employees to continue working from home until at least June 2021 [5]. TCS planning to allow 75% of its employees to work from home by 2025 [6]. Facebook founder Mark Zuckerberg had said that as many as 50% of his company's staff could work from home with the next five to ten years [7].

There are several user experience research methods & tools which researchers employ to meet the research objectives. User research methods involve varied setup, planning & infrastructure. Certain methods involve subjects (participants) and researchers (facilitators) to be co-located in physical space (context of product use) [8] such as contextual inquiry, ethnographic studies, focus groups, usability lab-studies etc. Having said that, the pandemic has forced researchers to think of some alternative methods that can be conducted remotely via digital collaboration or research tools. While this has allowed researchers to continue to gain insights, it has caused challenges and difficulties such as reduction in quality and richness of qualitative data. During in-person research sessions facilitators are usually maintaining eye contact and paying attention to facial cues, emotional reactions, physical behavioral cues. However, during remote sessions, researchers mentioned they are not able to pay as much attention to participants' videos, if they even have it turned on, and tend to focus much more on the screen they're sharing. Therefore, they miss out on important nonverbal communication which makes the qualitative data less rich than if they were physically with the participant [9]. Other challenges we learned about during this exploration are, reduced participant engagement, limited ability to evaluate physical products, professionals harder to recruit for research, efficiency impacted due to higher no-show rates and data loss due to technical issues [10].

2   Method

A total of 57 subjects participated in this study (avg exp & exp wise distribution to be added) by responding to the unmoderated online survey. The criteria used for selecting subject were a) subjects should be involved in & executing user research (UX research) activities professionally or academically.

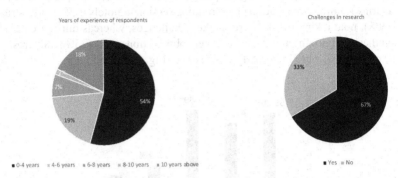

Fig. 1. Years of experience of respondents & challenges faced by respondents.

Primary goal of the online survey was to gather the participants responses related to user research planning & execution during working remotely due to COVID pandemic. Figure 1 shows the respondents years of experience wise counts, around 54% respondents were having up-to 4 years of experience, 19% with 4–6 years, 7% with 6–8 years, 2% with 8–10 years and 18% respondents with over 10% of experience in user research field. More than 66% respondents faced challenges in conducting user research remotely at 1 or more phases of overall research journey (Fig. 1). For detailed analysis overall user research journey was broke in to 5 phases, 'planning', 'preparation & setup', 'running & execution', 'data analysis & synthesis' and 'report & presentation' (Fig. 2).

Fig. 2. Phases of user research journey.

3   Results and Analysis

Most challenging stages of research were found as 'Running & Execution (57.89%)', 'Planning (55.26%)' and 'Preparation (47.37%). Researchers faced least challenges in 'Data analysis & synthesis' & 'Report or readout stage'. 'Running & execution' phase was the most challenging for researchers up to 4 years & 6–8 years of experience whereas 'planning' seems to be mainly challenging for researchers 6–8 years, and 10 years and above.

There was certain type of challenges reported by respondents considering a specific phase of research such as, stakeholder interaction has been identified as top challenge during 'planning'(71%) & 'Report & presentation' (66%), Ineffective communication

& discussions was identified as key challenges during 'planning'(47%) & 'preparation & setup'(44%) phase. User researchers faced challenges in participant recruitment (61%) & setting up research/testing on platforms (50%) during 'preparation & setup' phase. During running & execution phase running session remotely (63%), infrastructure setup (59%), note taking (45%) were the key challenges, whereas during 'data analysis & synthesis' digitizing the data (i.e. notes, observations etc.) (75%) and cross team collaboration (50%) were identified as key issues (Fig. 3, Table 1).

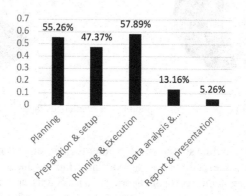

Fig. 3. Research journey phase wise challenges faced by respondents.

4 Findings

4.1 Extra Effort and Energy Overall

Majority of respondents mentioned that extra effort & energy is invested to overcome challenges in working remotely in terms of working in flexible hours, frequent internal team brainstorming, documentation etc. Choosing research methods was a challenging task reported by many respondents and they also had to explore alternate methods to replace some methods. Exploring best practices and usage of templates were helpful. Increase in design reviews and utilizing the secondary, historic research insights were reported by some of the respondents. To reduce the complexity, many researchers tried to reduce the scope of research and extend the project timelines. Many respondents faced issues in getting recording permission by participants while executing research remotely, so they have had to put additional effort in taking notes during sessions and inviting more note takers.

4.2 More Tedious Preparation

Due to limited control of infrastructure and working with less tech savvy participants, many respondents reported that they required an extra level of preparation of instructions to send it to participants in advance. Sometimes, running additional pre-session meeting with participants to check tools, internet bandwidth and other settings was also opted. Majority of respondents mentioned that extra effort was spent in multiple pilot sessions and checking the test setup.

Table 1. Research phase wise challenges faced by respondents

Challenges	Percept of participants faced
Phase 1 - Planning	
Stakeholder interaction was challenging	71.43
Ineffective communication & discussions	47.62
Cross team collaboration	42.86
Inefficient productivity	38.10
Getting customer/client/stakeholder buy-in for research activities	28.57
Reviewing research plan & getting feedback	23.81
Documentation, file management and sharing	19.05
Device & tech setup	4.76
Setup for voice based research	4.76
Phase 2 - Preparation & Setup	
Challenges in Participant recruitment	61.11
Setting up research/testing	50.00
Ineffective communication & discussions	44.44
Stakeholder interaction was challenging	33.33
Inefficient productivity	27.78
Getting customer/client/stakeholder/sales buy-in recruitment	27.78
Reviewing research plan & getting feedback	16.67
Choosing research methods was challenging	16.67
Cross team collaboration	11.11
Documentation, file management and sharing	5.56
Phase 3 - Running & execution	
Challenges in running session remotely	63.64
Challenges in technical infrastructure setup	59.09
Challenges in taking notes	45.45
Challenges in using research /usability testing tools	31.82
Challenges in executing few/some research methods	31.82
Challenges in convincing participants for recordings	22.73
Stakeholder interaction was challenging	18.18
Ineffective communication & discussions	18.18
Cross team collaboration	18.18

(continued)

Table 1. (*continued*)

Challenges	Percept of participants faced
Challenges in handling scripts	13.64
Inefficient productivity	4.55
Documentation, file management and sharing	4.55
Phase 4 - Data analysis & synthesis	
Challenges in digitizing the research data (i.e. notes, observations etc.)	75.00
Cross team collaboration	50.00
Inefficient productivity	25.00
Challenges storing/handling/managing participant data (recordings, responses, notes etc.)	25.00
Challenges in taking data backup from research tools	25.00
Challenges in using data analysis tools	25.00
Challenges in collaborative data analysis with team	25.00
Documentation, file management and sharing	25.00
Phase 5 - Report & presentation	
Limitations in being creative in presentation/insights walkthrough	100.00
Stakeholder interaction was challenging	66.67
Ineffective communication & discussions	33.33
Challenges in measuring impact of research	33.33
Challenges in convincing or persuading stakeholder/product team	33.33
Documentation, file management and sharing	33.33
Cross team collaboration	33.33

4.3 Productivity Loss

Productivity reported by respondents who faced issues working remotely during the pandemic is mean 3.55 (out of 5, standard deviation 0.84), where researchers who reported not facing issue reported slightly higher productivity as mean 3.73 (out of 5, standard deviation 0.86). This study was conducted several months into the pandemic so it's likely that respondents had already learned ways to increase their productivity while working remotely, like using remote collaboration tools, working during hours that normally would have gone into commuting to the office, or working longer hours in general. However, overall, respondents still felt slightly less productive being remote (Table 2)

Table 2. Productivity reported by respondents

Productivity	Challenges faced Yes	Challenges faced No
Mean	3.55/5	3.73/5
Standard deviation	0.84	0.86

4.4 Extensive Communication to Enable Collaboration

Exploration & piloting of new digital tools were also reported by majority of respondents during working remotely and running remote research. Many respondents mentioned that they had to put extra effort in having cross team collaboration and effective communication through various communication channels. Frequent reminders and follow-ups to maintain the success of communication. Many respondents claimed to use virtual or online white boarding platforms to analyze data and collaborate with others. Some respondents also utilized the recordings and other data to be creative in communicating insights (Fig. 4).

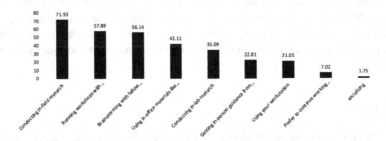

Fig. 4. Activities to be done when office resumes

4.5 Resuming Work from Office

Over 70% researchers reported 'Conducting in-field research' is what they most look forward to doing when they return to the office. 57% wanted to run workshops with stakeholders in person, 56% wanted to brainstorm with fellow researchers, 42% researchers wanted to use in-office materials like whiteboards/posters, etc. 35% wanted to conduct in-lab research. So, while there has been widespread adoption of remote collaborative technologies during the pandemic, there is still a strong desire for researchers to be able to conduct research in-person with participants in their own environments such as contextual inquiries or ethnographic studies. There is also a desire to be co-located with fellow research colleagues and stakeholders to brainstorm and have in-person workshops together. This would help with defining scope and timelines easier with stakeholders and with learning from other researchers on best methods to adopt for studies.

5   Conclusion

User experience researchers need to understand their stakeholder's needs, to frame appropriate research questions and goals. The tight collaboration throughout the research process are all important for research to maximize their impact with the project teams. Through this study we learned it is the collaboration with stakeholders during the planning, preparation and setup, and running and execution, where researchers face most difficulty in remotely working with their teams. The pandemic has forced researchers to find remote technology tools they may not have been using or using as frequently to facilitate these stakeholder conversations.

While user experience researchers have been able to adapt their research approaches and tools they use to overcome the challenges brought on by the pandemic, there is still a desire to conduct in-field research and it is the thing that researchers most look forward to being able to do when it is safe. Context, environment and non-verbal communication cues are so important for researchers to gain a thorough perspective and understanding of a user, their needs and pain points. There is also a lot of value in being physically located with the participant to help break the ice and have easy flowing conversations with them which result in deep insights about challenges they face, which they may not feel as comfortable revealing if the researcher hasn't been able to establish that rapport with them. So far, there doesn't seem to be a tool or method that can replace or provide the same value as in-field research. Perhaps, this is an area of further exploration and potential to build something new for the user experience research community all around the globe.

References

1. Ellie. H.: UX after Covid-19: What Can We Expect? UX Design Institute. www.uxdesigninst itute.com/blog/ux-after-covid-19-what-can-we-expect/. Accessed 22 June 2020
2. Tom, B., et al.: Are we measuring the same thing? Psychometric and research considerations when adopting new testing modes in the time of COVID-19. Alzheimer's Dementia **17**(2), 251–254 (2020). https://doi.org/10.1002/alz.12197
3. What Is UX Research? The Interaction Design Foundation. www.interaction-design.org/lit erature/topics/ux-research.
4. Elizabeth, G., et al.: Observing the User Experience a Practitioner's Guide to User Research. Elsevier, Amsterdam (2019)
5. Jack. K.: Google employees will work from home through next summer. Forbes Magazine. www.forbes.com/sites/jackkelly/2020/07/27/google-employees-will-work-from-home-through-next-summer/?sh=54df21c83268. Accessed 27 July 2020
6. Redefine Work Life: Automate Work from Home Process Using HRMS System. IT Consulting Services & Business Solutions. www.tcs.com/blogs/employees-remote-work-from-home-hrms-application.
7. COVID-19 Crisis: These companies allow employees to work from home 'Forever.' Business Today. www.businesstoday.in/current/corporate/covid-19-crisis-these-companies-allow-emp loyees-to-work-from-home-forever/story/418205.html. Accessed 8 Oct 2020
8. World Leaders in Research-Based User Experience: When to Use Which User-Experience Research Methods. Nielsen Norman Group. www.nngroup.com/articles/which-ux-research-methods/.

9. Remote UX Research: Advantages and Disadvantages, Part 2. UXmatters. www.uxmatters. com/mt/archives/2020/10/remote-ux-research-advantages-and-disadvantages-part-2.php. Accessed 19 Oct 2020
10. Scott, S., et al.: Pros and cons of remote moderated testing: considerations for ongoing research during COVID-19. Bold Insight. Accessed 1 Oct 2020

Sentiment Analysis on Substance Use Disorder (SUD) Tweets Before and During COVID-19 Pandemic

Avineet Kumar Singh[1] and Dezhi Wu[2(✉)] [iD]

[1] Department of Computer Science and Engineering, University of South Carolina, Columbia, SC 29208, USA
AS89@email.sc.edu
[2] Department of Integrated Information Technology, University of South Carolina, Columbia, SC 29208, USA
dezhiwu@cec.sc.edu

Abstract. This research aims to explore sentiment patterns on substance use disorder (SUD) before and during the COVID-19 pandemic, which has significantly challenged global healthcare systems and resulted in 2.78 million deaths based on CDC news as of March 2021. Because of social isolation, economic hardships, and fear caused by the lockdown orders, substance use has been strikingly increased including the youth. This is alarming because SUD causes long-lasting and permanent damages to human body and brains as significant health consequences. In this project, we extracted ten-month Tweet samples from May 2019 to December 2020 on Twitter related to SUD mentioning substance and consequences before and during the COVID-19, and then identified the sentiment patterns of the tweets mentioning the SUD. We found that the sentiment trends remained negative except in March and April of 2020, when the social restrictions were imposed, much more positive sentiment appeared in SUD-related tweets.

Keywords: Substance use disorder · SUD · Mental health · COVID-19 · Social media · Twitter · Tweets · Sentiment analysis · Social media · Social media analytics · Pandemic · Public health

1 Introduction

Substance use disorders (SUDs) are among the leading causes of mental health problems. Most addictive substances cause depression, anxiety, suicidal ideation, and bipolar disorder. Use of these substances at a young age could cause SUD later in life [1]. 15.2% of youth in US, who start regular drinking at the age 14, tend to develop alcohol abuse and dependence problems when they reach their adulthood as per results from the 2012 National Survey on Drug Use and Health [2]. And when these individuals experience

---

The original version of this chapter was revised: Additional acknowledgment and grant number were added in respective section. The correction to this chapter is available at
https://doi.org/10.1007/978-3-030-78645-8_82

periods of economic or psychological stress, they often consume more alcohol or other substances, resulting in increased symptoms of substance abuse [3, 4]. Being alone also increases the risk of overdosing, which may lead to death if no one is there to help [5].

Isolated environments were triggered during COVID-19 pandemic when stay-at-home orders were enforced. Many people lost their jobs and thus causing a tremendous economic and mental stress among people. Unemployment rate of youth (age 16–24) in the United States rose to 27.4% in April 2020 and was 12.5% in December 2020 [6]. Social isolation [7] is the risk factor in causing SUDs and younger generations are less capable of managing it compared to adults, when they had to face new challenging problems, such as closing of universities, attending classes from home, and losing part-time jobs. Kaiser Family Foundation (KFF) [8] has reported that throughout the pandemic, 56% of young adults have reported symptoms of anxiety or depressive disorder. Use of substances like alcohol, cannabis, opioids, nicotine, and other drugs reduces the lung function and develops comorbid health conditions, which make the body more vulnerable to COVID-19 infections which may lead to death.

Previous studies [9–11] have explored the SUD issues using traditional survey methods which are slow, time-consuming and expensive, thus timely tracking and understanding trends of substance abuse is challenging during the pandemic, because of unavailability of direct data sources, which further delay evaluating the effectiveness of the current public health policies and forming new public health policies in the context of social distancing and lockdown. Given approximately 3.96 billion people are on social media platforms worldwide, and 80% of the U.S. population had a social networking account [12], using social media data as an additional instrument has become a new way of extracting public opinions, trends, and monitoring the risk of human interactions in today's health and social media research [13, 14].

We aim to answer two research questions using Twitter data mentioning SUD related keywords: (1) What is the trend of Twitter usage in pre-COVID and during COVID-19 pandemic? (2) How does the sentiment change in SUD-related tweets during the pandemic?

2   Methods

2.1   Data Collection

In this study, we extracted tweets from twitter using specific keywords related to SUD, and then analyzed those tweets by checking how user account and tweet frequency changed monthly, and overall sentiment trends in pre- and during the COVID-19 pandemic. Word tokenization method was used to convert tweets into words and then the substance related words and hashtag counts were analyzed. We extracted historic tweets using 'Twint' python library by pairing a set of keywords on Twitter. A set of drug-related words were combined with health outcomes and emotion-related words, which resulted in 1860 pairs of keywords for data extraction. This dataset was collected from May 2019 to December 2020 resulting in a large corpus of 1.3 million tweets for analysis.

2.2 Data Analysis

At the initial stage of data cleaning, we removed tweets mentioning about alcohol usage as a sanitizer. The cleaned tweets were then grouped into two phases: (1) 'Before COVID' phase was from May 2019 to February 2020, and (2) from March 2020 to December 2020 was 'under COVID' phase. Thus, we obtained an equal time of 10 months before and during COVID tweets to analyze and compare their patterns. After data cleaning, we used TextBlob python library for sentiment analysis [15]. TextBlob is a Python library for processing textual data. It provides access to common text-processing operations through an API. The sentiment property returns a named tuple of the form Sentiment (polarity, subjectivity). The polarity score is a float within the range $[-1.0, 1.0]$, where 0.0 is considered as neutral sentiment and values below and above 0.0 are considered negative and positive sentiment, respectively. The subjectivity is a range of floats from 0.0 to 1.0, where 0.0 represents very objective and 1.0 means very subjective. After conducting sentiment analysis, we found that most of the tweets having polarity within the range of $(-0.2, 0.2)$ were inclined towards neutral sentiment. As such, we defined the range for negative sentiment to be $[-1.0, -0.2]$ and $[0.2, 1.0]$ for positive sentiment. This helped us further identify overall sentiment towards SUD associated with our targeted population. We also used a word tokenization method [16] to calculate the frequency of words in tweets and then studied its monthly trend.

3 Results

Figure 1 shows the frequency of the monthly SUD-related tweets from May 2019 to December 2020. It also shows the counts of users who tweeted them. We found that the counts of the tweets almost doubled in March 2020 and reached its peak in April 2020. This increasing trend remained constant during COVID-19 period. Similar increase was also observed in terms of the number of users talking about SUD.

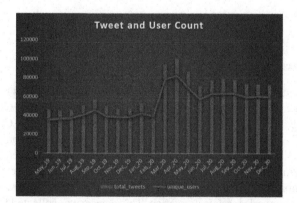

Fig. 1. Total tweets and unique users from May 2019 to December 2020

3.1 Sentiment Analysis

Sentiment of tweets towards drug usage remained negative before and during COVID-19 pandemic for maximum period (Fig. 2), but the positive sentiment tweets exceeded the negative sentiment tweets in the months of March and April 2020. Similar pattern was identified in September 2019, when another public health outbreak related to vaping occurred. As an example, *"March 2020: Okay, three essentials getting me through this quarantine - Netflix - Alcohol - Weed And that's on PERIODT. Okay and maybe school and working out and dancing too bahaha. YKTV"* indicates a positive sentiment in tweets, and *"March 2020: @Issuf_M @akreana_ Bathong 😣 😣how can parents both get into a car under the influence of alcohol knowing they have a child with them? So disappointed"* is categorized as a negative sentiment.

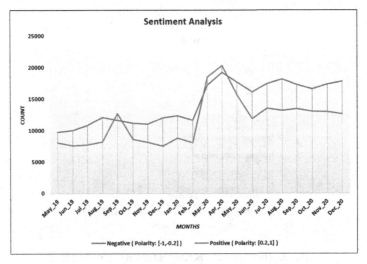

Fig. 2. Positive and negative sentiment towards SUD related tweets

3.2 Keywords and Hashtag Analysis

Table 1 shows different drugs which frequency in tweets increased significantly during COVID-19 as compared to the pre-COVID. Mentioning of 'Alcohol' and 'Tobacco' increased three times in the month of April 2020 as compared to February 2020. Interestingly, usage of 'Fentanyl' and 'Valium' in tweets increased by around 175% in August 2020.

Hashtags like 'cannabiscommunity' increased by four times as seen in Fig. 3. 'cannabis,' 'marijuana,' 'weed,' and 'cannabiscommunity' were used the maximum number of times as hashtags in SUD-related tweets. 'Dementia' had also shown a striking rise as compared to before COVID-19 period.

Table 1. Percentage increase in substance usage in tweets during COVID-19 as compared to pre-COVID period.

Substances	Percentage increase
Alcohol	94.96
Weed	88.7
Cocaine	44.41
meth	53.17
LSD	60.3
Valium	63.1
Adderall	114.9

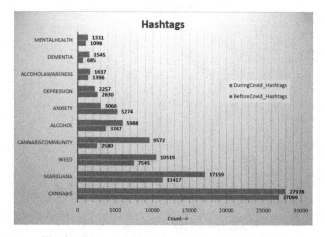

Fig. 3. Hashtag count before and during COVID-19

4 Conclusion

In this preliminary study, we successfully identified different trends in SUD-related tweets during COVID-19 period and demonstrated the SUD sentiment changes as compared to pre-COVID period. These trends indicate the increase on the posted tweets and user counts, different hashtags, and various substance-related words. In addition, we filtered tweets mentioning youth to understand the above trends, and found the patterns mentioning the youth indicate similar patterns to the overall trends. Tweet counts and unique users tweeting about SUD increased by 65% during COVID-19. Negative sentiment towards these tweets were always high as compared to positive sentiment, however, this trend changed during September 2019, March, and April 2020. We found this drastic change was triggered during the times when the deaths related to vaping (i.e., September 2019) were at its peak and the COVID-19 pandemic (i.e., March-April 2020) related restrictions were brought into effect. People seemed to be more inclined towards using these drugs during these unpredictable times. The increase in these drug-related tweets signifies the importance of monitoring such shifts in sentiment of the general population or youth for public health surveillance purposes to inform public health policies. The social isolation restrictions imposed, and the job losses had a great impact not only economically but also emotionally to the public. Future studies can be expanded on identifying different groups of users based on their tweet similarities using unsupervised machine learning methods. This will help us split the vulnerable population from the other user groups which will further facilitate creating appropriate intervention programs to support people who are in need of clinical treatments.

Acknowledgements. The authors would like to acknowledge the funding support provided by the University of South Carolina, Columbia, SC, USA [Grant No: 80002838], and partial support from the UofSC Big Data Health Science Center, a UofSC excellence initiative program [Grant No: BDHSC-2021-14]. We also would like to thank Dr. Phyllis Raynor for her clinical advice on keyword selections. The content is solely the responsibility of the authors and does not necessarily represent the official views of the funding agencies.

References

1. Jordan, C.J., Andersen, S.L.: Sensitive periods of substance abuse: early risk for the transition to dependence. Dev. Cogn. Neurosci. **25**, 29–44 (2017)
2. Substance Abuse and Mental Health Services Administration [SAMHSA] Report (2012). Results from the 2012 National Survey on Drug Use And Health: Summary of National Findings (NSDUH Series H-46, HHS Publication No. (SMA) 13–4795). Rockville, MD: Substance Abuse and Mental Health Services Administration. https://www.samhsa.gov/data/sites/default/files/NSDUHresults2012/NSDUHresults2012.pdf.
3. Wu, P., et al.: Alcohol abuse/dependence symptoms among hospital employees exposed to a SARS outbreak. Alcohol. Alcohol. **43**(6), 706–712 (2008)
4. Boscarino, J.A., Kirchner, H.L., Hoffman, S.N., Sarorius, J., Adams, R.E.: PTSD and alcohol use after the World Trade Center attacks: a longitudinal study. J. Trauma. Stress **24**, 515–525 (2011)
5. Volkow, N.D.: Collision of the COVID-19 and addiction epidemics. Ann. Intern. Med. (2020). https://doi.org/10.7326/M20-1212
6. https://www.statista.com/statistics/217448/seasonally-adjusted-monthly-youth-unemployment-rate-in-the-us/. Accessed 30 Mar 2021
7. https://www.apa.org/monitor/2021/03/substance-use-pandemic#:~:text=According%20to%20the%20Centers%20for,the%20onset%20of%20the%20pandemic. Accessed 28 Mar 2021
8. https://www.kff.org/coronavirus-covid-19/issue-brief/the-implications-of-covid-19-for-mental-health-and-substance-use/. Accessed 28 Mar 2021
9. Grossman, E.R., Benjamin-Neelon, S.E., Sonnenschein, S.: Alcohol consumption during the COVID-19 pandemic: a cross-sectional survey of US adults. Int. J. Environ. Res. Public Health **17**(24), 1–10 (2020)
10. Pollard, M.S., Tucker, J.S., Green, H.D.: Changes in adult alcohol use and consequences during the COVID-19 pandemic in the US. JAMA Netw. Open **3**(9), 1–4 (2020)
11. Coughlan, M., Cronin, P., Ryan, F.: Survey research: process and limitations. Int. J. Ther. Rehabil. **16**(1), 9–15 (2013)
12. https://www.statista.com/statistics/273476/percentage-of-us-population-with-a-social-network-profile/. Accessed 30 Mar 2021

13. Valdez, D., Thij, M.T., Bathina, K., Rutter, L.A., Bollen, J.: Social media insights into US mental health during the COVID-19 pandemic: longitudinal analysis of Twitter data. J. Med. Internet Res. **22**(12), 1–11 (2020)
14. Li, L., Ma, Z., Lee, H., Lee, S.: Can social media data be used to evaluate the risk of human interactions during the COVID-19 pandemic? Int. J. Dis. Risk Reduc. **56**(102142), 1–14 (2021)
15. Madhu, S.: An approach to analyze suicidal tendency in blogs and tweets using sentiment analysis. Int. J. Sci. Res. Comput. Sci. Eng. **6**(4), 34–36 (2018)
16. Ramachandran, D., Parvathi, R.: Analysis of Twitter specific preprocessing technique for Tweets. Procedia Comput. Sci. **165**, 245–251 (2019)

Analyzing COVID-19 Vaccine Tweets for Tonal Shift

Han Wei Tan[1], Chei Sian Lee[2(✉)], Dion Hoe-Lian Goh[2], Han Zheng[2], and Yin Leng Theng[2]

[1] CoHASS, Nanyang Technological University, Singapore, Singapore
HTAN092@e.ntu.edu.sg
[2] WKWSCI, Nanyang Technological University, Singapore, Singapore
{LeeCS,ASHLGoh,TYLTheng}@ntu.edu.sg, HAN019@e.ntu.edu.sg

Abstract. On November 09, 2020, Pfizer and BioNtech announced vaccine effi-cacy results, possibly providing hope during the COVID-19 pandemic. Corre-spondingly, vaccine-related information was shared on social media platforms, including Twitter. The present research aims to investigate tonal shift resulting from this important pandemic-related event using automatic text analysis of Twit-ter Tweets. We examined 209,939 tweets before, and 203,490 tweets after the vaccine announcement. Pennebaker's linguistic inquiry word count (LIWC) was used to detect tonal shifts via analytic thinking (which reflects logical think-ing), clout (reflects expertise), authentic (reflects disclosure), and emotional tone (reflects emotional valence). Results indicated a decrease in authentic score imply-ing a more guarded form of disclosure, while an increase in clout score suggests more sharing from expert users. The change was negligible for analytical thinking and emotional tone, suggesting users' mentality towards the pandemic was not affected. Overall, results suggest a minimal shift in tone on Twitter, even in the face of the good news about the vaccine announcement.

Keywords: COVID-19 · Vaccine · Twitter · Tonal analysis · LIWC2015

1 Introduction

As of March 08, 2021, the world has recorded over 116 million confirmed infection cases and 2 million death cases since the declaration of COVID-19 as a pandemic [1]. To combat the pandemic, the Director-General of the World Health Organization (WHO), Dr. Tedros Adhanom Ghebreyesus, called for a global coordinated effort and appealed to world governments in granting access to COVID-19 tests, treatments, and vaccines when available [2].

On November 09, 2020, Pfizer and BioNTech announced the first vaccine efficacy results, providing hope during the COVID-19 pandemic [3]. Correspondingly, vaccine-related information was shared on social media platforms, including Twitter. In the past, significant events were associated with changes in emotional reactions where positive events were discovered to produce negative sentiments [4]. This vaccine announcement

© Springer Nature Switzerland AG 2021
C. Stephanidis et al. (Eds.): HCII 2021, CCIS 1421, pp. 615–623, 2021.
https://doi.org/10.1007/978-3-030-78645-8_78

is an important event that is likely a positive turning point in the pandemic. This presents an opportunity to investigate the change in the tone of users' tweets on COVID-19. Thus, analyzing discussions on Twitter may provide some helpful insights into public reactions to the vaccine announcement.

The present research aims to investigate tonal shift resulting from an important event during a pandemic using automatic text analysis on Twitter Tweets. Here, tonal shift refers to the change in language style based on word choices [5]. There are three reasons for studying Twitter. First, microblogging platforms, like Twitter, are recognized as popular outlets for people to express their opinion [6]. Second, Twitter is known for sharing of health-related information and advice between users [7]. Third, to combat misinformation, Twitter has responded by updating its policies, in May 2021, to implement the use of labels in allowing users to fact-check tweets' content on the platform [8].

2 Related Work

The use of tweets as data sources were common in the analysis of sentiment and emotions of significant events, like disasters and emergencies, allowing researchers to understand public perception and provide recommendations to local authorities for improvement of measures [9]. The evaluation of tweets also provided potential insights on the communication pattern of users and may effectively reduce miscommunication, allowing Twitter to serve as a crisis communication channel between government officials and citizens when required [10]. Twitter was also evident to offer valuable information towards tracking sentiment on breaking news through assessing tweet frequency and time frame [11].

By analyzing language style and word choice, a better understanding of communication engagement in the online community may be obtained [12]. The language style adopted by users was also identified as a possible peripheral cue towards information sharing behavior [13]. This meant that the choice of words could also provide an overview of users' mentality and emotional state based on the information they consumed and shared on Twitter.

3 Methodology

3.1 Data Gathering, Pre-processing, and Analysis

The data analyzed was acquired from a multilingual actively collected Twitter dataset of COVID-19 tweets since January 28, 2020. Tweets were extracted, through Twitter's Search API using a list of keywords concerning the COVID-19 pandemic (e.g., "Covid-19", "Coronavirus", "Covid", etc.) [14]. As of March 08, 2021, there were over a billion Tweet IDs in the dataset, which is available on GitHub.

We selected 16 days of tweets, between November 01, 2020, to November 16, 2020 to examine. For each day, the number of Tweet IDs available ranged from 3,300,269 to 4,203,587. With the aid of R 4.0.3 and RStudio 1.3.1073, a random sample of 20% of Tweet IDs was picked. We then used the software, Hydrator, to hydrate the Tweet IDs to retrieve the full tweet content, providing between 288,418 to 380, 873 successfully hydrated tweets for each day [15].

Next, the dataset was split into two periods, "Before" (November 01, 2020, to November 08, 2020) representing the period prior to the vaccine announcement, and "After" (November 09, 2020, to November 16, 2020) representing the period after the announcement. We then selected a random sample of 500,000 tweets and removed non-English and duplicated tweets. The final dataset comprised 202,392 tweets for the "Before" and 194,806 for the "After" periods.

The dataset was further pre-processed to remove emojis, the "RT" text, blanks, spaces, links, and punctuation, which were unnecessary in the analysis of the textual content., Finally, word clouds of the tweets representing the two periods were created using the R-package wordcloud2.

3.2 LIWC Tonal Analysis

Pennebaker's Linguistic Inquiry Word Count (LIWC) is commonly used in social psychology and social computing analysis for uncovering psychological sentiment in text documents. For instance, the software is used in the classification of positive and negative sentiment to aid the coding of emotionality for quantitative sentiment analyses. In the past, by complementing the LIWC output with the help of human coders in analyzing tweets, intervention designs were proposed to tackle the issue of cyberbullying [16]. Moreover, sentiments detected by LIWC were also found to be consistent and linked towards identifying information-sharing behaviors [17]. Past research has also demonstrated LIWC's capability to identify changes in behaviors and moods of users across the day through a comparison of hourly tweets [18]. By using LIWC on Twitter, the outputs provide insights into users' reactions to events through analyzing textual patterns [19].

Hence in this study, we analyzed our Twitter dataset using LIWC to detect tonal shifts through four summary variables: analytical thinking, clout, authenticity, and emotional tone [20, 21]. The four summary variables are dimensions calculated through an algorithm developed from preceding published findings to provide standardized scores between 1 to 100.

- **Analytical Thinking.** A high analytical thinking score implies formal, logical, and hierarchal thinking [20]. The variable was developed by analyzing the usage of function words (e.g., pronouns, verbs, articles) [22]. For our case, analytical thinking was used to gauge logical thinking patterns, where an increase would suggest higher deliberation over the vaccine announcement by users.
- **Clout.** A high clout score indicates individual's portrayal of expertise and adoption of a confident style of writing [20]. The variable was developed by assessing first-person plurals (e.g., we, us, our) and second-person singular pronouns (e.g., you, your) [23]. Thus, clout would measure for a change in Twitter users' use of confident language style. An increase would suggest that users are portraying confidence towards their expressed perspectives on the vaccine through more.
- **Authenticity.** A higher authenticity score suggests writing with a more honest and personal disclosure [20]. The creation of the algorithm took into consideration of first-person singular and third-person pronouns (e.g., I, me), fewer exclusive words

(e.g., except, without), and negative emotion words (e.g., hatred, sadness) [24]. Thus, we used authenticity to examine the disclosure patterns among Twitter users, and an increase would suggest users' openness towards sharing their opinions on the vaccine.

- **Emotional Tone.** A score below 50 reflects a negative emotionality, while a score above 50 suggests a positive emotionality in the writing [20]. The emotional tone is tracked through the number of negative (e.g., hurt, sadness) and positive words (e.g., love, nice) in the texts [25]. Hence, we used emotional tone to detect emotional valence in the tweets, and to evaluate the sentiments expressed over the vaccine announcement.

4   Results

4.1   Word Cloud Analysis

By comparing word clouds across the two time periods, we noticed slight changes in the word frequencies (see Fig. 1). For example, an obvious increase in the word "vaccine" representing a higher count of users tweeting on vaccine-related topics (see Table 1). Words related to precautionary measures also changed substantially. An increase was observed for "mask", likely to encourage the usage, and a decrease for "lockdown", an indication of hope towards the reduction of this measure. The frequency change for words like "death" and "case" were also lower than expected.

"Before" – 01 to 08 Nov 2020	"After" – 09 to 16 Nov 2020
(a)	(b)

Fig. 1. Comparison of word cloud analysis between the two periods, "Before" and "After".

Table 1. Word frequency change between the two periods, "Before" and "After".

Word	Frequency	
	Before	After
vaccine	2460	11024
mask	8561	11229
lockdown	22723	13572
death	7604	6417
case	11222	10932

4.2   Results of LIWC Tonal Analysis

The LIWC analysis disclosed a shift for two of the summary variables, authenticity, and clout (see Fig. 2). We observed a decrease in the mean score of authenticity from 27.30 to 25.92, implying a potential guarded disclosure from the users after the vaccine announcement. This highlights a possible reduction in willingness to engage in open discussion. An increase in the clout mean score, from 60.88 to 61.26, may suggest users adopting higher confidence in their expression, meaning a shift in confidence towards the information or opinion shared in the tweets. The change was negligible for the mean score of analytical thinking, decreasing from 73.34 to 73.32, and emotional tone, from 41.49 to 41.47 (see Fig. 2). This points towards the possibility that users' attitudes and emotions towards the pandemic was largely unaffected by the vaccine announcement.

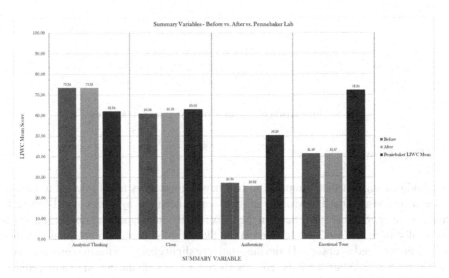

Fig. 2. Comparison of the summary variables between the two period, "Before" and "After".

To further explore the dataset, the tweets were analyzed by days. On the day of the announcement, the mean score of authenticity and clout dropped and remained low thereafter (see Fig. 3). The findings suggest the existence of open and confident tweeting pre-announcement, but users became reserved and portrayed anxiety after post-announcement of the vaccine. This exhibited a probable shift in willingness to share opinions over the vaccine and other COVID-19 related topics. The sentiments were also negative in both periods, despite an increase in positivity from the announcement. However, positivity was short-lived as the emotional tone returned close to "Before" levels. Analytical thinking was not affected by the announcement, indicating users were likely still undecided about the vaccine and efficacy results. Hence there was no shift in their thinking patterns.

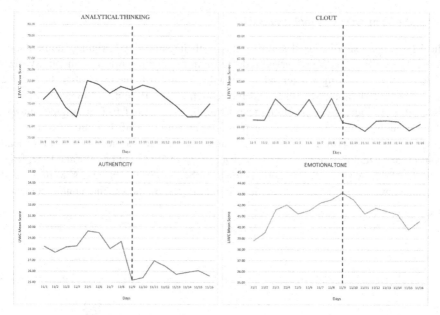

Fig. 3. Comparison of the summary variables across dates

5 Discussion

Our findings suggest that compared to bad news, good news tends to elicit a weaker societal response. The first vaccine efficacy announcement by Pfizer and BioNTech could be categorized as good news in the COVID-19 context, and yet results suggest a minimal shift in tone on Twitter. Even in the face of good news of a potential vaccine, users were unfazed as observed from the relatively slight change in mean scores between the "Before" and "After" periods. This seems consistent with the notion of a preference for negativity bias in news consumption where the reaction to good news is minimal compared to bad news [26, 27].

By comparing the results across individual dates, a pattern could be observed. The authenticity and clout score were notably lower and remained so compared to the "Before" period. This indicated that the good news of the pandemic could have instead produced anxiety and reduced the confidence in users. Yet, the increase in emotional tone score suggests a possible scenario of cautious optimism, where users might experience reduce confidence but higher optimism over the Pfizer-BioNTech vaccine results [28]. Alternatively, several regions were experiencing a second wave of infection in the same period, like Europe [29], this could have resulted in a loss of optimism over a potential effectiveness of the vaccine.

The minimal change in the analytical thinking score could have been confounded by other events that overshadowed the good news. One example is the discovery of mutated COVID-19 strains in minks reported on November 5, 2020 [30]. This could have accounted for the fluctuations in the mean scores. Similarly, users' reactions towards global infections surpassing 51 million could have been another confounding factor [31].

In the early stage of the pandemic, using text mining approaches, many researchers have uncovered various topics discussed on Twitter such as preventive measure, reports of new cases, and the like [32, 33]. While these studies provide some insights on what people concern during times of uncertainty, few of them have examined the language style people used for crisis communication. The current study contributes to the body of this literature by offering an alternative perspective through tone analysis, by investigating the change in language style and word choices used by Twitter users. Importantly, the results might help health researchers and authorities understand how communication patterns about COVID-19 vaccine changed on social media. Based on the tonal shift, targeted message interventions could be proposed to disseminate vaccine-related knowledge in the public.

6 Limitations and Future Work

Two limitations exist in the current study. The first is the use of tweets containing COVID-19 keywords, regardless of whether they were vaccine-related or not. There therefore could be alternative explanations of our findings due to where occurrences of other significant events, deemed by users. Next, we did not analyze tweets by geographical boundaries. Within the evaluated time frame, some regions (e.g., United States and Europe) were facing a spike in infection cases, while others (e.g., Asia) were much in control of the situation. These differences could have resulted in a canceling effect, as evidenced by minimal changes in our results across the "Before" and "After" periods.

Future research should consider narrowing to only vaccine-related tweets across a longer study time period. Tweets should be coded for geographical boundaries to provide a more nuanced understanding of reactions between regions. Next, extracting data from alternative social media platforms, like Facebook and Reddit, should be considered as this will increase the generalizability of the findings. Ultimately, the findings from this study will provide insights to practitioners and researchers on public sentiments to the COVID-19 vaccine announcement.

References

1. WHO Coronavirus Disease (COVID-19) Dashboard. World Health Organization (WHO) (n.d.). https://covid19.who.int. Accessed 8 Mar 2021
2. WHO's three messages for UNGA75. World Health Organization (WHO), 15 September 2020. https://www.who.int/news/item/15-09-2020-who-s-three-messages-for-unga75
3. Business Wire: Pfizer and BioNTech Announce Vaccine Candidate Against COVID-19 Achieved Success in First Interim Analysis from Phase 3 Study, 9 November 2020. https://www.businesswire.com/news/home/20201109005539/en/%C2%A0Pfizer-and-BioNTech-Announce-Vaccine-Candidate-Against-COVID-19-Achieved-Success-in-First-Interim-Analysis-from-Phase-3-Study
4. Thelwall, M., Buckley, K., Paltoglou, G.: Sentiment in Twitter events. J. Am. Soc. Inform. Sci. Technol. 62(2), 406–418 (2011). https://doi.org/10.1002/asi.21462
5. Pennebaker, J.W., Mehl, M.R., Niederhoffer, K.G.: Psychological aspects of natural language use: our words our selves. Ann. Rev. Psychol. 54(1), 547–577 (2003). https://doi.org/10.1146/annurev.psych.54.101601.145041

6. Pak, A., Paroubek, P.: Twitter as a corpus for sentiment analysis and opinion mining. In: Proceedings of LREC, vol. 10 (2010)

7. Scanfeld, D., Scanfeld, V., Larson, E.L.: Dissemination of health information through social networks: Twitter and antibiotics. Am. J. Infect. Control **38**(3), 182–188 (2010). https://doi.org/10.1016/j.ajic.2009.11.004

8. Roth, Y., Pickles, N.: Updating our approach to misleading information, 11 May 2020. https://blog.twitter.com/en_us/topics/product/2020/updating-our-approach-to-misleading-information.html

9. Jones, N.M., Silver, R.C.: This is not a drill: anxiety on Twitter following the 2018 Hawaii false missile alert. Am. Psychol. **75**(5), 683–693 (2020). https://doi.org/10.1037/amp0000495

10. Gascó, M., Bayerl, P.S., Denef, S., Akhgar, B.: What do citizens communicate about during crises? Analyzing Twitter use during the 2011 UK riots. Gov. Inf. Q. **34**(4), 635–645 (2017). https://doi.org/10.1016/j.giq.2017.11.005

11. Choi, D., Kim, P.: Sentiment analysis for tracking breaking events: a case study on Twitter. In: Selamat, A., Nguyen, N.T., Haron, H. (eds.) ACIIDS 2013. LNCS (LNAI), vol. 7803, pp. 285–294. Springer, Heidelberg (2013). https://doi.org/10.1007/978-3-642-36543-0_30

12. Thelwall, M., Buckley, K., Paltoglou, G., Cai, D., Kappas, A.: Sentiment strength detection in short informal text. J. Am. Soc. Inform. Sci. Technol. **61**(12), 2544–2558 (2010). https://doi.org/10.1002/asi.21416

13. Xu, W.(Wayne), Zhang, C.: Sentiment, richness, authority, and relevance model of information sharing during social Crises—the case of #MH370 tweets. Comput. Hum. Behav. **89**, 199–206 (2018). https://doi.org/10.1016/j.chb.2018.07.041

14. Chen, E., Lerman, K., Ferrara, E.: Tracking social media discourse about the COVID-19 pandemic: development of a public coronavirus Twitter data set. JMIR Public Health Surveill. **6**(2), e19273 (2020). https://doi.org/10.2196/19273

15. Documenting the Now: Hydrator [Computer Software] (2020). https://github.com/docnow/hydrator

16. McHugh, M.C., Saperstein, S.L., Gold, R.S.: OMG U #Cyberbully! An exploration of public discourse about cyberbullying on Twitter. Health Educ. Behav. **46**(1), 97–105 (2018). https://doi.org/10.1177/1090198118788610

17. Veltri, G.A., Atanasova, D.: Climate change on Twitter: content, media ecology and information sharing behaviour. Public Underst. Sci. **26**(6), 721–737 (2015). https://doi.org/10.1177/0963662515613702

18. Golder, S.A., Macy, M.W.: Diurnal and seasonal mood vary with work, sleep, and daylength across diverse cultures. Science **333**(6051), 1878–1881 (2011). https://doi.org/10.1126/science.1202775

19. Pope, D., Griffith, J.: An analysis of online Twitter sentiment surrounding the European refugee crisis. In: Proceedings of the International Joint Conference on Knowledge Discovery, Knowledge Engineering and Knowledge Management, pp. 299–306 (2016). https://doi.org/10.5220/0006051902990306

20. Pennebaker, J.W., Booth, R.J., Boyd, R.L., Francis, M.E.: Linguistic Inquiry and Word Count: LIWC 2015. Pennebaker Conglomerates, Austin (2015). www.LIWC.net

21. Pennebaker, J.W., Boyd, R., Jordan, K., Blackburn, K.: The development and psychometric properties of LIWC 2015. University of Texas at Austin (2015). https://doi.org/10.15781/T29G6Z

22. Pennebaker, J.W., Chung, C.K., Frazee, J., Lavergne, G.M., Beaver, D.I.: When small words foretell academic success: the case of college admissions essays. PLoS ONE **9**(12), e115844 (2015). https://doi.org/10.1371/journal.pone.0115844

23. Kacewicz, E., Pennebaker, J.W., Davis, M., Jeon, M., Graesser, A.C.: Pronoun use reflects standings in social hierarchies. J. Lang. Soc. Psychol. **33**(2), 125–143 (2013). https://doi.org/10.1177/0261927X13502654

24. Newman, M.L., Pennebaker, J.W., Berry, D.S., Richards, J.M.: Lying words: predicting deception from linguistic styles. Pers. Soc. Psychol. Bull. **29**(5), 665–675 (2003). https://doi.org/10.1177/0146167203029005010

25. Cohn, M.A., Mehl, M.R., Pennebaker, J.W.: Linguistic markers of psychological change surrounding September 11, 2001. Psychol. Sci. **15**(10), 687–693 (2004). https://doi.org/10.1111/j.0956-7976.2004.00741.x

26. Nguyen, V.H., Claus, E.: Good news, bad news, consumer sentiment and consumption behavior. J. Econ. Psychol. **39**, 426–438 (2013). https://doi.org/10.1016/j.joep.2013.10.001

27. Soroka, S., Fournier, P., Nir, L.: Cross-national evidence of a negativity bias in psychophysiological reactions to news. Proc. Natl. Acad. Sci. U. S. A. **116**(38), 18888–18892 (2019). https://doi.org/10.1073/pnas.1908369116

28. Wallston, K.A.: Cautious optimism vs. cockeyed optimism. Psychol. Health **9**(3), 201–203 (1994). https://doi.org/10.1080/08870449408407480

29. The Economist: The second wave of COVID-19 has sent much of Europe back into lockdown. The Economist, 7 November 2020. https://www.economist.com/briefing/2020/11/07/the-second-wave-of-covid-19-has-sent-much-of-europe-back-into-lockdown

30. Denmark wants to cull 15 million minks over COVID fears. AP NEWS, 4 November 2020. https://apnews.com/article/denmark-cull-15-million-minks-covid-19-37f57a303bbf738efca50918c35696de

31. International Update: Global Covid infections pass 51.4 million—100,000 cases per day in US. Pharmaceutical Technology, 11 November 2020. https://www.pharmaceutical-technology.com/special-focus/covid-19/international-update-global-covid-infections-pass-51-4-million-100000-cases-per-day-in-us/

32. Zheng, H., Goh, D.H.-L., Lee, C.S., Lee, E.W.J., Theng, Y.L.: Uncovering temporal differences in COVID-19 tweets. Proc. Assoc. Inf. Sci. Technol. **57**(1), e233 (2020). https://doi.org/10.1002/pra2.233

33. Hung, M., et al.: Social network analysis of COVID-19 sentiments: application of artificial intelligence. J. Med. Internet Res. **22**(8), e22590 (2020). https://doi.org/10.2196/22590

A Taste of Distributed Work Environments: Emergency Remote Teaching and Global Software Engineering

Simona Vasilache[✉]

Faculty of Engineering, Information and Systems, University of Tsukuba, Tsukuba, Japan
simona@cs.tsukuba.ac.jp

Abstract. During the 2020 Covid-19 pandemic, many academic institutions had to abruptly switch to online teaching, in what was termed emergency remote teaching. This work highlights some of the effects of this sudden switch to online teaching of a software engineering course and it shows how the online environment provided an opportunity to test mini-models of distributed teams in software engineering.

Keywords: Global software engineering · Distributed environments · Emergency remote teaching

1 Introduction

With the prevalence of globalization and internationalization in today's world, Global Software Engineering (GSE) as a discipline has been receiving growing attention. Courses on software engineering are now taking into account various global aspects and there is a large body of research dedicated to teaching and implementing GSE. In Japan, whereas GSE teaching may not be as widely present as in other countries, an increasing number of institutions pay attention to global aspects of teaching software engineering.

The 2020 Covid-19 pandemic forced many higher education institutions all over the world to cancel their face-to-face classes and move their courses online. While online teaching brings the flexibility of teaching anywhere, anytime, implementing this move had to be done at an "unprecedented and staggering" speed [1]. As many instructors quickly became aware, there is a difference between traditional online teaching and this sudden switch to online courses forced upon the academic world in the past few months. The new "emergency remote teaching" (ERT) term was coined, highlighting the current pressing teaching and learning conditions [1]. This poster will describe the effects of ERT on teaching an introductory software engineering course in Japan, in a multicultural environment. The following section will include details of the course, along with a description and discussion of the effects, and it will be followed by concluding remarks and future work.

© Springer Nature Switzerland AG 2021
C. Stephanidis et al. (Eds.): HCII 2021, CCIS 1421, pp. 624–628, 2021.
https://doi.org/10.1007/978-3-030-78645-8_79

2   Online Course and ERT Effects

2.1   Basic Course Description and Evolution

The observations and lessons described in this work are drawn from a course that the author held for the past 5 years at the University of Tsukuba in Japan. This course is aimed at graduate school students (mainly form the computer science department, but not limited to it), teaching introductory software engineering concepts (software development models and life cycle, requirements gathering and specification, system and user interface design, testing, project planning and management etc.). The course changed in its number of participants (made up of a mixture of local Japanese students and international students), as well as its format. In 2016, 15 students enrolled, followed by 26 students in 2017, 35 students in 2018 and 66 students in 2019. Finally, 35 students enrolled in the online, 2020 edition of the course. In terms of format, the 2016 and 2017 editions were mostly held in the classical lecture-style. Active learning was employed in the subsequent years, with an increasing number of class activities, mini-teams and a micro-project. Some of the lessons learned from the first four years of teaching this course were presented in our previous work [2].

2.2   Online Course Setting and Description

The evolution of the course structure between 2016 and 2020 is shown in Fig. 1. The latest edition of the course was held in spring 2020, in an online format (as explained above, due to the Covid-19 pandemic).

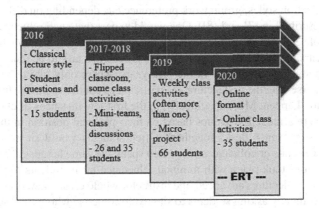

Fig. 1. Course structure evolution (2016–2020)

The lectures were held using two platforms: Microsoft Teams [3] (for the first lecture) and Zoom [4] (for the remaining lectures). The instructor held the lectures live during the designated days and times (as specified in the academic calendar and the course timetable); the lectures were recorded (and the recordings were placed on Microsoft Stream [5]) and then made available for the students to watch on-demand, with class materials and links to recordings provided in manaba [6], which is the learning management system currently employed by the university. Class activities and group work were managed using the breakout rooms feature of Zoom. The same breakout room was maintained during one lecture, but the componence of the rooms was changed with each new lecture.

2.3 Online Course Effects: Observations and Discussion

The number of students enrolled in the 2020 course was 35, with only 6 local Japanese students participating. This is the lowest number of local students since the course was first held in 2016 (and the highest percentage of international students, i.e. 82.8%). The instructor believes that there are two main factors determining this reduction in the number of students (from 66 participants in 2019 to 35 participants in 2020). The first and more obvious reason is the online format of the course, a novelty for most participating students (and for many instructors, as well). The uncertainties with regard to class structure, flow, evaluation etc. all contribute to the reluctance of enrolling in courses that are suddenly offered online only. The second reason is specific to this particular course; while we are not certain of the exact number, at least 10 students dropped the course within its first two weeks (which is the period allowed for making changes to course enrolment). During the first lecture of the course, the instructor explained that the remaining lectures would include extensive student participation and group work. Based on the author's previous experience, many local, Japanese students are reluctant to participate in class activities where they must express their opinions and where they must actively interact with students from other countries, in particular in situations where they need to speak English. As a matter of fact, there is a large body of research which deals with communication styles, group work preference etc. depending on different cultures (e.g. works described in [7] and [8]). One would expect that such reluctance would be present regardless of online or face-to-face classes. However, the author believes that, in previous years, the usual face-to-face classes proved this task to be much more easily achieved than students imagined. In the past years, where only two or three students dropped the course after the first lecture, the participants could experience first-hand how class interaction happen. More specifically, in the first few instances of class activities, the students were arranged in groups based on their physical position in the classroom (grouping 2, 3 or even 4 desks together). Often students would sit next to familiar faces, i.e. their friends or colleagues who often speak the same language. Thus, the first few class activities took place with minimal reluctance from students to participate in group work. As the lectures advanced, the instructor would create new, different groups, sometimes specifically asking students to sit next to someone whom they never sat next to before. The interaction with "new" people, with colleagues from a different culture or with colleagues with whom one can only communicate in English only, came later, when the students were, more or less, already familiar with most of the people around, when they were already aware that there is no particular pressure to speak out loud in English. Furthermore, even if they felt discouraged, it was already too late to drop the class, thus the students had no choice but to experience the novelty of being part of a group where they must express their opinions, where they must speak English and sometimes even (briefly) report in front of the classroom about the group's interaction and results.

Emergency remote teaching, with its "online" format, provided the opportunity to test mini-models of distributed teams in software engineering. With such a large number of international students and considering the pandemic situation, the students participated in the classes from various locations. Whereas most of them were in the city of Tsukuba in Japan (where the university is located), some students were in a different country (e.g. China), even on a different continent (i.e. Africa). This situation provided an excellent opportunity to experience a taste of distributed work environment, which is particularly important in the field of software engineering. The different locations often imply different time zones, each with different internet connection speeds and different technical specifications for their learning devices. The use of Zoom breakout rooms proved particularly useful to the instructor, who could assign specific group members to each room, making sure to create different groups every time. The group activities took place despite all these geographical and time-zone differences and the instructor believes that, while offering a mere taste of distributed environments, they were successful and they showed the students, through mini-activities and mini-teams, how a distributed software project could look like in the real world.

2.4 Students' Feedback

At the end of the course, the students provided feedback through a mandatory evaluation questionnaire (according to the university's rules), in which they rate how well the class was prepared and conducted etc. To give only two examples, most of the participants either agreed or strongly agreed that they were satisfied with the course (with only 3 students being neutral); similarly, the majority of the students felt that they achieved the course's objectives, with only one participant feeling that they achieved less than 40% of these objectives. When asked about the good aspects of the course, the responses included: "I like how everyone was able to contribute something to the class", "groupwork [...] useful for future job meeting", "good interaction with students, lots of hands-on opportunities", "it's relatable for those who have work experience", "a high degree of freedom to question the teacher and make group discussing [sic]".

In relation to the online aspect of the courses and possible drawbacks and improvements, several students pointed out that the instructor should be stricter with asking the students to show their face during lectures. (Bringing into discussion the "emergency" aspect of ERT, the instructor assumed that there might be technical difficulties, possibly reduced internet connection speeds, and thus the students were not strictly required to turn on their cameras). One participant stated: "I think there are too many disadvantages to taking lessons online. Lost the opportunity to communicate with the teacher face to face."

Furthermore, the management of the breakout rooms came into discussion: one student suggested"a strict approach" to this, in order to make sure that everyone in the room/group participates (again, having the camera on was pointed out as helping with an "increased focus"). Overall, the comments received from the students show that they appreciate the usefulness of class activities and discussions and, most of the time, they believe that these are feasible even in an online environment.

3   Conclusions and Future Work

This work highlighted how emergency remote teaching provided the opportunity to test mini-models of distributed teams in software engineering, during an introductory software engineering course held online. Most of the observations and conclusions drawn by the author were based on empirical observations gathered during lectures. In our future work we intend to gather quantitative and qualitative data which could help to prove (or disprove) the author's hypotheses; we also plan to survey the course participants and find out their perspective with regard to geographically distributed online classes as mini-models of distributed work environment.

References

1. Hodges, C., Moore, S., Lockee, B., Trust, T., Bond, A.: The difference between emergency remote teaching and online learning. Educ. Rev. **27**, 1–12 (2020)
2. Vasilache, S.: From an international classroom to a distributed work environment: student perspectives on global software engineering. In: 2018 IEEE International Conference on Teaching, Assessment, and Learning for Engineering, pp. 825–828. IEEE (2018)
3. Chat, Meetings, Calling, Collaboration|Microsoft Teams. https://www.microsoft.com/en-us/microsoft-365/microsoft-teams/group-chat-software. Accessed 17 March 2021
4. Zoom: Zoom Meetings & Chat. https://zoom.us/meetings. Accessed 17 March 2021
5. Microsoft Stream. https://www.microsoft.com/en-us/microsoft-365/microsoft-stream. Accessed 17 March 2021
6. manaba Homepage, https://manaba.jp/products/, last accessed 2021/03/17.
7. Tweed, R.G., Lehman, D.R.: Learning considered within a cultural context: Confucian and Socratic approaches. Am. Psychol. **57**(2), 89 (2002)
8. Mercier, H., Deguchi, M., Van der Henst, J.B., Yama, H.: The benefits of argumentation are cross-culturally robust: the case of Japan. Think Reason **22**(1), 1–15 (2016)

Operation Efficiency Study on a New Cooperative VR Whiteboard System

Jiangkun Wang[1] and Lei Jing[1,2]($\boxtimes$)

[1] The Graduate School of Computer Science, The University of Aizu,
Aizu-Wakamatsu, Japan
[2] Research Center for Advanced Information Science and Technology (CAIST),
The University of Aizu, Aizu-Wakamatsu, Japan
leijing@u-aizu.ac.jp

Abstract. Due to the COVID-19 pandemic, remote collaboration becomes widely needed. To this end, this research proposes a VR whiteboard system that facilitates multiple participants collaborate remotely using natural handwriting. Moreover, a controlled experiment is conducted to compare the operation efficiency of the VR whiteboard with two other whiteboards, including the physical whiteboard and electronic whiteboard. It shows that the VR whiteboard improves collaboration efficiency significantly compared to the mouse-based electronic whiteboard and even compatible with the traditional whiteboard.

Keywords: Remote collaboration · Handwriting input method · Whiteboard · Virtual reality · Working efficiency study

1 Introduction

Due to the widely spread of COVID-19, many people have to work at home, and many students have to take classes remotely. Remote collaboration becomes unprecedentedly important. The whiteboard is a piece of essential office equipment in most classrooms or offices, which facilitates people to collaborate locally. Nonetheless, the traditional whiteboards do not support remote collaboration, and the content written on the traditional whiteboard cannot be directly stored and shared digitally. The existed mouse-based electronic whiteboard supports remote cooperation [1]. Though, we found that writing with the mouse is inefficient and uncomfortable when tried to write some text with a mouse-based electronic whiteboard. A touch screen with a stylus is another widely used type of electronic whiteboard. However, it is not comfortable to write and read handwritten contents on a size-limited touch screen.

There has been a significant body of research on the cooperative electronic whiteboard. Some researches dedicate to digitizing the content on the whiteboard [2,3]. Some discuss the learning efficiency of natural handwriting whiteboards [4–6]. Rekimoto [7] proposes a public 2D touch screen whiteboard for information share. Mynatt et al. [8] design a 2D electronic whiteboard for office work.

© Springer Nature Switzerland AG 2021
C. Stephanidis et al. (Eds.): HCII 2021, CCIS 1421, pp. 629–636, 2021.
https://doi.org/10.1007/978-3-030-78645-8_80

Kukimoto et al. [9] develop a touch screen using HMD to assist thought share by annotating. "Zoom whiteboard" is a public whiteboard function in the remote conference software "zoom".

In recent years, the emergence of VR technology and VR device makes VR whiteboards possible. Users could write in a virtual space through HMD (head-mounted display) and controller. Virtual reality technology breaks the limitations of space and physical objects [10], and users can even write and draw more freely. However, it does not support remote collaboration, which is an essential function of the whiteboard. Due to VR equipment limitations, the existing VR whiteboard systems are mostly stand-alone systems with no collaborative functions. Sakuraba et al. [11] using HMD to serve 3D model design collaboration, and it does not support remote collaboration. "Dry Erase: Infinite VR Whiteboard" is a VR whiteboard game on Steam that supports free draw and writing in the VR space. It has no network connection function and does not support multiple users.

In this paper, we develop a virtual reality whiteboard system for remote collaboration with the natural handwriting input method. This system facilitates multiple people to collaborate at the same time through writing on the VR whiteboard. Specifically, the natural handwriting and remote collaboration function were implemented using the VR device and network service. Moreover, several controlled experiments were conducted to evaluate the system on collaboration efficiency.

2   VR Whiteboard System

This section introduces the implementation and operation manual of the VR whiteboard system. The VR whiteboard facilitates multiple people to collaborate using natural handwriting. There are three steps to implement it. First, build a three-dimensional virtual room and a virtual whiteboard with Unity 3D and HMD. Then it is excellent to have handwriting experience, so a controller is used as the input device and writes or draws naturally just like a real whiteboard becomes possible. Finally, to support remote collaboration, we need the network service to synchronize the written content in real-time.

2.1   Application Model

Figure 1(a) shows the application model of the VR whiteboard system. For example, user 1 is in Japan, and user 2 is in the United States. Due to some working problems, two people need to collaborate through a whiteboard as in a company conference room. At this point, these two people can use the VR whiteboard. The system consists of a server and several clients. The server is running on the cloud. In order to take part in the shared VR whiteboard, users will need a computer and a VR device kit. Here list some possible application scenes.

- You can show your ideas to your partners through the VR whiteboard as in a conference room.

- You can modify the prototype design of the product appearance or graphical user interface through the VR whiteboard with colleagues traveling in other places.
- Teachers can take remote dictation tests with multiple students at the same time. Students can write their answers on the VR whiteboard at the same time, just like in the real classrooms.

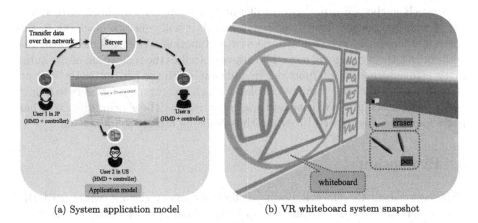

(a) System application model   (b) VR whiteboard system snapshot

Fig. 1. System design and implementation

2.2   System Implementation

The VR whiteboard system consists of three main modules. (a) PUN (Photon Unity Network) module implements a multiplayer synchronization function. (b) VRTK (Virtual Reality Toolkit) controls the VR devices. (c) InkPainter draws the writing trajectory. The system flow is as follows. First, the program connects to the Photon server and check whether there is a VR whiteboard room. If there is, enter the room. If not, create a room and then enter the room. Then the program will generate a pen and an eraser for each player. Finally, the program enters the data synchronization state, sends the current player's data to the server, receives data from other players from the server, and processes the data from the other two modules of the program.

2.3   VR Whiteboard GUI

A snapshot of the VR whiteboard system is shown in Fig. 1(b). There are virtual pens and erasers in the virtual space. The user could see this virtual 3D space after putting on the HMD and could move freely in the room-scale area. The specific using method, using process, and some necessary instructions of the system are as follows.

Turn on all related devices (computer, network, controller, etc.), execute the system program. After that, the users only need to wear the HMD and pick up the controller. The system will generate a pen and an eraser for each user entering the virtual space of the VR whiteboard as shown in Fig. 1(b). Users can walk and write with the VR controller on the VR whiteboard just as they write on the whiteboard with the mark-pen. The user holds the VR controller to take the pen in the VR whiteboard space by pressing the "Grip button" of the controller to release the pen by pressing the "Grip button" once again. The usage of the virtual eraser is the same.

Users hold the pen with the controller and write on the VR whiteboard. When the virtual pen touches the virtual whiteboard, it will generate black ink in the corresponding position to achieve the writing function. When the pen leaves the whiteboard, the writing will stop. The above describes the realization of the automatic stroke segmentation function. In addition, when the pen enters the writing state, the pen will change from red to black, which is convenient for users to adjust in real-time. Each user's writing and erasing actions will be synchronized to other participants via high-speed Ethernet, thus realizing remote collaboration.

3   Evaluation

This section evaluates the collaboration efficiency among the VR whiteboard, the traditional whiteboard, and the electronic whiteboard. We determined the three scenes of the evaluation experiment. Scene 1 is the traditional whiteboard (pen). Users write/draw on the traditional whiteboard with pens and erase content with erasers. Scene 2 is the electronic whiteboard (mouse). Participants use the mouse to select and control the writing tool to write/draw on the electronic whiteboard and select and control the erase tool to erase the content on the whiteboard. Scene 3 is the VR whiteboard (VR). Users put on the HMD and enter the virtual whiteboard space. Through the controller in hand, select and control the pen and eraser, writing/drawing, and erasing like a traditional whiteboard.

3.1   Efficiency Experiment Design

Experiment Task. The experiment tasks (Fig. 1(b)) include basic graphic elements such as straight lines, curves, squares, circles, and triangles, and ten different English letters. Each participant chooses a color and then the two participants collaborate to complete the drawing of graphics and letters in three experiment scenes. The line drawn cannot exceed the boundary of the template. The width of the template is fixed, which ensures acceptable writing accuracy, thereby controlling a variable of this experiment.

Experiment Participants. There are 12 participants in the experiment, with an average age of 25. All participants randomly team up, two people in each group. Finally, we get 16 groups (as shown in Table 2) in the evaluation experiment.

3.2   Experiment Process

1. Make each participant experienced through full pre-training and pre-test.

2. Each group completes the task in 3 experiment scenes with order as shown in Table 1 (Avoid sequence effect).
3. A stopwatch is used to measure the time cost and record stopwatch results.
4. Each participant completes the questionnaire.
5. Collect questionnaire and processing data.

Table 1. Experiment scene order

Group ID	Experiment order		
	1st scene	2ed scene	3rd scene
01	Pen	Mouse	VR
02	Pen	VR	Mouse
03	Mouse	Pen	VR
04	Mouse	VR	Pen
05	VR	Pen	Mouse
06	VR	Mouse	Pen
...	REPEAT IN ORDER		

3.3 Efficiency Experiment Result

We record the time cost to complete the experiment tasks, calculate mean and sd (standard deviation) and implement a statistical significance test (TTEST). Sixteen experiment groups (two participants in each group) completed at least two times collaborative efficiency evaluation experiment tasks in each whiteboard scene. To compare the three whiteboard scenes' collaboration efficiency, we uniformly take the last two data to Table 1.

The result of the collaboration efficiency experiment is shown in Table 2 for inspection. We calculated the mean and standard deviation of the results of the three scenes (Pen/Mouse/VR). The average time cost to complete the experiment task collaboratively is 60.9 s when using the traditional whiteboard, 119.4 s when using the electronic whiteboard, 57.0 s when using the VR whiteboard. It is obvious that the mean and standard deviation of the VR whiteboard scene is the smallest. The last two lines are statistically different TTEST. The larger the value of the calculation result, the smaller the difference between the two samples.

From Table 2, we see the experiment result for remote/Local collaboration efficiency of the VR whiteboard (Compared to electronic whiteboard).

– The average time spent on remote collaboration tasks using the VR whiteboard is smaller (extremely statistically significantly different).
– The time coat is more stable (sd is small).

The experiment results for local collaboration efficiency of the VR whiteboard (Compared to traditional whiteboard). The average and stability of the local

Table 2. Collaboration efficiency experiment result (time-cost of finishing task)

Group ID	Scenes			Group ID	Scenes		
	Pen	Mouse	VR		Pen	Mouse	VR
1	63	122	58	9	62	126	58
1	70	122	52	10	69	105	74
2	63	123	64	10	65	115	66
2	65	130	65	11	70	125	51
3	61	125	63	11	67	123	52
3	61	122	66	12	64	119	48
4	58	109	63	12	65	121	55
4	52	108	55	13	58	111	60
5	65	119	52	13	62	112	69
5	64	121	55	14	45	114	55
6	56	122	56	14	48	110	54
6	62	124	53	15	56	124	54
7	58	129	48	15	52	118	56
7	61	123	55	16	62	117	49
8	61	119	52	16	62	124	57
8	58	122	55	**mean**	60.9	119.4	57.0
9	63	118	53	**sd**	5.8	6.1	6.3
TTEST (VR_Pen)	0.01			P > 0.05: The two sets of data are not significantly different			
TTEST (VR_Mouse)	4.22E−46			P << 0.01: These two sets of data are extremely significantly different			

collaboration task time spent on the VR whiteboard are similar to those of the traditional whiteboard (no statistically significantly different).

The calculation method of efficiency is shown in Eq. 1. We take the reciprocal of the time cost as efficiency (as shown in Eq. 2).

$$Result(efficiency) = \frac{Efficiency(VR\ whiteboard) - Efficiency(electronic\ whiteboard)}{Efficiency(electronic\ whiteboard)} \times 100\% \quad (1)$$

$$Efficiency = \frac{1}{Time\ cost(s)} \quad (2)$$

3.4 Efficiency Experiment Conclusion

The VR whiteboard supports natural handwriting. The electronic whiteboard uses a mouse as an input device. Our VR whiteboards' collaboration efficiency is significantly higher than that of the electronic whiteboard for 52%. The local collaboration efficiency of the VR whiteboard is comparable to the traditional whiteboard.

4 Discussion

Combining the system performance and user feedback, we summarize some possible improvements in the VR whiteboard system as follows.

Although the VR whiteboard realizes the same natural handwriting input method as the traditional whiteboard, there is no physical feedback when writing. At present, we use the color change of the pen to indicate the writing state. In the future, we consider using the vibration of the controller to simulate physical feedback. This will make the VR whiteboard easier to use.

At present, VR devices are becoming more lightweight and comfortable, and there is a kind of wireless HMD that does not require cables, thereby reducing user fatigue and improving user comfort. Currently, the scene of the VR whiteboard system is occasionally misaligned. With the development of positioning technology, the stability of the system will be further improved.

5 Conclusion

This research developed a VR whiteboard system based on the VR device and photon unity network service. It facilitates multiple people to collaborate remotely using natural handwriting. Moreover, we implemented several controlled comparison experiments between traditional whiteboard, electronic whiteboard, and proposed VR whiteboard to learn the operation efficiency and obtained the following results. The average time cost to complete the experiment task collaboratively is 60.9 s when using the traditional whiteboard, 119.4 s when using the electronic whiteboard, 57.0 s when using the VR whiteboard. It shows that the VR whiteboard improves the collaboration efficiency by 52% compared to the electronic whiteboard and even compatible with the traditional whiteboard.

Here proposed some future research works based on the current experiment results. According to user feedback in the experiment, improve the stability and usability of the VR whiteboard system. Use the motion-capture glove designed by our laboratory as an input device for the VR whiteboard. Verify the learning curve of users about a new input method. Evaluate user fatigue during input and output.

References

1. McCanne, S.: A distributed whiteboard for network conferencing (1992)
2. Varona-Marin, D., Oberholzer, J.A., Tse, E., Scott, S.D.: Post-meeting curation of whiteboard content captured with mobile devices. In: Proceedings of the 2018 ACM International Conference on Interactive Surfaces and Spaces, pp. 43–54 (2018)

3. Ishii, H., Kobayashi, M.: Clearboard: a seamless medium for shared drawing and conversation with eye contact. In: Proceedings of the SIGCHI Conference on Human Factors in Computing Systems, pp. 525–532 (1992)
4. Karsenti, T.: The interactive whiteboard: uses, benefits, and challenges. A survey of 11,683 students and 1,131 teachers. Can. J. Learn. Technol. La revue canadienne de l'apprentissage et de la technologie **42**(5) (2016)
5. Wang, J., Endo, T., Lu, C., Jing, L.: A novel AR whiteboard system and usability study. In: 2019 IEEE 8th Global Conference on Consumer Electronics (GCCE), pp. 28–30. IEEE (2019)
6. Mariz, C., Stephenson, J., Carter, M.: Interactive whiteboards in education: a literature scoping survey. Austr. Educ. Comput. **32**(1) (2017)
7. Rekimoto, J.: A multiple device approach for supporting whiteboard-based interactions. In: Proceedings of the SIGCHI Conference on Human Factors in Computing Systems, pp. 344–351 (1998)
8. Mynatt, E.D., Igarashi, T., Edwards, W.K., LaMarca, A.: Flatland: new dimensions in office whiteboards. In: Proceedings of the SIGCHI Conference on Human Factors in Computing Systems, pp. 346–353 (1999)
9. Kukimoto, N., Ebara, Y., Furukawa, M., Koya-mada, K.: Experimental study on thinking support using handwritten annotation at collaborative works in the tele-immersive shared environments. J. Inf. Process. Society Jpn. **48**(6), 21532163 (2007)
10. Hastings, C., Brunotte, J.: Total immersion: VR headsets in language learning. 2016 PanSIG J. page 101 (2017)
11. Sakuraba, Y., Fujinaga, Y., Yamazaki, T., Watanabe, T., Kaneko, T.: A 3D Sketch-Based Modeling Interface for Cooperative Work 2012 (2012)

Conceptual Design of Working from Home Based on Behavior Change in New Normal

Sheng-Ming Wang and Shiau-Ting Wang[✉] [iD]

National Taipei University of Technology, Taipei, Taiwan
{ryan5885,ryan5885}@mail.ntut.edu.tw

Abstract. Nowadays, working from home has been the ideal working condition for people. Especially with the covid-19 pandemic, most of the office workers are forced to switch to work from home within a short period of time. This is no longer a temporary change but will be a huge change affecting our lives now and in the future. This research is based on human-centered design, at the very first part we do a widely-interview with people who work in different industries, the problems are not only mental health but also come from user's inner worlds, so we narrow down to make a deeper interview to our target user, digital nomads, the one who derives income remotely and online, rather than from commuting to an office. After it, we made the persona and user journey to find out the touchpoint, to define our problem more specifically, there're three main points (1) it is flexible but too fragmented at home, (2) inefficient working schedule, and (3) loss of connection to working partners. In addition, behavior change takes a big part here, which means when we find the right mode of working at home and persist on the basis of having a considerable level of satisfaction, it will become the new normal in the future. We come out with a conceptual application combining with smart home technology named Groovy, aims to let the user (1) reduce decision making time, the application will tell you what time is best for what to do, (2) observe and suggest better schedules for you, based on your working habits, and (3) reduce the feeling of loneliness. And next, we made the interface prototype and use Kano model for the evaluation to understand the services we provide are in which features.

Keywords: Work from home · Behavior change · User experience · Kano model

1 Introduction

As mentioned above, our work life at home varies from person to person, as technological advances allow us to keep in touch with our colleagues remotely, the new working style without going to the office is gradually changing our lives, not only breaking through the original framework of working hours, but also the original mode of using office space will also be facing changes. Working remotely is many people's hope before the covid-19 pandemic, but when we really experience the working from home situation, it's not that easy as how we think. After experiencing a few months of working from home, the ideal working pattern has slowly worn-out people's will, resulting in problems such as inability to unplug from work, time management problems, managerial trust problems, home health care, and worse working environment…etc.

© Springer Nature Switzerland AG 2021
C. Stephanidis et al. (Eds.): HCII 2021, CCIS 1421, pp. 637–645, 2021.
https://doi.org/10.1007/978-3-030-78645-8_81

2   Wild Interview and Aspects

Our interview was divided into two parts, we want to define the problem in the first part interview, therefore, tried to ask a wide range of interviewees, about any random ideas about working from home, or any tiny embarrassing problems they have experienced. Not only mental problems but also the physical unaccustomed is a problem that we often find. It is difficult to summarize the situation of each person in one sentence, but we find out some pros and cons about working from home.

2.1   Positive and Negative

The main pros should be that flexible schedule, we can flexibly plan all day, second is we save the time of commuting, no more traffic jams, don't have to wake up extra early, more time with family, or with the people that you live together. In another hand, though the pandemic was getting worse, people were suddenly forced to work from home, after a few months, Gensler U.S. in 2020 make a "work from home" survey, the data was collected from more than 2,300 anonymous U.S. workers, and the result shows 70% of people want to work in the office majority of their week, and more than 50% don't want to work from home anymore. The mental health is a pretty important reason in the negative aspects, because of the loneliness, and they don't talk with their colleges that much more, feels like just stay at home do all kinds of stuff alone, and the stress from work could cause depression.

3   Target User – Digital Nomads

Because of the limitations of the industry, it is impossible to meet the needs of everyone working from home, but in the future, we will have to get used to one thing, that is, working from home will be a normal part of life. In addition to that our target group of the research would be the digital nomads, they are people who can start their work just with a laptop and internet anywhere.

3.1   Interview II

These interviewees are all in the range of digital nomads, included human resources, designers, front-end engineers, product managers, and management positions. What we found interesting was that we saved a lot of time because we don't have to go to the office anymore. From this interview we found out that many people don't know what to do after a big change in behavior or environment. Especially, the working life changed from office to home.

3.2   Persona and User Journey

These Persona is a method used to describe a specific target object, after the interview of our target user - digital nomads, the persona was created as Fig. 1.

Fig. 1. "Persona, designer and developer were set, you can see the characteristics of these two types of person" create by this research

After persona, we made the user journey to know the specific problem, as you can see Fig. 2, the red area shows the touchpoints that have a big difference. For example, you could no longer see your colleagues in person, so communication became tougher. The meeting time could be longer because of technical problems. When you stay at home alone, you sometimes forget to take a break. Or the other way around, that you took too much of a break.

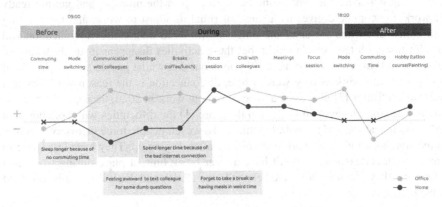

Fig. 2. "User journey of the persona" create by this research

4   Behavior Change

The process of behavior change is not a linear development, and the stickiness will depend on satisfaction of the new experiences [1], as Fig. 3. In other words, the journey to find out the new routines will not be smooth, when there are huge changes in life and new behaviors arise, in the process of finding out the new normal, people's stickiness to the new routine is proportional to the level of satisfaction with the experience gained, that is, when we find the right mode of working at home and persist on the basis of having a considerable level of satisfaction, it will become the new normal in the future.

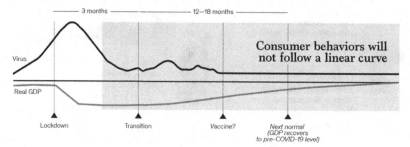

Fig. 3. "Behavior changes are not linear, and their stickiness will depend on satisfaction of the new experiences." by McKinsey & Company in June 2020

4.1 Invisible to Visible

In order to maintain a regular and efficient work status, a healthy and balanced life, we must start by establishing a strict life routine, in fact, this is the invisible part of we used to have in the office. While working from home, we often neglect to plan our schedules before and after off-work hours, thinking that we will work from home instead, and the stolen commute time gradually leads us into a mess, which in turn changes our daily behavior in our daily life. For example, getting up in the morning and getting ready for work, the commute gives us a sense of ritual to adjust to work, and the greeting with colleagues when we enter the office allows us to maintain communication and socialization with the outside world, but these activities disappear instantly when we switch to working from home. Paul [2] points out that whilst people say they're about as engaged with work as they were before, disconnection is the reason why they feel disengaged. Buffer [3] also done a state of remote work in 2020, the report shows the two unique struggles remain in the top three are (1) the difficulties with collaboration and communication, and (2) with loneliness. However, people force themselves to turn on the computer and go to work immediately after waking up. They have less space to interact with colleagues and don't have a clear break time or place during work, and after work, they feel like they have been at home all day and don't know how to get rid of the tiredness… etc.

4.2 About Focusing

Even though things didn't go as smoothly as we expected after we started working from home, there are many people who support working from home because it gives us the freedom to use our time. We can decide our own schedule anytime and anywhere, as long as we schedule it well. It is clear that before enjoying the flexible work from home life, we should set up a personal routine for working from home, so that our body and mind can adapt from inside out, not only the schedule at work, but also before and after starting work. Daigo [4] in 2016 have said, twenty-four hours a day are given to all equally. However, if you are able to harness the power of concentration, what you can achieve in those 24 h will make an overwhelming difference… The important thing is to focus on one behavior at a time and then habituate it, and by doing so, you will develop ultimate concentration. Therefore, we know that working from home has caused many changes and discomforts in our lives. It is not easy to find the right solution in one go or in a short time. The first step is to create the right concept, with the help of technology helps users to break the frame of their original working hours, they analyze the best working pattern and create a friendly working environment. And the most important part is to reduce the possibility of interference and decision from the outside.

5   How It Works

Since we save a lot of time commuting to and from work, and we can do what we want at the time we want, or we say at the "right" time. We found that IoT might be a good helper because most of the time we stay at home, and the furniture or spaces at home can best know our current state. The situation is based on having smart devices at home to observe and advise yourself on a better schedule. At certain times, a voice assistant will come out to ask you about your work progress and keep track of your status.

5.1   Problems and Goals

Therefore, the problems we want to solve with the application are (1) it is flexible but too fragmented at home, (2) inefficient working schedule and (3) loss of connection to working partners. And the application aims to help the users (1) reduce decision making time, the application will tell you what time is best for what to do, (2) observe and suggest better schedules for you, based on your working habits, and (3) reduce the feeling of loneliness.

6   Conceptual Application - Groovy

"Groovy", a self-improvement tool for working from home", for digital nomads to help them maintain a productive work-from-home routine and keep people who work together connected.

6.1   Schedule

User will see the to-dos of the day in this page. The color filled blocks and timeline emphasis which project should be done at the moment. The energy wave in the background is the system's prediction of user's concentration level throughout the day based on the data collection. The schedule is not only imported from the calendar, but also suggested according to the energy wave. So, when the wave is high, it is suitable for the work that requires a high level of concentration.

6.2   Office

It's a concept of virtual office, you can see the screen in the middle (Fig. 4), this user is working on a huge project called "boost", as the main designer, she often needs to check the progress with developers and the project manager. In this page, she can clearly see who she is working with and the status of her co-workers, through that she always feels connected and gain more motivation on work.

6.3 Learning

We provide users' daily or weekly review, some fun fact and the devices from expert, so user will have the opportunity to learn the reasons behind how Groovy gives suggestions in the free time, either from user's own behavior analysis or from expert advice. Through different categories, groovy hopes that everyone will actively learn to increase the motivation to change your behavior with visible growth and build a more sustainable routine.

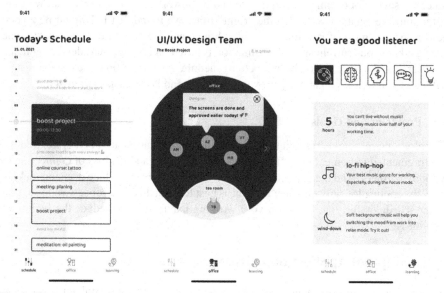

Fig. 4. "Behavior changes are not linear, and their stickiness will depend on satisfaction of the new experiences." by McKinsey & Company in June 2020

7 Evaluation

The Kano Model is used to analyses consumer preferences for different features and group them into multiple categories. This allows firms to identify which features they should focus on when developing a new product [5]. This research uses an online questionnaire, the questions were design from the three main functions, "Schedule", "Office" and "Learning", there're three questions of each function. Based on Kano model, so every question has positive and Table 1, the answers would be "I like it", "I expect it", "I am negative perspective at the same time, you can see the questions as neutral", "I can tolerate it" or "I dislike it". Total of 7 questionnaires were collected, all of them are valid, according to our persona, the test subjects are designer or developer. The template we used was provided by Harrigan Davonport [5].

Table 1. Kano model queationnaire.

S1-1	How would you think if we present your concentration in the form of waves?
S1-2	How would you think if we DON'T present your concentration in the form of waves?
S2-1	How would you think if we show the corresponding time beside the waves?
S2-2	How would you think if we DON'T show the corresponding time beside the waves?
S3-1	How would you think if we suggest the daily working schedule according to your energy waves?
S3-2	How would you think if we DON'T suggest the daily working schedule according to your energy waves?
O1-1	How would you think if we visualize the work status and progress of your colleagues?
O1-2	How would you think if we DON'T visualize the work status and progress of your colleagues?
O2-1	How would you think if we visualize the work and break status?
O2-2	How would you think if we DON'T visualize the work and break status?
O3-1	How would you think if we used the form of sliding to show different projects the user currently working on?
O3-2	How would you think if we DON'T used the form of sliding to show different projects the user currently working on?
L1-1	How would you think if we provide you with a daily/weekly review based on your usage?
L1-2	How would you think if we DON'T provide you with a daily/weekly review based on your usage?
L2-1	How would you think if we provide you the fun fact based on your usage?
L2-2	How would you think if we DON'T provide you the fun fact based on your usage?
L3-1	How would you think if we give expert advice for you based on your usage?
L3-2	How would you think if we DON'T give expert advice for you based on your usage?

Kano model classifies features into four categories, "Performance", "Must-be", "Attractive" and "Indifferent", depending on how customers react to the provided level of functionality. As you can see the result (Table 2), all the "Office" functions are in "Attractive" feature, there are unexpected features which when provided, cause a positive reaction, the only "Performance" feature is the function in "Schedule" which we provide the corresponding time beside the energy waves. In general, the develop priority of this category quadrant chart is "Must-be", "Performance", "Attractive" and "Indifferent" then, look back at the results of our data (Fig. 5), S2 and S3 in "Schedule" function are "Performance" features, they are the first priority to develop, the rest of others are the second.

Table 2. "Behavior changes are not linear, and their stickiness will depend on satisfaction of the new experiences." by McKinsey & Company in June 2020.

Feature	Must-be	Performance	Attractive	Indifferent	Category
Feature 1: Energy Wave	0%	14%	57%	29%	Attractive
Feature 2: Time beside the Wave	0%	43%	14%	43%	Performance
Feature 3: Daily schedule suggestion	14%	29%	14%	43%	Indifferent
Feature 4: visualized working progress of colleagues	0%	14%	57%	29%	Attractive
Feature 5: visualise work and break status	0%	14%	57%	29%	Attractive
Feature 6: show recent on-going projects	0%	14%	57%	14%	Attractive
Feature 7: provide daily or weekly review	0%	29%	29%	43%	Indifferent
Feature 8: provide fun facts	0%	14%	43%	43%	Attractive
Feature 9: export advices	0%	14%	29%	57%	Indifferent

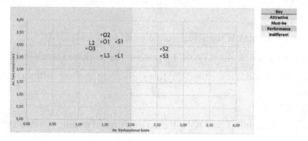

Fig. 5. "Functional and Dysfunctional score" data collected by this research and analysis template by conjoint.ly

8   Conclusion and Future Work

The daily schedule suggestion and the corresponding time beside the energy waves are the functions that the more we provide, the more satisfied our users become. People like the concept of virtual office, if we have this kind of function, they would be satisfied, and it also echoes the goal we mentioned earlier, to reduce the feeling of loneliness, transparent the status of colleagues could stronger the connection between them. Kano Model has the deeper analysis, it could show the importance of each function, but the data we collected was not enough to verify the result from most of the users, so we didn't do that part, for the future work, could consider the user in other fields.

Acknowledgment. Special thanks to Hsin-Tung Chen and Yi-Ruo Lin from The University of Applied Sciences Potsdam, this project was done by their support.

References

1. State of remote work 2020. Buffer, AngelList, 2020. https://lp.buffer.com/state-of-remote-work-2020.
2. Boutin, P.: Focus will shape the future of distributed work. https://blog.dropbox.com/topics/work-culture/economist-intelligence-unit-distributed-work-study. 13 Oct 2020

3. Sajal Kohli, B.T.V.F.S.M.V.: How COVID-19 is Changing Consumer Behavior –now and Forever. Mckinsey & Company (2020)
4. Focus, D.: Is your superpower: 18 learning weapons to control yourself and improve your performance (2016)
5. Davonport, H.: Kano Model of feature selection. Conjoint.ly. 22 Oct 2020

Correction to: Sentiment Analysis on Substance Use Disorder (SUD) Tweets Before and During COVID-19 Pandemic

Avineet Kumar Singh and Dezhi Wu (ID)

Correction to:
Chapter "Sentiment Analysis on Substance Use Disorder
(SUD) Tweets Before and During COVID-19 Pandemic"
in: C. Stephanidis et al. (Eds.): *HCI International*
*2021 - Posters***, CCIS 1421,**
https://doi.org/10.1007/978-3-030-78645-8_77

Acknowledgment section of the originally published version of chapter 77 was not complete. Additional acknowledgment and grant number were added in respective section.

The updated version of this chapter can be found at
https://doi.org/10.1007/978-3-030-78645-8_77

Author Index

Printed in the United States
by Baker & Taylor Publisher Services